THE WORLD IN
1971

This volume is dedicated to
the memory of Associated Press photographers
Henri Huet and Dennis Lee Royle,
who in 1971 gave their lives in performance of duty

THE WORLD IN
1971

History
as we
lived it...

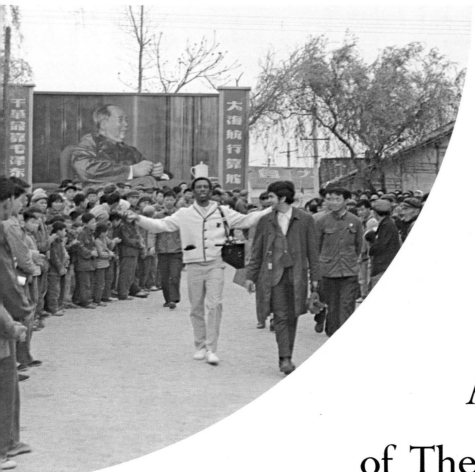

by the
Writers,
Photographers,
Artists and Editors
of The Associated Press

CONTENTS

Foreword

Many stirring events marked the worldwide news in 1971. Some of these were constructive occurrences, some were tragic and some were frightening in their reflection of human violence.

The China story developed with increasing drama, from the foot-in-the-door invitation of American Ping Pong players to President Nixon's surprise announcement that he planned to visit that country and, ultimately, to China's entry in the United Nations after two decades of isolation.

The Pentagon Papers and their publication demonstrated, perhaps more effectively than any previous example in the current century, the need for constant vigilance in preserving the constitutionally guaranteed freedom of the American news media to keep the public informed.

Late in the year President Nixon's new economic program, involving revaluation of the dollar and curbs on both wages and prices, went into operation. Its effectiveness in fighting inflation remained to be assessed in 1972.

Nature took its toll in tragic occurrences, including tornadoes in the southern states, tidal waves and floods in Pakistan, a disastrous earthquake in Southern California. While military action decelerated in Indochina and remained stalemated in the Middle East, armed conflict exploded in Pakistan. In the United States violence among individuals was epitomized by fatal outbreaks at Attica and San Quentin which offered stark evidence of what could happen within the American prison system. All these stories and more found Associated Press men on the job.

Whatever the nature of the news, THE WORLD IN 1971 has done its best to compile a wholly true record of what the year brought forth upon the earth—and even in space.

Wes Gallagher

Wes Gallagher

General Manager

Jan. 1, 1972

Troubled times for the United Nations ⟶

January

The United Nations-
Shaky After 25 Years?

The shadow of gloom had fallen upon its towering edifice;
"Nobody takes us seriously any more," one envoy said

NOBODY takes us seriously any more."
This plaintive remark by Saudi Arabia's veteran envoy, Jamil Baroody, pretty well summed up the uneasy feeling of most delegates as the United Nations passed its first quarter-century in an atmosphere of doubt that made one wonder if it would last out a second.

The slender slab of glass and steel towering beside New York's East River proclaimed that this was the home of the world forum of peace, a mecca for kings, presidents and sight-seers alike.

It was conceived as a symbol of hope, but after 25 years this lofty edifice was shrouded in gloom, its tenants beset with misgivings.

"Look at the visitors' galleries," said Baroody as he sipped coffee in the Delegates Lounge. "They used to be filled 10 years ago. But look at them today."

Gone was the romance, the air of excitement that once moved the late Adlai Stevenson to remind Americans: "Ours is the privilege of watching from the wings as the great dramas of our age unfold on the bank of the East River."

Actually the sense of disillusionment had begun to set in many years earlier, but it came slowly.

When the United Nations was founded in 1945, on high sounding principles enunciated by the Great Powers, millions of war-weary people around the world hailed it as the beginning of peace on earth.

But before a year had passed, the Soviet Union had cast its first veto and staged a boycott of the Security Council that forewarned of the struggle ahead.

In his booklined office at the Norwegian mission, Edvard Hambro, president of the General Assembly in 1970 and son of a former League of Nations president, shook his head at the memory of those early days.

"Many people thought at the beginning that the United Nations would usher in an era of understanding," Hambro recalled. "But those of us who were taking part in the undertaking in San Francisco did not entertain any such hopes. There were already signs that the cold war had begun."

Maybe so. But hope for the future had been reflected in the words of the U.N. charter ratified by the 51 founding members on Oct. 24, 1945, which included these four prime objectives:

—"To save succeeding generations from the scourge of war . . .

—"To reaffirm faith in fundamental human rights . . .

—"To establish conditions under which justice and respect for the obligations arising from treaties and other sources of international law can be maintained . . .

—"To promote social progress and better standards of life in larger freedom. . . ."

In the years that followed, the United Nations headed off some potential wars, but it stood helpless while others were fought. It had seen treaties flouted and freedoms stifled, while it cranked out endless resolutions that often seemed aimed more at mollifying everyone than at establishing the groundwork for peace.

Charles W. Yost, who stepped down in 1971 as chief U.S. delegate, once noted that the United Nations was weak in the fields where it should have been strongest: peacekeeping and peaceful settlements.

"The United Nations has no standing armed force," Yost said, "and it is obliged to rely entirely on national contingents in time of crisis and subject to withdrawal at any moment.

"It has no decisive power to control national armaments, limit national conflict or enforce peaceful settlements. Its principal organ for the maintenance of peace, the Security Council, is often immobilized by Great Power antagonisms and the veto. . . ."

Yost acknowledged that the United Nations had chalked up some notable successes in the peacemaking field. He might have added that they were usually accomplished when the United States and the Soviet Union both wanted peace.

Cooperation between the two super-powers enabled the United Nations to stop the Suez war of 1956. When the United States put in a resolution to the Security Council calling for an immediate end to the fighting, Britain and France—who had teamed up with Israel after it invaded Suez—cast vetoes. The council was paralyzed, until the Soviet Union backed the United States in invoking the famed "Uniting for Peace" resolution that dumped the issue into the lap of the General Assembly, where there is no veto. As a result, Britain and France pulled back their forces.

The United Nations succeeded in halting the Indian-Pakistani outbreak over the princely state of Kashmir in 1965, for the simple reason that both Washington and Moscow wanted the shooting stopped and threatened to cut off economic aid to both disputants unless they complied.

Looking back over instances where big power cooperation was lacking, one saw a very different picture. Prime examples were the Middle East, where fighting went on virtually unhindered for more than two decades, and Indochina, where the United Nations failed to exert any authority.

There were other military actions where the United Nations had not distinguished itself, such as the takeover of Tibet by Red China in 1959, which brought little more than expressions of concern from the world forum, or India's invasion of the little Portuguese enclave of Goa in 1961. In that case, a Soviet veto blocked a U.N. probe of what was going on.

The Security Council had its finest hour in 1950, when it

actually succeeded in sending forth into Korea the only major army that ever fought under the U.N. banner. But that was because the Russian timing was wrong. The Kremlin made the error of staging one of its Security Council boycotts just before hostilities began, and lost the chance to veto U.N., intervention. The Russians never made that mistake again.

One reason for the fading image of the United Nations was the tendency of the U.S. government in recent years to downgrade the organization and correspondingly decrease the status of its own U.N. representatives.

Gone were the days when the U.S. mission was recognized as the most powerful embassy on earth; so powerful that John F. Kennedy once referred to it as "my other State Department."

Those were the days when the mission was headed by some of America's most influential figures. One, Henry Cabot Lodge, informed the State Department that he took orders only from the White House. Others included Adlai Stevenson, whose stature at least equalled that of Secretary of State Dean Rusk, and Arthur J. Goldberg, who had held two of the nation's top jobs and was a personal friend of two presidents. James Wadsworth, Lodge's No. 2 man, filled the main spot in 1960 while his chief was running on the Republican presidential ticket with Richard Nixon. That was the stormy period when Soviet Premier Nikita Khrushchev and a galaxy of other world leaders descended upon the United Nations. The visit was climaxed when Khrushchev angrily waved his shoe in the General Assembly.

In one bitter exchange, Wadsworth noted that Khrushchev had likened the prestigious Security Council to a spittoon and then added, "in which he (Khrushchev) has been wallowing quite happily for some years."

For once, the voluble Khrushchev had no reply.

There were also colorful figures in the 10-member U.S. delegation named by the President each year to represent him during the three-month run of the General Assembly. This group included the four ambassadors attached to the mission plus two Congressmen; a Democrat and a Republican. The four remaining delegates usually were noted public figures, ranging from labor leaders such as George Meany to former movie stars such as Shirley Temple.

At times the United States had been placed in an awkward position by impromptu performances of these guest stars; such as the volatile senator who summoned newsmen one day and proceeded to denounce a famed Asian diplomat as "floor leader for the Communist bloc."

But most of the Assembly delegates acquitted themselves well. Richard Pederson, a former member of the U.S. Mission, noted that having prominent names on the delegation sometimes paid off.

"The fact that Dr. Charles Mayo of the Mayo Clinic made the final refutation in the U.N. of the Soviet Union's charges of germ warfare in Korea was certainly instrumental in bringing that particular propaganda campaign to a halt," Pederson said.

Most diplomats agreed that the United Nations made a notable contribution in bringing colonialism to an end in most parts of the world. Had this transition from subservience to statehood been won through insurrection rather than the orderly processes of the U.N. Trusteeship Council, the result could have been a string of bloody wars around the world.

The march to freedom had one ironic result, however. The ensuing parade of fledgling states—governed by inexperienced leaders—into the U.N. fold hampered the capacity of the General Assembly to act decisively on peace keeping, human rights and other vital issues.

Senior delegates complained privately that representatives from some of these young African states allowed their emotional involvement in racial issues and their distrust of the big powers in general to influence their decisions on other questions.

There was, for example, the African influence on the Assembly's Committee of Twenty-Four, charged with keeping vigil over progress of de-colonialism. Many Americans were disturbed by the committee's preoccupation with the status of Puerto Rico, which had chosen to remain part of the American community.

And there was the U.N. Subcommission on Prevention of Discrimination and Protection of Minorities. This group received orders about three years ago from its parent organization, the Human Rights Commission, to investigate any violation of human rights. The subcommission cited conditions in Haiti and Greece, but the probe suddenly backfired. It seemed that African and Asian members brushed aside the findings and charged that the United States and its allies were trying to divert attention from the racial policies of South Africa.

Members have expressed growing concern over the influx of ministates into the United Nations over the past decade. This also alarmed Secretary-General U Thant, who noted the "phenomenon of the emergence of exceptionally small new states into the world body."

Ethiopia's Lion of Judah, Haile Selassie, (Left) at 25th Anniversary session of United Nations delegates

U.S. Ambassador Yost and Senator Jacob Javits at Commemorative session

U Thant

"It appears desirable," Thant said in a statement to the assembly, "that a distinction be made between the rights to independence and the question of full membership in the United Nations."

Thant was referring to the fact that these small states, some of them little more than overgrown villages, had the same vote as the big powers. More than 70 of these ministates had smaller populations than the City of New York. An example was the smallest member, the Maldive Islands, a chain of Indian Ocean atolls whose 98,000 inhabitants could fit into Pasadena's Rose Bowl and leave room for 2,000 more people.

Thant warned that U.N. membership might eventually be granted to Nauru, an 8¼-square-mile former Australian Trust Territory in the Pacific with 3,000 inhabitants.

United Nations experts suggested some sort of system of weighted voting, based on population, to lessen the inequity. But the western nations were not too keen on that idea, mindful of the fact that Red China with its 700 million people might get into the United Nations before long.

Many delegates soured on the whole question of peacekeeping because these costly missions brought the organization to the brink of financial disaster. This was partly because the Russians defaulted $21 million in assessments on the $150 million Middle East force which was dissolved in 1967 and $40 million on the now defunct Congo operation which ran up a total bill of $369 million. France kept up its Middle East payments, but remained $17 million in arrears on the Congo.

The United Nations kept itself afloat through some intricate financial juggling that included a short-term loan from the U.N. Children's Fund and the sale of $200 million in U.N. bonds to member nations. The United States agreed to purchase $100 million worth of the bonds, if other nations would buy up the remainder.

The grave financial predicament moved U Thant to comment: "If the U.N. does not settle its past, it may not have much of a future."

In 1964, the United States threatened to invoke Article 19 of the U.N. charter against the Soviet Union. This would deprive the Russians of their vote until they paid up any assessment more than two years in arrears. But many members became so alarmed at the prospect of a head-on collision between the two super-powers, that they decided to avoid this risk by having the assembly hold a "silent" session for several months in 1964, with no votes cast (The World in 1964, 228–232).

The United States finally yielded to the fears of the others and withdrew its invocation of Article 19.

Despite drumfire criticism, the United Nations undoubtedly made Americans more world-minded, and this was reflected in the public opinion polls. They consistently showed 80 per cent of the American people behind the world organization. While some U.S. presidents were cooler toward it than others, the United Nations continued to enjoy the support of an overwhelming majority in Congress.

Whatever were its shortcomings as keeper of the peace, the world forum could take credit for launching an effort unequalled in history to raise the living standards in the earth's backward areas.

It made this giant stride through a farflung network of specialized agencies, notably the U.N. Development Program, the World Health Organization and the Food and Agricultural Organization.

The Development Program was created in 1959, and within three years it had grown into the largest technical cooperation program in the United Nations. Under Paul Hoffman, former president of the Ford Foundation, the volume of technical assistance soared to more than $80 million by 1964, and Hoffman set himself an eventual goal of half a billion dollars.

World Health, organized in 1946, sent its workers to plague-infested jungles and teeming slums to stamp out diseases, distribute serums and develop preventatives. It virtually wiped out malaria, once the scourge of the tropical nations.

The U.N. charter has borne much of the criticism aimed at the world forum. Many diplomats felt that the United Nations had become an unmanageable mammoth, likely to collapse under its own weight unless revision of the charter was made to keep pace with the times.

One demand was for a limitation on the Security Council, to see that the right of veto held by the major powers was limited to questions of war and peace. But with the recent tendency of the Soviet Union to be more restrained in its use of the veto, this problem appeared to become less pressing.

On the lighter side, a U.N. custom that threatened to get out of hand was the U.N. cocktail party, that fertile field of quiet diplomacy that played a role in solving some of the world's knottiest problems.

During the three-month run of the assembly, nearly all of the 131 member states had felt obligated to stage up to half a dozen social get-togethers each season. They ranged from cozy "working luncheons" for 20 diplomats to mammoth cocktail receptions and buffets for 800 or more guests.

Most governments had subscribed to the theory of the late Dag Hammarskjold that much could be accomplished at these more or less relaxed affairs that could not be dealt with on the assembly floor. A U.N. cocktail party played an important part in breaking the 1948 Berlin blockade. Former U.S. delegate Philip C. Jessup was chatting with Soviet Ambassador Jacob Malik at one of these functions when the Russian envoy dropped a broad hint that the Berlin problem could be solved by private talks.

Jessup got the message, and both diplomats were soon engaged in negotiations that ended the crisis.

Thus, aware of the importance of these sessions, U.N. ambassadors and their aides could usually wind up a day of wearisome debate by making the cocktail circuit, which might mean half a dozen parties in one evening.

Parties like this cost money—up to $10 a head for a hot buffet, not to mention the liquor—and a lot more for sit-down banquets. Such expense could be a strain on the coffers of the poorer governments.

There was also the ticklish problem of protocol, especially at evening banquets hosted by the secretary-general. As far as the business of the General Assembly was concerned, the United Nations adhered to the alphabetical system for seating delegates. But at social functions, a different yardstick was used, and the degree of cordiality existing between various governments was a key factor. For instance, the protocol staff would never dream of seating an Arab delegate within shouting distance of an Israeli.

The protocol staff still winces at the memory of one fateful banquet where two Latin American delegates whose governments were far from friendly found themselves assigned to the same chair. While the two ambassadors stood glaring at each other, U.N. officials feverishly checked the seating list. A crisis was averted when a waiter noticed that there was an empty chair on the other side of the table.

The flags of 131 nations dancing in the wind before the U.N. secretariat building always reminded the visitor that here was the host headquarters of the world's largest colony of diplomats. But this often seemed more of a burden than a distinction.

The ultimate responsibility for carrying out these duties as hosts fell on the U.S. Mission. The Mission staff tried to keep constant liaison with all members of the diplomatic community, some of whom waxed bitter at times over U.S. customs and laws.

As the years passed things moved more smoothly. New York and the diplomats learned to live together. But there were still some foreign envoys who ignored American laws, then took refuge behind a cloak of diplomatic immunity.

New York police have referred bitterly to this custom as a set of ground rules showing how much a foreign envoy could get away with. The list ran the gamut from double parking to murder. The same custom, which dated back centuries, applied to American diplomats abroad, but this didn't make the New York cops feel any better.

To make sure that American police did not forget the right of immunity, the government cited a statute which said that any officer is liable to three years in jail for trying to "imprison or offer violence to . . . those with diplomatic status."

A New Jersey cop ran into this head-on several years ago when a U.N. delegate spat in his face during an argument over a traffic violation. The angry officer hauled his assailant off to the stationhouse. But before he could book the diplomat, the latter had notified his mission and a representative of the U.S. State Department appeared waving a copy of the immunity statute.

The law settled for an apology, and only got that because the by then contrite diplomat offered it.

On the other side of the coin were Americans who took advantage of foreign envoys whenever they could get away with it.

Color discrimination had long existed in New York, and some delegates felt its sting. There was, for example, the young third secretary of an African mission who said that, when he telephoned in quest of an apartment, the rental agent, apparently charmed by his French accent, said there would be no trouble finding a suitable place.

"But when I went to see her personally, she took one look at my black skin," he recalled with a bitter laugh, "and then said that the place she had in mind was already rented."

Others told of being snubbed by head waiters, insulted by taxi drivers and otherwise mistreated. Since Africans made up a large percentage of the U.N. community, it was a big problem. But it was reduced somewhat by the efforts of Mayor John V. Lindsay's able U.N. commissioner, Mrs. John L. Loeb.

Mrs. Loeb, a niece of the late Sen. Herbert H. Lehman, sought to avert trouble by arranging for a representative to call on each newly arriving family to help find lodgings, schools and recreational facilities.

Other diplomats affected by the color problem complained that some hotels and restaurants tried to fleece well-heeled foreigners. But in the final analysis few of them were anxious to move the U.N. headquarters out of New York.

Saudi Arabia's Baroody who bemoaned the public's failure to take the organization seriously, also had some sharp words not long ago about pollution, high living costs and crowded living conditions in New York.

Baroody climaxed his remarks by proposing that U.N. headquarters pack up and move to a new location in Switzerland, France, or even Cyprus.

His suggestion met with almost total silence.

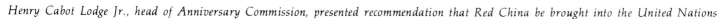

Henry Cabot Lodge Jr., head of Anniversary Commission, presented recommendation that Red China be brought into the United Nations

Victory, 16-13, Scored by Colts over Cowboys in Super Bowl Contest

W HEN THE Baltimore Colts trooped out to begin the second half of the 1971 Super Bowl, they trailed 13-6, and middle linebacker Mike Curtis was in a towering rage, reflected by a mouth moving infinitely faster than the Colts' offense.

"I was yelling at everybody," the guy they call The Animal recalled. "I used every four-letter word I could think of and some I invented. Our team was so uptight I couldn't believe it. If you can't gut it out for 60 minutes, you don't deserve to be in the game.

"Everybody was nervous, I guess. Everybody was overtense wanting to win so bad. I was screaming so much my mouth was dry and my legs were rubbery. I was that psyched up. I kept yelling and yelling, 'We can't let them beat us like the Jets did.'"

The Colts didn't let the Cowboys beat them like the Jets did. The Colts pulled from behind for a 16-13 victory and the championship of professional football in a bizarre game during which Curtis played a key role, both as a provocateur, inspiring his teammates, and, as an agent of destruction, fouling the Dallas offense.

But the 1971 Super Bowl, much as it will be remembered for Curtis' performance, likely will take its place in history as a game unlike any of the four previous Super Bowls—rapped before it was played for what it didn't have and rapped after it was played for what it did have.

What it didn't have was any of the aura surrounding the first four games—not the myth of invincibility that clung to the Green Bay Packers in Super Bowls I and II, not the cockiness of Joe Namath in Super Bowl III, not the haunting drama that underscored Len Dawson's efforts in Super Bowl IV.

It also didn't have the intense rivalry spawned by the friction between the American and National leagues in the first four games, matching this time two old-line NFL teams, Baltimore retaining that identification despite the fact it had moved into the American Conference in the first year of pro football's new realignment.

And what it did have was the bizarre—a totally unbelievable string of errors that left some question whether, of the 26 teams in professional football, these were the two who should be meeting in the sport's premier spectacle Jan. 17.

But what seemed to have been forgotten in all the prose that flowed before and after the game was that Super Bowl V was undeniably more exciting than the four that went before and, at the same time, offered three distinct heroes—an angry man (Curtis), an old man (Earl Morrall) and a young man (Jim O'Brien).

Curtis took his share of the limelight by receiving credit for jarring the ball loose from Dallas running back Duane Thomas in a play at the two-yard line and for making the interception that led to the winning field goal.

Morrall, the much-maligned goat of the Colts' stunning upset loss to Namath and the New York Jets two years before, took his share by steadying the Baltimore club after quarterback Johnny Unitas was injured.

And O'Brien, a mop-haired rookie from the University of Cincinnati, took his share as the shadows began to fall on the artificial turf of Miami's Orange Bowl Stadium by kicking the winning 32-yard field goal with five seconds remaining.

But it was Curtis who got the Colts started after a first half in which the Cowboys built their 13-6 lead on two field goals by Mike Clark and Craig Morton's seven-yard touchdown pass to Thomas.

The Colts had been able to counter only with a 75-yard touchdown strike from Unitas to John Mackey on a pass that was tipped into his hands by a Dallas defender and was hotly disputed at the time. Later in the half Unitas was injured, giving way to Morrall.

In between there were fumbles and interceptions that had the crowd alternately laughing and roaring, but always titillated by the action. Then, in the third quarter, the Cowboys pulled their forces together and moved toward another touchdown.

At the two-yard line, Morton handed off to Thomas, who cracked into the Baltimore line. Safety Jerry Logan came up quickly to make the first hit and then Curtis bounced over to help out, jarring the ball loose.

Jim Duncan pounced on it, the Colts had the ball and the Cowboys didn't have a touchdown.

"That undoubtedly was the big play of the game," Dallas coach Tom Landry said afterward. "If he scores, they have a lot of catching up to do."

As it was, the Colts needed only one touchdown to catch up, and Morrall had his opportunity to gain a measure of redemption for the loss to the Jets. He got it midway in the fourth quarter by leading Baltimore to a touchdown on Tom Nowatzke's two-yard run. O'Brien, who had missed the conversion after the first Baltimore touchdown, then tied it 13-13 with the extra point.

Each team had one opportunity to move the ball again before the series that wrapped it up for the Colts began with Dallas in control of the ball and just 1:52 remaining.

A plunge by Thomas and a holding penalty placed the Cowboys back on their own 32. Morton, trying feverishly to get Dallas into position for a field goal that would win it, then faded back to attempt a lob pass to running back Dan Reeves.

The play had worked successfully three times during the game for good yardage, but this time his pass flicked off Reeves' fingertips into the air. Curtis was there to intercept.

"On that type of play my job is to drop back and help the safeties," Curtis explained. "Then, when the play develops, I flow which ever way the quarterback moves. Morton has a

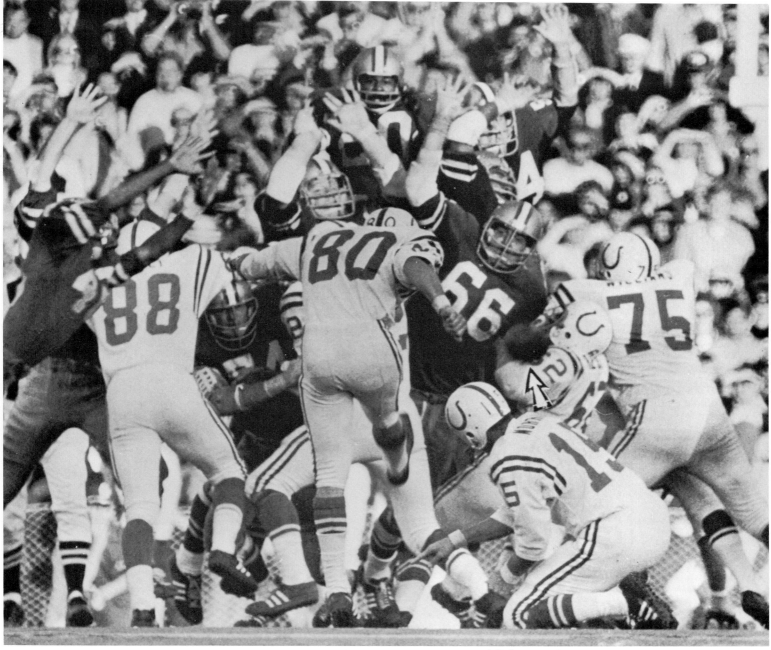

Melee: A field goal in the final second of the Super Bowl, booted by Jim O'Brien (80), earned Baltimore victory

tendency to look where he's throwing, so I was over there.

"The ball either was a hair too high for Reeves or he didn't jump a hair high enough."

That hair made the difference, and the ball fell into Curtis' hands.

"If I had dropped it," Curtis says, "I would have been the goat. I grabbed that ball so hard I almost squeezed the air out of it."

Curtis got the ball on the 41, and his first inclination, remembering the bizarre number of fumbles that had already occurred during the game, was to protect against losing the ball.

"I felt maybe I should just fall on the ground so I wouldn't fumble it away," Curtis recalled.

But instinct prevailed, and Curtis lumbered 13 yards to the Dallas 28. Then Morrall took over, calm, possessed, with 15 years' experience and the haunting specter of the Super Bowl defeat behind him.

His instructions from Coach Don McCafferty carefully under-

stood, Morrall went to the huddle with just under one minute remaining. He had been told to disdain any attempt at scoring a touchdown and instead merely position the ball for a field goal try while running down the clock so Dallas would have no chance to retaliate.

So Morrall sent Norm Bulaich into the middle of the Cowboys' line. The play gained one yard and wiped out 29 seconds. On second down, Morrall again handed to Bulaich. This time the play gained two yards but, more important, it wiped out another 21 seconds.

Just nine seconds remained as the Colts called time out. O'Brien trotted onto the field and swung his leg in a practice arc while Morrall knelt for the snap from center at the 32-yard line. The ball was snapped, placed down by Morrall, kicked by O'Brien and Baltimore had a 16–13 victory.

There never had been a more dramatic ending to a Super Bowl—all four previous games having been decided well before the game ended. This one took 59 minutes and 55 seconds to decide.

Many kids once had to hide such magazines as these

Nostalgia Victims Found New Life in Bygone Eras

Craving for atmosphere of the past created a fresh market for music, books, plays, other things popular years ago

GRANDMA, a tear or two glistening in her wrinkles, sat in her bedroom rocker flipping through the pages of *Those Were the Good Old Days.* In the living room Dad listened dreamily to Tommy Dorsey's melodies, re-recorded for up-to-date stereo systems. Mom and a neighbor's wife were on their way home from the 1970–71 revival of *No, No, Nanette,* a 1925 musical, in a New York theater.

Nostalgia was their hang-up. Even Junior caught the fever: he plastered the walls of his room with posters of Humphrey Bogart, W. C. Fields and a dozen other old-time stars.

This craving for the atmosphere of the past wasn't exactly new, but by 1971 it had created a burgeoning commercial appeal. For publishers, clothiers, movie houses, record companies and others it represented incomes of thousands of dollars.

Original copies of Superman comic books, published in 1938, were priced up to $400. Nineteenth century carvings of wooden cigarstore Indians drew $2,000 to $5,000 apiece. Almost everywhere collectors were finding a market for old maps, games, campaign buttons and the toys of children who had grown old. Even conventions were held for buffs fascinated by antique automobiles or such Disney creations as Mickey Mouse, Minnie Mouse and Donald Duck.

Most nostalgia sufferers simply sought comfort in sights, sounds, things—even odors—that recalled a bygone era. In a tumultuous age it appeared they wanted to get away from drugs, crime, the problems in the cities, the riots on campuses. Many middle-aged Americans felt that life was moving too fast, that their roots had been destroyed.

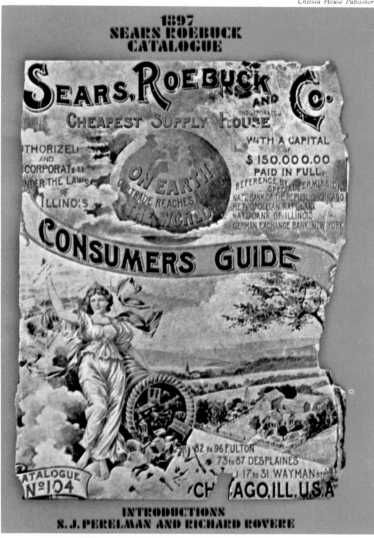

Seventy-four years ago—the Sears Roebuck catalogue

Fit for a princess

Among the discoverers of nostalgia as a commercial venture was the publishing firm Chelsea House. In 1968 it had issued a facsimile edition of the 1897 Sears Roebuck catalogue. Editor Harold Steinburg predicted the book would be bought mainly by libraries, as a reference volume. But 200,000 copies of the $14.95 facsimile were sold in a matter of months. Sears itself bought 10,000 copies as gifts and also sold the book through its catalogue.

To describe the firm's profusion of products, ranging from foot scrapers to autoharps, Chelsea House used the original copy that Richard Sears had written in 1897. His style, hard-sell and often humorous, headed such offerings as men's furnishings: "Shiftless he who shirtless goes."

Thereafter Chelsea and other publishing houses came out with other catalogues reflecting the years 1902, 1903, 1908, and 1927. They also offered such cartoon books as *The Collected Works of Buck Rogers* and *Arf, (The Life and Hard Times of Little Orphan Annie, 1935–1945)*. Steinburg said he published *The Celebrated Cases of Dick Tracy* because "he is part of the American consciousness: the fearless, tough cop that we seemed to have lost sight of."

Such reminiscent reading matter as *The Great Radio Comedians,* and *Whatever Became Of?* was accompanied by a somewhat bizarre and colorful collection of 50 full-length stories from the pulp magazines, edited by Tony Goodstone, also published by Chelsea House. The pulps originated around the turn of the

century and got their name from the type of coarse paper on which they were printed. The stories themselves dealt with adventure, mystery, science fiction and sex. However, the sex stories that a 16-year-old boy hid under the covers in the 1920s were nothing like those of 1971. Rather than printing detailed accounts of nudity and sexual acts, the pulps chose fiction that was more titillating and suggestive than it was realistic. For example:

"Through the gauzy thinness of the pajamas, Travis Bent could see the girl's heaving, panting breasts, twin ripe half-melons of cream-white flesh that strained at the pajama jacket like swelling mounds of enchantment."

The pulp magazines, the cartoons, the catalogues became a form of art in 1971, said Steinburg. "The value of pulling these things back is that what is an artifact in one period is an art form in another."

Many intellectuals agreed that people for generations had collected literary artifacts. John Cawelti, University of Chicago professor, put it this way: "People who would have called these things trash are the people collecting them now. But this is because this generation has grown up with this material, and they are seeking an identity with the past in a search to find themselves."

Many said they yearned for the past because, in retrospect, it seemed much less complex than modern times. What they seemed to need most was entertainment, not lectures on or visible examples of social injustice. They remembered the films of the 1930s featuring Bogart or Greta Garbo. They wanted films about heroes who flew their missions, saved lives and died for truth or love of country. They wanted to hear, and hum along with, songs like *Stardust* or to delight in the tap dancing of Bill Robinson. And they wanted once again to leave a theater romantically persuaded that man and woman found happiness in love for one another. And television did help Garbo and Bogart fans by showing limitless numbers of old movies.

Broadway resurrected for them *No, No, Nanette.* In its first few days it grossed $35,000. Its chorus of smiling girls and boys and its delightful songs featured 60-year-old Ruby Keeler, the song-

Bobby Van, Helen Gallagher in revival of No, No, Nanette

and-dance girl of the 1920s who had retired in 1929. She danced as if she had never left the stage. Tapping along with the number *I Want to be Happy*, the audience whispered its pleasure; when *Tea for Two* was sung in its old lulling and romantic fashion, everyone sighed. Even Busby Berkeley, the dance director of Miss Keeler's generation, made a comeback.

During intermission males of the audience recalled the days when they could go to a show and two or three nightclubs for as little as $10. But in 1971 scalpers were getting $50 for a pair of tickets to the revival of *No, No, Nanette*.

How did the young react to all of this looking backward? Largely with enthusiasm.

One woman said her daughter liked *No, No, Nanette,* then added: "The funny thing was that she thought the costuming was contemporary, but it's exactly what my mother used to wear."

When the midi and the maxi came out many fashion critics considered them a dirty trick the industry was playing on women. But was it only a way to make money or a strong desire for the past? Italian designer Valentino created his 1971 fashions in the mode of the Myrna Loy and Rita Hayworth look. He dressed his models in shirtdresses with waistcoats over them, or long torso dresses with wide, wide skirts that hugged the hips, with toppers and big swagger hats. All of this was displayed with the music of Tommy Dorsey and Glenn Miller in the background.

Teenagers went for both mini and maxi in a big way, but they soon fell for grandma's kind of style as well. Long granny dresses with ruffles, and steel-rim glasses, became a popular attire among girls of 20.

Many students took a serious interest in the past by examining its life styles through a course called popular culture. "By studying the big band era, or the movies made during the wars," said Russell Nye of Michigan State University, "we are able to make comparisons between the life styles of then and now. This study is good in another way because it teaches students something about history even if it's through the back door."

There were, however, the young and the hip that took nostalgia as a whim. Many of them spoofed the establishment by flaunting things of the past. Mickey Mouse, created during the Depression possibly as a symbol of optimism, came alive again when the hippies wore watches with the cartoon inscribed on the face.

The hippie culture was cited by some as epitomizing a preoccupation with the past. Professor Marshall Fishwick of Lincoln University said: "The hippies and the youth culture have not brought us anything new, but they have taken us back in time. They are a lot like the 1850 German romantics. They are disgusted with modern technology, and by going back in time they can deny themselves responsibility. They talk a great deal about Thoreau and Walden's Pond. Woodstock (the festival) in a way was supposed to be Walden's Pond, but the thing is that when they got there 3,000 people were there too, and these are the contemporary realities we have to deal with."

The nostalgia epidemic also became part of "camp" philosophy. Things often were sought because they were so banal or dated that they had become intrinsically entertaining. Posters with the face of Humphrey Bogart hung in college dorms all over the country. Young men greeted their girl friends with "my little chickadee" in the inimitable Fields fashion. Even merchants considered it "camp" to use old fashioned advertisements; Arrow, for example, sold its 1970 shirts with 1906 ads. Pan American Airways and the car renting Hertz Corp., used typefaces of the 20s and sepia toned photo prints.

The American portrait in 1971 was not always illustrated with modern technology, hard fast rock music, abstract art and progressive films. Merv Griffin and Johnny Carson on a number of occasions brought back the music of the swinging band era. Even clubs were created for nostalgia enthusiasts. The Nostalgia Book Club offered such works as *The Good Old Days* for its 12,000 members. And the Longines Symphonette Society sold records of earlier days through television commercials, with Jim Ameche giving the pitch.

For Halloween, it was estimated, 300 radio stations repeated the old Orson Welles narration of the *War of the Worlds,* the production that panicked most of its listeners into thinking the world was at an end. Some radio stations also replayed the old tapes from famous radio shows that made people laugh, cry and shiver with fright in the 20s.

Memories which were given monetary value seemed no longer memories to some and yet the nostalgia sufferers in this day and age excused the commercialization of it. To most of these nostalgic readers, listeners and collectors, the comfort and security of a memory from the past—whether free or paid for—was better than no comfort at all.

In Fort Collins, Colo., slates came back to fourth grade

SOCCER CROWD PANIC KILLED 66

Internationally, soccer had become more popular than any other sport. In the Americas to the south, in the British Isles and many other nations its fans were passionately—and often violently—enthusiastic. Unlike football in the United States, a soccer match sometimes ended in tragedy; this was not just a game but often a symbol of victory for avid fans among whom religious, political or racial differences were strongly evident.

For years the annual game between the Celtics and the Rangers in Glasgow, Scotland had been marred by religious strife. The Roman Catholics supported the Celtics, the Protestants the Rangers. A hundred arrests might be made during a game. In 1971, however, it was different. By the last quarter of the Jan. 2 match officials had reported only two or three incidents of violence in the crowd of 80,000 spectators. But one of the worst disasters in sports history came at the end of the game.

Sixty-six persons suffocated or were trampled to death and 200 others were injured when a steel barrier collapsed on the Ranger side of the stadium at Ibrox. With the score 0–0, minutes before the game ended, fans had started to leave the stadium. Suddenly the Celtics scored a goal in the last minute and the Rangers retaliated immediately. Hearing the crowd cheering, some Ranger fans who had already left the stadium tried to return on the stairway of exit 13, only to be met by departing fans. The result: the Ranger fans were engulfed by the others, the steel barrier gave way and suddenly hundreds were falling down 30 feet of stairway.

"I was leaving the match when I heard shouting and screaming," said a policeman at the scene. "When I looked back I saw a terrible sight—a pile of bodies about 10 feet high, all laid the same way with their faces toward us.

"The injuries of some of the people who had been crushed right under the barrier were terrible. We came away with our boots, socks and the bottoms of our trousers soaked in blood."

The police managed to push back 200 or 300 people and save them from dying. "I was about to fall when a policeman grabbed me and pulled me free, He saved my life," said a 14-year-old boy who identified himself as John. "The more you tried to move, the more you were crushed. I couldn't breathe at all. A fellow across from me shouted, 'I'm dying!' I saw him fall."

Of the 66 killed all were men and boys except one girl, 19-year-old Margaret Ferguson, who friends said was a Ranger fan. At Christmas she had made a doll for the baby daughter of Colin Stein, the Rangers' forward star, and had personally delivered it to his home.

Great Britain's worst previous soccer disaster occurred at Bolton, England in 1946. A barrier collapsed there too, and 33 died. More than 500 were injured. But the worst tragedy in the history of soccer occurred in Peru on May 24, 1964 (*The World in 1964, 93–95*).

Teams from Argentina and Peru were involved in an Olympic qualifying match. The crowd, angered by a disallowed goal, surged out of the seats, smashed and set fire to buildings. More than 300 died and 500 were injured.

Damaged barriers where 66 soccer fans perished in Glasgow's Ibrox Stadium

New York City's patrolmen ended a six-day wildcat wage strike after delegates for the Patrolmen's Benevolent Association voted 229–112 to go back to work. But the decision brought angry jeers from dissidents who wanted to keep the walkout going.

Workers siphoned off oil from slick that fouled up San Francisco Bay after two tankers collided in fog and one spilled more than half a million gallons of the black, sticky fluid into the water. Cleanup teams put out 4,000 bales of hay to soak up oil along the shore, and employed 10 tugs, 25 charter boats, seven oil-skimming barges, 30 vacuum trucks, 13 tank trucks and 20 dump trucks.

Cruise ship Antilles *burned in Caribbean but all 350 passengers were saved*

NO ONE LOST WHEN SHIP BURNED

Few of the 350 passengers aboard the *Antilles* paid much attention to the quickening wind or the rising waves, as the big French Line cruise ship ploughed through the Caribbean off the Grenadines.

No one seemed particularly worried when the ship crunched against a reef at about 4:20 p.m. Jan. 8. In fact, no one knew just what had happened. Someone said the ship had strayed from the regular lanes. Another said she was lying in 15 feet of water, ringed by jagged rocks.

But apparently few persons above deck were aware that the impact had torn a great hole in the hull of their pleasure vessel and touched off a fire that quickly engulfed the boiler room. The men in the engine room tried to put out the spreading blaze, but it was no use.

At about 5 p.m., Capt. Raymond Kerverdo gave the order to abandon ship. Within minutes his 340 crewmen had launched 16 of the *Antilles'* lifeboats and had tossed 13 liferafts overboard.

Officers feared that the abandon-ship order would touch off a panic, but everyone stayed calm, both passengers and crew.

Christiane Simon, of Caen, France, a freckle-faced young blonde who ran the ship's boutique, calmly tucked her money in the pocket of her blue jeans. But she retrieved nothing else before

she climbed into one of the lurching lifeboats. Most of the passengers also left their belongings behind.

Christiane said later that she had been convinced that this was only a precautionary measure and that she and the others would be back aboard ship by morning.

This optimism soon vanished, however. Looking back at the *Antilles,* the passengers saw the flames surge skyward as the ship went into her death throes.

Threading their way through towering waves, the lifeboats made it to the beach of Mustique, a tiny privately-owned island popular among members of the international set.

What could have been a disaster had been averted by the orderly evacuation, and all were saved.

"It was amazing," said Christiane. "The passengers were so noisy and excited all the time. But when we were told to leave the ship, everybody assembled quietly in their life jackets."

It might have been a different story. One sailor said that if the *Antilles* had not been caught on a reef, it would have gone down like a rock.

Meanwhile, the luxury liner *Queen Elizabeth II,* which had received the *Antilles'* distress call, was pounding toward the scene. Passengers and

officers aboard the vessel got a shock when they arrived and saw the *Antilles* ablaze and empty liferafts floating about the wreckage. They began a search, but found no one in the sea. They were all safely ashore on Mustique and the neighboring island of Bequia.

HASHISH SMUGGLERS SENTENCED

A three-judge panel in the Cretan court at Candia sentenced five Americans to a total of 49 years and fined them $90,000 after testimony that they planned to smuggle 1,426 pounds of hashish by plane from Lebanon to the United States.

Lebanese and Greek police arrested them last Aug. 29 when they landed on the island of Crete to refuel after a spectacular chase by air across the Mediterranean (*The World in 1970, 163*).

Prison terms of 10 years each were given John R. Moore, 51, the pilot, of Sacramento, Calif.; Kenneth H. Connell, 28, San Francisco; Robert Black, 29, and Philip Amos, 30, the co-pilot, of Sacramento. David Mantell, 30, of San Francisco was given 9 years.

SEN. RUSSELL TAKEN BY DEATH

When Sen. Richard B. Russell was a boy, his father, Chief Justice Richard B. Russell Sr., of Georgia, told him: "Son, marry your work if you are going into a public career." Russell died Jan. 21 at 73. As a bachelor he had heeded his father's words and had served more than half his life as one of the most respected men in the Senate.

President Nixon, in a eulogy, characterized Russell—a Democrat—as "a rare blend of courage, character, vision and ability that moved him indisputably into the ranks of those giants who have served in the United States Senate."

Mike Mansfield, Democratic leader of the Senate, said that if Russell had been from another part of the country, he would have become a president.

Russell entered the Georgia legislature at 23 and became the state's youngest governor at 33 before moving on to the United States Senate. Ultimately he was recognized as one of the most powerful men in Congress.

Although he was idolized by his own people and respected by the North and the West, advisers considered it implausible for Russell, as a Southerner, to seek the presidency. Nonetheless, he sought the Democratic nomination in 1952.

A top leader in the party told him, "Dick, I would support you if I could, but we just can't put a Southerner on top of this ticket." He lost to Adlai E. Stevenson and thereafter regarded himself as a victim of sectional prejudice. But he remained the master of parliamentary procedure and a formidable debater. A senator's senator, he spent his evenings at home studying Senate

The dean: Sen. Richard Russell

rules. He was chosen president pro tem of the Senate, chairman of the Armed Services Committee and chairman of the military expenditures subcommittee of the Senate Appropriations Committee. He served the Armed Services Committee for 15 years, resigning in 1969 to head the Appropriations Committee, a post he held until

he died. One of the leading congressional advocates of a strong military stance, Russell supported United States intervention in Korea and the Dominican Republic, and he urged President Kennedy to invade Cuba during the 1962 missile crisis.

"If we had struck and struck hard in Cuba I don't believe we would have had this situation in Vietnam," Russell once said. He termed Vietnam "one of the great tragedies of our history," and told the Eisenhower administration that it would rue the day it sent troops into Southeast Asia.

Offered the role of the Senate Democratic Leadership in 1953 he turned it down and supported Lyndon Baines Johnson for the post. Russell said, "I'm more concerned with my own thinking than with the Democratic party nationally."

His own thinking included a deep involvement with the fast fading Old South. He engineered the filibusters against anti-lynching legis-. lation in 1935 and later against civil rights as he grew increasingly critical of those he called the "South haters." The South, he insisted, had become a victim of conscious hate.

Despite his strong stand on racial issues, Russell won the respect of those who sometimes opposed him. "There have been times when we have looked at the issues in a different light," said Senator Edward Kennedy. "But everyone who has come to the Senate has to realize Senator Russell established a code of conduct that captured the essence of what this Senate is. He has given this body a tradition and tone that will continue for many years."

GUINEA CONDEMNED 92 TO DEATH

"You have the enemy in your hands. Crush the vermin! Traitors to the gallows!" And so be it, decided members of the National Assembly of African Guinea when they had considered the words of Ismael Toure, brother of President Sekou Toure.

On Jan. 24 the assembly condemned 92 persons to death by hanging. Sixty-six others were sentenced to hard labor for life, among them the Most Rev. Raymond-Marie Tchidimbo, Catholic Archbishop of Conakry, two West Germans, three Frenchmen and ten Lebanese. All had been tried for involvement in the abortive invasion of Guinea Nov. 22, 1970.

The attempted invasion apparently was the work of 300 Guinean exiles, backed by Portugal. The United Nations Security Council on Dec. 8 endorsed a United Nations mission which found the Portuguese had provided land and sea support.

President Toure ordered the executions despite appeals for clemency from the Vatican and Bonn, West Germany.

It was not certain how many were actually carried out. Guinea did confirm the hanging of five top government officials from a bridge on the main street of the capital. The Conakry radio described the executions as "a carnival," and said the people spat on the convicts and stoned their bodies.

Much of the rest of the world reacted to the sentences and executions with horror. Pope Paul VI maintained the Archbishop's innocence and a Vatican editorial said the "confessions of the

accused were heard by the judges through means of tape recorders. No defense, no foreign observers were admitted." The pontiff criticised the executions as a "blind and wicked vendetta in a collective explosion of hate and cruelty."

President Toure responded by saying that 500 people were victims of the aggressors and that the people had decided to provide punishment "in conformity with the demands of national independence and social peace."

SONNY LISTON FOUND DEAD

Charles (Sonny) Liston was an ex-convict who slugged his way to the world heavyweight boxing championship. Liston, one of 25 children, became a professional boxer in 1953 and won 33 of 34 battles before knocking out Floyd Patterson in 1962 to win the heavyweight title.

But on Feb. 25, 1964, he lost the crown to Cassius Clay when he was unable to answer the bell for the seventh round. He tried to regain the title in 1965, but Clay knocked him out after 1 minute 42 seconds of the first round.

At 18 Liston was serving time for robbery. His birth date was listed as May 8, 1932, but Ring Magazine always refused to verify any date.

His body was found in his Las Vegas, Nev., home Jan. 5 by his wife, but there were estimates Liston had been dead about a week.

Ex-champ "Sonny" Liston found dead in home

President Nixon, beginning his third year in office, delivered his State of the Union address in Washington Jan. 22, before Congress. He outlined proposals for a $16 million annual sharing of federal revenues with local and state governments and made known his plans for drastic revision of cabinet departments.

HOT PANTS with a male motif were featured in this outfit presented by Rome's Centinaro House. Model wore the hotpants with a man's jacket, black shirt and yellow scarf. The pants and jacket were of Indian Madras cotton.

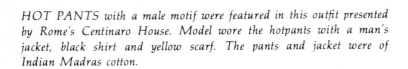

Digging out of the wreckage ⟶

February

Rescue workers dug and probed far into the night looking for quake victims

64 Died, 400,000 Shaken by Quake in Los Angeles

Loss reached hundreds of millions of dollars when freeways collapsed; 24,000 houses were damaged in a few seconds

warning. When it hit there was nothing human beings could do to fight it. And then aftershocks kept the ground in turmoil. These were weaker than the original, but each time one occurred there was no way of knowing that. Nearly two months after the main shock of the heavy earthquake in the Los Angeles area on Feb. 9, 1971, an aftershock of more than ordinary intensity smashed windows and dumped foodstuffs in an almost hopeless jumble on the floors of supermarkets and seriously damaged about 25 houses in the same area hardest hit by the far more severe main shock. It was normal that these follow-up jolts originated in the vicinity of the first and strongest shock.

Most earthquakes in the United States had taken place along the Pacific Ocean, mainly in California and Alaska. But in the past 100 years, according to U.S. government statistics, there had been quake damage and deaths in eight states and Puerto Rico. The death toll, including the Feb. 9 temblor in the Los Angeles area, was: California 999; Hawaii 234; Alaska 121; Puerto Rico 116; South Carolina 60; Montana 32; Washington 15; Oregon 4 and Utah 2. The South Carolina quake centered in Charleston in 1886. It was felt for a radius of 1,000 miles.

There was no large area of the earth that was permanently and entirely free of earthquakes. Aside from the Pacific belt, the U.S. seismic belts—that is, areas where earthquakes occurred and recurred—were listed by seismologists as the St. Lawrence River valley and the Appalachian states of east-central America.

In the five years prior to Feb. 9 no one in this country had died in an earthquake. That day, at 6 a.m., devastation struck in the Los Angeles area. In the initial and major shock the ground shuddered for only seconds. Yet 64 persons died. The federal government later said that, measured in terms of money spent for restoration and cleanup, it was the nation's greatest natural disaster. The total loss in public and private property was estimated at $600 million, but there was no official figure. Likewise unofficially estimated were injuries: at least 1,000. Experts calculated that 400,000 persons were subjected to a very strong shaking and another two million felt a moderate shaking. The U.S. government reported $437 million in grants and loans toward assisting the restoration of public property. The previous high was $253 million for a five-state area damaged by hurricane Camille on the Gulf Coast (*The World in 1969,* 156–161).

Hardest hit by the 1971 quake was the San Fernando Valley, a sun-kissed, semi-tropical land where families with backyard swimming pools were as common as two-car families in the rest of the nation.

Streets buckled. Water mains broke. Sewers were knocked out. Chimneys toppled. Roofs collapsed. More than 24,000 homes suffered damage; more than 1,000 had to be vacated because of major damage. So did about 100 school buildings. Just about everybody reported lamps knocked off tables and china broken.

Worried that a quake-damaged dam might collapse, the city ordered 80,000 residents from their homes for several days until the reservoir could be drained. Other thousands, afraid to return to their homes as aftershock followed aftershock, camped out in parks or on their lawns in tents. The Red Cross estimated 10,000 used its food and rest facilities.

Of the 64 dead, 45 were killed in the collapse of a 47-year-old Veterans Administration hospital at Sylmar, in the San Fernando Valley. Nine were heart attack victims. The others died under falling debris.

Perhaps most shocking was the death of two men killed when a freeway overpass collapsed on their truck as they drove to work. In Los Angeles public transportation was limited, and

T o live in California was to live with earthquakes. Some days there would be as many as 30, most of them so minute they could be detected only with delicate instruments. Perhaps one in 10,000 caused noticeable damage. But the potential for instant disaster always was present.

Generally, residents of the nation's most heavily populated state were aware of earth movement through little things. It was difficult at times to keep pictures hanging straight for more than a day. Small cracks appeared overnight in walls or in a concrete patio.

The federal government kept a record of quakes strong enough to be felt in the United States without instruments. There were 238 in 1970—130 of them in California.

On an average, a tornado in the Midwest or a hurricane on the East or Gulf coast was more deadly and caused more damage. There was this major difference: Unlike floods, forest fires or even tornadoes, an earthquake struck without the slightest

A tow truck hauling away wreckage of a truck smashed when the overpass in the background collapsed

the 65-mile-an-hour freeways and the family auto were virtually the only ways to get anywhere.

Damage to federal highways, streets and bridges exceeded $22 million and the state highway department listed its loss at $15 million. Most of this damage was to the freeway system, much of it part of the Interstate network.

Frank Carbonara, 64, lay under earthquake rubble for 58 hours at the veterans hospital. He was found when workmen lifted a concrete slab from debris. Rescue workers hadn't heard his cries for help and had assumed no one else was alive in the rubble.

Carbonara, treated for a broken hand, found he had lost 20 pounds. He had been preparing to clean a stove and had bent over a sink for some water when the quake came.

"I went right under the sink. That's what saved me," he said. "There was no light; everything was black. I slept on stones and dirt. I ate stones and dirt."

Said Dale Keith, 37, a patient on the second floor: "The first thing I saw was the nightstand roll over to the bed. By the time it hit the bed the roof hit it. That's what saved me from being crushed."

Chris Scott, 42, another patient on the second floor, said, "I heard a bump and felt like I was flying. The next thing I knew I was on the ground floor."

Scott and Keith were dug out with bruises only.

* * * *

When the Spanish explorers discovered California the San Fernando Valley was mainly desert. In the intervening years piped-in water enabled more than a million people to make

their homes there. It became a vast "bedroom area," mainly within Los Angeles but including a handful of independent cities.

The quake's epicenter was in Soledad Canyon, about 28 miles from downtown Los Angeles. Hardest hit were the 18,500 living in Sylmar, the 18,000 in the city of San Fernando, 10,000 in the Sunland-Tujunga area and 8,500 in the Newhall-Saugus area across the San Gabriel Mountains in an adjoining valley. Most damage was in a 40-square-mile area 15 miles long and two to three miles wide in the San Fernando Valley. Principal damage in the rest of Los Angeles involved buildings erected 40 years earlier, or older.

In the city of San Fernando, some residents were without water and sewage facilities for nine days until temporary lines could be installed. They received their water from 37 water trucks, carrying it home in any available type of container.

As quakes are rated on the universally used Richter scale, it wasn't a major one—registering 6.6. Some of the aftershocks were above 5.0. The scale, devised a quarter-century ago by Dr. Charles Richter, famed seismologist at California Institute of Technology in Pasadena, measured the release of energy, not damage. Thus a huge quake in a wasteland might do no harm; a smaller one in a populous area could cause great destruction.

The Richter Scale is logarithmic, so the energy rises rapidly with each higher number.

For example, a rating of 4, relatively small, indicates a release of 3,750 horsepower-hours of energy. A rating of 5 is 100 times as strong, and 6 is 100 times stronger than 5—or 10,000 times as much energy released as 4.

The greatest shock in modern times was the 8.6 quake in Assam

What the quake did to a Southern California freeway overpass

Scene of devastation after quake hit

in 1959. It was in an isolated area and caused little damage. The Feb. 9 quake in the Los Angeles area rated 6.6.

The destructive Alaska quake of March 7, 1964, was rated at 8.4. The San Francisco quake of 1906, recalculated long after the event, was 8.25. It was the worst in U.S. history, killing 700.

In most quakes a vertical crack, or fault, slipped, causing one side of the crack to move horizontally relative to another. California was laced from one end to the other with such faults. It was estimated that 90 per cent of U.S. quakes originated in this fault system.

The Feb. 9 quake differed from the usual in that it was of the thrust-fault type, with vertical movement as well as horizontal. Scientists said a piece of the earth's crust lying 10 miles below the surface suddenly slipped, causing a rupture in the surface and setting off an intense shaking. This shaking was due to (1) the type of quake, which localized its intensity in a relatively narrow area; (2) the alluvial soil in those valleys which did not provide a "bed-rock" foundation.

The slippage of the earth crust caused the San Gabriel Mountains—rimming the San Fernando Valley section hardest hit—to move upward three feet and southward another three feet. Experts said this was a normal part of the earth's mountain-building process.

Scientists could only guess as to what caused the earth crust to move Feb. 9 or what effect this had on California's major fault, the San Andreas, passing 20 miles to the east.

Over the years seismologists learned that the San Andreas was a great crack in the earth's surface 650 miles long, running north-south, from which most of the lesser California faults radiated. For eons the huge block of geography on the western side of the San Andreas had been creeping inexorably northward at a pace of about two inches a year. At some places along the faultline the movement would be only an inch, at others a half inch. Along the portion east of Los Angeles, however, there had been no movement at all for a century—the opposing faces of the earth pushed together too tightly to allow the earth to creep along and ease its strain.

Modern scientists knew such "frozen" sections could not resist more than 15 or 20 feet of the earth movement before they snapped forward, violently, to catch up with the rest of the great moving mass. When this happened there was a major temblor. Such a "snap" on the San Andreas caused the 1906 San Francisco quake.

When this happened in 1857 in Southern California, some 400 miles to the south, the extended Los Angeles area had few residents. By 1971 there were more than seven million in the city and environs.

Fear of this inevitable "great quake" caused some residents to move from California over the years, despite the lure of its bountiful sunshine and freedom from ice and snow. This was intensified to some extent after the Feb. 9 quake. Some went to specially set up discussion classes designed to calm their fears. But others, numbered in the millions, kept their optimistic, casual attitude toward the great forces of nature. After all, didn't more people lose their lives in automobile accidents in Los Angeles alone each year than those who died in ALL of California earthquakes?

The Feb. 9 quake was a scientific bonanza to researchers seeking to predict, prevent or lessen damage from earthquakes. No other ever was so well measured by batteries of instruments. Part of the data never was available before. It came from earthquake-sensing devices placed in Los Angeles skyscrapers to measure building motion induced by quakes.

"This is by far the most complete coverage ever obtained of an earthquake," said Dr. Donald E. Hudson, professor of earthquake engineering at Cal Tech, where some of the world's pioneering research on quakes was conducted. "Instruments were closer to the real center than ever before," he said.

"All the information on ground shaking that we obtained from these instruments will enable us to see how the designs of future buildings should be made," said Dr. George W. Housner, professor of engineering at Cal Tech. "By examining the buildings that survived, both the damaged and undamaged, we will have a greater understanding of the behavior of buildings under strong shaking."

The primary question was how and why elastic forces built up between two sections of earth and then suddenly were relieved, sending waves of energy through the crust strong enough to shake down buildings. If this could be determined, it might be possible to predict earthquakes as hurricanes and tornadoes have been predicted. By using data gathered from past quakes and field studies with sensitive measuring instruments, scientists learned they could say where an earthquake was likely. But not when.

* * * *

Next to the San Francisco quake of 1906, the most devastating in California was in Long Beach in 1933. That cost 120 lives. It also brought about wide revision of building codes. For the first time standards required new buildings to withstand lateral forces induced by earth motion.

No one knew how many buildings constructed before then —thousands of them still standing—were designed to bear only the vertical load of the building, not to survive the back-and-forth motion acceleration of a quake. Housner estimated there were 40,000 in Los Angeles County alone.

"We lucked out in Los Angeles this time because the tremor struck in early morning when most people were home," said Karl V. Steinbrugge, a University of California professor of structural design and head of an 11-member federal task force on earthquake safety.

The veterans hospital where most Los Angeles victims died was built in 1924. But two miles from it, the $23.5 million, 850-bed Olive View Medical Center, built to be earthquake-resistant and completed just a few months before, was wrecked. Both were in the foothills about four miles from the quake's epicenter.

The six-story, concrete, steel and glass Olive View facility didn't crumble. But, during the shaking, supporting columns on the ground floor failed, causing the rest of the building to list and settle. A recreation wing tipped on its side. One man died at Olive View, an ambulance driver crushed by a slab of concrete.

"The buildings were properly designed," said William Jensen, assistant chief deputy Los Angeles County engineer. "We've checked it out closely. It was built in compliance with county and earthquake-resistance standards."

No other large buildings were destroyed.

Cal Tech's Housner and Hudson, in a report on engineering aspects of the quake, said the Feb. 9 quake was of immense engineering significance because it was centered on the edge of a metropolitan area and involved such a variety of structures.

"The lesson is clear that certain buildings should be designed to be stronger than the minimum requirements of the building code," the report said.

Housner said the code "was indeed all right, at least for this type of earthquake." What about a larger one? "There would be more buildings that would end up in the shape of Olive View." Proposals to strengthen the building codes began immediately at various governmental levels.

As part of the stiffening of codes after the 1933 quake, a ban was imposed on any building above 13 stories in Los Angeles. The limit was lifted in 1959 and the city thereafter acquired several high-rise structures, some exceeding 50 stories. All came through the Feb. 9 temblor. Nearly all were built after designers put models through simulated stresses worked out with computer-analysis of quakes.

The architectural firm of Albert C. Martin and Associates pioneered in the design of Los Angeles skyscrapers to resist earthquakes. J. Edward Martin, a partner in the firm, said that only in the last few years breakthroughs were made in understanding ground motions of earthquakes and their effect on buildings.

"This is too recent to be reflected in the building codes, but it will," he said. "A code is a set of minimum standards by which the design and conduct of the builder should be mea-sured. Any good architect or structural engineer can improve on it in building a structure."

Among those who didn't think much of skyscrapers in earth-quake country was Richter, the world-famed seismologist. He said he didn't believe that such buildings would necessarily fall but that occupants on higher levels would be whipped about and endangered by toppling furniture.

He identified "old and poorly constructed commercial and public buildings, including schools," as California's principal earthquake danger, and estimated that 90 per cent of the loss of life and more than half of the property loss in earthquakes "is unnecessary and preventable." His solution: "By enforced inspection of privately owned as well as public buildings, fol-lowed by mandatory rebuilding or demolition when found un-safe, the state could remove most of the earthquake risk in California."

He also had this advice for individuals: "Just as some people have a fixed fear of cats, others have an excessive and un-reasonable fear of earthquakes. They should not try to live in California."

A five-story wing of Olive View Sanitarium lay on its side as a patient was removed from the area after the earthquake

Apollo 14 astronaut team (left to right): Edgar Mitchell, Alan Shepard Jr., and Stuart Roosa

Successful Apollo 14 Moon Trip Makes Up for Aborted Prior Flight

WHEN THE three Apollo 14 astronauts climbed aboard their spaceship atop a Saturn 5 rocket, they knew much was riding on their mission, perhaps the entire future of the space program. Fresh in the memories of everyone was the near-disaster of Apollo 13 nine months earlier. Another failure could deal a severe setback to U.S. manned space flight.

But astronauts once again were ready to challenge the moon —after a delay of several months while design changes were made in the spaceship to prevent a recurrence of the oxygen tank explosion that aborted Apollo 13 near the moon *(The World in 1970, 61–68)*.

Flying the critical Apollo 14 mission were Navy Capt. Alan Bartlett Shepard Jr., 47, who had been the nation's first space-man a decade ago, and two space rookies, Navy Cmdr. Edgar Deane Mitchell, 40, and Air Force Maj. Stuart Allen Roosa, 37.

Their job was to complete the Apollo 13 assignment: To land in the ancient and rugged Fra Mauro highlands to search for lunar material dating back 4.6 billion years to the convulsive birth of the moon and perhaps the solar system. While Roosa orbited the moon alone in the command ship Kitty Hawk, Shepard and Mitchell were to set the lunar machine they called Antares in a narrow valley nestled among hills, ridges, craters and rocks as large as automobiles.

As Shepard climbed into Kitty Hawk, pad leader Gunther Wendt jokingly handed him a cane as a reminder he was the oldest American yet picked for a space flight.

As he waited out the countdown, Shepard thought back to May 5, 1961, when he pioneered American rocket flight by riding his tiny Freedom 7 Mercury capsule on a 15-minute suborbital flight that took him 116 miles high and landed him in the ocean 302 miles southeast of Cape Kennedy.

For him, landing on the moon would be a personal triumph and achievement of a long-held dream.

Two years after his initial flight, Shepard was grounded by an inner ear disorder called Meniere's syndrome. Doctors said he couldn't even fly an airplane unless accompanied by another pilot.

The ear ailment finally was corrected in 1968 by a newly devised operation and he was returned to flight status. He campaigned hard for a seat on an Apollo flight and in 1969 was named to command Apollo 14.

While Shepard was on the sidelines, he met some wealthy Texans and joined them in several lucrative investments which made him a millionaire.

Shepard also was the last of the nation's original seven astronauts scheduled to fly, and thus Apollo 14 marked the end of an era in the U.S. space program.

Six of the original group made space flights. The only exception was Donald K. Slayton, grounded by a heart murmur. Four earlier left the space program to enter business. One was dead—Virgil I. "Gus" Grissom, killed in the Apollo 1 launch pad fire in 1967 *(The World in 1967, 8–13)*.

Shepard was the only one to get a crack at the moon. So this proud, sometimes arrogant pioneer had a lot to think about as the Apollo 14 countdown ticked methodically on Jan. 31. But, as the count reached the final minutes, dark clouds loomed to the west of Cape Kennedy and bore down on the launch area with heavy rain. Just eight minutes before the planned liftoff time, launch director Walter Kapryan called a hold in the countdown.

Every previous Apollo manned flight had been launched right on schedule. Was this a bad omen, a continuation of the jinx of Apollo 13?

The storm passed out over the Atlantic and the count resumed.

Astronaut Mitchell walks toward lunar module. The shadow is Shepard's

At 4:03 p.m. EST, 40 minutes late, the mighty Saturn 5 rocket broke its earthly bonds and thundered into space, propelling Apollo 14 into an orbit more than 100 miles above the earth. After circling the globe one and one-half times to make certain all systems were functioning, Shepard, Mitchell and Roosa refired their still attached third stage engine, increasing their speed from 17,400 miles an hour to 24,500 mph. They were on their way to the moon.

An hour later, they were in serious trouble.

After separating Kitty Hawk, Roosa turned the command ship around to extract the lunar module Antares from its perch atop the spent third stage of the rocket. Five times he edged his spacecraft toward the lunar vehicle, but Kitty Hawk's harpoon-like docking probe failed to catch inside the funnel-shaped lunar module receptacle.

Tension was high in Mission Control Center in Houston, Tex. The astronauts were not in danger, but if they could not link the two ships, the moon landing would have to be cancelled.

Experts on the ground worked out a solution. They told Roosa to give the command vehicle a sudden jolt forward. At the same instant, Shepard was to retract the balky probe. That way the astronauts would bypass three non-working latches on the probe and rely on two mated collars, one on each ship, to clamp together.

The maneuver worked. The two surfaces connected and were joined firmly together by 12 collar latches. Inexplicably, the three probe latches which had failed on the five previous tries also worked.

"We have a hard dock," called out an exuberant Roosa.

Later, the astronauts opened the connecting tunnel between the two ships and inspected and tested the probe latches. They found nothing wrong. Specialists theorized that some unknown foreign matter had lodged in the latches, preventing their operation, and that the repeated docking attempts had jarred it loose.

After running some tests on the ground, Mission Director Chester Lee gave the go-ahead for the lunar landing attempt. Even if the two vehicles could not dock after the moon exploration, Shepard and Mitchell could space walk their way the few feet back to the command ship, although this would be admittedly risky.

With the docking crisis over, the astronauts settled down to the relatively quiet three-day outward journey to the moon, a quarter million miles away.

The comparative calm was broken the day before they reached the moon when Shepard and Mitchell crawled through the tunnel into the lunar ship to check its systems. They discovered a slightly low voltage reading on one of two batteries in the ascent stage, the section that would lift them off the moon.

Mission Control feared that the battery might be bad or that it was being drained by a fault somewhere in the electrical system.

The only thing was to wait and see whether the voltage dropped lower. Several hours later Mitchell returned to the Antares cabin and reported it had not. Another crisis had passed. There were more to come.

Early on Feb. 4, Apollo 14 fired into an orbit ranging from 67 to 195 miles above the moon. Four hours later they again triggered their engine to shift into a path 11 to 68 miles above the surface, the closest approach yet by an Apollo command ship.

On the Apollo 11 and 12 landing missions, the command ships got no nearer than 65 miles. Purpose of the close-in maneuver was to give Shepard and Mitchell a better chance of achieving a pinpoint landing in the Fra Mauro highlands.

As the combined ships swooped low, barely eight miles above some mountain peaks, the astronauts were awestruck by their view of the barren, lifeless moon.

"Wow, this is really a wild place up here," exclaimed Shepard.

"Fantastic," chimed in Roosa.

"That's the most stark, desolate looking country I've ever seen," added Mitchell.

Hours later Shepard and Mitchell transferred into Antares, again checked the batteries and other systems, and cast off, leaving Roosa alone in the command ship to conduct photographic and scientific experiments for 40 hours until their return.

Then, more trouble. Mission Control noted that a spurious abort signal was popping up from time to time in the lunar ship's on-board computer. The trouble was traced to a faulty switch, but there was no way to fix it. If the signal was triggered after the astronauts ignited the module's motor for the descent to the moon, the computer would command an automatic abort, firing up the ascent stage engine to fling the astronauts back into orbit.

Experts at Massachusett's Institute of Technology's Charles Stark Draper Laboratory, which designed the computer, worked feverishly on a program that would instruct the computer to ignore the spurious signal. The information was radioed to Mitchell, who then fed 60 numbers into the computer's logic circuitry.

He won the race against the clock, completing the reprograming just 10 minutes before the descent was to begin. If there were a real problem situation on the way down, the astronauts would have to manually activate an abort.

Right on schedule, Shepard fired Antares' descent engine and they started down.

"That was really great work on the abort problem," Mitchell told Mission Control.

"That really saved the mission," Shepard added.

Suddenly, another shock. A landing radar failed to lock onto the surface at 30,000 feet altitude as planned. The spacemen prepared to abort.

"Come on radar, get a lock-on," Mitchell implored.

The ground radioed instructions to flip a circuit breaker on and off. It worked. The radar came on at 23,500 feet.

"Whew, that was close," said Mitchell.

They were at 7,000 feet, making their final approach.

"There's Cone Crater," Shepard shouted as he picked out a 1,200-foot-wide landmark near the landing site. "Right on the money."

At 4:18 a.m. EST, Antares, named for the star that helped guide the astronauts to the landing, touched down on the dusty lunar surface, just 87 feet north of the pre-planned target.

"We're on the surface," Shepard cried out happily.

"About the flattest place around here," Shepard commented as he looked out at boulder-strewn Fra Mauro.

Shepard and Mitchell immediately began preparations for the first of two excursions on the lunar surface. The cabin was depressurized, the hatch opened, and Shepard started down the ladder attached to one of the landing legs.

Shepard's footfall, the fifth human imprint in the ancient lunar dust, was recorded at 9:54 a.m. Feb. 5.

"It's been a long way, but we're here," were Shepard's first words as his foot gingerly tested the lunar soil.

"The soil is so soft that it comes all the way to the top of the footpad," he said.

Front view of the lunar module reflecting circular flare caused by brilliant sun

Tracks of the two-wheeled Modularized Equipment Transporter leading from the Lunar Module

Gazing around at the bleak landscape, he remarked: "It certainly is a stark place here at Fra Mauro. I think it's made all the more stark by the fact the sky is completely black."

Twenty minutes later, Mitchell joined Shepard on the surface. He reported that it was covered with a very fine brown dust, almost like talcum powder.

Their initial steps were relayed to earth by a black and white television camera. After the moonmen tested their ability to move about in the one-sixth gravity field, they took out another camera to give viewers 238,275 miles away their first sustained color view of the moon.

On the TV screens they looked like two ghostly figures as they prowled about seeking secrets of an alien world.

Among the first tasks was to implant an American flag, which stood out in the airless, windless world, held taut by a wire rod along the top.

Most of the first excursion was devoted to setting up a nuclear-powered science station intended to relay data to earth for a year or more on such things as moonquakes, meteor hits, radiation, the solar wind and the lunar atmosphere. They were aided by a first on the moon, a two-wheel pullcart on which they carried their tools and instruments.

Television viewers got an idea of the undulating terrain when the astronauts began to disappear as they passed over a small crest and walked down the far slope.

"You're visible from the armpits up," Mission Control told them.

"Nothing like being up to your armpits in lunar dust," Mitchell quipped.

In a new experiment, Mitchell laid out a 310-foot electrical cable to which three sound-recording geophones were attached —one at each end and one in the middle.

He walked along the cable with a four-foot-long device called a thumper, designed to discharge firecracker-like explosives when he pressed it to the surface every 15 feet. The resulting shock recorded by the geophones told scientists listening on the ground about the firmness of the upper few feet of the moon's crust.

As they walked back to the landing craft, Shepard and Mitchell gathered about 40 pounds of rocks, including two the size of footballs.

After more than 4½ hours on the surface they climbed back into the lander to rest, eat and replenish the oxygen and water in their back packs.

They were to have slept 10 hours, but they were anxious

Shepard shades eyes from the brilliant sun

to return to the surface. They requested, and received, permission to start their second moon walk two hours early.

The excursion was primarily a geology field trip to gather interesting and varied samples, make observations and measure the moon's magnetic properties. The focus of the traverse was Cone Crater, gouged out of the top of a 400-foot-high ridge. Along the rim, the astronauts hoped to find ancient lunar bedrock dating back 4.6 billion years to the creation of the moon. The oldest rocks returned by the Apollo 11 and 12 astronauts in 1969 ranged between 3.2 and 3.7 billion years.

The walk started out easily and the explorers, pulling their cart, stopped often to collect a rock, drive a core tube a foot or more into the surface or dig a small trench. But they soon found it difficult to get their bearings in the gullies they had to cross. Moreover, the slope leading to the rim of Cone Crater proved steeper than anyone thought, and it was strewn with huge boulders that slowed the astronauts.

"The grade's getting pretty steep now," Shepard reported. Exertion showed in the heavy breathing and gasping sentences of the astronauts. About halfway up the slope Shepard slumped against a large rock to rest. He doubted they could make it to the top unless they took their time, which would mean eliminating some of the planned field trip.

"Aw, gee whiz. Let's give it a whirl," Mitchell urged him on.

They pressed on, but both men soon were huffing and puffing and when their heartbeats nearly doubled, to around 150 beats a minute, Mission Control told them to forget the rim and start back toward Antares, more than half a mile away.

"I think you're finks," Mitchell protested.

Geologists on the ground estimated later, after viewing pictures and talking with the astronauts, that they had approached to within 75 feet of the crater rim. Rocks gathered that close could still be the oldest on the moon, they said, but months of study and analysis would be required to be certain.

The trip down the hill was considerably easier and the moon walkers soon regained their spirits as they went about their geology tasks. Back at the landing craft, they loaded aboard the 92 pounds of rocks they collected. But before re-entering the cabin, Shepard had a surprise for television viewers.

He pulled out two golf balls and a makeshift golf club he had smuggled aboard. "I'm trying a sand trap shot," he joked as he swung at the first ball, spraying lunar dust.

"Looked more like a slice to me, Al," quipped Mitchell.

The second shot apparently was more successful.

"There it goes," Shepard exclaimed. "Miles and miles and miles."

They were back inside Antares at 7:50 a.m. after another 4½-hour excursion.

At 1:48 p.m. they fired their ascent engine and blasted away from the moon after a record stay of 33½ hours. For two hours they skillfully guided the ship in pursuit of Roosa in the command ship.

The caught the Kitty Hawk right on schedule and maneuvered for the critical docking. Thoughts of the initial docking failures six days earlier were on the minds of everyone in Mission Control.

But the operation went smoothly and the two ships linked on the first try.

"We have capture," Roosa announced.

"Beautiful," replied Shepard.

The moonmen returned through the tunnel to the command cabin and jettisoned Antares, which ground controllers signaled into a crash-landing to excite a seismometer the astronauts had left at Fra Mauro.

At 8:37 p.m. that night, the astronauts fired their main engine to break away from lunar gravity and to start the nearly three-day homeward journey.

In contrast to the problem-plagued outward leg, the homeward voyage was trouble-free.

Shepard called the mission a "smashing success" and said their ability to overcome problems showed the value of manned over unmanned space exploration.

"I can intuitively tell from what we've done, what we've seen, that we're bringing back a wealth of information, photographically and geographically, and we've left another science station on the moon sending back information," Shepard said.

At 4:05 p.m. Feb. 9, Apollo 14 recorded its second bull's-eye landing, splashing down in the South Pacific less than four miles from the main recovery ship, the helicopter carrier *USS New Orleans.*

Next stop was Houston's Lunar Receiving Laboratory, where the three adventurers were quarantined until Feb. 26 on the remote chance they returned to earth with lunar germs.

As scientists eagerly began the months-long task of examining the treasure chests of rocks and soil samples, Dr. George Low, acting administrator of the National Aeronautics and Space Administration, said:

"Alan Shepard and his crew demonstrated that man belongs in space, that man can achieve objectives well beyond the capabilities of any machine that has yet been devised."

They also had wiped away much of the disappointment of Apollo 13 and restored confidence in America's manned space flight program.

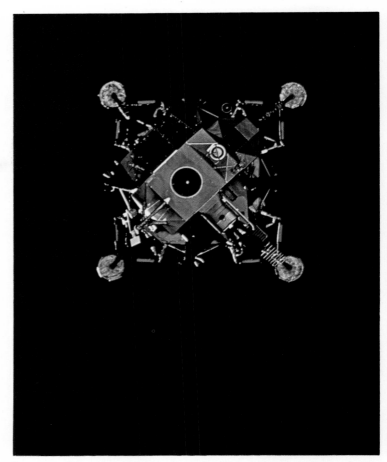

Lunar module returning to space craft after mission

Para-rescueman helped Apollo 14 lunar module pilot Edgar D. Mitchell from spacecraft during recovery operation in the South Central Pacific

Gone With the Wind—
117 Lives in Four Hours

EVEN ON a perfect winter day, the Mississippi Delta presented a drab and colorless face to the world. With the previous year's cotton crop long picked and the stalks plowed under, the brown sea of barren fields was broken only by the small farm towns, each with its inevitable gin, a deteriorating main street and rows of clapboard Negro shanties.

And Sunday, Feb. 21, 1971, was anything but perfect. Shortly after midnight a warm front blew in from the Gulf of Mexico, bringing thunderstorms and an oppressive blanket of humidity. It was a bleak, wet, lifeless day.

At the same time, but hundreds of miles to the west, south central Texas residents were experiencing another kind of weather front, an intense low pressure center with a trailing line of bitter cold.

Weather forecasts called for the warm southerly winds and rain to continue throughout the delta all day, but the low front in Texas began moving to the east, and by late morning the Jackson, Miss., weather bureau meteorologists knew the two would meet somewhere along the Louisiana-Mississippi border in a textbook condition for tornadoes.

Their conclusion proved deadly accurate. In the span of four hours, 117 people in Louisiana and Mississippi were dead. Four small towns ceased to exist. More than 1,600 homes were destroyed or damaged, and millions of dollars in property had been lost.

At the Jackson weather bureau, the first warning went out at 11:55 a.m., when many were in church. The warning was repeated throughout the day, but few, if any, residents left the area.

At 3:23 p.m., the first twister touched down, shredding a frame house in Delhi, La., 20 miles across the Mississippi River from Vicksburg. It lifted the house from its foundation, chewed it up and spit out the pieces. Six died in the vortex. Another four were killed in the small town.

From Delhi the storm moved across the river and spent the remainder of its life in the Mississippi Delta, producing the most deadly natural disaster in that area's history—107 dead in seven rural counties.

Nearly 1,100 were injured in Mississippi, Louisiana and the southeastern corner of Tennessee. More than 1,000 were left homeless. The tiny farm communities of Inverness, Delta City, Pugh City and Little Yazoo were flattened.

President Nixon declared the delta a national disaster area and hundreds applied for free food stamps, government-owned mobile homes and low interest home and business loans. Thousands more joined the victims in the massive job of clearing debris, and columns of smoke from huge bonfires hung over a dozen towns.

Numerous twisters were involved in the storm, but experts said most of the deaths and destruction were caused by four or five tornadoes, which hopscotched across the delta.

Allen Pearson, director of the severe storm forecast center at Kansas City, called the Mississippi tornadoes some of the strongest ever recorded. One, which first touched down at Cary in Sharky County, bounced all the way to Oxford, a distance of about 125 miles, before dying out, making it "some 100 times stronger than an average tornado," Pearson said.

Another single twister, Pearson said, was responsible for the destruction of both Delta City and Inverness, about 25 miles apart.

Bill Keating, a meteorologist at the Jackson Weather Bureau, said barometer readings in the center of the low front as it hung over Mississippi fell to 29.10 inches of mercury, compared with 28.94 in the eye of hurricane Camille, which devastated the Mississippi Gulf coast in 1969 *(The World in 1969, 156–163).*

"It was incredible," Keating said. "The low was pulling in the warm air and it was shooting straight up. The tops of the thunderstorms went up to 55,000 feet."

According to weather bureau records, it was the worst tornado disaster to hit the state since 100 persons were killed in a twister that struck Lamar and Wayne counties in the southwest corner of the state in April 1908. In Mississippi's most deadly tornado 317 persons were killed at Natchez in May 1840.

*   *   *   *

Survivors of the 1971 storm told stories ranging the emotional spectrum from incredible luck to heroism and despair.

Wayne Creel of Little Yazoo and his bride of two days were spending their first night in a newly-furnished house.

"It hit at 5:30 because I remember the clock broke," Creel recalled as he helped his father clear rubble from the family's destroyed lumber supply business next door to his own demolished home.

"We had just moved our new furniture in. We were in there hanging the curtains. My brother-in-law, his wife and daughter were visiting. They were leaving, standing at the door kidding us about the first night in the house and all.

"My brother-in-law opened the door and we heard the noise. It was a roar. I threw my wife on the bed and fell on top of her. An inside wall fell on us. That little wall was the only thing that saved us.

"We had just bought the furniture. We hadn't cooked anything on the stove and hadn't eaten anything off the table," Creel added, walking through the ruins of his home.

But like many others, Creel "thanked the Good Lord we were not killed."

The tornado that smashed Creel's house and everything else in Little Yazoo roared down the middle of U.S. Highway 49, splintering trees and decorating the barren hulks with twisted pieces of metal.

Tom Jeff Pittman of Pugh City said he lived through a tornado that killed 75 people near Greenwood, Miss., in 1942, but nothing in his existence compared with the twister of that February Sunday.

"I knew I had to run," he remembered. "I said, 'Lord, take care of me,' and then I watched it hit. I saw mules going down the road 100 miles an hour."

W. A. Keene of Belzoni said he and his family were watching television when his wife "heard this loud noise."

"I told everybody to get in the car and, just as we did, the danged thing started pushing us up the road," Keene said. "I guess it shoved us about 200 yards, and I never even got the car started. Finally it turned the car over but we all managed to get out."

In one of the most harrowing tales, Skipper Campbell, a first aid instructor traveling from Rayville, La., to Greenville, said he sat out the Inverness tornado, the most deadly twister of the storm, in his car without even getting his hair ruffled.

Left, Wayne Creel sits amid wreckage that was his home in Little Yazoo. Right, after a tornado hit Inverness, Miss., killing at least 13 persons

"It was a droning noise like a gigantic bunch of bees," Campbell said. "It was like I was sitting in a bottle floating in a rough sea. I watched the houses on both sides of the road being destroyed—they just completely caved in or exploded out. I could have sworn I saw a body flying through the air."

Campbell drove into Inverness after the tornado passed, set up a first-aid station and gave some of the victims everything in his suitcases.

"Everyone in town must be wearing my shirts and my coats," he said.

From the air Inverness looked like a town ravaged by war. The tornado smashed some businesses and homes into mountains of brick and lumber. Others exploded, throwing shredded bits of lumber into the cotton fields which surround the community of about 1,800.

* * * *

The character of the people of the delta was perhaps best expressed by Mrs. Ruth Sylvester, a 76-year-old "grandmother" to all the children of Delta City.

Mrs. Sylvester lived alone in the farmhouse in which she was raised. She was born in another house on the same 35-acre plot of land. In the fall she gathered pecans from her own orchard, and eight years ago began teaching impromptu kindergarten in her home when the last of her immediate family died.

She was in the kitchen eating dinner, "a little boiled ham and eggs and some ice cream and cake for dessert," when the tornado struck at 4:30 p.m.

She lived through it unscratched, standing in a corner. But her home was demolished and the pecan orchard, which she remembered watching her father plant, was stripped and broken.

"My nephew doesn't want me to build back," she said. "He wants me to come to Meridian and live in a house trailer. But I couldn't do that. I'll build another little house here. This is my home."

Mrs. Sylvester still had her "piece of land and a little income" from her cotton crop. Others were left with nothing—the poor, black field workers whose winters were hard in the best of times.

Emergency housing was initially denied 129 mostly black families because they were too poor to comply with federal regulations. The problem—they had no utilities, running water or sewerage, a prerequisite for receiving one of the hundreds of mobile homes which were shipped into the area by the federal government. It was several weeks before they were able to leave emergency shelters in schools and community centers which were established all across the delta in the wake of the storm.

In some cases plantation owners provided alternative sites with utilities, and in other instances some of the regulations were compromised. Officials said all were finally housed.

Mrs. Johana Mae Anderson, whose husband worked at the Inverness gin when it was in operation, sat in the corner of an emergency center at Indianola and described what it was like.

"We don't have a place anymore," she said, soothing two small children. "My husband is working with the men at Inverness, but he ain't getting paid nothing. We ain't got no money. I think The Lord he spared us. But I just don't know what we're going to do."

Tornado turns a trailer park into a garbage dump at Oxford, Miss.

February's Varied Scenes

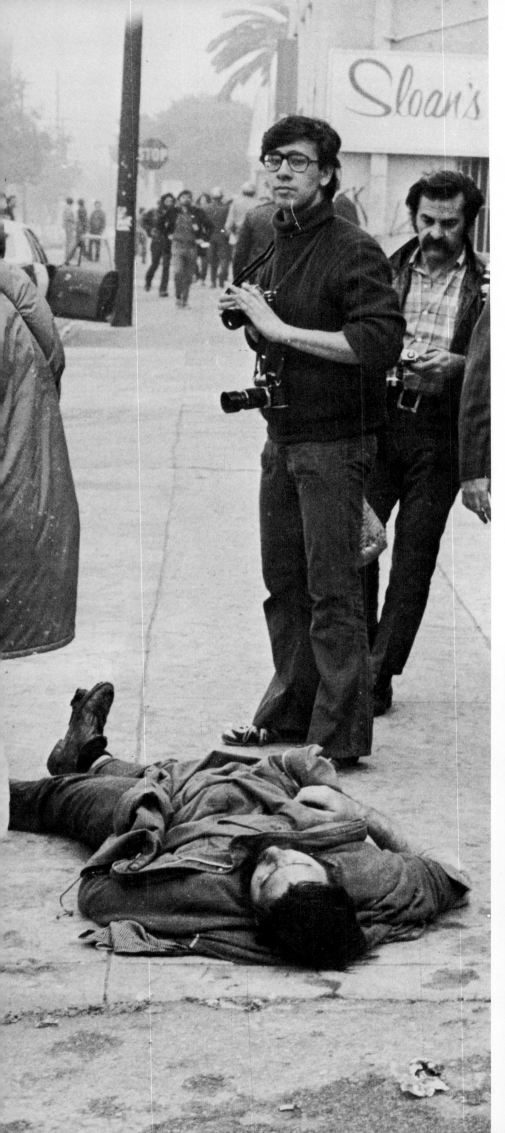

(Left) The body of a Mexican-American youth lay on a Los Angeles sidewalk where he was shot during an outbreak following a rally protesting alleged police brutality. (Below) Flames shown rising from the waters of the Gulf of Mexico during a fire which gutted an oil rig. (Top right) Former luxury liner Queen Elizabeth sailed from Port Everglades, Fla., for Hong Kong to be outfitted as a floating university. (Bottom right) Seattle disc jockey Don Clark had a final frolic with Tony and Tanya, tiger cubs he had befriended at a Seattle zoo. Clark decided that, at seven months age, "the time has come to leave them alone."

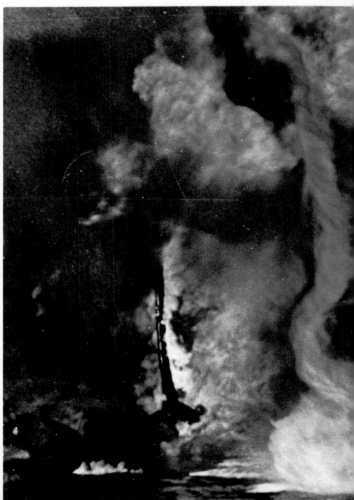

Fireman sift through the wreckage of a chemical plant near Brunswick, Ga., ripped by an explosion that killed at least 28 persons

FLARES PLANT BLAST KILLED 28

A heavy-set and graying woman entered a one-story cinder block building of the Thiokol Chemical Corp. near Brunswick, Ga.

Approaching a group of officials who uneasily shuffled their feet and looked away from the woman's gaze she said, "I'm here looking for my sister-in-law."

Two men escorted her inside. As she walked along a row of bodies she spotted that of her sister-in-law and fell to her knees, weeping.

"Oh God, oh God, my sweet Jesus help us; tell me it's not so."

Her sister-in-law was one of 28 people who lost their lives Feb. 3 when an explosion and fire leveled a munitions building at the Thiokol Chemical Corp. Thirty-two persons were hospitalized.

Of the building only a concrete wall and twisted metal remained. Shredded clothing lay in the blackened wreckage. A rescue worker pushed aside debris to expose a pair of scorched and muddy overalls and a work shoe.

"That's all there is left," he told a reporter.

The steel-reinforced structure had housed the manufacture of magnesium trip flares for use in Indochina. The blaze spread to three other buildings and at least 10 wooded acres.

A makeshift morgue was set up nearby. Those injured were evacuated by 17 airplanes and eight helicopters that used a taxi strip three miles away.

WOMEN TURNED DOWN AS VOTERS

The margin was close, but it was enough to cost women their long-awaited right to vote in the pocket-sized principality of Liechtenstein, nestled between Switzerland and Austria.

In December the 15-member two-party Parliament had decisively approved voting rights for women. But in a referendum Feb. 28 the all-male balloters reversed this action.

The Fatherlandish Union, popularly known as the Reds, polled 2,007 ballots against the women, just 28 votes more than those cast by the Progressive Citizens party, or Blacks.

Liechtenstein—population 20,000—thus remained the one area in the western world where women were not allowed to vote. The only exceptions were a few Arab countries that also had held out against women's suffrage.

Switzerland granted women the right to vote in federal elections Feb. 7. Women there also got the right to hold federal offices. In Liechtenstein the Catholic Church had supported the women, but the principality's ruler, Prince Franz Josef II, remained silent on the subject.

Political experts said some of Liechtenstein's older citizens held the view that following Switzerland's example so quickly would be interpreted as slavishly copying their larger and stronger neighbor.

Liechtenstein was separated from Austria after World War I. It grew prosperous in ensuing years and acquired a close customs and currency union with Switzerland, which thereafter handled the bulk of the principality's trade with other countries. After achieving its independence, Liechtenstein developed such diverse business activities as a large false teeth factory and a thriving tourist trade. It also became a tax haven for numerous worldwide enterprises.

One probable factor in the failure of women's suffrage in Liechtenstein: The women citizens outnumbered the men.

Wreckage of a train that burned inside a tunnel near Zenica, Yugoslavia, on Feb. 14, killing 34 persons and gutting the engine and nine passenger coaches

FUTURE OBSCURE FOR BLACKS

As with most surveys, the picture that emerged was not a clear one. The figures appearing in the 1970 U.S. census survey projected a bright future for the American black, or a bleak one, depending on what category he fell into.

One finding showed that government programs for the disadvantaged had boosted dramatically the median income of young Negro couples in the North to $8,900.

Another contained disturbing news that nearly a third of America's 4.7 million black families consisted of broken homes headed by only one parent, usually the mother. For this group, 53 per cent were trying to subsist at below the $3,800 poverty level.

The outlook for the two groups differed sharply in 1971.

Better schooling for young blacks in the northern states, manpower training programs and more job opportunities were seen as largely responsible for their rise from incomes that averaged 78 per cent of what their white counterparts made in 1960 to 91 per cent a decade later.

"We're seeing gradual progress," said Herman P. Miller, director of population studies for the Census Bureau.

"What the figures suggest is that younger, better-educated blacks in the North have been able to get jobs, maintain stable marriages and vastly narrow the income gap."

What about the other group, the one with the large percentage of broken homes?

Authorities were concerned by the fact that 27 per cent of America's black families were headed by women in 1970. This compared to 22 per cent only 10 years earlier and 17 per cent in 1950.

These families were usually the poorest of all, and the result had been a grim paradox. The dire poverty of such families had prompted the father to give up the struggle and leave home. His absence drove them still farther down the economic ladder.

Said George Wiley, director of the National Welfare Rights Organization: "The failure to be able to provide for your family when that's what society expects of you is an assault on your manhood. So, it's a natural reaction when things get tough to bug out."

The divergent lot of those two groups had a marked effect on population trends, Miller noted.

"As Negro families succeed," he said, "they move out of the depressed areas. As a result, there is a concentration of misery in our largest cities."

Three of the biggest—Washington, Newark and Atlanta—were more than half black. This was partly because the black families in these cities were steadily multiplying, but largely for the reason that blacks at the poverty level or below were funneling up from the South into urban centers, while white families headed for the suburbs in increasing numbers. Three examples of such population shifts over the past decade:

—New York City: the white population dropped by 617,000 while the blacks increased by 579,000.

—Chicago: white population decreased 505,000, blacks went up 290,000.

—Baltimore: whites dropped 131,000, blacks rose 95,000.

The census refuted, incidentally, the widely accepted belief that the migration of Southern blacks northward had tapered off. Actually the rate remained fairly constant over the past three decades. But the problems were becoming more acute.

More than 75 per cent of the 1.4 million black migrants who left the Southland over the past decade headed for five large states where the mounting cost of welfare posed a crucial problem.

The biggest increase was measured in New York, which gained 396,000 black migrants in the 1960–70 decade. California gained 272,000, New Jersey attracted more than 100,000 and Illinois and Michigan each gained roughly 120,000.

Figures might not lie, but at first glance they could certainly mislead.

Measured in percentages, the movement of Negroes to some suburbs seemed astronomical, but the growth actually was small compared to the increase of whites in those same areas.

In the suburbs of Cleveland, for instance, Negroes increased by 453 per cent between 1960 and 1970. But in actual figures this meant that the number of blacks rose from 8,000 to 45,000. Over that same period, suburban Cleveland's white population soared by 239,000. As a result, Negroes were still only 3.4 per cent of the total suburban population.

If the current trend continued, population experts foresaw an America whose cities were largely black, ringed by nearly all white suburbs.

GOMULKA OUT AS PARTY LEADER

In certain ways Poland in 1956 was not much unlike Poland in December 1970. In both years workers and farmers with economic demands staged riots. In 1956 the question of full Russian domination was still open, although a communist government had been set up some 10 years earlier.

Wladyslaw Gomulka, long time revolutionary and an active member of the Communist party, was brought in during 1959 as party chief. Gomulka was attuned to the peasants' desire that Poland remain independent from Russia. After securing his position he set up voluntary religious education in the schools and declared Poland would not partake in collective farming. Economic conditions gradually improved under his five-year governmental program.

But late in 1970, after widespread price increase riots, Gomulka was succeeded on Dec. 20 by Edward Gierek, who accused Gomulka of following the same policies for which Gomulka had blamed his predecessors. Gomulka had proposed, 15 years earlier, "to reestablish contact with the masses and win the confidence of the worker." Gierek similarly pledged himself to close a communications gap that he claimed Gomulka had opened.

Gomulka told a Central Committee meeting in Oct. 1956 that "there should be a clear delineation of the roles of the party apparatus and the state apparatus." Gierek likewise insisted that party and state responsibilities be kept separate. He said it was the party's interference in government functions that created much of the chaos late in the Gomulka regime.

On Feb. 7, 1971, Gomulka was suspended from the party's Central Committee and lost his seat on the 12-member Politburo for what Gierek called his "serious mistakes" leading to the December riots in which 45 died and 1,165 were injured. "The improper methods applied during the crisis make the further participation of Comrade Gomulka impossible in the work of the Central Committee," Gierek announced over a nationwide television broadcast. He added that Gomulka's orders to send in police and army units against the demonstrators only worsened the conflict.

Observers speculated that, had Gomulka not been too ill to testify at his hearing, complete expulsion from the party would have followed.

Arnold and William Holiman, 12-year-old twins lay on thin ice of New York City's Central Park lake on a February day, as helicopter moved into position to rescue them after a ladder attempt failed

FOR THE RECORD

SIGNED. By the Soviet Union and the United States on Feb. 11, a treaty barring nuclear weapons from the ocean floor. The treaty was drafted to prohibit, upon ratification, any nuclear weapons, launching installations or other facilities specifically designed for storing, testing or using such weapons from the seabed beyond 12 miles from shore. President Nixon called the pact a modest step toward broader agreements in the control of nuclear arms.

RECEIVED. By Senator Edward M. Kennedy on Feb. 8, renewal of a driver's license revoked for one year following a Massachusetts accident on Chappaquiddick Island in July 1969. Kennedy pleaded guilty to leaving the scene of the accident, which resulted in the drowning of Mary Jo Kopechne, a Washington, D.C., secretary. Kennedy also received a suspended sentence of three months in jail.

APPROVED. By the Senate on Feb. 8, John B. Connally as the new Secretary of the Treasury. Connally, formerly governor of Texas, was the first Democrat in President Nixon's cabinet. He succeeded Chicago banker David M. Kennedy, who was confirmed as an ambassador at large in the State Department with duties in international finance.

Ali hits the canvas ⟶

March

Jubilant Muhammad Ali had just received the word that the Supreme Court reversed his conviction for draft evasion

And Then the Mountain Caught up with Muhammad

Ali's loss gave Frazier the heavyweight title all to himself

IT WAS more than just another fight born in a promoter's office. It was borne from the political divisions which for years had divided the nation. It was a match-up, many believed, in the classical "good vs. evil." It attracted international interest as had few fights before it, and when it ended it had attracted more money than ever before and had decided who was the champion.

"Float like a butterfly, sting like a bee," was Muhammad Ali's philosophy, but it didn't work this time.

"Kill the body and the head dies," was Joe Frazier's, and it worked. He had the world heavyweight championship all to himself.

Nearly four years after boxing's hierarchy lifted the crown

from Ali for his refusal to accept military induction, and barely a year after Frazier won almost universal recognition as the new champion, the two undefeated fighters finally met to settle things.

"If Joe Frazier beats me," Ali bellowed at the pre-fight weigh-in, "I'm gonna crawl across the ring and look up at him and say, 'You are the greatest. You are the champion.' Then I'm gonna crawl back across the ring and go home."

Frazier was, as usual, less talkative. He saved his performance for the Madison Square Garden ring and the 20,455 fans who paid an indoor record $1,352,961 to see it in person.

An estimated 300 million others around the world also saw the fight on closed-circuit television or on home TV via satellite, paying what promoter Jerry Perenchio said would be a gross of $20 million or more.

For their hour in the ring, each fighter received $2.5 million. When it was over, the right side of Ali's face was grotesquely swollen and Frazier's was a mass of lumps.

And Ali had his first defeat in the ring while Frazier finally had the championship.

The fight lived up to its advance billing. Ali danced around Frazier, lashing out with lightning combinations to the head while Frazier plodded unrelentingly forward, bombarding Ali's midsection. By round four, however, Ali wasn't dancing. He stood flat-footed to conserve his strength for what he knew would be a long battle.

In the end, it was Ali's years out of the ring that determined the outcome. By mid-fight the legs which had enabled him to flit around earlier foes were heavy and rubbery.

Frazier backed him against the ropes and into the corners and bludgeoned him with left hooks. He stood back and, employing one of Ali's old tactics, dropped his hands to his sides and tauntingly dared Ali to hit him.

Ali had held his own in the first 10 rounds—but the rest belonged almost exclusively to Frazier. Ali raged back briefly in the 14th round—and burned himself out.

In the opening seconds of the 15th, Frazier reached back and unleashed a devastating left hook that sent Ali crashing to the canvas.

He scrambled up at four, took the mandatory eight count, then fended off Frazier or clinched the rest of the way. There was no question about the outcome.

Referee Art Mercante had Frazier the victor by eight rounds to six with one even. Judge Artie Aidala had it 9–6 and judge Bill Recht 11–4 to make it unanimous. The Associated Press scored it 9–5–1.

"He said he would crawl across the ring on his hands and knees if I beat him," Frazier sneered. "Well, I didn't make him do that . . . I don't think he wants a rematch. Not right now, anyway."

But the champion also had words of praise for his fallen foe. "That man takes some punch. I hit him some shots and he took the best of them." Referring to the knockdown punch, he said: "I reached back for that one. That one came out of the country."

Referee Mercante agreed—but split his praise. "The way they were hitting each other I was surprised that it went 15," he said. "But it was a beautifully fought fight and they threw some of the best punches I've ever seen."

Ali wasn't saying anything. He was in Flower Fifth Avenue Hospital having his jaw X rayed. It had ballooned in the 11th round when Frazier landed a particularly damaging left hook. The jaw was massively bruised but not broken.

His assistant trainer, Drew "Bundini" Brown, faced the writers. Brown would later be suspended by the New York State Athletic Commission for sending a spray of water across the ring at his downed fighter.

"We'll be back," Bundini told the writers. "Three years ain't gonna be three years no more. The car was in the garage three years, but all the bumps and clinks are out now."

He was referring to the 3½ years during which Ali never entered a ring for a match, the idleness enforced by the rulers of the sport who, outside the ring, had done what nine men had been unable to do in it—lift Ali's championship.

Ali tried to protect his face from Frazier's punches

Ali began his quest for that title as a light heavyweight in 1960, winning the gold medal in the Olympic Games in Rome. That was when he was still known as Cassius Marcellus Clay.

Then, after 19 professional fights—15 of them knockouts—he earned the shot at the title held by Sonny Liston.

Few observers figured the "Louisville Lip" could win against the dour man he called the "big ugly bear," just one of the phrases in his collection of pre-fight histrionics and poetry.

But on Feb. 25, 1964 in Miami Beach, the boxing world watched a cool, precise 22-year-old fighter toy with Liston for six rounds and win the crown when the champion, muscles torn in his right arm, failed to answer the bell for the seventh.

Soon after, he changed his name from Clay to Ali and became a Black Muslim minister—and much of the nation began choosing up sides.

He had been called for military duty once when he called himself Cassius—but the Army turned him down for having a low I.Q.

When, with lowered standards, the draft called again, the fighter had changed, too. Now known as Ali, he refused to serve on religious grounds and said: "I ain't got no quarrel with them Viet Congs."

He was called a draft-dodger and worse by some, a persecuted symbol by others. The government tried and convicted him for refusing military service. His title was taken away and, as he sought a license to fight, state athletic commissions would turn him down.

Finally he got the chance in Georgia, which had no state agency to regulate boxing. Atlanta granted him permission to fight and, more than 43 months after he had last defended his title, he fought Jerry Quarry.

Shortly after Ali scored his three-round knockout, the courts ruled that, by turning their backs on him, the state athletic commissions were illegally depriving him of earning a living.

Ali was back in action. He toiled for 14½ rounds before knocking out Argentine Oscar Bonavena Dec. 7 in New York. Three weeks later, the appeal on his draft conviction still a long way from being settled, he signed for the final step in his remarkable comeback, the Frazier fight.

Finally, however, on June 28, the Supreme Court cleared Ali. It ruled 8-0 that the Justice Department had misled Selective

Fourth round: Ali against the ropes

Service authorities by advising them that the boxer's claim as a conscientious objector was neither sincere nor motivated by religious beliefs. Justice Thurgood Marshall, who had been Solicitor General, or chief government prosecutor, when Ali was being tried, abstained on the court vote.

Ali was already the world champion when Frazier won his gold medal as a heavyweight at the 1964 Olympic Games in Tokyo. The former slaughterhouse butcher then turned pro and, like Ali, won 19 in a row—but with 17 by knockouts. Then the confusion began. With the heavyweight title vacant, Frazier and Buster Mathis fought a one-shot elimination bout March 4, 1968, and, on an 11th-round knockout, Frazier was recognized as champion by New York and four other states.

The World Boxing Association, recognized by most of the other states as well as many other nations, was holding its own elimination series, won by Jimmy Ellis, a former Ali sparring partner.

Two years later, after Frazier had defended his share of the title four times, he won the rest of it by bludgeoning Ellis into submission in five rounds on Feb. 16, 1970. And on Nov. 18 he demolished Bob Foster in two rounds as the light heavyweight champion tried unsuccessfully to step up to the heavyweight division.

But Frazier still had his doubters and Ali had his backers. After all, they said, Frazier had never taken the title from Ali. Indeed, no one had—and until someone did, a lot of people would still recognize Ali as the champion, regardless of what boxing's rulers decreed.

Ali, still the alternately brash-and-humble headline grabber he had been in his championship days, led the verbal barrage for a showdown. On Dec. 30 he and Frazier signed for it—and Ali shifted into high gear.

"Joe Frazier will be a punching bag. Frazier don't even look like a champion—too short . . . Frazier's got to cut. I'll tag him —pow, pow!—and then dance away.

"Nobody can go without cuttin' after six or eight rounds," added Ali, who predicted on the night of the fight that he would win it in six rounds.

Frazier, who said he would dispose of Ali in one to 10 rounds, explained: "He can't stay in the ring with me. He can't run fast enough to keep away from me." And although Frazier would, indeed, be repeatedly tagged by rapier jabs and combinations, he kept Ali from getting away—and finally the mountain caught up with Muhammad.

Ali, of course, thought he had beaten Frazier. "I think I won the fight on points. I think I won a good nine rounds. . . . If I knew that by playing around with him I would lose those (middle) rounds, then I wouldn't have done it."

Turning philosophical, he added: "In a way it was good that I lost. You have to learn how to conquer defeat. The man who is successful is the one who can learn how to cope with upsets."

He also decided he knew how to cope with Frazier. "I'll run more for the next fight," he said. "Next time I'll be in better condition."

But would there be a next time? No one seemed to know for sure—least of all Frazier.

At first he said he was retiring, then said he would give Ali a rematch.

Then he checked into a Philadelphia hospital and the rumors began to circulate, rumors that he had suffered eye damage, that he was in serious condition with pneumonia—and worse. A week later, the treatment for his kidney infection complete, he was back in circulation. But it was still to be quite a while before he would say definitely if his future plans included Ali.

Thomas E. Dewey shortly before his death

Good Winner, Good Loser

Heart attack closed career of Thomas E. Dewey, three times governor of New York and twice a presidential nominee

A POLITICIAN'S stock in trade is the image he projects. One observer likened Thomas Edmund Dewey to the "little man on the wedding cake," but he was best known as a towering figure in the Republican party who served three terms as New York's governor and almost captured the presidency.

Dewey's career of public service spanned a generation and projected many images over the years.

To the racketeers he sent to jail while serving as special prosecutor for New York State in the 1930s, he was the determined gangbuster who declared war on the underworld.

To New York voters who sent him to Albany three times, he was the efficient administrator who unfurled a 550-mile ribbon of concrete between Buffalo and New York City and established one of the world's biggest university systems.

To his colleagues in the Republican party, Dewey was the relentless campaigner whose tireless efforts won him the distinction of making two tries for the White House.

To his adversaries in the elective process, he was a principled opponent, a man whose differences posed worthy challenge, yet a man unafraid, voicing agreement when he felt agreement was in the common good.

His life ended at 68. Apparently in good health after a checkup at a Miami hospital, Dewey played a round of golf in the morning of March 15 and scheduled an afternoon of other activities. But his failure to appear thereafter puzzled his friends. His body was found in his room. He had suffered a massive heart attack.

* * * *

Thomas E. Dewey was born in Owosso, Mich., March 24, 1902. He was the son of a weekly newspaper publisher and a distant relative of Adm. George Dewey, the hero of Manila Bay in the Spanish-American War.

Dewey's administrative prowess began to show when he was 13. He took charge of a citywide magazine agency, employing older boys to help with the work. His early musical talent took him to New York City, where he was encouraged to study

In 1948 President Truman and Gov. Dewey shook hands as they squared off for the White House race

voice. But ultimately his tutor decided that he sang too "in-telligently" to succeed in the operatic world. Dewey thereafter was graduated from the University of Michigan and studied law at Columbia University.

While serving as a clerk in a Chicago law office he married the former Miss Frances Eileen Hutt, of Sherman, Tex. In the early 1930s he found himself an interim post as U.S. attorney for the southern district of New York. That appointment was the beginning of his career in public life.

Success came quickly. His first attempt at prosecuting figures from organized crime resulted in a 10-year prison sentence for Irving Wexler, alias Waxey Gordon, a well-known Brooklyn beer runner. Income tax charges iced Wexler away.

Briefly, Dewey returned to private law practice, but it wasn't long before the call to public service was made again.

In 1935 a New York County grand jury probing rackets urgently asked Gov. Herbert Lehman to appoint a special rackets prosecutor. Dewey accepted the appointment. It was reported at the time that he was earning about $50,000 a year in his private practice. The prosecuting position offered about one-third that amount.

During the next three years, Dewey compiled an amazing record of 72 convictions in 73 cases brought before the courts. Some of the biggest names in the underworld fell before his meticulous and relentless investigations. Among them were Charles "Lucky" Luciano, overlord of vice and narcotics, and James J. Hines, Tammany District leader and reputed protector of policy rackets operated by Arthur Flegenheimer, alias Dutch Shultz.

The name Dewey and the term racket-buster had become synonymous. Organized prostitution was smashed; gone was an illicit web of crime that included loan sharking, bail bonding and trucking rackets. Headlines in daily newspapers heralded his efforts.

Thrust into the public eye, and with demonstrated ability as a determined taskmaster, Dewey became ideal political material. His aspirations to elected office began on a sour note with a defeat in his first try for the governor's chair, but concluded with victory, then reelection to that same office.

Dewey was regarded as the modern saviour of the New York Republican party when he made a breakthrough in 1942 with a resounding victory in the gubernatorial election. His try against Gov. Lehman in 1938 had fallen 64,000 votes short among some five million cast. His victory marked the first time in two decades that a man of his political persuasion had managed to occupy the chief executive's office in Albany. Democrats had rattled off nine straight victories.

Two years later he was called upon by the National GOP to challenge President Franklin D. Roosevelt just as World War II was winding down and an Allied victory was virtually assured. Dewey lost the election, but came closer to victory from a standpoint of popular votes than any other defeated candidate in 25 previous years.

Two more years passed, and Dewey was on the gubernatorial campaign trail again, trekking across New York State preaching the merits of "progressive Republicanism" to the old line state GOP. The result was reelection by an increased margin. But once again, Dewey was called from the governor's mansion to strike out against the Democrats and bring the White House back to Republicans. This time his opponent was President Harry S. Truman in the election of 1948.

Most of the polls taken in advance of the election showed Dewey a clearcut winner by a landslide. And as early returns began pouring in from the East Coast, that pattern began to emerge.

Dewey went to bed thinking he was a President; he awakened a loser.

So certain seemed the results that night, that some newspapers and magazines on deadline proclaimed Dewey the winner.

"I have been graduated at a relatively early age to the role of elder statesman, which someone has aptly defined as a politician who is no longer a candidate for any office," Dewey exclaimed in his first major speech following the Truman victory.

And with that, he returned to Albany, disavowing any future plans to seek the GOP presidential nomination. In 1950 he announced that he would not seek reelection as governor. After 20 years of public life, he said, he was tired and run down.

In less than two months, however, he reversed himself and decided to run for reelection. His about-face, he said, was due to the Korean War and the demands it made on the residents of his state.

"The people of New York are being asked to make sacrifices for our defense in the face of deadly peril," he said. "In good conscience I cannot ask others to serve unless I am equally willing to serve." He won reelection, but it was the last elected office he would seek.

When Dewey finally left office he said he had allowed his family's financial affairs to slip and he was going to rectify that situation. Since 1955 until his death he served as senior partner in the prestigious New York City law firm of Dewey, Ballantine, Bushby, Palmer and Wood.

* * * *

Dewey's career as governor matched in determination and degree of accomplishment his crime-busting days in New York.

His most visible achievement was the 550-mile New York State Thruway between Buffalo and New York. The superhighway still bore his name in 1971. He also pushed through the legislature the establishment of the state university system, now one of the largest in the world.

His resourcefulness and farsightedness in fiscal management quickly became evident. During the Korean War, when building material was scarce, Dewey tucked away surplus tax revenues in a reserve fund. When the war came to an end he ladled out the money in great sums for a politically attractive capital improvement program, while holding taxes down and keeping state budgets balanced.

He used his influence to prod the Republican-controlled state legislature to move from stand-pat conservatism to social innovation and was especially proud of the "sickness disability benefit" program he established. Under that plan workers received sustenance payments for wage losses due to illness.

Following his loss to Truman, during his last term as governor and in his years after leaving public office, Dewey emerged as the figurative head of Republican politics. In that role he spoke out on the issues of the day, made a European tour of nine nations and spoke with world leaders. He disagreed often with some policies of the Truman administration, but was quick to voice agreement with others he considered sound.

President and Mrs. Nixon at Dewey funeral

A strong internationalist, Dewey agreed with the Marshall Plan for the relief of war-torn Western European nations and added his backing to the Atlantic Pact that gave Truman the authority to establish America's defenses against Russia in the heart of Europe.

While many in his party were launching barrages of criticism against Secretary of State Dean Acheson during the Korean War, Dewey declared that the United States was in a state of emergency and "this moment is not the time for further criticism" of administration handling of foreign affairs.

Dewey clearly differed on matters of foreign policy with many GOP leaders, including Sen. Robert A. Taft of Ohio and former President Herbert Hoover. He took to task Republican floor leader Sen. Kenneth Wherry of Nebraska for the latter's resolution banning transport of troops to Europe without congressional approval.

In matters of national security and issues close to the heart of the nation's well being, Dewey preached a clear-cut bipartisan line.

A few weeks before the Russian-trained North Koreans invaded South Korea, Dewey warned:

"Before any Republican rejoices for the possible shipwreck of the foreign policy of the Democratic Administration, he should remember that we are all in the same boat."

But the strength of his belief in national unity and bipartisan approach to critical foreign affairs often took another direction when he felt that Washington wasn't measuring up to the task.

He once charged that the nation should stop watching Communist successes "with the calm of a Buddha contemplating his navel," claiming that Washington at the time conveyed "the impression of fiddling while freedom burns."

So the mustachioed figure, who reportedly was described by Alice Roosevelt Longworth as "the little man on the wedding cake," remained a tough and viable force in the national eye. His appearance at subsequent GOP national conventions continued to spark applause and cheers comparable to the days when he stood on the nominating platform himself amid the wild exhilaration of his own nominations.

And it was from that platform in 1948 that he described a problem for Americans and cited a hope that implied the theme of his long public service career:

"Our problem is not outside ourselves. Our problem is within ourselves. We have found the means to blow the world, physically, apart.

"Spiritually, we have yet to find the means to put together the world's broken pieces, to bind up its wounds, to make a good society, a community of good will that fits our dreams."

British Economy Heavily Hit by Mail Strike and Collapse of Rolls-Royce

Striking postal employes also rejected 9 per cent raise offer

"Hanged" in effigy: Bill Ryland, acting Post Office chief

IN THE YEAR 1571, Queen Elizabeth I of England received her mail as fast as a messenger on horseback could ride. Special delivery sometimes meant a week's hard gallop. Four centuries later, in 1971, the Royal Mail could no longer guarantee that same speed of service, not even for her direct descendant, Queen Elizabeth II, despite the jet planes and electronic computers at its disposal.

The reigning monarch, like the lowest of her subjects in the British Isles, had to wait nearly seven weeks for some personal letters. For the first time since it was created a crown monopoly by Elizabeth I, in the days when William Shakespeare was writing plays, the Royal Mail ground to a halt.

The first postal strike in British history lasted 47 days. It was the longest national work stoppage of any kind since 1926 in a country where strikes had become as common as the cold and a major symptom of an ailing economy. And still, when the mail strike finally ended March 7, the nation faced yet another new malady, "postman's hangover." Millions of bills, undelivered since the strike began Jan. 19, descended on a public that had managed to escape nasty reminders of reality, like bank account statements held up in the mail. Embarrassed Britons, usually dedicated family budgeters, found they had overspent in a glow of artificial affluence. "It was like Christmas all over again while it lasted," one chain store executive said. "But it will be a horrible Easter."

John Newman, a London businessman with a wife and two children, agreed. "It'll probably take us months to make up the excesses of the past few weeks," he admitted. "I've probably overspent by 300 pounds ($720)."

The 230,000 postal workers themselves returned to their jobs emptyhanded, with no increase in their basic pay rates of between $36 and $66 a week, despite the hardships of the long strike that had forced them to use up savings or borrow. They had sought pay increases of 15 per cent, and rejected an offer of 9 per cent, but in the end, when the money ran out, they returned to work to await the decision of an impartial commission formed to sort out the pay dispute.

Postal workers are among the lower paid in Britain. They could not afford to hold out. Only family men got social security benefits during the strike, lower than their regular pay. Their meager union strike fund provided only $4.20 a man before it went broke. Fellow unions offered to help with loans the postmen could not afford to repay, instead of the straight cash grants desperately needed.

No public outcry emerged from the inconvenience, no general demand that the post office give in to the strikers. The public made do with telephones, or private messenger services, telegraph and telex lines, or bill-free shopping sprees, leaving all the pressure on the postmen themselves. "The rent is due on Monday and I don't know how I'm going to pay it," London postman Brian Cook said early in the strike. "We'll have to sell the kids," his wife, Doreen, quipped bitterly. At least 30,000 postal workers defected during the stoppage and returned to their jobs, allowing a skeleton service to continue in some areas. Cook stuck it out. "We've got to have a raise, and the strike is the working man's only weapon," he explained. "Prices keep going up. As fast as the money comes in this hand it goes out that one."

By contrast, the government-run post office could afford to wait, spared the wage bills of the costly mail service during the strike, but still running the profitable telephone operations. The strike cost the post office $595.2 million in lost revenue, but it had saved more—the $624 million that would have been paid out to striking workers.

Prime Minister Edward Heath's Conservative government, facing rampant wage inflation and a rising cost of living of 9 per cent a year, had stood firm against the postal workers in a test case. He won that battle, if not the war. Strikes remained an economic sore and the key domestic political issue of the year. They lost the nation a record 11 million man-days of work in 1970, cutting millions of pounds off the vital export orders by which the British island trading nation lived. More work days were lost by strikes in the first four months of 1971 alone than for the whole preceding year. The government's top priority bill, a controversial measure to curb strikes that kept Parliament up through all-night sittings, was expected to become law by summer. But no one could predict with certainty that it would work in the face of overwhelming trade union opposition. Militant labor leaders called a series of one-day national work stoppages and vowed they would "kill the bill." Ford Motor Company workers, striking at the same time as the postmen, held out for a 32 per cent wage boost over two years, and won. The company warned that Britain's strike fever would force it to build new plants elsewhere, and the chairman, Henry Ford II, told Heath, "There is no stability in Britain." The huge Ford settlement quickly touched off a new wave of strike threats and inflationary wage demands before the bill could become law.

Sociologists found deeper causes for the industrial chaos. Some believed the legacy of Britain's class system continued to inhibit upward social mobility and helped breed trade union militancy as the best way to improve working conditions. Most British working class children left school at age 15, with no chance for the further education that could lead to better jobs.

There was also a suspicion that the unions had missed their chance for a larger share of the national wealth in the days when they were weak and the British empire was a rich, world power. The working class was by this time demanding a larger share it considered overdue, but the economic pie was smaller. While they were more affluent than before, and covered by a wide range of social welfare benefits such as the free national health service, they still got paid less than their counterparts in much of Western Europe.

By March 1971, however, no one could blame all the nation's economic ills on strikes any more. The month before, the rock of Gibraltar of British industry, Rolls-Royce Ltd., had collapsed into government receivership. Management had miscalculated the cost of building the RB-211 engine for America's Lockheed Tristar jet plane and could no longer meet its contract commitments without bankrupting the company, bringing down a world status symbol, the profitable automotive division, as well. Britain's Fort Knox had seemingly gone bust. The government had to step in to save it because the company made engines for 48 national air forces, including Britain's, and 112 civil airlines, contributing a key to the defense of the west and the maintenance of two thirds of the world's air transport. There had been no similar collapse since the fall of the house of Krupp.

In the weeks that followed, devoted to saving the company, the contract, and tens of thousands of dependent jobs, officials on both sides of the Atlantic tried to piece together what went wrong. No one blamed the British trade unions. Rolls-Royce management, encouraged by the former Labor government, had won a $2 billion bonanza in the RB-211 contract, a cornerstone to keeping Britain a heavy industrial world power, instead of a lesser exporter of goods like Scotch whisky and knitted wear. To get the contract, management promised to build a revolutionary new kind of engine at deadline speed that would meet all specifications, and allow a profit, all at a lower cost than any rival bidder. In the end, it couldn't be done. Management in Britain was forced to take a searching look at its efficiency too.

In colonial days, with captive markets and sources of supply, British firms felt little need to compete with other foreign powers. All that vanished with the empire by the 1960s. One American management consulting firm in London estimated that British managers were now 50 years behind their American counterparts in the techniques of competing in world markets. By 1971 the British economy had almost stopped growing, with a rise of less than 1 per cent predicted for the year in the gross

Daniel Haughton, Lockheed Aircraft chairman, in London for re-negotiation of contract with Rolls Royce Ltd.

national product. Investment was at a low since World War II and unemployment nearing a postwar high level. British cars, long a major export winner, were losing ground to foreign rivals, even in the British market. All British automotive companies spent less per worker on plant and equipment than their European competitors. A comparison with another island trading nation, Japan, was instructive.

Ten years earlier Britain produced 24 million tons of steel a year and Japan 22 million tons. Since then British production rose slightly to a total of only 28 million tons while Japan's skyrocketed to 93 million tons. In Japan 12 steel plants each produced more than 5 million tons a year. While Britian did not have a single plant with that much capacity. Its defeated rivals in World War II, West Germany and Japan, had long before outstripped Britain in the postwar economic battle for world markets.

By the end of March, Heath's government acted in an attempt to revive the sagging economy. The annual budget, the first since his administration was elected in June 1970 (*The World in 1970, 117–120*) provided major tax cuts for industry to stimulate investment in plant and machinery. It projected a 3 per cent growth rate target for the year, triple the current estimate. At the same time, government hopes were pinned on the anti-strike bill and Britain's bid to join the faster developing economy of the European Common Market. Only time would tell whether any of these efforts would succeed.

The effects of the post office strike, however, were clear sooner. For one thing it forced the British, nearly 95 years after Alexander Graham Bell's invention, to accept the telephone completely. For decades, British lawyers, businessmen and even police had preferred to communicate by post when possible and housewives to chat by mail. Britain had a population 25 per cent as large as the United States in 1971, but normally made less than 5 per cent of the number of daily phone calls in the United States. During the postal strike telephone use jumped 50 per cent. Firms found they could often phone long distances more cheaply than the cost of paying a secretary to type a formal letter.

Companies chartered planes to the continent to post overseas mail, and rented security agency trucks for inland correspondence. In some cases they found the makeshift services quicker, more efficient and worth the extra cost. About 50 private postal services, authorized by the government during the emergency, made quick profits charging up to 30 times the normal postage rates. Some employed school boys and housewives and issued their own stamps. At best they handled a million of the 35 million letters and parcels normally carried by the post office every day.

Hardships were kept to a minimum. Postal workers volunteered to keep special counters open during the strike to pay state pensions and other benefits. The fear of a wave of bankruptcies never materialized among smaller businesses, not even among the hard-hit mail order firms which coped with the situation by arranging central collection points and gave employes time off. The queen missed her private mail, but still got state papers delivered.

Individuals suffered, of course. Lady Zoe Hart-Dyke, a silk farmer, found herself stuck with five million silkworm eggs she could not mail to her customers. A playwright and director, Lord Ted Willis, glad to miss all the mail he never liked to read anyway, said he drank a toast every night to Tom Jackson, head of the striking post office workers union, and millionaire J. Paul Getty told inquirers the strike was a "blessed relief from begging letters."

Torture, Terror, Death in Brazilian Prisons? Authorities Denied it

BRAZILIAN AUTHORITIES angrily branded them as lies, but the reports persisted. They told of beatings, torture and even mass rape, of the killing of political prisoners and others who had run afoul of the military regime.

—A young Italian Roman Catholic priest told a military court that Brazilian political police had tormented him with electric shocks and threatened other tortures after his arrest on charges of antigovernment propaganda.

—An American staff member of the U.S. Naval Mission, located on the same floor as Brazil's navy ministry in which political prisoners claimed they were tortured, said, "I have been hearing groans and screams for about two years."

—Tanya Chao Charters, a young Canadian woman arrested in Rio on charges of subversion, testified in a court hearing that after she was tortured with electric shocks, and lay half-naked on a concrete floor, a live alligator was placed in her cell.

—No less a figure than Archbishop Paulo Evaristo Arns of Sao Paulo charged that a young woman church secretary or social worker, had been picked up by political police and tortured "in an ignominious manner."

At first the charges of mistreatment came from fugitive Communists and other rebels. People abroad took them with a grain of salt. But when Catholic leaders, editors and respected intellectuals joined in the swelling chorus of protest, people began to listen.

The government responded by clamping a tight lid on both press and television. It broadened the list of punishable "offenses" by the media to include talking or writing in terms that had a hidden meaning. It was seen as an attempt to halt the flow of double entendres that Brazil's political opposition and journalists had long used to ridicule those in high places.

But the protests would not be silenced. If suppressed at home, they were spirited across the border and published abroad.

The result was a sign of recognition in official places that mistreatment of prisoners did exist in Brazil. It happened last February, when Sao Paulo police announced that they were investigating the torture charges made by Archbishop Evaristo Arns. This marked the first time a government agency had acknowledged accusations that political prisoners might have been tortured in Brazil.

No longer could Brazil, birthplace of the samba, pose as an oasis of tranquillity in a continent of violence. Any such image had been shattered by the wave of unprecedented violence and terror.

On the surface there was still little evidence of turmoil. No extra large police or army detachments regularly patrolled the streets of Rio or other cities. Antigovernment slogans were quickly painted over on university walls, and the muzzled press carried few reports of political unrest.

The country had achieved one of the highest growth rates in the world in the previous two years, with the economy booming at the rate of a 9 per cent GNP growth a year. The record-setting Rio stock market moved into the third position in the world for volume of shares traded.

But the violence was there. It flared forth in bank holdups, gun battles between terrorists and police and the arrest of political suspects in their homes or offices. News of the latest seizures and beatings might not appear in Brazilian papers, but it spread among friends by word of mouth and by documents and circulars distributed by various clandestine opposition groups.

Even the complaints of some high church leaders were censored by the press, and military officials tried to debunk the charges. One general, addressing army recruits in Sao Paulo, declared: "You must unite and organize yourselves to participate in the struggle to defend moral and ethical principles. Our enemies are conditioned to kill in cold blood, rob banks and kidnap men, women and children."

Emilio Garrastazu Medici, a career general who became president of Brazil in 1969 (The World in 1969, 194) was plainly ruffled by the recurrent rumors of torture and repression of opponents of his regime. People who spread such stories, said the president, were "bad Brazilians, Communists and subversives."

Such words were new in this largest of Latin American countries which had long prided itself on being a civilized nation that did not go in for bloodletting like some of its neighbors. Unlike those neighbors, Brazil had had no bloody war of independence, and few people were killed in the scattered revolutions that did erupt, including the one that brought the military to power in 1964 (The World in 1964, 66).

Strikes and street demonstrations had not been uncommon, but acts of terrorism and reports of torture in jails were rare.

The turning point came in September 1969, when terrorists kidnaped U.S. Ambassador Charles Burke Elbrick and held him for three days until the Brazilian government released 15 political prisoners and flew them to a safe haven in Mexico (The World in 1969, 194). Incensed authorities reacted by restoring the peacetime death penalty in Brazil.

Theodomiro Romeiro dos Santos, a 19-year-old student turned terrorist, was the first Brazilian to be sentenced to death in recent times. He was convicted of killing a policeman during an escape attempt.

But the threat of capital punishment did not prevent the kidnapings of the Japanese consul general in Sao Paulo, and the West German and the Swiss ambassadors. All were released by terrorists after the government set free a total of 130 political prisoners and flew them to political asylum havens in Mexico, Algeria and Chile.

Actually, Brazil's baptism of violence came a good deal earlier. It began with the appearance in 1958 of the Death Squad, a vigilante group believed made up of policemen dissatisfied with the pace of justice in their land and determined to compensate for the absence of the death penalty for nonpolitical crimes. The Death Squad was held responsible for an estimated 1,200 "executions" after it went into action 14 years ago.

Its victims ranged from petty criminals to cop killers who usually were strangled by a nylon cord or cut down in a hail of gunfire and their bodies left in the countryside. Near the bodies squad members customarily left drawings of a skull and crossbones, one of the trademarks of the organization. The bodies of some victims were dotted with cigarette burns, indicating that they had been tortured.

After the appearance of the Death Squad reports began cropping up about the Communist Hunters Command, a clandestine rightwing group believed made up of military officers who concentrated on breaking up opposition gatherings. They also were accused of an occasional political assassination.

Acts of terrorism, guerrilla warfare, mass arrests and the first reports of torture of political prisoners came after the 1964 revolution. Student demonstrations were harshly put down, and Brazil's congress was closed for 10 months, then reopened as a powerless body.

Last year a university student charged with terrorist activities, testified in a military court that he had been beaten, had two ribs broken, was put through a mock hanging and had electric shocks applied to all parts of his body.

With the harsh new restrictions under the military regime, many militant leftists went underground to wage an armed struggle and a campaign of terrorism. Extremist groups turned to bombings, assaults and bank robberies.

The Brazilian government denied in May 1970 that there were tortures in Brazilian jails. But it refused a suggestion that the denial be confirmed by letting newsmen visit jails.

Seven months later, Education Minister Jarbas Passarinho admitted that there was torture of political prisoners in Brazilian jails, but he denied that tortures were systematic.

Censorship of Brazil's newspapers was relaxed after Medici became president in 1969. But authorities continued a system of self-censorship, stepping in occasionally to warn against publication of a specific item.

At the end of 1970 the entire nine-man staff of the satyrical weekly O Pasquim (The Lampoon) was arrested and held for weeks. In December 1969 the government struck at the foreign press by expelling French newsman Francois Pelou, who, authorities claimed, did not turn over to police a terrorist message he had received.

Further government pressure was brought to bear in April 1971 against the afternoon daily Jornal da Tarde and its sister publication, O Estado de Sao Paulo, after O Estado published an editorial that apparently hit a raw nerve of the military-backed regime.

The censors let the papers publish after O Estado agreed to follow a policy of rigid conformation to censorship norms.

It was not known to what degree the charges of torture in the prisons were true, but most observers agreed that Brazil was still a long way from being a free-wheeling democracy.

In 1971 the situation was generally brighter than it was two years earlier, when writers and teachers were being muzzled, many of them denied their political rights. The man in the street felt that things were better and he showed little sympathy for the terrorists who kidnaped diplomats, robbed banks and hijacked planes.

"They just make things worse," said a shoeshine boy in Rio de Janiero.

Victims of a Death Squad "execution"

LANDSLIDE VICTORY IN INDIA

Jubilant shouts rose from the milling crowd of bearded Moslems and turbaned Sikhs as the results went up on the election scoreboard in New Delhi. "Indira Gandhi, leader of our country," they chanted.

The enthusiasm swelled when it became clear that Mrs. Gandhi and her New Congress party had scored a landslide victory, taking district after district from the Vale of Kashmir to the jungles of Assam.

When the final returns were in, Mrs. Gandhi's party had won 350 of the 515 contested seats in the lower house of parliament.

It was a stunning triumph for the daughter of the late Jawaharlal Nehru who was embarking on her third term as prime minister, or one less than her celebrated father.

The lopsided victory, which surprised even her most enthusiastic supporters, gave the 53-year-old leader the power to pass what bills she wanted without having to make what she considered debilitating compromises with regional factions in parliament.

Bolstered by the sweeping mandate, Mrs. Gandhi shook up her cabinet, dropping seven ministers including Dinesh Singh, a former foreign minister and once one of her closest confidants.

The results carried the prime minister's influence into areas that had been strongholds

Prime Minister Indira Gandhi addressed thousands in campaign for her party's victory

for the opposition. Such a one was the state of Mysore, where the New Congress party won all 27 seats and announced that it would form a local government there.

It was a heady triumph, but predictions that Mrs. Gandhi would start enacting at once reforms that make up the basis of her platform brought appeals for patience from the prime minister herself.

"Economic measures by themselves don't really take you anywhere," she told a news conference. "They have to be accompanied by certain social changes and changes in the people's thinking."

Yugoslavia's President Josip Broz Tito was greeted by Pope Paul VI in first formal visit by a communist head of state

AVALANCHE TOLL 250 IN PERU

It began with a slight earth tremor, but it set off a chain reaction that left more than 250 persons dead or missing in the Andes Mountains of Peru, still recovering from a massive quake 10 months earlier that had killed an estimated 50,000 (The World in 1970, 84–91).

The tremor was severe enough to knock off part of a mountain peak and topple it into Lake Yanahuarina, projecting a wall of water over its banks. The flood sent tons of rocks and mud crashing down on Chungar mining camp, which produced lead and copper ore, about 10,000 feet up the side of Mt. Puajanca 62 miles northeast of Lima.

Residents of the camp were in the middle of their morning routine when the slide engulfed them. The camp school was swept away along with a teacher and dozens of children registering for classes.

Mine watchman Isodoro Lasadera, who managed to shepherd nine children to higher ground, said he stood in awe as boulders and earth rained down from the mountain 900 feet above them.

"I felt powerless as the earth trembled and a gigantic wall roared toward the camp destroying everything in its path," the mine watchman recalled later.

Rescue workers who spent eight hours plodding to the disaster site expressed fear at first that up to 600 persons had perished. But as survivors began turning up in the days that followed, the figure was revised to an estimated 256 dead or missing.

Peruvian miner carries body of a child, an avalanche victim

POOR HAD THEIR DAY IN COURT

America's poor had their day in court, and the nation's highest tribunal handed down two milestone decisions in their favor. On March 2, the Supreme Court ruled that the needy were entitled to cost-free divorces and that no one could be jailed merely because he was unable to pay a fine.

Only one court member dissented from the ruling that people who wanted to end a marriage but were too poor to pay filing fees and court costs must be given cost-free divorces by the states. Justice Hugo L. Black, 85, denounced the decision as one that would use taxpayers' funds to encourage divorce.

Black indicated his displeasure at seeing such an innovation spring from a court on which President Nixon had placed two "strict constructionists:" Chief Justice Warren E. Burger and Justice Harry A. Blackmun.

"If ever there has been a looser construction of the Constitution in this court's history, I fail to think what it is," said the justice.

There was no dissent on the other decision that people could not be put in jail simply because they were too poor to pay fines. The decision erased the power that American judges have wielded for more than three centuries to sentence poor defendants to "$30 or 30 days."

The second ruling created a right to be applied to the poor alone. An affluent person could be put promptly in jail for failing to pay a fine, but some other method of collecting fines from the poor—possibly installment payments—would have to be tried, the court held.

ONE MORE COUP IN ARGENTINA

At best, Argentina could be described as a politically unstable country. In the 16 years since Juan D. Peron had been ousted in 1955, this land of 23 million people had undergone five coups, two of them led by Gen. Alejandro Agustin Lanusse, gray-haired commander of the army.

On March 26, Lanusse took over as president of Argentina, four days after spearheading a coup against his predecessor, Gen. Roberto Levingston. The changeover marked the latest power struggle within the military clique which had ruled Argentina since civilian Arturo Illia was overthrown as chief of state in 1966. It

also marked the second president that Lanusse had unseated for dragging his feet on restoring constitutional government.

Lanusse, 52-year-old career officer and a member of Argentina's landowning aristocracy, had toppled President Carlos Ongania in June 1970, accusing him of increasingly autocratic and authoritarian methods. He especially pinpointed Ongania's failure to make good on his promise to hold elections (The World in 1970, 124).

Lanusse and his military colleagues then chose Levingston, an obscure brigadier general, to succeed Ongania. But a rift developed when the new president began advocating a waiting period of four or five years before calling elections.

Lanusse had been the key member of a three-man junta that had "cogoverned" with Levingston. It had been expected that the chiefs of Argentina's navy and air force would team up with Lanusse in a triumvirate. But when the army chief took the presidential oath, it became clear that his two fellow chiefs, while serving on a junta, would definitely be under his orders.

The people, accustomed to coups, hardly seemed to notice the latest change in government. They were too busy protesting the government's decree of a series of one-week bans on beef consumption in this cattle country. "People don't care when a government goes," said an aroused housewife, "but when you take the beef away, that hurts everybody."

After Argentine coup: Center, Lt. Gen. Alejandro Lanusse, army, named himself president; his aides: Left, Adm. Pedro Gnavi, navy: right, Brig. Gen. Carlos Alberto Rey, air force. Lanusse said they fired President Roberto Levingston

Law enforcement men sifted through debris in a restroom after bomb explosion in Capitol at Washington

CAPITOL DAMAGED BY BOMB

In 1814, during the War of 1812, the British set fire to Washington's Capitol. Through the ensuing 157 years various acts of violence were perpetrated there. A bomb damaged the structure's Senate reception room in 1915, almost exactly a century after the fire. Then, on March 1, 1957, Puerto Rican fanatics, firing from the visitors' gallery, wounded five congressmen on the House floor. Precisely 17 years later to the day, a powerful bomb went off in a men's lavatory on the Capitol's ground floor, just beneath the Senate chamber.

The 1915 bombing was admitted by Frank Holt, a young instructor opposed to United States arms sales to World War I allies. The congressmen wounded in 1957 all recovered. But the explosion March 1, 1971 caused the most serious damage to the Capitol since the 1814 fire. That building was reconstructed in 1819.

* * * *

At 1:32 a.m. a heavy explosion reverberated in the Senate wing, unoccupied except for security personnel and a few others. Seven rooms, including several used by lawmakers for ultra-private conferences, were severely damaged. The unmarked lavatory, located on a small cor-

ridor rarely used by the public, became a pile of rubble.

Elsewhere doors were blown off their hinges and plaster was knocked down. Some of the building's brick supporting arches were lifted, but most settled back into place. No one was hurt.

Half an hour earlier a telephone caller had warned the Capitol switchboard. James Powell, chief of Capitol police, told newsmen a male voice informed the operator: "This building will blow up in 30 minutes. . . . This is in protest of the Nixon involvement in Laos."

The FBI took charge of the investigation. Its agents, with other law enforcement officers, sifted through the wreckage of the lavatory. The consensus of Capitol police was that a time bomb had been planted in the lavatory before 4:30 p.m. the previous day, the closing hour for the customary Sunday parade of tourists.

Almost immediately a flood of protesting statements and demands for tighter security issued from shocked members of executive, legislative and judicial branches. Said Sen. George S. McGovern, D-S.D., "The massive bombardment we are continuing year after year against the peoples of Indochina has its counter-

part in the mounting destruction of human values in our own land. It is not possible to teach an entire generation to bomb and destroy others in an undeclared, unjustified, unending war without paying a terrible price in the derangement of our society."

President Nixon, on a speaking engagement in Iowa at the time, said in a statement that the bombing was intended by "the violence people" to scare him into staying in Washington and to force the closing of governmental buildings to the public. "It won't work," he said. While he echoed the call for more stringent protective measures, he also stated the opinion that citizens have a right to visit such buildings and that this privilege should not be canceled.

On the day of the bombing the Capitol remained closed during the morning to expedite the official inquiry. But in the afternoon most corridors were open again to tourists. Any packages they carried, however, were examined by police.

The next day The Associated Press received a long letter in which responsibility for the explosion was claimed by "The Weather Underground."

A day before he died, Whitney Young swam in the Gulf of Guinea with Sen. Edmund Muskie

WHITNEY YOUNG'S CIVIL RIGHTS CAREER ENDED BY DEATH

Whitney Moore Young and his more militant black brothers sought the same thing: equality for the American Negro. But unlike some black leaders Young saw no need for unruly protest or violence. Instead, in a quiet, direct and determined fashion, Young sat among presidents and corporate giants, getting the thing he thought blacks needed most: jobs.

Young was regarded by some as "Uncle Whitey" or an "Oreo cookie"—black on the outside, white on the inside. Yet, upon his death March 11 at 49, the widely shared image he left was that of the nation's most productive —and much misunderstood—civil rights leader.

As part of his strategy, Young clung to the belief that, in order to get what he wanted, he had to take it from someone who had it to give. Since in most cases that was the white man, he believed in building a rapport that was keyed to the needs of his own people. One day on his way to work from his suburban home in New Rochelle, N.Y., he mused: "Should I get off this train this morning and stand on 125th street cussing Whitey to show I am tough? Or should I go downtown and talk to an executive of General Motors about 2,000 jobs for unemployed Negroes?"

The choice wasn't hard for Young to make. Before he became executive director in 1961 the National Urban League had the reputation in some quarters of being a lax job placement bureau for the middle class Negro; a research-minded organization sometimes deaf to the cries of ghetto Americans. Young moved in with a quiet but stern hand. He opened 35 new chapters, increased the professional staff from 300 to 1,200. In two years he found 40,000 new jobs for unemployed blacks and 8,000 better jobs for those already employed.

Born in Lincoln Ridge, Ky., he was the son of the president of Lincoln Institute, a Negro boarding high school. He was graduated from Lincoln at the age of 14 and received a B.S. degree from Kentucky State at 19.

Young's intention had been a medical career, but World War II intervened and he found himself in the Army. He was often subjected to discrimination until officers became aware of his scholastic record. Within two weeks he was promoted to first sergeant. He spent most of his time in Europe working with an all-black unit, building roads. It was then that he got his first lessons in mediation between Negroes and whites, an art he was to use effectively later in closing the gap between the militant and the conservative blacks. Poet and playwright Imamu Amiri Baraka (Le Roi Jones) said of Young: "There is a loss here that a lot of black people aren't aware of. Whitney Young had become a kind of bridge between that part of the community which is activist and that part which is mainstream. He unified all forces."

As the civil rights movement changed so did Young. Despite fears that white contributors might cut off aid, the league's board of directors agreed to participate in the 1963 March on Washington. At that time Young was a main coordinator. He had once supported the war in Southeast Asia, but when he decided that it was stifling the nation's efforts to help the poor—some of whom had lost the jobs he had procured for them—Young not only became active in several marches but also met with many Washington officials.

After receiving his master's degree at the University of Minnesota, he became dean of the School of Social Work at Atlantic University from 1954 until he became director of the Urban League, with an income of $45,000 a year. He served on seven presidential commissions and won the Medal for Freedom, the nation's highest civilian award. He was president of the National Association of Social Workers and turned down numerous offers of public office.

When the world learned of his death while swimming at Lagos, Nigeria, where he was attending the African-American Dialogue, thousands paid him tribute. His body lay in state in New York, and dozens of dignitaries attended the burial service in Lexington, Ky. Among them was President Nixon, who said, "I have lost a friend, black America has lost a gifted and commanding champion of its just cause and this nation has lost one of the most compassionate and principled leaders it has had in all the long centuries since whites from Europe and blacks from Africa began building toward the American dream."

But of all the eulogies none perhaps was as appropriate as the words he himself once spoke: "I tell people I can't guarantee you a monument in stone. Your monument will be people helped in moments of distress, people given hope when they had every reason to feel despair. I'm not anxious to be the loudest voice, or the most popular. But I would like to think that, at a crucial moment, I was an effective voice of the voiceless, an effective hope of the hopeless."

He was.

FOR THE RECORD

SIGNED. By President Nixon, a bill increasing Social Security benefits across the board. But the President called on Congress to vote the money at once to pay for it, arguing that putting through such an increase without providing the financing could be inflationary. Nixon also called on the legislators to act promptly on a proposal to raise the income base on which 5.2 per cent Social Security taxes are paid from $7,800 to $9,000.

MARRIED. Prime Minister Pierre Elliott Trudeau, of Canada, one of the world's most eligible bachelors, to 22-year-old Margaret Sinclair. Though Mrs. Trudeau was not a well known figure in government circles, some members of Parliament remembered her as a small girl they saw in the Commons gallery, waving to her father, James Sinclair, a Liberal party cabinet minister in the 1950s. The 51-year-old Trudeau met his bride on a holiday in Tahiti, three years earlier. March 4, in Vancouver, B.C.

Did table tennis breach China's wall?

大海航行靠舵

April

China: Ping Pong Puzzle

"You have opened a new page in the relations of the Chinese and American people," premier told U.S. table tennis team

THIS IS my first dispatch from China in 22 years. The news I have to report would have been incredible only a few weeks ago: Americans are welcome in the People's Republic."

So began the chronicle of an astonishing and puzzling week in the history of American relations with Communist China. The man who filed the dispatch was John Roderick of The Associated Press Tokyo bureau, an "old China hand" and one of only three American newsmen permitted to enter Communist China to cover a tour of a U.S. table tennis team.

It had happened with dazzling suddenness. The characteristically subtle Chinese employed all the subtlety of a sledgehammer to drive home Peking's message: The time had come to smile upon Americans.

But not all Americans. Not official Americans. Not the U.S. government. China's suave and able premier, the elegant Chou En-lai, made it as clear as he could that the smiles were for the American "people." The Peking press and radio continued daily to blast Washington as a nest of "bloodthirsty gangsters."

April had brought its happy hint of spring after the harsh winter of northeast China. How much of a thaw did the April events promise in the long-frozen relations between the Communist regime and the United States? Americans would be a long time assessing the full meaning of those developments, but it was all so deliberate on the Chinese side, so obviously planned and directed from the pinnacle of the Peking regime, that there had to be something deeply significant about it for the future of U.S.-Chinese relations and for the future of vast China's role as a major power in a shrunken world.

It had begun in Nagoya, Japan, during the 31st world table tennis championships, a fact warily noted by the Japanese, weighing their future economic and political relations with the Communist giant on the mainland of Asia. The Chinese, who

Newsmen returned to Hong Kong after tour of Communist China (from left): John Roderick, Associated Press; Hiromasa Yamanaka, John Rich and Jack Reynolds, all of the National Broadcasting Company

have some of the world's greatest table tennis players, of course had a team on hand, and there was also a team there from the United States.

A young man named Chuang Tse-tung—was it an accident that he bore the same given name as Chairman Mao?—started the Ping Pong ball bouncing. Chuang, the Chinese table tennis champion, struck up an acquaintance with an American team member, 19-year-old Glen Cowan of Santa Monica, Calif., whose long hair and flamboyant garb proclaimed him representative of the youthful American avant garde. In what would seem to have been an offhand manner, Chuang casually suggested that the American team might like to make an all-expenses-paid tour in the People's Republic. Indeed, most of the Americans would, and 15 of them jumped at the idea.

"To quote Chairman Mao," Cowan would say later, "I seem to have struck the spark that started a prairie fire."

The spark burst into a warming flame. Chuang's suggestion to Cowan soon became a formal, official invitation delivered orally by Sung Chung, secretary general of the Chinese contingent in Nagoya, to Rufford Harrison, deputy leader of the U.S. delegation. Arrangements soon were ironed out in a meeting between the Chinese group's leaders with Graham B. Steenhoven of Detroit, Mich., head of the U.S. delegation, along with Harrison and Tim Boggan, a player-official with the American team. The U.S. State Department, wondering what was going on, had no objections. It hardly could have, since only a few weeks before it had removed restrictions on Americans' travel in Red China.

Lights burned late in the foreign offices of the world's capitals as experts sought to fit together the pieces of this new Chinese puzzle. Was this a major breakthrough? Was it, indeed, something of enormous importance taking place, despite the fact that its confinement to Ping Pong might make it all seem curiously trivial? The use of sport as an instrument of policy is not unusual in diplomacy. The Russians, in fact, had done likewise in the days immediately after Stalin's death, when they seemed about ready to break out of Stalinist isolation.

China had been in isolation, too—the more so because of three years of violence known as the Great Proletarian Cultural Revolution. Now the cultural revolution was over, for the most part. China had calmed down. There had been little possibility between the years 1966 and 1969 to reduce tension between China and the Americans because of the mighty power struggle that was taking place in Peking, but now Mao's foes, headed by the aging President Liu Shao-chi, were destroyed and in disgrace. A new constitution made Mao the ruler for life as "Great Leader." Lin Piao was officially anointed in the constitution as Mao's successor. A measure of stability was returning to the huge nation. China could afford to take cautious steps into the outer world.

Washington was cautious, even though the first reaction was to view this sudden Ping Pong approach from Peking as heralding perhaps a more flexible attitude, at least on the people-to-people level. Moscow growled and didn't like the development at all. To the Kremlin, Peking's gesture was an "unprincipled" flirtation with the Americans.

As the plans went forward quickly to get the American delegation members into China, lightning struck again, this time in the form of a telegram to the Tokyo Bureau of The Associated Press:

"John Roderick, Associated Press of America, Tokyo:

"Visa granted only for the purpose of covering U.S. table tennis team visit to China. Please contact China Travel Service, Hong Kong, for necessary arrangements.

"Information Department, Ministry of Foreign Affairs, People's Republic of China."

Similar messages went to John Rich, another "old China hand," and Jack Reynolds, both of the National Broadcasting Company in Tokyo. These three newsmen would be the only Americans permitted to cover the history-making table tennis tour.

An unlikely group of unofficial diplomats, the American table tennis group—eight were players, five officials and two the wives of officials—flew to Hong Kong and gathered at the Lo Wu border station on April 9, there to begin the adventure of their lives. Their leader, Steenhoven, was a gray-haired, solidly conservative executive of a U.S. motor company. Their deputy leader, Harrison, was an easy-going chemist from Wilmington, Del. The delegation included a university assistant professor, an IBM programmer, a psychology student from Cincinnati University, an employe of a Wall Street bank, a black who was employed at the United Nations, an immigrant from the Dominican Republic, two housewives and two teen-age girls. Their ages ranged from 15 all the way to the 59 years of leader Steenhoven.

The bright, hot springtime sunshine made the tin roof of the covered bridge glisten as the Americans walked across it from Lo Wu to the territory of Communist China. On the other side at Shumchun they were cordially greeted by uniformed Chinese officials who checked them through quickly and escorted them to the railway station, where a gleaming, spotless cream and blue train was waiting to take them the 23 miles to Canton—the Chinese called it Kwangchow—the first leg of their journey inside the Communist realm. As they sped through a land of lichee trees, banana groves and rice terraces they saw innumerable giant-size portraits of Mao Tse-tung beaming benevolently down at them from billboards along the tracks. No matter where they looked, there was Chairman Mao, on posters, in sculptures, on billboards and on buttons in the lapels of millions of blue-jacketed Chinese. Martial music blared from station speakers, interrupted frequently for the intonation of quotations from the little red book of *The Thoughts of Chairman Mao*.

At Canton's new and hardly used international airport, named White Cloud, a Russian-built Ilyushin-18 plane waited for the party. With them was an official of the Chinese table tennis organization, constantly solicitous for their comfort.

The newsmen would not be far behind. Their notification of a 10-day visa approval had arrived at about midnight in Tokyo on Easter Saturday. Within eight hours they were on their way to Hong Kong. They crossed from the British crown colony into China at 10:30 a.m. on a sunny Easter morning.

For the 56-year-old Roderick, it was his first glimpse of the China mainland since his 1945-1948 assignment, when he had been stationed in the country to cover the civil war between the Communists and Chiang Kai-shek's Nationalists. He had met Mao and Chou and other top Chinese Communists in the cave city of Yenan in remote Shensi Province, Mao's headquarters ever since his famed "Long March" in flight from Chiang's forces in the mid-1930s.

With Roderick and the two NBC men, Rich and Reynolds, were four other newsmen: John Saar, an Englishman who headed the Time-Life bureau at Hong Kong; Frank Fischbeck, a West German photographer for Time-Life, and Jose Schlesinger and Bob Whyte of the Canadian Broadcasting Corp. Only Rich and Roderick had been in China before the Communist takeover.

At Canton, cradle of Sun Yat-sen's 1911 Republican revolution, an automobile took the correspondents through the teem-

London telephonist Pamela Gee about to connect the first commercial call from England since Communist China suspended service

ing streets of the city of 3 million, threading its way in and out of a flow of bicycle, pedicab and pedestrian traffic which was otherwise disturbed only rarely by a scant few motor vehicles.

"The new airport, built four years ago, seemed to exist only for us," wrote Roderick from Canton. "We newsmen . . . and a clutch of Chinese were the only passengers in the four-engined Ilyushin-18, held over from its usual 2 p.m. departure time for us. The last thing we saw when we took off at 5:15 p.m. was Mao smiling up at us from an enormous portrait in front of the airport building. Inside, a smaller picture faced us and a printed quotation: 'People of the world unite and defeat the U.S. aggressors and their running dogs.' "

The American table tennis delegation by that time already was comfortably ensconced in the Hsinchiao Hotel in Peking, a six-story concrete mass originally designed for tourists and usually set aside for foreign guests. There was only the slightest trace of spring in the air of the capital, where winter lingers long. But if the skies were drab, the red-carpet treatment of the Americans more than made up for that. The meals were lavish and enormous—tray upon tray of hors d'oeuvres followed by course upon course of Chinese dishes ranging all the way from sharkfin soup and century-old eggs to the Chinese-style meal topper, a rich and meaty chicken soup for dessert.

The delegation's tour began with a visit to the ancient and fabled Great Wall, built to keep out the barbarian. The occasion seemed symbolic. China had been isolated for 21 years,

and now, as Roderick put it, a "hole has been made in the once impenetrable wall."

Before 18,000 cheering Chinese Ping Pong enthusiasts, garbed monotonously in blue and green jackets, the Americans played an exhibition match with a Chinese team. It was not a first-string Chinese team and the Americans had the impression that this was a display of Chinese tact. A first string team could have humiliated the visitors. As it was, the scores were fairly close. The Chinese men won, 5-3, and the Chinese women, 5-4, in what were billed as "friendly matches."

Table tennis long had been a solemn business for the Chinese Communists. The Chinese considered themselves the best in the world when it came to table tennis, and with considerable justification. They had done extremely well in world tournaments, although during the cultural revolution they had encountered some political difficulties with Ping Pong players. The trouble had arisen when some nefarious Chinese table tennis official back in 1966 had permitted publication of an article saying that the main factors in the Chinese players' successes had been experience and training. This report, said the newspaper People's Daily, "filled the team members with anger" because the article failed to attribute all the success to the thoughts of Chairman Mao. Thenceforward it was the rule to "place emphasis on the decisive role of Mao Tse-tung's thinking in winning victories at table tennis," and Peking's entry went on to win six of seven titles at stake in the 1966 tournament.

(Above) A path flanked by trees, for Red Chinese workers in a commune

(left) Canal traffic, laden with foodstuffs, through Red Chinese commune

It had been the custom for the team to go into a match reading aloud a quotation from Chairman Mao, but on the occasion of the exhibition match with the Americans this formality apparently had been adjudged unnecessary. A banner was stretched across the vast, modern gymnasium welcoming the Americans, who took part in the ritual preliminaries. This involved marching, hand in hand with the Chinese opponents, into the arena to the martial tune of *Sailing the Seas Depends on the Helmsman, Making Revolution Depends on the Thought of Mao Tse-tung.* Young Cowan, with his long hair and bell bottoms, was a crowd favorite, not so much because of his play as because of the red band he wore to keep his copious locks under control during the match.

The table tennis itself, however, was just a sidelight so far as the watching world and, probably, official Peking were concerned. The big event came the next day. Premier Chou En-lai received the group in the huge, red-carpeted reception room of the Great Hall of the People. Austerely garbed, as usual, in the gray Mao-style tunic affected by all Chinese leaders, Chou told the U.S. delegation: "You have opened a new page in the relations of the Chinese and American people. I am confident that this beginning again of our friendship will certainly meet with the majority support of our two peoples. . . . You have made a start here and I believe that in the future more American friends will come to China."

It had been 23 years since Chou had laid eyes on AP's Roderick, but the premier recognized the correspondent and singled him out.

"Mr. Roderick," said Red China's 73-year-old indispensable man, "you have opened the door."

In the future, said Chou, more American correspondents would be visiting China. "They will come in batches," said the smiling Chou, and he also suggested that he would not mind making a visit to North America, a continent the widely travelled Chou had never seen. He did not specifically say he wanted to visit the United States, but the broad hint was there.

Chou proved himself a stick-in-the-mud, old-hat conservative from the point of view of the world's far-out youth, by his comments on the hippie movement. Perhaps, he said in a grandfatherly way, youth was dissatisfied with things at present and wanted to seek truth. But, he counselled young Cowan, the young should "always try to find something in common with the great majority. . . . One must get the agreement of the majority of the people."

Evidence that Chou was in earnest about future visits by correspondents came with a Peking decision, announced as the table tennis group was winding up its tour, that Tillman Durdin of the New York Times would be permitted into Red China for one month as a correspondent. Roderick, meanwhile, was permitted to stay on an extra three days after the table tennis delegation, surfeited with exotic food and drink and overwhelmed by Chinese hospitality, left by the route it entered, through Lo Wu.

On Saturday, April 17, the American delegation, all smiles, walked back across the bridge to British territory. It had been quite an adventure. They had seen the Forbidden City of Peking. They had seen teeming Shanghai and Canton. They had visited Chinghua University and the Great Wall and a rural commune and a factory, and they had gaped in awe at the Manchus' exquisite Summer Palace in the capital. They had seen and chatted informally with one of the world's most celebrated Communists, Premier Chou. As one of them said upon leaving Canton, "It was an experience I will remember all my life."

The excitement was over. Now was the time for sober assessment. Just what had taken place? What did it mean for the future of Chinese-American relations? Was there really a hole in the wall?

The answer to the last question seemed to be a cautious affirmative. Chou and the Chinese organs of propaganda had continued to make the careful distinction between government and "people," but this could be read as a need to let the Chinese people know there had been no direct approach to Washington. After all Peking had said about official Washington, to change tune suddenly might involve loss of face. In Communist parlance, however, "people" was equated with those who did not oppose the Communists who, by dogma, were called the "vanguard of the people." Anyone who opposed "the people" therefore was automatically called "anti-people" or "enemies of the people." By this time the literate public in Communist countries, particularly party members, were fully aware of the distinctions.

But there had to be something to the developments with regard to government-to-government relations. Nothing like this in a Communist regime could conceivably have happened by accident. The whole episode thus brought into focus a new concept of a struggle in the world at three corners of a triangle of great powers—and China by now surely was to be considered a great power along with the Soviet Union and the United States. Apart from the sheer weight of her numbers—800 million or more people—China was a full member of the nuclear weapons club and possessed nuclear-tipped missiles. She could not be ignored in any assessment of world power relations.

For a long time China's leaders had suggested that the big question on their minds was: Are the Americans and Russians getting together to quarantine China and keep her isolated?

Now the question on the Soviet mind might be: Was Peking —still feuding with Moscow and vowing enmity for the current Soviet rulers—attempting to align itself with the United States and thus isolate the Russians in the big power alignment?

And a question on the American mind could be: Were the Chinese really interested in opening a door, or were they using the prospect of it as a weapon in their political-propaganda warfare with the Russians?

The Ping Pong exchange had produced a black mood among Soviet officialdom. A Soviet commentator, giving voice to Kremlin misgivings, sniffed that the episode—"this insignificant step" —was "being used by the U.S. press for noisy propaganda of a clearly anti-Communist and anti-Soviet nature." The Kremlin's suspicions were deepened by a Nixon Administration announcement, obviously well timed while the table tennis delegation was in China, easing regulations governing trade with China and lifting currency restrictions.

Peking's propaganda against the United States, both for domestic and foreign consumption, continued harsh. The Peking press and radio hailed reports of disturbances in America and called for violent revolution in the United States. Peking continued to appeal for armed "revolutionary struggle" throughout non-Communist Southeast Asia. It continued, too, to denounce the United States in the most searing terms on the Vietnam issue. And in spite of all this, Moscow sniped angrily at the Peking leaders, accusing them of pursuing a policy aimed at "helping the imperialists" at the expense of communism.

The Ping Pong episode of 1971 brought fresh knowledge of China to the West. The West learned a good deal from the reports of correspondents lucky enough to be chosen to enter Red China. But the episode also left many questions unanswered. To what extent would the people-to-people contacts be permitted to develop into relations on a government level? How earnest was Peking about building a bridge to the United States?

Chou's options remained open. He had spoken only of the desirability of good relations between "peoples." He could not be accused of having asked Washington for anything at all. And yet his words had been carefully chosen as if to hint that a new chapter in Chinese-American relations need not be as grim as the last had been.

And so the Ping Pong episode did in the long run suggest a possibility of purposeful dialogue. It might be difficult to bring about. It might be laborious going. But there were good reasons in this last third of the 20th Century why the two huge nations should talk together seriously.

The day of friendly relations still seemed distant. Peking had long held to a posture of deep hostility to Washington. The United States had long been nervously suspicious toward and hostile to Peking's intentions. It would be no small matter, on either side, to open the door wide. But at least, in 1971, it seemed that the door had opened just a crack, enough to let a small ray of sunlight show through.

The My Lai Massacre: Calley Found Guilty

Verdict was first-degree murder in slaying of 22 South Vietnamese but General O'Connor later reduced life sentence to 20 years

Lt. William Calley Jr.

Bodies of women and children lay in roadway leading to My Lai

Life Magazine photo, copyright 1969

L T. WILLIAM L. CALLEY JR.'s task force commander called the operation of March 16, 1968, in Vietnam an American search and destroy mission "well planned, well executed and successful." But the world called it the My Lai massacre. During a few hot and humid morning hours in that Asian hamlet, American military might was misdirected, sophisticated American weapons misaimed. The result was scores of unarmed, unresisting Vietnamese civilians slain—men, women, children, babes in arms.

Estimates by villagers ran as high as 527 (*The World in 1969, 257*).

During an intermittent four months beginning Nov. 12, 1970, Calley stood trial in a small, neat courtroom within Building No. 5 at Fort Benning, Ga. There the whys and wherefores of My Lai were minutely examined through the testimony of 91 witnesses, and by means of depositions, documents, maps and photographs.

At the end of March 1971 a jury of six of his senior officers convicted the 27-year-old Ft. Benning graduate of the first-degree murder of at least 22 villagers and sentenced him to life imprisonment. All six jurors were combat veterans, five of them with decorations won in Vietnam.

Nearly 5 months later at Fort McPherson, Ga., Lt. Gen. Albert O. Connor, commanding general of the Third Army, reduced Calley's sentence to 20 years. Calley thereby became eligible for parole in six or seven years.

A native of Miami, Fla., Calley described his boyhood as cheerful and active. But over the years there was established a pattern that was to persist—of an individual always seeking, never quite achieving his aims. He flunked out of junior college. He held a succession of unimpressive jobs. Finally he enlisted in the Army to avoid being drafted.

Selected for Officer Candidate School at Ft. Benning, Calley reported on March 16, 1967, to that home post of the infantry, spread across 285 square miles of rolling hills in west central Georgia. My Lai was exactly one year away.

Calley graduated in the bottom third of his class. But the fledgling 5-feet-3 lieutenant, with the widow's peak of darkly reddish hair whence his nickname "Rusty" was derived, swelled with pride when the gold bars were pinned on his shoulders.

On the following Dec. 1, Calley landed in Vietnam. He was 24 years old, a member of Charlie Co., 1st battalion, 11th Brigade, 20th Infantry regiment, Americal division. His company commander was Capt. Ernest Medina.

Charlie company was assigned to Quang Ngai province on the shores of the South China sea. Ill trained, more attuned to obedience to orders than to the rules of warfare as outlined in the Geneva convention of 1949, Charlie company made a series of fruitless forays in quest of the Viet Cong enemy. They never closed with the foe. But they had evidence of his presence—in casualties inflicted by sniper fire and mine ambushes.

On Jan. 27, Charlie company was assigned to Task Force Barker, named for Lt. Col. Frank A. Barker Jr., who was to die at the age of 40 in a helicopter crash that occurred three months after My Lai.

Calley led Charlie company's first platoon, a spearhead unit in the March 16, 1968, attack on My Lai. Before noon the sweep was completed. My Lai was a village ablaze, its L-shaped drainage ditch red with civilian blood. Calley's platoon took only one casualty—a GI who shot himself in the foot, either by design or accident.

Before noon also, there was awareness that all was not right about Charlie company's mission.

Maj. Charles Calhoun, executive and task force operations

A break in the proceedings: Calley conferred with Richard Kay, civilian counsel, as they walked to lunch from courtroom

officer, relayed a message from Barker to Charlie company to make sure the infantry troops "weren't hurting any civilians or doing any unnecessary burning."

A helicopter pilot, Warrant Officer Hugh Thompson, returned from My Lai to report to his commander that "I thought something was wrong out there because I couldn't foresee any way of how the bodies got in the ditch."

Thompson's misgivings were relayed through Barker to the brigade commander, Col. Oran Henderson, and on up to the Americal division's assistant commander, Brig. Gen. George H. Young. The division's commander was Maj. Gen. Samuel Koster, who was over My Lai that late spring morning in a helicopter.

But in the words of a subsequent House Armed Services subcommittee report, "it can reasonably be concluded that the My Lai matter was 'covered up' within the Americal division."

Criminal charges of covering up were dismissed against Koster and Young. But, six weeks after Calley's conviction, both were censured and had their Distinguished Service Medals revoked. In addition, Koster was demoted to brigadier general. They were accused of failure to conduct a more intensive investigation of My Lai.

It was in a confidential combat action report filed March 28, 1968, by Col. Barker that the My Lai assault was described as "well planned, well executed and successful."

There the matter rested for exactly one year.

Then a Vietnam veteran named Ron Ridenhour entered the picture. He had not been at My Lai. But he had been with the men of Charlie company earlier in Hawaii as a member of the 11th brigade.

About a month after My Lai, as Ridenhour encountered some of his old comrades, he began putting together scraps of their conversation about "Pinkville," as the GIs referred to My Lai because the area was colored pink on military maps. On March 29, 1969, Ridenhour mailed 30 copies of a letter to President Nixon, various senators and representatives, top military brass and the State Department. In the letter he documented his belief that "something rather dark and bloody did indeed occur sometime in March 1968, in a village called 'Pinkville' in the Republic of Vietnam."

With surprising accuracy Ridenhour detailed the role played by Calley, referring to him as "Lt. Kally," and adding "this spelling may be incorrect."

As word of the My Lai massacre now spread for the first time beyond the Americal division, Calley was indicted for first-degree murder. His was not the first case disposed of, however.

First to go to trial was S. Sgt. David Mitchell, 30, one of Calley's squad leaders. He was acquitted on a charge of assault with intent to murder 30 civilians at My Lai, following a court-martial at Ft. Hood, Tex. Also acquitted in a subsequent court-martial at Ft. McPherson, Ga., was Sgt. Charles Hutto, 22, a machine gunner in Charlie company's 2nd platoon. He was charged with assault with intent to kill six villagers.

Dominating the prosecution case against Calley were five of its 36 witnesses. The first of these was Paul Meadlo, 23 at the time of My Lai, where he was a PFC and a rifleman in Calley's platoon.

A former Indiana farm boy, Meadlo had large hands and broad shoulders. He also had only one foot. The other was blown off by a land mine the day after My Lai—a maiming he took to be punishment inflicted by God.

On network television Nov. 24, 1969, Meadlo laconically admitted his role at My Lai, in words and phrases that shocked the world into its first deep realization of the ghastly scope of the village massacre.

Meadlo told Calley's military jury that as the first platoon entered My Lai he helped round up about 35 or 40 Vietnamese men, women and children who were herded at rifle point to a clearing where two trails crossed within the village.

Calley came up to the scene and Meadlo said he directed, "you know what to do with them, Meadlo."

"I assumed he meant guard them and I said yes," Meadlo went on.

Calley was distracted by another errand but was soon back on the scene and Meadlo's testimony continued:

"He says, 'How come they're not dead?' I said I didn't know we were supposed to kill them. He said, 'I want them dead.' He told me to help shoot them."

The witness said he and Calley stood side by side and pumped M-16 automatic fire into the massed captives from a distance of about 20 feet. The government claimed at least 30 Vietnamese died at the trail.

Meadlo then carried his recital to the eastern edge of My Lai and the L-shaped drainage ditch that was to become notorious during the trial. The government claimed at least 70 villagers were slain there.

Q. What was Lt. Calley doing at the time?

A. I don't remember.

Q. Were there any Vietnamese there with him?

A. Yes, there was Viet Cong (sic) there. I estimated 75 to 100. He said to me "We got another job to do, Meadlo." Lt. Calley started shoving them off and shooting them in the ravine.

Q. (Under cross-examination) Did you form any opinion of Lt. Calley while he was at those places?

A. I thought he was a man who was doing his duty and doing his job.

Meadlo was followed to the stand by Dennis Conti, 21, a truck driver from Providence, R.I., long-haired, utterly mod, and with an air of ineffable boredom. It was his fifth appearance as a witness at various My Lai inquiries, and he seemed fed up with the entire subject.

Conti testified he had helped Meadlo guard the Vietnamese on the trail and saw Calley fire upon them as "they screamed and yelled." He said Meadlo began to weep and tried to get him to join in the massacre. But, Conti added:

"I said, 'If they're gonna be killed, let Lt. Calley do it. I'm not gonna do it.' Lt. Calley fired on 'em and killed 'em one by one."

Then, at the ditch, Conti said he watched Calley and Mitchell firing at the massed Vietnamese cowering there.

Q. What were the people doing?

A. A lot of them were trying to get up. Most were just screaming. They were shot up pretty bad. I looked down and seen a woman trying to get up. I seen Lt. Calley fire and blow the side of her head off.

Meadlo had testified Calley instigated the massacre and took part in it. Conti claimed to have actually seen Calley's M-16 rifle bullets kill. Now it was Charles Sledge's turn.

Sledge, 23, of Sardis, Miss., of medium build, with a small, neat mustache, was Calley's radio-telephone operator at My Lai. He told of seeing the Vietnamese killed on the village trail. Then he said he proceeded to the drainage ditch and watched more villagers die, their screams cut short by the automatic rifle fire.

Near the ditch was a man in white robes similar to those worn by Buddhist monks. Illustrating with his palms pointed up—fingertip to fingertip in an attitude of prayer—Sledge testified:

"The priest would say, 'No Viet,' and he held his hands in this shape. Calley asked him a few more questions and he bowed his head and he still said, 'No Viet.' Then he hit him with the butt of his rifle in the mouth."

Q. What did the priest do?

A. He didn't do nothing but fall back, doing this with his hands again, sort of like pleading. Lt. Calley took his rifle at point blank and pulled the trigger in the priest's face. Half his head was blown off.

Sledge then testified regarding a child of about two, saying: "Someone hollered, 'There's a child.' You know it was running back toward the village. I don't know whether it was a boy or girl. It was a little baby. Lt. Calley grabbed it by the arm and threw it into the ditch and fired."

He couldn't be sure, Sledge added, that Calley's fire actually struck the child. And he conceded it was possible the monk-like man might have had a weapon concealed in his robes, and that his prayer-like gesture covered an effort to reach it.

Nonetheless, Sledge had proved a crucial witness for the prosecution. The shooting of the monk and the child were an integral part of the case against Calley, spelled out in the military equivalent of his indictment. Sledge was the only witness to substantiate this phase of the Army's case.

Following Sledge on the witness stand was Thomas Turner, a 24-year-old student at the University of Nebraska, who had been a rifleman in Calley's platoon at My Lai.

It was Turner who put before the jury a picture of a methodic murder-by-assembly-line operation, as the government sought to refute the idea that whatever Calley did at My Lai was unpremeditated, conceived on the spur of the moment.

Again the scene was the ditch as Turner testified:

"As I looked into the ditch I saw a pile of bodies. They were old men, women and children. They were covered with blood. Lt. Calley began firing into another group standing and kneeling in the ditch. There was a variety of people there—men, women and children. . . . There was being brought up small groups of people and they were being placed in the ditch and Lt. Calley was firing into it."

Q. How long did this last?

A. Approximately an hour and a half.

The defense vainly sought a mistrial, calling Turner's testimony "devastating." On cross-examination the witness testified that as Calley reloaded his weapon again and again, GIs of his platoon "brought up various groups at different times, maybe five or 10 groups."

Q. Which direction were they coming from?

A. They were coming from the village.

The last of the five GIs whom the court-martial judge Col. Reid Kennedy called "obviously key witnesses to the facts in this case" was James Dursi, 23, tall, sideburned, another of the riflemen in Calley's platoon. He came to Ft. Benning from Brooklyn, where he worked for an electrical manufacturing firm.

Dursi told of herding villagers ahead of him to the ditch and of seeing Calley arrive on the scene. The witness continued:

"He came across first and he was followed shortly afterwards by Meadlo. Meadlo was shook up. He was crying. Lt. Calley said to Meadlo, 'We have another job to do.' And he told us to start putting people in the ditch. We moved the people into the ditch with our rifles at port arms position. Some started crying and they were yelling. I was ordered to shoot."

Q. By whom?

A. Lt. Calley. I can't remember the exact wording, something like start firing, something like that. Then Lt. Calley and Meadlo started firing into the ditch. Meadlo turned to me shortly after the shooting began and said, "Shoot! Why don't you fire?" He was crying and yelling. I just said, "I can't, I won't" and looked down at the ground.

Q. Why did you not fire?

A. I couldn't go through with it—these defenseless men, women, kids.

It was one of the few notes of compassion voiced during the trial for the victims of My Lai. It also was strong corroboration of Meadlo's damning prior testimony against Calley.

It was Feb. 23, 1971, when Calley took the witness stand. Only his combat infantryman badge was affixed to his green army tunic. Missing were the Purple Heart and Bronze Star medal he was entitled to wear.

Shifting about in the witness chair, leaning first on one arm and then on the other, Calley denied he ever was in the vicinity where Vietnamese civilians were massacred on the trail. Nor, he testified, did he ever throw the fleeing child back into the ditch and shoot it, or shoot the man in monk's robes.

However, Calley admitted telling Meadlo in the vicinity of the ditch that "if he couldn't move the people to waste them."

Then what happened, Calley was asked. He testified:

"Then I came out of the woodline and saw my troops shooting the people in the ditch. I fired into the ditch, told my men to hurry up and get on the other side and get into position."

Q. How many shots did you fire?

A. Six to eight, sir.

Q. Do you know if you hit any of them?

A. No sir, I don't.

Q. How far were you from them when you fired?

A. The muzzle would have been five feet, sir.

Calley attributed everything he did that day at My Lai to orders from Capt. Medina, commander of Charlie company. One exchange highlighted his contention:

Q. Now why did you give Meadlo a message or an order that if he couldn't get rid of them to waste them?

A. Because that was my order, sir. That was the order of the day, sir.

Q. Who gave you that order?

A. My commanding officer, Capt. Medina, sir.

Q. How many times did you receive such an order from Capt. Medina?

A. The night before in the company briefing, platoon leaders' briefing, the following morning before we lifted off and twice there in the village.

From the witness stand, Medina denied he ever ordered women and children killed at My Lai. He said of his briefing to his company the night before the assault:

"One of the questions that was asked of me at the briefing was 'Do we kill women and children?' My reply to that question was, 'No, you do not kill women and children. You must use common sense. If they have a weapon and are trying to engage you, you can shoot back, but you must use common sense.' "

After the village was cleared, Calley testified he joined Medina and the other platoon leaders at lunch.

Q. Did you tell Capt. Medina that you had shot the people in the ditch?

A. Yes sir, I did . . . It wasn't any big deal.

Medina swore under oath that he never had lunch with Calley that day.

Calley's testimony that he ordered and participated in the shooting at the ditch closed one avenue the defense had been pursuing—that the deaths there might have been caused by helicopter gunship or artillery fire in connection with the My Lai mission.

Now the defense was forced to fall back on two factors that lay strictly within the realm of the psychiatrists, who proceeded to take over the witness stand.

An order from Medina to kill unresisting villagers would have been an illegal order. The question the psychiatrists disagreed on was whether Calley had the understanding to recognize the order as illegal and to reject it, and whether his mental capacity had been so diminished by the stresses and strains of combat that he was unable to premeditate murder.

Col. Kennedy, an amiable, sharp-witted jurist, gave the case to the six-man panel at 9:25 p.m. EST Tuesday, March 16, 1971—the third anniversary of My Lai.

For the next 13 days the jurors were secluded in their deliberation room, a dingy 12-by-27 feet cubicle across the hall from the courtroom. At night they were locked up together under guard in a bachelor officers' quarters on the post.

The indictment charged Calley with the premeditated murder

Court martial chief judge: Lt. Col. Reid W. Kennedy (left); Capt. Aubrey M. Daniel III, prosecutor

of 30 villagers on the trail, 70 at the ditch, plus the fleeing child and the man in monk's robes—102 in all.

At 4:29 p.m. Monday, March 29, the jury filed back into the courtroom with its verdict. Standing at stiff attention directly in front of the panel, Calley heard the foreman and ranking officer, Col. Clifford Ford, 53, the only member not a veteran of Vietnam, announce the findings.

Calley was convicted of the premeditated murder of at least one unresisting Vietnamese on the trail, at least 20 at the ditch, plus the man in the monk's clothing—a total of at least 22. He was found guilty of assault with intent to kill the fleeing child, on the theory the bullet could have missed.

The defendant snapped a crisp salute in Ford's direction. A short time later he was imprisoned in the officers' section of the post stockade, sharing his quarters with a young second lieutenant accused on bad check charges. There Calley awaited the trial jury's decision on the penalty—either death or life in prison.

On the following afternoon, March 30, Calley took advantage of his right to address the jury personally. Standing in front of them, he told the six officers:

". . . I'm not going to stand here and plead for my life or my freedom . . . I've never known a soldier, nor did I myself wantonly kill a human being in my entire life.

"If I've committed a crime, the only crime I have committed is in judgment of my values—apparently I have valued my troops' lives more than I did that of the enemy. When my troops were getting massacred and mauled by an enemy I couldn't see, I couldn't feel and I couldn't touch, that nobody

(Below) Lt. William Calley Jr.: Waiting for the verdict

"You crucified him," said Mrs. Hildagad Crochet at Calley rally

in the military ever described as anything other than Communism.

"They didn't give it a race, they didn't give it a sex, they didn't give it an age. They never let me believe it was just a philosophy in a man's mind. That was my enemy out there and when it became between me and that enemy, I had to value the lives of my troops and I feel that it is the only crime I have committed.

"Yesterday you stripped me of all my honor. Please, by your actions that you take here today, don't strip future soldiers of their honor, I beg of you."

Calley ended his plea in a breaking voice, tears filming his eyes. The six jurors appeared utterly impassive.

This time, the jury deliberations took only until 2:28 p.m. the next day, Wednesday, March 31. Calley was sentenced to life imprisonment, dismissal from the Army and forfeiture of pay and allowances totaling $773.10 a month.

Calley sagged at the pronouncement, his jaw slackened and he managed only a limp salute for Col. Ford. Then he was led back to the stockade. When he awoke the next morning he was at the center of a new storm.

Vietnam hawks and doves found themselves united in protesting Calley's punishment. Antiwar groups deemed him a scapegoat in a conflict they considered immoral. The pro-war faction saw in him a symbolic abandonment by the nation whose flag he had served.

The clamor rapidly reached all the way to the White House, where letters ran 100 to one against the Calley verdict and sentence. On Thursday, April 1, from San Clemente, Calif., President Nixon ordered Calley released from the Benning stockade and moved to house arrest in his post apartment.

Thus Lt. Calley began the long wait for an appeals process under which his sentence would be reviewed, and possibly softened or even overturned. As solace, he had an announcement on Saturday morning, April 3, by Nixon aides, who said:

"Yesterday the President made the decision that before any final sentence is carried out in the case of Lt. Calley the President will personally review the case and finally decide it."

This was the President's prerogative anyway, as commander in chief of the Army. But the announcement aroused Capt. Aubrey M. Daniel III, 29, the handsome blond and green-eyed Army prosecutor, who observers agreed had made a brilliant if at times petulant case against Calley. His opponent was chief defense attorney George Lattimer, 70, an erect, crane-like Mormon, as courtly as Daniel was curt.

Daniel wrote Nixon in part:

"I would have hoped that all the leaders of this nation, which is supposed to be the leader within the international community for the protection of the weak and the oppressed regardless of nationality, would have accepted and supported the enforcement of the laws of this country as reflected by the verdict of the court and not made any statement concerning the verdict until they had had the same opportunity to evaluate the evidence that the members of the jury had. . . .

"I have been particularly shocked and dismayed at your decision to intervene in these proceedings in the midst of the public clamor."

Nixon's only reply was to characterize Daniel as "a fine officer."

Col. Kennedy, 50, the trial judge, concurred with Nixon's action in releasing Calley from the stockade and added:

"The trouble with Daniel is he's a purist. He's a very intelligent young man, but he only sees good and evil. As you get a little older, you realize that most people are between the two extremes."

Within a few days Daniel became a father for the second time. Finishing out what was left of his Army tour, he departed the service April 28. Shortly thereafter it was announced he was joining the Washington law firm of famed trial lawyer Edward Bennett Williams.

Stravinsky: At 88 a Vast Musical Loss

Composer Igor Stravinsky at 83, during a recording of one of his works

IGOR STRAVINSKY was less than a year old when Richard Wagner died in 1883. Their barely overlapping lifetimes were dedicated to music; otherwise their careers and their personalities bore no resemblance beyond the fact that each had dominated his century in a mutual field of endeavor.

In the opinion of Alex Leger, French Nobel Prize winner and diplomat, "Europe was under the spell of Wagner. We had to be liberated, not so much from Wagner as from Wagnerism. Stravinsky appeared as a man of great technical genius and the mysterious instinct of the creator. We have been taking Stravinsky for granted for a long, long time. He is a giant, a great keystone and a far-reaching influence."

Early in his career the impact of Stravinsky's unconventional and, at times, violent music jolted the world. Later his work acquired a frigidly unemotional quality which some critics termed more classical than that of Bach. Of one of his religious works Igor once said:

"This is cold music, absolutely cold. There are no women's voices. They are by their very nature warm; they appeal to the senses."

He had used 50 male voices and an orchestra composed solely of 10 woodwinds.

Many musical pedagogues assailed both phases of Stravinsky's work, as well as his experimental forays in the realm of jazz. But, however bitter these attacks were, he always emerged ahead of his detractors: The more they vilified him the less they could afford to ignore him.

* * * *

Stravinsky was born at Oranienbaum, near St. Petersburg, Russia on June 18, 1882. He died April 6, 1971, in a recently purchased New York apartment, where his few final pleasant hours were spent. Lillian Libman, the composer's personal manager, said the last words she can remember that Stravinsky spoke were associated with these new living quarters overlooking Central Park: "How lovely; this belongs to me, it is my home."

The son of Feodor Stravinsky, a noted basso who preceded Chaliapin at the Imperial Opera, was a born musician. Only five-feet-four in height, Igor's fragile, birdlike appearance was deceptive. Although he had been frail physically for many years, he had attained the age of 88 when he succumbed unexpectedly a week after his release from a hospital.

"Two and a half months ago," Miss Libman said afterward, "he was playing the piano and composing—orchestrating two preludes from Bach's *Well-Tempered Clavier.*"

In the hospital he had been treated for circulatory and respiratory disorders. The immediate cause of death, physicians said, was failure of his overtaxed heart.

However troublesome his health had been, Stravinsky was esthetically indomitable through more than two-thirds of the 20th century. Irving Kolodin, music critic and associate editor of the Saturday Review, said Stravinsky conceived "a world of rhythmic, sonorous and harmonic combinations which effectively bypassed almost all Wagnerian associations."

Pierre Boulez, chosen to become musical director of the New York Philharmonic Orchestra in the 1972 season, commented: "The death of Stravinsky means the final disappearance of a musical generation which gave music its basic shock at the beginning of this century and which brought about the real departure from romanticism.

"Something radically new, even foreign to western tradition, had to be found for music to survive, and to enter our contemporary era. The glory of Stravinsky was to have belonged to this extremely gifted generation and to be one of the most creative of them all."

At 20, after abandoning law courses at the University of St. Petersburg, Stravinsky made a critical and lasting choice: He began studying music with Nikolai Rimsky-Korsakov, composer and orchestrator. Just after Rimsky-Korsakov's death in 1908, the young composer wrote *Fireworks*, a successful orchestral fantasy, for the marriage ceremony of his teacher's daughter. In the same year Stravinsky produced his *First Symphony* and *Le Faune et la Bergere*, which brought his name to the attention of Serge Diaghilev, of the Ballet Russe.

Thus began a close and noteworthy association, a happy and fortunate blending of talents that produced the most colorful period of the composer's career. At 27 Stravinsky was commissioned by Diaghilev to write an original score, *The Firebird*, based on a Russian legend, and after its Paris premiere in 1910 Diaghilev said of the composer, "Mark him well. He is a man on the eve of celebrity." *The Firebird* ultimately was rated by most as Stravinsky's first masterpiece.

But the ballet *Petrouchka*, scored by Stravinsky for Diaghilev in the following year, was even more successful. It was followed in 1913 by *The Rite of Spring*, a further departure from academic tonal and rhythmic values. Stravinsky found himself an international musical personality.

Nonetheless, its premiere in Paris indicated that *The Rite of Spring* was somewhat ahead of its time. For the French, at least, its music was savage and primitive. A near-riot ensued, members of the audience battering one another with their canes and fists. Police hauled dozens to jail. Stravinsky himself, forced to flee, climbed through a window and jumped into an alley at the rear of the theater.

Pierre Monteux, then Ballet Russe conductor and later a fast friend of Igor, said that when he first heard Stravinsky play music from *The Rite of Spring* on the piano in Monte Carlo, he thought that the composer was mad.

Stravinsky too found fault with the premiere of *The Rite of Spring*, notably its choreography. This was created by the great dancer Waslaw Nijinsky, and it did not please Stravinsky. Fully aware of Nijinsky's genius as a dancer, the composer complained afterward that "the poor boy knew nothing of music."

Vindication was to come for Stravinsky. In the following year *The Rite of Spring* won acceptance as a departure from the sentimentality and romance of music in the prior century.

*   *   *   *

In the years to come Stravinsky was to make a hundred or more important musical contributions. Between 1918 and 1923 a group of typically Russian compositions included *L'Histoire du Soldat; Mavra*, a one-act opera, and *Les Voces Villageoise*, introduced by the Ballet Russe. But early in the post-World War I era a change became evident in Stravinsky's musical concept, a trend away from Russian Folk themes and toward strictly classical treatment.

Reviewing the later decades of Stravinsky's career, Kolodin wrote after the composer's death, "The Twenties were the 'neo' decade . . . in which neoclassicism led him backward to absorption dance music of Pergolesi and even further back to the Greek associations of *Oedipus Rex*. In the Thirties there was a spiritual rebirth of the Catholic orientation to which he had been born, musically embodied in the *Symphony of Psalms*, one of his most expressive orchestral works.

"In the Forties the symphony absorbed him, first in the *Symphony in C* and then in the work titled *Symphony in Three Movements*. In the Fifties he stood sponsor for a return to the classic Mozartean opera in *The Rake's Progress*. And in the Sixties he applied himself to the counter-revolutionary precepts of Schoenberg and Webern. The musical outcome was not remarkable but the attitude was endearing."

Stravinsky and Arnold Schoenberg had, for years, been regarded as the leaders of contemporary musical composition: Stravinsky heading the tonal devotees whose techniques—dissonant or not—remained within the bounds of harmony; Schoenberg and his followers consisting the 12-tone group.

Shortly after *The Rake's Progress*, an opera first performed in 1951, Stravinsky himself became a 12-tone composer who, as the New York Times expressed it, "based each work on a series of notes stated as a 'tone row' in the opening measures."

Agon, a ballet commissioned by the New York City Ballet, came along in 1957 and was premiered on Stravinsky's 75th birthday. But many of his works in later years were religious, including *Canticum Sacrem* in 1956 and *Threni* in 1958.

*   *   *   *

Stravinsky's ability as a conductor, a talent he particularly enjoyed, was overlooked by many who held his composition in high regard. He was also a naturally capable pianist. His first American tour was made in 1925, as conductor of his own works with the New York Philharmonic and as pianist with the Boston Symphony. His ballet *Apollon Musagetes* was first performed in Washington, D.C., and in Paris the same year he introduced another ballet, *Le Baiser de la Fee*. His *Symphony of Psalms*, written for the 50th anniversary of the Boston Symphony, was completed in 1930, and in 1937 he made another American tour featuring *Card Party*, a ballet on a poker game, produced at the Metropolitan Opera House under his baton.

In 1939 Stravinsky delivered a series of lectures at Harvard University, where he held the Charles Eliot Norton chair. His *Symphony in C* was introduced in 1940. Yet another tour was undertaken by the composer, at 79. He conducted in Africa and, a few months later, in America, in several countries of central Europe, in Israel and in Russia. Four days before his 80th birthday his initial score for television was presented.

*   *   *   *

Stravinsky had left Russia in 1914, at the beginning of World War I, and his 1962 tour of that country marked his first return. For years he had lived in Paris, and had become a French citizen in 1934. His first wife was Catherine Nossenko, to whom he had been married in 1906. They had four children. She died of tuberculosis in 1939.

In 1940 he came to the United States. Vera de Bossett, a painter, had become his second wife in that year, and both received American citizenship in 1945. They settled in a modest house overlooking Los Angeles, near Beverly Hills. By this marriage there were no children.

In 1959 Stravinsky and his wife left the West Coast intending to reside in Paris. Instead they ended their journey in New York, where they made their home thereafter. While they were in California, however, not even Stravinsky could fail to take note of the motion picture industry. He shunned films completely as a musical outlet, once refusing $100,000 a year to compose three scores annually for the screen.

"To turn out one worthwhile piece of music a year is enough," he commented. "To guarantee three is to make a deceit of art." Thus he never achieved great wealth, although he lived in financial comfort.

Basically, he criticized the secondary role allotted to music in motion pictures, particularly on the ground that films could be "a powerful instrument for advancing the appreciation of good music." Stravinsky had always objected strenuously to the "interpretation" given his compositions by other conductors. He was particular about the way his works were performed, and he annotated his scores with elaborate directions for the conductor. This perfectionism was largely responsible for his refusal to work for Hollywood.

On the other hand, Stravinsky held no prejudice against movies as part of popular entertainment. After all, he had composed a polka for the dancing elephants of the Ringling Bros.-Barnum & Bailey Circus; the *Scherzo a la Russe* for Paul Whiteman, *Ballet Scenes* for Billy Rose and a "small concerto" for Woody Herman. The latter composition was recorded in 1946, under the title *Ebony Concerto*, by Herman's band, with Stravinsky conducting.

Ebony Concerto was not his first venture into the field of jazz. In 1918, fascinated by the rhythms of Negro origin in American dance music, he wrote *Ragtime* as "a portrait of jazz," followed by *Piano Ragtime Music*. By 1948 Stravinsky had been imitated even by the exponents of "bebop," a radical and usually formless projection of jazz. At the same time Dizzy Gillespie and Stan Kenton, then leaders of the "bebop" or "progressive" school, "admitted" that Igor used "some of the same sounds and rhythmic devices."

* * * *

Stravinsky was meticulous and immaculate in his personal habits and his well ordered routine of work and relaxation in his hillsite house. He was sensitive to drafts, and usually wore a scarf or sweater—sometimes both—indoors. But he also was an advocate of sunbathing, as nearly nude as possible, on his sequestered terrace at breakfast time.

His wants and his privacy were devotedly respected by Vera. An intense worker, he liked good food and good wine when he rested, and he cultivated roses in his garden, played interminable games of Chinese checkers with his wife. His neighbors, most of whom he ignored, gazed wonderingly as he came and went in sandals, slacks and sport shirt, his arms laden with groceries from a nearby store. Only rarely did he attend parties, contending he met too many people who thought they knew all about music—particularly his music—and he found insincerity or stupidity intolerable. But when the company was good he was a gay and animated conversationalist.

His study, a magnificent hodge-podge of books, gadgets, theater programs, sketches of him by Picasso and Cocteau, drafting table, desk, two pianos and a sofa for his inevitable afternoon nap, was cited by composer Nicolas Nabokov as the best equipped workroom any composer ever had. Stravinsky had a weakness for pencil sharpeners, cigarette lighters, colored pencils, various stationers' supplies and nicknacks in general. The walls were soundproof and one piano was muted "because it makes me nervous if anyone can hear me." Mornings were his favorite time for composing, but when deeply engaged he frequently devoted the night hours as well to his work.

In *The Poetics of Music*, published by Harvard University Press in 1947, Stravinsky undertook to explain his musical technique. He referred to himself as an inventor, and delineated his motivation perhaps better than did any of his analysts when he said: "This appetite (for composing) is not at all a fortuitous thing like inspiration, but as habitual and periodic as a natural need."

According to his wish, Stravinsky's funeral service in New York was Russian Orthodox, the faith in which he was baptized. Fulfilling another of his requests, interment took place in the Russian corner of the cemetery of San Michele, in Venice, Italy, where Diaghilev was buried in 1929.

George Balanchine, head of the New York City Ballet, a fellow Russian who had been Stravinsky's longtime friend, said:

"I feel he is still with us. He has left us the treasures of his genius, which will live with us forever. We must have done 20 ballets together, and I hoped to do more."

Stravinsky funeral procession on canal in Venice, Italy

Gas Chamber Decreed for Manson and Three Women of His Hippie Family

Grisly 1969 slayings of actress Sharon Tate and six others resulted in death sentences after trial lasting 9½ months

Hands cuffed and legs chained, Manson was led back to Los Angeles cell after two days of processing at San Quentin

IT WAS a morning for disaster. At dawn the earth had rumbled, quaked and tossed Los Angeles into a state of terror. A few hours later, in a courtroom dusty with broken plaster, a tall and slender brunette struck the most shattering blow to the defense in the stormy Sharon Tate murder trial. Susan Atkins, in a soft husky voice, confessed that she killed the blonde pregnant actress and that she wasn't sorry.

"It was a happening," she sighed. "You know, an earthquake *(pages 23–28)* is a happening."

Then, in a grotesque pageant of abberation, the two other women on trial followed her to the stand to tell their own grisly tales. Calmly, they spoke of stabbing terrified strangers in their homes, of ignoring pleas for mercy, of sopping up blood with towels and using it to scrawl words on walls. And through it all, they said, they felt "nothing" because they were "stoned" on LSD.

As if by rote, each repeated that Charles Manson, the glib and persuasive ex-convict who had adopted them as members of his hippie style "family," was innocent *(The World in 1970, 255)*.

To the jury, which sat in stunned silence, the confessions were merely a shock of confirmation. After seven tumultuous months of trial, the seven men and five men had deliberated and found Mason and the three women guilty of murder and conspiracy in the slayings of actress Sharon Tate and six others.

The confessions at the trial's penalty phase could influence only one verdict—the decision of life or death for Manson, 36, Miss Atkins, 22, Patricia Krenwinkel, 23, and Leslie Van Houten, 21.

The women's attorneys, clinging to shards of their shattered defense case, said their clients had testified over their objections and that the confessions showed the three were mentally ill. They were, said the attorneys, "sick little girls," deranged by LSD and Manson's mesmerizing influence.

An angry prosecutor said the women were trying to cover up for Manson. Manson's attorney, appropriately, said he believed the women; Manson was innocent and should live.

The jury would reach a different conclusion.

But before that climax of decision, the trial would stretch to 9½ months, the longest murder proceedings in California history and perhaps in the nation. It cost the county of Los Angeles nearly $1 million.

The confessions, however, were the fitting denouement to this real-life drama so incredibly bizarre that it drew gasps even in nearby Hollywood where Sharon Tate and her friends lived in a film world inured to fantasized horror.

Star witness Linda Kasabian.

It had begun in August 1969 as the most savage "Hollywood murder" in the city's flashy history *(The World in 1969, 242-245)*. Found slain at a hilltop mansion in plush Benedict Canyon was Miss Tate, 26, beautiful wife of film director Roman Polanski. Also slain with her—their bloody bodies scattered about the estate—were hair stylist Jay Sebring, 26; Polish playboy Wojieiech Frykowski, 37; coffee company heiress Abigail Folger, 26; and Stephen Parent, 18, a friend of the caretaker. The murder scene was weird—one body hooded, two joined by a rope, the word "Pig" scrawled in blood on a door.

The next night, 10 miles away in the upper middle class Los Feliz district, a wealthy market owner and his wife, Leno and Rosemary LaBianca, were found slain in "copycat killings" marked by makeshift hoods and bloody scrawlings on walls.

It was December in 1969 when police announced the arrests of an odd band of roaming hippie types led by a shaggy-haired little man whom disciples called "Jesus" "Satan" and "God." His name was Charles Manson.

With the opening of the trial in June 1970, the Tate murder case was transformed into a testing ground for legal procedure and a laboratory for dissecting generation gaps, drug problems, hippie communal life styles and sex habits of the young.

The trial's 23-week guilt phase featured lurid testimony about Manson—supervised sex orgies and drug "trips" at the clan's communal home, the Spahn movie ranch. The state's star witness was Linda Kasabian, 21, a pig-tailed former family member who said she went along and witnessed the killings but didn't kill anyone herself. Indicted with the others, she walked out free, given immunity for her testimony.

The four defendants carved bloody "X"s on their foreheads, said they were "Xed out of society" and refused to cooperate

in an orderly trial. Shouting, chanting and insulting the judge, they were ejected from the courtroom repeatedly and listened to much of the trial from adjoining rooms.

And, after dozens of strange twists had turned the trial topsy turvy—after the defense had rested without calling a witness, the women had demanded to testify then retracted the demand, and Manson had taken the stand to deliver a dramatic monologue declaring his innocence—a defense lawyer disappeared into the wilderness never to return.

As 1970 drew to a close the trial stalled while a new lawyer caught up on the case. Then, in final arguments, attorneys told the jury that Manson and the women were innocent, that others had committed the killings, that the state case was a plot to prejudice society against the hippie life style.

The prosecutor, Vincent Bugliosi, said the women were "robots" and "zombies" manipulated by Manson, "a dictatorial maharajah of a tribe of bootlicking slaves." He called the killings a "classic textbook example of premeditated murder" and demanded guilty verdicts.

After eight days of deliberation, jurors filed into court on Jan. 25 and delivered verdicts of guilt against all. The defendants, led into court for the first time in weeks, were uncharacteristically quiet and decorous. But Manson managed to throw in a punchline after the verdicts were read. Looking at the jurors, he said, "I think they're all guilty." Then he shouted at Superior Court Judge Charles H. Older: "We're still not allowed to put on a defense! You won't outlive that, old man!"

The chief defense attorney, Paul J. Fitzgerald, told newsmen: "We lost the case when we lost our change of venue." He and other attorneys claimed pre-trial publicity had prejudiced jurors against the defendants, and the trial should have been moved out of Los Angeles.

The penalty trial opened on Jan. 28 with hints that it would be even livelier than the guilt phase. Manson, complaining of the long-winded tactics of his attorney, Irving Kanarek, shouted, "I can't communicate with you!" and punched the attorney in the arm and side as they sat at the counsel table. Manson was ejected before testimony began, shouting at the judge: "You've already convicted me for something I didn't do . . . There's no justice here. Dammit, man, look at it . . . What good is a courtroom if it's one-sided?"

The state called only three witnesses, relying on its 84 witnesses and 290 exhibits in the guilt phase to tell its story. The defense, saying it would now present the case scuttled in the guilt phase, began calling witnesses in its fight for life sentences rather than the only other possible sentence—death in the gas chamber.

First, and most moving, were the divorced parents of Miss Krenwinkel and the mother of Miss Van Houten. Tearfully, they told of middle-class childhoods, of Easter egg hunts, trick-or-treating on Halloween, singing in the church choir. Where did their daughters go wrong? They just didn't know. Of her daughter, Dorothy Krenwinkel said, weeping, "No one will ever tell me she did anything terrible or horrible."

From the street corner outside the Hall of Justice, where they camped throughout the trial, came still faithful women members of Manson's raggedy tribe. Freckled-faced Lynette "Squeaky" Fromme, 21, testified in vivid detail of the genesis and wanderings of the Manson clan. She said Manson gathered his flock of mostly women in 1967 in the Haight-Ashbury district of San Francisco, piled them in an ancient school bus and cruised the California coast picking up runaways along the way.

"We were riding on the wind," said Miss Fromme. "We'd

meet kids begging on the streets. All they wanted was to get away from one kind of life that was beating them around." Manson, she said, offered them love. Sandra Good, 26, told of communal life and the birth of babies named "Sunstone Hawk," "Pooh Bear," and "Zeezo Zozee Zadfrack." Others spoke of Manson's "miracles," saying he played with rattlesnakes and brought dead birds back to life.

Then, suddenly, the women defendants, halting their defense case, insisted on taking the stand.

Miss Atkins, her eyes wide with excitement, began the confessions, saying she stabbed Miss Tate to death. "I killed her," she said. "I stabbed her and she fell. And I stabbed her again. I don't know how many times I stabbed her and I don't know why I stabbed her . . . She was pleading with me, 'Please don't kill me.' And I said, 'Shut up. I don't want to hear it.' " She told of the pregnant Miss Tate begging to have her baby, then said, "She kept begging and pleading and begging and pleading and I got sick of listening to it, so I stabbed her."

She said the killers were under the influence of hallucinogenic drugs—"I was stoned, man, stoned on acid."

After more than two days on the stand, during which she also confessed to the slaying of a Malibu musician in another case, Miss Atkins declared, "I feel no guilt for what I've done. It was right then and I still believe it was right." An attorney asked, "But how can it be right to kill somebody?" Miss Atkins replied dreamily, "How can it not be right when it's done with love?"

Miss Krenwinkel, plain looking and emotionless, confessed that she killed Miss Folger on the lawn of the Tate estate, then stabbed Mrs. LaBianca the following night. Of the Folger killing, she said, "I had a knife in my hand and she ran out a back door . . . I chased her through the door and onto the lawn and I stabbed her and I kept stabbing her and I looked up and there was blackness and that was all." What did she feel? "Nothing . . . It was just there, and like it was all right."

The next night, she said, she and Miss Van Houten stabbed Mrs. LaBianca with kitchen utensils while, in another room, a clan member killed her husband. Later, Miss Krenwinkel said, she carved "WAR" on LaBianca's chest, stuck a fork in his stomach and used his blood to scrawl on walls. Did she feel remorse? "I don't even know what that word means." She too said she was on drugs, explaining, "I've taken so much acid that I am acid."

Miss Van Houten, the youngest and prettiest defendant, told cheerfully of her teen-age years as a homecoming princess, then her introduction to drugs and life as a dropout. With the Manson group, she said she found "a feeling all my life I'd been looking for."

Yes, she had joined Miss Krenwinkel at the LaBianca house, "stabbing and cutting up the lady." She told of Mrs. LaBianca crying for mercy, trying to fend off her killers with a lamp. "She grabbed for the lamp shade again and I took one of the knives that Patricia had and we started stabbing and cutting up the lady. I stabbed her. I don't know if it was before or after she was dead but I stabbed her."

Was she sorry? "Sorry is only a five letter word," she said. "It can't bring back anybody."

As a postscript, the women offered a possible motive for the killings. A family member, Robert Beausoleil, had been charged with murder in another slaying marked by bloody scrawlings. They felt if they did "copycat killings" police would believe they had the wrong man in custody and release Beausoleil. (He was later convicted and sentenced to die).

The defense changed course. No longer able to deny their clients' guilt, the women's attorneys set out to prove the killings resulted from two powerful forces—LSD and Manson. Manson's attorney called few witnesses, noting that evidence hadn't shown Manson killed anyone, though the state claimed he gave the orders.

Four psychiatrists—all specialists in hallucinogenic drugs—testified that the women could have been changed by LSD and because of it might have obeyed orders to kill. One said that with LSD, Manson could have run a successful "school of crime."

The only psychiatrist to interview all three women, Dr. Joel Hochman, said he believed they were mentally ill, their problems rooted in an unsatisfied yearning for love. "All three girls," he said, "have a history of a search for something, someone to fill their psychological needs. . . . Mr. Manson seems to fit their psychological needs better than anyone."

Were they insane when they killed? None of the doctors could say for sure.

Manson, disturbed by the psychiatrists' comments, muttered derogatory remarks, then altered his appearance drastically. Shaggy-haired through most of the trial he showed up one morning nearly bald, later shaved off his beard and finally changed the "X" on his forehead to a swastika. He explained his new hairstyle in a note saying, "I cut my hair because I am the devil and the devil always had a bald head."

The defense rested its case on March 16, having called 29 witnesses. In the interim, further complications concerning the "family" had arisen in other courts. Manson and Miss Atkins were indicted on an eighth murder charge in the slaying of the musician, Gary Hinman. Manson was charged along with two male clan members with a ninth killing, that of a stuntman whose body hadn't been found. Five Manson followers were indicted on charges stemming from the alleged kidnapping of a state witness to Honolulu during which she was dosed with an LSD-spiked hamburger. They pleaded no contest and got 90-day sentences on misdemeanor counts.

Charles "Tex" Watson, 24, originally indicted with the others and later sent to a mental hospital was declared fit to return to Los Angeles to stand trial, but his case was postponed while his attorney arranged for psychiatric tests. He later pleaded innocent by reason of insanity.

The Tate trial jurors, sequestered in a hotel for seven months of trial, were allowed to go home nightly through most of the penalty phase when they said it was becoming a hardship to stay away from home. But they were ordered locked up again as final arguments began.

In final argument, the prosecutor described Manson and the women as "human monsters" for whom the death penalty should be automatic. "If the death penalty is to mean anything in the state of California other than two empty words, this is a proper case," he said. Waving gory photographs of the victims, he recounted the bloodiness of the killings, called Manson "one of the most evil, satanic men to walk the face of the earth," and demanded the death penalty.

Manson's attorney said his client was "possibly innocent," and, if nothing else, should be saved as a specimen for psychiatric study. Kanarek read from the Bible and said, "Mr. Manson is being treated the same way as Christ."

Miss Atkins' attorney, Daye Shinn, cited her cooperation with the district attorney's office in cracking the case, claimed officials had reneged on a promise to not seek the death penalty for her, and said the prosecutor would forever be haunted by "the voice of Miss Atkins crying out for justice."

Maxwell Keith, who took over Miss Van Houten's case

when her attorney vanished, cried out to the jury, "How insane these young girls must have been!" He blamed Manson for the corruption of Miss Van Houten, saying, "Can you see the incomprehensible horror of it . . . the destruction of a lovely young girl before your eyes?" Should the women be put to death, he said, they would be "human sacrifices."

Fitzgerald, last to address the jurors, asked with tears in his eyes for "the gift of life" for the defendants. "Don't condone the very crime we seek to punish," he said. "We have had enough killing." He called the crimes "the first of the LSD murders" and suggested more study of the drug.

Then, in an emotional climax, Fitzgerald described in excruciating detail the imaginary execution of the women—the octagonal green gas chamber and official farewell. "The warden enters the cell, leans over and shakes their hands and says, 'Goodbye Patricia, goodbye Susan, goodbye Leslie.'" He told of dying convulsions, of spittle drooling from their mouths, and finally death. Such a day of execution, he told jurors, would be "a day of crucifixion as well as retribution . . . In the warped and lonely persons of Patricia Krenwinkel, Susan Atkins and Leslie Van Houten, the son of man has been crucified again."

The three women, pale and thin in drab blue prison uniforms, dropped their usual chatty demeanor as he spoke of their deaths. For the first time in the long trial they sat frozen, silent in their seats.

Jurors deliberated only 10 hours this time. Later they would say there was little doubt of the verdict; they just took time to dutifully review the evidence. As they were finalizing their work on the morning of March 29, word came from the rugged wilderness of Ventura County that a body, later identified as that of missing defense attorney Ronald Hughes, 35, had been found in a creek. Torrential rains had taken his life. Outside the Hall of Justice, Manson's faithful women followers showed up with their heads shaved bald and sat cross-legged like monks threatening to immolate themselves if death was the penalty. They later changed their minds.

At mid-day jurors rang a buzzer to signal a verdict, and filed into the courtroom, their eyes averted from the defendants. But the four didn't stay long. Ousted for angry shouting,

none was present to hear the decree—death in the gas chamber for all.

"You don't have no authority over me. You're not nearly as good as me," shouted Manson before being evicted. The women, their long hair cropped short, heard Manson's penalty read, then shouted at the jury. "You've all judged yourselves," said Miss Krenwinkel and Miss Van Houten. And Miss Atkins cried, "It's gonna come down hard. Lock your doors. Protect your kids . . . Remove yourselves from the face of the earth; you're all fools."

One juror said later: "We wanted to protect society . . . You just can't go into a person's house and butcher them up."

The prosecutor said he felt the verdicts reflected "community feelings." Fitzgerald said, "I fail to see how it helps anything . . . The country that kills its problem children denies itself the access to insights, solutions." He said he anticipated appeals in the case would take another five years and might go as far as the U. S. Supreme Court.

Ronald Hughes was buried a week after the verdict, with other attorneys in attendance and Fitzgerald eulogizing his colleague. Authorities said Hughes was the victim of a natural disaster—killed in torrential rains which swept the area where he had been camping.

On April 19, the judge, who had the power to reduce the penalty and spare the defendants' lives, sentenced them to death, saying: "Not only is the death penalty appropriate but it is almost compelled by this case."

The three women came for sentencing with their heads shaved bald in imitation of Manson. An emaciated Manson, looking shrunken in baggy prison blues, asked to speak. With his head bowed and voice quavering, he told the judge: "I have always lived in the truth of your courtroom. I have always done what I was told . . . I accept this court as my father . . . I accept the judgment of my father."

For once the judge had the last word.

"After 9½ months of trial all of the superlatives have been used . . . All that remains are the bare, stark facts of seven senseless murders—seven people whose lives were snuffed out by total strangers for motives that remain known only to them."

(Left) Manson, as he listened to verdict (Right) Defendants in Sharon Tate murder trial, with "X" marks cut into their foreheads (left to right): Susan Atkins, Patricia Krenwinkel, Leslie Van Houten

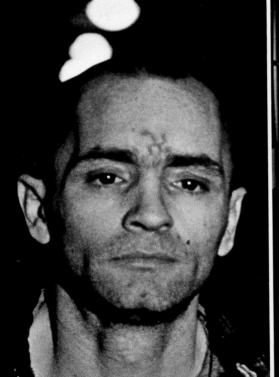

FIRST AID FOR SOVIET MEDICS

When the fathers of Soviet Communism drew up the blueprint for their "workers' paradise," they may have overlooked the medical profession. As a result, Russian doctors were among the poorest paid citizens, earning less than skilled factory workers.

Leonid I. Brezhnev, leader of the Soviet Communist party, decided to improve the lot of Soviet doctors, 72 per cent of whom were women. He told a party congress in April that the new five-year plan envisioned more pay for both doctors and school teachers.

With the spotlight turned on the medical pro-

fession, the government also decided to adopt its own version of the Hippocratic oath.

The oath, to be administered in the presence of professors and health officials, combined traditional medical ethics with a specific reference to Communism and an emphasis on duty to society. The physician would swear that he would "preserve medical confidences." This closely followed the oath attributed to Hippocrates, the Greek physician. That oath says "Whatsoever things I see or hear which ought not to be noised abroad, I will keep silence thereon, counting such things to be sacred secrets."

The Soviet physician under the new oath would undertake "to guard and develop the noble traditions of Soviet medicine to be guided in all actions by the principles of Communist morality. . . ."

The organ of the Soviet medical profession, Meditsinskaya Gazeta, declared that the new oath would "help raise considerably the doctor's prestige and enhance his sense of responsibility for the performance of his duty."

With virtually no private practice in the Soviet system of free medical care, they had to subsist on what the state allotted them.

SON, 19, HAITI'S PRESIDENT FOR LIFE ON DUVALIER'S DEATH

Francois Duvalier, a slight, gray-haired kindly looking man, wanted people to regard him as a simple country doctor beloved by his countrymen in Haiti. But his 14-year rule was the embodiment of terror, marked by mass arrests and mass executions, and it ended only with his death April 21 at 64.

Papa Doc was the affectionate title he went by, harking back to his days as a physician. But there was little benign about his ruthless dictatorship, which eliminated political opponents almost casually by imprisonment, exile or execution.

His private army of thugs, known as the Tontons Macoute, bogeymen hidden behind sunglasses, stalked the streets on the lookout for any whisper of opposition.

Duvalier's enemies claimed that these bullies operated torture chambers in the basement of the presidential palace and liquidated the president's foes.

But Duvalier, who made himself president for life in 1964, wanted to project the image of a beloved leader. Huge likenesses of the president were plastered on walls in Port-au-Prince and from time to time truckloads of citizens were hauled into the capital dutifully screaming "Viva Papa Doc!"

On one thing everyone agreed. Duvalier was an expert in survival in a land where presidents were not noted for dying peacefully. He remained under the constant guard of a 600-man force in the palace, 350 soldiers in the adjacent Dessalines Barracks, some 5,000 militiamen—and the dreaded Tontons.

He also used superstition as a political instrument. A Roman Catholic by upbringing, Duvalier became a student of voodoo, which Haiti had inherited from West Africa. In 1944 he published a book on it, and after his rise to power he circulated rumors that magic made him and his family bullet-proof. He also suggested that the spirits living in plants and animals were all working for him.

The son of a teacher and local magistrate, Duvalier studied medicine in the United States after graduating from Port-au-Prince schools and the Lycee Petion. In 1934 he was licensed by the University of Haiti medical school. Later he won a fellowship to study at the University of Michigan School of Public Health.

In Haiti he joined a U.S.-backed clinic which was working to wipe out yaws, a disease which caused sores to break out on the body and which then afflicted 80 per cent of all Haitians.

Duvalier campaigned against the disease, building a valuable reputation as a dedicated doctor who helped the suffering. He became

minister of health and labor in the 1950–56 regime of President Paul Magloire. But he soon began building his own political machine and was forced into hiding when Magloire became suspicious.

An important base of support for Duvalier was an organization of drivers of public vehicles who later could be relied upon to paralyze the country by strikes.

With his term running out in 1956, Magloire's government was rocked by scandal after scandal, and battles erupted in the streets between police and opponents of the regime.

Duvalier called on his drivers to strike at the critical moment and the combined opposition brought Magloire down. He fled the country. Duvalier had joined forces with Daniel Fignole in the Workers and Peasants Movement. With an interim president unable to rule, Duvalier and Fignole threw their support behind an army junta which they later ousted and replaced with Fignole.

Duvalier let Fignole restore order, then sent an army unit against the presidential palace and forced his ally to flee to New York.

The army, which believed that Duvalier could win financial support from the United States, produced new election rules requiring peasants to make ballots in advance and deliver them to the polling booths.

The result: Of the 900,000 ballots cast, Duvalier had 680,000. He took office Sept. 22, 1957.

Papa Doc quickly dropped the mask of humility and became the incredible ruler of a nation of five million of the poorest people in the hemisphere. It was a nation where life expectancy was below 35, where 90 per cent of the people could not read or write and where the per capita income was about $75 a year compared with the Latin American average of about $400.

Duvalier had a seemingly callous contempt for his people. He did not even bother to speak Creole, the nation's language. He spoke French, which only about 10 per cent of Haitians could comprehend.

Since a slave revolt in 1804 made Haiti the world's first black republic, a succession of governments had brought the fertile land closer to the brink of ruin, and Duvalier did little to halt the slide. After 14 years in office, little had changed. Almost 90 per cent of the people were still illiterate, the income level was as low as ever and the people were still plagued by yaws.

The last amendment Duvalier made to the 1964 constitution repealed a requirement that the president of Haiti must be 40. That was because Papa Doc, seeking to found a dynasty, had announced that his playboy son, Jean Claude, 19, would succeed him as president for life.

Haitian President Francois Duvalier resting hand on shoulder of son, Jean Claude

BREZHNEV'S PRESTIGE ADVANCED DURING SOVIET PARTY CONGRESS

It began March 31 with six hours of oratory by Leonid I. Brezhnev, burly, 64-year-old chief of the Soviet Communist party. Eleven days later, the 24th Party Congress ended with nearly 5,000 delegates rising in ovation for Brezhnev, who appeared to have emerged as the nation's No. 1 leader.

The cheers echoing through Moscow's huge Palace of Congresses marked the greatest show of adulation since Nikita Khrushchev had been ousted from the premiership in 1964 and replaced by a collective leadership.

The demonstration was in sharp contrast to the previous party congress in 1966 when Brezhnev had shared equal honors with Premier Alexei N. Kosygin.

This time, Kosygin was placed in the shadows. His three-hour speech was carried only in edited excerpts on radio and television, whereas Brezhnev's blockbuster was broadcast in its entirety.

It took the Congress 16 seconds to give unanimous endorsement to the progress report that it had taken Brezhnev six hours to deliver and 46 delegates five days to praise.

Brezhnev had clearly expected as much. A few minutes before the actual vote, he told the audience that "merging with the voice of the delegates is the voice of the entire Soviet people."

Brezhnev then confided that more than 250,000 letters and telegrams had been received since he had spoken six days earlier. Needless to add, they all praised his report.

Observers noted that when Brezhnev, in a closing speech, read the names of the new Politburo, he placed that of President Nikolai A. Podgorny—whose post was regarded as largely ceremonial—second after himself, with Kosygin in the third spot, reversing the previous order of president and premier. Later the official news agency Tass put out the names in alphabetical order, but the question of rank had been raised.

The Politburo was expanded from 11 to 15 members, with three of the new ones apparently protegés of Brezhnev. The indication that Podgorny had been given a boost upward intrigued

Party leader Leonid I. Brezhnev revealed Soviet power lineup

Kremlin watchers. He was a holdover from the Khrushchev days, and in 1964 had been regarded as a possible heir.

Those who kept tabs on Soviet affairs also noted that Andrei A. Gromyko, the veteran Soviet foreign minister, had once again been bypassed for membership in the elite Politburo. They reasoned, however, that Gromyko didn't make it, because he was considered too valuable where he was.

As a Politburo member, Gromyko would have had a role he had never played in the past, a say in the making of policy. He would have had to leave the day to day job of carrying out that policy to a successor at the head of his ministry.

Brezhnev's massive report to the congress

reflected great confidence, but he left the impression of being a juggler with too many plates in the air at once. On domestic affairs, Brezhnev stressed the civilian view that higher living standards were of great importance. In foreign affairs, he called for a conference on nuclear and general disarmament, a proposal reminiscent of one presented years earlier by Khrushchev.

Inside the Communist bloc, Brezhnev conceded that "some difficulties and complications have continued to appear."

Moscow's ideological war with Peking obviously worried Brezhnev, and he denounced Communist China for what he described as its divisive tactics. He also singled out what he called renegades, including veteran Communists in France, Italy, Austria and Venezuela.

Brezhnev hinted that one method of keeping heresy in check would be to form a sort of international Communist directorate. More international Red parleys, he said, would promote cohesion of the movement.

It was clear that other Soviet leaders were concerned over disunity among the world's Communists. So were the leaders of communist parties in other nations.

"We highly value the principle of the independence and sovereignty of every Communist party," said Georges Marchais, deputy chief of the French party. "At the same time, we hold that unity of action of all Communist parties on the basis of Marxism-Leninism is a sacred duty and an imperative condition of success of our entire struggle."

For the average Soviet housewife, the party congress probably meant little. But one spinoff benefit delighted everyone. Such rarities as hothouse cucumbers, white and red grapes from the Caucasus and bouquets of tulips and carnations in Moscow shops became available during the congress. Smiling women emerged from the stores, their string bags bulging with ducks and chickens imported from Poland and Belgium and oranges from Morocco.

"There hasn't been such stuff in the stores since the 50th anniversary of the revolution," said one Muscovite.

George Smith Watchetaker, Oklahoma Comanche, did a ritual rain dance in Texas, and by the time he finished it was pouring

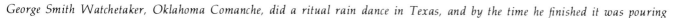

FIFTH TERM FOR MAYOR DALEY

In Chicago, the Old Guard remained in power as expected, but it was a different story half a continent away in the California community of Berkeley, where three acknowledged radicals won seats on the city council.

In other results of April 6 balloting Oklahoma City became the largest metropolis in America with a woman mayor, and Kansas voters gave landslide approval to an amendment to the state constitution granting the vote to 18-year-olds in state and local elections.

In Chicago, Richard J. Daley, the nation's most successful big city organization politician, was elected to a fifth term as mayor by a huge margin. Daley had faced what appeared to be the most serious challenge in his long mayoral career from Richard E. Friedman, energetic Democrat turned Republican.

But less than three hours after the polls closed, Daley pushed his way through throngs of clamorous admirers at his campaign headquarters to claim victory. Friedman ran as tough a campaign as Daley had seen in his 16-year-reign. But, like the legendary gunfighter in the Old West who took them all on, the veteran mayor came up a winner by a wider margin than even his staunchest supporters had expected. Daley had won 70 per cent of the votes.

"The overwhelming vote was a mandate to us to make Chicago a better city for all people," said the 68-year-old Democrat.

Friedman drew a different conclusion.

"We made some waves today," he said, "and they're going to be hitting shore."

In Berkeley a crowd of 1,500, mostly longhairs, jammed the Community Theater and watched the stage intently as a crew of workers fed figures into a bank of computers and flashed figures on a pair of movie screens.

At 11:45 p.m., a new set of numbers went up on the screens and the crowd rose, some waving red flags and raising clenched fists. The radicals had scored a significant victory.

The insurgents had won three of four available seats on the city council, bringing it to an even 4-4 split between leftists and moderates. And Warren Widener, 33-year-old former council member and a supporter of the radicals, became Berkeley's first black mayor.

But Berkeley's radicals suffered one defeat. The voters overwhelmingly rejected their proposal to split the Berkeley police into three departments controlled by councils in the black, white and student neighborhoods. Police officials had warned that 90 per cent of the force threatened to resign if that proposal was approved.

In Oklahoma City, Mrs. Patience Latting had planned to sleep late after celebrating her election as mayor. But at dawn the telephone began ringing. People called from all over the country to praise her, she said, for "striking a blow for women's liberation."

"Please don't make me out a women's liberationist," said the 52-year-old mother of four.

Victorious Mayor Richard J. Daley of Chicago

Berkeley Mayor Warren Widener

END OF AN ORDEAL IN NEWARK

The strike pitted the 4,400 members of the militant Newark Teachers' Union against the black community of a city long torn by racial strife. It kept half of Newark's 80,000 students out of school for 11 weeks in the longest such walkout that ever gripped a major American city.

The dispute seemed a paradox in itself. The teachers' union, 60 per cent white, had struck for changes they claimed would improve ghetto education. But their toughest opposition came from the blacks who accounted for nearly 80 per cent of the public school enrollment.

Money was never a real problem in the marathon stoppage. That issue was settled in the early stages with a provision for a $500 pay boost in the second year of a teacher's two-year contract. The major sticking point was the range of professional chores allotted to the teachers; such jobs as monitoring students in the cafeterias or keeping an eye on youngsters in the playgrounds.

The teachers asserted that the city should hire "paraprofessionals" to do such tasks. But the five-man black and Puerto Rican majority on the school board insisted that teachers should be required to do such chores because they involved the "more human aspect of teaching." Teachers who would not do such jobs, the black leaders declared, were "insensitive to the needs of black children."

The board received strong vocal support from Le Roi Jones, the black poet-playwright who usually appeared on the scene when race became an issue in Newark.

A member of Jones' Committee for a Unified Newark said that the teachers lived in Newark's suburbs and that, acceding to their demands, would be "like having a foreign country" dictate policy.

Many Newark residents felt the differences that touched off the strike actually boiled down to a struggle for control of the city's schools between the teachers' union and the white community on the one hand and the black community and the school board on the other.

"This whole messy business has become a racial fight," Newark's Negro mayor, Kenneth A. Gibson, told an interviewer at one point in the dispute. "There are people who always turn every issue into a racial fight."

The prospect of a racial struggle was just what people dreaded in this volatile city where four years earlier riots had raged for five days in the Negro community, resulting in 26 deaths.

For a while it looked as if their fears would be confirmed. One day after the strike was called on Feb. 1, about 15 teachers were attacked outside the headquarters of their union. The victims claimed that they had been assaulted by 25 men, all Negroes. Later, another teacher was stabbed.

But violence was no novelty in Newark, a city with the greatest percentage of slum housing and the highest per capita rate of crime in the nation.

The strike finally came to an end April 18, when the board of education and the Teachers' Union accepted a contract proposed by the mayor.

The plan included a compromise on the disputed nonprofessional chores and placed them largely on a voluntary basis.

When the acceptance was announced it caused a stir among the 300 spectators in the conference room of the board of education, most of them black.

"Sellout!" cried several in the audience.

"I don't think anybody scored a victory," said the board president, Jesse L. Jacob. "I say children got kicked in the teeth."

FOR THE RECORD

PROMOTED. Navy Capt. Alan B. Shepard Jr., 47, America's first man in space, and Navy Capt. Samuel L. Gravely Jr., first black to command a U.S. warship, were named rear admirals. Shepard began his career in 1959 when he was chosen as one of the seven original astronauts. He went aloft in a Mercury space capsule May 5, 1961, on a trail-blazing 15-minute suborbital flight. He was also commander of the Apollo 14 crew which landed on the moon Feb. 4, 1971 *(pp. 30–36)* Gravely, 48, was skipper of the guided missile frigate *Jouett* which saw duty off the Vietnamese coast.

REELECTED. South Korean President Chung Hee Park won a third term by a wide margin. Park, 53, a candidate of the Democratic Republican party, defeated National Assemblyman Kim Dae-jung of the New Democratic party. Park, an army general who took over after a military coup in 1961, won his first presidential term in 1963. He campaigned this time on the economic gains and political stability achieved during his first two terms as president.

ACQUITTED. Capt. Eugene M. Kotouc was cleared of guilt by an Army court martial in the maiming of a Vietnamese prisoner at My Lai 4 three years earlier. Kotouc said he had cut off part of one of the prisoner's fingers by accident when he thrust a knife at him during an interrogation. A jury of seven career officers deliberated less than 60 minutes before freeing the defendant, who was one of the planners of the Army assault on the Vietnamese hamlet on March 16, 1968 *(The World in 1969, 257).* The maiming occurred a few hours after the assault.

War medals, other awards littered the Capitol grounds ⟶

May

Antiwar Demonstrators Arrested by Thousands on Washington Streets

THEY CALLED themselves the Mayday Tribe, and they trumpeted warnings that if the United States would not stop the war in Indochina they would bring the government to a standstill. The result was a stormy week of disorders in the federal capital that sent shock waves across the nation. At one point 7,000 demonstrators were in custody.

The youth culture revolutionaries behind the massive protest wheeled out a new weapon for their cause—Gandhi with a clenched fist. The famed Indian leader's image was everywhere on buttons, posters, flyers and even on the Mayday tactical manual designed to explain the special interpretation of organized civil disobedience behind the campaign.

Revolutionaries who believed that the youth culture would provide the cutting edge for radical change in America had been casting about for tactics that would have dramatic appeal to the free-wheeling and anti-authority "freak" population. The image of Mohandas Gandhi seemed to be the answer.

The Mayday protest climaxed three weeks of antiwar dissent in Washington. It had begun April 18 when a group called the Vietnam Veterans Against the War set up camp on the Mall below the Capitol and picketed the Supreme Court. They were followed by an estimated 200,000 demonstrators who staged a peaceful march on April 24.

The following week the Peoples Lobby sat in on Capitol Hill, at Selective Service headquarters and around other Federal agencies.

Then came the Mayday tribe, most of them longhaired white radicals from the East. From 12,000 to 15,000 of them mobilized and tried to tie up Washington traffic. They armed themselves with clubs, bricks and bottles, but nonviolence seemed to be the motif. Few of the demonstrators attacked any others, including the police.

They came to protest a war and paralyze the city of Washington, but it didn't work out that way. The youngsters displayed weaknesses that proved to be police strengths.

Demonstrators' techniques ranged from simply littering in roadways to throwing boards studded with nails. Another tactic was to drive or push a car into the middle of a street, then abandon it.

But at times the army of demonstrators seemed to be without direction or communication. When thousands were arrested, no replacements appeared to fill the breach.

In contrast, it appeared that expense had not been spared in preparing police communications, transport, troop support and other logistical details vital in coping with the antiwar offensive.

The Nixon administration had charged Washington's 5,100-man police force with one mission that week: to keep the streets clear of protesters so that the government could run smoothly.

The policemen carried out their mission, but in the process they provoked charges from the other side that they had failed to live up to their reputation as one of the most restrained departments in the nation.

Spectators asserted that authorities had made liberal use of tear gas when dispersing the largest groups, and it had hung in the chill spring air for hours. Military helicopters had hovered above, sometimes landing troops to deal with demonstrators.

On May 3 Washington police rounded up 7,000 persons—the largest lockup in a single city on a single day in American history. The action brought accolades from President Nixon and cries of protest from the American Civil Liberties Union, which charged that U.S. authorities had skipped over the U.S. Constitution.

Federal troops, called in to prevent disruption of government machinery, had strict orders to use "minimum necessary force."

Critics vented their ire mainly against the police. They accused them of making indiscriminate arrests, rounding up innocent spectators as well as actual participants in the demonstrations.

The action began Sunday morning, May 2, when 750 helmeted police carrying batons confronted thousands of rock musicians and demonstrators in a local park and forced them from their campsite. The protest leaders watched sadly as their troops drifted away, bedrolls in hand. Some went to remote points throughout the city, disorganized and out of touch with their leaders. Others left town altogether.

When the remainder of the protest group moved toward their targets Monday, authorities closed in before they could assemble. The police charged, with clubs swinging, and lobbed scores of tear gas cannisters. The local jails and a temporary detention camp on a football field were quickly filled with thousands of arrested demonstrators. The courts proved unable to handle such numbers and declared many of the arrests illegal anway.

All over the city brief dramas were unfolding. At the intersection of Connecticut Avenue and L, a young man with short hair began throwing construction sawhorses at disrupters who were trying to use the equipment to block L Street.

"Get the hell out of here, you idiots," he shouted.

Two blocks away a couple of protesters talked earnestly with a middle aged hardhat.

This demonstrator against war cried when she was arrested and searched in Washington

"Were you ever in the service?" the hardhat asked. The demonstrators shook their heads.

"Well, if everyone joined the army and we all went over there, we could end it in a hurry."

The protest drive reached a straggly end Thursday, May 6 when a handful of about 50 demonstrators showed up for one last outburst at the South Vietnamese embassy. It was a far cry from the 15,000 who had jammed the capital a few days earlier.

The backgrounds of leaders of the Mayday tribe made interesting reading. They included:

—Rennie Davis, mild-mannered 30-year-old bespectacled revolutionary who had been among the five defendants convicted in the turbulent Chicago conspiracy trial of inciting rioting during the 1968 Democratic National Convention (*The World in 1970, 34-37*).

—Sidney Peck, 44, a veteran activist on leave from Case Western Reserve University where he was an associate professor of sociology.

—Michael Lerner, 27, radical theoretician and former assistant philosophy professor at the University of Washington.

—John Froines, 32, a veteran militant who had been acquitted in the Chicago conspiracy trial.

Not all of the protesters were young longhairs. In the group was a great grandmother, Nannie Leah Washburn, who spent her 71st birthday in jail. She had journeyed to Washington wearing an army fatigue jacket. She hadn't been there long when she was arrested for lying down in the middle of a traffic circle. And, like many of her young compatriots, she voiced complaints about the District of Columbia's legal system.

Participant in Washington peace rally, wrapped in flag

Antiwar demonstrators used Washington's Mall as a campground

Girl protesting war lost her placard to irate Madison, Wis., man

"I didn't hear any of the charges against me," she told a reporter upon her release after a day in custody.

There were complaints from other quarters. Doctors who had treated demonstrators spoke of crowded jails. Dr. Ronal D. Gregor told a news conference that the packed cells at the federal appeals courthouse "looked like a monkey cage at the zoo" with demonstrators climbing the bars to make room for others to sit down.

The police found it was no bed of roses either. For officer Harvey Keck it meant living out of a bus, eating cold sandwiches, drinking warm soda pop, postponing his son's baptismal party and spending long hours coping with the protesters. But neither Keck nor Roger Davis, a patrolman, blamed the police department—or the protesters, for that matter—for their mode of existence during the week of demonstrations.

The two policemen claimed that no one in their bus had used tear gas.

"It wasn't necessary in our case," said Davis. "We didn't use more force than was necessary. I think the majority of the kids were out here for the fun and games and didn't want to hurt anyone. I asked one of them what they would be doing if the war ended tomorrow. He said he would be right back with another cause."

The antiwar rallies were followed by another demonstration that also took issue with the White House but for different reasons. About 15,000 persons calling themselves Patriots for Victory appeared on the scene and heard the Rev. Carl McIntire urge the President to repent his Vietnam policy and "use the sword as God intended."

The two groups could not have been less similar. The antiwar group with the beards and trappings of Street People had been eager to challenge authority and seemingly anxious to be arrested. The Rev. McIntire's people were normally dressed, middle-aged. There didn't seem to be among them a man with a beard or a girl without a bra.

From the platform one speaker declared that "54,000 boys have given their lives so we can surrender to the Communists. That's the policy of the White House."

The McIntire group was peaceful for the most part and gave the preacher a big hand when he had some kind words to say for J. Edgar Hoover, FBI chief.

When the dust had finally settled, one prominent figure had praise for the police and a few brickbats for the antiwar group. Atty. Gen. John N. Mitchell compared the protesters to Hitler's brownshirts and said "nothing else could have been done" except to make the mass arrests that swept them off Washington's streets by the thousands.

"I am proud of the Washington city police," said Mitchell. "I am proud that they stopped a repressive mob from robbing the rights of others."

There was one aftermath that gained considerable attention. Yippie leader Abbie Hoffman was arrested in New York, accused of participation in the Washington protests. He was indicted on a charge of crossing state lines to incite a riot.

Said Hoffman, "I had about as much to do with the demonstrations in Washington as the Capitol bombing or the earthquake in Los Angeles, which I also expect to be indicted for."

Arrested demonstrators were marched to buses at DuPont Circle

Sanford Katz, defense counsel, and Joan Bird, one of 13 Black Panthers acquitted of bomb and murder conspiracy in New York

Major Victories Scored by Panthers in 3 Trials

In New York 13 acquitted of conspiring to kill police, bomb buildings; kidnaping-murder conspiracy charges in New Haven dismissed, and in Detroit case 12 found innocent of murder

THERE WERE distinctive differences between Black Panther trials that took place in New York City, New Haven, Conn., and Detroit during May and June in 1971. But when these cases were concluded the results were quite similar: Although many accusations had been made against the Panther Party in recent years, prosecutors in New York and New Haven had failed to convince the juries that the defendants were guilty of any charge.

In Detroit 12 Panthers were acquitted on murder and conspiracy charges. Three of them were convicted of felonious assault alone, the only failure the defense suffered in any of the trials. The New York trial involved 13 of 22 Panthers indicted on charges of conspiring to bomb public places and to kill policemen. Most of the 13 had been in jail since April 1969 because of high bail.

Pretrial hearings strained the patience of New York State Supreme Court Justice John M. Murtagh. Often he turned his swivel chair to present his back to the defendants, finally commenting that he had been called a racist pig once too many times.

Court attachees termed the eight-month trial the longest in the state's history and by far the most expensive, costs exceeding $2 million. In spite of repeated disruptions of courtroom procedure by defendants and their supporters, all of those indicted emerged unpunished, including two who fled to Algeria.

The jury, including five blacks and one Puerto Rican, retired May 14. Both defense and prosecution anticipated many days of wrangling among them to pass thereafter, but, to the amazement of all concerned, the jurors returned in three and a half hours with a verdict of innocent for all, on each of 156 counts.

The jubilant defendants and spectators reacted by screaming "Power to the people!" and "Right on!"

The prosecution was stunned. Its attorneys had based their case primarily on the testimony of four undercover agents who infiltrated the party in 1968 and 1969. These agents had testified that they heard the defendants plan to bomb police precincts, department stores, railway and subway stations and the Bronx Botanical Gardens; they also told of attending classes, conducted by the Panthers, at which instructions were given on weapons, making bombs and conducting guerrilla warfare.

Panther lawyers had attacked the credibility of the undercover policemen who, these defense lawyers said, were under pressure to justify their roles by getting incriminating evidence. They said the prosecution's case was compounded of innuendoes, out-of-context statements, irrelevancies and appeals to racial fears and bias.

Joseph Gary, one of the five black jurors, commented: "I don't fault the undercover agents; they were doing their job where society put them, but nobody really saw anybody do the things they talked about."

The acquitted defendants were Lumumba Shakur, 29, and his wife Afeni, 24; Walter Johnson, 26; John J. Casson, 30; Robert Collier, 34; Curtis Powell, 35; Alex McKiever, 21; Clark Squire, 34, Joan Bird, 22; William E. King Jr., 33; Lee Roper, 24; Michael Tabor, 25, and Richard Moore, 26.

Tabor and Moore fled to Algeria in February, forfeiting bail of $150,000 and $100,000 respectively, while the trial was in progress.

In New Haven things had gone a little differently during the trial of Panther national chairman Bobby Seale, 34, and local party leader Ericka Huggins, 23, before Harold M. Mulvey, a state Superior Court judge. Both Panthers were charged with kidnaping resulting in death, aiding murder and conspiracy to kidnap and to murder, in connection with the slaying of party member Alex Rackley (*The World in 1969, 224*).

Rackley's body had been found in a river bog near Middletown, Conn., in May 1969. George Sams Jr., the state's chief witness against Seale, was a former Panther. Sams testified in the Seale-Huggins trial that he heard Seale order Rackley slain as a suspected police informer. The prosecution maintained that Mrs. Huggins had known of the impending killing and had aided and abetted it. Rackley had been slain at Middlefield, near Middletown.

However, witnesses testified that Sams was a chronic liar who had hated Seale and vowed he would "get even" with him after the Panther leader expelled him from the party for stabbing another member in the leg. Sams was allowed to testify only

after two court-ordered psychiatric reports found him competent to be a witness.

The defense blamed Sams for Rackley's murder and attacked his credibility and motives.

The defendants, had they been found guilty, could have faced the death penalty. But instead, when the jury of five blacks and seven whites could not reach a verdict on May 24, the judge declared a mistrial. The following day he dismissed the charges, and the prosecutor said neither defendant could be reindicted.

The judge noted that some 1,500 persons had been considered for jury duty in four months of jury selection, and that the panel finally selected was not convinced the defendants were guilty. In addition, Seale and Mrs. Huggins had already spent more than two years in jail, he said.

"With the massive publicity attendant upon the trial just completed, I find it impossible to believe that an unbiased jury could be selected without superhuman efforts, efforts which this court, the state and these defendants should not be called upon either to make or to endure," Judge Mulvey said.

Although pro-Panther demonstrations just off the Yale University campus brought this trial a great deal of publicity, court proceedings were peaceful and were cited by opposing attorneys as extremely fair.

Another witness in the case with Sams was Panther member Warren Kimbro. Before the trial both Sams and Kimbro had pleaded guilty to second-degree murder in the Rackley slaying, but sentencing was deferred until the Seale-Huggins trial was concluded. Thereafter they drew the automatic sentences of life imprisonment.

It was also Judge Mulvey who, in 1970, presided at the trial of yet another Panther, Lonnie McLucas, charged with kidnaping resulting in death, conspiracy to kidnap and murder, and binding with criminal intent, all involving Rackley.

On Aug. 30 of that year McLucas was found guilty of con-

Acquitted Panthers: Curtis Powell and Joan Bird after acquittal of bombing and murder conspiracy with 11 others in New York trial

Huey Newton, cofounder of Black Panther party, in his Oakland, Calif., penthouse after a jury failed to agree in his manslaughter retrial

spiracy to murder. His sentence was 12 to 15 years. He was acquitted on the other charges, which carried heavier penalties.

* * * *

In Detroit, the murder and conspiracy to murder charges involved a black policeman slain during a gun battle at Panther headquarters in the fall of 1970. The three convicted of felonious assault on a second officer were Erone Desaussure, Benjamin Fondrun and David Johnson.

The jury verdicts were rendered on the last day of June, following an 18-day trial during which the prosecution presented 18 witnesses. They told of shots being fired at policemen from the Panther headquarters. But none could identify any Panther alleged to have fired the shots. The defense rested its case without calling a single witness.

As had happened in New Haven, a jury failed to agree after six days' deliberation in the Oakland, Calif., manslaughter retrial of Huey P. Newton, a cofounder of the Black Panther party *(The World in 1970, 103)* and a mistrial was declared on Aug. 8.

In New Orleans, a jury decided in favor of 12 Panthers charged with the attempted murder of five policemen in a shootout at a housing project. The jury of 10 blacks and two whites deliberated for one and one-half hours on Aug. 6 and the 12 were acquitted.

* * * *

The course of the Black Panther party had been a stormy one almost every year since two black friends, Huey P. Newton and Seale, founded it in 1966 *(The World in 1968, 191)*.

Panthers drew national attention in May 1967 when they entered the capitol in Sacramento, Calif., carrying guns to demonstrate against proposed gun control legislation. It should be legal, they said, for members of minority groups to defend themselves against the injustices of the police and other authorities. Thereafter many law enforcement agencies accused the Panthers of gun carrying and revolutionary tactics. Their warlike assertions stirred fear throughout the nation, among whites and moderate blacks, authorities said. In 1970 FBI director J. Edgar Hoover called them the "most dangerous and violence-prone of all extremist groups," and the government repeatedly blamed them for bombings, murder and attempted assassinations.

But some of the ideals and practices of the Panthers were found worthy by many non-members. Free breakfasts for children and their community projects against drug abuse won considerable respect in major cities.

In 1969 police resistance began to damage the party. The Panthers contended the police sought to wipe them out, and claimed far more of their members were killed in police shoot-outs than were policemen. But in 1971 fresh attacks on police were attributed to the black militants. Panthers began to lose members to prisons, death or exile. Members seldom were seen selling the party newspaper on the streets or passing out leaflets. News conferences were rarely called, and there was less talk about free breakfasts and free medical clinics. In such major cities as Los Angeles, New Orleans, New York, Washington, Boston, Denver and Chicago, and in the San Francisco Bay area where the party was founded, there were reports that offices had been shut down.

Stokely Carmichael, who had been involved in a running dispute with the Panthers, said during an interview with the New York Times that the Panthers were finished. He contended the Panthers had been victims of their own rhetoric, which he said forced them into positions they could not defend.

In the wake of the 1971 Panther courtroom experiences, however, many police authorities felt that the party was not in any way finished; that its members simply were relaxing temporarily to devise new strategies.

Panther Ericka Huggins wins freedom in murder trial at New Haven

Panther leader Bobby Seale

Was Israel Closer as a Haven for Soviet Jews?

Death penalty in Leningrad jet hijacking attempt shocked the world, and sentence was commuted for two who tried to flee

AFTER THE FREE STATE OF ISRAEL was proclaimed in 1948, the Soviet Union rushed to become among the first to recognize the new government. But at home Zionism was looked upon as inimical to the Soviet brand of Communism. A short time after the war between Israel and the Arab states ended in 1949, Jews in the Soviet Union were being warned against adopting an attitude of "bourgeois nationalism," which in effect meant loyalty to anything non-Soviet.

In the 20 years that followed, thousands of Soviet Jews petitioned for the right to migrate to this new homeland, but most of their appeals were in vain.

The campaign against Zionism, which dated back to the era of the czars, reached a peak of bitterness near the end of Joseph V. Stalin's reign. During the years that followed, such manifestations were fitful, but in 1970 the anti-Zionist drive came to life again, as the Kremlin sought to persuade the world that Israel held no very strong attraction for Russia's Jewry.

On Christmas Eve in 1970 most of the western nations were deeply shocked when two Jews in Leningrad were sentenced to die by hanging for an attempted hijacking of a plane bound for a small town near the Finnish border.

The two condemned men, Mark Dymshits and Edward Kuznetsov, were members of a group of 12, of whom 10 were

Jews, who were charged in the case. Dymshits, the captain, had testified that their intention was to fly the plane to Sweden, then proceed to Israel. He said he had been planning the escape for two years.

All 12 had been tried under articles of the Soviet criminal code which held that attempts to flee the country were treasonable. Nine of the defendants were given from four to 15 years each in prison, at hard labor.

The reaction of other nations was immediate. Even some in communist-ruled eastern Europe questioned the equity of the two death sentences. In Jerusalem, 11,000 Jews demonstrated at the Wailing Wall. Mrs. Golda Meir, a native of Russia and Israel's premier, told the Knesset the efforts of Russian Jewry were not against the government but rather a "national awakening," a fight "for the right to join their own people." She said the defendants' only crime was that they "dared approach the Soviet authorities to let them go to Israel. Woe to this big power that it has to use such means as the Leningrad trial."

In Washington, D.C., 1,000 persons took part in a candlelight procession to the White House. Similar protests to the government were made by Jewish organizations across the United States. Through diplomatic channels the U.S. government appealed to the Soviet government for clemency. So did the United Nations. Demonstrations and protests also took

In Jerusalem, immigrants protested trial of Jews in Leningrad plane hijacking

place in Switzerland, France, Great Britain, West Germany and elsewhere.

Finally, on Dec. 31, 1970, the Russian supreme court conceded that the hijacking had never actually taken place. The death penalties were commuted. Dymshits and Kuznetsov each got 15 years at hard labor, but Kuznetsov's sentence included "specially strict" treatment—which meant a bare subsistence diet and only one visit yearly by relatives—because he had been armed when the arrests were made outside the plane June 15, 1970.

Pope Paul VI received the news with "relief and joy." Mrs. Meir expressed satisfaction. In New Rochelle, N.Y., Rabbi Philip Weinburger said, "We have learned our lesson; we will never remain silent in the face of injustice, intimidation and suffering against our people or against any people."

The sentence commutations were the dramatic climax of 1970 and earlier conflict between Soviet officials and Jews seeking asylum. On March 4, 1970, a news conference had been called by prominent Jews, including Veniamin E. Dymshits, a deputy premier and the only Jew in a high Russian post (no relative of the convicted captain). He told the conference that "Soviet Jews are protected from discrimination by the U.S.S.R. constitution." And, on March 9 of that year, the government newspaper Izvestia printed a statement by Moscow's chief rabbi that "the real motherland of Soviet Jews is our native Soviet Union."

In rebuttal, 39 Jews sent to Leonid M. Zamyatin, chief of the foreign ministry's press department, a denial that all Soviet Jews were anti-Israel, pro-Arab and happy to stay in their homeland. Their declaration said they were "ready at any minute, leaving behind everything, whatever it may be, to make our way to the State of Israel, even on foot."

A few months later another letter, signed by 21 Jews, contended the Kremlin maintained an anti-Israel policy and asked permission to leave the Soviet Union. Those Jews in Russia who had denounced the Israeli effort and supported the Russian cause, the letter said, were Jews only because their passports said so. "We are the real Jews, with a deep feeling for Jews wherever they are—in the Soviet Union or Israel or America."

As 1970 drew to a close, the Soviet Union canceled what was to have been the first American tour of the Bolshoi opera and ballet troupe after a number of assaults had been made on Soviet citizens visiting the United States. Izvestia blamed the cancellation on "Zionist extremists" who "not only create obstacles to the implementation of official functions by Soviet establishments in the United States and jeopardize performances in the field of cultural exchange but threaten the personal security of Soviet citizens." Russian newspapers often condemned Zionist organizations and the press in the United States for any dissension, largely because the Soviet Union insisted that in Russia "the Jewish question" did not exist.

In turn, the party newspaper Pravda charged that Zionists were trying to recruit Russian Jews. Its argument was that, among the youth in capitalist countries, the appeal of Zionism was dwindling.

"Few young people," said Pravda, "take the Zionist bait in developed capitalist countries, and fewer and fewer young Jews express the will to 'return' to Israel to 'develop' the temporarily occupied Arab lands. . . ."

The situation flared up again in May 1971 when a Leningrad court convicted nine Jews who had hoped to emigrate to Israel. They received sentences ranging from one to 10 years on charges stemming from the attempted air hijacking of June 1970.

Rabbi Meir Kahane, Jewish Defense League leader

The most severe sentences were meted out to an engineer and a doctor. A sentence of 10 years was given Gilya I. Butman, 38-year-old engineer described by the prosecution as one of the originators of the plan to fly 12 passengers out of the Soviet Union in a hijacked plane and make their way to Israel. Mikhail L. Korenblit, 34, a physician, also accused of playing a leading role in the attempt, got seven years.

Israeli officials promptly denounced the verdict.

Also in May, four Latvian Jews were sentenced in Riga to serve prison terms from one to three years for slandering the Soviet State. The offense of the "criminal group," Tass reported, was to have reproduced and distributed to fellow Jews "anti-Soviet publications from Tel Aviv and slanderous material."

The three-year sentence was imposed on Arkaday Shpilberg, a 34-year-old engineer who had pleaded innocent and had claimed he was arrested only because he wanted to emigrate.

Mikhail Shepshelovich, 29, a locksmith, was sentenced to two years. Boris Mafster, 25, an engineer, and Ruta Alexandrovich, 25, a nurse, each received a one-year sentence.

In June, there was an aftermath to the Leningrad trial. The Moldavian supreme court found that all nine Jews tried at Kishinev in connection with the alleged attempt to hijack the plane were guilty of anti-Soviet actions. They were sentenced to prison camp terms ranging from one to five years. However, the principal charge against the nine appeared to be alleged involvement in a group that coordinated information about Jewish life with other groups in Leningrad and Riga, Latvia.

In 1971 diplomatic relations between Russia and the United States were weakened by a small but militant organization, the Jewish Defense League, based in New York. Its estimated 12,000 members were led by Rabbi Meir Kahane, who had adopted the slogan "Never again," a reference to the extermination of Jews in Germany under the Nazis. In their demonstrations the league's supporters carried such signs as "No Russian is safe in New York" and "Two Russians for every Jew." In January seven of its members, including its leader, were charged with assault, inciting to riot, rioting, criminal mischief and burglary. Four months later they were arrested by U.S. Treasury agents and charged with conspiracy to violate federal gun and bomb regulations.

The Russian news agency Tass accused Kahane's JDL of stirring up anti-Soviet feeling in the United States and said the American press was "striving to slander the Soviet government to aggravate world tension."

A bomb exploded outside the Russian cultural building in Washington, D.C., on Jan. 8, and on Jan. 15 a brick was thrown through a window of a Russian airline's ticket office in New York. Also on Jan. 15 Russia retaliated with the threat that, if such violence continued, American citizens in the Soviet Union would be treated accordingly.

When 750 world Jewish leaders assembled in Brussels Jan. 13 to discuss the problems of Soviet Jewry, the Soviet Union called the conference proceedings "anti-Soviet slander" intended to "divert the attention of the world public from continuing aggression in the Middle East and Indochina."

Rabbi Kahane was barred from that conference and ultimately was expelled from Brussels. Yet many of those who attended remonstrated nonetheless, indicating a split between liberal and conservative Jewry. But, at the meeting's conclusion, 600 of the 750 delegates signed a declaration of "solidarity with our Jewish brothers in the Soviet Union," and called upon the Russian government to "recognize the right of Jews who desire to return to their homeland in Israel."

* * * *

During the 27th annual session of the United Nations Human Rights Commission at Geneva in February 1971, the United States and Israel formally accused Moscow of discrimination and urged the Soviet Union to permit the emigration of those who wished to leave. In reply, Nikolai K. Tarassov, the Russian delegate, described the United States as a "racist Babylon," guilty of genocide in seeking extermination of 20 million American Negroes and the people of Vietnam. Thus neither of the meetings in Brussels or Geneva had brought Jews and Soviet authorities any closer to an understanding.

In addition, hope for improving U.S.-U.S.S.R. rapport grew fainter as unsavory occurrences continued in both countries. American newsmen in Moscow reported acts of vandalism, particularly against their automobiles, and incidents in which their personal freedom was impaired by Soviet agents.

In Washington, D.C., 800 persons chanting "Freedom now!" were arrested for blocking an intersection near the Russian embassy on March 21. The demonstrators were part of 2,500 protesters who had arrived in 28 buses from New York, Newark and Philadelphia. Their leader, Rabbi Kahane, and other speakers urged intensified harassment of Russians in the United States, and called upon President Nixon to break off disarmament, trade, space and cultural talks with the Soviet Union.

"We are going to make the life of Russians hell all over the country," the rally was told by Yossi Templeman of the Student Activists for Soviet Jewry. "Every single day during World War II 10,000 Jews were gassed and turned into soap and lampshades, and nobody did anything. We stand guilty and condemned for doing nothing. Never again."

Russian officials repeatedly fell back on the claim that Jews would be allowed to emigrate more freely when the Arab-Israel conflict was terminated, thus lessening Soviet fears of swelling Israeli army ranks. There were, of course, some exit visas issued to Jews each year. But these had taken time to obtain—often many years—following the filing of applications. One of the more recent cases, spanning two years, exemplified the fortunate cases:

In February 1969 Yosif Kazakov wrote a letter to Premier Alexei N. Kosygin, asking permission to leave Russia for Israel, with his family. He told his friends he was optimistic. If Kosygin saw the request, Kazakov said, he would surely grant it immediately.

But time passed, and Kasakov's confidence turned to despair.

"On Feb. 12 I was fired from my job as an electric line engineer," said Kazakov, 45. "No reason was given. I have tried 15 times to get another job. But each time they say they will hire me, each time they check with my old employer, each time they say 'Nyet.'

"Now my family is starving. There is nothing; we still want to go to Israel, but we will never make it alone. I know that now."

Things were not quite as bad as Kazakov thought. Earlier in that month one of his sons had managed to get a student visa to attend Haifa Polytechnic Institute in Israel. There a Jewish organization got him a temporary permit to visit the United Nations in New York. The true motive of his sponsors, however, was propaganda; he staged a nine-day fast in front of the U.N. Building as a protest against Soviet treatment of his father and other Jews.

Nothing happened for a year. Then, on Feb. 14, 1971, five households were granted permission to leave Russia for Israel. Kazakov's family was one of them.

In greeting the families, Mrs. Meir said: "There is nothing in the world that can defeat a Jew as long as he wants to remain a Jew."

These Jews from Moscow, Kiev and Riga arrived in Tel Aviv after winning right to emigrate

Thereafter, wrote William L. Ryan, Associated Press special correspondent, the issuance of exit visas increased until they averaged about 200 a month. The number of Jewish citizens in the Soviet Union had been estimated as three million.

Although Soviet authorities had maintained that a Jewish problem did not exist, Ryan suggested it was possible that, on the contrary, the problem had become too big to handle.

* * * *

For 2,000 years the Jewish peoples of the world had been persecuted and occasionally praised, discriminated and plotted against. For 2,000 years they had struggled to preserve their identity, find their freedom and establish an independent state with a united society. The hope that burned with each new century, that lingered with each moment of peace and then waned with each recurrence of tragedy was at last fulfilled. Yet from the time of its birth in 1948, the new nation found itself embroiled in a struggle for survival with the Arabs, sworn enemies of Zion and of the state of Israel.

Israel's declaration of independence read: "The State of Israel will be open for the emigration of Jews from all countries of their dispersion." Jews in a steady stream left their many birthplaces. But those in Soviet Russia found themselves facing a bitter predicament: Since the revolution that followed World War I, Soviet authorities had shown little sympathy for Jew or Gentile who tried to leave that country.

Under Communist rule at least some Jews would concede that they fared better than they had under the czars, when thousands were eliminated in massive pogroms.

Yet as late as Stalin's regime, tolerance was minimal. In 1952–53 the campaign reached alarming proportions as repeated articles appeared in the Soviet press assailing Zionism. Jews were referred to by implication as "homeless cosmopolites."

Shortly before Stalin's death in 1953, an anti-Jewish campaign was in full swing. Stalin accused Jewish doctors of being among those plotting against the lives of Politburo members. A number of Jewish doctors were arrested, and they were not freed until months after the dictator's death in March 1953.

In his final months, Stalin dismantled the autonomous Jewish state of Birobidjan, supposedly set aside in the Far East for Jews. He also severely persecuted those who sought to create a haven in the Crimea for Jewish refugees who had managed to escape from the German Nazis during World War II.

Although the Soviet constitution purported to extend religious freedom to all, the official policy supported atheism. By 1971 there were only about 90 synagogues in all the Soviet republics. Many difficulties impeded the practice of the Jewish religion. No school anywhere in the Soviet Union taught Hebrew or Yiddish. Sporadically there was official and unofficial interference with such activities as the manufacture of matzoth for the holidays or the performance of sacred Hebraic rites.

Because of this denial of Jewish traditions and the added intensity of the Israeli cause, many religious Jews sought to leave Russia.

Many who were born Soviet Jews unquestionably had been sovietized and did not practice the religion of their forebears. But many others doubtless did; and those who remained religious eagerly sought permission to leave the U.S.S.R.

In New York, members of the Student Struggle for Soviet Jewry and the Jewish Defense League burned a Soviet flag

The Idle Rich:Gone Forever

Symbol of a bygone era: Newport, R.I., mansion of the late financier, Arthur Curtiss James

THE IDLE RICH don't exist any more," said Mrs. Stephen "Laddie" Sanford over a round of cocktails in her ornate New York apartment. "Children just cannot afford to live like their parents. Taxes have taken care of that."

Col. Serge Obolensky voiced agreement as he gazed moodily out of the window of his midtown office.

"You might call the Idle Rich the new breed of vanishing American," said the 81-year-old former Russian prince. "There is no leisure class today."

In interviews with The Associated Press, Mrs. Sanford and the colonel left no doubt that they were well qualified to speak for the wealthy class—or what remained of it.

In the course of his long life the slim, elegant Obolensky had been married to daughters of Czar Alexander II and John Jacob Astor. At 81, he was regarded as dean of the International Set.

"It's all very Middle Class today," said Obolensky. "The Labor Class has become middle and so has Society. I suppose it's a good thing.

"Besides," he added, "you cannot have a leisure class without servants, and no one wants to be a domestic any more. The whole style of living has changed. The offspring of the rich in this country simply do not want the vast estates and huge homes their parents had. They want to spend their money on pleasure, not upkeep."

It was an interesting commentary from a man whose family in czarist days had owned seven large houses in St. Petersburg, plus estates covering more than 50,000 acres of farmlands, forests and game preserves.

Mrs. Sanford echoed Obolensky's complaint about the scarcity of household help, but admitted that she had been fortunate. The seven who staffed her Palm Beach estate had been with the Sanford family for years.

The attractive, vivacious wife of retired sportsman "Laddie" Sanford had long been regarded as one of the leaders of society in Palm Beach, that glittering 14-mile strand founded in the 1890s by Henry Morrison Flagler, a partner of John D. Rockefeller.

It was a dwindling class, this favored few. But they still had more diamonds, more limousines, more yachts, more mansions and more works of art than 95 per cent of the population.

Where were such fabulous figures as the late Harrison Williams, whose wife for years held the title of America's Best Dressed Woman? His Long Island estate was run by 30 house servants and 100 gardeners, and there were four chauffeurs and 10 cars to drive Williams and his spouse here and there. Most such employes were part of the past.

There were some holdovers from the old days, however. Mrs. Merriweather Post continued to make do with a staff of about 60 at Mar-A-Lago, her Palm Beach palace. Mrs. Sanford herself occupied an ocean front Palm Beach home that had an 80-foot reception room adorned with the heads of big game she and her husband had bagged over the years.

Robert David Lion Gardiner was the 16th lord of the manor. The manor consisted of 3,300 acres he shared with his sister on Gardiner's Island, lying between the forked eastern tips of Long Island, N.Y.

The extremely wealthy had other distinctions. Eccentricity was one.

"Most rich people have a screw loose somewhere," said Mrs. Sanford, who, as actress Mary Duncan, once worked for a living. "I knew one person worth millions who saved string. Another enormously wealthy woman allows her daughter only one paper handkerchief when she sneezes.

"Or take Pat Lanahan, with his yacht, private plane and everything. And no car! Good Lord, he could be driven home by some drunk after a party and get killed. But he thinks it's great not to have a car."

The wealthy socialite had another distinction. His reactions were often quite different from those of the average man. There was the case of the young man who was telling fellow guests at a fashionable dinner party how his pocket had been picked while he was sipping sherry late one night at a local tavern. Our hero was warming up to his story when an elderly gentleman at the table fixed him with a cold, disapproving eye.

"Why were you drinking an aperitif at that late hour?" the oldster demanded.

There were other differences about this group of mortals known variously as the Very Rich, The Regal Society and the Beautiful People. Said Stephen Birmingham, who made a career of chronicling their activities, the breed had a different "look" about them; a simple, tweedy mode of dressing that never seemed to go out of style and a special accent that typified the flat New England "a" blended with a touch of soft southern drawl.

These people attended what they fondly referred to as the "right" schools, played the "right" sports and shopped in the "right" stores to outfit themselves for the long hard year of benefit balls.

These were the people who dined in the best restaurants, often as much to be photographed as nourished, but who drove American cars because they felt that only parvenu types tool around in those prestigious foreign models.

The Very Rich clung together because only in their company could they feel really comfortable.

They migrated seasonally in herds: Palm Beach in the winter, Aiken in the spring, the Hamptons in the summer and New York in the fall.

With the passing of the years, Society had changed its image somewhat. No longer was there the obsession among matrons

Mrs. Jacqueline Onassis leaving London's posh Claridge Hotel

Charlotte Ford (center profile) danced at her debut ball

to marry off their daughters to titled Europeans. And there was less interest in tracing one's ancestry, possibly because some had done so with unhappy results.

One thing had not changed. Money was still the prime ingredient for anyone who wanted to play the social game, no matter how impeccable his other credentials might be. But one had to be discreet about one's worldly possessions. It might not be sinful to have a lot of money, but it seemed wrong to enjoy it openly.

This sensitivity to ostentatious wealth was especially evident among those with political ambitions. Many remembered how Nelson Rockefeller had campaigned for the governorship wearing an ancient overcoat with frayed sleeves. Richard Nixon had never been classed with the Very Rich, but he too was sensitive about ostentation. It was recalled that he used to send word ahead to local groups planning his campaign motorcades; "No Cadillacs."

This did not mean that there was no ostentation. In fact, it prompted some students of the contemporary scene to make a differentiation between New Wealth and Old Wealth. The Old Wealthy, said social observer Lewis Lapham, recognized each other by small, elusive signals, such as a name in common, or a summer spent at Fisher's Island. But the New Rich often recognized each other by comparing possessions, like youngsters swapping bubblegum or photos of ball players. They would specify the size of a house or the price of a cruiser, in contradiction to the maxim of the late J. P. Morgan that anyone who had to think about the cost of a yacht had no business owning one.

The Old Rich carried this theory a step farther, giving small tips or reaching slowly for a restaurant check, apparently in the hope of convincing everyone that they were not made of money and therefore not fair game for swindlers.

To the New Rich, said Lapham, the world was a department store. To the Old Rich it was a conspiracy of thieves.

In 1971 the rich may have had time on their hands, but idleness was no longer the *IN* thing. Some ran boutiques, stocked with costly baubles, raised huge sums for charity and built and decorated palatial villas which they sold off to one another. Others worked long hard hours increasing their wealth or protecting their fortunes against the inroads of taxes.

A good example of the modern rich man was J. J. Mascuch, the inventor who put in a 10-hour day running his electronics

empire in New Jersey, then went happily home to a pink villa stocked with such rarities as a priceless Holbein, a Rembrandt sought by a score of museums, a cluster of Ming vases and a $200,000 swimming pool with 24 karat gold tiles.

Mascuch liked to shepherd visitors through his treasure-filled castle in Milburn, N.J. He made no secret of the fact that he thoroughly enjoyed the fruits of an income derived from more than 150 inventions in the automotive, aeronautic and space fields. But he had not become obsessed with wealth for its own sake.

"Riches are not an end in life, but an instrument in life," he told an interviewer.

A still more radical change in the 1970s was noticeable among young businessmen bent upon making their first million. Many worked seven days a week, whether it meant promoting a rock group or marketing an invention. And many were far more keenly aware of the injustices of the social system than their predecessors ever were. The American system had made them rich, but it still had produced no solution for the poor.

"We've learned to make it in the system, but that doesn't necessarily mean we like that system, and we're looking for ways to change it," said one self-made young man.

There were still links to the old days, but they were more for tradition than anything else, like the order of Colonial Lords of the Manors, which held its 60th annual meeting in New York last May. The Order didn't have as much business to transact as it did in the old days, when a succession of British rulers bestowed 10 manorial patents in New York.

Forefathers of the organization had the right to collect taxes and rents, appoint clergymen and convene judicial courts. By 1971 things had changed somewhat. The only member who still owned a large tract of land was David Gardiner, lord of Gardiner's Island. The main reasons for the continuance of the order were to research, study and publish information about the manors, and to meet once a year to talk over the good times.

The leisureliness of any nation's aristocracy had always been based on the almost total absence of leisure among members of that nation's working masses. So-called aristocratic elegance in the old sense was predicated largely on the fact that, willing or not, kitchen maids were capable only of scouring pots 12 to 14 hours a day. In the same category were the gardeners who manicured velvety lawns or tended formal gardens from dawn till dusk. In America those days evidently were gone forever.

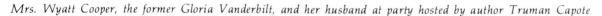

Mrs. Wyatt Cooper, the former Gloria Vanderbilt, and her husband at party hosted by author Truman Capote

WAR HERO AUDIE MURPHY KILLED

The U.S. Marines and the paratroops rejected Audie Murphy in 1942 because he was too skinny, but the freckled-faced Irish kid from Texas persisted. Concealing the fact that he was not quite 18 he got into the Army and went on to become the most decorated American hero of World War II.

The baby-faced son of a sharecropper ran up an incredible record fighting through Italy and France, killing an estimated 240 Germans and winning 24 decorations from the Americans, three from the French and one from the Belgians.

He became a legend, this shy youngster who did not drink, smoke or swear. This was Audie Murphy, who rose to the rank of lieutenant and made a victorious stand on a blazing tank destroyer fighting off scores of Germans and six German tanks.

Holding a .50 caliber machine gun, he stood there exposed on three sides, firing into the German lines. For more than an hour he continued shooting, despite a leg wound. He killed or wounded some 50 Germans. For this he won the Medal of Honor, America's top award.

The luck of the Irish stayed with Murphy throughout his military career. Enemy gunners wounded him in both legs and the hip, but he survived.

Texas went wild when Murphy finally came home in 1945. Thousands turned out to give a royal welcome to the green-eyed kid who had helped support his family since he was 12.

He seemed an unlikely hero, this youngster who stood 5 feet 5 inches, and weighed only 134 pounds and was so shy he did not give his name to the welcoming committee waiting in San Antonio.

Associated Press writer William C. Barnard was on hand that day, and on a long drive through Texas Murphy gave him his thoughts about the war.

"They talk about bravery," Murphy told Barnard at one point. "Well, I'll tell you what bravery really is. Bravery is just determination to do a job that you know has to be done. If you throw in discomforts and lack of sleep and anger, it is easier to be brave."

They made a big fuss over Audie Murphy. His handsome face on the cover of Life maga-

zine won him a film contract and he made acting his new career. His biggest success was *To Hell and Back,* based on his wartime exploits. But in later years, after a series of westerns and a television series that failed, he declared bankruptcy in 1968. Thereafter he recovered his losses to some extent.

Murphy was flying from Atlanta to Martinsville, Va., to scout an investment prospect with two business men, Raymond Prater of Chattanooga, Tenn., and Jack Littleton of Fort Collins, Colo. Their chartered plane crashed and burned on Brush Mountain, near Roanoke, Va. The wreckage was found May 31, after a two-day search.

Also aboard were Claude Crosby, 48, of Atlanta; Kim Dody, 29, of Fort Collins, and Herman Butler, of Denver, the pilot. All were killed.

Murphy's business manager, Lincoln Carle, said Murphy had just completed a motion picture, *A Time for Dying,* in which his son Terry also had a role.

At the age of 46, the fabulous luck of Audie Murphy finally had run out.

PROFILE OF A HERO—AN AMERICAN TRAGEDY

When Skip Johnson was a skinny kid, the bullies in Detroit's Corktown sector used to chase him home from school. In Vietnam nearly two decades later, Sgt. Dwight Johnson won the Medal of Honor, America's top award, for valor. Last April the pendulum swung again, and the 23-year-old soldier was shot to death as he tried to rob a neighborhood store.

News of Johnson's death and the circumstances shocked and saddened Detroit's black community.

They remembered a November day in 1969 when President Lyndon B. Johnson had pinned the prestigious medal on Johnson. They also remembered a Detroit dinner honoring the sergeant the following February.

Gen. William Westmoreland had attended the

dinner and declared that "the unsurpassed heroism of this Medal of Honor winner has reserved for him a special permanent place in the annals of history."

Johnson was decorated for extraordinary courage under enemy fire near Dak To in South Vietnam. The citation said he had been serving as a tank driver when the enemy struck.

With his tank pinned down by North Vietnamese regulars, Johnson jumped out of the vehicle armed only with a .45 caliber pistol and proceeded to gun down seven of the enemy while under heavy fire. Out of bullets, he jumped back into the tank, picked up a submachine gun and attacked again.

When the second weapon ran out of ammunition, Johnson leaped aboard another tank,

helped a wounded GI out, then began firing the tank's cannon until it was out of shells.

Johnson left the service in July 1969, but he re-enlisted in November to serve as a recruiter in Detroit's inner city. Later he was to enter Valley Forge Army Hospital near Philadelphia to undergo psychiatric treatment. He was on convalescent leave in Detroit when he entered the store owned by Charles Vandendeghem armed with a gun.

The store owner tried to wrestle the gun from Johnson but was wounded in the left arm, authorities said. Vandendeghem then produced a gun and shot Johnson three times in the chest and once in the face. The soldier who had braved the enemy in Vietnam and saved the life of a comrade died three hours later.

Three black colonels became brigadier generals (from left): Roscoe C. Cartwright, 49, Kansas City; Oliver W. Dillard, 44, Margaret, Ala., and James F. Hamlet, 49, Alliance, Ohio

TURKEY MAINTAINED ITS ANNUAL QUOTA OF DEADLY EARTHQUAKES

An orphaned child sat amid the wreckage caused by the quake that struck Burdur in southwest Turkey

For six straight years at least one major earthquake had brought death and destruction to Turkey, and 1971 was no exception. Tremors ripped open the earth in the opium-growing country around Burdur on May 12, killing 57 persons and virtually flattening Burdur, in Western Asia Minor.

This was only a taste of things to come. Just 10 days later the earth shifted again, this time in eastern Turkish Asia Minor, just as residents of the town of Bingol were retiring for the night. Within minutes, 90 per cent of Bingol lay in ruins and about 1,000 persons were dead. Stunned survivors groped through the darkness in the mountain town of 17,000, looking for friends and relatives.

"It's horrible," shouted a telephone operator in a call from a town near the disaster center, then broke off. From Bingol itself, a state radio operator came on the air, his voicing breaking with emotion.

"It's horrible," he too shouted. "Everyone, mothers, fathers, children, are milling around in streets blocked by rubble, looking for dead relatives. Families are desperately searching the ruins for their children."

Turkish rescue teams, well trained after years of such tragedies, began funneling supplies into the stricken area. Mobile hospitals were included, as well as soup kitchens and thousands of tents for the homeless. Supplies of food and water were rushed in.

Since 1966, the quakes have been hitting with deadly regularity along the Anatolian Fault, a half moon extending from the Burdur region northward from the Aegean Sea, east along the Black Sea and south into the mountains.

Turkish Premier Nihat Erim visited the disaster area a day later, accompanied by his top ministers. He said that the toll had been high because most of the houses in the area were made of sun-baked brick which could not withstand the earth shocks.

"Our sorrows today are high," said Erim.

Turkey's 1970 earthquake—at Gediz near Istanbul and also on the Anatolian Fault—occurred March 28, taking 1,089 lives and leaving about 90,000 homeless. Then, on May 31 of that year, an estimated 50,000 persons died and hundreds of thousands of dwellings were destroyed or damaged beyond habitation by a massive quake in Peru, centered along the 80-mile Huaylas Canyon in the Andes *(The World in 1970, 84–91).* In May 1971 more than 20,000 of these Peruvians were still living in the disaster area's provisional shelters.

CUT IN NATO KILLED BY SENATE

From the moment that Mike Mansfield, affable Democratic majority leader of the Senate, made his pitch for a cutback of U.S. forces in Europe, the White House stood fast against any such move.

To bolster its case, the Nixon Administration recruited a potent coalition of elder statesmen and generals prominent in Atlantic alliance activities, plus two former Democratic presidents, Harry S. Truman and Lyndon B. Johnson. Their presidential assignment was to lobby on Capitol Hill against the Mansfield proposal.

The White House strategy paid off. By a vote of 61-36, the Senate turned thumbs down May 19 on Mansfield's plan for a 50 per cent reduction in the 300,000-man U.S. European force by the end of 1971.

Many senators believed that a significant factor in the outcome had been the offer by the Soviet Communist party leader, Leonid I. Brezhnev, to enter exploratory negotiations with the United States and countries of the Atlantic alliance on mutual troop reductions in Central Europe.

All through the debate, supporters of the administration had stressed that any unilateral cutback action would undermine the bargaining position of the United States and its partners in the North Atlantic Treaty Organization in negotiating with the Communist bloc.

Vice President Spiro T. Agnew sat in the chair as the ballot time came, ready to cast his vote in case of a tie. But the administration never came close to needing him. The majority vote was all one way—President Nixon's way.

Mansfield said after the balloting that his fight had at least succeeded in increasing awareness of the problem. But he expressed regret that "there has been no hint of an understanding from downtown, the White House or overseas."

The White House had gone to great lengths to spell out its conviction that results of Mansfield's proposal would be disastrous. Secretary of State William P. Rogers had asserted that it would "signal the end of NATO." And Nixon himself had declared that a NATO troop cut at that stage would be "an error of historic dimensions."

But, even though Nixon succeeded in routing the effort to force a cut in U.S. troop strength in Europe, a significant majority of the Senate took a stand in favor of some change in the European status quo. This conclusion stemmed from analysis of the voting, which showed no individual troop cut proposal received more than 36 votes, but about 60 of the 100 senators voted either to require a cut or to urge one.

Others made clear during the debate that, while they felt it would be a rebuke to Nixon to support any of the reduction proposals, they also believed that America's European allies should take on a greater share of the NATO defense burden.

In Brussels, a NATO spokesman voiced gratitude that the Mansfield proposal had failed.

FINAL CURTAIN FOR THE SST?

For all the ballyhoo surrounding it, the ambitious plan to develop an American supersonic transport plane never really got off the gound. And, on May 19, the U.S. Senate delivered the presumably fatal blow. By a thumping vote of 58 to 37, it buried attempts made in the House with President Nixon's encouragement to restore development funds for the SST.

The vote was an anticlimax, however, after all the heated arguments over possible effects of such a plane on the ecology and environment of America, as well as its impact on the economy.

The plane project apparently had been doomed, despite the House move to restore $85 million in development funds. William M. Allen, chairman of the Boeing Company, made that clear when he declared that $85 million was unrealistic. Allen had estimated that it would cost from $500 million to a billion dollars to get the project moving again. He added that his company would also require another $2 billion of government funds to start up an SST production line.

Conceding defeat, White House Press Secretary Ron Ziegler said one stumbling block had been Boeing's insistence on development of a new, quieter SST engine which alone would have added $350 million to the overall costs.

A few days after the May 19 vote, the Office of SST Development made a last ditch effort to save the plane. William M. Magruder, chief of the SST Office, made three attempts to find financial help. He went first to James R. Mitchell, vice president for aerospace at the Chase Manhattan Bank in New York; to the three major SST contractors—Boeing, General Electric and Fairchild-Hiller—and finally to George P. Shultz, director of the Office of Management and Budget. But his efforts were in vain.

Ahead of the United States in the SST trend were three foreign countries. A prototype of the supersonic Concorde—a project undertaken jointly by France and Great Britain—flew French President Georges Pompidou from Paris to Toulouse May 7 in 75 minutes, including a 16-minute interval over the Atlantic Ocean at 1,315 miles per hour. Russia's supersonic TU144 was in production.

EGYPT-U.S.S.R. PACT SIGNED

Egypt and the Soviet Union signed, on May 27, a 15-year pact of friendship that caused reverberations on both sides of the Iron Curtain. It was viewed by some western observers as a master stroke of Soviet diplomacy.

Presidents Anwar Sadat of Egypt and Nikolai V. Podgorny of the Soviet Union signed the historic agreement after three days of talks in Cairo's Kubbeh Palace and followed it with speeches depicting the United States as a warmonger bent on scuttling any peace attempts in the Middle East.

Said Podgorny:

"The Americans will not object to a so-called peaceful settlement so long as it is the kind of settlement which would enable the Ameri-cans, through Israel, to impose their will and maintain regimes" they favor in the area.

The pact drew a mixed response from Israel. Premier Golda Meir told a news conference in Stockholm: "There is, as far as I can see, nothing really new" in the pact.

But Mrs. Meir's deputy, Yigal Allon, said in an interview in Jerusalem that he viewed the pact as a "first class diplomatic success" for the Kremlin. Said Allon, the pact not only bolstered the Soviet position with Egypt, but aided the Russians in their global struggle with the United States.

In Moscow, western diplomats said terms of the agreement appeared to extend to Egypt the doctrine of Soviet Communist party chief Leonid I. Brezhnev. That doctrine claimed the right of the Soviet Union to intervene if a Socialist state was threatened. Memorably, that doctrine was applied in Czechoslovakia in 1968 when Soviet tanks rumbled into Prague.

The pact signed in Cairo provided more Soviet military, economic, political and scientific aid to Egypt. Some observers in the Egyptian capital also felt that it committed Moscow to deeper military involvement, if the Egyptians went to war again with Israel.

Western diplomats did not fail to note that the pact was signed in the wake of Sadat's purge of pro-Soviet officials in his government, a move that had appeared to weaken Cairo's ties with Moscow, if anything.

BABIES ALLOWED WEDDED WACS

Having become used to women in its ranks, the U.S. Army decided to change the double standard. New regulations went into effect in May permitting married members of the Women's Army Corps and Army nurses to have children.

The edict said that both female officers and enlisted women "who are pregnant, have had terminated pregnancies or who become parents" could remain in the Army. Hitherto automatic discharge from the service followed pregnancy.

Apparently fearful that the Army might turn into a giant nursery, a military spokesman hastened to note that the new policy did not mean "a wholesale opening of the doors" to mothers in uniform.

"The mere fact that a woman is married and pregnant and wants to stay on are not the only grounds," he declared. "She must also meet the other requirements."

These included a statement from the expectant mother's commanding officer that the child would not interfere with her work or that her service would not "result in neglect of the child."

In addition, enlisted women must also provide an explanation of "the circumstances involved" in a pregnancy.

The army was clear on another point too: Unmarried women who became pregnant would be discharged, as in the past.

LONG WALK TO FIGHT HUNGER

There were four million of them and they ranged from statesmen to hippies and children. Through 600 cities in 50 countries they marched to raise money for the world's hungry.

In the United States alone more than 600,000 —most of them youngsters—walked through about 200 towns during the weekend of May 8-9 and raised $5.1 million.

Singing and exuberant despite sore feet, the young Americans hiked up to 30 miles in the march formed by the Freedom-From-Hunger campaign organized by the U.N. Food and Agricultural Organization.

Sponsored by individuals and organizations that had pledged sums ranging from a few cents to $10 a mile, the hikers slogged through lashing rain in the eastern part of the United States, leaned into gusty winds in the Middle West and strolled under balmy skies in the Far West.

They carried litter bags, lunches and cards that were stamped at checkpoints along the way to verify the number of miles walked.

In Rome, the marchers set out in groups of 800. That was to symbolize the 800 deaths the FAO said occurred from hunger in the world every hour.

The 16-mile hike through winding streets of the Eternal City was climaxed by a special greeting from Pope Paul VI. The pontiff praised the initiative of the marchers as "an eloquent sign of a new conscience maturing in the world."

It was hot and muggy in Rome, and many marchers held their noses as they passed heaps of garbage piled up because of a city employes' strike.

U.N. Secretary-General U Thant also had words of praise for the drive. He called it a "constructive people's movement to mobilize world public opinion . . . to eliminate hunger and poverty wherever they exist on earth."

Sky and earth turned a sullen red as flaming rivers of molten rocks spewed from Mt. Etna volcano

FOR THE RECORD

SIGNED. An agreement by Canadian Prime Minister Pierre Elliott Trudeau and Soviet Premier Alexei N. Kosygin. The pact called for regular high-level contacts to improve "friendship, good-neighborliness and mutual confidence." Canadian officials said that the agreement had been drafted at Soviet initiative and that it provided a convenient framework for discussion of such bilateral questions as preserving common Arctic areas, along with more general problems.

RELEASED. Raphael Minichiello, 21-year-old AWOL U.S. Marine from imprisonment in Italy where he had served 18 months for hijacking an airliner at gunpoint from California to Rome (*The World In 1970, 231*). Minichiello told newsmen that he did not want to return to "my second country," the United States, where he faced a possible death sentence on charges of air piracy. "I don't hate Americans," the decorated Italian American Vietnam war infantryman said after his release from Rome's Regina Coeli Prison. "I don't hate anyone. It's just that they don't understand me."

A country chapel wreathed in fog ⟶

June

The snow-clad majesty of Mt. Rainier, 14,410-foot dormant volcano in Washington

Through Foreign Eyes, A New View of America

What does America look like to its foreign visitors? Peter Arnett and Horst Faas, veteran Associated Press correspondents abroad, made an extensive tour of the United States to find out. Operating as a reporter-photographer team, they prepared this account for The World in 1971. Arnett grew up in Riverton, on the southern tip of New Zealand's south island. Faas was born in Berlin.

FACES of America . . . faces you remembered of the thousands that passed by in a three-month tour . . . faces of 1971.

There was Lola Pepion, 17, a Blackfoot Indian girl waiting on Fisherman's Wharf for a boat to take her to the old prison island of Alcatraz across San Francisco Bay that was occupied by Indian militants. "I am not an American," she shouted, "I am an Indian," and she stamped her dainty foot on the planking as a trio of bearded braves nodded approvingly.

There was Dan Morin, 26, standing tall at the bar at Trixie's Roadhouse in Western Montana, his cowboy hat pushed to the back of his head, his spurs scraping idly at the wooden foot rails. "I served my time in Vietnam and I saw Hong Kong and Bangkok," the lean cowboy said. "But this is where I belong," and he waved across the snow-flecked pines to the distant ridgelines, the icy streams and the one-room log cabin he called home.

There was Chicago detective Joe Stachula, expertly lifting the veil of anonymity from the crowded pavements. We drove past a black walking along the sidewalk and Stachula commented, "Look out for him; he's been some time in the pen."

"How can you tell?" we asked.

"Did you notice he was taking short steps? You learn that kind of walk only in jail, inside a cell."

There were many other faces of America.

Angie Solari, with her sister the only inhabitants of the ghost town of Indian Gulch in the Mother Lode country of California. At age 87 she was still driving trespassers off her land with a walking stick.

A picturesque character encountered on a city street

"I don't know who will die first, me or Indian Gulch," she sighed, stabbing gnarled fingers at the dilapidated, abandoned jailhouse, the crumbling adobe saloon and the once-red frame church that stood buckled against the prevailing wind on a hillside golden with the colors of autumn.

There was Big Red. Stubble sprinkled his chin and his jacket was soiled, but in that Los Angeles street of broken men he carried himself with an air of assurance. We piloted him into one of Skid Row's sleazy bars but he preferred coffee, saying that he was seeking out some old friends. "When I start drinking I hit the bottle for five, six and seven days and on that ride I want company that I like." Big Red called himself a "snowbird." He said, "I come south in the winter like those birds. I'll go back north when the weather gets warmer, and I'll ride the rails."

And there was Anna Magallon, stooping painfully over a row of strawberries in the Salinas Valley of California. As we approached she stood upright and massaged her back with her hand. She smiled through her eyes, the only part of her face not bandaged against the wind and dust. "We are slaves no more," she said in a lilting voice, and talked of a new contract signed with the fruit growers.

There were many other faces, the land etched deeply into some, others just anonymous visages on the passing parade of America. Some of those faces stayed fixed in our minds, and as with the faces so with the landscape. We found that America still had beauty. If you looked for it.

Much of America was still so young. When westward pioneers were pushing through northern Utah along the Oregon trail more than a century ago, their wagon wheels bit deeply into the surface of the empty land. North of Salt Lake City those wagon ruts were still visible on the hard desert floor, and the land itself seemed the way the pioneers must have first seen it — stark, majestic and still empty.

America was congested, America was polluted. But it was America's emptiness, and her beauty, that most impressed us. We saw that California sprawled in a jerrybuilt suburb from San Francisco to Los Angeles by way of the San Joaquin Valley. But take Route One, the coastal highway. It navigates the Big Sur Country where bulging promontories cut man down to mortal size as he nervously hugs the winding, narrow ribbon of highway.

Or north, to the Olympic Peninsula that thrusts into the Pacific past busy Puget Sound, its loins shielded by roadless rain forests and skirted by rocky, windswept beaches. Watch Indian tribesmen digging clams on the beaches or hunting in the forests, still masters of the northwest paradise of salmon-filled rivers and glaciered mountains.

Drive along Route Two across Washington State, and see where man worked his will on the Coulee Country, erecting there the largest concrete dam in the world. But man's engineering pales beside that of nature herself, who carved vast, rock-walled valley mazes with her rivers. The Grand Coulee Dam in that environment looks like a peanut caught between the knuckles of the earth.

Beyond the Coulee country the scenery changes bewilderingly, telescoped by the Interstate highway. Drive through sandy scrublands of what could be the Sahara Desert, enter the rocky, purple plains of Algeria, and roar through the snow-tipped Swiss alps, wheels sliding on the Great Divide snow. Finally, it is into the Steppes of Russia in Montana—all in just one day of driving.

Or fly to Las Vegas and, like us, hire a station wagon with cans of drinking water sloshing in the back. Drive across into Death Valley, where in summer the long, dramatic sweep is the hottest and driest place in America. In autumn, however, the valley is cool and still. Jet streams from aircraft flying out of Los Angeles streak the distant sky but there is no noise and you can stand at Zabriskie Point and ponder the geometrically split mud-hills in peace.

Death Valley spills into Nevada, and as you climb out of those purple depths your automobile might bump and skid on the gravelly road as the terrain gains even greater drama. Bold, jagged escarpments tumble like waterfalls into the naked valleys, sculpture fantasies by a whimsical God.

While there was much spectacle in beautiful America, such as the dramatic depths of the Grand Canyon, we discovered in our journey that there was much subtle beauty as well. Sunset silhouetting fishnets draping a rotting jetty on a north Maine beach in late autumn; sunrise bathing the South Carolina swamps in a golden hue that glazed the mud and set the old oaks afire.

It was the solitude of the Old Euphrata Cloisters in the rolling Pennsylvania Hills, and the joy of bright flowers framing a religious statue in the garden of the Carmel Mission on El Camino Real. It was also the pristine loveliness of the snow flowers flirting on snow-clad Mt. Rainier; the old print reflection on a Cajun plantation house in the still water of the Bayou Teche.

But only two hours away from the bayous was Baton Rouge, dirty and unkempt, a noxious haze drifting over it like a devil's halo. That too, alas, was America.

There were other aspects to America, 1971, that surprised us,

Lonely lighthouse on Maine's rockbound coast

in addition to the extent of the pollution. We had landed in San Francisco carrying the expectations and prejudices of foreigners who had grown up with Export Americana: Hollywood movies, slick news magazines, popular music, Coke red, Pepsi blue.

Our image of America, too, was a mirror of those we met abroad—assured American tourists gawking at the wonders of the world. Generous American aid officials ploughing vast outlays of cash into remote corners of the world. Brave Americans dying far from their shores.

But the qualities of generosity and confidence so apparent among Americans abroad seemed to us lacking in Americans at home. Most Americans we met here were openly dissatisfied with the quality of their lives. Compared with the rest of the world, we found in America so much to be happy or even contented about. Yet we met few Americans who would admit to either sensation.

Our stereotypes of the people proved false. Americans seemed generally uncongenial at home. This trait surprised us because we had the reverse impression abroad. If people at home were agreeable at all it was often grudgingly, and then only after we had gotten to know them.

We anticipated this attitude in the ghettoes and were not disappointed. "What do you expect?" commented our social worker guide when stones rained down on us as we walked through East Los Angeles in the Mexican-American ghetto. "You should be lucky they are not shooting at you. . . ."

But we did not expect it in coastal Maine where, on stopping to photograph an old automobile built into a cabin-house, we were chased away by a man wielding a gun. Or in the Mother Lode country of California where a cattle farmer commented sourly to us, "There are just too many strange people poking around these parts."

There were some other aspects of America that we disliked in 1971. We discovered a nasty geographical streak. People on the Eastern seaboard were scornful of California. "They are kooky over there, idiotic," commented a Philadelphia bus con-

Flowering cactus in the Big Bend country of Texas, land of vivid contrasts

lightly across the land. It peeled off easily to expose the diversity underneath. This diversity in people, in life style and in attitudes was the major pleasant surprise of our journey. We thought the cowboy had long ago ridden to his last roundup, dusted off only when required by the movies or for cigarette commercials. But as we drove west of the Great Divide we met the real thing spurring his horse through the first snows of another long winter. And even some of the very old exhibited the sense of power, drive and dynamism we had expected. There was Fred McCay, 89 years old but still young enough to be self conscious about his three missing upper front teeth, which he hid shyly with his fingers when he talked. Fred purchased his ranch in California in 1911 and remembered the roar of gunfights along the Hornitos trail, and the rustlers who sometimes came at night to steal his pedigreed Aberdeen Angus cattle.

The farther out from American cities we travelled, the more faith we found in the country's future, and Fred was typical when he commented, "This is a great country, and it will be greater."

The rich ethnic diversity of American cities surprised us. We had vaguely imagined the fabled "American melting pot" boiling away eccentricity and individuality and rebuilding the residue into First Class American. But the Poles and the Slavs in Chicago, the Irish and Italians in Boston, the Jews in New York

ductor. In the central states we found people despised New York. On the West Coast they did give the East some due ("New York is one half of the world, Southern California the other," a Los Angeles reporter told us) but they acted as though the Midwest did not exist.

Fences crowd the Far West and march across some of the prettiest countryside. They are obviously a necessary addition to private property yet there seemed something overpoweringly sinister about the fences of rural California because they were so numerous. So many "no trespassing," "no hunting," "no shooting," "no smoking," "no burning" signs adorned a lengthy stretch of farmland that we felt totally intimidated. Standing one bright afternoon on a dusty road between the gold rush towns of Hornitos and Mariposa in the Mother Lode country we looked with satisfaction across the land where no human or animal stirred. Then we saw a sign nailed firmly to a tree: "No loitering." And even free spirit Jack London was imprisoned at last, his grave in the Valley of the Moon surrounded by a fence.

But there was much in America that we liked. We came with great expectations because the impact of American power and technology upon the world has been immense. Just as youths from the outlying provinces flocked to powerful London of the late 19th century, half expecting to find the streets paved with gold, so did the visitor to America expect to find an efficient uniform life style befitting the technological expertise of the first country to unlock the atom and to place man on the moon. And the efficiency was here, even though we heard it frequently questioned. The telephone system was a marvel compared to the archaic systems overseas. The fantastic technology was evident also in the Wall Street brokerage houses where we saw computers that digest the markets, determine the dividends, write the letters and lick the envelopes. Those sleek, purring automatons housed in the dust-free air conditioned inner sanctums of the Wall Street financial temples were as pampered by pretty girls as Indian fertility gods.

We saw much uniformity and blandness in America, as we had expected. But we found it was a veneer painted only

Mudhills formed geometric pattern in California's Death Valley

retained some of the language and many of the customs from the old countries. We wondered at what point a person stopped being an Italian, say, and started being an American. How many people regarded themselves as Italians with the right to live in America, or Americans with a taste for Italian food and customs?

We found a diversity amongst the blacks. We expected every black we met to be militant. Many were, in Watts, in Harlem, in Chicago. But we did see another side where we least expected it: Atlanta, Ga., where a black middleclass seemed satisfied with the way things were. "I can visit any town in Georgia and eat lunch there in a public restaurant if I want to," explained a charming black lady we met as we strolled through the campus of black Atlanta University taking pictures of pretty girls on a sunny day. Her comment surprised us. We had just spent three days in north Georgia where the hospitality was wonderful—as long as you were not a revenue agent looking for moonshine stills. Or you weren't black. The lady explained patiently. "Naturally, we only eat at a Howard Johnson's or some other national chain where we'll get served without the backchat. But we don't mind. We are doing fine. We love it here in Atlanta."

We discovered diversity in America's cooking pots: Oysters steamed in the shell in the old paint buckets in South Carolina,

Sweeping view of Big Sur, California, from atop a cliff

Spanish moss in South Carolina's bayou country near Beaufort

Hutterites, religious sect in Montana, retained the dress of ancestors

$1.50 for five dozen; oysters in thick black gumbo in the bayous of Louisiana. We were in the Olympic peninsula on the night of an ebbing tide and the Quinnault Indians brought in tons of razor clams. Pan fried, as the wind howled outside and the rain beat on the roof of our tiny motel kitchen, they were delicious.

Horst discovered that the Amish had brought with them to America secrets of sausage and cheesemaking that had died in the old country of Germany long ago. We loaded up our rented station wagon with a half a dozen varieties of meat and cheese, topped with shoo-fly pie and apple cider, that saved us from the franchise restaurants all the way to New York. We discovered the succulence of Southern cooking at a table groaning with chicken and dumplings and pies at a roadside restaurant in Dahlonega, Ga.

The quality we most expected was American self reliance, and there was much of it, particularly on the land. Farmer Jim Wright steered his plough across the hard, early winter pasture in remote Blackfoot Valley, Montana, frozen hands on the wheel, his weathered face peering back sometimes at the perfect furough behind him. The temperature could go to 50 below up there, but the cattle would stay outside. They were hardy, like the men.

Amidst all the diversity of America, you suddenly came upon what you expected to find all along. We met a gray haired hunter standing knee deep in snow in a mountain pass in eastern Washington state. He told us he had spent five seasons hunting a male elk in those mountains and had not gotten close enough to fire a shot.

"He's a cunning devil," said the hunter. "He knows I am stalking him. Only one has been shot in these parts in years, but I will get one or the mountain will get me first." He trudged off towards a distant ridgeline as the snow and the wind closed in. That hunter somehow represented to us all we used to envision about America. The hunter was bold and determined, but generous in battle, certain of direction, and persevering. But we had to climb a mountain to discover those truths.

After more than four months of travel we learned that nothing was simple about America. There were Americans to suit all tastes and budgets. Everyone we met in America seemed to have firm opinions. And if our accents did not get us into arguments then almost any choice of words did. Bright Berkeley youths derided the fear and indecisiveness of their elders; the wise old men living in the quiet retirement of the countryside scorned the brashness and arrogance of the young.

But there were places where the pressures of America 1971 just didn't seem to apply. We found the most relaxed people of America in California's Napa Valley and neighboring areas, the wine growing country. Their happiness might be attributed to the soothing qualities of the grape. "We're still trying to wean America off soft drinks," commented a Berringer Brothers vineyard manager as he rummaged behind some old casks in a limestone cave and produced several bottles of 1965 Cabernet Sauvignon to convincingly reinforce his arguments that California wine compared favorably with the French product.

The pressures seemed also far away from the town of Mullen, wedged in a wooded valley in northern Idaho's Coeur D'Alene mining region where we asked an elderly street cleaner for directions. He led us to a little clapboard police station, removed his leather cap and plumped himself behind the desk. "I'm also the police chief," said Gunnar Johnson. Later he revealed he was also chief of the volunteer fire brigade—a one man city hall in this prosperous mining town of 1,400 people.

The quietude of rural America, the spectacle of the remote deserts and valleys were what we most liked about America. But we realized that more people lived in the cities than in the countryside, that America was an urban civilization. What New York was in the present might well be like what all the cities of the world would be like in the future.

So as visitors, we were not anxious to cast final judgment on America of 1971. And we preferred to think that the harsh edges we found in American society would get blunted by time, not more jagged or cutting.

White House bride: Tricia Nixon in her wedding gown

Rain Threatened Garden Wedding at White House

President's wish: That Patricia Nixon and Edward Cox would spend lives outside the "merciless glare of publicity"

". . . This moment is the beginning of a new day. In the evening of their lives together, may they be able to look back and say how splendid the day has been." Chaplain Edward G. Latch of the House of Representatives expressed this wish in his prayer during the marriage of Patricia Nixon, 25, and Edward Finch Cox, 24.

In the nation's capital rain threatened through the morning of June 12, and the weather bureau reported a 30 per cent chance that it would fall that afternoon. Even when the drizzle started, Tricia, eldest daughter of President and Mrs. Richard M. Nixon, was determined that her wedding would take place in the White House Rose Garden as she had planned—the first outdoor ceremony of its kind in the 171-year history of the mansion.

The rain delayed the ceremony for a half hour. It was still sprinkling when the rite started at 4:30 p.m. The first of eight groomsmen stepped from the Diplomatic Reception Room into the garden setting upon which the bride-to-be had insisted.

Flowers were in abundance: White roses, peonies, lilies and petunias, purple delphinium and heliotrope, potted trees and white planters filled with cascading petunias and ivy.

Best man for the bridegroom was his brother, Howard Ellis Cox Jr., 27. Preceding the bride came her four bridesmaids: Julie Nixon Eisenhower, the matron of honor; Mary Ann (Mazie) Cox, 25-year-old sister of the groom, the maid of honor, and Tricia Nixon's two cousins, Amy Nixon 13, and Beth Nixon, 11, junior bridesmaids. They wore soft matching hats and layered silk organdy gowns of mint green and lilac, with fluttering necklines and hems.

The bride-to-be, who 15 minutes earlier had shown her disappointment with the weather, became dazzling and radiant when, to the music of Purcell's *Trumpet Tune and Voluntary,* her father escorted her down the curving South Portico stairway.

Tricia's petite size 4, five-feet-three figure was clad in a fitted sleeveless gown, its exterior featuring layers of translucent white silk organdy embroidered with lilies of the valley and trimmed with rose-petal Alencon lace, worn over a white crep slip. Her blonde tresses were drawn back beneath a pearled Juliet cap from which veils flowed to her feet. The dress was created by Priscilla of Boston, who also designed the wedding gowns of Luci Johnson Nugent (*The World in 1966, 146-148*) and Julie Nixon Eisenhower.

The bridal bouquet carried by Tricia consisted of lilies of the valley, small white sweetheart roses, baby's breath and Baker's fern.

The President brought his daughter to the flower-decked white wrought-iron pavilion, where the groom and the minister waited. Nixon kissed her softly on the cheek and took his seat. The 70-year-old Mr. Latch, a Methodist, conducted the marriage service, a blend of Episcopal, Methodist and Catholic ritual assembled largely by Tricia herself. There were no "I do's" and no promises to obey.

The platinum wedding ring was set with 30 flashing full-cut diamonds and bore inside the inscription "Ed-Trish, June 12, 1971." After the groom had placed it on the bride's finger he kissed her tenderly on the cheek. When the 8½-minute ceremony ended the couple paused to receive the congratulations of their parents. Tricia kissed her mother, fa-

President Nixon escorted Tricia to Rose Garden for her wedding

Mr. and Mrs. Edward F. Cox as they walked from the altar

ther and in-laws, and the bridegroom shook hands with his father and the President. The couple then led the 400 guests into the White House for the reception.

Although Nixon had been in Congress 14 years, no congressmen were present but the guest list included cabinet members, a few of the bride's former beaus, top officials, wealthy businessmen, entertainment personalities and religious figures. Charles G. Rebozo, a close friend of President Nixon, came from Key Biscayne, Fla. Ralph Nader attended, invited by the groom, who had worked with him in the summer of 1968.

Other well-known personalities included the Rev. Billy Graham, F.B.I. Director, J. Edgar Hoover and the Rev. Norman Vincent Peale, who married Julie Nixon to David Eisenhower in 1968 (The World in 1968 p. 263).

Mrs. Nugent and Mrs. Lynda Bird Robb (The World in 1967, 244–245) also were there, along with Ethel Waters, Art Linkletter and Mrs. Bob Hope. From the publishing world came William Randolph Hearst Jr., the Norman Chandlers of the Los Angeles Times and Hobart D. Lewis of the Reader's Digest. Mrs. Dwight Eisenhower was the only overnight guest at the White House for the wedding. Her grandson, David, husband of Julie Nixon Eisenhower, was on sea duty in the Mediterranean at the time.

Also present was Mrs. Alice Roosevelt Longworth, 87, daughter of President Theodore Roosevelt. A White House bride herself, Mrs. Longworth frequently had been a guest at weddings there.

From Italy came the Baron and Baroness Guido Zerilli Marimo and one of the eight groomsmen, Charles Robert Horsburgh Jr., flew in for the wedding from his station with the

President Nixon and the First Lady as they left the wedding scene

Bridal couple and parents: Center, Tricia Nixon and Edward Cox; left, President and Mrs. Nixon; right, Mr. and Mrs. Howard Ellis Cox

Newlyweds cut the bridal cake

Peace Corps in Iran. The bridegroom, a law student at Harvard University, was graduated from Princeton with Horsburgh in 1968.

Guests and the wedding party danced and drank champagne of California and New York vintage and watched as the couple cut the first piece of a somewhat controversial 250-pound, seven-tier, seven-foot lemon-flavored pound cake.

The cake displayed royal white icing, blown and spun sugar lovebirds, white roses and pink-tinged cherry blossoms, its top layer crowned by a sugary model of the domed wedding gazebo surrounded by cherry blossoms. It was created by two White House chefs, Henry Haller and Heinz Bender, and by a decorating expert, pastry chef Maurice Bonte, of New York. The recipe had caused some consternation when the White House revealed it some weeks prior to the wedding, and a few newspaper food writers tested it in their kitchens. Some came up with uncomplimentary results and opinions. The wedding guests seemed to like the grand concoction. But there were some reports that the cake was a bit dry.

During the reception Tricia tossed her bouquet to the groom's sister, Mazie Cox, who had just graduated from Yale's School of Architecture. The newlyweds then departed by the front door of the White House and sped off in a black limousine, their destination a secret. Their honeymoon spot turned out to be Camp David, the presidential mountain top retreat in western Maryland.

Tricia had met Cox at a Christmas dance seven years earlier, while she was attending Chapin School in New York City. He was the son of Howard Ellis Cox Sr., the senior partner of a New York law firm, and Mrs. Anne C. D. Finch Cox, a descendant of Robert R. Livingston, 18th century chancellor of New York who had helped Jefferson, Adams and Franklin to draft the Declaration of Independence. The Cox family, wealthy and socially prominent, maintained an apartment in New York and a summer home at Westhampton Beach, on Long Island.

In 1964, three years after their meeting, Tricia and Cox started dating. By then she was attending Finch College in New York City, and Cox was her escort to the International Debutante Ball, where she made her debut. In the two years preceding their marriage they met far more frequently. Cox often was a guest at the White House or the Nixon homes in San Clemente, Calif., and Key Biscayne, Fla. On other occasions Tricia went to the Cox family's Long Island home. Both were determined to avoid public attention as long as possible.

Some of their friends regarded Tricia as strong willed but reticent, and perhaps the most conservative member of the Nixon family. To those acquaintances Cox seemed much more liberal. After graduating from Princeton, Cox worked for a summer with Nader's Raiders and was co-author of a blistering report against the Federal Trade Commission. He also spent a summer writing for the weekly New Republic magazine.

Tricia and Eddie kept their engagement secret for two years. Shortly after the President's inauguration Cox had asked her to marry him, but it wasn't until about six months before the wedding that he sought the permission of her father. The announcement of the approaching wedding was made March 16, 1971 during an Irish evening in the White House, marking Mrs. Nixon's birthday on the eve of St. Patrick's Day.

Tears were visible among the guests who watched the couple ride away from one of the gayest weddings in White House annals. "Regretfully, I don't have anymore daughters," the President remarked. But he added that he hoped Tricia would fulfill his main wish: to live a life of her own, out of the "merciless glare of publicity."

111

Youths trying to reach festival setting got the "thumbs away" signal from a Louisiana state trooper

A Festival or a Fiasco?

Louisiana Rock "Celebration of Life" closed early, marred by three deaths and by sanitation, dope, financial problems

THE FESTIVAL is legally off," promoter Kenny Lind told a crowd of several thousand youths milling around a Louisiana plantation. "The stage is being dismantled. I want you to disperse. It's over, man, it's over."

Lind's plea was unavailing; many in the crowd simply slipped around a blockade at the entrance of the festival site, in rural Pointe Coupee Parish. They weren't going to leave, they said, until they had a show.

"What are we going to do to stop them?" one trooper asked. "We can't go out there and start busting these kids' heads. This is all the politicians' fault."

Ultimately, three young people died.

On June 18 U.S. District Court Judge E. Gordon West in Baton Rouge refused to hear an appeal of the State District Court decision blocking the rock festival on the grounds that no health permit had been obtained from the parish unit.

But the youths refused to move from the 700-acre site between the Mississippi and Atchafalaya rivers, in central Louisiana. Thousands had been camping along highways, sleeping on private property and in cars that caused a massive traffic congestion. During the day they spent restful hours basking in the 90-degree sun or swimming nude in the Atchafalaya River.

Walter Pelange Jr., a member of the parish council of New Roads, said his constituents had flooded him with telephoned protests since the day the festival was conceived.

"It doesn't bother me so much, but it bothers my people; they are very adamant against it, presumably because of the fear of not knowing anything about it (the festival) and the consequences of what might happen," Pelange said.

On June 20 the Fifth U.S. Court of Appeals in New Orleans ruled that the State District Court had erred in refusing to give the promoters a hearing on their request to hold the festival. The promotion firm, Cambridge Investment Corp., said in an appellate court brief that it had spent or owed some $500,000, and that the money would be lost unless the injunction was granted.

In the meantime the local grocery store enjoyed a thriving business until the food ran out. Farmers began donating bread and canned goods, maintaining a kind of rapport with the kids.

"They are good people," a local resident declared. "They are respectful and put their trust in God." But he added: "They don't wear much clothes, and I don't like that."

One of the rock fans said he offered to share his marijuana cigarette with a farmer. The youth said the farmer tried it, but decided he'd stick to beer.

On June 22 State Health Department officials finally approved sanitation facilities and the festival was ready to start. Rain and mud delayed the opening for another day. But instead of the originally conceived eight-day menagerie of rock singers, circus acts, fireworks and handicraft bazaar, it became a fiasco. Excessive heat and dust, inflated food prices, bad sanitation facilities and low quality music finally became unbearable.

Dr. William Abruzzi, in charge of the festival medical staff, said 1,000 to 1,500 persons were treated daily, including 150 to 200 suffering from excessive use of drugs. Reports of motorcycle gangs beating and robbing some festival celebrants prompted a step-up in police protection and a standby notice to the National Guard.

Three days after the "Celebration of Life" festival began two youths trying to cool off drowned in the Atchafalaya River. On the same day one young man was shot in the leg while involved in a hassle with a narcotics agent.

A witness said: "The narcotics officer arrested a young couple and they began screaming 'get the pigs.' A crowd surrounded the officer and began throwing various objects at him. Two men on motorcycles fired pistols, and the officer fired warning shots . . ." The final tragedy, on June 27, was the death of a 20-year-old Ohio youth from an overdose of drugs. This was the only reported drug fatality, said Capt. Russell Hebert, a narcotics division field supervisor, who added: "But there have been a lot of freaked-out kids. Every drug in the spectrum is available here, and there have been a lot of overdoses."

On the same day promoters announced for the last time that the festival was over. The ultimatum came with increased police pressure on narcotics violations and after the Internal Revenue Service had filed a lien against ticket sales.

The festival, scheduled for eight days, had lasted for only four.

After the festival Jim Ortege, the attorney for the promoters, charged that unreasonable financial and health demands by government agencies had a lot to do with its premature closing. He added that officials denied workers access to the site and wanted demands met so swiftly that the event was unable to continue.

Governmental officials, however, said that promoters brought the trouble on themselves. Dr. Andrew Hedmeg, chief officer of the Louisiana Health Department, said promoters had been warned after the festival opened that waste disposal, water supply and food service did not meet state standards, and that if they were not immediately improved the festival would be closed.

"They have no reason to plead they didn't know the health requirements. We've dealt with them before," Hedmeg said.

Walter H. Claiborne, president of the governing body in the parish, said the festival brought "every form of depravity and obscenity."

"Our lives have been disrupted, facilities overburdened, public expenses escalated, farm roads ruined and our poor parish turned into a garbage dump . . . Many young people lured to this 'Garden of Eden' are disappointed, broke, hungry and stranded," he said.

"Yes, it was a bad trip," said one young fan. "I'm glad I went, but that's the last rock festival I'll go to."

The festival promoters earnestly maintained their position.

"It is unfortunate that the political climate in this country is such that a gathering of 50,000 of America's young people could not be allowed to take place without unwarranted, government interference," Ortege said.

While courts debated opening of festival grounds, thousands set up temporary shelters nearby

On the porch of her shotgun shanty Lelia Johnson, 78, bridged the generation gap with a new cycle of longhairs

Smoke and flames belched from store set afire by Trinidad rioters in Port of Spain

Unrest Stirs Many of Poor in Caribbean

ALL THROUGH the Caribbean and its fringes it was the same story. Social unrest, political upheavals and racial disturbances were sweeping one lush isle after another; islands where tourism had brought some of the world's most affluent whites into contact with some of the poorest blacks. The evidence:

—Frowning youngsters brandishing clenched fists in Black Power saluted as a white tourist walked nervously past. That was Tobago.

—An idyllic spice island turned into a political pepperpot, terrorized by police agents and the seeds of one-man rule. That was Grenada.

—A sugar-plantation economy in which less than 1 per cent of the farms occupied 56 percent of the total acreage. That was Jamaica.

—A young black militant proclaiming "tourism is whoreism. The white man is your enemy." That was British Honduras.

—An 18-story condominium sitting empty for months as work permits for men needed to install the elevators were turned down. That was the Bahamas.

—Young blacks demanding complete independence from Britain sought to hoist the flag of liberation over a traditional honeymoon haven and tourist mecca. That was Bermuda, on the outskirts of the Caribbean.

—The luster suddenly worn off a 25-year-old industrialization program long hailed as a showcase of how an island short of resources could lift itself out of poverty. That was Puerto Rico.

The program, cited as a model for developing nations in the Caribbean, was Operation Bootstrap, conceived for Puerto Rico in 1946. Its lure to hundreds of foreign investors had been an offer of 10 years of freedom from corporate taxes and a seven-year exemption from personal income tax on dividends.

But there were disturbing signs in 1971 that Bootstrap was being rejected because of the nationalist attitudes of Caribbean leaders and intellectuals attracted by the "Third World" theme.

Critics of the ambitious program charged that it had only succeeded in expanding the gap between the living standards of the relatively small group of privileged workers and those still on the farm.

Advocates of Black Power were becoming increasingly vocal throughout the Caribbean. And many were substituting action for oratory.

Some Government officials and hotel owners tried to laugh it off, but demonstrations and riots sweeping the islands gave visitors a bad scare and did little for the image of the Caribbean as a paradise of tranquillity.

Some officials blamed the disturbances on Communism and outside influences, but it had become clear that a spirit of nationalism and anticolonialism had gripped the island populations.

Not only did tourism bring the Haves into abrasive contact with the Have-nots; there was the fact that the visitors were nearly all white, while the hosts were for the most part black.

Tourism had tripled in the Caribbean in the 1960s, reaching four million visitors in 1969 or close to a quarter of the population of the islands themselves. It was still growing in 1971 but at a slower rate.

Thus tourism had become the major industry, and at the same time a target of resentment which often translated into a racial cause. The gleaming beaches, turquoise waters and palatial hotels were still there, but a few streets away anger mounted.

Ironically, it began at a time when blacks, not whites, ruled in much of the area. Said Lynden O. Pindling, black prime minister of the Bahamas, "The reincarnated forces of the 1930s have stepped onto the . . . scene and are moving like a mighty avalanche."

The avalanche swept not only islands that remained colonial outposts of Britain, France and the Netherlands, but also those that had won independence in the 1960s.

It was the worst period of social unrest to visit the Caribbean since the trade union disturbances of a generation earlier.

Tiny Tobago, which depended largely upon its tourist indus-

try, probably suffered more from unrest than any other area. Trouble had started there in 1970, when thousands of Tobagonians marched on major tourist spots, urged on by Black Power leaders. In the riots that swept Trinidad and Tobago a good part of the army mutinied and four persons perished.

Before the spotlight swung to Trinidad and Tobago, rioting had plagued Willemstad, capital of the Dutch Antilles, killing two persons and causing more than $20 million worth of damage.

Some militants regarded tourism as a demeaning influence in which the offspring of black slaves were waiting on whites. This feeling was pointed up by the fact that rich white visitors tended to concentrate in the luxury hotels or housing areas where the natives felt excluded. The division also involved affluent blacks living on the islands.

In Jamaica, a sugar-plantation economy in which less than 1 per cent of the nation's farms occupied about 55 per cent of the total acreage, the sharp cleavage between rich and poor had continued even after the country won independence from Britain in 1962. In the same land dwelled prosperous and well-educated blacks and mulattoes in comfortable homes and impoverished, ill-educated blacks whose unemployment rate reached 50 per cent in some areas, according to a Time magazine survey.

Different islands had different problems, but the unrest was there in varying degrees.

The U.S. Virgin Islands had a healthy economy to all out-

U.S. pacifists and Puerto Rican activists tried to pull board away from U.S. Marine on Culebra Island off Puerto Rico

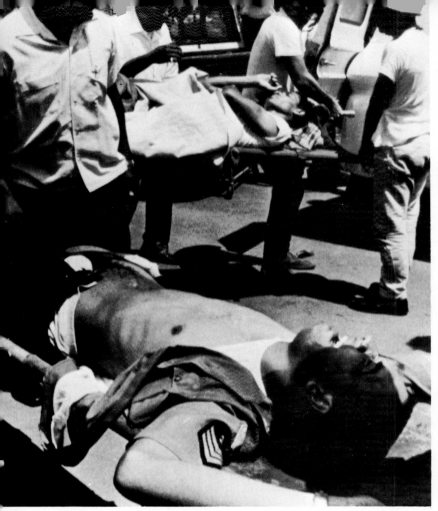

Police sergeant and student wounded in University of Puerto Rico riots

Jamaican women searched for arms in a Kingston street

ward appearances, with unemployment down to a 1¾ per cent and a per capita income of $2,800, the highest in the Caribbean. But even those islands were beginning to pay the price of prosperity, with crime on the rise and the undermanned police force hard-pressed.

Some of the crime suspects had links with a Black Power organization, but police insisted that they were acting on their own. The white population of the Virgin Islands made up only 15 per cent of some 80,000 inhabitants, so it stood to reason that many of those involved in crime were black.

Black Power made little headway in the Barbados, Anglophile Isle whose coral beaches were washed by both the Atlantic and the Caribbean. This was explained by the fact that the transplanted Africans of Barbados were in sharp contrast to the more volatile and aggressive peoples in neighboring, intercultural islands like Trinidad.

But there were rumbles in Barbados too. The University of the West Indies, for instance, experienced a sitdown strike in 1970 in sympathy with the uprising in Trinidad and Tobago.

In the Bahamas there was trouble also. How much Black Power had to do with it was uncertain, but the chain of idyllic islands fanning out from Florida seemed to be more in gloom than bloom.

In 1967, it had looked as if the Bahamas might become a paradise for the Bahamian when a black government in a nation 85 per cent black took power for the first time in 300 years. But the new rulers had little experience in running a government. They replaced English civil servants who had kept the mechanism operating smoothly.

As a result unemployment rose, foreign investment dropped off, slowing construction, and money became tight.

Bermuda, haven of pastel-hued villas and gleaming beaches, seemed as near to being an earthly paradise as any of the islands. Who could find fault with a colony where there was no

income tax, no unemployment and only a minimal property levy? The black militants could and did.

Bermuda's militants called themselves the Black Berets, and in style they resembled the Black Panthers. With blacks making up about 60 per cent of the population of the island cluster, the Berets were a force to reckon with.

"Our aim is to organize black people in order to achieve our freedom," Beret leader John H. Bassett told a reporter. "Because it's necessary to deal on a power basis, we must control the island's institutions."

The Black Berets said they wanted to see better social conditions and better education for blacks in order to prepare them for other than busboy or waiter jobs in the resort hotels.

The governor of Bermuda, Lord Martonmere, took a different view. He insisted that the local militants were being influenced by "outside black power."

"The problem would not be so bad if the Bermudians were left alone," he said.

To the tourist, Grenada was still a picturesque spot, adorned with sandy beaches and miniskirted women. But opponents of the government in power claimed that the tiny island had turned into a miniature Haiti, with a political police force and a trend toward one-man rule.

Grenada's Premier, Eric M. Gairy, a Negro himself, brushed aside the Black Power movement in his land and declared, "What we need is brain power."

Opposition leader Herbert Blaize took a similar view. He declared that there was "no real Black Power menace in Grenada." Blaize went a step farther, however, and accused Gairy of using public alarm to justify a dictatorship.

Advocates of Black Power in the Caribbean ranged from religious fanatics to devotees of the thoughts of Mao Tse-tung. But their cause was rooted in one common explosive element: the mounting friction between the Haves and the Have-nots.

When drawbridge tenders struck they left the bridges open on Harlem River, tangling New York's rush-hour traffic

78 KILLED IN 2 PLANE CRASHES

One day apart, two plane crashes on the nation's east and west coasts took the lives of 78 persons.

Air West flight 706 to Salt Lake City, Utah, left Los Angeles International Airport at 5:50 PM, June 6. Skies were relatively clear, yet 18 minutes after takeoff the DC9 and a Marine Corps Phantom jet fighter collided, killing all 49 aboard the airliner and the captain of the fighter plane. The collision occurred over Southern California's San Gabriel Mountains, 25 miles northeast of Lost Angeles.

"I heard a boom and saw two flaming objects going behind the mountain," said Jim Frisbe, who lived about three miles from the scene. Moments later he heard a second blast.

First Lt. Christopher Schiess, 24, of Salem, Ore., parachuted safely to the ground, the only survivor.

Schiess said the airliner hit the fighter plane and "we tumbled violently four or five times . . ." He said that he thought the pilot also had ejected himself and parachuted.

The tail and right wing of the Marine jet slashed through the left front section of the jetliner, said George R. Baker, who headed the National Transportation Safety Board investigation. He added, "I'm not saying who hit who."

The Federal Aviation Administration said the fighter, on a navigational training flight from Fallon Naval Station in Nevada to the Marine airbase at El Toro, Calif., was flying by the "see and be seen" rule, which meant it had not filed a route plan with radar air traffic controllers. The DC9 was following a specified route under radar control, the FAA said.

On June 7 an Allegheny Convair 580 coming

Marine Lt. Christopher Schiess, sole survivor of air collision that killed 50 persons.

in from Groton, Conn., with 31 persons aboard attempted an instrument landing in fog at the Tweed-New Haven airport. The airliner struck a row of vacant beach houses along the Connecticut coast, killing 28 of the passengers. No one on the ground was hurt.

The three who survived the crash were James Walker, 45, co-pilot, of Memphis, Tenn., and passengers Janet McCaa, 28, of Washington, D.C., and Norman Kelly, 38, of Waterford, Conn.

Airport manager James Malarky said he believed the accident would not have occurred if proposed electronic landing control equipment had been installed at the New Haven airport.

NONUPLETS ALL DIED IN A WEEK

It had been a week of tragedy for Mrs. Len Brodrick, 29. She lay in bed at the Royal-Hospital in Sydney, Australia, after having given birth to the world's first record nonuplets.

Of the five boys and four girls, two boys were stillborn. But the mother had hoped desperately for the survival of the tiny seven who remained. The heaviest weighed only two pounds, two ounces, the lightest a mere twelve ounces when they were delivered naturally but 12 weeks prematurely, in 32 minutes on June 13.

The only baby Mrs. Brodrick saw was the smallest and the one who survived the longest —six days. The others had been kept in incubators. Three died of respiratory problems on the night of their birth. Two more died on June 14 and June 15, leaving only the smallest and the largest.

The heaviest, a girl, died June 18, and the chances of the only remaining child seemed very slim. No larger than a man's hand, the baby had received a blood transfusion because of liver complications and Mrs. Brodrick saw him twice daily in his incubator. On June 19 he died.

Mrs. Brodrick, a former nurse, was the mother of two other children, 4 and 5, by Caesarean section. She had been given a Swedish fertility drug thereafter, to regulate a hormone problem. Three weeks before the multiple births Mrs. Brodrick had been admitted to the hospital because doctors had foreseen a multiple birth.

Just before leaving the hospital to return to Canberra with her husband, Mrs. Brodrick said she would not hesitate to use the fertility drug again if necessary, although she would prefer a confinement without resort to fertility stimulants.

SOME KIDNAP VICTIMS FREED

During the 1970-71 rash of political kidnapings, particularly in South America, the story was pretty much the same: A diplomat was usually abducted on his way to or from work. The terrorists identified themselves, then accused the government involved of imperialism, police repression and torturing prisoners. The ransom was set and, if paid, the victim was released.

The question of payment, however, made the abductions less than routine. They often became a frightening gamble for both the victim and the governments involved. The decision to refuse payment in some cases meant death.

During the summer of 1970, the Uruguayan terrorist group, the Tupamaros, kidnaped three people: Dan A. Mitrione, U.S. adviser to the Uruguayan police; Aloysio Mares Dias Gomide, a Brazilian consul, and an American agronomist, Claude L. Fly. The Tupamaros asked for the release of all political prisoners, totaling more than 150. President Jorge Pacheco Areco, with the endorsement of the United States, refused. Uruguay won and lost the gamble. Mitrione, of Richmond, Ind., was killed two weeks after the president refused payment *(The World in 1970, 249-251).* Dias Gomide was released Feb. 21, 1971, and Fly was freed March 2.

Fly, a native of Fort Collins, Colo., had been in Uruguay as a private consultant to the Uruguayan agriculture ministry. When released he was left on a stretcher at the British hospital in Montevideo after having suffered what was described as a mild heart attack.

The Brazilian government decided not to gamble on the life of Swiss Ambassador Giovanni Bucher, who was kidnaped Dec. 7, 1970. For his freedom Brazil agreed to release 70 political prisoners. On Jan. 14, the prisoners were flown to Chile, a country under the leadership of Marxist President Salvador Allende.

The 70 exiles said kidnaping Bucher was a "legitimate defense" against the torture they had suffered in prison on orders of Brazilian authorities.

"They hung me by the feet," said Antonio Expedito Perera, a lawyer. "Later they attached electrical connections to all the sensitive parts of my body. My body was kept wet so the shocks would hurt more."

"One time they brought my wife in to see how I had been tortured."

Nancy Mangabeira Unger, a 22-year-old who said she had dual United States and Brazilian citizenship, commented "almost anyone who expresses ideas against the government in Brazil goes to prison." Though she was not tortured she said in English that she spent a month in solitary confinement at the Recife women's prison and saw other women being tortured.

Forty-eight hours after the 70 exiles arrived in Chile, Bucher was released.

On Jan. 8, 1971, Uruguay's Tupamaros struck again, kidnaping British Ambassador Geoffrey

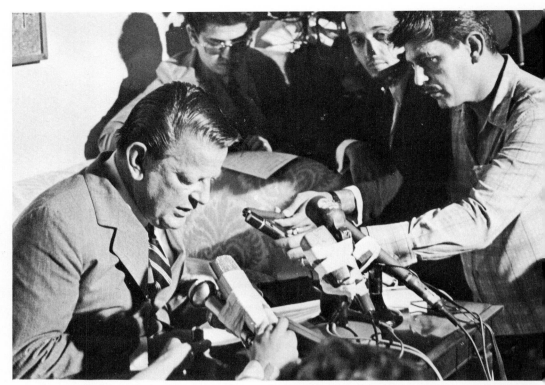

British Ambassador Jackson told London news conference about his abduction and release by Tupamaro guerrillas in Uruguay

Jackson in his own limousine. This time there was no immediate ransom demand.

Jackson was released Sept. 9 after eight months' confinement.

On March 4, a kidnaping occurred far from the Western Hemisphere. In troubled Turkey, leftist guerrillas seized four American airmen and demanded a thumping $400,00 ransom. The Turkish government refused to pay, however, and the terrorists released their captives four days later without receiving any money.

Flown back to the United States, all four airmen said they had feared for their lives when they heard how much ransom was being demanded.

"When we heard they wanted $400,000 in ransom, I frankly didn't think much of our chances," Airman 1C Richard Caraszi of Stamford, Conn., told newsmen.

Released with Caraszi were Sgt. James Sexton of San Angelo, Tex., and Airmen 1C James M. Gholson of Alexandria, Va., and Larry J. Heavner of Mayville, W. Va.

The Tupamaros made headlines again March 10 when they seized one of their own countrymen, Uruguay's attorney-general, Guido Berro Oribe. He was released March 23 without payment of ransom.

On May 17, guerrillas struck again in Turkey. This time they abducted Israeli Consul General Efraim Elrom, demanding the release of political

prisoners as the price for his life. Again, the Turkish government refused to comply, but this time the guerrillas carried out their threat and killed Elrom five days later.

As police moved in on the terrorists, two of them captured the 14-year-old daughter of a Turkish army major and held her hostage, threatening to kill the girl unless they received safe passage out of the country. After a tense two-day siege, police closed in. Wearing bulletproof vests, they stormed the apartment where the girl was being held. One guerrilla was killed and the other wounded in a blazing gun battle, but the girl was rescued.

Kidnaping did not invariably figure in political terrorism involving government officials or former officials. On June 13, in Santiago, Chile, left-wing extremists Roland Rivera Calderon, 24, and his brother, Arturo, 20, died in a four-hour gun battle with police. They had been accused of killing an ex-minister of interior, Edmondo Perez Zukovic, on June 8. The brothers, armed with machine guns and grenades, were shot when police stormed a private garage. Six other persons, including three women, were arrested near the garage, apparently a munitions warehouse.

Another suspect in the same case, Heriberto Salazar Bello, burst into police headquarters June 16, killed two detectives and then ended his own life with a grenade.

NIXON-BRANDT TALKS ON BERLIN

West German Chancellor Willy Brandt and President Nixon met at the White House for what Press Secretary Ronald L. Ziegler termed a "very full and cordial discussion" of Berlin's status and the prospects for East-West negotiations to reduce the number of troops in Europe.

Brandt spent five days in the United States.

Ziegler said that, in their June 15 conference, they considered enlargement of the Common Market in Europe, Strategic Arms Limitation Talks with the Russians, the Middle East situation and the costs Germany would bear for continued maintenance of U.S. troops in that country.

On the question of mutual troop withdrawals,

the press secretary said, "I think there is basic agreement between this government and the German government regarding this matter."

He also pointed out that Soviet Premier Leonid Brezhnev had mentioned the possibility of improved relations within the divided city of Berlin.

NO JURY TRIALS FOR JUVENILES

A U.S. Supreme Court ruling that juveniles held no constitutional right to trial by jury was described by Justice Harry A. Blackmun as a necessity in maintaining the "intimate, protective proceedings" sought by the court under the juvenile system.

The 6 to 3 decision June 21 ended a 23-year trend during which the court had extended Bill of Rights privileges to juveniles in a succession of cases.

A dissenting opinion by Justice William O. Douglas held that courts and law enforcement officials sometimes considered juveniles not as delinquents but as potential criminals. Since some courts had used juvenile proceedings to prosecute youths for crimes and to confine them, these juveniles should be entitled to the same constitutional protections available to adults, he said.

The judgment was made on cases originating in Pennsylvania and North Carolina. In Philadelphia, two 15-year-old boys had sought jury trials when brought up on delinquency charges. In Hyde County, N.C., similar trials were requested by 46 black youths arrested during demonstrations.

Justice Blackmun, Chief Justice Warren E. Burger and Justices Potter Stewart, Byron R. White, John M. Harlan, and William J. Brennan Jr. constituted the majority in the Pennsylvania case. Dissenters with Douglas were Justices Hugo L. Black and Thurgood Marshall. In the North Carolina case, Brennan also dissented.

In 34 other states and the District of Columbia, existing laws and court rulings barred jury trials in juvenile courts, Blackmun said.

Secretary of State William P. Rogers, signed a treaty restoring Okinawa to Japan; Japanese Ambassador Nobuhiko Ushiba sat beside him

PACT ON OKINAWA SIGNED

After a bloody campaign of 83 days and the loss of tens of thousands of Americans and Japanese, the United States took possession of Okinawa and the 72 additional Ryukyu Islands on June 21, 1945, during World War II. Twenty-six years later, on June 17, the governments of Japan and the United States simultaneously signed an agreement giving Okinawa and the other islands back to Japan in 1972.

The agreement called for the United States to turn over to Japan 47 military base facilities on Okinawa, while retaining 88 such facilities there.

After the evacuation the United States would no longer be able to launch air or ground military operations from Okinawa without Japanese government approval.

The signing brought violent street demonstrations in Japan and protests in Okinawa. Scores of participants and at least 30 riot police were injured in clashes in Tokyo. The students and workers who demonstrated claimed that the agreement permitted a continuing U.S. military presence and did not provide specifically for stripping Okinawa of nuclear facilities.

The island had been converted into a strategic military base considered the keystone for the military defense of the Eastern Pacific. In 1952 the United States had recognized Japan's "residual sovereignty" over the islands and promised they would be returned eventually.

Under the 1971 pact Japan would pay the United States $320 million, including $70 million for the removal of nuclear facilities.

Casualty records showed that the World War II campaign on Okinawa cost the lives of 159,222 combatants, 49,151 of them Americans.

The Death of Actaeon, *Titian's 400-year-old masterpiece, sold at Christies in London for* $4,032,000

Asuncion de la Virgen, *an El Greco painting stolen from a Madrid mansion in 1936, was recovered in Manhattan; its value was estimated at $1 million by the FBI*

FREEDOM SOUGHT FOR NAMIBIA

Namibia, a huge area of plateau lands and coastal plains, rich in diamonds, lead and zinc, and inhabited by Hottentots, Bantus and Bushmen, had been administered since World War I by the adjacent Union of South Africa. This occupation ultimately had been endorsed by a League of Nations mandate, but later the United Nations General Assembly declared the mandate invalid, and in 1968 appointed an 11-nation council to take over Namibia and lead it to independence.

South Africa refused to recognize the council's authority. By 1971 Namibia—also known as South-West Africa—had become a major concern of the U.N. Security Council, which asked the International Court of Justice in The Hague to review the situation.

On June 21 this court ruled that the Union of South Africa should immediately terminate its "illegal occupation" of Namibia. However, the ruling was advisory, having no binding force, and again the Union refused to comply. Its prime minister, John Vorster, termed it an "international political vendetta" against his country, and added: "It is our duty to administer South-West Africa so as to promote the well being and progress of its inhabitants."

Other South African spokesmen asserted that any withdrawal from the territory would bring about an inevitable breakdown of industry, trade and public utilities.

In supplementing its June ruling, the World Court said member states of the United Nations should avoid economic, diplomatic and other actions that might imply support or recognition for South Africa's administration of South-West Africa.

The court declared that member states were "under obligation to abstain from entering into treaty relations with South Africa in all cases within which the government of South Africa purports to act on behalf of, or concerning, Namibia," but it made an exception for multilateral treaties of a humanitarian nature.

FOR THE RECORD

NAMED. Vernon E. Jordan Jr., as director of the National Urban League, succeeding the late Whitney M. Young Jr., on June 15. Jordan said that he would seek to maintain "consistent dialogue" between black and white people, and that he did not believe in endorsing any political candidate. He previously was executive director of the United Negro College Fund. In 1961 he had attained nationwide recognition by leading a Negro, Charlayne Hunter, into the University of Georgia through a crowd of white protesters. Jordan was graduated from Howard University School of Law. During his career as a civil rights leader he had been field director in Georgia for the National Association for the Advancement of Colored People and director of the Voter Education Project for the Southern Regional Council.

RESIGNED. Stanley R. Resor on May 21 as Secretary of the Army, a post he had held for six years. On June 15 President Nixon named as Resor's successor Robert F. Froehlke, who had been serving as Assistant Secretary of Defense for Administration. Resor returned to private life.

A different way of life: a maker of moccasins ➞

July

(Above) Living communally the urban way: Members of a city commune in Seattle. (Left) Alone with nature: Young man meditated at Sheep Ridge Ranch near San Francisco Bay

The Alternative Society

UTOPIAN COMMUNAL EXPERIMENTS in the United States originated in the 19th century, among them the New Harmony colony in 1825 and Brook Farm in 1844. But the movement reached massive proportions in 1971, when thousands left the privacy of their homes in flight from the "straight" society which, they felt, was decaying in its own materialistic values. Dehumanizing, in their view, was the nine-to-five-o'clock doctrine that only hard work and possessions led to happiness.

One of these believers, an anonymous New York suburban housewife, told an interviewer: "I'm splitting. I'm afraid of that world. It's dying, smothering in its own corruption, and I'm not going with it."

She and countless others had joined in forming communes, occupying old and delapidated farmhouses, ramshackle city apartments or self-made dwellings to follow the distinctive life form of the Alternative Society, with their own institutions, values and religions—a society far removed, in most cases, from that of their parents.

The National Institute of Health estimated that approximately 3,000 such communes were scattered across the nation, and that the number was growing. These included groups which some students of the trend regarded as offshoots of the Beatnik and hippie congregations in the 1960s, such as those in San Francisco's Haight-Asbury district. There, some members—the foolish, depressed or weak—maintained they had no other place to go. Others, perhaps, were free-spirited young folk who sincerely sought to develop artistic or literary talents in an atmosphere of brotherly love.

But, among the more perceptive, few felt they could find the satisfaction they sought in such a mixed environment. These fled to the country to live as families, away from exhibitionists, tourists and the hip mania. A common goal united them: a joyful interpretation of life, a desire to love oneself and one another, and the will to return to the simpler ways of civilization. To these such was possible only if men and women worked together in building, organizing and learning to survive apart from the mother culture, a culture they considered hostile and doomed.

"We are trying to create a whole new culture with its own economics and values," said Tom as he dished out vegetables and bread to his fellow members of the New Haven commune.

Feeding a commune usually was a financial problem. Agricultural communes often attempted to support themselves by growing their own food, but fertile land was not always available, and farming techniques were unknown to many country dwellers with city backgrounds.

Some cities set up barter stores in which food and household products were traded for whatever commune members had to give.

"We had no restrictions on what people could take, so they took everything," said a young lady at a free store in Albuquerque, N.M.

The Alternative Society worked to establish its own institutions to provide free medical care, free education and free legal advice.

Allen, a 30-year-old physician, worked hard to build a free medical clinic in Seattle, but he admitted there were not many like him. In a graduating class of 72 doctors, he was the only one who planned to devote his career to free medicine. Other Alternative Society professionals—teachers in free schools and lawyers—found it difficult to separate themselves completely from the conventional society since to do so would break their contact with colleagues upon whom they were dependent for continuing education in their fields.

Donations helped to keep the alternative institutions alive, but the hard cash had to come from the "straight" society. In addition, communal members who did not have a specific craft had to depend on random jobs. But in remote areas of the country such employment was scarce, forcing commune members to travel as far as 80 miles to work. This often was impractical, and communes so located had to disband.

*   *   *   *

The idea of communal living was based on the principle of sharing. Food stamps and whatever money came in from jobs, welfare or unemployment checks, were shared by the whole family; even by those who proclaimed themselves "house poets" and who stayed home to write material that was seldom published.

Communes had contacts, to one degree or another, with various communications media, including news services, radio stations and even underground newspapers. The Portola Institute put out a publication called the Whole Earth Catalogue, which supplied information on camping equipment, clothes and other items needed for communal living.

Another publication, The Modern Utopian, a quarterly published in Berkeley, Calif., carried lists of communes throughout the country, stating their religious orientation, if any, their sex policy—little, some or much—and the extent of drug usage.

This system helped to strengthen unity and to pass on the communal philosophy, a philosophy which many advocates said was part of the counterculture. "Wherever we are we live communally, whether it is in a commune or not," said Yvonne Jaffee, a former commune resident. "We visit friends and stay with people. Friends drop in here (her home) any time they want, and everyone contributes. This comes out of a consciousness of understanding the kind of life we want to live."

Even so, the practice of sharing and the extension of good will often contributed to the downfall of a commune. All types sometimes moved in, including the addict looking for junk, motorcycle gangs that harassed the "freaks" or the "ripoff" artists whose thefts all but killed the hospitality of the crash pad. This led many communes to seek isolated locations wherein a small unit sometimes remained apart even from its own culture.

Many critics felt that it was impossible for individuals to live so closely together when they hadn't been conditioned to it at an early age.

"It's difficult enough to live in a one-to-one relationship," said John McGrane, of Ecology Action in Cambridge, Mass., and a veteran of two communes. "Our divorce rate suggests that, and it's improbable that more than two people can live together unless they are very mature and very tolerant. I tend to be tolerant, but many people are not tolerant and tend to get disturbed over small things."

He added, "In a commune, life tends to polarize along the lines of the cleans and the sloppies, and it isn't easy to handle. You have to remember that a lot of people in the youth culture have really deluded themselves into believing they are really beautiful people, when in reality many of them are mirror images of their parents. So, when the real conflicts develop, it is utterly impossible to arbitrate the hostilities. They are transformed into political dialogues. They become very abstract kinds of conflicts that are very seldom brought to personal levels, and an explosion of one kind or another becomes inevitable."

Some communes tried to find a solution to the tension of living together, like the Christian-oriented Brothers for Com-

Motherhood In a Commune: Rena, wife of former singer Lou Gottleib, nursed their baby at Occidental, Calif.

mon Life in New York, a group who shared all their money equally but who were not required to live together.

"For 20 or 30 years some of these people lived under the values of their parents, who advocated a nuclear family existence. You have to remember that it is going to be very hard for them to simply cast away these values and feel happy living in an environment they have never known before," said the elder of the brothers, John Swanson.

One communal family in Seattle expected conflicts and learned to handle them in many cases.

"You know it is not going to be easy," said Joy, a 27-year-old sculptress from Milwaukee. "But you also know the people around you dig you, and know that everyone around wants to help everyone else. When something goes wrong, we pick it up quickly and have it out in the open. You can do it because you know people are with you, and are not going to come down on you."

*   *   *   *

Most members agreed that the only way communes could survive was to maintain a policy of complete honesty. If one member concealed hostility or any other problem, the result often was "bad vibes" (vibrations), an environment that could destroy the family.

Dan Boyle, bothered by what he called a discharge of nega-

tive energy, told the group in his Albuquerque commune: "I'm going to go up to my room and close the door and sit on my bed and send out such vibes that whoever is doing what they're doing is gonna get blown out the door."

In another Albuquerque commune, where the same sort of situation prevailed, a member who gave his name as Kirby said he told a friend: "I'm trying to help you, and you won't let me. You're hiding something from me, and I'm the kind of guy that isn't going to let you. I'm going to keep at you until I find out what it is."

The success of a commune also depends on the strength of a common commitment. In the Woodlawn commune at New Haven, Conn., a young woman who was dissatisfied by life there said, "The people . . . wanted to have all their own personal things, and they wouldn't give up their individuality for the good of the group. There was no sense of togetherness and the desire to know and love one another."

Certain communes had strong religious affiliations—Yogi, Christianity or others. Even spiritualism was found to be a salvation for some.

"I was a drug addict, a smacker; then Jesus came in. A 30-second heroin cure and with no cold turkey; it just takes that long with Jesus. Praise the Lord," such was the testimonial of Dennis, a resident of the Taos, N.M., commune.

Others tuned in on "cosmic energy." Yoga fanatics sat cross-legged on a mountain's edge, looking for spiritual insight.

Hare Krishna followers, heads shaved and their clothing orange in color, chanted on street corners and opened communes in every major city. Sorcery and Satanism cults reappeared in the exotic atmosphere of California.

Paranormal experiences were common in the extended family. One member of the Libre commune in Gardner, Colo., "Peter Rabbit," reported that while hunting deer he spoke to one of a group asking him to sacrifice himself, vowing that the energy gained from his flesh would be used for creative and constructive pursuits of Libre. Without fail Peter said one deer would move from the others remaining still until shot.

The notion that "mental vibrations" can influence crops, the weather, animals and people was taken for granted.

The use of I Ching, Tarot cards, the Ouija Board and astrology were part of the daily existence for some.

Many Christian-orientated communes attempted to revive the concept of loving and giving which their members said had been smothered by capitalism. "I saw the death of Christianity due to economic reasons," said John Swanson, president of the Brothers for a Common life. "They spend all this money building buildings and making all sorts of plans and doing nothing for the poor in the meantime. I looked into some way of avoiding all that, and the best way seemed to be to start a community and to incorporate it so we wouldn't have to pay taxes. By pooling all our money we have something left to do our real work with."

*   *   *   *

Drugs were a part of communal life, although many of the members reported that the use of hard drugs and mind expanding drugs was on the wane.

"We got to where we wanted to go with the use of drugs, and now we don't need them any more; we can do it on our own," said a young woman. "Grass is taken for granted, I guess, like the business man and his martini."

Life in a commune was often physically perilous. Three cases of bubonic plague were reported in one commune in New Mexico over the past two summers. All three victims survived. Hepatitis was a chronic problem, especially when there was a scarcity of water. Sanitary conditions were often primitive. The hippie infusion into commune territory could be dangerous, as was the animosity of some local inhabitants who made attacks on their new neighbors and sometimes raised the question of land rights.

In many sections of the country the straight world feared communes. "Straight people have a negative attitude about communal living because the hippie is attacking their major values, the very core of their existence," said John, of a New York commune.

The straight society often regarded communes as places for massive sexual orgies, initiated with the extensive use of drugs. Many thought all partook in group marriages, when in fact that practice was not common.

Ken Hartnett of The Associated Press, in an in-depth study of the Alternative Society, wrote: "Sexual permissiveness varied from commune to commune. Promiscuity seemed most common in those that used an extensive amount of drugs and who tried that life style for kicks. It was less common in the more stable communes, particularly those organized around a specific task or political or spiritual goal."

The hope of the Alternative Society was children. Communards and straights alike saw them as beautiful and free spirited. Dr. Eva Wailen, of the Bernalillo County Health Depart-

ment in New Mexico, was impressed by the care children were given.

"Amazingly, their children seem to be—at least the ones I've come in contact with—extremely bright, barefooted, brown-skinned from the sun . . . On the whole the ones we see are round and fit and happy looking."

She also said most communards seemed to come from homes lacking warmth or loving parental care. That may be one reason they turned to the commune—to create the happy family they never had, she suggested.

Some communards would not think of bringing up their children in any other atmosphere.

"In the straight society it is considered bad when you simply don't want to have your children around," said a young woman in a New York commune. "But when you are living communally it is an accepted thing, and you are not ashamed to have someone else take over your duties once in a while."

"I couldn't imagine raising children with just one other person," said a former suburban housewife, now living in a Madison, Wis., commune. "Collectively, it can be done in a way that is probably healthier for the children."

A mother of two reported that she simply told them they were much more fortunate than their playmates, who had only one father. They had dozens of them, all who took a transitory but real interest in the children.

In a few communes, particularly those favoring group marriage, women admitted they made love with a number of men so that the father of the conceived would be unknown. In others childbirth was ritualized: The father delivered the baby in front of the whole group, out in the open air.

Although natural childbirth and breast feeding were common practices, not all deliveries were made at the communal

Not all communal activity was confined to the United States: Thousands of Flower Children gathered on Britain's picturesque Isle of Wight

(Above) Young worshipper holding infant joined singing of Hare Krishna group in New York's Central Park

(Left) Barefoot couple in front of their tepee at Occidental, Calif., commune

site. Many went to local hospitals and some believed in parents alone caring for their children.

The mother of a little girl at the Pulsa commune in Connecticut, who had her child in a New Haven hospital said, "I don't believe in sharing the care of my child. I take care of her 90 per cent of the time, and I feel this gives her a feeling of security."

Some of those hippies living within the straight society scoffed at their contemporaries in communes.

"Most of them are lost, immature and looking for kicks," said a young artist. "What good does it do anyone to drop out of things? They say they are serious about group living, loving and sharing when summer comes. They preach it and try to practice it, but then they find that they have the same hassles as everyone else, that things are no different. Come bad weather, they split."

*   *   *   *

The Wall Street Journal in an editorial said most communes, other than those that produced products to sell to the straight world, were total failures.

"Most contemporary commune members are confused, listless and quite helpless people," the Journal said in part. "Communes themselves for the most part are disharmonious

places that usually survive no more than a year. As utopian solutions most are dismal failures. Nevertheless, many are valuable as transition points, temporary places, where people undergoing radical personal changes can experiment with new life styles in sympathetic surroundings."

Yale's Prof. Kenneth Keniston viewed aspects of the Alternative Society as inspiring to those who shared its values but who plunged into the larger society nonetheless. He called these people infiltrators.

"You are beginning to see a lot of people with new culture values but old culture skills, people who really agree with the most radical criticism of the society but at the same time are learning an awful lot about urban management or are going into medicine and becoming public health professionals," he said.

"My own view is that social change is more likely to come about through infiltration than through a commune in Colorado, although the commune may be important because it provides inspiration for the infiltrators."

Another view: "This counter-culture has made its mistakes and in many cases communal living doesn't work," said a New Haven commune member. "But for some it is fulfilling, and for our children we have provided a whole new life style, rich with values that they will remember their lives long and will hopefully carry on to their children."

A Waif at 13, Armstrong Became the King of Jazz

His trumpet and his gravelly voice were stilled at 71 by a Heart attack, and the world's modern music lovers mourned

IT WAS SAID that when he sang, it sounded like "a piece of sandpaper calling to its mate."

But when he played . . .

There was no question then why Louis Armstrong was called King. There would be no crown prince. There never really was. For, more than any other man, Armstrong lifted jazz from the bawdyhouses and gin mills of New Orleans and made it an American art form heard around the world.

Armstrong didn't invent jazz. No one did. But when he died of a heart attack in his sleep in his New York home July 6, two days after his 71st birthday, he had already become a legend. He was a former waif whose face, voice and trumpet had become worldwide landmarks; a scarcely educated boy who became a genius in the language all men can understand—music.

The New York Times said in an editorial: "No one else played so creative or enduring a role in the evolution and development of jazz or in insuring its survival."

There were tributes too from leading musicians of the day who had known Armstrong. They included Duke Ellington, Gene Krupa, Earl (Fatha) Hines, Tyree Glenn and Eddie Condon.

Ellington commented: "if anybody was Mr. Jazz, it was Louis Armstrong. He was the epitome of jazz and always will be. He is what I call an American standard, an American original."

"He could play a trumpet like nobody else," Condon said, "then put it down and sing a song like no one else could."

His remarkable career was all the more remarkable considering his origins. Daniel Louis Armstrong was as old as the century—born in New Orleans July 4, 1900. His father, who stoked furnaces in a turpentine factory, left the family when Louis was an infant. As he grew up Louis sold coal to warm prostitutes' cribs in the old Storyville area, stole food from hotel garbage cans and sold that and sang for pennies on the street.

Fate stepped in when Louis was 13. He was arrested for firing a .38-caliber pistol in the air on his birthday and was sent to the Colored Waif's Home for Boys.

"Pops, it sure was the greatest thing that ever happened to me. Me and music got married at the home," he said.

He was taught bugle and cornet by Peter Davis, an instructor at the home, and became a member of the boys' band. When he was released after 18 months, Armstrong's formal education (he never finished fifth grade) was over, but the groundwork had been laid. The boy began playing in honkytonks and was befriended by Joe (King) Oliver, who taught him and gave him a cornet.

In 1918 Oliver moved to Chicago and Louis replaced him as cornetist in the band of Kid Ory, the tailgate trombonist and one of the few jazz giants of the time to survive Armstrong.

Louis "Satchmo" Armstrong in a relaxed pose about a year before his death

Louis also played in the city's traditional marching brass bands and on river boats on the Mississippi.

Then, in 1922, Oliver called Louis to Chicago to take the second horn chair in his Creole Jazz Band. Old records of that band show Louis already blowing driving harmonies and brief, brilliant and biting breaks behind his mentor's cornet. It was only a matter of time before Louis went on his own way. He went to New York two years later to play with Fletcher Henderson and also appeared in an all-Negro review on Broadway in which he introduced Fats Waller's *Ain't Misbehavin'*.

But it was in Chicago beginning in 1925 that Louis cut the records that were to make him king. These were his Hot Five including Lil Hardin, a pianist he ultimately married. Later he added a tuba and drums, recording as the Hot Seven. That they were. Armstrong could take even the tritest of tunes and transform it into a classic with cascades of notes that could hardly wait to get out of his horn. His extensive solos were a departure from the more traditional ensemble playing. The burnished tone, drive and bursting genius of his improvisations made them record collectors' items despite the crude recording equipment of the time. They were high-water marks of recorded jazz, and Armstrong became an international star.

He gave up the mellow cornet for the flashier trumpet, with which he would soar like an acrobat through the upper register. His small recording band had been replaced with a larger one, and some purists felt that Louis had traded gold for silver. But to Armstrong music was music. "I never did want to be no big star. It's been goddam work, man," he said years later.

Eventually he went on tour abroad. This was the first of many he would take, including several postwar playing trips for the State Department that earned him the unofficial title of "Ambassador Satch" (For Satchelmouth, a nickname).

After his death, a State Department spokesman said "his memory will be enshrined in the archives of effective international communications. The Department of State, for which he traveled on tours to almost every corner of the globe, mourns the passing of this great American."

Never one to be impressed by royalty, musical or otherwise, King Louis once played before the British Royal Family in a command performance and growled to King George V in his fogbound guttural voice: "This one's for you, Rex."

Years later, he also played for the king's granddaughter, Princess Margaret, saying "we're really gonna lay this one on for the princess," thereby striking up *Mahogany Hall Stomp*, a jazz classic that took its title and perhaps some of its spirit from a New Orleans bawdyhouse.

Louis toured all over the world after World War I, generally with a small band that included such famous sidemen as Jack Teagarden, Edmond Hall, Barney Bigard and others. He had become more of a showman by then, and some of the stamina and sustained creativity had diminished. But his voice was as croaky as ever. He had several best-selling records in his later years, among them *Hello Dolly* and *Mack the Knife*.

Louis was a familiar figure on concert stage and on TV, wiping away beads of sweat from his glistening forehead with an endless supply of handkerchiefs and keeping his precious lips dry.

"If you don't look out for your pipes and chops, you can't blow the horn and sing," he said.

His health slowly began to fail, and he made his last public appearance in March 1971 at New York's Waldorf-Astoria. He said he had played for three generations. "The old cats, their children and their children's children, I love my audience, and they love me, and we just have one good time when I get up on stage," he said. "It's such a lovely pleasure."

His end came peacefully, and he was buried quietly in New York, far from New Orleans and its marching brass funeral bands. He lay in state for one day in Manhattan, visited by 25,000 mourners, then was taken back to his own neighborhood for burial.

Celebrities—Mayor John Lindsay, Gov. Nelson Rockefeller, Ella Fitzgerald, Dizzy Gillespie and Benny Goodman—were among those who sat in his local church along with musicians and friends. Peggy Lee sang the *Lord's Prayer* and Al Hibbler sang *Nobody Knows the Trouble I've Seen*.

So the King was dead. But his music knew no grave.

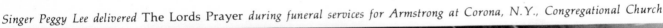

Singer Peggy Lee delivered The Lords Prayer *during funeral services for Armstrong at Corona, N.Y., Congregational Church*

Armstrong giving horn a workout at New York home while colleague Tyree Glenn joined in on trombone

Extortion: A New Hazard to World Airlines, Long Imperiled by Hijackings

BY MID-1971 a new element—extortion—had joined the tribulations of the world's airlines, financially pressed and long subjected to simple hijackings by non-paying passengers who just wanted to go somewhere swiftly.

Fireworks, parties and heat-escaping trips to resorts occupied millions of Americans during the long Fourth of July weekend. One, however, wanted ransom—plus 7,650 miles and 43 hours of transportation to other countries—badly enough to hijack a jetliner.

On July 2, a Braniff 707 from Acapulco, Mexico with 110 passengers and crew members aboard was preparing to land at San Antonio, Tex. A bearded man stepped up to a stewardess, Jeanette Crepps, 21, of Oklahoma City, and pushed a pistol against her ribs. He ordered her to tell Capt. Dale S. Bessant, of Grapevine, Tex., to turn the plane around and head for Monterrey, in Nuevo Leon, Mexico. Bessant complied.

The hijacker, later identified as Robert Lee Jackson, 36, whose last address was in Maryville, Tenn., then announced: "Don't anybody try to be a hero. If you do, this is going to blow us all up." He pointed to a suitcase he held with one hand, claiming it contained a pint of nitroglycerin.

Accompanying him was Lydia Lucrecia Sanchez, a 23-year-old native of Guatemala, who also carried a pistol. Miss Sanchez was a resident of Mexico.

After landing in Monterrey, Jackson freed three crewmen and all but one of the 102 passengers. In exchange for the life of that one, Monica Amparo Garza, he demanded $100,000. Jackson and his companion chose Algeria as their final destination, hoping they would be granted political asylum there. He told a stewardess he had been charged with a crime he did not commit.

The money, in unmarked bills, was supplied by the Nuevo Leon state government and delivered to the plane in an armored car. Mrs. Garza was then freed.

She said the hijackers gave her $1,000 of the ransom. "He said the money was to pay for the shock and compensate for my attitude." She added that she turned the money over to a representative of the Mexican attorney general because "I don't think the money belongs to me."

After the plane was refueled it took off for Lima, Peru with its hostage crew, Bessant, co-pilot William R. Wallace and flight engineer Phillip L. Wray, both of Dallas, Tex. The hostesses were Tina Garcia and Susan Harris, both of Corpus Christi, Tex.

In Lima a volunteer crew of four and two hostesses took over. The plane was refueled and provided with food and pep pills.

At Rio de Janeiro the air police were waiting on the taxiway to the civilian side of the big airport. Evading them, the hijacked plane taxied toward a military hangar, only to discover that scores of military police awaited the jetliner there. But, before the soldiers could block the runway with jeeps and trucks, the big plane turned again and took off for Buenos Aires.

There they encountered more police and soldiers, who surrounded the aircraft. Jackson wanted to continue to Algeria but the police, backed by Argentine President Alejandro Lanusse, refused to refuel the jet or to send food aboard. The plane's tires were flattened.

Conferences began. United States embassy officials in Buenos Aires and Harry Marples, Braniff vice president in Argentina, said they urged the Argentine government to allow refueling for the 11-hour flight to Algiers. But near midnight on July 3 the Argentine government formally announced that the aircraft would not be allowed to depart.

Soon thereafter Marples said Jackson showed signs of weakening. Once Jackson started down the staircase from the plane, but changed his mind and went back. Then, two minutes later, he emerged and surrendered.

By this time the FBI in San Antonio had charged Jackson with air piracy and assault with a deadly weapon. A spokesman for the embassy in Buenos Aires said the United States would seek to extradite him. The Mexican government said it was preparing to ask for extradition.

But Argentine officials said extradition would not be possible because of the seriousness of Argentina's charges against him: kidnaping and theft of an aircraft.

Hours before Jackson had surrendered his woman companion walked off the plane and was taken into custody. Police declined to discuss her role in the hijacking except to say that she had a pistol in her purse and that she had slept frequently during the 21 hours Jackson held out inside the plane. Jackson had not slept in two days.

*   *   *   *

On the evening of June 11 a tall, thin black man pushed his way into a TWA 727 trijet being loaded at O'Hare Airport in Chicago. The plane was eastbound to New York. Stewardess Catherine Culver, 24, of Fond du Lac, Wis., asked the intruder for his boarding pass. He had none. She ordered him to get off.

Instead, he drew a gun and demanded that TWA fly him to New York and then to North Vietnam. But he also ordered that the airline give him $75,000 and a machine gun.

At the sight of the gun Miss Culver screamed. Crew members in the cockpit looked into the cabin through the peephole. One of them opened the door, saw the weapon and slammed the door shut again.

Capt. Robert E. Elder then used the intercom to speak to the

(Left) Hijacker Robert Lee Jackson of Townsend, Tenn., made victory sign as police led him away at Argentina's Ezeiza Airport (Right) Lydia Lucrecia Sanchez, 23, a Guatemalan, went to court in Buenos Aires to answer charges in connection with the hijack of a Braniff airliner over Mexico

hijacker, later identified as Gregory White, 23, of Harvey, Ill., married and father of two. Elder asked him to allow the 20-odd passengers to disembark, and White agreed.

As they filed off the plane one passenger, Howard Franks, apparently trying to retrieve his coat, turned and approached the hijacker, whose gun still was pointed at Miss Culver. Witnesses assumed that White considered Franks a threat.

"He took the gun away from my head just long enough to kill the passenger," the stewardess related afterward. "Then he returned it to my temple, saying 'You're next!'"

But Franks, struck in the head, was still alive. The hijacker permitted Franks to be taken off the plane. He died on the way to a hospital. After the shooting the remaining passengers fled from the cabin.

Franks, 65, of Darien, Conn., had boarded the plane at Albuquerque. He had recently bought a house there and was returning to Darien to plan the move with his wife, who did not accompany him to New Mexico.

White had insisted that Miss Culver, Capt. Elder, 42, of Stamford, Conn.; First Officer Ronald J. Dupuis, 31, of Sparta, N.Y., and Flight Engineer Don E. Weishimer, 34, of St. James, N.Y., remain aboard the plane as hostages.

On the field but outside the plane, U.S. Deputy Marshal Joseph Zito, 39, was examining luggage with a magnetic detection device when he got a phone call that there had been a shooting aboard a plane and that a thin man was needed to crawl into the plane's cockpit. Zito, about 5-feet-6, put on a pilot's uniform, grabbed two pistols and wriggled through a small window. From the cockpit he watched through the peephole while the hijacker kept the gun at Miss Culver's head.

By the time Zito entered the plane the stewardess had relaxed White somewhat and had persuaded him to sit down and talk to her. At this point the plane took off for New York.

Some time later Zito reported to the captain that White had left his seat and gone to the tail end of the plane. "I think I can get him now," Zito said.

With Elder's consent, Zito opened the door, stepped out and fired twice.

"He fell behind the seat—I don't know whether I hit him—and I ducked behind a seat," Zito said. "We lay there the whole flight, him watching me and me watching him."

As it turned out, White was not hit at that time.

Zito said he had given one of the pistols to Dupuis, who, without effect, also took "a couple of shots" at White.

The stewardess had taken cover under a seat between the two men.

After the plane landed at Kennedy Airport in New York, White agreed to let the stewardess and the rest of the crew leave the cabin by means of the escape chute, Zito said.

William Mullaly, an FBI agent, was waiting beside the plane on the ground when the hijacker pegged a shot at him. An FBI spokesman said that Mullaly fired back, hitting him in the left arm.

White then told the airport tower by radio that he had had enough and was coming out unarmed.

The plane had been surrounded by FBI agents, who took the hijacker into custody. The next morning White, a processing clerk for the Illinois Central Railroad, was held in $200,000 bond to face homicide and air piracy charges in Chicago and an assault charge in New York.

Zito was not one of those U.S. marshals who had been assigned to travel aboard planes as security guards. "It was my first flight, and I was very scared," he told newsmen in New York.

* * * *

When an Eastern Airlines 727 landed on Nassau in the Bahamas on May 29 only two persons walked off the plane. One, a passenger, held the arm of the other, the second officer.

Approaching them with his right arm extended to shake the passenger's hand was a large man wearing grease-stained work clothing, apparently pretending to be a member of the Irish Republican Army. But the passenger ignored the greeting and stepped briskly ahead, still clinging to the arm of the second officer, Robert Condon.

"That was his big mistake," the would-be welcomer said later. "He walked past me and I gave the signal and jumped him."

The "mechanic" was, in reality, 230-pound John O'Neill, vice president and chief pilot of Eastern Airlines, and the plane had been hijacked to Nassau from LaGuardia Airport after the passenger had demanded $500,000 and a woman as ransom. Police identified him as James Bennett, 39, of Commack, N.Y.

Bennett, who had said his waist was strapped with explosives, was headed for a fake ransom package when O'Neill tricked him. The vice president's signal alerted 30 other men who jumped out of hiding places and swarmed over Bennett, forcing Condon to the bottom of the heap with a small bottle "jammed into my stomach," Condon said. The hijacker had told him the bottle contained acid.

"I started shoving and pushing like mad and finally managed to kick it away," Condon said.

O'Neill had specifically flown to Nassau to stop the hijacker.

The Bahamas police reported that the "large quantity of explosives" around Bennett's waist was nothing more than a few packages of mints.

Bennett, 39, who had been with the New York Police Department from 1955 until 1970 when he was discharged for "medical reasons," had boarded the New York-bound plane in Miami.

Approaching stewardess Janet Wesley, he pulled out the bottle, which, he told Condon later, contained acid, and demanded to see the captain, Eugene K. Sullivan. Bennett told the captain he wasn't sure where he wanted to go, so the plane proceeded to the Marine Terminal at LaGuardia Airport, about a mile away from the regular passenger terminal.

The 131 passengers in the economy class said most of them were "in the dark" about the incident until they were escorted off the plane and a policeman remarked that the man was carrying explosives.

Bennett's wife and young son were brought to the airport, at Bennett's request. They tried unsuccessfully to persuade him to give up the hijacking attempt.

Bennett repeatedly conceded that he was very unstable and emotional. At first he said that he wanted to land at Shannon Airport in Ireland and that he wanted a representative from the Irish Republican Army to meet him there. He also demanded $500,000 from Eastern. When the captain explained the plane hadn't enough fuel for a transatlantic flight, he then demanded to be flown to Nassau to pick up the money. To this Eastern agreed.

After his capture in Nassau, Bennett was arraigned in Brooklyn and held in $50,000 bail for a mental examination.

* * * *

Flight 755 of Qantas, Australia's national airline, had taken off for Hong Kong on May 26 when Sydney International Airport received an anonymous phone call reporting that a bomb was stored in an airport luggage locker. Airline personnel quickly found the unconnected gelignite missile in the designated locker, and they also found three notes:

One said that aboard the Hong Kong flight was hidden a similar barometric bomb, set to detonate upon the plane's descent to an altitude of 20,000 feet.

The second note explained how the bomb could be defused.

The third announced that, upon payment of $560,000 by the airline, the location of the bomb on the plane would be disclosed. Instructions for delivering the money to a "Mr. Brown" were included.

Sydney's airport at once passed the word to Capt. William G. Selwyn aboard Flight 755. He was instructed to have his crewmen hunt for the bomb, packed in a small box. Selwyn also was told to turn back to Sydney and to circle the airport at a safe altitude if the box and bomb were not found meanwhile.

Qantas officials then set about collecting the extortion fee, and Capt. James Ritchie took it in two suitcases to the airline's office in downtown Sydney. At 5:45 p.m., a small yellow truck drew up, and the driver identified himself as "Mr. Brown." Ritchie hastily thrust the two suitcases into the van, and "Mr. Brown" sped away.

Shortly after the payoff another phone call to the Sydney airport advised Qantas that there was no bomb aboard Flight 755, and that the search for the small box could be abandoned.

By this time the plane had been circling Sydney for six and one-half hours and its fuel tanks were nearly empty. Capt. Selwyn was told to descend, and the landing was uneventful. An immediate inspection of the aircraft confirmed that nothing —not even a box—had been hidden aboard.

One of the 116 passengers commented, "There was no panic at all. Everyone was remarkably calm. The captain and his crew were very efficient; we were given a drill on emergency procedures while the crew searched under the carpets."

TWA stewardess Catherine Culver wiped way tears while Deputy U.S. Marshal Joseph Zito described gun battle with a hijacker as plane was en route from Chicago to New York

Others said that, although crewmen did not disclose the nature of their search, nearly all of those on board were convinced that a bomb had been planted.

While the plane was circling, Qantas had made elaborate preparations for a major disaster. Eight ships of the Royal Australian Navy, including two submarines and three destroyers, had been rushed to Botany Bay, on the fringe of the airport. Ambulances, firemen and police had been summoned to the field.

Authorities held the view that the lucrative hoax was a "gang job," probably inspired by the movie *Doomsday*, shown in Sydney March 2. The film's plot resembled the extortion plan in that it involved a barometric bomb set to explode at a certain altitude. In the picture the pilot landed safely by choosing a city—such as Denver—situated at an altitude exceeding 5,000 feet.

Those who saw "Mr. Brown" at the payoff said he appeared

to be in his mid-20s and wore what looked like a false beard.

Nothing further developed for more than two months.

On Aug. 4 two Sydney men were arrested—Peter Pasquale Macari, 36, a driver, and Raymond Jans Poynting, 28, a barman —and Inspector V. Taylor, police prosecutor, said $27,061 of the extorted money was recovered. Both signed admissions of involvement, police said, and both appeared the next day on charges of demanding money with menaces (extortion). On Aug. 7 $154,000 was found when police knocked down a brick wall of a shop in a Sydney suburb.

A third man, Francis William Sorohan, 21, a miner of Mount Isa, Queensland, was arrested and charged with being an accessory before the fact, in relation to the three notes sent to Qantas.

By mid-December no formal plea had been taken from Macari. Poynting, having formally pleaded guilty, awaited sentence. Charges against Sorohan were dismissed.

SOVIET SPACEFLIGHT TRAGEDY

"This is Amber. Everything is in order on board. We feel fine. We're ready for landing."

The radio message to earth came from Lt. Col. Georgi Dobrovolsky aboard Soyuz 11, the Soviet spaceship. The colonel and fellow cosmonauts Vladislav Volkov and Viktor Patsayev had just completed an unprecedented journey of nearly 24 days in the sea of space and were returning to the Soviet Union.

For more than three weeks the trio had orbited the earth in their huge space station, performing scientific experiments, joking with ground control crews and even celebrating a birthday aboard.

All systems aboard the spaceship and the attached shuttle craft had seem to function flawlessly, and when the cosmonauts were finally ordered to return to earth there was little cause for apprehension.

Their arrival was awaited eagerly by millions of Russians who, from the beginning, had honored their spacemen to a degree rivaling sainthood.

Soyuz 11 made a normal landing June 30 on the steppes of Soviet Kazakhstan and a recovery helicopter prepared to touch down alongside the cavernous ship. Members of the recovery crew unfastened the hatch and swung it open. The three cosmonauts were still strapped in their seats.

All three were dead. The triumphant Russian space mission had ended in stunning tragedy.

The news sent Russian officials and civilians into deep mourning. Men and women in the streets of Moscow seemed dazed. A bakery shop clerk wiped her eyes, an elderly woman wept quietly, and workers talked in subdued tones on their way to office and factory jobs.

Most Soviet citizens had felt a close identity with the cosmonauts. During their long period in space the three men had appeared daily on television, explaining their life in orbit and cracking jokes about weightlessness. Messages of condolence poured in from all over the globe. Those expressing grief included President Nixon, Pope Paul VI and U.N. Secretary-General U Thant.

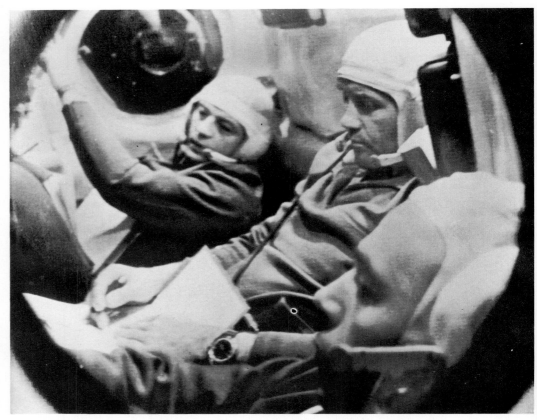

Training picture of the three doomed cosmonauts (from left): flight engineer Vladislav Volkov, Commander Georgi Dobrovolsky, test engineer Viktor Patsayev

In Cape Kennedy, Fla., Astronaut David R. Scott commander of the Apollo 15 Moon Mission learned the news while jogging on Cocoa Beach early in the morning.

"Oh my God," was his only comment.

The flag-draped ashes of the cosmonauts were borne on gun carriages through the streets of Moscow, to Red Square. The urns were entombed July 3 in the Kremlin Wall, the nation's most sacred place of interment. Marching with Soviet cosmonauts in the funeral procession was

U.S. astronaut Thomas Stafford, who represented President Nixon at the funeral.

The nagging question remained: What caused the deaths? Nearly two weeks later the answer came. A terse report by a government commission said a pressure leak had developed in the spacecraft half an hour before landing.

Western experts theorized that the cosmonauts' blood had ebullated—boiled off—after their cabin pressure was lost. They probably had died without pain in 12 to 16 seconds.

AIR DISASTER OVER JAPAN

Sgt. Yoshimi Ichikawa, a 22-year-old student pilot, was pushing his F86F fighter plane along, 28,000 feet above the rugged mountains of northern Japan on July 30, when he suddenly spotted a giant Boeing 727 jetliner approaching from the rear.

Ichikawa's instructor, Capt. Tomotsu Kuma, 31, shadowing his student in another F86F, also saw the All Nippon Boeing 727 and barked an order: "Pull up, right turn!"

Ichikawa tried frantically to veer out of the path of the oncoming jetliner, but he didn't make it. A moment later the two planes had collided, killing 162 persons in what was to be listed as aviation's worst disaster.

Ichikawa's plane began to plummet earthward, but he managed to bail out and land safely.

Pilots flying in the vicinity heard the commander of the stricken airliner, Capt. Saburo Kasai, say in a tense voice, "Emergency, All

Nippon . . . unable to control . . . oh, oh, oh."

Then there was silence over the airwaves as the big Boeing screamed downward, a plume of white smoke streaming from one wing. As it neared the ground the plane began to disintegrate. The jetliner slammed into a wooded mountain slope with a deafening roar, carrying 155 passengers and seven crew members to their deaths.

Tadashi Yasumoto, who ran an iron works in Shizukuishi near the site of the crash, said later he had heard a "big booming sound which sounded like the eruption of a nearby volcano." Yasumoto dashed out of the house and saw the plane coming down in pieces.

A school teacher in the vicinity also saw the tragedy. He said he saw a rain of debris showering down on a nearby mountain after a sound like a giant thunderclap.

A search was ordered as soon as news of the

disaster reached authorities. They dispatched an army of 620 policemen and 2,300 defense troops who spent the night scouring the wooded terrain. By morning they had recovered all 162 bodies. Parts of the plane were scattered across an area of 4.5 square miles.

Among the passengers aboard the ill-fated plane were 125 members of the Bereaved Family Association, made up of relatives of men killed in World War II. The plane had been bound for Tokyo from Sapporo on Hokkaido, Japan's northernmost main island.

There was also one American aboard. He was identified as the flight engineer, Dom M. Carpenter, 30, of Miami, Fla.

It was the second major air crash that Japan had suffered in one month. On July 3, a YS11 of the Japanese TOA Airlines had crashed into a mountainside in the northern part of the country, killing all 68 persons aboard.

MOROCCO, SUDAN COUPS FAILED

Westerners had always been baffled by the intricate political maneuverings in the Arab world, where revolution was a way of life and Arab justice was harsh.

No exceptions were Morocco and Sudan, where revolts in July exploded within a week's time and were quickly crushed. Each entailed a bloodbath of reprisals that shocked the outside world.

In Rabat King Hassan II, once one of the better known playboys in the Middle East, decided to throw a lavish party to celebrate his 42nd birthday on July 10. Attired in red slacks and a flowered shirt, Hassan greeted 500 guests at the white summer palace, where a lavish buffet included such delicacies as lobster, smoked salmon, roast sheep and couscous.

No one paid much heed to the first rattle of gunfire, believing it was fireworks. Then a wounded man staggered onto the terrace where the guests were dining by the swimming pool.

Suddenly the gay lucheon took a grim turn as rifle shots rang out and the crump of mortars and grenades joined the clatter of machineguns. Rebellious officers in Hassan's 50,000-man army had decided to topple his pro-western regime, and 30 truckloads of mutineers were lined up before the palace raking it with gunfire.

As rebels surged into the palace, people were pushed against a wall and shot. Hundreds of guests on the patio were ordered to lie down in the flower beds.

Hassan slipped into the throne room and held a hasty conference with Gen. Mohammed Medbouh, commander of the king's military household and nominal leader of the coup. Minutes later, Medbouh was shot dead, apparently accidentally, by one of his own guards.

Within two and a half hours nearly a hundred guests and members of the royal household had been killed, including Belgian Ambassador Marcel Dupret and three French doctors.

Suddenly, the picture began to change. A young soldier nervously approached Hassan, kissed the king's hand explained that the invaders were mostly cadets from a military school who had entered the palace under the impression that they were protecting the monarch from a plot against his life.

Soon loyal troops arrived at the palace and outgunned the rebels, who then surrendered. Reprisals followed swiftly. Within two days four Moroccan generals, five colonels and a commandant had been tied to stakes and gunned down by firing squads. Within a week the governments of Egypt, Libya, Syria and Sudan had angrily condemned Hassan for "executing without trial" the leaders of the abortive coup.

Undismayed, Hassan continued to clean house, firing his cabinet and promising to rid his country of corruption.

The spotlight swung next to Sudan, which was in the grip of a searing heat wave with temperatures soaring to 120 degrees. Because of the weather, most office workers were taking a siesta when the rebels made their move July 19.

Maj. Hashem el-Ata, supported by the presidential guard and an armored division, moved tanks into position in Khartoum and swiftly took over the capital from the premier, Maj. Gen. Jaafar al Numairi. For three hours he consolidated his hold, virtually without opposition. It looked like a bloodless coup.

Then the other side acted, and within a few days the coup had been smashed in a hail of

Mourners crowded around military truck carrying coffin of a victim of Moroccan coup attempt

Sudan's leader, Major Gen. Jaafar Al Numairi showed Communist party leader Abdel Khalek Mahgoub a document accusing him of masterminding abortive revolt

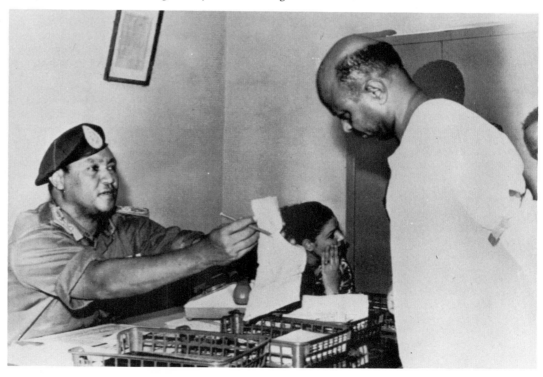

gunfire. Fighting raged through Khartoum, littering the streets with dead and filling the hospitals with wounded. By week's end Atta and three other rebel officers had been shot as Numairi set up four tribunals for swift justice.

Later, Sudanese firing squads shot two officers who had been hauled off a British plane by Libyan authorities and handed over to Numairi. One, Lt. Col. Babakr al Nour, had been named leader of the rebel government that was to have taken over.

Shortly afterward the head of the Sudan's

Communist party, Abdel Khalek Mahgoub, was also found guilty of treason and hanged. By the end of the week 14 accused leaders of the coup attempt had been executed.

The reprisals aroused indignation in Moscow, which had supported the dissidents. The Kremlin warned Khartoum against what it called "the impermissibility of resorting to extreme measures".

Retorted Numairi: "If they (the Russians) want to choose that path, we will have no alternative."

LIBERIA'S TUBMAN DEAD AT 75

Liberia's late president, William V. Tubman

His fellow Liberians fondly referred to the old man as "Uncle Shad," and he ruled with total authority for 27 years in the African nation founded by freed American slaves.

William Vacanarat Shadrach Tubman, who died July 23 at the age of 75, was a dapper, portly man with a taste for Havana cigars and Scotch whisky. He was also a tireless executive who came to power in 1944 and spent six presidential terms obliterating internal differences and fostering the economic health of Africa's oldest independent republic.

Tubman preached to other West African nations the need for cooperation among them. He called on his fellow Africans to avoid stubborn nationalism, bigotry and class hatred, and the wasting of energy on ancient quarrels. The venerable president appealed also to the great powers to listen to the voice of the small nations.

Tubman's Methodist preacher father was descended from slaves and emigrated from Augusta, Ga., in 1834. His mother, born in Atlanta, Ga., went to Liberia in 1872. Tubman rose from county revenue collector to become in 1928 the youngest senator in Liberia's history. Regarded as the most energetic figure ever to appear on Liberia's political scene, he was up each day at 6 a.m., no matter how late he was out the night before. By 8 a.m. he was on the job, and he usu-ally stayed at work for 11 hours or more, dictating letters, seeing callers and mapping orders to aides.

As president-elect, Tubman came to the United States at the invitation of Franklin D. Roosevelt during World War II, accompanied by the outgoing chief of state, Edwin Barclay. They became the first blacks to spend a night at the White House and the first to be entertained in the Executive Mansion since Booker T. Washington lunched there in 1901.

Iron, rubber and Tubman brought Liberia to the fringes of the modern World. With efficient management, the president turned his homeland from a primitive state to one with 500 miles of new roads, a dozen modern hospitals, an air-conditioned hotel, a water system and a modern sewage-disposal plant for Monrovia.

Tubman introduced a civil service system for Liberia, income tax laws and women's suffrage. A gregarious man, Tubman liked to spend his evenings calling on friends or entertaining them over a highball in his presidential mansion. Although he and most of his friends were descendants of freed American slaves, Tubman took offense at the designation "Americo-Liberians" for his country's leading families.

Outlawing the phrase, Tubman declared "we are all Liberians."

AGNEW STUCK STRICTLY TO BUSINESS ON THIRD WORLD TOUR

On his third world tour of Africa, Asia and Europe Vice President Spiro Agnew epitomized the traveling businessman, isolating himself from each country's ordinary way of life and attending solely to the tasks President Nixon had assigned him.

When asked by the press why he saw only the leaders of the nations he visited, Agnew responded: "If I come to play a constructive and a rewarding role on this trip it will be due to what I do in the set meetings rather than out in the street or at some housing project."

Certain meetings, however, did not go quite as was expected. After leaving the United States

Kenya President Jomo Kenyatta, assisted by Foreign Minister Njoroge Mungai (center), gave Vice President Agnew a monkey skin cloak

June 27 his first stop was Seoul, South Korea, where he was scheduled to stay six days. Besides attending the third term inauguration of President Chung Hee Park, Agnew was expected to discuss with the president such major issues as reduction of American troop strength and the United States' increased warmth toward China. However, as days went by it became obvious that these topics would not be considered. After leaving the country Agnew conceded that President Park "quickly made known to me in our first conversation that he had no intention of going into substantive matters on this trip."

The rest of Agnew's 31-day tour included Singapore, India, Kuwait, Saudi Arabia, Ethiopia, Kenya, the Congo, Spain—where he stayed a week—Morocco and Portugal. His wife Judy met him in Spain, and in each country he delivered President Nixon's regards and his hopes for peace and good will.

Unlike his other world trips, Agnew did not brief the press on the flight home. He did conduct seven press briefings including two only in the final three weeks. The last one, on July 17 between the Congo and Spain, stirred a domestic political storm due to his comment on U.S. black leaders. These he compared unfavorably to such African statesmen as Ethiopian Emperor Haile Selassie, Kenya's President Jomo Kenyatta and Congolese President Joseph D. Mobutu. Earlier on the trip Agnew twice fired off blasts at familiar targets—the communications media and press publication of the Pentagon papers.

The vice president, who had voiced reservations about some aspects of the Nixon Administration's hopes to thaw relations with China, refused to comment on the President's proposed trip to Peking, and some White House officials said Agnew had not even known about it in advance of the public announcement.

DEATH CAME IN A CAN OF SOUP

On a hot night last June, banker Samuel Cochran, 61, and his 63-year-old wife, Grace, of Bedford Village, N.Y., served for dinner chilled vichyssoise from a can.

The following morning Cochran complained of double vision. In a short time he had trouble speaking. By the time he was admitted to a hospital later that day he had difficulty moving his arms and legs. Shortly before midnight he was dead. His wife, also admitted to the hospital, was gravely ill but she survived.

Both were victims of botulism, a deadly form of food poisoning.

The tragedy in the Cochran family triggered a hunt throughout America and abroad for other canned products of Bon Vivant Soups, Inc., a small Newark, N.J., canning company.

State and federal health authorities ordered the recall of all products prepared by Bon Vivant, which turned out numerous soups, sauces and other foods under its own name, as well as under some 33 other private brand labels.

Then came the revelation that the Bon Vivant soup plant in Newark had not been inspected by the Food and Drug Administration for more than four years—nor by the New Jersey Health Department for close to five years—before botulism was traced to the can of vichyssoise. Officials blamed a lack of manpower for the long gaps between inspections.

An intense inspection was ordered. Of the first 324 cans of Bon Vivant vichyssoise recalled and tested, five were found contaminated with botulism infections. There had been earlier scares.

In April 1970 a nationwide hunt was launched for 80,000 frozen pizzas believed to contain mushrooms tainted by botulism. In 1963 a total of 14 Americans died in two botulism epidemics, one caused by infected canned tuna fish and the other by infected smoked fish.

Botulism was, in effect, the poisoning of the nervous system by what many scientists considered the deadliest known toxin, produced by the spores of the bacterium Clostridum Botulinum

as it germinated and reproduced. A few ounces of the toxin, scientists said, could kill all human beings on earth.

Botulism could be prevented by cooking, since high heat both killed the germs and inactivated the toxin, but the spores were resistant and required prolonged application of a high temperature.

It had been found that symptoms of botulism

normally showed up in 18 to 96 hours after the infected food was eaten. Those who died were usually victims of paralysis of the respiratory system or of heart failure, since the poison primarily attacked the nervous system.

On July 26, less than a month after Samuel Cochran died Bon Vivant Soups, Inc., filed for bankruptcy, declaring that it was "unable to meet its obligations as they mature."

More than 1.2 million cans of Bon Vivant Soup Company's 97 products were recalled after vichyssoise soup caused a man to die of botulism

TROUBLE IN COMMUNICATIONS

Unrest, long brewing in the postal and telephone services, approached a climax July 1 when the semi-independent U.S. Postal Service took control of the nation's mail system.

President Nixon hailed the postal reorganization as "one of the major achievements of my administration." But the ink was hardly dry when a $750 million pay increase offer by the postal service was rejected by union negotiators. In New York the 27,000-member Manhattan-Bronx Postal Union and other locals voted overwhelmingly to call a strike if they deemed it necessary.

Two weeks later, about 400,000 members of the Communications Workers of America did launch a nationwide walkout against the giant Bell Telephone system. The union branded as inadequate a company wage offer of about 30 per cent. Despite the strike, however, service remained virtually unimpaired. It was maintained by the supervisory staff of 300,000 who manned the largely automated switchboard sys-

tem and who performed emergency repair and installation services.

By July 20, the trouble appeared to have passed. Communications workers and the Bell System agreed on a contract calling for a 33.5 per cent increase in pay and fringe benefits over three years which would cost Bell about $4 billion.

At the same time, a Labor Department spokesman said negotiators for the Postal Service and representatives of seven postal unions had reached accord after haggling for six months. The settlement gave 750,000 workers 20 per cent in pay increases over the ensuing two years. It would cost the Postal Service about $1 billion.

RABBI KAHANE FINED $5,000

"Every Jew a .22," shouted Rabbi Meir Kahane, head of the militant Jewish Defense League, in addressing a group of his supporters upon leaving a courthouse in New York. He had just been fined $5,000 and given a suspended sentence of

five years on conspiracy charges, to which he had pleaded guilty.

Kahane admitted to overseeing the making of bombs at a JDL camp in Woodbourne, N.Y., last year and utilizing instructions from left and right-wing pamphlets.

Judge Jack B. Weinstein suspended the term July 23, on condition Kahane would have nothing more to do with guns or explosives.

"In this country at this time it is not permissible to substitute the bomb for the book as the symbol of Jewish manhood," the judge commented from the bench.

Kahane told his cheering sympathizers that there was no obligation on his part to cooperate with the court. "I didn't ask for mercy, I cannot compromise my principles with expediency. Some time or other, there is no other way than violence."

Given three-year suspended sentences were one of Kahane's aides, Chaim Bieber, 41, who also was fined $2,500 and a third defendant, Stewart Cohen, 19, who was fined $500 and given three years' probation.

CHILE'S RECURRENT NIGHTMARE

The quake struck with an estimated force of 10 million tons of dynamite and ripped across the populous north central region of Chile, killing 90 persons and causing damage estimated at $250 million.

The wonder was that the loss of life had not been higher. It was part of a continuing nightmare for Chileans, whose homeland lay in the "circle of fire," a ring of volcanoes and seismic fault lines that encircled the Pacific Basin.

"This is the second time we've been left

homeless," muttered one man in the town of Llay Llay, 66 miles northwest of Santiago, as he gazed at the shattered ruins of his adobe hut. An earthquake that killed more than 400 persons in March 1965 (*The World in 1965, 67*) had destroyed the man's earlier home.

The 1971 quake did not do much damage to Santiago, but it hit the port city of Valparaiso hard enough to topple the main tower and part of the roof of the Roman Catholic cathedral. Bridges collapsed and pavement was buckled

along the Pan American highway terminating in southern Chile.

President Salvador Allende flew to the farm regions of Illapel and Salamanca, both hard hit. What he saw stunned the president.

"It was dreadful," he said after visiting Hierro Viejo, a village of 5,000 persons where virtually every building had been reduced to rubble.

Chile had suffered more heavily in the past. About 3,000 Chileans were killed in the 1906 earthquake, 30,000 in 1939 and 5,000 in 1960.

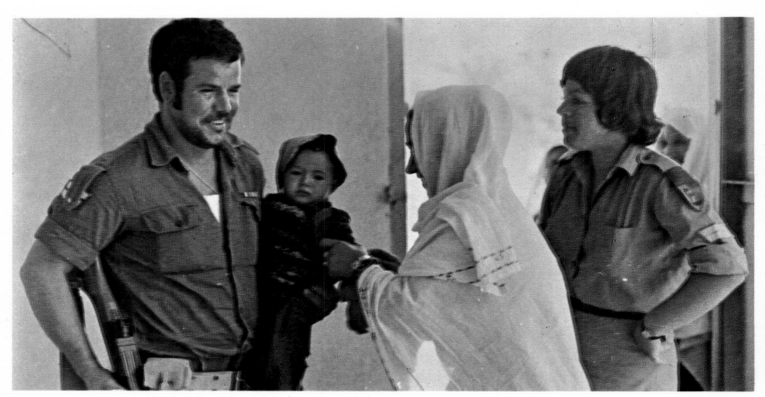

The Israeli soldier, left, got a peculiar guard-duty assignment: Holding a baby while its Arab mother was searched by an Israeli woman trooper and then told that babies were not allowed in the courtroom where guerrillas were being tried in the Israeli-occupied Gaza Strip

38 OF 50 STATES RATIFIED NATIONAL VOTING AMENDMENT

The states had moved with astonishing speed, taking only three months and seven days to ratify the 26th Amendment granting voting rights to 18 to 20-year-olds. It became a fact on June 30, when the Ohio House of Representatives—by a thumping vote of 81-9—made it the 38th state to approve the amendment. That was enough for ratification.

Six days later the measure was officially certified by President Nixon, while more than 500 members of a singing group known as Young Americans in Concert, looked on in the East Room of the White House.

Why such alacrity in ratifying the amendment? To some extent, the Vietnam war had been a factor. The argument that people old enough to die were old enough to vote had been persuasive. That was the primary consideration when Georgia, in the midst of World War II (1943), became the first state to give 18-year-olds the vote in state elections.

A more important reason in 1971, however, was the confusion that would have resulted from the need for most states to maintain separate election rolls for state and federal balloting. In New York City alone, it was estimated that the

additional cost would have totaled some $15 million a year.

Commenting on the dispatch with which ratification was handled, Nixon said: "Some 11 million young men and women who have participated in the life of our nation through their work, their studies and their sacrifices for its defense are now fully included in the electoral processes of our country. I urge them to honor this right by exercising it."

Glancing around the room at the sea of blue blazers and starched white blouses Nixon said he was sure the young singers, who were about to embark on a tour of Europe, would "represent America well abroad and that the 11 million new votes will do well for this country at home."

Political commentators were quick to state that the President hoped to capture many of the new voters in the 1972 presidential election.

The lowering of the voting age to 18 by constitutional amendment had been necessitated by a Supreme Court decision in December 1970, modifying a law previously passed by Congress that had given citizens over 18 the vote in all elections.

The court ruled that Congress had overstepped its powers by setting voting standards for state and local elections as well as national elections. It upheld only the granting of national voting rights to the teenagers.

FOR THE RECORD

RESIGNED. Dr. Glenn Seaborg, chairman of the Atomic Energy Commission. Dr. Seaborg, a Nobel Prize chemist, terminated his 10-year appointment July 21 to return to the University of California at Berkeley. As his successor, President Nixon nominated James R. Schlesinger, an assistant director of the White House Office of Management and Budget.

RETIRED. During a deadlock of the Paris Peace talks, David K. E. Bruce, chief American delegate. For reasons of health, the 73-year-old diplomat withdrew July 29, after delivering a final protest to North Vietnamese and Vietcong delegations. He accused Hanoi of having increased its military activity in and around the demilitarized zone and of having built a road through its western section. Bruce was replaced by William J. Porter, previously ambassador to South Korea.

Apollo 15: headed for the moon ⟶

August

Astronauts of Apollo 15 Toured Moon Three Days

*Fourth landing expedition used weird surface vehicle to make
Scientific experiments and hunt for ancient rocks*

*(Left) Plaque left on Moon by Apollo 15 crew listed U.S. and Soviet spacemen who perished in development of the program (Right) Astronaut Scott
shooting pictures near base of Apennine Mountains*

As Apollo 15's Saturn rocket and spacecraft rolled from the Cape Kennedy assembly building to the launch pad in May, mission commander David R. Scott gazed up at the towerlike 36-story-tall stack and declared: "There is more scientific equipment and capability contained in this one vehicle than man has ever conceived before. Apollo 15 will be the most singular, significant scientific expedition ever conducted."

Early Apollo missions had been primarily engineering flights, to perfect the hardware for extended lunar exploration. But by August 1971 four expeditions had landed a total of eight men on the moon *(The World in 1969, 141-152, 229-233).*

Its equipment having been perfected, Apollo 15 was designated the first moon vehicle whose primary purpose was scientific exploration.

Astronauts Scott, James B. Irwin and Alfred M. Worden trained for months so they could make meaningful geological observations and operate a complex array of equipment, including a moon car, during record stays both on the surface and in lunar orbit.

Experts selected one of the most scientifically-interesting landing sites on the moon—a narrow valley hemmed in on three sides by the 15,000-foot-tall Apennine Mountains, highest on the moon, and on the fourth by a mile-wide canyon named Hadley Rille.

"We really have a 5-in-1 geology site at Hadley-Apennine," Scott explained. "We have the mountain front which may contain original lunar crust; we have the mysterious rille, which could have been formed by lava flow or volcanic gases. We have a cluster of craters believed formed by the impact of material thrown out by a larger crater; we have craters which may have been volcanoes, and we have another mare (flat plain) for comparison with the mare visited by the Apollo 11 and 12 crews."

Emphasizing the scientific nature of the mission, the astronauts named their command ship Endeavour, after the first vessel to sail the seas for science—British Capt. James Cook's ship which explored the South Pacific in 1768.

Col. Scott, Lt. Col. Irwin and Maj. Worden, all Air Force officers, selected Falcon, the Air Force Academy mascot, as the name for the lunar landing craft.

Scott, 39, was a veteran of two previous earth orbit/space flights, Gemini 8 and Apollo 9. Irwin, 41, and Worden, 39, were making their first trip. They set forth right on time at 9:34 a.m. EDT July 26 on the pulsating power of the Saturn 5, which hurled them into orbit more than 100 miles high. After circling the globe for nearly three hours, they re-fired the still-attached third stage of the rocket and streaked toward the moon at more than 24,500 miles an hour.

Several times during the three-day outward voyage, the astronauts grappled with nagging problems—a short-circuit in a switch, a water leak and a broken glass cover on a meter. But they were able to overcome them, and they had a smoothly operating pair of spacecraft when they fired into lunar orbit on July 29.

The threesome had been relatively quiet on the translunar trip, but perked up as they circled the strange, alien world of mountains, craters and plains.

"It's fantastic," exclaimed Irwin.

"This is absolutely mind-boggling," said Scott.

"Why, it's just unreal," added Worden.

The next day, they had a brief scare. As Scott and Irwin prepared for the descent to the surface, they were unable to separate the Falcon from the Endeavour.

"Houston, we did not get a separation," Scott radioed.

Worden and the ground quickly diagnosed the problem, and the command module pilot scurried into a tunnel connecting the two vehicles. He tightened a loose electrical cord, and Scott reported all was now well with the undocking mechanism.

Minutes later Falcon separated and began the dizzying dive that took it over the peaks of the Apennines and into a steep descent to the plain below. With Scott piloting and Irwin calling out the altitude, the four-legged craft moved steadily downward.

"I see a good spot," Scott called out as he steered Falcon like a helicopter toward a smooth landing site in the cratered valley.

"Contact," he exclaimed as they touched down. "The Falcon is on the plain at Hadley."

Astronaut Irwin with Lunar Roving Vehicle and St. George Crater in the background

Ninety minutes later, the astronauts donned space suits, depressurized the cabin and opened the top hatch. Scott thrust the upper half of his body outside to survey the landing site, to help geologists at Mission Control Center plan the three driving excursions on the surface.

"Oh, boy, what a view," the commander shouted as he observed the mountains towering around him.

After a night's sleep, Scott and Irwin were ready the next day, Saturday, July 31, to begin their exploration. Scott was the first down the ladder, the seventh man to leave his imprint in the dusty lunar soil. As he gazed at the dazzling, incandescent light of the lunar morning and absorbed the stark and lonely beauty of the scene, he commented:

"As I stand here on the wonders of the unknown at Hadley, I sort of realize there is a fundamental truth to our nature. Man must explore. And this is exploration at its greatest."

Irwin bounded from the last step of the ladder, saying: "Oh, boy, it's beautiful out here. It reminds me of Sun Valley."

Then they turned their attention to a machine the world was waiting to see—the first man-driven vehicle on the moon. As a television camera relayed strikingly clear pictures to earth, the moonmen operated cables which slowly lowered the $8 million jeep-like vehicle to the surface. Its hollow, wire-mesh wheels snapped into place, and the astronauts assembled seats and other parts and loaded aboard their geology tools.

As Scott climbed into the driver's seat he discovered a problem. The front-wheel steering did not work. But it was designed to operate on either front- or back-wheel drive, and the rear system was working perfectly. So they set off for the Apennine front two miles to the south.

"Man, oh man," cried Scott as the moon buggy bounded over the undulating plain at top speed of about eight miles per hour, dodging craters and rocks. "This is really a sporty driving course. What a Grand Prix this is!"

Both were strapped in with seat belts, but Scott cautioned: "Hang on."

"Buckin' bronco!" yipped Irwin.

But their commentary could also be sophisticated, and they gave pleased geologists back at Houston a graphic running description of the terrain as they bumped along. At their first stop, Elbow Crater, on the rim of 1,200-foot-deep Hadley Rille, the astronauts dismounted to collect rocks and soil, radioing detailed descriptions of their finds as they placed them in numbered sample bags. The television camera, mounted on the front of the rover, relayed every step of their exploration whenever they stopped. Viewers watched in fascination as they moved about with a kangaroo hop in the one-sixth gravity of the moon.

Scott and Irwin found the base of the Apennines in this area to be a gentle slope and they were able to drive several hundred feet up the incline to St. George Crater, a large pit resembling a shellhole.

Mission Control noted they were running behind schedule, and told them it was time to head back to Falcon. The geological pickings were so good that Scott regretted leaving. "I wish we could just sit down and play with the rocks for awhile," he said. "Just look at those babies—so shiny and sparkling." But back they drove to the landing craft, having logged about five miles on their first excursion.

About 300 feet from the lander, they carefully set up a nuclear-powered science station intended to relay data for a year or more on such things as the lunar atmosphere, moonquakes, radiation, magnetic fields and the solar wind. Scott had trouble drilling three 10-foot holes in a new experiment intended to gather subsurface samples and to measure the heat flow from the moon's interior. After drilling one hole of five feet, the commander found that no matter how hard he pushed on the electric drill, he could not make the second hole any deeper than 3½ feet.

"I'll tell you one thing," he said. "The base at Hadley is firm."

Because Scott was working harder than expected, he was rapidly depleting the oxygen supply in his back-support pack. Unwilling to take a risk, Mission Control ordered the astronauts back into the Falcon, about half an hour earlier than intended. They had been outside 6½ hours. During the night they rested, ate and recharged the oxygen supplies in the back packs. On Sunday morning they were ready to explore again.

Overnight the wizards at Mission Control figured out a possible solution to the rover's front-wheel steering problems. They directed Scott to throw some switches in the electrical system.

"It works," reported a happy Scott as he made a test drive.

Then he and Irwin headed for the Apennine foothills, about four miles to the southwest. Once again they were able to drive partway up the slope. They stopped at two areas to gather samples, to dig up soil and to drive core tubes three feet into the surface. On the return trip they stopped at a crater they named Spur, the most geologically-rewarding stop of all.

"This crater is a gold mine," radioed an exuberant Scott, who was rock-hunting so intently he fell twice, requiring Irwin's assistance once to regain his feet. Suddenly Scott announced: "Guess what we just found? I think we got what we came for!"

"Crystalline rock," explained Irwin.

"Yes sir, you better believe it," bubbled Scott. "Plag in there. Oh, boy, I think we might have ourselves something close to anorthosite, because the crystals are almost all plag. What a beaut—that is really a beauty!"

While this was hardly guaranteed to excite the average television viewer, scientists took immediate notice. Many of them believed that anorthosite rock, which contains the mineral plagioclase, or plag, formed the original crust of the moon. Thus, the rock collected by the astronauts might well be 4.6 billion years old, dating back to the creation of the moon.

The rocks gathered by Apollos 11, 12 and 14 date back 3.2 to 3.8 billion years. They were gathered from either the flat plains or the low highlands. The Apollo 15 site was selected because of the possibility of finding the most ancient material in the area of the mountains.

"They may indeed have found it," commented one Houston scientist. Others immediately dubbed the find the "Genesis rock."

"Make this bag 196, a special bag," Scott radioed as he

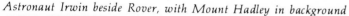

Astronaut Irwin beside Rover, with Mount Hadley in background

tucked the bauble away by itself. Back at the Falcon, the astronauts tackled the drill again, this time succeeding in boring a core sample tube eight feet deep. But they were unable to extract it. Fearing overexertion, Mission Control told them to leave it until the next day. The moon-farers did so gladly, carried out the traditional flag-raising ceremony and retired to the landing craft cabin after nearly seven hours outside.

Refreshed after a night's rest, Scott and Irwin attacked the balky drill once again. Working together, they managed to jerk it out of the soil, but they had difficulty breaking it into foot-long sections. They were becoming exasperated and ready to abandon the project.

"Hey, Joe," Scott radioed capsule communicator Joseph Allen, "you never did tell me that drill was that important. Just tell me it's that important and I'll feel a lot better."

"Quite seriously," Allen, a scientist-astronaut, replied, "that's the deepest sample out of the moon for perhaps as long as the moon itself has been there."

The astronauts, using a vise, managed to separate some of the sections. They were able to reduce all parts to a small enough size to place aboard the spacecraft. Besides revealing much about the moon, the core might provide a record of the activities of the sun. Had it flared up during the past few billion years? Had its fires ever diminished? By studying the microscopic tracks left by the bombardment of cosmic rays in each layer of the core, and by looking for traces of an element like argon—which was blown from the sun to the moon on the solar wind—scientists could possibly get the answers.

The target for the third rover drive was the rim of Hadley Rille, little more than a mile away. While the buggy's TV camera, remotely operated in Mission Control, followed them, the astronauts walked slowly about 100 feet down the gentle upper slope of the 1,200-foot deep gorge.

"This is a spectacular place," Scott said as he reported spotting at least two major layers of material on the far vertical wall. One of the layers, he said, contained at least 10 subordinate layers. Television watchers had a brief fright when the commander suddenly tumbled over a rock and fell on his right arm and shoulder. But he was helped unhurt to his feet by Irwin and vowed: "This time I'll look and make sure I don't fall over some silly rock." Later Scott was on his knees again, intentionally, using a hammer to chip a large piece off a big boulder which he believed was a chunk of the moon's bedrock.

The rocks and pictures returned from the rille were intended to help scientists determine how the canyon was formed—whether by a single lava flow, a series of flows or by a faulting action.

It was time to end the exploration and pack up for home. As a final task, Scott drove the rover about 330 feet away from the lunar module and pointed it so the television camera would give earthlings their first look at a blastoff from the moon. Nearly four hours later, Scott and Irwin fired their ascent engine and on the TV screen Falcon suddenly leaped up like a jack-in-the-box and disappeared from sight in less than two seconds. Left behind on the surface was the descent stage,

Apollo 15 command module hitting Pacific waters after bold mission

Astronauts Worden, Irwin and Scott appeared before a joint session of Congress with House speaker Carl Albert and Senate president pro tempore Allen J. Ellender in background

its gold insulation foil shredding and scattering in the engine's blast. The moonmen immediately began flying the complex rendezvous maneuvers that would take them back to the mother ship Endeavour, where Worden had been a busy man for three days, operating a $17 million array of cameras and scientific instruments. With them, he was photographically and chemically charting about 20 per cent of the lunar surface, including much of the hidden backside.

Using one of the devices, a laser altimeter, Worden measured the lunar contours with such precision that he proved something theoreticians long had suspected—the moon was lopsided. The altimeter showed that the front surface which always faced the earth, was 1½ miles lower than it would be if the moon were perfectly round, and that the back face was three miles higher. This could be associated with tidal flows on earth. The instruments also detected an eruption of carbon dioxide gas and traces of hydrocarbons on the far side, possible indication of continued volcanism deep within the moon.

Even after the Falcon crew was successfully reunited with Endeavour, the scientific tasks continued. Instead of heading immediately home as past Apollo crews had, Apollo 15 remained in lunar orbit an extra two days to gather as much data as possible. On their 74th and final orbit, they jettisoned a 78.5-pound satellite into lunar orbit. It carried devices to send data for a year or more on magnetic, electrical and gravity fields.

"Tally ho! That's a very pretty satellite out there," Scott exclaimed as he watched the payload spin away.

Then, behind the moon, out of radio contact, the astronauts fired their main engine to start the three-day journey back to earth.

"Endeavour is on the way home," the commander reported as the spaceship emerged from behind the moon.

The following morning, Worden executed man's first walk outside a speeding craft in deep space. He opened Endeavour's hatch and, bundled in a protective suit, moved on handrails about 15 feet back to a service compartment at the rear to retrieve two film cassettes from cameras which had mapped the moon. The stroll, 200,000 miles from earth, was necessary because the service compartment would be jettisoned before

reentry and would not return to earth with the astronauts. With Irwin standing halfway out the hatch, paying out the lifeline that attached Worden to the craft and operating a TV camera, the space walker easily collected the cassettes, with a total of nearly two miles of film.

"I'm enjoying it," Worden reported. Glancing back at Irwin, silhouetted against the moon, he said: "Jim, you look absolutely fantastic against the moon back there. That is really a most unbelievable, remarkable sight."

After 18 minutes, Worden was safely back in the cabin and the spacemen prepared for a generally relaxing final two days.

Television viewers had a ringside seat Saturday, Aug. 7, as Apollo 15 returned to earth, dangling beneath three huge orange and white parachutes as it floated toward splashdown in the North Pacific just seven miles from the recovery carrier USS Okinawa.

Suddenly, one of the chutes collapsed a few hundred feet above the water. But the system was designed so the spaceship could land safely on two chutes. The only complication, and it was minor, was that Endeavour landed slightly harder than it would have on three parachutes.

Forty-one minutes after splashdown the three astronauts walked briskly across a red carpet on the deck of the Okinawa while a band played the Air Force song. Worden summed up the feelings of the threesome when he said: "We've just finished the most fantastic 12 days I've ever had in my life."

Doctors said they were slightly more tired than previous crews because of their heavier workload, but reported them in good physical condition.

Back in Houston, scientists eagerly received the 171 pounds of rocks, the film and other data returned by Apollo 15. All agreed that this was the most scientifically-productive of all the Apollo missions.

But much work lay ahead as experts tried to learn the origin of the moon and perhaps the earth and the entire solar system from the material returned by the astronauts. Said Dr. William Phinney, chief of the Manned Spacecraft Center's geology branch:

"It will be years before this mission can be analyzed to the point that will permit people to begin putting it together."

(Above) Victim of the fighting between East and West Pakistan, this child sat in a refugee camp on Assam border (Right) Elderly man fleeing from the fighting crossed over into India at a point about 70 miles from Calcutta

For East Pakistanis, a Harvest of Suffering

At least seven million Bengali exiles streamed into India in flight from Death, Pestilence, War and Famine

WHEN THE TIME of the gathering of harvests came to the Ganges delta in East Pakistan—Golden Bengal—the world could only marvel, and weep, at the immense strength of suffering the proud Bengalis displayed and wonder how much more they could endure.

Hundreds of thousands had died the previous November in a cyclone that ravaged their bountiful rice crops (*The World in 1970, 226–227*). Other hundreds of thousands fell to the shot and shell of West Pakistanis, countrymen in name only, when civil war reduced East Pakistan's cities to rubble the following spring, at planting time. The summer monsoons arrived as ex-

pected but when they did the weary Bengalis were without homes. Cholera stalked their flooded refugee camps. By August what little harvest there was to gather lay rotting in the fields, because the numbed Bengalis—no fewer than seven million of them—were pouring across their borders into India in endless processions of sorrow, seeking escape from all of the apocalyptic four: Death, Pestilence, War, Famine. "Bengali refugees," said Dr. David L. Weiner of the International Rescue Committee, "must now form the largest group of displaced persons in the world."

Relief for so many desperate exiles, a massive task under the

146

best of circumstances, was further complicated by the realities of geopolitics. Pakistan still remained divided after its civil war, and India was providing surreptitious support of Bangla Desh, as the secessionist Bengal nation was known. Should India continue its support of Bangla Desh guerrillas, the president of Pakistan warned, "I shall declare a general war—and let the world take note." The world could hardly fail to, for Pakistan was an ally of China, India and of Russia.

Pakistan, with its separate eastern and western regions, was unique among the nations of the world, an artificial marriage of the Middle East and Southeast Asia with their only conjugal bond a tenuous Moslem majority in both regions—surrounded by India's sea of Hindus. Indeed, East Pakistan and West Pakistan were separated not only by 1,100 miles of Indian terrain but by widely divergent, even hostile, cultures and histories.

West Pakistan: Tall, light-skinned people, Punjabis, descendants of Aryan hordes who swept into the subcontinent in the second millenium B.C., speakers of Urdu, a tongue synthesized from Persian and Hindi and written in Arabic characters; sturdy people, aggressive people, whose sparsely populated region of desert and snowcapped peaks was the frontier of the British empire in Kipling's day.

East Pakistan: Slight, dark-skinned people, speakers of Bengali, a language of Indo-Aryan origin with traces from the Dravidians whom they subjugated, industrious growers of rice and jute on rich alluvial fields carved out of verdant forest; gentle people, whose favorite pastime was *adda*—conversation—carried on end-lessly under the banyan trees in the villages and in the coffee-houses of Dacca and the wharves of Chittagong.

The improbable marriage between these two cultural opposites came in 1947. In a self-determination election the subcontinent decided to partition itself along religious lines. Five provinces with Moslem majorities split away from Hindu India. The result was the political absurdity of Pakistan, a divided nation.

From the beginning East Pakistanis felt themselves oppressed by their western brethren. As one Bengali leader said, "We have never been anything but a colony of the west." Though it contained only one-seventh of the land area of all of Pakistan, the eastern wing, a region about the size of Florida, contained half the country's population and contributed about 70 per cent of the country's foreign-exchange earnings. Bengal, in short, paid Pakistan's bills. Yet West Pakistan regularly devoured as much as 75 per cent of foreign aid and 60 per cent of export earnings, and Punjabis, in control of the country since its founding, held 85 per cent of the government jobs. More ominous in Bengali eyes was the added fact that Punjabis constituted 95 per cent of Pakistan's 275,000-man army.

Not surprisingly, talk about separatism always found eager ears in Bengal. Support for the party known as the Awami League, which advocated autonomy for Bengal, was widespread. The leader of the Awami League was Sheik Mujibur Rahman— "Mujib" to his adoring followers—a popular, leonine, 51-year-old political figure and fiery orator who once had spent 10 years in prison for urging more freedom for Bengalis.

Armed civilians and Freedom Fighters roved the streets of Jessore, East Pakistan, about 25 miles from Indian border

147

Bengal's destiny, however, was in the firm grasp of General Agha Mohammed Yahya Khan, a blunt and intensely nationalistic man who took over the government when the avuncular Ayub Khan stepped aside in March 1969. Yahya (pronounced Ya-*hee*-uh) imposed martial law and declared, "I'll be damned if I'll see Pakistan divided." Though Yahya discarded his military uniform in favor of civilian clothes when he assumed the presidency, he nonetheless occasionally carried a swagger stick, giving credence to the old Pakistani saying, "A general galloping upon a stallion is slow to dismount."

On the other hand Yahya at first gave believable evidence that he did not seek power. He decided to move ahead with plans not only for national elections but for a new constitution as well. The elections, first in the 23-year history of the country, were held Dec. 7, 1970, just three weeks after the devastating cyclone in Bengal. After that disaster, which took half a million lives, Yahya had been shockingly slow in the eyes of the distressed Bengalis to send aid; tons of grain sat undelivered for days in West Pakistan warehouses, and Yahya himself waited a fortnight before visiting the stricken area.

Thus when Bengalis went to the polls in the national elections they were chafing over yet another grievance against the West.

Sheik Mujibur Rahman, leader of Awami League, holding news conference

Further goaded by Mujib's oratory, the Bengalis voted in such numbers that Mujib's Awami League won 167 of the 169 seats allotted the East in the 313-member national assembly. That gave the league a solid majority and assured Mujib the post of prime minister of Pakistan.

That was a turn of events Punjabi politicians simply had not anticipated. West Pakistan's most popular political leader, the left-leaning Zulfikar Ali Bhutto, flatly refused to participate in the new parliament and President Yahya abruptly postponed the opening of the assembly indefinitely. Within hours of Yahya's decree, Mujib called a general strike in East Pakistan.

Eventually Yahya flew from the West Pakistan capital of Islamabad to Dacca for discussions with Mujib. He wanted to find out just how much autonomy Mujib wanted for Bengal. Mujib actually was not calling for full independence, but rather for a program that would allow East and West each to control its own taxation, trade and foreign aid. Even that was unacceptable to Yahya and the half dozen generals who were his closest advisers.

While Mujib and Yahya talked, Yahya's military commander in East Pakistan, Lt. Gen. Tikka Khan, quietly began a covert troop buildup in Bengal, flying in reinforcements from the West in Boeing 707s commandeered from Pakistan International Airways. By March 25 Tikka Khan had doubled his forces in Bengal to 60,000 men. That same day Yahya broke off his talks with Mujib. He left Dacca, flew back to Islamabad and outlawed the Awami League. Five hours later Tikka Khan unleashed his troops.

Tanks crashed through the streets of Dacca. Flamethrowers set sections of the city ablaze and machineguns mowed down fleeing civilians. The campus of Dacca University, a hive of separatists, was reduced to a bloody shambles. In cities throughout Bengal—Khalishpur, Chittagong, Jessore, Kushtia—the destruction and carnage were repeated. In country villages Bengalis were shot down in the fields and their bodies dumped into community water wells. By mid-April the campaign was complete. Estimates of the number of dead ranged from 200,000 to more than half a million. In Dacca, even street names were changed to eliminate vestiges of Bengali culture. Shankari Bazar Road became Tikka Khan Road.

Bengali resistance was sporadic, and at times fierce. At the Rajabagh Police Barracks 1,000 surrounded Bengali policemen fought to the last. Throughout Bengal elements of the Mukti Bahini, the Liberation Army, said to number 25,000 fighters, conducted sabotage raids—blowing up power stations in Dacca, severing the railroad at the port city of Chittagong—and tried to organize into an effective guerrilla army. There was evidence, too, that not all the bloodletting was done by the Punjabis. Some reports filtered out of the villages telling of Mukti Bahini raids that left suspected collaborators slaughtered in their beds.

And so throughout the month of August Bengalis by the weary millions trudged across their borders into India and scattered into some 1,500 refugee camps. The United States government committed $70.5 million to their aid and private American organizations—the International Rescue Committee, UNICEF, Catholic Relief Services, Americans for Children's Relief, among others—quickly raised $1.8 million and 45 other countries added $73.5 million more.

By mid-August more than 360,000 tons of food grains were on their way to beleaguered Bengal. But the suffering remained indescribably severe and it showed in the hollow faces of the refugees.

As one doctor said, "The people are not even crying any more."

Unlucky Start for New Rail Passenger System

*Complaints about service, two work stoppages and a wreck
That killed 10 persons marred Amtrak's initial year*

MISFORTUNE PLAGUED the inauguration of a new railroad passenger network in the United States. Within its first 40 days the system was criticized for substandard service and equipment, paralyzed by a nationwide strike and then beset by a grinding, flaming wreck that took 10 lives.

A second strike took place in July and August.

The Illinois Central's renowned City of New Orleans left Chicago at 8 a.m. on June 10, with 200 passengers in 13 coaches drawn by four diesel locomotives. It was due in New Orleans at 1:30 a.m. the next day, but by early afternoon the train was a mass of shattered coaches, some threaded by broken rails.

The derailment occurred three miles northwest of Salem, in southern Illinois, while the train was traveling more than 90 miles an hour. Seven cars, overturned, skidded along the roadbed. Ripped-up rails were twisted into grotesque patterns. Rescuers using acetylene torches cut their way through barriers of steel to reach the injured, who numbered 94.

Charles Baker, of Brinkley, Ark., said he witnessed the wreck from the truck he was driving about six blocks away. "I saw a rail shoot out from the side of the train," he said. "Then the cars started piling up and fire and smoke started boiling up."

Illinois Central officials said the accident probably resulted from the sudden locking of wheels on the lead locomotive.

Even during its organization the new system was opposed by many congressmen, some labor unions and much of the public. But it was apparent that the individual railroads wanted to drop their passenger service as unprofitable unless financial aid was forthcoming. Congress authorized the formation of the National Railroad Passenger Corp., a quasigovernmental corporation which on April 19 chose Amtrak as the name of the nationwide service in preference to Railpax, the original nickname, on the ground that Railpax was too closely associated with the deteriorating system which was being replaced.

Amtrak went into operation May 1. Its aim was faster, more efficient, more comfortable service, but passengers on the New Orleans to Los Angeles run, aboard rolling stock which Amtrak inherited almost immediately, reported coaches that smelled of sweat and unflushed toilets, of dim lighting, of air conditioners that failed to work in 101-degree heat and of roomette doors that rattled and popped open. Improvements were to come, however.

During its organization Amtrak had eliminated about 175 trains, some of them long-distance flyers that had become part

Sister Ann Joachim, attorney and nun at Siena Heights College in Adrian, Mich., who made futile attempt to save the Wabash Cannon Ball, waved to crew of the historic train as it made a final journey through Adrian

The City of New Orleans passenger train, twisted and smoking, after derailment in Illinois, a wreck that took 10 lives and injured 94 persons

As many train schedules were blanked with the advent of AMTRAK, a Chicago passenger anxiously sought a substitute train to take him home

of the national heritage. The Wabash Cannon Ball and the Manhattan Limited were examples. On the eve of Amtrak's debut, many of the expiring trains made their final runs in an aura of champagne farewells.

Union leaders and passenger groups had opposed Amtrak for a variety of reasons, among them job losses and cancellation of so many trains. Critics in Congress had cited one problem: Amtrak held the license, but the trains actually were operated by the railroads, and the train crews were still employes of the individual lines. Some contended that Amtrak had inherited work rules and attitudes of workers that had contributed to the decline of passenger train travel in recent years.

On May 16, 10,000 signalmen, representing only 2 per cent of the 540,000 U.S. rail workers, struck for more pay and set up picket lines that halted the nation's rail operations. The result was a mass layoff of thousands of workers in mines and factories and hardship for millions of commuters across the land.

President Nixon called upon Congress to do something about the stoppage, which had taken place during a week designated by the White House as a period saluting "Transportation; Filling the Needs of a Growing America." Within two days Congress had rushed through a special law aimed at curbing the walkout and giving the signalmen an interim pay boost of 13.5 per cent.

Amtrak was back in business, but only temporarily. Critics continued their attacks. They claimed that the service would not be able to attract sufficient patronage from the trains' major competitors—speedy airliners on long routes, automobiles over shorter distances.

Rail officials took the complaints in stride, declaring that growing congestion of highways and airways would turn more riders to trains.

"Success will depend on the American people and how they respond," said Secretary of Transportation John A. Volpe. "They will be our boss."

Labor acted again in July, launching a walkout that lasted 18 days and froze service on 10 carriers, including five major lines: the Union Pacific, the Southern, the Southern Pacific, the Norfolk and Western and the Santa Fe.

The strike also affected more than 150,000 rail workers and more than half of the freight traffic in the nation.

Wheat from the Midwest piled up on sidings or was stacked in huge mounds in the main streets of some towns. Produce lay rotting in southern yards and chickens went hungry for lack of corn. In Appalachia, coal choked the pit heads, shutting down many mines.

The California Growers Council reported that farmers in that state, providing 40 per cent of the nation's produce, suffered a $35 million loss on their crops. Agriculture spokesmen estimated that field hands and allied business lost $100 million. Local markets were glutted with melons, and lettuce was plowed under when growers ran out of emergency storage space.

The damaging strike ended Aug. 2, with the signing of a contract calling for pay boosts totaling 42 per cent over 42 months, and the United Transportation Union called off its pickets. Established in the new contract were some work rule changes that the railroads had been seeking for years, such as the right to institute longer train runs for crews.

In October, passengers were reporting improved service and some trains were being added.

Time of Crisis Loomed for Aircraft Industry

Production problem with Lockheed TriStar airbus, along with Financial woes of other companies, held the attention of Administration and Congress for months

THE U.S. aerospace industry could look back on 1971 as a year of travail, a time of crisis—particularly for the Lockheed Aircraft Corp. But not for Lockheed alone. The problem of production of the Lockheed L-1011 TriStar airbus in the wake of Rolls-Royce receivership *(pp. 52–54)* and the threatened ending of the RB-211–22 engine program occupied the attention of the Nixon Administration and Congress for months. Lockheed also suffered a $200 million loss on its contract for the Air Force C-5A super-transport.

Lockheed had plenty of company in misery. Seattle's Boeing Co. sustained a severe setback in the cancellation of a supersonic transport prototype development program that had been making progress until the Congress cut off further funds. Cancellations and slowdowns in 747 jumbo jet orders from an undernourished airline industry also hurt the Boeing-based economy.

The Grumman Corp. came under General Accounting Office audit after the company notified the Navy of possible cost overruns on the $11.5 million F-14 twin-engine carrier-based fighter. Grumman said it might lose up to $35 million on an initial 48-plane order alone. A Congressional group headed by Sen. Mark Hatfield, R. Ore., denounced the F-14 as a mediocre plane outclassed by advanced Soviet fighters, and recommended cancellation of the program. The Defense Department looked into possible contract modifications.

Continuing sharp aches and pains from runaway cost increases and declining traffic were reported by the aircraft industry. Permission from the Civil Aeronautics Board to increase domestic fares alleviated their plight only to a degree.

Some airlines chose the merger as a solution of their difficulties. Trans Caribbean Airways blended into American Airlines. American and Western also sought marriage, with Continental, a disappointed suitor for Western, as a major opponent. Long-ailing Northeast Airlines, locked out of one CAB-approved merger by Northwest Airlines' refusal to accede to CAB-imposed restrictions, signed a merger agreement with strong and healthy Delta Air Lines and began anew the long process of trying to gain federal government permission. Eastern took over the management of Caribbean-Atlantic Airlines on a temporary basis, with a view to eventual acquisition. Aloha and Hawaiian Airlines twice agreed to merge and then disagreed.

Allegheny and Mohawk airlines also awaited CAB approval for a merger as well as Northwest Orient and National Airlines. Under the agreement in principle, one share of National would be exchanged for 0.85 of a share of Northwest.

Airline employes pitched in to help. TWA's 4,000 pilots set up a program through union chapters to generate business and improve service for their airline. Eastern's 3,660 pilots volunteered to fly overtime at straight rates with payment deferred until January 1972, and to defer up to 50 per cent of their vacation time until 1972, to give the airline greater flexibility in meeting unexpected bursts of business. Alaska Airlines asked its employes in May to take temporary cuts in pay to help the company meet its bills.

Even so, in July several airlines made known to the CAB their concern over the costs-versus-earnings picture. United disclosed it had cut back its order and options for the $16.5 million McDonnell-Douglas DC10 airbus by 28 planes, and had deferred delivery on four of the $23 million 747s from 1971 to 1973. TWA's President F. C. Wiser said that airline might have to let some of the costly 360-seat jumbo jets sit on the ground unused for lack of the passengers and cargo to warrant their use. "Although this is a fine airplane, it is simply too big for today's markets," Wiser said.

On the transatlantic routes the airlines acted to fill half-empty planes, at very low profit margins, introducing youth fares as low as $199 for the New York-Europe round trip. One result was a flood of youthful Americans invading tourist centers all over Europe during the summer months.

With all its other concerns, some elements of the airline industry were frank in expressing relief that at least for the present they were not faced with the prospect of having to buy SSTs, the 1,800-mile-an-hour supersonic airliner that Boeing and General Electric had been developing for the Transportation Department.

SST production sources were selected in 1966, and the program to develop and flight test two prototype planes got under way in 1968. With budget demands pressing in from all sides, the Congress voted in March to discontinue the project. The House of Representatives made a last-ditch effort to revive the SST in May by voting $85.3 million for continued development, but the Senate voted a week later to appropriate $155.8 million in termination funds (p. 99). Attempts to find private financing, headed by Fairchild Hiller President Edward G. Uhl, a major subcontractor, were without success.

Sen. Warren Magnuson, D. Wash., calculated that the costs of ending the SST program totaled $677 million, against about $478 million that would have been needed to complete two prototypes. With $864 million already invested in the program, he said, the U.S. government stood to lose some $1.5 billion. William M. Magruder, director of SST development for the Transportation Department, called the outlook for U.S. industry frightening in view of Lockheed's difficulties, the Boeing $1 billion debt, a McDonnell-Douglas debt of $1.5 billion, and in view of continued flight testing of the other SSTs, the Soviet TU144 and the Franco-British Concorde.

Lockheed's British relationships dated back to a vigorous competition in 1967 and 1968 for the contract to develop engines for the L-1011 trijet. In what was hailed as one of the greatest triumphs in British manufacturing history, Rolls-Royce won the contest with its RB-211 over strong competition from General Electric and Pratt & Whitney (p. 53).

In mid-1969 Lockheed's bankers extended a $400 million line of credit mainly to finance the TriStar program. By November 1970, engine development costs were said to have risen from an original estimate of $168 million to $324 million, Rolls-Royce had reported a six-month operating loss of $7.4 million, and the British government had announced the grant of $213.6 million for the RB-211 development program.

Rolls-Royce Ltd., Britain's 64-year-old engine manufacturer, went into receivership Feb. 4. Said Daniel J. Haughton, Lockheed's chairman, who was in England at the time studying the program: "We had been aware of technical, funding and scheduling difficulties that we had been assured could be solved without major impact on the total program. But we were completely surprised and appalled at the precipitate decisions made by the Rolls-Royce board of directors and the sudden withdrawal of the British government's financial support for this key industrial firm."

The British government acquired Rolls-Royce assets essential to continuation of activities important to national defense, to joint programs with other countries, and to air forces and civil airlines around the world. But the government said it had no liability with regard to the Lockheed engine contract.

Lockheed and U.S. airline officials, in a series of talks with British representatives, called for British government assurance of support for the Rolls engine program, through successful operation for the next 20 years, to reestablish the reliability of Britain's intent to develop, produce and service the commercial engine for the world's airlines. They said thousands of jobs and billions of dollars in investments in the United States, Britain and Canada, hinged upon fulfillment of the Rolls-Royce commitments. The British in turn demanded assurances of U.S. support of the Lockheed program.

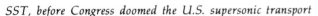
SST, before Congress doomed the U.S. supersonic transport

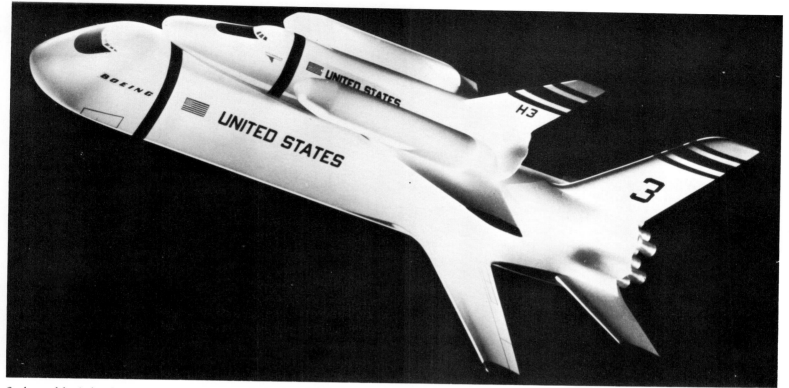

Scale model of the Grumman-Boeing Space Shuttle configuration which was under study for use in conjunction with a "heat sink" type booster of spacecraft

Secretary of the Treasury John B. Connally Jr., announced May 6 that the White House had agreed to support his request that the Congress enact legislation to guarantee a $250 million bank loan to Lockheed, to carry the company during the period of stress in its TriStar production program. Connally said $1.3 billion had been spent to develop and build the L-1011 as a competitor for the DC10 and the 747. In addition to Lockheed's own investment of $375 million and bank loans totaling $400 million, the figure included $240 million in advance payments from the airlines, and $350 million invested by Lockheed's suppliers. Connally said a Lockheed failure could have serious adverse effect on the general economy and on business and consumer confidence at a time when healthy economic expansion was essential.

In a lengthy prepared statement, Fred J. Borch, chairman and chief executive officer of General Electric, assailed Lockheed and its airline customers for selecting the Rolls "paper engine" bid, at an unrealistic price, from a company lacking experience in making large engines incorporating advanced technology.

Borch charged that in competing for the engine business the British government backed Rolls-Royce by providing subsidies in the form of long-term credit for U.S. airlines, thus establishing new dimensions in international competition against which no U.S. manufacturer could compete.

"The airlines ordering the Lockheed airbus were given 10-year loans for 90 per cent of the total engine cost, at 6¼ per cent at a time when prime rates in the U.S. were at least two points higher," Borch said.

"This subsidization was done despite understandings between the U.S. and Great Britain not to use their finances to support exports into the other's country."

Borch said that, if GE had won the competition and failed to meet its commitments as Rolls-Royce did, GE stockholders would have been liable for several hundred millions of dollars in penalties and Lockheed would not have needed U.S. government assistance. Nor would Lockheed have been in its serious financial difficulties if the British government had honored the Rolls contracts, he said.

"The British government position nets down to the fact that it will not stand behind its own British company, but it insists that the U.S. government stand behind the U.S. company," Borch said.

"This position is all the more difficult to accept when one recognizes that it was the poor performance of the British company that put the U.S. company in trouble on the airbus.

"If it accepted this British Rolls-Royce position, the U.S. government would in effect be endorsing: (1) the unsound tactics employed by Rolls-Royce in its original negotiations; (2) the British repudiation of the original Rolls-Royce contract and the heavy penalties entailed; and (3) the British subsidization that influenced U.S. airlines in the first place."

While the House considered federal guarantees of $250 million in loans to Lockheed, the Senate Banking Committee proposed a broader approach: Authority for up to $2 billion in federally-guaranteed bank loans where business failures could be so great as to adversely affect national or regional economics, with a maximum guarantee of $250 million for a single company.

On July 30 the House approved—by the tight margin of three votes—a compromise on the loan plan. Three days later, on Aug. 2, the Senate by a single vote approved identical legislation. The bill made the federal government a cosigner for $250 million in private loans to Lockheed. It established a permanent three-man board which could grant government backing on private loans to any company whose collapse might damage the economy. However, the measure was tailored specifically to Lockheed. On Aug. 9 President Nixon signed the bill.

A consortium of 24 banks, on Sept. 13, approved a $50 million loan to Lockheed, the first advance under the government's $250 million guarantee.

Summertime In Places Near and Far

Top right: British Prime Minister Edward Heath, center, shown at the helm of his yacht Morning Cloud during the Admiral's Cup yacht race at Cowes, Isle of Wight; below: The newly-crowned Miss Universe, Miss Georgina Rizk of Lebanon, center, pictured with her runners-up, left to right: Elaine Parreira of Brazil, Beba Franco of Puerto Rico, Toni Hayward of Australia and Pirjo Laitila of Finland. Below, right: Three youngsters tugging at tails and fins of whales that tried to beach themselves on the island of Gasparilla, off the Florida gulf coast

REVOLT NO. 185 FOR BOLIVIA

To the United States, Bolivia's political platform in the last ten months had appeared alarming. President Gen. Juan Jose Torres, striving to meet leftist demands, had nationalized mines owned by interests in the United States, and Russian influence had become stronger as Bolivia approved various Soviet projects in mining and oil exploration.

The right wing faction in that country also regarded the situation as perilous. Leftist concessions by Torres, the right wing claimed, had brought Bolivia to a point of economic crisis.

What was becoming almost a historic tradition in that country had been planned carefully in the six months before Aug. 19. On that day a military coup, the 185th in 144 years of independence, had taken place in the eastern Bolivian city of Santa Cruz and later spread to the capital of La Paz, where Torres' military position steadily crumbled with the Bolivian air force going to the rebel side.

The revolt had been inspired primarily by three top military leaders; Col. Hugo Banzer, who later was made president; Gen. Jaime

Florentino Mendieta and Col. Andres Selich, who was appointed interior minister. They had been supported by businessmen, rural proprietors and conservative politicians. Torres, who had taken control in a coup ten months earlier, (The World in 1970, 205), was supported by elements of the army and by the powerful central labor organization.

On Aug. 22 the rebels took over the presidential palace.

With 10 dead, another Bolivian government had been born.

FINCH PAROLED IN WIFE MURDER

Ten years ago the front pages of the major newspapers displayed sensational details revealed in the third and final trial of Dr. Bernard Finch and his sweetheart, Carole Tregoff, for the death of the physician's socialite wife Barbara.

Finch was convicted of first-degree murder and conspiracy to commit murder. His former receptionist, Miss Tregoff was convicted of second-degree murder and conspiracy to commit murder. Both were sentenced to life in prison.

Finch in 1961 became a model prisoner. He was the tennis champion of San Quentin Prison, an honor inmate and a clerk to a Protestant chaplain. Later he was moved to a minimum security institution at Chino, Calif. When, at 53, he made his second bid for freedom in 1971 he was granted parole on Aug. 17, effective Dec. 6. His girlfriend had been paroled in 1969. She returned to West Covina, Calif., took another name and was employed in the medical records department of a hospital. In 1971 she was 34.

Henry Kerr, chairman of the eight-member California Adult Authority Board that paroled him, said that Finch had been approached about jobs in Missouri, Nebraska and Maryland. The Missouri offer was from a small rural community which wanted him to operate a small hospital and clinic.

Finch's wife had been found lying on her back in a neighbor's lawn by a cruising police patrolman on the moonlit night of July 18, 1959. She had been shot, her skull was fractured and the body showed numerous scratches and bruises.

The prosecution told the jury Finch and Miss Tregoff wanted Finch's attractive wife "out of the way" so they wouldn't have to share $750,000 in community property Mrs. Finch had described in a divorce suit.

Dr. Bernard Finch paroled from life term; his sweetheart Carol Tregoff was paroled in 1969

Finch and Miss Tregoff contended Mrs. Finch pulled a gun when they met in the garage of the Finch home and died when it accidentally fired as Finch and his wife struggled for the weapon.

Those on the Adult Authority Board who opposed Finch's freedom "were somewhat concerned about the factors that came out at the time of the crime that this was a deliberate, premeditated case of murder," said Chairman Kerr.

CRIME GAINED 176% IN DECADE

The 1971 report of the Federal Bureau of Investigation showed that serious crimes increased 176 per cent during the 1960-70 decade. However, Atty. Gen. John N. Mitchell said in releasing the report that the rate of crime incidence in 1970 gained only 11 per cent over that of 1969. The gain in 1969 over 1968 had been 12 per cent and, in 1968 over 1967, 17 per cent.

Mitchell added that the 1971 report showed almost all areas of the United States were involved in the statistics—northern, southern, eastern and western states, cities, suburbs and

rural regions—and that all showed increases in 1970.

Cities led the list in the number of offenses, but the rate of increase was higher in suburbs and rural areas, the report said. The increase rate for cities was 6 per cent, against 14 per cent for suburbs and 15 per cent for the countryside.

Law enforcement officers slain in the line of duty numbered 100 in 1970, and in each case a suspect was arrested (The World in 1970, 176-178). In 1969 the number of such deaths was 86. The number of serious crimes—including

murder, forcible rape, robbery, burglary and aggravated assault—totaled more than 5.5 million in 1970.

Miami, Fla., was reported to have the highest crime rate while the San Francisco Bay area was second and New York City was third. In last year's findings the San Francisco Bay area ranked first, Albuquerque second and the Los Angeles-Long Beach area third.

Police were able to solve only one in five crimes through arrests in 1970. This compared with a solution rate of nearly one in three in 1960.

HORSES HIT BY SINISTER VIRUS

The disease was known as VEE and it swept into Texas from Mexico at the end of June. During the 2½ month epidemic that followed, a total of 1,447 horses died in Texas. The Texas Animal Health Commission, however, said that only 89 of the deaths were confirmed by laboratory tests to be caused by VEE.

Within hours after it struck, a grim battle was under way against the sinister virus, Venezuelan equine encephalomyelitis, a form of sleeping sickness.

In Texas alone, more than 570,000 horses were vaccinated for the disease, and wide areas of the south Texas coast were sprayed in a drive to kill mosquitoes carrying VEE.

New Mexico, Louisiana and Florida closed their borders to horses, mules, donkeys and burros from Texas. And the state animal health commission halted all intrastate movement of horses. The U.S. Agriculture Department declared a national emergency to provide funds for combating the dread disease.

There was another ominous aspect. The VEE virus was so highly infectious that the U.S. Army had at one time selected it as one of the seven kinds of biological weapons for development and stockpiling as germ warfare agents—out of thousands of other known disease-causing organisms, even though it was not particularly lethal to humans.

By coincidence, at the height of the VEE plague in Texas, the Army, acting on a 1969 presidential order to destroy all stockpiled biological weapons, began destroying its supplies of VEE virus.

In humans, VEE caused symptoms like influenza, treatable mainly with rest and aspirin. Symptoms included fever, diarrhea, vomiting, convulsions, headaches, muscular pain and dry cough.

Among a small number of VEE victims, the disease inflamed brain tissues, and about 2 per cent human died. Generally, however, humans who contracted the virus recovered in 24 hours to a week.

With horses it was another story. One to two days after infection a horse's temperature would rocket to 105 degrees. This was followed by loss of appetite, rapid pulse and, finally, prostration. About 50 per cent of the afflicted horses died.

Mexican officials disclosed in late July that the VEE epidemic had killed 10,000 horses and mules in the states of San Luis Potosi and Vera Cruz alone, and that 90 per cent of the 5,000 persons in Rio Verde, Mexico, were afflicted. They also revealed that five humans had died of the disease.

VEE was first diagnosed in Venezuela on the Colombia border in 1936, and the specific virus was identified two years later. By 1943 the disease had swept the island of Trinidad.

Outbreaks of Venezuelan equine encephalomyelitis in horses also occurred in Panama, Colombia, Ecuador and Peru.

Stricken colt on a horse ranch near Rio Hondo, Tex., struggling to get up

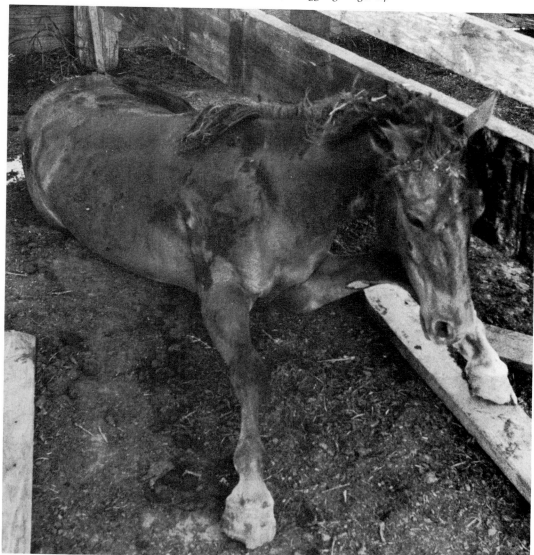

FEDERAL KENT INQUIRY DROPPED

In October 1970 the President's Commission on Campus Unrest concluded that rifle fire by members of the Ohio National Guard during demonstrations on the Kent State University campus was "unnecessary, unwarranted and inexcusable."

Nearly a year later Atty. Gen. John N. Mitchell announced that he would not order a federal grand jury investigation of occurrences which ended in the death of four students.

Mitchell's announcement on Aug. 13 said a Department of Justice review "persuades me that there is no credible evidence of a conspiracy between the National Guardsmen to shoot students on campus and that there is no likelihood of successful prosecution of individual guardsmen." He added that it was doubtful if a further investigation would produce any new evidence justifying federal grand jury action.

Following Mitchell's announcement, a statement by parents of the slain students said in part: "The shock of learning of the decision . . . is nearly as great as the shock that came when our children were killed."

After the campus deaths in May 1970 an Ohio grand jury had exonerated the guardsmen.

Robert I. White, president of Kent State, told a news conference that the grand jury's report not only was inaccurate but also represented an attack on all free universities (*The World in 1970, 187–190*).

WELFARE RESIDENCY LAW CURBED

Cost of the New York State welfare program was a record $3 billion in 1970. With rising problems and costs in housing, narcotics control, education, health, environmental protection and crime suppression in the budget crisis of 1971, one of the corrective attempts was enactment of a statute requiring one year's residence in the state by all welfare applicants.

The residency law became effective June 22. Within the next month 211 relief seekers were rejected in New York City and about 100 others elsewhere in the state. During that period the New York Civil Liberties Union challenged the residence requirement, citing the case of Pedro Lopez, a Florida migrant worker.

Lopez, his wife Maria and seven children came to New York State June 26 and, when he could not find work, he applied for welfare aid on June 29. He was turned down. But by July 22 a restraining order had halted enforcement of the residency law.

Thereafter a hearing on constitutionality of the residency provision was taken before a panel of three federal judges in Buffalo, N.Y. Judge Paul R. Hays of the Second Circuit Court of Appeals and U.S. District Court Judges John T. Curtin and John O. Henderson found the residency statute "unconstitutional under the equal protection clause of the 14th Amendment to the United States Constitution." After oral arguments their decision had required only four minutes of deliberation. Marvin K. Karpatkin, counsel for the C.L.U., held in his argument that in 1969 the U.S. Supreme Court had declared residency requirements in welfare cases violated constitutional rights of travel and equal protection. The 1969 case involved Connecticut, Pennsylvania and the District of Columbia (*The World in 1969, 162–163*).

DEATH TOLL IN FERRY FIRE: 26

Dawn was breaking over the southeast coast of Italy Aug. 28 when a raging fire swept through the crowded Greek ferryboat *Heleanna*, creating a panic that drove more than 1,000 persons, many in nightclothes, into the Adriatic. At least 26 lost their lives.

"I saw people jumping into the sea with no lifejackets," said Jean d'Heibonnez, 41, a French surgeon. "There was no assistance from the sailors to coordinate the exit."

But in Piraeus, Greece, the owner of the 11,232-ton vessel, Constantine Efthymiades, said the crew of 92 offered all assistance possible. He acknowledged that there were only 12 lifeboats aboard, but added that scores of inflatable liferafts capable of carrying hundreds were available.

A gas explosion in the *Heleanna's* galley started the fire.

"Nobody told us there was a fire on board," D'Heinbonnez related. "Nobody told us to abandon ship. We had to do everything ourselves. . . . We all assembled on the sundeck. There was no announcement from the loudspeakers."

Hans Gold of Salsburg, Austria, his wife and three teenaged children, saved themselves by jumping overboard in lifejackets. "I have been at sea many times, but I never witnessed such mad scenes," he said.

A crewman who refused to give his name said he lowered two lifeboats, but only with difficulty, because their cables were rusty. Only two others were lowered, he added.

The *Heleanna* burned for six hours. Merchant ships and fishing boats in the vicinity reported they picked up 1,151 survivors, one of whom died later in a hospital. But Efthymiades claimed only 1,128 were aboard. About 70 were listed as missing.

An Italian pilot flying overhead said he saw rows of automobiles tumble into the ferry's hold as flames licked up through the deck.

The day before the fire the *Heleanna* had left the Greek port of Patras. Two days later its captain, Demetrios Antipas, was arrested in Brindisi, Italy, where the survivors were taken. The charges against him: Multiple homicide and neglect. Officers said he had tried to leave Italy on a ship headed for Greece.

Antipas also was accused of sailing without adequate fire-fighting and lifesaving equipment, and with leaving the ferry while "numerous passengers were still aboard." The captain denied these accusations and said he was the last person to leave the vessel.

But Piergiuseppe Fiorito, a Milan engineer, countered: "The captain was among the first to abandon the ship, and he was immediately followed by the crew. I saw them with my own eyes."

Greek ferryboat Heleanna, gutted by fire in South Adriatic with at least 26 lives lost

FOR THE RECORD

RESIGNED. For personal reasons, John S. D. Eisenhower, son of the late President Dwight D. Eisenhower, from his post as ambassador to Belgium, on Aug. 16. President Nixon, a close friend, accepted his resignation with regret. The President stated in a letter that Eisenhower had carried out his responsibilities with exceptional competence and in so doing had contributed significantly toward strengthening the long-time friendship between the United States and Belgium.

Medical aide in blood-stained smock leaving
Attica prison after helping wounded ➤

September

Violence in Prisons: I
43 Slain Inside Attica

Detective atop an Attica building kept watch through binoculars and the scope of an AR16 rifle

JACKPOT ONE, take off and vector off the north wall, go out half a mile and circle. Do not fly over the yard. . . ."

"Jackpot 2, on your first crop, make sure you cover 'Times Square.'"

An all-night rain had stopped. The $1,275,000, highly porous concrete outer walls of New York's Attica state prison looked as if they were bleeding. It was 9:42 a.m. (EDT), September 13, 1971.

"All forces in position."

9:43 a.m. "Cut the power! . . . The first detail near the fire apparatus, charge those hoses! . . . Contact the sheriff and have him get all available ambulances to the northeast gate."

9:45 a.m. "Zero in on your targets, and wait for the drop . . . Jackpot Two, become airborne and launch your mission . . . RA, you are not to take action until the drop. The officer in charge will give the order on hostile action."

Two sharp cracks, the voice of a .270-magnum rifle.

9:46 a.m. "Move in! Move in! The drop has been made."

*   *   *   *

The narrative in the State Police radio transmissions had announced the end of the beginning for America's bloodiest, most violent prison revolt.

One guard already had died.

By 9:48 a.m. that Monday, 97 hours after 1,241 prisoners at the "maximum security" correctional facility exploded in a fury of beatings, burnings and territorial war, another 42 men were dead or fatally wounded.

Pathologists determined that three white inmates had died sometime during those 97 hours, of an unusual pattern of multiple stab sounds.

Some of the victims died at the prison infirmary, others en route to or at hospitals 10 to 45 miles away. Ten days later, another prisoner died of his wounds; two days after that, another. A month after the riot's eruption, another guard died.

The body count: Correctional officers, 7; accounting clerks, 2; industrial foremen, 2; prisoners, 32; total, 43.

The dead prison employes, all of whom—except the first, who was injured fatally during the initial riot—were among 39 hostages seized by the rampaging inmates on the first day, died of gunshot wounds, pathologists determined. A few also had lacerations on their throats and necks.

The casualties included 25 wounded hostages, five wounded state troopers and up to 100 wounded prisoners.

"Attica"—the word alone almost instantly became a part of the American's short-form language—erupted from the unknown of green, trimmed Wyoming County, N.Y., into the deceptively familiar of dinner-table and barstool knowledge, 18 days after George Jackson, Soledad Brother, died at San Quentin Prison, San Rafael, Calif., in what authorities there said was an escape attempt. The Attica population of 2,254 complete with a contingent of politicized blacks like Jackson, heard the news that August Saturday.

The next day, the long-unsettled institution served its usual Sunday morning breakfast. Only a few, if any, of the convicts ate.

"It was the weirdest thing . . ." recalled Sgt. Jack English, a guard, white like all the 396 guards there. "But nobody picked up a tray or a spoon, and nobody took any food.

"They just walked through the line and went to their seats and they sat down. They looked straight ahead and nobody made a sound . . . Then we noticed that almost all had some black on them. . . . It scared us because a thing like that takes a lot of organization, a lot of solidarity, and we had no idea they were so well organized."

The second breakfast shift less than three weeks later, on Sept. 9, evolved into the shouting, pipe-wielding vanguard of the rebellion, a rebellion whose organization became starkly evident as the rebels established their territorial imperative over a cellblock and a half for four days, complete with their own work details, jail, asylum, cabinet and "people's central committee." According to accounts given by prisoners during their occupation of Cellblock D and parts of Cellblock B, to reporters they invited in, the immediate spark of the riot was struck on the flint of an incident in an exercise yard the afternoon before.

To a veteran guard, it looked like a fight as he stepped through a door into A Yard. He approached the pair and grasped the black man on the shoulder. The inmate wheeled and swung, striking the guard, an act—in the context of the prison subculture—comparable to high treason.

The white man then vigorously defended the black man and, the accounts continued, the guards decided not to press the issue. But that night, the prison grapevine had it, unidentified guards dragged the two prisoners away—to "the box" isolation cells, their fellows presumed. These prisoners said the two were beaten as they were taken from their one-man cells, and a Puerto Rican inmate was said to have thrown a glass at a guard escorting one prisoner, cutting the guard's face.

What happened the next morning, Thursday, remained unclear. Two accounts with credibility were offered: One said the 94 men on 5 Gallery refused to line up for breakfast's second shift when their escort guards unlocked the cells—because one unlocked cell contained the unidentified Puerto Rican who threw the glass. Outmanned, the guards relented and opened the cell, this account went, and the inmates joined the second shift of about 700 men.

But when they left the mess hall en route to the exercise yard, they found the door to the yard locked. The guard told them, "No yard today." The riot was on.

The other account held that the 5 Gallery prisoners were walking to breakfast at about 8:50 a.m.—"Brother Richard" Clarke, a Black Muslim minister who later served as a leader of the rebels, among them—when they burst into rebellion, surging through the cellblock, overpowering the first five guards in their way and racing throughout the compound, freeing galleries, destroying doors and gates, storming the 15-feet-high covered-corridor catwalks separating the four yards and converging at "Times Square" and its fenced-in guard shed overlooking the interior.

The guard there, William Quinn, 28, had his skull fractured in two places as he fought the prisoners with his only weapon, a nightstick. Reports persisted that he was thrown from the catwalk after being subdued.

Raiding parties moved from Times Square throughout Cellblocks B, D and C; the mess halls where—a Wyoming County deputy sheriff said—pipes were hidden under loaves of bread

Shotgun carrying State Police passing a gate at Attica about two hours after troopers and other officers stormed the area

Left, Attica inmates raised their fists in salute as they voiced their demands in a negotiating session with Commissioner Russell Oswald. Center, Corrections Commissioner Russell Oswald listened as a prisoner shouted demand that he also be kept hostage until inmates' demands were met. Right, prison guards showed sharpened spears they took from Attica inmates

on trays. Outside the blocks they spread into the machine shop, the chapel and the school, setting fire to the three buildings but also gathering raw materials and such tools as grinding wheels, as they roamed.

Injured guards stumbled through the gates, some wearing only blankets. The prisoners captured the metal shop, where another ascendant leader was working at the time: Herbert X. Blyden, also a Muslim, who had a 72-count indictment standing against him for his alleged role in a 1970 uprising at the Tombs detention house in New York City.

The Attica population was mustered in the corridors and yards, with Cellblock D swiftly shaping into the command post, as the farthest from the administration building and the nearest to the shops. For four hours the convicts ran free within the walls, looting, seizing hostages, setting buildings to the torch, fortifying, making weapons from clubs and pipes, loading two teargas guns and "liberating" E block, which was separate from the main compound and housed old, infirm convicts. Clarke and Blyden had assumed their positions of authority. Shortly after noon the ranks of the State Police that sped to the scene had swollen to about 250 riot-equipped men.

The assembled troopers heard this directive from Capt. Henry F. Williams, head of the Bureau of Criminal Investigations for that region in western New York: "If somebody on the other side gets killed, well, that's the way it's gotta be. You're to take no crap from anybody. Don't lose your weapon and don't lose your buddy."

Flying to Albany to take charge was the reform-oriented state correctional services commissioner, who had taken office just eight months earlier and had met with Attica prisoners just a week before to hear their grievances. Outside, the families of guards and other employes not yet heard from began their agonized vigil. Guard Quinn's family sped to a Rochester hospital where a sheriff's deputy had driven him when Clarke —persuaded by the blood dripping from the unconscious guard's ears—had him passed through the new "no man's land" to officials and aid.

The 39 hostages were thrown into a circle in D Yard—some of them beaten, all of them stripped, bound, then dressed in prison garb and blindfolded. Black Muslims stepped in as

self-appointed guards of this human collateral, fending off other inmates with "scores to settle."

The leaders established a secretariat at a makeshift table near the wall. Shortly after 2:30 p.m., Herman Schwartz, a Buffalo law professor, and State Assemblyman Arthur O. Eve, a black, were allowed through the corridor under the catwalk—already a ruin of glass and barricades, guarded by turbaned, helmeted inmates—into the rebel territory to hear demands.

The rebels demanded that Commissioner Russell G. Oswald—who the week before had used the session with Attica inmates to announce sweeping, controversial reforms in prison life—hear them out.

Either Oswald or Gov. Nelson A. Rockefeller, they demanded. The governor was notified by a telephone at his Pocantico Hills estate. That night he would dispatch T. Norman Hurd, a top advisor and director of state operations.

Oswald, against the advice of Warden Vincent Mancusi and other aides there, went in, returning with 15 demands to which he already had responded favorably: Application of the state minimum-wage laws to prison shop work, freedom of political activity, religious freedom, an end to censorship of publications, more liberal communication with the outside, a full release without parole when an inmate reaches "conditional-release" status, judicial resentencing of parole violators rather than administrative resentencing by jailers, training for guards, more fruit and less pork, a more modern school, a full-time physician, a prisoners' grievance committee, more recreation time and less cell-time, one exercise yard instead of four.

That evening Oswald returned to the floodlight-bathed yard, now a tent city with camp fires, bringing with him a "pool" of reporters the rebels demanded.

The prisoners called for a committee of outsiders to act as intermediaries—among them attorney William Kunstler, known nationally for his defense in 1970 of the Chicago Seven (*The World in 1970, 34–37*); Tom Wicker, columnist and associate editor of The New York Times, who had written what many considered sympathetic columns upon's Jackson's death; Huey P. Newton, the Black Panther party's "defense minister," who was a co-founder of the Panthers in California.

They sought also a federal court injunction against any "physical and mental reprisals" for their acts. This was drafted late Thursday night in Warden Mancusi's office by Oswald, Professor Schwartz and a rebel representative. Schwartz flew with it to a judicial conference in Vermont, for Judge John T. Curtin of U.S. District Court in Buffalo to sign, and returned with it Friday morning.

The rebels called it inadequate. Apparently forgotten was the paper Oswald had given them Thursday night at the height of tension: his signed statement of "No administrative reprisals against prisoners for activities of Sept. 9, 1971." The governor's office had rapidly qualified it, anyway, pointing out that amnesty for criminal acts was impossible; no one had that authority.

Officials began rounding up the outside mediators on Friday, after the commissioner, having been threatened at a morning meeting with inmate leaders, decided not to return to Cellblock D's yard.

Those named by the prisoners were sought, and the governor added to the list, sending his secretary, Robert R. Douglass. Others were U.S. Rep. Herman Badillo, D-N.Y., the first Puerto Rican elected to Congress; Alfredo Mathew, a Manhattan school superintendent; retired Maj. Gen. Almerin C. O'Hara, head of the state Office of General Services; regional legislators and those involved with prisoners as chairmen of committees and study groups.

The observer-mediator committee met with the leaders and their constituents. Anyone who wished could "get it off his chest" at the open microphone before the seated committee, but the standing, alert "secretariat" periodically cleared the air of rhetoric and drove home their real demands. Suspicion was the second hand on every watch.

The outsiders' committee and the press pool observing them Friday night did not leave D yard until 4 a.m. Saturday—the last time a working newsman entered the prison in that capacity until late Monday afternoon.

One faction drew up the proposals as agreed upon. A three-man committee was dispatched to negotiate with Wyoming County Dist. Atty. Louis James, who would handle any subsequent prosecutions for the state.

Over a pancake breakfast, Wicker, Publisher Clarence Jones of The Amsterdam News, a Black weekly, and Julian Tepper of the National Legal Aid and Defenders Association softened an adamant James enough to secure a signed promise of no "indiscriminate mass prosecutions," each case on its merits.

Back in the stewards' room, Kunstler objected, on the grounds the statement would have an adverse affect on the inmates' attitude if its ramifications were explored. The committee agreed the promise would be relayed without comment, and they set about structuring a final draft of the demands in the afternoon and into the evening.

At mid-afternoon, with the outsiders closeted away, the rebels released a middle-aged hostage, Anthony Sangiacomo, who apparently had suffered a heart attack. And a black inmate fought his way through the rebel's security lines into trooper territory. Oswald and the State Police thus had two new sources of information about the activity in D yard and sources inherently friendly to them, as some mediators were not.

From Sangiacomo had come a week later the first stories of inmates and "maybe one or two hostages" already dead, of beatings, of mutilations.

The mediators, although visibly exhausted, spoke optimistically. Kunstler told reporters Oswald had agreed "on most of the other" demands, except full amnesty, transfer to another county, the demand for elimination of the catwalks and two demands requiring legislative action: a minimum wage for shop work and an end to the present parole system.

Shortly before dusk Black Panther National Chairman Bobby Seale arrived from Oakland, Calif. Ninety minutes before, at 4:30 p.m., Quinn died at Rochester's Strong Memorial Hospital.

Seale was not passed through the gates upon his first arrival. Instead, he was driven around the driveway to the road that passes the prison, on the other side of which was a parking lot for a bar that closed when it heard Seale might come. Gathered there were about 50 young radicals bannering empathy with the prisoners.

"If anything happens to those guards, the state and the governor should be charged with murder," Seale told the cheering demonstrators. He told reporters the sight of armed troopers and insistent reporters made him nervous; then he left.

An hour and a half later, he returned under State Police escort and was passed through the gate with Kunstler. His aides passed out a statement from the Panther central committee:

"The prison guards, called 'hostages,' have actually in reality been placed under arrest by the 1,280 prisoners who are rightly redressing their grievances concerning the harassing, brutal and inhuman treatment to which they are constantly subjected. . . . A promise of amnesty is the first thing that must be done to start negotiations of the prisoners' 27 demands. This is the only bail the arrested guards can have, from the analysis of the Black Panther party."

Seale, with objections to his presence overruled, functioned as a member of the outsiders' committee for two hours, saying little. Publisher Jones was left in D Yard with the delicate task of relaying to the equally edgy rebels the proposals—demands drawn by the committee with wording designed to be acceptable to all combatants. Things were not going well for Jones, he later said. He reported he sensed the convicts felt they had been sold out, although there was no violent response as he presented the 28 proposals Oswald had signed as "acceptable (to him) at this time."

The agreed-upon proposals included an ombudsman for the prisoners, "true religious freedom," political activity; such innovations as a Latin library and a narcotics-treatment program; more black and Spanish-speaking guards; inmate participation in institutional policy-making through an "inmate grievance commission"; recommendations to the legislature in line with the demands that required statutory changes; improvements in daily living conditions, the visitation environment and rehabilitation programs.

The prisoners were standing firm on the questions of total amnesty, the firing of Mancusi and the removal of the prison's two doctors, who served them part-time only.

And Oswald, according to briefings he later gave congressmen, was ready to give the orders to smash the rebellion that afternoon. He delayed in deference to the observers' pleas as they sought to buy time by appealing directly to Rockefeller, who had cancelled his trip to the national governors' conference in Puerto Rico. But he issued a statement that said, in partial reference to the amnesty question, "I do not have the constitutional authority to grant such a demand and I would not, even if I had the authority, because to do so would undermine the very essence of our free society—the fair and impartial application of the law."

Shortly after 1 p.m., Oswald told the committee he was drafting an ultimatum:

". . . I urgently request you to release the hostages unharmed, now, and to accept the recommendations of the committee of outside observers, whose recommendations were approved by me, and join with me in restoring order to this institution.

"Only after these steps are taken am I willing to meet with a five-member committee chosen by you to discuss any grievances you may have and to create a mechanism by which you can be assured that the recommendations I have agreed to are implemented. . . ."

Wicker, publisher Jones, Badillo and State Sen. John Dunne, whose committee supervised state prison affairs for the legislature, spent 40 minutes on the telephone with Rockefeller, who already had the backing of President Richard Nixon.

The four pleaded with the governor to come to Attica. He said he would not. They persisted. He said he would reply through his secretary—a reply that took the form of Oswald giving them, several minutes later, a copy of the ultimatum already being read in D Yard.

The committee left the yard at the end of the afternoon that had begun with the stabbing deaths of prisoners Kenneth Hess and Michael Privatera—deaths not confirmed until after the prison was secured.

Outside, the mediators made their desperation public, issuing this statement:

"The committee of observers at Attica prison is now convinced that a massacre of prisoners and guards may take place in this institution. For the sake of our common humanity, we call on every person who hears these words to implore the governor of this state to consult with the observer committee so that we can spend time and not lives in an attempt to resolve the issues before us."

Rockefeller answered:

"From the beginning of the tragic situation involving riots and hostages at the Attica Correctional Facility which imperil the lives of many persons, including 39 innocent citizens and dedicated law-enforcement officers, I have been in constant direct contact with Commissioner Oswald and my representatives on the scene. Every effort has been made by the state to resolve the situation and to establish order, hopefully, by peaceable means. . . .

"The key issue at stake, however, is still the demand for total amnesty for any criminal acts which may have occurred. . . . In view of the fact that the key issue is total amnesty . . . I do not feel that my physical presence on the site can contribute to a peaceful settlement. . . ."

Seventy trucks of Army National Guard troops and chemical-warfare equipment were bivouacked 10 miles away, under a cloak of secrecy and official denial of their call-up that lasted well past the last shot the next day. But Rockefeller had signed the order sometime Sunday.

Oswald left the prison for less than four hours. His face when he stepped from the state limousine on his return showed no sign of sleep. He agreed to reissue Sunday's ultimatum, with a one-hour time limit.

The day shift of State Troopers came on, masks and rifles at the ready, ponchos and grey riot helmets on. The night shift did not come out. At 8:30 a.m., Oswald's spokesman handed press copies of the ultimatum. The helicopters cleared their engines after a night of rain.

Brother Clarke asked for an extension until 9 a.m. Granted.

Trench fortifications erected the night before were filled with liquid fuel, mostly gasoline. Barricades were reinforced with more barrels, doors and chairs, and with stakes to impale assaulters going over them.

The hostages were taken from their protective circle and, in a hurried fashion, parceled out to other inmates randomly chosen as "executioners."

Twelve hostages were dumped in the gasoline-filled middle trench. The booby traps of volatile peat moss and oil, wired with time charges, and the crude catapult-type rocket launchers were checked. The grinding wheels that had been going all night, fashioning knives and spears and other makeshift hand weapons, stopped their whir. Inmates gestured with what appeared to be knives at the throats of the blindfolded, supine hostages. Then they pulled them out of the ditches, pits and trenches and marched eight across the yard to the catwalks they controlled.

It was 9:11 a.m. when the radio reported, "Yes, the four hostages are at each corner of 'Times Square' with knives at their throats."

The foot-soldiers were in position. Riflemen were ready.

Walter Dunbar, a deputy corrections commissioner for

*Above, bedclothing and other debris made a shambles of Attica yard.
Right, bullet-shattered windows overlooking courtyard after the siege*

human rights, was in the A block corridor facing down the rebel security guards. Oswald was at his desk waiting for a telephone call for him, The News reported in its copyright series.

The hostages were standing, their necks arched, on Times Square, inmate wrists cocked at their throats with what appeared to be knives in photographs seen later. The helicopter with the bullhorn was airborne, checking the weather. The rain had stopped.

Five squads of troopers were coiled at the doors to the catwalks from Cellblocks A and C. One squad of 25, armed with shotguns loaded with buckshot, had attached to it two guards, to identify their comrades, outfitted by the rebels in prison garb.

The squad of 27 was termed the "force rescue squad" by trooper Maj. John Monahan, who said he gave his men two objectives in "this hazardous chore": "to obtain, to effect the rescue of the hostages and, two, to regain control of the correctional facility."

Jackpot Two, a CH-34 helicopter, was on the way.

Within a second, the concentration of tear gas, pepper gas and mustard gas was dropped right on top of the makeshift sheet-shelter on Times Square under which the hostages and "executioners" stood.

The firing began—the rescue squad bursting through one catwalk door, the first squad of catwalk-assigned riflemen through the other—blasting through the obstacles erected 50 yards down the path, picking off 11 or 12 inmates and, preliminary evidence suggested, at least two hostages on Times Square.

The rescuers dropped their ladders into D Yard, having wiped through the convergence as a squad of riflemen manned each quarter of the catwalk, firing below into the yards as they thought necessary—"a crossfire," Rockefeller later said.

Troopers involved reported most prisoners among the 1,240 in the D Yard area did not resist.

The rescue strike-force members say it took them a minute and a half to break the "obstacles" on the catwalks and get into the yard, another two and a half minutes to achieve their objective, the rescue of the hostages. And that was how Monohan would measure his men's success, by the fact that 29 hostages were now safe.

They were bloody when brought out for an ambulance ride to a town or city outside, or to succumb in the prison infirmary with dying, bloody prisoners.

The dead and injured hostages' blindfolds had fallen, red with blood, around their necks. The deed that all non-prisoners had been primed for was believed now, and it spread like wildfire—slashed throats.

Reporters relayed the slashed-throats "fact," some with attribution but none with substantial skepticism.

Prisoners were being rounded up from their prone surrender, stripped and herded through yard doors into other yards, through lines of troopers and guards with hickory billy clubs. Oswald's aides four days later admitted that lawmen had "firmly prodded" inmates through the door and down the lines that, inmates and some of the observers later charged, some in court, were beatings-by-gauntlet.

Fifteen hostages had passed through the front gate. Capt. Williams had dispatched his identification men to D block.

"I want 10 bureau men. . . . Needless to say, they're to get as much as possible on those homicides, and take them to the morgue." This, at 10:21 a.m., was the first word of death behind the walls.

Oswald and his spokesman, Jerry Houlihan, were walking from the administration to the gate to the gate-side ropes, to read a statement to the reporters captive behind police lines on the wall side of the roadway. It was 10:41 a.m.

"For the past four days I have been doing everything humanly possible to bring this tragic situation to a peaceful conclusion," Oswald said.

". . . As you know, during this ordeal I have personally met with inmates on several occasions in areas under their control. I brought together a citizen's observer committee most of whom were requested by the inmates, to assist me in bringing a peaceful resolution," Oswald continued.

"I understand and am sympathetic to many of the grievances expressed by the inmates . . .

"A federal court injunction demanded by the inmates to guarantee that no administrative reprisals would be taken was obtained overnight.

"In spite of all these positive efforts towards peaceful resolution on my part, the inmates have steadfastly refused to release the hostages and meet with me on neutral ground for a final settlement. . . .

"This morning I made a final attempt to resolve the situation without resort to force. The inmates were requested to release the hostages unharmed immediately and to join with me in restoring order to the Attica Correctional Facility.

"Additional time was asked for by the inmates, and the request was granted. It proved to be only a delaying tactic this morning. The leaders never returned but callously herded eight hostages within view with weapons at their throats. This is the way they chose to give me their decision. . . .

"A few moments ago, state police troopers moved into the unsecured areas of the institution to restore order, under specific orders to only use force to meet force, to protect the lives of the hostages. At the same time, a riot-control gas was dispersed by helicopters in an effort to immobilize persons in the unsecured areas." He added:

"The action now under way was initiated with extreme reluctance, only after all attempts to achieve a peaceful solution failed. To delay the action any longer would not only jeopardize innocent lives but would threaten the security of the entire correctional system in this state. Armed rebellion of this type we have faced threatens the destruction of our free society. We cannot permit that destruction to happen.

"It has been an agonizing decision."

And Oswald, 62, returned inside the fortress, without responding to questions.

Houlihan, although unprepared for the harshness of the voices or the substance of the queries, remained for that. 11:29 a.m.

There were the routine, the obvious questions.

How, Jerry? How did the hostages die? Who killed them, Jerry? What about slashed throats? We have several reports of slashed throats, Jerry; can you confirm them? "I have no information on that." Why not? Did they or didn't they have slashed throats? We have a right to know! The public has to be told these things!

It became the inquisition of a mob trying an already condemned man. The same questions, the same non-response for 10 minutes.

Then, exasperated, Houlihan let out the same hearsay he had gotten and not confirmed, that reporters were then trying to confirm with the "official spokesman" tag: "Several of the hostages had their throats slashed."

Which was true, if "several" meant the three that reporters independently confirmed first-hand? Those three survived. None of the nine—later, ten—who died that day were killed by a throat laceration, three forensic pathologists determined.

Dr. Michael Baden, New York City deputy medical examiner, later called in to examine all the bodies, criticized those handling the aftermath for the chaos that resulted in both the exaggerated horror stories, stemming from the expectations of savagery that were built up, and an improper handling of the bodies from a pathological-examination point of view.

But, he said a month afterwards, "thus far there have been no indications that any of the inmates died of neglect following bullet wounds. Their injuries in and of themselves were sufficient to be fatal."

At 1:16 p.m., Houlihan came out again, met once more by pushing and shoving as he sought a clear area on the lawn that had been turned into a field of cars, reporters and litter.

"According to the doctors' reports, we now have 37 dead, nine hostages and 28 inmates," he said.

A man collapsed, his face a grotesquely poignant portrait of the pain the citizens of Attica would experience for years to come.

A stir at the gate. The committee was coming out, all who were not legislators scheduled for a tour an hour or two later.

The door closed behind Wicker, his exhaustion showing. A guard hissed, "You people will never again be allowed inside this facility under any circumstances."

"Speaking for myself, I think any event where 37 persons are dead can be termed a tragedy," Wicker said. "Some way, we should have found a way to settle this. . . ."

It was time for the first press pool to pass through the gates since before dawn Saturday.

Oswald met them after troopers and guards displayed the eight boxes of primitive weapons picked up in the yards. Oswald led the tour, repeating the tales of atrocities, recalling the agony of decision-making in crisis.

The details of mutilations, casualty figures and prisoner barbarism were calmly relayed to the pool reporters.

Before noon the next day, that scenario had crumbled under the findings of Dr. John F. Edland of Rochester, the Monroe County medical examiner: all nine hostages died of gunshot wounds, no castrations, no mutilations beyond evidence of early beatings, no slashed throats among the dead.

Shortly after 5 p.m., the director of correctional accounts came out in Houlihan's place, to announce a 9 p.m. news conference with Oswald inside the walls.

Oswald came to the portable podium at 10:50 p.m. and read his statement: "We would like to explain to you what apparently has been a misstatement of facts, the origin of which facts were unfortunately given to the press.

"The two statements at variance initially suggested that all hostages died as a result of cut throats. The second statement suggested that the deaths of all hostages resulted from gunshot wounds. The true facts—now verified—are these:

"A physical inspection of the deceased bodies shows slash marks on throats and backs of necks, puncture wounds, apparent broken arms, blackened eyes, broken face, abrasions on nearly every hostage and some hostages only with puncture wounds; albeit the forensic pathologist who did the examinations reported that the cause of death in each instance was gunshot wound. We thought you should, however, have this additional information.

"The first question we must answer is why the exact cause of death was not known until this late hour. The second question that must be resolved is how any of the hostages could have died by gunshot.

"In response to the first question, on the lateness of the actual cause of death, there are a number of factors that could have contributed to the erroneous report of slashed throats: (1) For four days preceding the restoration of law and order, the inmates had threatened on numerous occasions that they would kill all hostages the instant that any force by authorities was applied. . . . (2) Several correctional officers and other individuals who viewed this action positively stated that they had seen hostages drop as their throats were apparently cut. (3) In the confusion that existed during the evacuation of casualties, various individuals who were assisting in the evacuation and who were not qualified to identify whether the evacuee was a hostage or an inmate reported that a number of those evacuated did have slashed throats.

"This fact has been verified since there are two hostages now in the hospital known to have lacerated throats.

"And finally, at the instant of the move to regain the total facility, several eyewitnesses verified that hostages were being held at what appeared to be knifepoint at so-called 'Times Square' within the prison compound. . . .

"In summary, it was possible from all of these reports, rumors and facts for some unauthorized reports to be made to the effect that all hostages had died of slashed throats. . . .

"The second question to be answered is 'How could any have died of gunshot wounds?' and there are several answers to this.

"The most important and obvious answer is the fact that the inmates had dressed all hostages in prison garb to insure difficulty of identification between inmate and hostage. Additionally, the hostages could very well have been used as shields or forced forward into gunfire to suggest that they were not hostages and could have been mistaken for such because of their prison garb. The pathologist told us that all of those he examined had their feet and hands bound. . . ."

The stream of ambulances, one every 15 minutes Monday, had gone. The majority of the state troopers, by the time Oswald, began to speak, had gone home.

Commissions would flourish for a period of time that no one could estimate.

Words of comfort for the relative of a dead hostage outside the walls of Attica

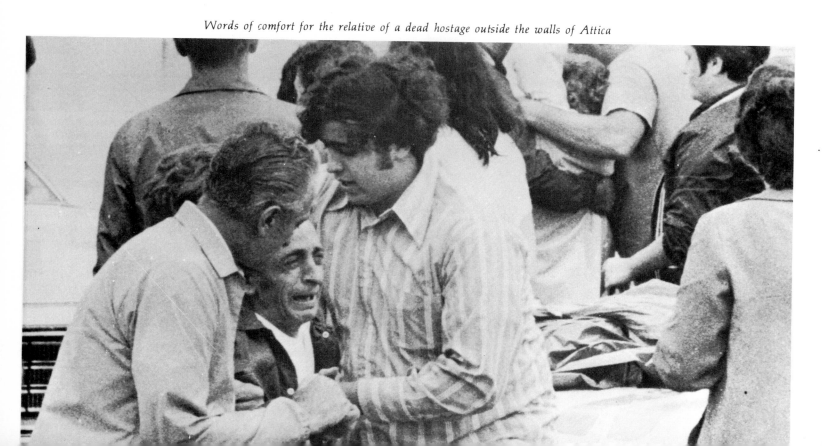

Violence in Prisons: II
Six Died at San Quentin

F OR 117 YEARS a buff-colored mausoleum-like fortress had dominated the shoreline of a peninsula jutting into San Francisco Bay, visible from passing sailboats. This was San Quentin Prison. From its towers the San Francisco skyline loomed, 12 miles to the south, on fog-free days.

August 21 was a quiet, sunny Saturday afternoon. The only outward signs of what had taken place there were a flashing red roof light and the arrivals and departures of maroon hearses bearing the dead: Three white guards, two white "honor" inmates and black convict George Lester Jackson, one of the Soledad Brothers.

In numerous court appearances during the previous year, the Soledad Brothers had become symbols to black militants and their supporters as victims of all that was wrong with a prison and judical system run by whites. Jackson had spent 10 of his 28 years in prison for a $71 service station robbery.

Warden Louis S. Nelson got a standing ovation from the Rotary Club a month after the slayings when he blamed the violence on revolutionaries "dedicated to proving that our judicial system will not work."

Looking back over 1971, Nelson said San Quentin officials "had seen the dark clouds on the horizon."

On Jan. 7 a convict ambling back to his cell after dinner was stabbed in the back and killed. When four more stabbings followed, Nelson ordered the first prison-wide lockup in two years.

The stabbings continued and on July 21, Leo Davis, 38, became the first guard to die at San Quentin in 19 years.

Warden Nelson said the "Q" grapevine reported the killings and knifings were retaliation among black and white prisoners amid racial tension.

"The stabbings resulted from the same kind of thinking of inmates who pick up revolutionary rhetoric and decide that killing is a glorious way to bring about a new world," said Associate Warden James L. Park as the prison took count: 6 deaths and a total of 29 stabbing incidents.

On Aug. 17 some 570 convicts staged a one-day strike and refused to go to work assignments. Guards looked in a wastebasket and found a written list of 14 demands including permission to wear mustaches and long hair, a minimum hourly wage of $1.84 for prison work, lower canteen prices and better food.

Park called the demands "old hat."

Four days later, weary and his eyes filled with tears, Park met anxious newsmen at the East Gate and told them San Quentin had suffered "its blackest day." Authorities gave this account:

Attorney Stephen Mitchell Bingham, 29, arrived at San Quentin about 1:15 p.m. to visit Jackson.

The attorney handed his briefcase to a guard inside a tiny stationhouse and the officer sifted through it, but failed to open an expanding brown envelope and the case of a small portable tape recorder.

Prisoners lay stripped and handcuffed on the grass and armed guards stood watch while a search for arms went on inside the San Quentin adjustment center

Dead "Soledad Brother:" George Jackson, who was killed in the San Quentin break attempt

searched again, then locked inside the "A" visiting room with Bingham. The only furniture in the 10-by-7 foot room was a table and chairs. There was nothing to prevent the two from passing objects to each other.

During the hour-long visit, guards watched the pair through glass windows but not constantly and at no time was Jackson alone in the room without Bingham.

About 2:25 p.m., Bingham stood and left, carrying the case, walking back past the guard station, then along a sidewalk for about 1,000 more feet, signing out at the East Gate at 2:30 p.m.

Officer Frank P. DeLeon, 44, escorted Jackson back to the Adjustment Center and prepared to frisk the black convict. But another guard noticed that Jackson's Afro hairdo looked different than it had when the convict had left.

Authorities claimed that when Jackson was asked about it he whipped a black Afro wig from his head under which he had been hiding a 9 mm foreign made automatic pistol and live cartridges.

"Jackson got the drop on the officer and grabbed the gun," said Park.

Jackson yelled: "This is it!"

He ordered all the officers in the main lobby, where he was standing, to lie face down on the polished concrete floor. At 2:50 p.m., Sgt. Jere Graham, 39, walked into the Adjustment Center to get DeLeon for another detail. An unidentified guard unlocked the door for Graham, and this guard was grazed in the arm by a bullet fired through the glass door. He ran for help.

Jackson ordered one guard to stand up, walk to the end of the cell blocks and, with his key, automate an electronic switch on the wall which opened the doors of all 34 cells on the first floor, loosing 27 convicts.

Among them were the other two Soledad Brothers, Fleeta Drumgo and John Clutchette, and another black, Ruchell Magee, accused with Angela Y. Davis in the Aug. 7, 1970 San Rafael courthouse slayings of four. *(The World in 1970, 153–157).*

It was unclear exactly what took place during the five minutes or so when three white guards and two white inmates were killed.

They were officers Graham, DeLeon, Paul Krasenes, 52, and two inmates who had been loose and working on the first floor: John Lynn, 29, convicted of murder, and Ronald L. Kane, 28, serving time for car theft and attempted escape.

Two died of gunshot wounds to the back of the head. The others were killed by convicts "sawing" their necks with a dull razor blade melted into a toothbrush handle, Park said.

Sgt. Kenneth McCray, 39, was slashed in the throat and dragged from the lobby area to Jackson's 6-by-7 foot cell, about 20 feet away on the north side of the Adjustment Center.

Convicts flung three dead men on top of McCray, in a bloody pile, in Jackson's cell.

"This probably saved his life," said Park. "Since he was on the bottom, they probably didn't know he was still alive." McCray survived.

Two officers had been bound hand and foot and parts of their drab, green uniforms had been removed.

Alarm sirens were screaming by this time.

Armed with the gun, Jackson dashed out the door of the Adjustment Center with black convict Larry John Spain, 22, convicted of murder in Los Angeles.

In the sunlight they sped about 75 feet across a landscaped courtyard towards a 20 foot high tan brick wall. There Jackson was cut down by rifle fire—from sharpshooters in one or two guard towers.

Bingham walked through a metal detector and was handed his briefcase back. The dark-haired attorney then walked along about 50 feet across a plaza to a three-story tan building that housed a prison visiting area on the first floor.

Inside the open door, he signed a registry at a guard's desk. Another guard went to fetch Jackson, who was in his cell about 100 feet away in the concrete gray Adjustment Center, where the most dangerous convicts were housed, including Sirhan B. Sirhan, convicted of killing Sen. Robert F. Kennedy. *(The World in 1969, 72–76).*

The guard ordered Jackson to strip naked, bend over and spread his legs apart, stand, rub both hands briskly through his hair and open his mouth. This type of "skin search" he and other dangerous prisoners always went through before seeing visitors.

Jackson dressed again in his denim blue pants, shirt and jacket and was brought by a guard to the visiting area,

Police from surrounding Marin County towns beefed up the already heavy guard outside San Quentin's main gate following the abortive break

One bullet hit his left ankle, the other hit his back and traveled up and out the top of his head. He staggered about 10 feet, then collapsed dead on the black asphalt. It was 2:55 p.m.

Spain, uninjured, leaped and hid behind waist-high green shrubbery and was later dragged out.

None of the guards on the ground had weapons—only those in the towers were armed. But, with the alarm sirens sounding, officers ran and armed themselves with submachine guns, carbines, pistols and rifles.

Capt. D. R. Weber and six men entered the Adjustment Center heavily armed and fearing convicts might have had a grenade, explosives or more guns.

Other men came in and carried the bodies of their dead and wounded fellow officers and the convicts to the prison hospital.

Meanwhile, the other convicts huddled inside cells at the opposite end of the Adjustment Center.

"We have hostages," one called out.

"It won't do you any good," Weber yelled back. He was observing a San Quentin rule that officers shoot to kill any convict who takes a hostage within the prison, even at the risk of killing the hostage.

He fired his submachine gun down the 50-foot corridor—hitting the wall—and the two hostage guards ran up the corridor to freedom.

The inmates were ordered to strip naked, raise both arms high and come down the corridor one at a time, walking backwards.

"We told them one funny move and they'd have 50 pounds of lead in them," said Weber.

Each inmate then was handcuffed, his feet shackled and all were ordered to lie face down outside on the lawn. Officers shaved the convicts' scalps in a search for more contraband.

A prisonwide shakedown turned up a "zip" gun barrel inside a two-pound block of cheese, some 410 gauge shotgun shells embedded in bars of soap and cheese and 17 live .38 caliber shells. Officials claimed a store-bought Afro wig was found flushed down a toilet.

This led authorities to believe Jackson had engineered a large scale breakout plan with many convicts escaping in the uniforms of guards.

Raymond Procunier, State Department of Corrections director, said discovery of Jackson's gun may have forced the black convict to trigger his plan prematurely. Procunier said rumors of a massive attempt by "revolutionary types" had been circulating for months in California prisons. Officials also said they had managed to get a copy of a letter in which Jackson detailed an escape plot and advised various friends and relatives to smuggle him weapons and explosives during visits.

Park said it was his "personal theory" that the gun was smuggled to Jackson in a small tape recorder case during a visit.

A month later, Bingham was charged with five counts of murder.

The scion of a rich, prominent New England family and a Yale graduate whose grandfather was the former Connecticut governor and U.S. Senator Hiram Bingham, young Bingham had worked for civil rights causes such as voter registration in the South and the farm workers' grape strike in California.

"There is no other way Jackson could have gotten the death gun but during his visit with Bingham," said Marin County Dist. Atty. Bruce Bales.

Authorities said that the gun Jackson used was purchased by a Black Panther member and that a black woman—who had accompanied Bingham but was not allowed inside San Quentin that day—gave her address as the Black Panthers Oakland headquarters.

Hours before Jackson's funeral, terrorist bombs rocked two California prison offices. A letter to news offices called it "one outraged response to the assassination of George Jackson."

Ten months before he died, Jackson had written his way to the underground's best-seller lists with his book *Soledad Brother: The Prison Letters of George Jackson.*

"If I leave here alive, I'll leave nothing behind," he had written in one letter. "They'll never count me among the broken men, but I can't say that I'm normal either. I've been hungry too long, I've gotten angry too often. I've been lied to and insulted too many times.

"I know they will not be satisfied until they've pushed me out of this existence altogether. I've been the victim of so many racist attacks that I could never relax again."

The book was dedicated to Jackson's younger brother Jonathan, to black revolutionary Angela Davis and to Jackson's mother, Georgia Bea Jackson.

At 17, Jonathan was killed a year before in the Aug. 7, 1970 San Rafael courthouse shootout. As a black kidnaper-accomplice yelled that he wanted "the Soledad Brothers released by 12:39" Jonathan, armed with guns, allegedly tried to take hostages to exchange for his older brother's freedom. The attempt was cut short in a blaze of gunfire that left Jonathan, a Superior Court judge and two other men dead.

The Soledad Brothers were accused of slaying a white guard at Soledad Prison in January 1970, three days after another white guard killed three black convicts during an inmate fracas.

Angela Davis, accused of helping plot Jonathan's aborted attempt to free the Soledad trio and recipient of several letters in Jackson's book, was awaiting trial in a San Rafael jail less than five miles from San Quentin when George Jackson was killed. She wrote his death meant "the loss of an irretrievable love."

On Aug. 28, Jackson's body, clad in the Black Panthers dress uniform of black leather jacket, black beret and blue shirt, was buried in Mt. Vernon, Ill., next to Jonathan.

Jackson's mother said she believed her last son was purposefully murdered by guards who dragged him into the prison yard to make it look like an escape.

State Rep. Julian Bond of Georgia called it Jackson's "assassination" and "the expected outcome of his constant attacks on a vicious system which was unable to crush his spirit or his body."

Congressman Ronald V. Dellums, D-Calif., said the death "raised serious questions with respect to a penal system which produces such tragedies" and added his voice to others calling for an investigation.

"The people in the street are saying this is an execution, that it's ridiculous Jackson could hide a gun in his hair," said California Assemblyman Willie Brown.

Guards and state officials blamed pressure from liberals and "dilettante revolutionaries" for persuading them to relax tough prison rules. They announced a clampdown on visitors and said inmates no longer could read the incendiary Black Panther newspaper, which was then headlining: "George Jackson Lives!"

They called for a doubling of the 350-man guard staff at San Quentin after eight guards resigned and one remarked: "I see no future in laying my life on the line for a convict."

John Arms, who had been a guard at San Quentin for 20 years, quit his job the day before Jackson's funeral.

"My insides are torn out," he said. "I've seen all the useless, needlesss bloodshed I can see and still live with myself."

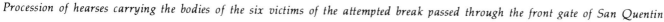

Procession of hearses carrying the bodies of the six victims of the attempted break passed through the front gate of San Quentin

Financial Problems Hit Schools and Colleges; Teacher Job Market Cut

IN 1971 HARD TIMES hit the nation's public and private schools at all levels with sledgehammer force. Unemployed holders of doctorate, master and baccalaureate degrees were counted in the tens of thousands. Public and private universities and colleges, large and small, were scrambling to avoid deficits. Those already in the red were cutting corners in the hope of not sinking deeper into a financial mire.

Bankruptcy had become a reality for some small four-year colleges. Private elementary and secondary schools were closing at an alarming rate. Public school districts were cutting back on programs and services.

One college president briefing his faculty on the financial crisis said:

"First, I'll give you the good news: things are bad. Now the bad news: They're going to get worse."

Yet on July 12 of this year President Nixon signed H.R. 7016, the largest educational appropriations bill in history, and gave education a federal bankroll of $5.1 billion, nearly $1 billion more than was available the year before. In most areas local and state expenditures on education were at an alltime high but voters were turning down—in a high percentage of cases—new school bond or tax issues.

Seriousness of the crisis was underscored by Dr. Earl F. Cheit of the University of California, who estimated that two-thirds of the nation's colleges, enrolling three-fourths of the nation's students, were in financial difficulty or headed for it.

Cheit reached this conclusion after a survey of 41 schools that were illustrative of the major types of educational institutions. His study resulted in the Carnegie Commission on Higher Education book, *The New Depression in Higher Education* (Mcgraw-Hill 1971).

After the prosperous days of the Fifties and early Sixties, educators began worrying about finances three years ago.

"I was deeply concerned with a university deficit which I feared was increasing from less than $1 million in 1967-68 to perhaps $2.5 million in 1969-70." Dr. Allan Cartter, chancellor of private, prestigious New York University, told Congress: "In fact, despite the most rigorous internal economy measures, last year's deficit was $4.5 million and is destined to top $7 million in 1970-71."

The dramatic change in university finances the past three years could, in Cartter's opinion, be traced to seven basic causes:

—Elimination of draft deferments for graduate students had sharply cut graduate school enrollment—down 2,000 in six NYU graduate schools, reducing income $5 million.

—A sharp reduction in federal grants for research and development.

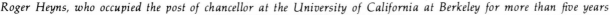

Roger Heyns, who occupied the post of chancellor at the University of California at Berkeley for more than five years

—Medical school costs rising dramatically, as health personnel costs rose at a rate double the national average.

—Spiralling construction costs. (NYU planned four new buildings in 1965-66 which in 1971 were costing $52 million instead of an anticipated $37 million).

—Increased use of university funds ($2 million at NYU) to help financially disadvantaged students attend school.

—Inflation: insurance rate quintupled in three years; labor contracts called for increases from 10 to 20 per cent; more costly supplies.

—Many private colleges were pricing themselves out of the market with steadily rising tuition rates.

—Dr. Cheit summed up the "nightmare of the small liberal arts private college president" this way: "His school opens next fall but no freshmen show up. In competition with other types of institutions, his school has been priced out of the market."

This was not unlikely. One Georgia school normally had 350 freshman applicants and in 1971 reportedly received only seven. And private schools in Missouri reportedly had 7,000 vacant seats at a time the state university was rejecting qualified applicants for lack of space.

The major private universities were the first hit. Such illustrious schools as Yale, Harvard, Princeton, Stanford, Columbia and NYU were faced with red-ink balances running into the millions of dollars.

Each had taken emergency measures and most were making long-range plans to stabilize the financial picture. Stopgap steps included cutback in programs, halting new construction, bypassing maintenance, academic and non-academic staff cutbacks and increased tuitions.

But the financial crisis was not limited to the private sector. Dr. Wilson Elkins, president of the University of Maryland and the National Association of State Universities and Land Grant Colleges, said, "the financial crisis now buffeting U.S. higher education very definitely includes public universities and colleges."

"A great many of these institutions," he said, "have been forced by the financial squeeze to resort to stopgap measures which could irreparably damage the fabric of public higher education in this country."

The concensus among college administrators was that the federal government must help with "institutional grants," unrestricted funds which schools could spend as needed and which also would help financially in the construction of new facilities.

The gloom that hung over the nation's higher education campuses wasn't any darker than that wrapped around the nation's public and private elementary and secondary schools.

Again the answer to their problems, educators maintained, was more federal dollars. The government had contributed about seven per cent to the nation's $60 billion school bill with local, county and state governments putting up the rest.

Plight of the private and parochial schools was especially desperate, as was that of the large urban inner-city public schools.

John B. Geissinger, president of the American Association of School Administrators, said the government had to come forth with supplementary financial assistance "to halt the devastating cutbacks of educational programs, and school closings."

Citing conditions in large cities, Geissinger said Philadelphia had eliminated all extracurricular activities, Chicago had kept schools closed 12 extra days at Christmas and New York and Detroit had been forced to take similar drastic steps to meet dollar shortages.

Unless help was forthcoming, he said, "American education will suffer the irreparable damage of continuing deterioration and uncertainty."

The National Education Association, 1.1 million-member teacher organization, had long insisted that the federal government should finance one-third the cost of public elementary-secondary education.

With voters turning down school bond and school tax issues with increasing frequency, and inflation eroding the school dollar, public schools faced a bleak future but not nearly as grim as the one facing the Roman Catholic elementary-secondary school system, second in size only to the public schools.

On June 28, 1971, the U.S. Supreme Court struck down as unconstitutional the use of tax dollars to assist church-related elementary-secondary schools in meeting operating expenses for secular education.

The court upheld a massive program of construction grants to church-affiliated colleges but said no to Pennsylvania and Rhode Island programs authorizing teacher subsidies for elementary-secondary parochial schools. Voting 8 to 0 in the Pennsylvania case and 8 to 1 in the Rhode Island case, the court held that the teachers' salaries supplement in Rhode Island and the purchase of instructional services program in Pennsylvania were unconstitutional "because as we see it they involve excessive entanglement between church and state."

This did not ban states from extending help to parochial schools in such areas as school lunches, transportation and use of textbooks.

The decision was a blow to church leaders who felt that these programs were the only avenues of relief of their desperate financial situation.

Since 1966, nearly 1,400 Catholic parochial schools had closed their doors and pushed into public school systems more than one million students. This had had a chain reaction on some local school districts. St. Albans, Vt., a community of 9,000, had two Catholic high schools and one elementary school shut down and 800 students moved into the public system, forcing the school tax rate to jump from $3.38 a hundred in 1968 to $5.50 a hundred in 1969.

The Rev. C. Albert Koob, president of the National Catholic Education Association, said in an interview that all 150 Catholic dioceses "are in trouble" and "about 75 per cent are in dire trouble with a massive debt piled up." In some areas the churches were spending more than 50 per cent of their income on church schools.

And what had the financial mess meant to both the private and public school students, the college student?

At all levels it had resulted in cutbacks in educational programs and options, increasing the teacher-student ratio, reduced supplies and—some educators maintained—lowering the quality of education offered to young Americans.

As the money squeeze worsened, many colleges and universities, both private and public, had been increasing tuition and fees and with each increase bringing more students into the category of needing financial help to continue their educations.

Dr. Cheit said that "the president of a large private university told me recently that the median parental income of students applying for financial aid at his institution is now well over $16,000 a year."

For teachers, from kindergarten to graduate school, the profession was in the grips of the worst job market since the Great Depression 40 years earlier.

Hardest hit was the elementary school market, with the NEA

predicting that colleges and universities would be turning out 100,000 to 150,000 teachers a year more than the number of job openings.

The high school job situation had been tight, but the real squeeze there was expected in the mid-1970s. NEA's research department predicted that there would be no relief during the current decade in the elementary market and that the 1971 teacher surplus will double by 1976.

What caused it? Educators said the crest of the post World War II baby boom had passed the public school level. No doubt the pill had been a potent factor in reducing the baby crop. And the school districts were cutting back on programs, with the net result that the number of teachers needed was lessened.

Said the NEA:

"The situation is completely unlike anything we have faced since the Great Depression of the 1930s. Not only beginning teachers but persons with above average experience and qualifications are unable to find vacancies for which to apply."

Things were so bleak that Syracuse University's School of Education sent a letter in June to students enrolled in elementary education, outlining future job prospects and suggesting they might want to consider changing career goals "before you get so far into a program that it's impractical to change."

Some of the statistics Syracuse cited: less than half the 1971 graduates had jobs lined up for September; 70 per cent of the State University of New York teacher graduates hadn't found jobs; the Solvay school district near Syracuse had 400 applicants for six openings and Liverpool over 300 job seekers for each of its vacancies.

This shortage of openings was much the same from Maine to California and Chicago to New Orleans. "Go where the jobs are," advised Dr. A. C. Murphy, director of placement at the University of Texas. "There is no way a graduate can continue to be selective over such matters as climate, geography and money."

But an NEA official in California said he advised friends to look for jobs in the California mountains, and when they returned they reported: "they're not hiring out there, either." And Los Angeles, which in the past sent recruiters across the nation looking for teachers, now had a long waiting list.

NEA said the teacher surplus would disappear and a shortage reappear if schools would reduce the teacher-student ratio and inaugurate new programs. But creating jobs "would cost a great deal of money," the NEA rationalized, "and in the present economic situation it would be unrealistic to hope that any (proposed programs) would be, at best, more than partially implemented."

Three years ago a doctorate was an almost irrevocable pass to a good job and a top starting salary. This bubble had broken, and students winding up eight years of study were finding in many cases that they were "overeducated" for open jobs.

The Cooperative College Registry, originally organized by a group of schools to seek out young doctorates, was now trying to find jobs for unemployed PhD holders. Mrs. Elizabeth S. Fisher, executive director of the agency, said 34 per cent of the more than 6,000 PhDs who had registered were still jobless by late summer. Those holding the master degree were in even greater number.

"Many of these people are having to settle for less," she said. "They have the qualifications to teach at university level but many are having to accept junior college and high school jobs, and others are turning to business.

"One man began driving a taxi rather than teach at a level below his credentials," she said.

*   *   *   *

In comparison with the deadly violence that swept the nation's campuses after the Cambodian incursion, most of the nation's schools were almost as orderly as a church picnic (The World in 1970, 186–189). The big question was: Would this be merely a lull or a definite change in student attitudes?

There was no pat yes or no answer. Student leaders mostly described the calm as frustration and a state of looking for a cause that could bring the various student factions together under a united banner.

"The biggest problem on campuses is the inability to articulate feelings and to mobilize around an action," said David Ifshin, former president of the National Student Association.

The elements for a revival of the stormy campus protests were still present. Ifshin expressed the belief that more students were being radicalized, and Playboy magazine's 1971 survey of student opinion reported that 46 per cent of the students said they would join some protest group, although 36 per cent also said "I would protest now but not violently."

Students, educators and administrators agreed that there were a number of elements in the campus cooling: The economy—employers were no longer lined up at the campus with job opportunities—winding down of the Vietnam war, a general revulsion to such violence as took place at the University of Wisconsin, and a renewed effort to work within the system because of the 18-year-old vote.

One thing was apparent. Students were not rushing blindly to support overt demonstrations. John Froines, one of the Chicago Seven defendants, showed up at the National Student Association Congress in Fort Collins, Colo., seeking support of another May Day type demonstration in Washington.

"What we do this fall is to go back to Washington and commit the crime again," he urged. But students didn't follow his course as they had the year before at St. Paul, when radical leader Rennie Davis proposed to shut down the federal government.

After four years of turbulent student protest activity, the University of Wisconsin had experienced a complete turnabout. It was here in 1970 that a bomb exploded in Sterling Hall, killing a physics teacher. State Street, one of the university's main streets, was largely boarded up. But near the end of 1971 visible signs of State Street trashing were gone. Students again turned to football and campus life.

The University of California at Berkeley, where it all started, was without a major issue or controversy. A writer in the Daily Californian commented:

"The level of life in Berkeley has degenerated. The despair of the junkie pervades much of the community. We sit around smoking dope or drinking or thinking of new stereos. . . . all too many people are just waiting for life rather than living."

A University of Michigan professor of social work, John L. Erlich, said: "The calm is deceptive. The open marching, chanting, demonstration approach has subsided because administrators have learned to deal with it. New tactics are constantly emerging, attracting less attention perhaps, bur causing significant change."

The Michigan educator conceded that "large numbers of students have become discouraged and alienated but larger numbers are still committed to change."

Whether the calm would continue through 1972 was moot, but one thing was certain: Campus administrators harassed by student disorders welcomed the respite to try and find solutions to perplexing financial problems.

Nikita S. Khrushchev

Khrushchev in a relaxed mood during happier days

He Left a Duller World

THE WORLD might not have been any the worse for having lost Nikita Sergeyevich Khrushchev, but it would surely have been a duller place without him. Outside the Soviet Union, nobody had known much about Khrushchev in the days of Joseph Stalin. He seemed just a pliant bureaucrat in Stalin's service, ready at all times to do the dictator's bidding, never questioning the leader's dogma or infallibility.

But after Stalin died in 1953, Khrushchev exploded into prominence as the man to beat in the Kremlin sweepstakes. He lasted at the top of the heap for 11 years before being toppled by a cabal of plodding, colorless Communist party warhorses who distrusted Khrushchev's pyrotechnics—as they seemed to distrust everything unorthodox—and joined forces to pull him from his high perch.

Even in retirement and until he died at the age of 77 on Sept. 11, 1971, Khrushchev overshadowed the personalities of those who succeeded him and who seemed dull and unimaginative by contrast. They had called him "hare-brained" and a bungler in domestic and foreign policy, but he got in his last licks even when relegated to the obscure status of "merit pen-

sioner" on $600 a month. Whether with his permission or not, what passed for his memiors *(Khrushchev Remembers)* was published in a blinding blaze of world publicity. What was in those remembrances of things past reflected little credit on the coterie of leaders who had surrounded Stalin and who now had succeeded to power in a mutually protective collective.

With Orwellian logic the new collective seemed to want it to appear that Khrushchev hadn't really existed at all. They expunged his name from the Soviet history books. They deprived him of credit for whatever good he might have accomplished and didn't even blame him by name for the bad. They blamed instead "subjectivist errors," which became the new synonym for Khrushchev. The former premier and first party secretary was officially an unperson.

But Khrushchev's impact on contemporary history, Soviet and international, was enormous. It was Khrushchev who led the first post-Stalin peace offensive in an attempt to show the world a different Soviet face from the terrifying one to which it had been accustomed. It was Khrushchev who "de-Stalinized" Soviet life and gave Russian intellectuals the first breath of freedom—however slight and fleeting—they had experienced since Stalin rose to total power.

It was Khrushchev who blustered his way around the world shaking the Soviet fist, threatening and cajoling, tossing verbal thunderbolts as he progressed. It was Khrushchev who, after making a spectacular journey to the United States in the name of peace, then set the nerves of the world on edge by rattling H-bombs and steaming up a tense crisis over Berlin. It was Khrushchev who moved the two great superpowers to the brink of nuclear war with his attempt to install offensive missiles in Cuba.

But it also was Khrushchev who collaborated efficiently with the United States to achieve such a significant landmark as a partial ban on nuclear weapons testing, who withheld nuclear missiles from Red China at a time when to do otherwise could have spelled disaster in Asia. It was Khrushchev whose innate caution—belying his outward bluster—so outraged the Chinese Communist leadership that the resulting ideological schism did irreparable damage to the international Communist movement.

When the rotund peasant, a leader in war and politics and a preeminent figure in Byzantine palace plotting, passed to his reward, his successors denied him the final honor accorded other top Russians: Burial in the Kremlin wall.

But in spite of them the Khrushchev era was likely to be remembered by historians outside the Communist orbit long after the memory of the current leaders had faded away. Alongside his successors, Khrushchev was as a brilliant sky-rocket compared to sputtering firecrackers.

A prototype of the eternal Russian peasant, the round and garrulous Khrushchev probably was the most popular ruler either Russia or the Soviet Union ever had, for he was neither Czar nor frightening dictator nor cold-blooded functionary. Unlike the other leaders, he was all proletarian. He personified the common touch. He could make people feel he was one of them—as he indeed was. He was a product of the Kursk region, born April 17, 1894, to a coal miner's family. Khrushchev, too, worked in the mines as a boy, then in factories, and then tended sheep and cattle.

"I began working when I learned to talk," he would say in later years. "Life did not pamper me."

He was no pre-Revolution Bolshevik, like the other early leaders, but joined the Communists only after the October coup. Self-taught, he managed in his 20s to beat his way into a technical school in Moscow run by the party, and was lucky enough to come to the attention of gruff, tough Lazar Kaganovich, known as the "Iron Commissar" of the Ukraine. At the time Kaganovich, the only Jew on the Politburo under Stalin, was the party chief of Moscow, and as his protege Khrushchev helped supervise the building of the Moscow subway. That started him on his way up the ladder, and he became secretary of the Moscow party committee—boss of Moscow—in 1932. By 1938, after Stalin spilled the blood of many thousands and sent millions to living death in labor camps in the great purges, Khrushchev was a palace favorite of the dictator. Evidently he had given Stalin yeoman service in carrying out the purges in the Ukraine, where by that time Khrushchev was boss of the provincial party committee. A new reward came in 1939, when he was given full membership in the Politburo, nerve center of Stalin's power.

Through World War II, Khrushchev served on several fronts and held the rank of lietuenant-general. He distinguished himself particularly in the Battle of Kursk, one of the greatest tank battles of all time, a critical engagement which helped break the back of the Nazi invasion.

After the war Khrushchev emerged as an agricultural specialist for Stalin, carrying out the master's whims without question and thus doing irreparable harm to Soviet agriculture, which suffered not only from lack of mechanization but from all manner of other ills, not the least of which had been Stalin's own directives.

When Stalin died, Khrushchev had ranked only fifth in the hierarchy after him. It was a moment of terror for most Politburo members. The secret police chief, Lavrenty Beria, almost had Moscow—and the nation—in the palm of his hand by virtue of his command of a vast police network and army. No man's life was safe at that moment. Guardedly, the successors formed a collective leadership in which Georgi Malenkov emerged as premier. Khrushchev took on the chore of "first secretary" of the party. But that was a key position.

Beria was successfully surrounded, arrested, accused as a "spy" for the United States and executed. The "collective leadership" lasted only a year after that. When he was strong enough in the party, Khrushchev maneuvered Malenkov out of the premiership early in 1955 on charges of incompetence. Nikolai Bulganin, the gray-bearded, dignified political general who had headed the defense ministry, became premier, but by this time it was obvious that in the Kremlin it was Khrushchev who called the shots.

The team of "B & K" became world renowned for globe-trotting performances on state visits, with the "K" of the team always in the limelight. They went to India together, and Khrushchev learned how to roar the Hindi word for "brother" at the fascinated mobs. They travelled to Britain and were nonplussed by a cool reception. "Call me a pot, but don't put me on the stove," bellowed Khrushchev, who disliked being roasted in free-speaking Britain.

But it would be as the symbol of de-Stanlinization that Khrushchev would be remembered the longest, both in Russia and abroad.

On a bitter cold day in February 1956 during the 20th Congress of the Soviet Communist party attended by delegates from around the world, Khrushchev mounted the rostrum to make what was to be a secret speech. To the consternation of his audience, Khrushchev launched on an hours-long indictment of Stalin as a butcher, a murderer of good Communists, a blunderer in war and peace, a man who had done enormous harm to Mother Russia. At times Khrushchev sobbed as he detailed Stalin's crimes, one after another.

The speech got out quickly and rocked Communists in all corners of the world. De-Stalinization meant to some inside the Communist orbit that now there might be more freedom, and it produced rioting in Poland and, finally, open rebellion against Communist rule in Hungary. Moscow rescued the fallen Communist regime with a brutal and massive military suppression of the rebels.

Khrushchev was in trouble and plots were afoot against him. The plotters included Kaganovich, his old mentor and patron, and V. M. Molotov, the perennial Old Bolshevik foreign minister. Khrushchev proved his adroitness as a politician.

Enlisting the aid of Marshal Georgi K. Zhukov, the hero of Berlin, and the use of military planes to summon the party central committee to an emergency session in Moscow, Khrushchev arranged for the majority of the Politburo members to be voted down in an attempt to remove him. It was a first in Soviet history. Now Khrushchev was able to label his enemies the "anti-party group."

"We took the black sheep by their tails and threw them out of the party," he would say later of his coup.

Not satisfied with that, he also turned on Zhukov, had him removed as defense minister and packed off in semi-disgrace. He removed Bulganin from the premiership and took that job for himself. For the first time since Stalin's days, one leader held the reins of both party and government in his hands. Khrushchev was the boss of the U.S.S.R.

Americans who came in contact with Khrushchev during his visit to the United States would have reason never to forget it. It was a wild two weeks from the time Khrushchev landed in Washington until he left for home. Everywhere he went there were, inevitably, Khrushchevian fireworks. His performance on an Iowa farm produced a scene of rural havoc as the Soviet leader bellowed threats at hordes of cameramen and journalists chasing him through cornfields. He stood Hollywood on its ear with his earthy aphorisms. He visited a San Francisco supermarket and the horde of chroniclers followed in his wake and reduced it to wreckage.

That was not his last visit to the United States. The impact of the second, in fact, may have been considerably more memorable for many Americans.

Khrushchev had, after his return home from the first trip to America, been outraged early in 1960 by the disclosure that American U-2 planes had been spying on Soviet territory. One was shot down. Khrushchev, at what was to have been a British-American-French-Russian summit in Paris, blisteringly denounced President Dwight D. Eisenhower to his face as "my false friend." In a speech full of ominous threats, he broke off the summit before it could start.

It was against that inauspicious background that he made his second journey to the United States, this time, in late 1960, to attend a special session of the United Nations General Assembly along with top leaders from many of the world's nations.

Khrushchev turned it into a memorably noisy session. There he launched his blockbuster propaganda proposal: "General and complete disarmament." There he blustered and shouted at any who disagreed with him. And, finally, he shook the diplomatic community to its striped pants.

When one speaker particularly annoyed him, Khrushchev leaned over, slipped off his shoe, and used it to pound upon the desk in front of him. Ever-obedient to the boss, the entire Soviet and Communist contingent began also to pound on their desks in rhythm. Never had the U.N. seen such a performance in the past, nor was it likely to see such a performance again.

Khrushchev's brand of "peaceful coexistence" could blow hot and cold. In 1961 he had met the new young President of the United States, John F. Kennedy, in Vienna, taken his measure and decided that Kennedy might be pushed. Consequently, Khrushchev embarked upon a scheme to gain the upper hand in the game of power politics. He would install offensive missiles in Cuba, newly under Soviet Communist domination.

Khrushchev guessed wrong. Kennedy was not to be bluffed into accepting such a situation. In a showdown, Khrushchev was faced with a demand that he withdraw the missiles. A misstep at that moment could have spelled calamity for the world. But Khrushchev backed away and agreed to remove the weapons. For consolation he had wrung from Washington a promise to remove American missiles from Turkey.

Many in the Soviet politburo had looked on all these years in disapproval while Khrushchev's performance, however menacing it might have seemed at the time, commanded a lion's share of world attention.

Finally on Oct. 14, 1964, while Khrushchev was away from Moscow on vacation, eagerly awaiting news of a newly launched space fight, his political foes made their move. They used against Khrushchev the tactics he had employed against others. They pushed him out and branded him a hare-brained incompetent who was responsible, among other things, for domestic economic troubles, problems in agriculture and the widening rift with Mao Tse-tung's China *(The World in 1964, 194-201; 241)*.

Khrushchev retired to obscurity with his wife, Nina Petrovna, and his memories of days of glory, his days of total power over an immense land mass and a quarter of a billion people. If he sought for consolation, perhaps he had found it in the knowledge that nothing his successors had been able to do had suggested that they would ever outshine him in any of the fields in which they had called him a failure.

A final farewell from Khrushchev's widow during burial ceremonies

PACT UNIFYING ARABS RATIFIED

The agreement was known as the Federation of Arab Republics. It united Egypt, Libya and Syria in what appeared to be a revival of Arab militancy against Israel and received nearly unanimous endorsement Sept. 1 in referendums called in the three Arab states.

Each member country retained her national sovereignty within the federation, but the new political entity brought together 42 million of the Arab world's 100 million people.

Earlier Egypt's president, Anwar Sadat, hailed formation of the union and made clear that it was primarily intended as an Arab bulwark against Israel.

Sadat stressed that he and the Libyan and Syrian leaders had agreed to channel the resources of their countries toward the liberation of all Arab territories occupied by Israel.

"There will be no negotiations or peace agreement with Israel, no abandoning of one inch of Arab territory and no relinquishing or bargaining on the rights of the Palestine case," Sadat declared last April when the union was agreed upon.

TITO, BREZHNEV ACCORD SEALED

A four-day visit by the Soviet Communist party leader, Leonid I. Brezhnev, to Yugoslavia ended with the signing in Belgrade of the new "Belgrade declaration." The document, reaffirming Yugoslavia's political independence and her right to develop Communism in her own way, was negotiated by President Tito and Brezhnev.

Signed Sept. 25, the pact was Brezhnev's endorsement of a 1955 declaration in which the late Nikita Khrushchev attempted to restore ties disrupted by Joseph Stalin's expulsion of Yugoslavia from the Communist family in 1948.

This 1955 declaration spelled out the right of the Yugoslav Communists to follow their own methods and guaranteed Yugoslavia's sovereignty, integrity and right to noninterference.

Belgrade-Moscow relations had worsened sharply after the 1968 Soviet incursion of Czechoslovakia. Regional feuds developed in Yugoslavia, for which that country blamed the Soviet Union. A persistent dispute over Macedonia by Yugoslavia and Moscow's ally, Bulgaria, also contributed to the growing tension.

SANCTUARY IN BUDAPEST LEFT RELUCTANTLY BY MINDSZENTY

It was a bitterly disappointing outcome for the frail, bent clerical figure who stepped into a waiting car. Leaving an embassy in Budapest that had provided him sanctuary for 15 years, he traveled out of Hungary determined never to return.

For 79-year-old Jozsef Cardinal Mindszenty it was a humiliating finale to the drama that had held the world's attention for many years. It was a drama that began the day after Christmas in 1948, when he was arrested by the Hungarian Communists on a charge of antistate activities, tried and sentenced to life imprisonment.

For seven years the cardinal languished in a state prison. Then he took refuge from Russian troops in the American Embassy after Freedom Fighters had liberated him in the short-lived 1956 uprising.

For 22 years the prelate had vowed that he would never leave his homeland until he was cleared of all charges against him. But on the morning of Sept. 28 he departed from the gray stucco embassy in Budapest's Freedom Square and drove to Vienna, accompanied by three fellow churchmen. One was Msgr. Giovanni Cheli, an official of Pope Paul's Secretariat of State and a specialist on Eastern Europe. The monsignor was believed to have brought back to Rome several weeks earlier Cardinal Mindszenty's letter to the Pontiff accepting the solution to the deadlock that he had resisted for so long.

· "I am ready to say goodbye to my favorite country and continue a life of prayers and penitence in exile," the primate had written.

The letter was published after his arrival in Rome.

From Vienna, the cardinal continued by plane to Rome's Fiumcino Airport. From there he drove by car to the Vatican, where he was embraced by Pope Paul. It had been Pope Paul who appealed to the primate to "make the hardest sacrifice of your life."

Cardinal Mindszenty's departure from Hungary climaxed an exchange of views between the Vatican and Hungary which began in 1962, when the regime of Janos Kadar offered the cardinal safe conduct out of the country if he agreed never to return. But the iron-willed churchman had refused any solution that did not include his full rehabilitation.

Observers noted that the communique issued on the primate's departure by the state-controlled Hungarian press agency used the word "cardinal" in announcing the event. Thus, they held, by tacitly acknowledging the prelate's position the Hungarian government was rescinding the 1949 verdict.

The heroic cardinal had proved to be something of a problem for both Washington and the Vatican. Without wishing it, he had become an impediment to improved relations between the United States and Hungary and to reapprochement between the Vatican and Budapest.

It was no secret that the Holy See was anxious to get Cardinal Mindszenty out of Hungary. Several times over the past few years Franz Cardinal Konig of Vienna had been dispatched to Budapest to try to persuade his colleague to quit asylum in the U.S. Embassy and leave Hungary. The Vatican, obviously, was anxious to improve relations with Hungary and thus gain closer contact with Catholics of other Iron Curtain countries.

After years of adamant refusal, Cardinal Mindszenty finally relented. It was a sad conclusion for the religious leader who, in 1956, had stood forth as the heroic symbol of the outraged people of Hungary. But he accepted it, the Vatican paper said, "as a token of my limitless love for the church."

Shortly afterward the cardinal left Rome to establish residence in Vienna.

Pope Paul VI gave warm greeting to Josef Cardinal Mindszenty when the famed primate of Hungary arrived at Vatican City

MEDINA FREED OF ALL CHARGES

After listening to nearly two months of testimony, the jury of five combat officers arrived at a verdict. On the afternoon of Sept. 22, they found Army Capt. Ernest L. Medina innocent of all charges of involvement in the killing of 100 or more civilians at My Lai 4.

It was a complete vindication of the officer who had commanded Charlie Company on the bloody morning of March 16, 1968, and whose bearing and manner radiated pride of uniform and rank.

The trial was held at Fort McPherson, Ga., and the verdict was reached after 60 minutes of deliberation. Medina had been charged with premeditated murder in the killing of a Vietnamese woman, with involuntary manslaughter in the killing of about 100 Vietnamese civilians and, on two counts, with assault against a prisoner.

The darkly handsome captain controlled his emotions with difficulty when the court president, Col. William D. Proctor, announced the verdict. He saluted the court, walked back to his seat at the defense table, blinked his eyes and gulped down a glass of water. Plainly struggling to keep his feelings in check, the captain averted his gaze from his German-born wife, Barbara, who had been weeping on the shoulder of a friend since the verdict announcement.

A few minutes later, the couple embraced in the witness room. Medina then told newsmen that, although he had always had "complete faith in military justice," he was determined to quit the service.

It had been a long ordeal. From the day the

Capt. Ernest Medina burst into a grin—he was acquitted

trial opened on July 26 until the announcement of the verdict, the 35-year-old officer had heard himself denounced by the prosecution as one who abrogated his responsibility and who "like Pontius Pilate cannot wash the blood from his hands."

Medina had also heard himself described in the summation of the defense as "no filthy felon" but "a disciplined commander who honored and loved the uniform he wore and the company he represented."

Only six days before the verdict, the military judge had reduced to involuntary manslaughter the original charge against Medina of premeditated murder of the 100 civilians during the sweep through My Lai. The court also had thrown out a charge that the captain had killed a small boy.

The jury had to consider whether Medina had been guilty in the slaying of the woman, an incident described by defense counsel F. Lee Bailey as "justifiable battlefield homicide."

Medina was cleared, and with his acquittal the government closed the legal books on participants in the assault. Five officers and men had stood trial, charged with crimes of assault and murder at My Lai. But only Lt. William L. Calley Jr. had been judged a mass murderer. Calley had been sentenced to life imprisonment in March but five months later the sentence had been reduced to 20 years *(Page 68)*.

After the Medina verdict, one of the jurors in the case issued a statement saying: "we feel that justice has been done." He added: "I am certain war crimes were committed. In the case of Capt. Medina, the jury was convinced he committed no war crimes."

Earlier, at Ft. Benning, Ga., a Calley juror had said:

"When you conjure up a mental picture of men, old men, women, children and babies, that was a rather harsh treatment for them. This is not the way the American soldier is taught to fight. You don't round up civilians and kill them."

IMMUNITY CONTROL RATE LOWER

The discovery of a vaccine against the virus disease measles in 1963 lessened the number of cases and deaths year by year thereafter. But in 1971 the lines of the graphs started upward again, a trend which experts said was common to many infectious diseases.

With measles, as with the cases of many other diseases such as polio and diphtheria, Americans often ignored available immunization vaccines. Public health officials in Washington considered the trend tragic because otherwise the diseases assumably could have been virtually eradicated by vaccines.

Though the immunity to diphtheria remained approximately level in recent years, it had been low enough to permit some serious outbreaks, mostly in poverty areas. The outbreaks, although limited to a few communities, were dangerous because, one expert said, the germ that caused the serious illness was extremely difficult to eliminate from the population as a whole.

Immunity to polio, too, had been declining in recent years. In 1970 there were only 33 reported cases of polio and 20 the year before.

Then findings began to show that the immunity percentage among American youngsters below the age of four was dropping steadily, even though these youngsters once had been adequately immunized against this treacherous disease. One report put the figure at 79 per cent of this age group in 1966 and only 65.9 per cent last year.

One of the problems of immunization, researchers said, seemed to be that parents often forgot the importance of a disease simply because there had been no major recent outbreaks. Another contributing factor was that national efforts to vaccinate against one disease seemed sometimes to have usurped the impetus needed to complete the work against an older disease. A case in point was the major national effort made to fight rubella, or German measles, which took attention away from the efforts to control common measles, a disease similar to rubella.

"It is apparent that race, resistance and riches are factors affecting immunization status," said Dr. J. D. Millar of the Center of Disease Control in Atlanta, Ga., at their annual meeting.

The communicable disease most seriously out of control in the United States in 1971 was gonorrhea because there was no vaccine available to prevent it. Syphilis was also on the upsurge but not to the extent of gonorrhea.

PRISON TERM FOR LADY FLEMING

It was an embarrassing moment for members of the Greek regime who decided they had to sentence Lady Amalia Fleming, widow of the famous Scottish scientist who discovered penicillin, to 16 months imprisonment. But Lady Fleming had said she had played a part in the attempt to free Alexander Panagoulis from prison, where he was serving a life term for trying to assassinate Premier George Papadopoulos in 1968 *(The World in 1968, 194)*.

"I did it for humanitarian reasons," insisted 62-year-old Lady Fleming, who added that she was informed through reliable sources that Panagoulis was being tortured and that she "couldn't sleep nights imagining Panagoulis was going through agony."

Friends said that she was convinced Pana-

goulis was a *tyronoktonos* (in the ancient Greek sense, a man who killed a tyrant) and therefore "the conscience of Greece" had to be saved.

Lady Fleming, who held dual citizenship in Great Britain and her native Greece, was sentenced on Sept. 28. She was tried with four other persons. Their names and sentences were: Athena Psyhogios, 42, Minneapolis, Minn., 14 months; Constantine Androutsopoulos, 30, Athens, 15 months; John Skelton, 26, Yardley, Pa., seven months suspended, and a Greek soldier, Constantine Bekakos, 13 months.

Skelton said Lady Fleming had "misused" him, taking him to the prison on the night of the attempted escape without his knowledge that something illegal was taking place.

Skelton had been in Greece attending the Athens University theology school on a scholarship from his church in Yardley. By Sept. 29 he had started his trip back to the United States. Bekakos, 21, was accused of failing to disclose a prisoner's escape plans to his military superiors.

Panagoulis was imprisoned at a Greek military police training center in an Athens suburb. He had planned, according to the government, to give his guard sleeping pills in a soft drink, then make his way to the edge of the military camp under cover of darkness and jump the fence to join the others.

The government said its investigation revealed that Panogoulis' brother, Stathis, set up the escape plans during two visits to Athens.

Shortly after sentencing, Lady Fleming's term was suspended for eight months, due to illness, and she was released. Then, in mid-November, Lady Fleming was stripped of her Greek citizenship and required to board a London-bound plane, her attorney said.

EAST-WEST BERLIN PACT SIGNED

The Four Powers had been haggling over Berlin for 26 years, but ambassadors of the four took pen in hand Sept. 3 and, in 20 minutes, signed an agreement designed to end confrontation over the divided former capital.

The signing, ironically, took place in Berlin's neoclassical Allied Control Council Building where a Russian walkout in 1948 had triggered division of the city. But more than two decades later the mood was jovial. As the envoys shook hands, Soviet Ambassador Pyotr Abrasimov said with a grin; "All's well that ends well."

Under the terms of the pact, the Soviet Union promised that it would not interfere with civilian traffic across East Germany from West Germany to West Berlin. The western allies agreed that West Berlin was not a constituent part of West Germany, but declared that ties between the two would be maintained. Moscow pledged to improve communications between West Berlin and East Germany, including visits by West Berliners to the East, and diplomatic representation in West Berlin was granted to the Soviet government.

Four-power talks over the future of Berlin had been going on fitfully since the end of World War II, but until the agreement was reached Sept. 3, the exchanges had produced little. The reason? Apparently the Soviet Union and the three Western powers had felt that the time was not ripe for compromise.

Problems over Berlin arose when the four victorious powers split the capital of defeated Germany into four sectors. The historic city was part of German soil occupied by Soviet troops, 100 miles from the occupation zones of the West.

The western powers had neglected to insure free surface access to Berlin, and when attempts at four-power rule broke down and the Russians withdrew from the quadripartite government in 1948, the question of land routes into Berlin became a critical issue.

The Russians attempted to seal off Berlin from the west with a blockade in 1948 and nearly succeeded in doing so. But an allied airlift broke their grip on the city 11 months later, in May 1949.

A four-power foreign ministers' conference convened in Paris, also in 1949, agreed that all restrictions imposed on access to Berlin by the Soviet government would be removed. But in October 1949, the Soviets violated the city's four-power administration status by proclaiming Berlin the capital of Communist East Germany.

By 1949 Berlin had been divided politically with separate city governments for the east and west sectors. Despite the division, however, servicemen of the United States, Britain and France continued to cross over into East Berlin by military jeep and car without being checked, although they performed no official function in that sector. It was one of the last remaining four power rights, upheld by both sides.

The climax of the running east-west dispute over Berlin came in August 1961 when the Communists began erecting a wall dividing the city physically as well as administratively.

Late in 1969, the Western allies proposed new talks over the divided city and they began in March 1970. By October 1970, the talks seemed hopelessly stalled, and nearly broke down until President Nixon personally took up the matter with the Soviet Union.

American diplomatic sources disclosed that the President intervened by conferring with Soviet Foreign Minister Andrei A. Gromyko who was in the United States at the time. Soviet Ambassador Abrasimov had refused to discuss with the west the question of access to West Berlin, insisting that it was a matter of East German rather than Russian interest.

The diplomatic informants said that Nixon had been keeping in touch with the Berlin situation, discussing it regularly with U.S. Ambassador Kenneth Rush.

In the agreement, the Russians did not give outright guarantee of a right of access to West Berlin, but they said they and the East Germans had agreed to allow unimpeded transit traffic through East Germany.

LOOK LEAVES MAGAZINE FIELD

The announcement came during National Magazine Week, sponsored by the Magazine Publishers' Association. In the ballroom of the New York Hilton on Sept. 17 Gardner Cowles, chairman of Cowles Communications, Inc., told the press that Look magazine would cease publication with its issue of Oct. 19, in its 34th year.

Look, one of the country's last mass-circulation picture and text journals, had been a victim of an unstable economy, said Cowles.

Although the magazine's circulation was 6.5 million, Cowles reported that "the economy went sour, and Look, after 21 consecutive years of profitability, became unprofitable. As the recession worsened, so did Look's troubles. But the economy is not the whole answer, of course. Television, particularly network television, cut deeply into our advertising revenues. And the costs keep rising. Major costs are out of our control. Postal rates in particular have risen dramatically and they are due to go still higher."

During the last two years the Cowles organization closed or sold five newspapers and divested itself of all book publishing and magazine ventures, retaining three television stations, two radio stations, a travel magazine and the Des Moines Register and Tribune newspapers. Cowles Communications had no connection with the Minneapolis Star Tribune, owned by John Cowles Jr., nephew of Gardner Cowles.

Bronze bust of John F. Kennedy dominated the grand foyer of the Washington Center for the Performing Arts

October

Freedom of the Press–

Scene in New York Times city room after a federal judge ordered the paper to suspend publication of a series of articles based on Pentagon study

and the Pentagon Papers

THE SUPREME COURT of the United States ordinarily moved at the pace of a very deliberate snail. The two cases hastily inscribed on its docket June 25, however, were not ordinary cases. Thus the justices agreed on one day to review the cases —Nos. 1873 and 1875—and scheduled oral arguments for the very next day, agreeing to extend the normal court term for the first time in 14 years in order to decide the matters promptly.

Basic elements of the cases were these:

Does the government have a right to prevent publication of information it deemed vital to the national interest?

Does the constitutional guarantee of freedom of the press extend to publication of secret government documents obtained from unauthorized sources?

Throughout the night lawyers for both sides labored over briefs their opponents would barely have time to study; nor, indeed, would the court even have time to more than scan the documents in question. When the ruling came, it broke no new legal ground. By a vote of 6 to 3 the court reaffirmed a fundamental American liberty and blocked the government's attempt to suppress in advance publication of the material.

The reason the cases took on historic proportions was the prestige of the litigants and the significance of the material in question. In past cases involving the First Amendment guarantee of a free press, including a landmark 1931 decision, the court had ruled on the illegality of a state law shutting down a scandal sheet. Cases Nos. 1873 and 1875, however, involved the executive branch of the United States government, for the first time in history, attempting to suppress publication of a major article in two of the country's greatest newspapers, the New York Times and the Washington Post. It would be difficult to imagine a clearer confrontation over the sanctity of First Amendment Freedoms. As if to underscore that fact, each of the nine justices, for the first time in memory, submitted a separate opinion. Reading them closely, it was clear that the press's victory was far from unqualified.

The articles the two newspapers sought to publish were based on a top-secret government study titled: History of the United States Decision-Making Process on Vietnam Policy. It consisted of 47 typescript volumes bound in cardboard covers. The Times labeled them simply the Pentagon Papers.

Robert McNamara commissioned the study during his last days as Secretary of Defense in the Johnson Administration. Working in an office adjoining McNamara's, 35 researchers, including experts from the Rand Corporation, assembled documents dating as far back as the Truman Administration when the argument was over whether or not the U.S. should aid the French in their vain effort to put down Communist uprisings in Vietnam.

When it was finished, the study contained 4,000 pages of documents, 3,000 pages of analysis and 2.5 million words. McNamara's successor, Clark Clifford, said he never took the time to read it. Neither did one of the scholars called in to help with the project, Harvard's Henry Kissinger, who became President Nixon's national security adviser and chief White House strategist on the war. As for the President himself, he didn't even know the study existed—until the New York Times of Sunday, June 13, landed on his doorstep.

There was nothing sensational about the headline. It said, dryly: "Vietnam Archive: Pentagon Study Traces 3 Decades of Growing U.S. Involvement." The story began on Page One and jumped to six inside pages where the reader could find support for the allegations made in the article—column after column of cables, position papers and memoranda. It was clearly the most massive leak of secret documents in U.S. history, and it laid bare many of the choices, assumptions, guesses and, at least in the Times writer's view, deceptions, that attended America's deepening involvement in the Indochina quagmire. Moreover, it fed a growing American appetite to find villains, someone to blame for the divisive war.

Most prominent in that category, according to the Pentagon Papers, was Lyndon B. Johnson. The documents suggested that far from being caught off guard by the Gulf of Tonkin incident in 1964, and reacting to that incident by escalating the war, President Johnson had made the decision to escalate months before and had even drafted a Congressional resolution supporting it. They also said that when the Administration decided in April 1965 to commit U.S. ground troops, he ordered the decision kept secret and, when put into effect, be made to appear "gradual and wholly consistent with existing policy." In fact, the day he made the decision, the documents attested, the President himself told a news conference that he knew of "no far-reaching strategy that is being suggested or promulgated."

The following day, Monday, when the Times published its second installment, the Nixon Administration reacted. The President was said to have been angered not so much over the content of the documents as the fact that they were disclosed at all. It seemed to him, according to an aide, that the sanctity of government was under attack, that one such breach might lead to more and thereby undermine the government's ability to conduct foreign policy in confidence. When Attorney General John Mitchell proposed moving against the Times to stop publication, the President agreed.

Mitchell wired the Times asking "respectfully" that it voluntarily stop publishing the papers, citing a provision in the espionage law that carried a possible 10-year sentence or $10,000 fine for anyone convicted of willingly revealing secret information that could jeopardize the national safety. Further disclosures, said Mitchell, would "cause irreparable injury to the defense interests of the United States." The Times duly noted in a Page One news story the Attorney General's request, and went ahead with its third installment.

That night, in Washington, Robert Mardian, the Attorney General's chief of internal security, assembled a group of department lawyers who worked through the night preparing a lawsuit seeking an injunction against the Times. Next morning, Tuesday (the Times's Tuesday edition, containing the third installment, actually was printed Monday night), Mardian was in New York before Federal Judge Murray Gurfein, a 63-year-old jurist who had been appointed to the federal bench just five days earlier. Judge Gurfein scheduled a hearing on the injunction for Friday, but meanwhile temporarily restrained the Times from further publication of the Pentagon Papers.

What followed was a series of events the government lawyers clearly had not forseen.

On Friday, the very day the hearing began in New York before Judge Gurfein, the Washington Post began publishing its own version of the Pentagon Papers, quoting liberally and verbatim from quite obviously the same set of documents the Times had possession of. The Times' articles and the Post's articles were distributed, condensed, around the world by The Associated Press and other news services.

"The readers of the New York Times alone in this country are being deprived of the story," argued Yale law professor Alexander Bickel before Judge Gurfein on behalf of his client newspaper.

That was not quite so, for in a curious journalistic anomaly the Times was in fact printing The Associated Press's reports taken from the Post's series. The government moved against the Post. While the Times case was still in court, Federal Judge Gerhard Gesell in Washington refused to grant even a temporary injunction against the Post on the grounds that the government had no right "to impose a prior restraint on publication of essentially historical data." The government rushed an appeal to a three-judge appeals court in Washington and won a 2 to 1 decision which at last halted further publication in the Post. In New York, Judge Gurfein refused a permanent injunction against the Times but kept in force his temporary restraining order until the U.S. Appellate Court could rule on the case.

Dr. Ellsberg testifying before an unofficial House subcommittee

Frank Stanton, president of the Columbia Broadcasting System, talking with Chairman Harley O. Staggers, D-W.Va., left, before a Washington hearing on the Pentagon documents

In its arguments before the various courts the government repeatedly claimed it was simpy trying to recover "stolen" documents essential to national security.

Stolen by whom? A fortnight after it all began a man named Daniel Ellsberg, who had participated in compiling the 47 volumes, surrendered to U.S. marshals at the old Boston federal building and announced that he was indeed the source of the leak.

"I felt as an American citizen, a responsible citizen," Ellsberg said, "I could no longer cooperate in concealing this information from the American people. I took this action on my own initiative, and I am prepared for all the consequences."

Ellsberg, a nervous, intense, 40-year-old scholar, had participated in the Vietnam study as a member of the Rand Corp., the California-based think tank which had participated in numerous Pentagon studies. His background fitted him well for the job. He graduated from Harvard summa cum laude in 1952 and eventually won a doctorate with a thesis on the nature of the decision-making process. He did a stint in the Marine Corps, and in 1964 went to the Pentagon as a special assistant to Assistant Secretary of Defense John McNaughton. Later he went to Vietnam as an intelligence agent, then was put in charge of evaluating the new pacification program. He returned to Rand in 1967.

All this time Ellsberg was a confirmed hawk on the Vietnam war. Gradually, however, he began to have doubts. At length he became a confirmed dove and gradually came to regard all who did not actively work against the war as "war criminals." By 1970 he realized that his views were becoming an embarrassment to Rand and resigned, accepting a fellowship at M.I.T. The invasion of Cambodia in 1970, he said, finally impelled him to release the Pentagon Papers.

The very day he turned himself in, prepared, as he said, to take the consequences, the government handed up a two-count indictment against Ellsberg accusing him of having "unauthorized possession of . . . documents and writings related to the national defense" and of putting copies of these documents to "his own use." Conviction on either charge could bring a maximum sentence of 10 years in jail and $10,000 in fines.

Ellsberg did not conceal his pleasure at the outcome of the Times and Post cases before the Supreme Court. Indeed he explained that his failure to surrender himself for two weeks was not to evade prosecution, which he said he had anticipated, but to keep himself available to see that the purloined papers somehow got before the public.

With the favorable Supreme Court verdict there was no stopping publication. Both the Times and the Post resumed where they had left off, and the Times later published its entire series in a paperback book.

The Times and the Post won their immediate battle: The right to publish the Pentagon Papers; but the victory, as articulated by the justices, was far from an ironclad guarantee of the freedom from prior censorship in all circumstances. Only two members of the court, Justices Hugo Black and William O. Douglas, both well known for their belief in the First Amendment's inviolability, felt that prior censorship was flatly ruled out; a majority of the justices said they could conceive of a circumstance when it might be permitted.

The overriding importance of the Pentagon Papers cases, which Justice John M. Harlan called "as important as any that have arisen during my time on the court" (16 years), seemed to be this: Whether or not the American press could set itself above the law, it was plain that the American government could not set itself above the Constitution.

THE PRESS VS. CENSORSHIP

The following are excerpts from five of the nine opinions handed down by the Supreme Court in the government's cases against the New York Times and the Washington Post. The five represent both sides.

Justice Hugo Black, concurring:

"I believe that every moment's continuance of the injunctions against these newspapers amounts to a flagrant, indefensible, and continuing violation of the First Amendment . . . Now, for the first time in the 182 years since the founding of the Republic, the Federal courts are asked to hold that the First Amendment does not mean what it says, but rather means that the government can halt the publication of current news of vital importance to the people of this country.

"The press [in the Founding Fathers' view] was to serve the governed, not the governors. The government's power to censor the press was abolished so that the press would remain forever free to censure the government. . . . Only a free and unrestrained press can effectively expose deception in government. And paramount among the responsibilities of a free press is the duty to prevent any part of the government from deceiving the people and sending them off to distant lands to die of foreign fevers and foreign shot and shell. In my view, far from deserving condemnation for their courageous reporting, the New York Times, the Washington Post, and other newspapers should be commended."

Justice Potter Stewart, concurring:

"In the absence of the governmental checks and balances present in other areas of our national life, the only effective restraint upon executive policy and power in the areas of national defense and international affairs may lie in an enlightened citizenry—in an informed and critical public opinion which alone can here protect the values of democratic government. For this reason, it is perhaps here that a press that is alert, aware, and free most vitally serves the basic purpose of the First Amendment. For without an informed and free press, there cannot be an enlightened people."

Justice Byron White; concurring:

"I do not say that in no circumstances would the First Amendment permit an injunction against publishing information about government plans or operations. . . . But I nevertheless agree that the United States has not satisfied the very heavy burden which it must meet to warrant an injunction against publication in these cases. . . . To sustain the government in these cases would start the courts down a long and hazardous road that I am not willing to travel at least without Congressional guidance and direction."

Justice John M. Harlan, dissenting:

"With all respect, I consider that the Court has been almost irresponsibly feverish in dealing with these cases. . . . Pending further hearings in each case conducted under the appropriate ground rules, I would continue the restraints on publication. I cannot believe that the doctrine prohibiting prior restraints reaches to the point of preventing courts from maintaining the status quo long enough to act responsibily."

Chief Justice Warren Burger, dissenting:

"In this case, the imperative of a free and unfettered press comes into collision with another imperative, the effective functioning of a complex modern government and specifically the effective exercise of certain constitutional powers of the executive. Only those who view the First Amendment as an absolute in all circumstances—a view I respect, but reject—can find such a case as this to be simple or easy.

"This case is not simple for another and more immediate reason. We do not know the facts of the case. . . . I suggest we are in this posture because these cases have been conducted in unseemly haste . . . due in large part to the manner in which the Times proceeded.

"To me it is hardly believable that a newspaper long regarded as a great institution in American life would fail to perform one of the basic . . . duties of every citizen with respect to the discovery or possession of stolen property or secret government documents. That duty I had thought—perhaps naively—was to report forthwith, to responsible public officers. This duty rests on taxi drivers, Justices and the New York Times."

Mrs. Katherine Graham, publisher of the Washington Post, and Executive Editor Benjamin C. Bradlee, looking over reports of the 6-3 Supreme Court decision which permitted the paper to publish stories based on the Pentagon papers

Daily Mirror
BRITAIN'S BIGGEST DAILY SALE

• Dateline: Westminster, Oct.
• Time: 22-16 hours
• The historic decision is made

'YES' TO
EUROPE!

MAJORITY: 11?

LAST NIGHT THE HOUSE OF COMMONS PASSED THE FOLLOWING MOTION

That this House approves her Majesty's Government's decision of principle to join the European Communities on the basis of the arrangements which have been negotiated

FULL ST
BACK P

Left, opponents of British entry into the European Economic Community demonstrated outside the House of Commons on the eve of the vote. Right, reproduction of the front page of the mass circulation London Daily Mirror carry the news of the vote to join the Common Market

Britain Voted Admission to Europe Common Market

Parliamentary decision conceded that, after 900 years, nation no longer could afford to pursue private power status

ON THE NIGHT of October 28, 1971, high atop the white cliffs of Dover on the southeast coast of England, former British Prime Minister Harold Macmillan ignited a giant bonfire with a lighted hand torch. Once again a fiery signal there marked a major turning point in European history. The first one, four centuries ago, warned that the Spanish Armada was coming. The destruction of the great Spanish fleet then meant Britannia ruled the waves. This time the fire Macmillan lit had a far different meaning. Moments before, parliament had adopted its most important peacetime decision in this century, to take Britain into the European Common Market. The decision signalled a recognition that, after more than 900 years of independent power status, Britain could no longer afford to go it alone and was now ready to help build a united Europe. Finally, and somewhat reluctantly, Britannia had waived the rules.

Across the English Channel 21 miles away in Calais, France, crowds celebrating on a diet suitable for the occasion—scotch whisky and french fried potatoes—answered with a bonfire of their own. Channel fog obscured the smoke signals but the message was clear for both sides.

The British Parliament, in a democratic vote, had brought closer the age-old dream of a united Europe than the armies of Charlemagne, Napoleon or Hitler ever advanced by force. It brought the nations of Western Europe to the threshold of their strongest union since the countries involved were last tied together as part of the Roman Empire of the Caesars, 15 centuries before. This time they were moving together by choice, on relatively narrow economic grounds at first, building a base for a new political superpower in world affairs.

The British were the first applicant nation to accept terms for Common Market entry offered by the six founding members—France, West Germany, Italy, Belgium, The Netherlands and Luxembourg. Three other applicants—Ireland, Norway and Denmark—were expected to follow suit. Together the enlarged 10-nation community would form the world's most powerful free trade area. Its gold reserves and annual exports would surpass those of the United States, the Soviet Union, Communist China or Japan. It would have a larger population—some 250 million people—than any other major power except China. The new Europe's gross national product per capita would be higher than any other power except the United States.

Ultimately a politically united Europe could rival both Washington and Moscow as a third force influencing world affairs. But all sides agreed that prospect likely was still a generation away at least. It had taken over a decade just to agree on the simpler question of terms for British entry into the Common Market. To many, that alone was a major accomplishment. To an 82-year-old Frenchman named Jean Monnet, rightly called the father of the Common Market, it was the crowning of a life's work. Monnet, who watched Parliament make its historic decision from a gallery in the House of Commons, said later: "This is what I have been waiting for during the last 25 years."

It was Monnet in the early 1950s who put together the direct forerunner of the Common Market, the European Coal and Steel Community, that turned wartime enemies like France and Germany into peacetime partners. In the middle 1950s Monnet was instrumental in expanding the coal and steel pool into a wider customs union, the Common Market. The British, still stronger than their continental neighbors at the time, refused entreaties from Monnet and others to join at the outset.

The Common Market was born in 1958, with the six member nations gradually abolishing trade restrictions among themselves and building common tariff walls against the outside world. German machine tools, Italian shoes, Belgian textiles and French fashions moved across frontiers duty free, much as goods crossed state lines in America. Each country enjoyed access to a wider home market, and all prospered, while Britain began to falter.

By 1961 Macmillan was applying to join Europe and naming Edward Heath as his chief Common Market negotiator. It was a major turning point in British foreign policy in this century. Since World War II the British had based their policy on twin pillars of a special relationship with the United States and with the Commonwealth nations, their former empire. Neither saved Britain the humiliation it suffered at Suez in 1956. By 1962 Europe had replaced the Commonwealth as Britain's biggest export market. At the same time both the United States and the Commonwealth were shifting their trade from Britain toward the New Europe.

But former French President Charles de Gaulle still saw the British as intruders, building a bridgehead in Europe as a Trojan horse for U.S. influence on the continent. In 1963 and again in 1967 De Gaulle vetoed Britain's application. Yet even De Gaulle once admitted privately that Britain would probably join one day, most likely when Heath was prime minister.

From the moment of his election in June 1970, Heath made Common Market membership the cornerstone of his foreign policy (*The World in 1970, 117-118*). By May of 1971 he had agreed in Paris with De Gaulle's successor, Georges Pompidou, that the political will was there to make the entry negotiations succeed. They did a month later in Luxembourg.

Heath then faced a tough battle at home to convince British public opinion that Britain's future did rest in Europe. Strong objections came on both economic and political grounds.

By October the cost of living in Britain was rising by more than 10 per cent a year and higher food prices from Common Market membership threatened to touch off even worse inflation. Unemployment at a 30-year high of almost a million men out of work raised fears of losing even more jobs to cheaper labor on the continent. The collapse earlier in the year of the proudest name in British industry, Rolls-Royce, shook confidence in predictions that British technology would lead the way in Europe. To all these arguments the pro-marketeers in Britain could only reply that the long-term benefits of access to a market four times the size of Britain's would eventually raise the standard of living well above the short-term entry costs. They had no guaranteed figures to prove their case, only the conviction that Britain would suffer more by staying out.

On the political side, opponents charged Britain would lose sovereignty by joining Europe. Pro-marketeers argued there could be no meaningful sovereignty in economic weakness outside Europe.

The public remained largely unconvinced by arguments for entry. Opinion polls throughout the year showed the majority of the electorate against. Former Prime Minister Harold Wilson's opposition Labor party, which had favored joining Europe while in government, decided to reject entry on the terms negotiated by Heath's Conservatives. It demanded a general election on the issue, hoping that the anti-market public would vote Labor back into office.

But Heath repeatedly made clear that Parliament would decide, refusing all bids for an election or a referendum. After a six-day debate Parliament voted on Oct. 28, 1971, for Europe by a substantial majority. The decisive ballot in the House of Commons in favor of entry in principle was 356 to 244, with 22 abstentions. It was a major personal triumph for Heath, who had built his political career on joining Europe.

"Many millions of people across the world will rejoice that Britain will be taking her rightful place in the true European unity that we are going to build," Heath said after the vote. And indeed their leaders did. President Nixon and West German Chancellor Willy Brandt were among the first to hail Parliament's vote as a historic turning point.

Heath won that vote with the help of 89 opposition Labor lawmakers who either voted "yes" with the government or abstained, despite demands from their party leadership to vote "no." Among them was Roy Jenkins, Labor's influential deputy leader and an ardent marketeer. Jenkins refused to change his mind on the issue and voted "yes," despite charges of "traitor" from Labor colleagues. Heath's Conservatives were also split, with 39 of them voting against the government and the Common Market.

A year-long political battle remained to approve detailed legislation aligning Britain's laws with Common Market rules before Britain could actually join the community on the target date of Jan. 1, 1973. Should Labor unite solidly against these bills and the Tory rebels continue to vote "no," the government could fall over them and the Common Market application with it. But most commentators saw this as unlikely. One said it was as illogical as accepting the 10 Commandments as a whole and then breaking them individually. Europeans also saw the chance of a subsequent defeat as remote. "Britain is not a country that gives its word and then takes it back," French Foreign Minister Maurice Schumann said.

Generally the British public accepted the parliamentary vote in principle. A public opinion poll showed that 49 per cent of the British public opposed entry while only 30 per cent favored it and 21 per cent were undecided. Significantly, the same poll said 84 per cent believed the country would join anyway and 65 per cent thought the parliamentary battle on the issue should stop after the first vote. The Daily Express, an influential national paper with a circulation of over 4 million copies, had strongly opposed joining Europe, and called the first vote "A great mistake." But it said this verdict of the nation's freely-elected representatives should be accepted and the time had come to promote British interests in Europe. The paper conceded defeat and said it would no longer fight to keep Britain out. Pro-market journals also took the first vote as a final. The normally sober Economist called the House of Commons approval in principle for entry "The most momentous peace-time decision of its history."

European leaders also made clear there would be much wider consultation between Britain and the Common Market nations well before Britain actually joined. All were already members of the North Atlantic Treaty Organization—NATO—and all had been driven closer together this year by a series of American policy decisions.

All lined up against the United States behind a formula for resolving the trade and monetary crisis President Nixon touched off Aug. 15. All demanded an early end to the U.S. 10 per cent import surcharge. All urged a devaluation of the American dollar against gold as part of a general realignment of the free world's leading currencies. All expressed concern about signs that America could withdraw from world affairs and pull its troops back from Europe, sentiments that gained credence when the Senate voted to end the U.S. foreign aid program. All were consulting over U.S. demands that Europe assume a bigger share of the burden for western defense. A European summit meeting was being considered for early 1972 to discuss these and other questions.

There was perhaps a note of irony in it all for the United States. It was America which first encouraged the West Europeans to get together after World War II, beginning by forcing them to cooperate to get the aid provided in the postwar Marshall Plan for economic recovery. Every American President since then praised each step along the way to a united Europe, working in a transatlantic partnership with the United States. With Britain in the Common Market, throwing its influence from support for the United Nations to support for Europe, there appeared to be little doubt that Europe would speak with a stronger voice. But it remained to be seen whether this voice would speak as a transatlantic partner of the United States or as a political and economic rival.

British negotiator Geoffrey Rippon, left, and French Foreign Minister Maurice Schumann at Common Market discussions in Luxembourg

Pittsburgh Pirate pitcher Steve Blass leaped high in the air after first base umpire called Merv Rettenmund (14) of Baltimore out to end last game of the series

World Series Grabbed by Pirates in Seventh Game with Surprised Orioles

Whenever people recalled the 1971 World Series and Pittsburgh's stunning comeback victory over Baltimore, they remembered the exploits of Roberto Clemente.

But Manager Earl Weaver of the Orioles always would have difficulty forgetting Steve Blass.

"As great as Clemente was," Weaver said after the Pirates had won the Series in the decisive seventh game, "it was Blass who beat us. This was the guy who knocked us off. If it hadn't been for Blass we might be popping the corks (champagne). Steve Blass was Mr. World Series."

Make that "Steve Blass of the No-Name Pitching Staff." For that was the identifying phrase Blass coined after he and a fuzzy-faced kid named Bruce Kison had turned Baltimore's booming bats to brittle toothpicks, pitching the Pirates to their first World Series triumph since 1960.

It was difficult to believe what had happened even after it had happened.

But it was virtually impossible to foresee it happening before it did happen.

The Orioles, champions of the American League, had be-

189

come only the second team in baseball history to win 100 games or more in three consecutive seasons and the first in a half-century to have four 20-game winning pitchers.

The line-up was a modern Murderers' Row, the assassins including Frank Robinson, Boog Powell, Brooks Robinson, Merv Rettenmund and a collection of others that were the envy of many of their competitors.

The Pirates, champions of the National League, had Clemente, major league home run leader Willie Stargell and 19-game winner Dock Ellis. But only Clemente would play an important role during the Series.

What then were the Pirates' chances?

About as good as they were in the first two games as the Orioles, labeled the best team in baseball history by Weaver, responded to the appellation with 5–3 and 11–3 victories in which they lashed 24 hits.

Then it began to turn around—and the man who began to turn it around was Mr. World Series.

Driven from the mound in the playoffs against San Francisco and reduced to the No. 3 spot in the starting rotation, Blass held the Pirates' hopes in his beleaguered right arm as the site of the Series switched to Pittsburgh.

The 29-year-old right-hander of the No-Name Pitching Staff put his name in headlines with his performance, baffling the Baltimore batters with an assortment of fast balls, curves and sliders resulting in a three-hit, 5–1 victory.

The Pirates now had hope, but they didn't seem to have much else when Luke Walker went out to the mound for

Pirates' pitcher Blass stuck out his tongue as he delivered during seventh game

Game 4 and had to be relieved in the first inning after allowing the Orioles three quick runs.

Danny Murtaugh, the wily cigar-chomping Pittsburgh manager, immediately called for Kison, who just a year earlier had cut his classes at Central Washington State College to see the World Series on television.

Now the kid was coming in to pitch in the glaring spotlight of an audience of some 60 million watching via television the first night game in World Series history. And pitch he did for the next 6⅓ innings, allowing the Orioles just one hit.

The Pirates, meanwhile, scored two runs in their half of the first inning, tied the score with a run in the third and then started a rally in the seventh inning when, with one out, Bob Robertson and Manny Sanguillen singled.

One out later, Murtaugh decided to pinch-hit for Kison, sending up reserve catcher Milt May, like Kison a 21-year-old rookie and a product of the 1968 draft. May responded with a line single to right field that brought in the winning run in a 4–3 victory.

The teams were now even, and Pittsburgh's Nelson Briles took center stage for Game 5. Acquired in a trade with St. Louis, the 28-year-old right-hander had struggled through an undistinguished season that left him with an 8–4 record.

But when he came to bat in the eighth inning he received a standing ovation. This tribute, he admitted later, left him in tears.

"When I got that big ovation when I came to the plate, it was like a flashback," Briles said after the game. "All I could think of were the many people who had been so helpful to me. It was the culmination of a two-year struggle."

Briles, who literally fell flat on the ground when he pitched and figuratively had fallen flat on his face since winning 19 games in 1968, received the ovation en route to a performance that topped the efforts of Blass and Kison.

For Briles pitched a two-hit, 4–0 shutout that gave the Pirates the lead three victories to two and sent the clubs back to Baltimore with Pittsburgh needing only one victory in the final two games to reign as the world champion.

And how things had turned around. Now the entire emphasis was on the Pirates, who were in position to become the first team in Series history to win four in succession after falling behind 0–2.

But, back in their own ball park, the Orioles bounced back with a 3–2 victory in 10 innings, Frank Robinson sliding home with the winning run after tagging up from third base on a short sacrifice fly by Brooks Robinson.

So they went to Game 7—and Blass went out to pitch for Pittsburgh against Mike Cuellar.

In the fourth inning, Clemente gave Pittsburgh a 1–0 lead with a home run—his 12th hit in the Series, finishing with a .414 batting average and the feeling that "now people in the whole world know the way I play."

Clemente, 37, a major league star for 17 years, went into the Series having decided in his own mind that his talents had not been fully appreciated and he was determined to show the big crowds and national television audience.

"They say I am a .300 hitter but I can't pull the ball," Clemente explained, talking about his detractors. "It's always 'but' or some other sarcastic thing. They never want to give me credit. But this is what I want people to know—how I play, not that I am a hypochondriac."

People now knew. But it still was up to Blass.

The Pirates got him another run in the eighth inning on a single by Stargell and a double by Jose Pagan, and Blass had only six more outs to get and had allowed just two hits. But there was trouble in the Orioles' half of the eighth.

Two singles, a sacrifice and a grounder produced one run before Blass pitched out of trouble and went back to the bench to rest before trying for the final three outs.

But nervousness overcame him and he had to rush to the clubhouse, sick to his stomach. There he vomited, but pulled himself together for the ninth inning—facing Powell, Frank Robinson and Rettenmund.

They went down 1–2–3 as Blass preserved the 2–1 victory and clinched the Series for the Pirates, leading to the traditional champagne celebration in the clubhouse that Weaver felt would have been the Orioles if the Pirates hadn't gotten the clutch pitching of Blass.

And that's where Blass, undeniably happy, coined the phrase No-Name Pitching Staff.

It was there also that the phone jangled in Murtaugh's managerial cubicle. The caller was President Nixon.

Murtaugh accepted the call with the same stoic manner he had maintained throughout the Series, and was even chided by the President for his manner.

"He told me he thought I was rather calm on the bench for a situation like this," Murtaugh related. "It's a tremendous boost when the President can take time out from his worldly duties for a baseball game."

Nixon then had his call shifted to the Orioles' dressing room to speak to Weaver. Weaver listened, then responded:

"Mr. President, you couldn't have called at a better time. It means so much more now than it would at any other time."

Weaver probably never would forget that call. But as much as the name Nixon remained in his mind, it was the name Blass he would have to live with.

Pirates' Willie Stargell starting slide for plate as Orioles' catcher Ellie Hendricks waited for the throw in the final game

Nixon in Crisis Halted Gold Sales for Dollars

The Floating Dollar: French photographer in commentary on President Nixon's decision to suspend the dollar's convertibility into gold, showed a U.S. banknote afloat in a Paris fountain

Extra 10 per cent duty ordered on most imports, and foreign nations told to readjust their currency value

THE WORLD'S worst money crisis since the Great Depression of the 1930s came up like a thunderstorm in the night—and almost anybody who was awake knew it was coming. But for the great sleeping majority the first alarm was the cataclysmic cancellation of the dollar's gold value, the thundering fall of the world's strongest money.

Actually, as hot days bring a storm, this one had been incubating for more than 25 years. Its origins went back to the end of the Second World War, when the United States, the richest country in the world, held some $35 billion of the $40-odd billion monetary gold in the world.

Being so rich in gold, the United States had considered it its duty to help others. Loans to devastated countries, grants to poor ones, heavy spending on armies overseas, all these looked small compared to that $35 billion.

And even if the outflow of gold was not balanced by an equivalent inflow, there was no apparent need to worry. One of the sweeter fruits of that period of international cooperation at the end of the war had been the Bretton Woods agreement on money.

"Bretton Woods" had become almost a synonym for mystery and high finance. But actually it was not at all complicated. Finance ministers of most Allied powers, soon to be victorious, met at a mountain resort called Bretton Woods in 1944. In a brief three weeks, they worked out a world money system which was to serve international trade well for 25 years.

This was the system:

All the member countries, all the major ones except those in the Communist bloc, were to put up capital to form the International Monetary Fund. The contributions were partially in gold, partially in each country's currency. Voting in the Fund was in proportion to the money put up, so the United States, which put up the most gold and dollars, had 22 per cent of the votes.

The Fund was to lend money, short-term, to countries having a temporary financial difficulty. If India had a drought and had to import wheat and couldn't export jute, the Fund would lend money to balance the import-export account until the rains came again.

There was another proviso which proved the weak link in the system and nearly caused its collapse. Dollars and gold were to be the reserves backing each country's own money. A dollar was to be worth 1/35 of an ounce of gold. Other countries were to express the value of their currency in dollars—the pound then was to be $4 and the mark about 24 cents and so on.

There was not enough gold in the world to support the expected volume of foreign trade, so the dollar was made equal to gold. A country owing another could pay in either gold or dollars. And the United States promised to buy all the dollars anybody had for $35 an ounce. That made the dollar "as good as gold."

The system was a good one and it brought some regularity into the world's money, which had been pretty chaotic since the Depression. At that time many countries stopped giving gold for their money, a move called "going off the gold standard." Even the United States, in raising the price of gold from $20 to $35 an ounce in 1934, had barred its citizens from owning gold. The ban was originally aimed at keeping people from making money on the devaluation of the dollar, but it effectively kept them from putting their funds into gold coins.

For a while, all went well. The end of the War led into the greatest world-wide boom in history. By using the dollar as international money, there was plenty of credit to go around, causing the so-called "international liquidity." This meant there was enough money in circulation to finance the increased trade.

But early in the 1950s the heat began, the buildup of the hot wave that led to the storm. The United States went into the Korean War and financed it out of general revenues. There were some special war taxes, but not enough to pay for the action. More dollars flowed out of the country than came back for exports.

This was not exactly "printing press money"—it was a credit on the books. If Germany sold the U.S. so many Volkswagens that cattle hides exports to Germany didn't pay for them, there was a credit to Germany and a debit to the United States. Germany had this credit of so many dollars to use as backing for its own issue of marks.

After the Korean War, things got better. The United States was still spending a lot of money overseas on defense, both for itself and for other countries, but the import-export balance was good. The U.S. was selling more abroad than it was buying and this covered some of the deficit in the defense spending.

But during the 1950s the gold was flowing out and the U.S. stocks had been cut in half by 1960. It had only $17 billion left by Jan. 1, 1961. Other countries were building up their stocks of dollars but they were also taking a lot of gold, selling their dollars back to the U.S. for gold.

This steady drain on gold continued during the 1960s: the stock was $16 billion in 1962, $15 billion in 1963 and so on. By the end of the decade, the stock was down to $11 billion. This was just about the minimum working balance, because the United States had to have, by law, a dollar's worth of gold in the Treasury for every $4 in paper money circulating in the country. And the country couldn't get along with less than $40 billion in paper money and coins to make change.

There was another sign that the money weather was getting sultry enough for a storm. During the 1960s the trade balance kept getting smaller and smaller. In 1960, for instance, the U.S. bought $15 billion worth of imported goods and sold almost $20 billion. But by the end of the decade this favorable balance was down to $2 billion a year.

Things rapidly got worse. By April 1971, there wasn't any trade balance any more. The U.S. was a net importer and the curve of rising imports had risen above the curve of exports. The spending in Vietnam was being cut, but not as fast as imports were rising.

That was the bad year, 1971, the worst yet. The U.S. was in the position of a man who had been living on his capital. He had spent most of it, owed a lot more, and was not cutting down his living expenses.

The first sign that the strain was so great that something would break came in early May. One of the provisos of the Bretton Woods agreement was that each country was responsible for keeping its currency at the fixed value of the dollar. It had to buy dollars when they were pushing up currency values, or borrow and sell when the currency was falling.

Germany, during this time, was prospering. Her people worked hard, strikes were rare, her steel was cheap and her automobiles were popular. She had a highly favorable trade balance, meaning she was selling more abroad than she was buying.

This had made her money worth more, and twice during the 1960s the mark had been revalued. That meant that its official value in relation to the dollar had been changed. In 1961 it went to 4.2 marks to the dollar and in 1969 it went to 4 marks. Each time people who had had the foresight to stock up on marks made money—the mark they had bought for 24 cents, for instance, suddenly became worth 25 cents.

With continuing prosperity, the mark was a favorite candidate for another revaluation. And there was plenty of money loose in Europe to take advantage of the opportunity. These were "Euro-dollars," dollars owned overseas, either by banks or private investors. Early in the year the pool of Eurodollars was estimated at around $5 billion, but it grew rapidly. By May there was an estimated $50 or $60 billion in Eurodollars available. This huge sum, about as much as all the currency in circulation in the United States, was enough to overwhelm any country.

About the first of May, the dollars started to flood into Germany. The German central bank bought tens of millions of dollars worth, then hundreds of millions as the flood continued. By May 9 the central bank was completely inundated and had to give up the fight. It notified the International Monetary Fund, the IMF, that it would have to breach the rules on maintaining the mark's low value. It turned the currency loose to "float," to have its value set by the old law of supply and demand.

Germany's objection to the dollar flood was that it would set off inflation in that country. Since it had to pay out marks for dollars, there were too many marks in circulation. Germany's own stability was threatened by the release of the billions of marks.

The German action relieved the pressure for a little while. The mark floated up to about 27 cents and hung there. This was a break for the U.S., because the more expensive mark meant that it took more dollars to buy 400 marks to pay for a ton of steel beams. It also took more dollars to buy a Volkswagen, so fewer people bought the foreign car. So imports were down—but only a little. And, since marks would buy more dollars, American computers could sell for less in the German market, thereby increasing exports.

Unfortunately, the relief was only temporary. There was still that huge pool of Eurodollars sloshing around Europe, ready to flood over national boundaries in search of a quick profit. Once they had made their profit on the mark, they were ready to go somewhere else.

By the middle of July, the French franc and the Swiss franc seemed likely candidates for revaluation. The dollars started to flood into the Paris money markets, buying francs. But the French, learning from the German lesson, were a little more ready. They slapped controls on purchases of dollars, lowered interest rates on bank deposits arising from dollar sales.

Money flows were worse than a nervous horse. Any accident could scare them into a panic. The French action really scared them. Dollars became hard to sell to provincial banks and exchange houses. Tourists found difficulty in selling their dollars. For the first time, foreigners were afraid to buy and hold dollars.

Meanwhile, the Germans were trying to get rid of their surplus of dollars, trickling them into the market whenever the rate rose a little. These dollars were available to go to France

Susie Drucker of Wilmette, Ill., (left) and Diane Erpelding of Denver exchanging foreign currency for U.S. dollars at Kennedy International Airport upon return from Europe

Treasury Secretary John B. Connally declared that the United States was under no compulsion to get a solution to the money crisis "this week, this month or this year"

or Switzerland, and meanwhile the dollar sales in Germany kept the exchange rate from settling. The Swiss also took defensive action against any dollar flood.

This made the situation extremely ticklish. Two international finance experts told Barron's, a financial magazine, in the third week in July that there would be trouble within 90 days. And they meant serious trouble, a worldwide depression or a wholesale collapse of exchange rates. As it turned out, it was the exchange rate collapse, and it happened in a whole lot less than 90 days.

Two major events crystallized the crisis. The tension had been building up, the experts had warned that it was dangerous. Then almost simultaneously the two things which triggered the storm came in the first week in August.

One was a forecast by the Morgan Guaranty Bank estimating that the American trade deficit in the second quarter would be in excess of $7 billion. This would have been the largest in history and it showed that the German float had not permanently cured the world's trade illness.

The other was a report released by the Joint Economic Committee of the U.S. Congress. This said the dollar was "over-valued," meaning that it was not worth 1/35 of an ounce of gold. It said the International Monetary Fund should increase the value of all other currencies. If the IMF did not act, the committee report said, the U.S. should halt its conversion of dollars into gold for foreign governments. (The gold conversion for private holders had been cancelled earlier as the U.S. gold stock shrank.)

The committee report was the final straw. The stock market had dropped after the Morgan Guaranty estimate, as investors

sold stocks and prepared to send their money abroad. The committee recommendations caused a wholesale movement out of the dollar, into any foreign currency available.

The committee report was published in the Sunday papers of Aug. 8. The next week was a wild one as tourists found their dollars refused and owners of Eurodollars tried to change them into other currencies.

The rate for the dollar dropped in Europe and sales rose sharply. By Tuesday the sales were running at the rate of $200 million a day. Marginal currencies like the Portuguese escudo and the various Scandinavian crowns and krones were rising fast.

Trade was reduced because importers did not know what their dollar would buy when the goods were delivered. Exporters in other countries had been reluctant for some time to quote prices in dollars for future deliveries.

This was the situation when President Nixon went on the air Aug. 15 to deliver what aides had said would be a speech on economic matters. But they indicated it would deal with domestic economy, inflation and unemployment and so on.

And that was what he dealt with, until the final minutes of his speech. Then, in his dry, lawyer-like manner, unemotionally, he announced the most drastic, radical, far-reaching changes in America's money matters since President Roosevelt devalued the dollar in 1934.

* * * *

America, President Nixon said, would no longer sell gold for dollars. An extra 10 per cent duty was put on most imports. All countries were called on to readjust the value of their currency in true relation to the dollar. Americans were given tax cuts if they bought American goods in some cases.

All these had been discussed in the previous weeks as possible steps the government might take.

"We knew he had to do something," Barron's said later. "What we didn't expect was that he would do everything."

American money experts in many cases applauded the action. The most important immediate result, one banker said, was a restoration of faith in the dollar. Not that it was actually any stronger, he explained, but President Nixon had shown that America intended to defend it and keep it from disaster.

It also gave the government a negotiating weapon, explained another. By putting on the extra import duty, the surcharge, he could bargain to take it off if other countries would revalue their money.

The importance of this lay in an apparent paradox in foreign trade: The cheaper a money unit was, the better for the country using it. If the dollar was worth 660 yen (as it was then) it would take 6600 yen to buy a $10 Japanese radio. But if the dollar was worth only 600 yen, then it would take $11 to buy that radio. The radio cost more, so not as many of them would be sold. On the other side of the ledger, at 660 yen a $3 bushel of soybeans would cost 1980 yen. But at 600 yen, the cost would be only 1800 yen per bushel. So the Japanese would buy more soybeans.

Thus it was to America's interest to raise the value of other currencies. Equally, it was to their disadvantage for other countries to revalue. And their exports were hurt by the surcharge on the import duties.

But there was general sympathy and understanding overseas for the American position. The Japanese held out for a week, but finally stopped intervening in the foreign exchange market and let the value of the yen rise. The number required to buy a dollar dropped gradually from 660 to 630. The Germans sold a few dollars when the dollar rate went down too much, but they held the change to about 10 per cent.

More important, there was no retaliation in the import-export picture. Other countries did not put higher prices on American goods in reprisal.

However, events did not follow the script entirely. The price of imported goods did not go up at once, since most dealers continued to sell what they had in stock for the old prices. One said that it would take several months for the new goods, at the new prices, to reach the market.

Another unexpected event was that the dollar did not go down as much as expected. Some experts had thought it might fall as much as 15 per cent. Instead, it went down only 2 per cent in the two weeks after it was cut loose from gold. One reason, of course, was that some countries bought or sold dollars to keep the fall within bounds, what a German banker called "a dirty float" because it was not entirely left to market forces to fix the value.

Still another piece of action that did not fit the script was the comparative weakness of gold. Instead of rising as had been expected, its value hung steady around the $42 free market price it had reached before President Nixon's action. This, the experts explained—but not until after it happened—was because it had already risen 20 per cent above the $35 mark and nobody expected the dollar to be devalued this much.

And another curious effect was that American tourists began buying their foreign money in the U.S. before they set off on their travels. The demand was so heavy that one foreign exchange dealer had to set up special air transport arrangements to bring in enough francs and marks and pounds and lira.

But these events were sideshows, not the main event. That was the meeting of the directors of the IMF. By accident, the annual meeting of the fund had been scheduled for the end of September, before the crisis became acute. This gave an opportunity for the finance ministers around the world to get together and settle the problem.

But before this happened, there were preliminary meetings of the money men of the major industrial countries, the so-called "group of 10," in Europe. It was at this meeting that the main outlines of a likely settlement came to light. The other countries said they were willing to revalue if the U.S. would cancel the surcharge. The U.S. said it would cancel the surcharge if the others revalued. There was the basis of an understanding right there—it was just a question of timing.

Yet there was one stumbling block which came to light at the IMF. The others wanted the U.S. to devalue the dollar officially, by raising the price of gold. The U.S. said this wasn't necessary, because it wanted to reduce the use of gold as money.

The IMF delegates set up machinery for further negotiations. The Group of Ten arranged for a meeting of deputy finance ministers in October, to draft general terms for revaluation. A full-dress ministerial meeting was planned for about Nov. 20, but later was postponed.

There was optimistic talk of a solution by the year-end—a general realignment of currencies, an agenda for dismantling of barriers against U.S. goods, a specific plan for removal of the surcharge.

But nothing moved, for months. October's meeting ended in deadlock. So did a cabinet-level trade conference in Washington of Japanese and American officials. Europeans warned that world-wide recession was setting in, caused largely, they contended, by uncertainties raised by the U.S. actions.

To meet the U.S. overall goal quickly—a $13 billion swing in the U.S. balance of payments, from the deep deficit to a surplus—would wreck Europe's economies, the Common Market said. The U.S. indicated the shift could be spread over a period of two or three or four years.

The other countries wanted more specifics: Exactly what was the U.S. price for removal of the surcharge? How soon and by how much should their protective barriers be reduced, and by how much should their currency values be increased?

American negotiators showed no haste about getting down to specifics. The President's chief economic spokesman, Secretary of the Treasury John B. Connally, told reporters the U.S. was "under no compulsion to get a solution this week, this month, or this year."

Europeans did not disguise their suspicions that the Nixon Administration wouldn't mind retaining the surcharge—in effect, a new protective tariff—indefinitely. Some countries began building up their own trade and exchange restrictions. Denmark imposed a surcharge of its own. The French and others hinted bitterly of retaliation. Connally held to his tough bargaining stance saying: "Retaliation is a two-way street."

As chairman of the Group of Ten ministers, Connally had responsibility for fixing date and place of their scheduled November meeting. Instead, on Nov. 10, the Treasury announced it was "exploring dates in early December."

"After evaluating the views and statements of others, prospects for progress did not appear sufficient to warrant a meeting at an earlier date," said the Treasury statement. "More time for preparation appears useful. No date has been set."

And the statement warned against "either optimism or pessimism about the results of a single meeting."

BODIES OF 25 FARM WORKERS
UNCOVERED IN ORCHARD GRAVES

They were lonely men. Their free hours—when they had them—were spent sitting in the Skid Row sections of small towns, drinking wine in doorways, sleeping on sidewalks, dreaming of relatives and friends far away. When the season was good these drifting farm laborers from as far east as Atlanta, Ga., toiled in the fertile fields of the California valleys, picking peaches, prunes, tomatoes, plums—whatever the soil produced.

In the height of the peach harvest they could make 75 cents for thinning a small tree, $1.50 for a large one. But the workload was heavy for those who had never done it before, and jobs were scarce.

Nobody has paid much attention to these migrant workers. Nearly every day one or more turned up dead beside a remote railroad track or in a dank alley.

Because of Yuba City, a Sutter County town in the Sacramento Valley, the nation became more aware of the lives of such men when a mass murder of 25 laborers was uncovered. Police said 25 male bodies had been dug up in Jack Sullivan's orchards along the Feather River. Some had been dead 48 hours, others for two months. Law officers were puzzled by the lack of any inquiries from relatives or friends.

The first body was found May 21, when a farm worker on a nearby ranch noticed a newly dug hole. That afternoon, when he saw that the pit had been filled, he notified officials. Then the body of Kenneth E. Whitacre was exhumed.

The second corpse was revealed when a tractor driver noticed a suspicious mound. Sheriff Ray D. Whiteaker began a systematic search that required a full month before all 25 victims were revealed.

One by one the bodies were taken from graves three to six feet deep in the orchards and along the banks of the Feather River. Each had been stabbed in the chest repeatedly, their backs hacked, in the shape of crosses, with a machete or axe, their arms pulled over their heads and their shirts covering their faces. All were white except one, a Negro, all apparently between the ages of 40 and 63.

On May 26 local authorities visited a newly built $20,000 tract home on the edge of town and arrested 37-year-old Juan V. Corona, handsome, six-foot father of four daughters.

Subsequently he was indicted on 25 counts of murder. Corona, who barely spoke English, claimed a few days later that he had no idea why they had arrested him.

Roy Delong, a friend of one of the victims, Sigrid (Pete) Beierman, reported that he last saw Beierman getting into a yellow-and-white van owned by Corona, deputies said.

Corona had been frequently seen transporting men to and from their jobs in his new yellow van or in an old school bus. For 16 years Corona had been a farm labor contractor supplying workers for growers, taking the traditional 10 to 15 per cent from their pay and selling them food, according to Yuba City residents.

In one of the graves, Sutter County law officials reported, were found two receipts from the Del Pero Brothers meat company, made out to Corona, and in Corona's cellar police came upon an 18-inch machete showing bloodstains and hair.

* * * * * * * * * * * * * * *

In 1955 Corona had followed two older brothers, Natividad and Felix, from Jalisco,

Juan Corona, accused of slaying 25 men and burying their bodies

Mexico, to Sutter County. Later two younger brothers, Pedro and Alvaro, joined them. All except Alvaro became farm labor contractors. Juan Corona became the Sullivan ranch contractor. The foreman, Raymond E. Duran, said of Corona: "He was far and away the best contractor we ever had. He would never cheat the ranch."

When Corona bought his new home in 1968 he paid $5,000 cash and easily obtained a mortgage from the Wells Fargo Bank. He also owned a 1970 sedan and the new van. An old friend said that whatever Corona owned he got because he was "hard working, determined and industrious."

A few months after he arrived in Sutter County the Feather River flooded, killing 37 persons in Yuba City. Early in 1956 Corona's brother, Natividad petitioned to have Juan, then 22, committed to a mental institution.

"He believed that everyone in this area had drowned in the flood," Natividad said. "He reads the Bible and writes all the time."

Two local doctors then examined Juan and found him "confused, disorientated" and suffering from "delusions and hallucinations." They gave a tentative diagnosis of schizophrenia and recommended treatment in an institution. The court ordered him sent to DeWitt State Hospital in Auburn, where he was released three months later as cured.

Following Corona's arrest, Det. Sgt. John Purchell said in an affidavit that the subject was

"known to have fits of temper such that his family had to take ropes and tie him down until he became quiet again."

Corona's last year as a contractor, 1970-71, had been a difficult one. The rains came early and cut the harvest time. Mechanization had replaced most of the tomato harvesters. Now mechanical peach pickers were being used. The Sullivan ranch had bought one. Early in 1971 Corona applied for welfare at the Sutter County office but was turned down when an investigation showed that he had more than the $600 in personal property allowed by law.

On June 2 Corona pleaded innocent of murder. His lawyer, Richard E. Hawk, said that the only really hard elements of evidence were the two meat receipts with his name on them. "Would he have left calling cards like that behind if he really killed those men?" Hawk asked.

As Corona sat in jail he worried about his wife and children. They were No. 1, he told reporters in an interview. "There is no one to support them now. And the four children have to go to school and there is nobody who can give them clothes, food."

When one brother of Juan's was told of his arrest he simply said, "He was the best brother I ever had."

Corona's physical condition weakened while he awaited trial. He was hospitalized for two mild heart attacks, one in the middle of June and one late in August. A change of Venue from Sutter County was denied in October.

Iran's 2,500th Anniversary

Above, Iranian army troops dressed as Persian warriors of yore paraded before a dais which seated a glittering gathering of the world's royalty and heads of state. Right, The Shah, Mohammed Reza Pahlavi officially inaugurated the observance of 25 centuries of Persian royal rule. Below, scene inside the imperial dining tent during a gala banquet given by the Shah and Empress Farah Diba

SOVIET SPY SUSPECTS EXPELLED

When his name first appeared in British newspapers he seemed fairly inconsequential—a Soviet garment buyer, Oleg Lyalin, who had failed to appear before a London court to answer charges of drunken driving. What the press didn't know, until the British Foreign Office released a report, was that Lyalin was in reality a Soviet KGB agent (The Committee for State Security) who defected from Russia, blowing the lid off a spy ring.

The result was the expulsion of 105 Russians with British diplomatic passports.

The British government said that, upon defection, Lyalin handed over documents and secret plans detailing espionage activities and confirming existing suspicions about the agents involved.

There were 550 Russian diplomats and attaches in Great Britain at the time. Of the 105 Russians asked to leave, some were Aeroflot airlines officials, representatives of the Moscow Bank, or members of trade delegations. Their positions, the government said, indicated a trend toward industrial as well as military espionage.

In a formal statement informing Moscow of the expulsion on Sept. 24, the Foreign Office in London said the defector, Lyalin, "an officer of the KGB, brought with him (to the Foreign Office) certain information and documents, including plans for infiltration of agents for the purpose of sabotage."

Part of this information, the New York Times said, included a Soviet plan for infiltration of the navy. A particular target was the secret research establishment at Portland, on the English south coast, from which secrets were stolen between 1955 and 1961 by a spy ring headed by a Soviet agent, this account said.

British officials pointed out that a quieter form of diplomacy had been attempted to stop Soviet espionage when Foreign Minister Sir Alec Douglas-Home wrote Moscow on two occasions, one in December 1970 and the other August 1971, acting on individual cases in London. However, the Kremlin made no reply.

The Soviet Union charged the British were acting with "anti-Soviet hysteria" and making "false accusations" basing them on the information given to them by a playboy who was a minor officer in the KGB. Britain's intention, said the Soviet government, was to wreck the Soviet-sponsored plan for a European security conference, one of Moscow's prime foreign policy objectives.

On Oct. 8 the Soviet government expelled four British diplomats and a businessman, and denied entry of ten other Britons into Russia. Nine of the ten were former British embassy staff members and one was a scholar. The Soviet announcement said the British who were ordered to leave or denied entry were "dealing in activities incompatible with their official status, which would harm the interests of security in the Soviet Union."

The British government said the KGB had conducted a wide variety of security operations. Many of these had no link to international espionage.

The KGB had made a name for itself in the past. There was the famous Col. Rudolf Abel, who spent nine years in the United States running a spy network that may have covered most of North America. He was given back to Russia in exchange for Gary Powers, who was shot down near Sverdlovsk in the U2 incident in 1960.

But the KGB had had its failures too, the most classic being an attempt to buy an entire French-built Mirage fighter plane from a Lebanese Air Force officer for $2,000,000 in 1969. The pilot exposed the plan.

BRITISH PLANE CRASH TOLL 63

Sixty-three persons aboard a British European Airways plane were killed Oct. 2 when, witnesses said, its turbo-prop engines exploded near Tielt, Belgium. Observers reported that the Vanguard came in low, grazing some red-tiled houses, hit a tree and plunged into the ground, exploding on impact.

The plane, used occasionally to fly into Belfast, Northern Ireland, was en route from London to Salzburg, Austria. In addition to eight crew members, the plane carried 37 Britons, eight Austrians, six Americans and four Japanese.

One witness, Jose De Witte, 24 a son of a nearby farmer, said "onlookers rushed to the site, swarmed all over it and started pillaging wallets and other personal belongings."

BEA officials said later they could not understand why a 10-year-old Vanguard had been used on a flight to Austria. "Normally they are used for domestic flights" in the British Isles, a spokesman said.

The last major plane disaster in Belgium, in 1961, was the crash of Sabena Boeing 707 near Brussels airport, on a flight from New York, killing all 73 passengers and crew.

ANCIENT SKULL FOUND IN CAVE

A human skull which anthropologists said might be more than 200,000 years old was found in congealed sand in the floor of a Pyrenees cave by a group of French paleontologists.

The New York Times gave this account of what was said to be the first clue to the facial appearance of the man who inhabited Europe in that era preceding the Neanderthal man. The nearly complete skull had massive eyebrow ridges, a remarkably flat forehead, more horizontal than vertical, and a narrow elongated

brain case. Despite his small brain there were indications that this creature was a potent hunter. Surrounding him were numerous rhinoceros and horse bones, as well as bones from bears, panther, a form of elephant, turtle, deer, a big archaic cow, wolf, rabbit and birds.

Not much was known about man who lived 200,000 years ago except that he was a toolmaker, as evidenced by stone implements that were found in Britain and the Middle East dating back to that time.

But anthropologists hoped to determine from the skull that the European Neanderthal man who lived 90,000 years ago evolved independently of his contempories in Africa and Asia.

The skull, which was classed by the French as belonging to the so-called Tayacian culture, was found last summer in a cove above the village of Tautavel near Perpignan, in the Eastern Pyrenees. The discovery was made by a group working under Henry de Lumley, a geologist at the faculty of sciences of the University of Ais-Marseilles, and his wife, Marie-Antoinette de Lumley.

Japan's Emperor Hirohito midway through his tour of European capitals visited the London zoo with Prince Philip. The emperor was a keen marine biologist

MURDER MARRED ITALIAN RALLY

A canopy of plastic streamers—red, white and green, the colors of homeland Italy—had been hung overnight across Manhattan's Columbus Circle. From Italian neighborhoods throughout New York City thousands of residents were assembling beneath the tall statue of Christopher Columbus in the plaza.

Red, white and blue American flags, complementing the colorful streamers above, flew from the sidewalk stalls that encircled the throng, in county fair fashion. An army of vendors offered sweets, ices and prideful lapel buttons expressing dual respect for both nations. Everyone talked at once, in competition with the amplified organ music.

The occasion was the second annual celebration of Unity Day, sponsored by the Italian-American Civil Rights League, and the day was a humid, hot June 28. Just as the formal observances were about to begin, Joseph Colombo Sr., 48, nattily dressed and beaming, pushed his way through the crowd, shaking hands, answering questions and posing for photographers.

Colombo was one of the founders of the league. Among other things, he had sought to improve the image of Italian Americans as loyal and law-abiding U.S. citizens. At the same time he had evidently expected to aid the Mafia by prevailing upon the U.S. Department of Justice not to use the terms Mafia and Cosa Nostra indiscriminately, and by inducing the makers of *The Godfather,* a film based on the Mario Pusso novel, not to use them at all.

But it appeared that Colombo had also angered some Mafia leaders by drawing attention to their traditionally secret way of life. In the Justice Department files Colombo was listed as the reputed leader of one of the five Cosa Nostra families in New York City. And, during his tour of greeting in Columbus Circle on the morning of June 28, ample reason for speculation about his true vocation was suddenly and violently created:

A volley of shots momentarily silenced the music and the talk. Colombo fell to the pavement on his back, bleeding profusely from the head and neck. He had been hit, but not fatally, by three bullets.

Moments later the suspected gunman was dead, shot by another who disappeared in the crowd.

Colombo's attacker was later identified by police as 24-year-old Jerome Johnson, a black photographer who only minutes before the shootings had been photographing Colombo with a movie camera.

With bullets in his brain, neck and jaw, Colombo was taken to nearby Roosevelt Hospital, where he underwent five hours of surgery. Doctors said he had a 50-50 chance to survive. For two months he remained in critical and comatose condition. On Aug. 28 he was discharged, still semi-comatose but physically recovering, and taken to the home of a son. But at October's end his condition remained basically unchanged, police said. No arrests had been made in Johnson's slaying.

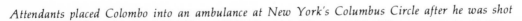

On the day of the shootings the most recent incident upon which the Colombo family had drawn attention took place April 30, 1970, when the senior Colombo's son, Joe Jr., was arrested and accused of melting coins into silver ingots. His father bailed him out, hired the best lawyers. Joe Jr. was acquitted. In the following month the senior Colombo picketed the FBI, claiming his family was being harassed by agents. Later that summer the Italian-American Civil Rights League was organized, and Joe Sr., with numerous demonstrations, achieved repression of unrestricted use of Mafia and Cosa Nostra, at least by federal officers and *The Godfather* filmers. "The Mafia," he once observed during an interview, "what's the Mafia?"

Although Joe Colombo Jr. insisted that his father had nothing to do with the underworld, police linked the senior Colombo's slayer to one of the New York "families." Johnson was born in New Brunswick, N.J., and had acquired a record of seven arrests, including peddling, attempted rape and burglary. His only conviction was for peddling in Los Angeles, for which he received three months' probation. He had established an unsavory reputation in New Brunswick, where he made himself a nuisance to Rutgers University coeds, who referred to him as the "Pisces man" because of his constant and often frightening discussions of astrology.

The New York Times said that one unidentified woman had told its reporter that after meeting Johnson at Rutgers he frequently visited her New York apartment and finally persuaded her to live with him. She said he would sometimes beat and rape her, or threaten her with a dangerous weapon. He was a strong admirer of Italians, and referred to himself as "God," she said.

Chief of Detectives Albert Seedman told a news conference that Johnson hung out in an after-hours joint in Greenwich Village controlled by Paul DiBella, reputed "soldier" in the "family" of Carlo Gambino. "Johnson," said Seedman, "associated with people known to be connected to the Gambino 'family'."

Deputy Police Commissioner Robert Daley said it appeared that Johnson was "hired by the Italian underworld community" and that he was the victim of a doublecross. But Daniel P. Hollman, chief of the police Joint Strike Force to Combat Organized Crime, said he considered the attempt to kill Colombo was the work of a psychopath, not part of any struggle among underworld factions. It was not the style of organized crime, he said, to give "a job like that to someone not in the organization." Seedman disagreed. On Aug. 31 federal sources announced that Joseph Yacovelli, ostensibly a $100-per-week trucking employee, was the new leader of the Colombo family.

Accounts of reputed strife between Colombo and other "families" over the years were numerous and speculation was endless in the months that followed the shootings. Included in the guesswork was the fairly widespread opinion that police were hesitant in taking positive action for fear of starting a bloody "family" war.

Attendants placed Colombo into an ambulance at New York's Columbus Circle after he was shot

H. RAP BROWN FINALLY FOUND?

A 1968 photograph of H. Rap Brown, who police said was wounded in an attempted bar holdup

For 17 months the name of H. Rap Brown was on the Federal Bureau of Investigation's ten "most wanted" persons list. Many authorities believed he had left the country in April 1970 when he didn't appear for his trial in Bel Air, Md., on charges of inciting to riot and arson in disturbances that destroyed much of a Negro section of Cambridge, Md., three years earlier.

Others believed him dead; killed in a bomb blast that wrecked a car and killed two of his friends at Bel Air on March 9, 1970 *(The World in 1970, 58).*

Then, on Oct. 16, 1971, New York City police reported that the 28-year-old militant black leader and three other accomplices had robbed a upper West Side bar during early morning hours. In a hospital bed with two abdominal wounds was a man whose fingerprints, officials said, identified him as H. Rap Brown, but the patient insisted his name was Roy Williams.

This account of his arrest was given by investigators:

On a phone tip, police went to the bar where Brown and three others, later identified as Sam Petty, 23, and Arthur Young, 25, both of St. Louis, and Levi Valentine, 24, of Chicago, had made 25 black patrons lie on the floor to be robbed. Officers arrived just as the four were leaving, and opened fire. Chasing them into an apartment building, the police captured three men on the stairs. Brown, wounded in the stomach, had rushed to the roof of the building where he was cornered by Patrolman Ralph Mannetta, 26.

Two patrolmen in the hunt were wounded: Gerald Hunt, 21, in the chest and Salvatore Rosato, 29, in the hand.

In a bedside arraignment, Brown was held in $250,000 bail and charged with attempted homicide, robbery, and possession of a dangerous weapon. The other three, similarly charged, were held on $100,000 bail each.

One of the trio that accompanied Brown—Sam Petty—became Brown's body guard about three years ago.

William Kunstler, who represented Brown on the Maryland riot charges, maintained that the man authorities said was Brown was not necessarily him. When Criminal Court Judge James M. Yeargin tried to designate Kunstler as Brown's attorney at his bedside, Brown told the judge: "I never said he could represent me."

In May 1967 when Hubert Geroid Brown took over the chairmanship of the Student Non-violent Coordinating Committee its former chairman Stokely Carmichael introduced him by saying "you'll be happy to have me back when you hear from him—he's a baaaad man" *(The World in 1967, 142, 184).*

Brown's fiery speeches brought him the nickname of Rap as audiences shouted "Rap it to 'em baby." He frequently made appeals to blacks to take militant action in their fight for equality with white citizens.

DEAN ACHESON TAKEN BY DEATH

He had been a key figure in the monetary reforms of the 1930s, but it was as Secretary of State during the last four years of the Truman Administration that Dean Acheson came into his own, exercising a deep influence on U.S. foreign policy.

When he died Oct. 12 at his farm in Sandy Spring, Md., at the age of 78, Acheson was hailed by President Nixon as "one of the towering figures of his time."

As a member of the State Department almost continuously from 1941–53, Acheson left his mark on American destiny. During the last four years of that period he was the major factor in formulating the North Atlantic Treaty Organization, signing the peace treaty with Japan, outlining the political strategy of the Korean war, determining U.S. attitudes toward the Communist regime in China and resisting the onslaught of the McCarthy group at home.

Some of Acheson's other outstanding achievements were:

—The Bretton Woods agreement which led to the establishment of the World Bank.

—The Truman Doctrine of assistance to Greece and Turkey.

—Groundwork for the Marshall Plan for bolstering Europe.

—Creating and rearming West Germany.

—Bipartisanship in foreign policy.

Acheson, a Connecticut-born aristocrat with a sharp tongue and haughty manner, had a virtually free hand in diplomatic affairs under Harry S. Truman. He used it to establish the basic U.S. Cold War strategy.

Working on the premise that the Soviet Union was a major threat to world security, Acheson formed a series of alliances designed to surround Russia with enough military and economic might to deter thoughts of aggression.

The Secretary of State also pressed hard for the Marshall Plan aimed at rebuilding war-shattered Europe.

Confronted with the takeover of China by Mao Tse-tung, Acheson had doubts about the viability of the Nationalists, but he promoted a policy of nonrecognition of Mao and aid to Chiang Kai-shek in Taiwan.

One of the major crises in Acheson's career came when Alger Hiss, a friend and former State Department associate, was accused of being a Communist. He refused to disavow his friendship for Hiss, who later was convicted and sentenced to prison for perjury in denying he had been a Communist.

Acheson, as architect of U.S. foreign policy in a troubled era, came in for brickbats from both sides of the fence. Sen. Joseph McCarthy accused him of being soft on Communism and harboring security risks in State. Others said he was blind to the reputed advantages of dealing with the Kremlin. And to historians in the 1960s, he became known as the father of the Cold War who exaggerated Soviet world ambitions and promoted the United States as a supercolonial power. To Truman, however, he was "among the greatest secretaries of state this country had."

Acheson stood for the Vietnam policies of Lyndon Johnson. He later recanted some of his views, claiming that he had been misled about the real situation in Indochina. But he supported Nixon's Vietnam policies. A reading of his many books and articles showed Acheson as a man of warmth, understanding and loyalty.

Acheson with President Harry Truman after South Korea was invaded by the Communist North in June 1950

Celebrating
Seniors

Left top, British novelist P. G. Wodehouse at celebration of his 90th birthday. Left bottom, conductor Leopold Stokowski, 89, acknowledging congratulations of friends celebrating the 10th anniversary of the American Symphony which he founded. Below, artist Pablo Picasso watching a bull fight at Frejus on the French Riviera with his wife, Jacqueline; he became 90 on Oct. 25

Red Chinese delegates took their seats in U.N. General Assembly

November

China In, Taiwan Out After United Nations Vote Upset U.S. Plans

WHEN THE VOTE flashed on the electric tally board in the great hall of the U.N. General Assembly, the Tanzanian delegates did an impromptu jig in the aisles, the Algerians embraced and the Albanians shook hands. But George Bush, freshman chief of the U.S. delegation, sank back in his seat, the picture of dejection.

By a decisive margin, the Assembly decided Oct. 25 to seat the Communist government of China, a nuclear power comprising nearly 800 million people who had been isolated from the outside world for 22 years. It also voted to expel the Nationalist government of Chiang Kai-shek, who had fled to the island of Taiwan with two million followers in 1949 when the Reds took over the mainland.

The action dealt a stinging blow to the United States, which had laid its prestige on the line in a vain effort to keep the Nationalists in the United Nations even though it had dropped its opposition to Peking's entry. It was the first time in the history of the peace forum that the United States had suffered such a major defeat and it sent shock waves echoing from New York to Washington.

Incensed by the spectacle of U.N. delegates rejoicing over this setback to U.S. foreign policy, Republican leaders exploded in wrath. Sen. Barry Goldwater of Arizona called on the United States to pull out of the United Nations and banish its headquarters to "some place like Moscow or Peking." And Senate Minority Leader Hugh Scott of Pennsylvania spoke derisively of "hot-pants principalities" that had opposed the United States.

Two days later President Nixon's press secretary, Ron Ziegler, denounced "the shocking demonstration and undisguised glee among some of the delegates following the vote" in the Assembly.

Actually, the ballot that had provoked so much jubilation was the one that defeated the perennial resolution declaring that the China issue was an "important question" to be decided only by a two thirds majority. It was a device the United States had used since 1961 to bar Peking from the United Nations. Only this time the aim was to prevent the expulsion of Taiwan. Approval of the "important question" resolution by a vote of 59-55 with 15 abstentions decided the issue, and when

Taiwan's Foreign Minister Chow Shu-kai walked out of the hall just before the decisive vote seating Peking

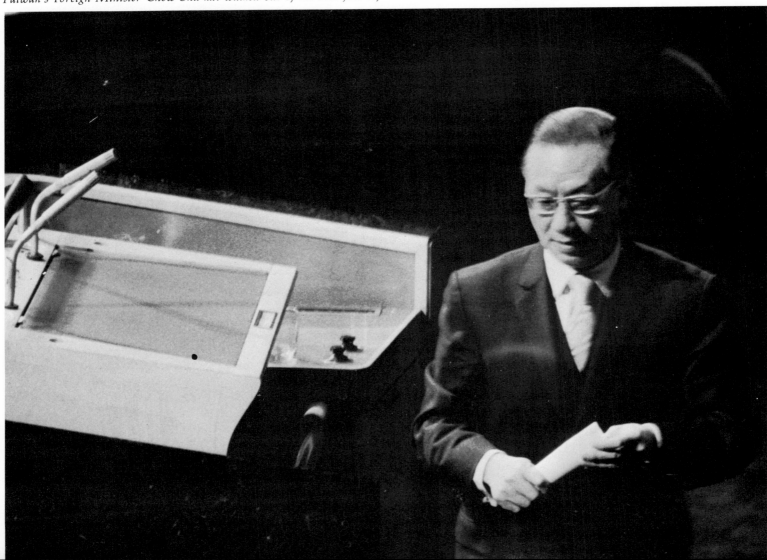

the Albanian resolution to admit Peking and oust Taiwan was approved 76-35 with 17 abstentions about 90 minutes later, it was something of an anticlimax.

With the admission of Red China, the United Nations rang down the curtain on the longest debate in the history of the United Nations. It began late in 1949, when Chou En-lai fired off a telegram to the United Nations demanding that it expel the fugitive regime of Chiang Kai-shek and replace it with that of Communist boss Mao Tse-tung.

No action was taken that year, but the seating of the Chinese Reds was formally proposed in the General Assembly by India in 1950. For the next decade India played the role of Peking's sponsor, but the United States, with strong backing from other western nations, managed to prevent the question from even being placed on the agenda of the Assembly. Then, after she got embroiled in a border squabble with Peking, India abandoned her advocate role.

In 1961 the United States changed its strategy. It agreed to permit a vote on China but insisted that it be regarded as an important question.

In 1965 the pro-Peking resolution—which was by then being put forward by Albania—got as far as a tie vote. Arthur J. Goldberg, then chief U.S. delegate, acknowledged that the controversial issue had become the subject of "innumerable conferences" at home and abroad.

Peking advanced another step in 1967 when Richard Nixon wrote in the quarterly publication Foreign Affairs: "We simply cannot afford to leave China forever outside the family of nations."

In 1969 the resolution to seat Communist China saw 51 nations voting in favor of Peking with 49 against and 25 abstaining. But the demand for important question status already had been approved, and Peking remained outside the Glass House beside New York's East River.

In February 1970, Nixon declared that more than 750 million Chinese mainlanders "should not remain isolated from the international community." He added that the United States would "maintain its treaty commitment" to Taiwan, thus broaching a two-China policy which both Taipei and Peking had vowed they would not go along with.

Nixon's declaration set the stage for a debate that diplomats predicted would be the most crucial in the history of the China Question.

The debate, ironically, opened Oct. 18 on a note of dissension between Nationalist China and its staunchest supporter, the United States.

Bush and Nationalist Foreign Minister Chow Chu-kai both urged the Assembly to refrain from ousting Taiwan. But Chow denounced the actions and policies of Peking and omitted any mention of the American-sponsored resolution for dual representation.

Chow, his voice breaking with indignation, stood at the lectern in the Assembly trying to spell out why Peking should not be allowed to replace his government. But the reception was one of general boredom among the listeners, and many of Taiwan's opponents refused to stay in the hall when he spoke.

Bush made an impassioned appeal on behalf of Taiwan that some spectators said reminded them of Billy Graham. Most delegates agreed that it was an effective speech.

As expected, the Soviet Union ridiculed the American proposal to have two Chinas in the United Nations and charged that the U.S. effort to prevent the expulsion of Taiwan was an "unsavory policy intended to sever Taiwan from the People's Republic of China." Britain's Sir Colin Crowe served notice that his government would vote against the appeal to keep the Nationalists in. Crowe asserted that the U.S.-backed resolution would only delay the admission of mainland China.

The pro-Peking countries had made their opening moves early and created an aura of confidence that left the United States on the defensive. Albania and 16 cosponsors had put in their resolution to admit Peking back in July instead of the eve of the assembly as usual. When the United States finally issued its counter-proposal in September it had trouble getting cosponsors. The 21 it finally mustered were small nations, with the exception of Australia, Japan and New Zealand. This did not help the U.S. cause. The willingness of important countries to put their names behind a resolution had always carried considerable impact in the United Nations, especially in wavering states which wanted to be on the winning side.

Peking, which in previous years had usually managed for some reason to kill its chances of admission with a belligerent statement or aggressive action on the eve of the vote, switched tactics this time and did some effective lobbying.

The Red Chinese established diplomatic relations with more than a dozen nations in the months before the assembly decision and each of them cast their ballot for Peking. The Chinese also made some farsighted deals, such as agreeing to buy fish meal from Peru and rubber from Malaysia. Tanzania and Zambia both sided with the Chinese, who were building a $400 million railroad linking the two African countries.

As the debate went into its final week, the American side still exuded optimism. Said Taiwan's foreign minister, Chow: "We are confident we will win." And the U.S. delegation continued to predict a narrow victory right up until the morning of the vote.

But, as the crucial moment approached, a number of small nations began switching their allegiance from the United States in an obvious effort to get onto the band wagon. As the speeches droned on during the fateful evening of Oct. 25, it became increasingly plain that the U.S. side was in trouble.

Peking's backers saw the support shifting and moved in for the kill. Yet few outside the Assembly hall realized that the moment was at hand. The television networks were set for live coverage the following day, when they had expected the vote. Official Washington turned in for the night.

In the Assembly Hall the Albanians and their colleagues pressed for action, realizing that to delay a day might give the United States time to muster new support and turn the tide against them. Saudi Arabia's Jamil Baroody, in an apparent effort to help the U.S. cause, moved for adjournment of debate overnight. But the Pro-Peking forces voted him down and pushed on for a ballot on the vital "important question" resolution. When they defeated that proposal, it became clear that the United States was unable to muster a majority. With the final hurdle cleared, Peking went on to victory.

Moments before the decisive vote on admission, the Nationalist delegate, Liu Chieh, announced that his government would take no further part in the proceedings. The delegation led by Foreign Minister Chow received a round of friendly applause as they walked out of the great hall. Outside, Chow told newsmen that Peking, in taking over his government's place, would subvert the world organization.

"It will surely transform the United Nations into a Maoist battlefield for international subversion," he declared.

With the historic vote, mainland China had finally burst forth from the isolation imposed on her by the United States and its allies a generation earlier; an isolation that Peking itself had seemed to prefer for years.

Above, Red China's Chiao Kuan-hua welcomed to United Nations by America's George Bush. Right, Chiao Kuan-hua making maiden speech before General Assembly Below, Peking's Chiao Kuan-hua arriving at U.N. headquarters was greeted by protocol chief Sinan Corle (right)

Nationalist authorities in Taiwan took the defeat philosophically. They conceded that Taiwan's sudden demotion from one of the five Big Power members of the U.N. Security Council to that of non U.N. member had not done its status any good. However, they said, the situation was "tough but not irreparable."

"We are not going to draw back into a shell," Tsai Wei-ping, Taiwan's vice minister of Foreign affairs, told Tillman Durdin of the New York Times. "Our approach will be positive and outgoing. . . . We are prepared to have relations wherever we can, and they will be extensive."

Six days after the vote, Red China advised U.N. Secretary-General U Thant that she wanted to be listed as "China, Peoples Republic of." The following day the mainland's red flag with five gold stars was run up in front of U.N. headquarters along with the banners of the 130 other member states.

On Nov 2 Peking sent word that Chiao Kuan-hua, a long-time confidant of Chou En-lai and a deputy foreign minister, had been chosen to head the nine-man delegation. As regular head of the mission, the Chinese named Huang Hua, then ambassador to Ottawa and one of their senior diplomats.

About a week later the Communist delegation booked in at New York's Hotel Roosevelt, long known as national headquarters for Republican presidential candidates.

The delegation informed the Roosevelt kitchen staff that it was fond of fresh fruit, well done meat and fish, and had a weakness for German potato salad. For a beverage it asked for mugs of plain hot water, startling waiters used to serving glasses tinkling with ice cubes.

The new envoys seemed quiet and showed little emotion. They even watched outwardly unperturbed while several hundred singing, shouting demonstrators milled in front of the hotel and screamed "Kill Mao Tse-tung."

On Nov. 15 Peking's delegation made its formal entry into the United Nations General Assembly and caused some consternation with an acceptance speech which diplomats had predicted would be in a low key.

After a welcoming ceremony which lasted five and a half hours and featured speeches from delegates of 56 nations, Peking's Chiao Kuan-hua took the rostrum. Removing his glasses and gazing out over the crowded chamber, he launched a biting attack against the United States, accusing it of aggression by sending U.S. naval forces into the Taiwan Strait and by its military intervention in Vietnam, Cambodia and Laos.

The speech brought a sharp retort from the United States. A terse statement issued by Bush accused Peking of using "intemperate language" and "empty cannons of rhetoric."

For better or worse, the United Nations had entered a new phase in its 26-year history. If it did nothing else, the admission of Peking injected new life in an organization that had ceased to attract much public interest.

DRUGS:
Their Supply and Use
in Southeast Asia

*Addiction to and protection of narcotics by thousands
of American troops created critical problems*

A silhouetted American serviceman smoking marijuana through a Vietnamese water pipe in South Vietnam

THE SAP of the seeded Papaver pod began its tortuous journey in the Himalayan fields where the opium poppy grew. Harvested by mountain tribesmen in the area it moved over a complex pipeline, was converted into heroin along the way and finally sold to U.S. servicemen in the bars and back alleys of Saigon.

Formidable obstacles confronted U.S. authorities in their effort to stem the tide of heroin flowing to their troops in Vietnam. Prodded by the White House, American officials applied heavy pressure to curb the traffic, but found themselves bucking a way of life that had flourished for a century and was tolerated if not encouraged by Asian officials and military leaders.

An Associated Press survey of how drugs found their way into American hands in Southeast Asia disclosed that the vast traffic was controlled by a Chinese "Mafia" which operated a family-style network out of a dozen Asian cities. These Chinese overlords greased the way for the drug traffic by paying off military rebels whose caravans gathered the opium gum, soldiers who guarded the remote heroin refineries along mountain streams, officials at customs checkpoints as well as fishing boat owners and truck drivers in Indochinese villages. Also on the receiving end were some South Vietnamese generals who allowed the traffic to continue in their command areas.

American attention had centered on the ancient Oriental opium trade only in recent years because of the alarming spread of heroin among U.S. fighting men. As a result, it had little to go on.

"We didn't give a damn about the drug business as long as only Asians were using the stuff," commented an American investigator in Saigon. "Now that American GIs are hitting heroin, we just don't have enought hard facts to adequately crack down."

United States officials, trying to combat drug traffic in Laos, South Vietnam and Thailand, said despairingly that even though they had learned some "hard facts" about the system, it was quite a different matter to break through the wall of protection and obtain names and evidence.

Efforts to crack the ring were stepped up, however. In the first three months of 1971, U.S. military authorities apprehended 1,084 users, or almost the same number as they had taken in the whole of 1970. The estimates of GI users ranged from 12,000 to as many as 37,000 among the 250,000-man American force in Vietnam.

Once concerned mainly with opium and smoking heroin supplied to Asians, the traffic in narcotics had become a major industry upon which many people depended for their living. So sophisticated had the racket become in Southeast Asia that some officials were convinced that it was ready to expand and follow the American serviceman home should Middle East and European sources in the United States dry up.

The flow of drugs to GIs in Vietnam was something to reckon with. Col. Lee Doc Huong, head of the narcotics investigation for South Vietnam, said that on the basis of the seizures the traffic had reached an estimated 50 kilos a week, a kilo equaling 2.2 pounds. This amounted to about 150,000 doses a week.

In Newport, a Saigon port area with the largest remaining

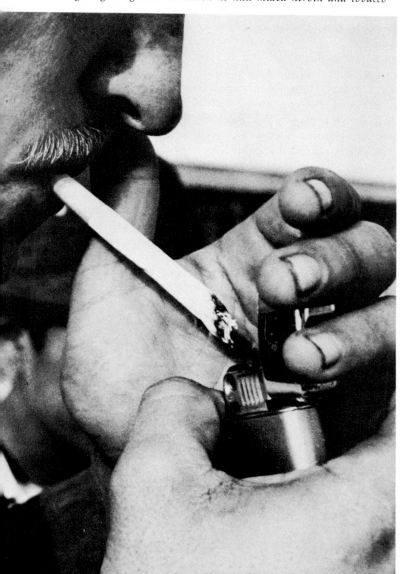

A GI lighting a cigarette in which he had mixed heroin and tobacco

A GI in Vietnam holding an empty vial that had contained heroin

American logistics installation, a military police sergeant watched groups of GIs walking into the mess halls.

"We all use the stuff openly here," he claimed. "The officers are in on it; the MPs are in on it.

"See those guys who just walked in the gate?" the sergeant asked, pointing to a group of young GIs in wrinkled tropical fatigues. "I'll bet you they've got heroin vials on them. But you know something? Why should I bust them? If I bust them, I'll have to bust nearly everyone in the place, and who the hell wants that?"

The friendly MP said there were about 300 servicemen on duty at Newport's dock loading and maintenance facilities. He estimated that 200 of them were "using something or other, and nearly 100 are on heroin."

"Many of the MPs, my own guys, are on the stuff," he declared. "There are officers on it. I know them."

At the entrance to the maintenance compound was a guard box and inside sat a young bleary-eyed soldier, a loaded M16 automatic beside him. The youth looked up and his lips moved, but the words that tumbled out were incoherent.

"He's never off drugs," said the MP sergeant, shaking his head.

One conduit of the heroin pipeline to Vietnam originated in the Laotian town of Ban Houei Sai, a sleepy Mekong River hamlet with a single dusty street. Wild bananas and bamboo clumps pushed against the wooden frame houses, perched on stilts because the muddy Mekong River flooded its banks annually. With the river swirling on one side and steep mountains rising on the other, remoteness made Ban Houei Sai a perfect opium town. And narcotics agents of half a dozen nations claimed that it was a major drug center.

But the town had an innocent air. Meo tribesmen milled around the marketplace mingling with women with embroidered skirts flopping at their bare ankles and feet. The Meo people grew the opium poppies, scraping off the sap to sell to itinerant Chinese traders, who passed it on to rebel military bands. The bands assembled each year large caravans of pack mules to carry the opium to Ban Houei Sai.

In the Laotian capital of Vientiane American officials disclosed that big caravans had pulled into the hills north of Ban Houei Sai last April and May, unloading tons of raw opium. A Chinese store there offered mute evidence of the local industry; rows of molded bronze opium weights in the shapes of ducks and lions. They were used by traders to measure the harvest brought in by the Meos.

A report by the U.S. Central Intelligence Agency said the largest heoin refinery in all Southeast Asia had been located in a village on the edge of the town. It was capable of processing 100 kilos of raw opium a day, enough heroin to provide the total estimated GI demand in Vietnam. However, investigation disclosed that the refining and storage buildings had been burned to the ground.

"The Chinese who control this stuff deliberately burned down that refinery a week ago," said an American informant. "It was, you might say, one result of our pressure. But they moved out all the apparatus and the dope before the fire, and are now in business a few miles upriver." The pipeline drew its supply from peaceful-looking hamlets in Burma, Laos and Thailand. In such places the Meo families developed the opium crop. A family often had as much as two acres of opium poppies under cultivation, yielding 33 pounds of raw opium in a year. Chinese traders paid from $20 to $40 per kilo for the stuff, but prices soared along the route and in Saigon a kilo of heroin brought $10,000.

The journey from these rural points of origin wound through mountains and valleys, and snaked along hidden pathways—all leading to the processing plants near the borders of Thailand and Laos.

The big drug dealers of Southeast Asia played an active role in assembling caravans of up to 300 pack mules. These dealers were the Chu Chow Chinese, sharp businessmen who came from the Fukien coast of China and moved as families into the neighboring countries.

The next payoffs along the drug route were made to customs officials, local military garrisons and to police. Large amounts of money also changed hands at the processing plants throughout remote country areas. Here raw opium was refined into morphine blocks and into heroin of different grades. Payoffs were made at such plants to provide troop protection. Appearance in 1970 of the new, movable processing plants near the poppy fields tipped narcotic agents to the fact that the drug business was expanding. It came as little surprise that the new market proved to be Saigon.

The next major payoffs came after the processed base of heroin was trucked through the complex of roadblocks along Thai highways to the coast, or by plane to Vientiane. American intelligence reports had charged repeatedly that members of the Royal Lao Air Force carried opium and heroin from Ban Houei Sai and an air strip in the Laotian Shan states.

From the Thai coast narcotics were transported by fishing trawler to Vietnam. From Vientiane they were flown to Saigon and Nhatrang, with a stop at the southern Lao town of Pakse.

In Asian nations the public attitude toward the drug traffic was far more tolerant than in the West. Asians had always held a different view about narcotics. Even though the death penalty for opium processing had been in effect in Thailand for a decade, Americans stationed in that country said drugs rolled through Thai border checkpoints and roadblocks and on to waiting trawlers. The narcotic traffic had become so deeply woven into the social and economic fabric of Southeast Asia that it was actually a native industry on which many depended for a living. Thus, when narcotics agents seized a huge cache of drugs at the Vietnamese coastal town of Rach Gia last July and arrested two sailors guarding it, an incredible confrontation between the Vietnamese army and navy ensued.

A police official disclosed later that three South Vietnamese navy speedboats tried to free the two sailors and to take the drug haul for their own profit. The agents called on the army for help and the local military commander sent two infantry companies to the canal where the trouble had erupted. With 100 infantrymen lined up on either side of the waterway, the navy boats finally backed off, and the seizure was carried out without further interference.

Holding little hope of stamping out drug traffic, or even making much of a dent in it, U.S. authorities began working from the other end. It warned GIs against the perils of drug usage and brought pressure to bear upon the Saigon government to put teeth in their drug supression laws.

Saigon responded with a bill instituting the death penalty for importers and peddlers belonging to organized rings. But the outlook was still discouraging.

"To effectively stamp out heroin," said a veteran U.S. official, "we would have to change the economic patterns of Asia. The governments of Laos, Thailand and South Vietnam are run by officials who are required to scoop out large doses of cash from the system to buy allegiance and pay political favors. At this stage of the game, with Americans getting out of Vietnam, we have less leverage than ever before."

British troops patroling troubled Belfast

Northern Ireland Beset by Urban Guerrilla War

N o one in his sane sense," William Cardinal Conway said in Belfast, "would try to bomb a million Protestants into a United Ireland." Sane or not, that was precisely the objective of the guerrilla gunmen of the Irish Republican Army, and they pursued it with chilling ruthlessness through a violent year. Bombings, gun battles and assassination became the daily diet of Belfast and Londonderry, Northern Ireland's two main cities, and spread inexorably through the province.

By October the year's known toll had topped 150 and was increasing daily. It was the North's worst year since 1922, when 232 were killed in the birth throes of partitioned Ireland.

The IRA promised to wreck Belfast by Christmas. Prime Minister Brian Faulkner, backed by 14,000 British troops, promised in turn to wreck the IRA. The origin of this orgy of violence lay deep in Ireland's centuries old struggle of the Orange and the Green (The World in 1969, 164–170). The Protestant settlers concentrated in the North. The Catholic Gaels' common aim was to make the island one nation once again. The more recent trigger was the claim of Northern Catholics that for years they had suffered discrimination by the Protes-

tant majority, getting a second best deal in jobs, housing and even votes.

Those issues sparked the civil rights campaign of 1968, a nonviolent exercise quickly infiltrated by the IRA and assorted leftists. Riot and insurrection followed in 1969, continued through 1970 and in 1971 developed into fullscale guerrilla war. Reforms designed to meet the grievances of the Catholic third of the North's 1.5 million population now held little relevance: The IRA's claim was unity or nothing. Its slogan: "Get the British out." Its method: "Killing soldiers, one by one."

British troops first went on to the streets of Londonderry and Belfast in August 1969 to head off Protestant-Catholic clashes that came close to civil war. Despite the months of riot casualties were comparatively light. Not one soldier was killed until February 1971. By October, 35 troops were dead and the two-year death roll of military and civilians together was heading for 200. Many hundreds more had been wounded, and opinion polls showed the British across the water were getting tired of the battle. Looking back to Aden and Cyprus, some British politicians and even top soldiers had their doubts

Above, mourning father carrying coffin bearing remains of his 18-month-old daughter killed in a terror attack. Left, an elderly woman watched apprehensively as a British army sharpshooter took up position on her doorstep in Belfast's Market area

whether urban guerrilla warfare in modern western conditions could ever be defeated.

The IRA had a guerrilla tradition lasting more than 50 years. It had access to seemingly unlimited supplies of gelignite, ferried in for the most part from across the mainly unmarked border with the Irish republic. It had expert marksmen, skilled enough to pick off soldiers through the neck. It had ample funds, the product of repeated bank raids in Ireland and Britain and the support of Irish-American sympathizers across the Atlantic. It lacked, however, advanced weapons of the mortar and rocket type, and these it set out to get.

David O'Connell, a 32-year-old leader of the IRA's high command, left for Europe with a pretty Dublin student, Maria McGuire, as interpeter and assistant. British agents had wind of their purpose and tipped off counterparts in Western Europe. O'Connell and the girl were traced to Amsterdam—and at the Dutch capital's Schiphol airport police found more than three tons of modern arms consigned from Communist Czechoslovakia to a mysterious "Mr. Dougan." Back in Dublin, O'Connell and the girl admitted their role in the mission that failed, and Miss McGuire was mainly concerned to assure the world that nothing "improper" had taken place in their Amsterdam hotel rooms.

Another arms consignment was picked up in Cork, second city of the Irish Republic, having been shipped from the United States as baggage aboard the *Queen Elizabeth 2*, pride of Britain's merchant fleet. This was mainly light arms, clearly intended to replace the hundreds of weapons seized by British troops in their nightly searches of Belfast's Catholic areas. One consolation for the British was that the bizarre collection of carbines, Thompson submachine guns and assorted pistols turned up by the searches proved that the modern stuff, by October at least, had not filtered through to the IRA's front line.

But the gelignite was getting through and causing untold damage. Early in the year a bomb wrecked the Belfast plant of the British-based Daily Mirror. That bomb alone—50 pounds of gelignite costing the equivalent of 25 dollars at commercial rates—did damage estimated at two million pounds sterling, or $5 million. Compared with 150 explosions in all of 1970, bombings were now running at 150 a month, hitting stores, bars, factories, public utilities, army posts and police stations. The center of Belfast, with department store windows shattered and replaced by hardboard, looked like something from the blitz of World War II. "Business as usual," proclaimed the posters along Royal Avenue, but it wasn't.

By night the city center was silent except for the rustling of thousands on thousands of starlings that perched along Royal Avenue. Soldiers with blackened faces crouched in doorways or crossed and recrossed the street at the double in a deliberate bid to draw sniper fire. Restaurants and movie theaters reported zero business. One of the city's two live theaters stayed gamely open and sometimes had more people on the stage than in the audience. The Grand Central Hotel, headquarters for visiting businessmen and industrialists, closed its doors for the last time, beaten by two years of insurmountable losses. The bright spot, and surprise, was that the province's industrial production kept expanding, counter to the trend in the rest of the United Kingdom. Given a year of peace it might at last break into its chronic unemployment figures, but peace looked far away. The only thing solved so far was Belfast's parking problem: People stayed home whenever they could.

Politically, Faulkner's Protestant-based Unionist government and the mainly Catholic opposition had hit collision course

back in July, just when it seemed they might be reaching an accommodation. Faulkner took the premiership in March, when James Chichester-Clark quit in despair at the mess around him and bitter that the British would not answer his call for tougher action against the then re-emergent IRA. Faulkner's strategy was to try to associate Catholic moderates like Londonderry's John Hume with the machinery of government, and so undercut their complaint that for 50 years Protestants had monopolized political power. He offered to give opposition members of the Provincial Parliament a direct role in planning and overseeing social and economic policies. Hume and other members of the Social Democrat opposition gave the scheme a guarded welcome. Before the month was out they had quit parliament altogether, announcing plans to set up a rival assembly. The ostensible reason for the boycott was failure to stage a public inquiry into the shooting of two men by British troops in Londonderry. The real reason, Protestants charged, was intimidation by the IRA, which made boycott of parliament a prime plank of policy on both sides of the Irish border. In August, with bombings and shootings growing daily worse, Faulkner took off for London on a supposedly secret mission. With him was Gen. Sir Harry Tuzo, the British commander in the North. They returned with British permission to deploy the 1922 Act which gave Northern Ireland governments sweeping powers to upset habeas corpus and order arrest and internment without trial.

In the small hours of Monday, Aug. 9, the great sweep began. More than 300 supposed IRA men or supporters were taken from their beds and hustled first to army camps, then to the prison ship *Maidstone* in Belfast docks or the gray-walled jail on the Crumlin Road. The reaction from Catholic backstreets was furious. Within 24 hours 14 persons were killed and scores wounded in the worst single outbreak since the killing started in August 1969. Property damage ran into millions. Whole streets burned in West Belfast, where Protestant families on the fringe of Catholic areas fled their homes, setting them alight as they left. Newry and Londonderry were like cities under siege. Catholic mothers and children by the thousand quit the battle areas and found refuge in the republic.

"We are at war with the terrorists," proclaimed Faulkner. "There aren't jails enough to hold us all," cried Bernadette Devlin, leftist figurehead of Catholic militancy, who two weeks later produced a daughter weighing six pounds, two ounces, making her the first unmarried mother to sit in Britain's mother of parliaments.

The extent of the internment sweep was itself testimony to the growth of the IRA. Only in February government members had said that to "lift" 50 men would break the core of the Northern IRA—and IRA veterans supported that view. Now more than 300 were inside, though both wings of the organization, leftist "Officials" and nationalist "Provisionals," claimed cheerfully that their leaders had escaped the net. Joe Cahill, 51-year-old Belfast boss of the Provisionals, soon demonstrated his own freedom by calling a news conference under the noses of British troops in West Belfast. He next turned up in England and after a grilling at Manchester Airport was to most people's surprise sent back not to Belfast and internment but to Dublin, where open campaigning and parading by IRA leaders went on through most of the year with little check from the republic's legitimate government.

Cahill took off for the United States on a fund-raising tour but was refused admission on the ground of his prison record. In 1942 he and five other IRA activists had been sentenced to death for the shooting of a police officer. One was hanged; the

The Rev. Ian Paisley, militant Protestant leader

other sentences were commuted. Cahill served seven and a half years of a theoretical life sentence. Deported from New York Sept. 9, he went straight to the steps of Dublin's historic Post Office, centerpoint of the 1916 uprising against British rule, and told a cheering crowd: "We want England to get the hell out of our country. The next time I speak here will be at a victory rally in a free Republican Ireland. Nothing will now stop us."

Soon allegations of brutality and systematic torture by British-controlled security forces began to seep out of Belfast's Crumlin jail. Their main source was Seamus O'Toole, who as ex-editor of Dublin's United Irishman was a professional propagandist of the IRA. His dispatches, supposedly smuggled from his Crumlin cell, told of men being thrown from helicopters which they thought were high in the air, of repeated beatings and barefoot marches over broken glass, of men kept for days without sleep, their heads in bags while the room was filled with unnerving noise.

O'Toole was promptly released and sent back to Dublin, a decision which he denounced as cynical. But his allegations, first printed in Dublin newspapers, were taken up by the Lon-

don Sunday Times and seemingly were becoming a cause of governmental embarrassment, if not outright scandal. Faulkner denied flatly that any brutality had occurred, and insisted that internment should be judged not just by the furious response it evoked but as a long-term weapon. As the weeks rolled by the numbers arrested under the Special Powers Act topped 900, of whom many were released after questioning or eventually brought before the normal courts on criminal charges. More than 250 were interned at Long Kesh, a disused airstrip outside Belfast, sleeping 40 to a hut in what their supporters called the only concentration camp in Western Europe. Many were veterans of internment during previous IRA campaigns of 1938-40 and 1956-62. At least one claimed to have served 23 years with the British Army. Cases of father and son interned together testified to the IRA's family tradition. John Curry, from Belfast's Lower Falls, was paroled for two days to attend the funeral of his 18-year-old daughter Rose, blown to pieces while helping her boy friend build a bomb.

Throughout August and on into the fall the bombings went on. The year's worst single incident had taken place back in February, when a landmine killed five technicians on a lonely road leading to a British Broadcasting Corp. television mast. The IRA said that one was a mistake; the bomb had been intended for an army patrol. In March three young Scottish soldiers, off duty and in civilian clothes, were enticed to a bar on the outskirts of West Belfast, then shot down in the lane outside. From then on soldiers off duty in Belfast were confined to their makeshift barrack rooms in disused linen mills and warehouses, spending their four-month tour of duty with no outside recreation of any kind. The bombing teams apparently delighted in placing their charges just where security might be thought impenetrable. One blast blew in the doors of Crumlin jail in the sunshine of a Sunday afternoon, killing a high ranking prison officer. Others were planted inside police stations, and when security there was strengthened the bombs were planted in neighboring buildings. A double charge planted on each side of a station on Belfast's Ormeau Road wrecked a pub and a boutique, killing three persons and injuring more than 30. The bombing team pulled guns on the pub's customers and gave them just 10 seconds to get out before the 50-pound charge brought the roof down.

Cardinal Conway, Belfast-born Roman Catholic Primate of all Ireland, had long before denounced the bombers: "These people have absolutely no mandate; their action is completely unjustified." He had been equally stern in condemning internment as totally one-sided and aimed exclusively at the Catholic community. "An army," he said, "is a very blunt instrument for maintaining civil order in this part of the world."

Blunt instruments, said the cardinal, should be kept out of sight when not in use—indicating he thought the army's search and patrol operations in Catholic areas were provocative. But as the year wore on the soldiers pushed ever more frequently into the Catholic enclaves, setting off as they arrived a cacophony of clattering sound from trash can lids hammered on the sidewalks by vigilante women warning their wanted menfolk to go to ground.

Politicians charged that the army, once welcomed in Catholic areas, now was regarded as an oppressor, the tool of the Orange regime. More charges of one-sidedness came when Protestants of Sandy Row and the Shankill Road were allowed to police their own night-time barricades aimed at keeping out the bomb teams. Catholics remembered only too well that their own barricades were immediately pulled down.

Ivan Cooper, a Protestant oppositionist who was from the

beginning a supporter of the Catholic civil rights campaign, charged that troops had shot innocent people, had refused to acknowledge mistakes and had split the community as never before. He called for a phased withdrawal and said: "If they do not go they should be treated as the plague. It is now clear that the troops are not operating against the IRA but against the whole Catholic community." To neutrals in the middle-road Alliance party it seemed equally clear that, if the troops did go, Belfast would erupt into a bloodbath of communal strife, with the long forecast Protestant backlash sweeping into militant action. To the IRA and even to a moderate like John Hume all talk of Protestant backlash was mere bluff, the Orange card which British Tories first used nearly a century ago in thwarting a United Ireland.

In this poisoned atmosphere, three prime ministers met in the search for some sort of political gesture to calm the storm. Britain's Edward Heath was host to Northern Ireland's Faulkner and the Irish Republic's Jack Lynch at Chequers, Heath's country residence west of London. They achieved little except agreement to talk again at some unspecified date. Lynch, beset by militant defections from his Fianna Fail (Soldiers of Destiny) party, did deliver on a promise to tighten control of gelignite within his borders. In return he could claim to have won British recognition that his government had a right to a voice in northern affairs—a claim which Faulkner would never admit.

As Christmas approached, the unsettled Irish question raised its turbulent head in American politics. Sen. Edward Kennedy, conscious of his Irish background, called for the British Army to get out. Faulkner dismissed the speech as a mere irritant. Others denounced it as a cynical appeal to the Irish-American vote, something Kennedy's supporters might reasonably claim to have sewn up anyway. A reader of the London Times wrote to point out that in the first six months of this year Northern Ireland had had fewer than 70 killings, while New York had 700. By Kennedy's reasoning, he said, the logical course would be to urge the cops to quit New York.

November came in with more bombings, more murders of police, more killings of soldiers and civilians. The military charged that the IRA, hurt by casualties and internment, was bringing out girls and schoolkids to join its depleted frontline gunmen. British politicians, and not only in the opposition Labor party, began to talk of disbanding the Northern Ireland parliament. Their theory was that a period of direct rule from London might defuse the situation and perhaps persuade Protestants to accept some as yet undefined agreement with Dublin as a step to Irish unity. Faulkner's answer was: "Hands off." The Protestant majority, he said, would fight to preserve its parliament, and direct rule would bring direct civil war. The older Ulster slogan of "No surrender" was back to the fore-front of basic policy.

Women picked their way through rubble on Belfast's Farringdon Avenue past rows of gutted homes set afire by fleeing Protestants in a "scorched earth" action

Nation Jolted by Nixon
With Wage-Price Freeze

*President's plan to strengthen economy followed U.S. budget
deficit totaling $23.2 billion at end of fiscal year*

PRESIDENT NIXON had said 1971 would be a good year and 1972 a great year. As things turned out, 1971 was just a fair year and by the time it ended—after a nerve-jangling juggling with the dollar and the first wage-price freeze in peacetime history—people weren't too sure what 1972 would bring.

For the first 7½ months trouble rained down on a country which, the President promised in January, would be entering an era of prosperity without inflation. Production rose but not high enough. Inflation slowed but stayed too high. Unemployment clung to the near-recession rate of 6 per cent. The President's official forecast of national output for the year, on which he based the federal budget, was $1.065 trillion. Economists scorned it and journalists derided it and, sure enough, it proved to be far too high. The outcome was around $1.050 trillion, and the gain was half inflation.

The fiscal 1971 budget, for which Nixon had projected a tidy $1.3 billion surplus, began a long skid into deficit at the rate of $2 billion a month. The president wound up at the fiscal year-end on June 30 with an enormous $23.2 billion shortfall, only $2 billion less than that of Lyndon B. Johnson's 1968 deficit—the biggest red-ink blot in peacetime history, on which Nixon had blamed much of the nation's current inflationary ills.

In his January budget message Nixon announced the nation was adopting the "full employment budget for fiscal 1972." The real budget would be $11.6 billion out of balance, he estimated, but there would be a "full employment balance." The full employment budget is an accepted tool of economic planning, designed to measure the amount of federal spending stimulus needed to spur a lagging economy. It is "balanced" if spending does not exceed the amount of tax revenue that would be generated if the economy were running at a full employment rate.

Thus there would be an actual deficit but, according to the theory, it would be properly stimulative and—if the full employment budget was in balance—would not be inflationary. Nixon restated his policy position: The basic guideline "which we should never violate" is not to let the full employment balance slip into deficit; that would indeed be inflationary."

The 1972 budget did slip; with the fiscal year only one-half over in December, it was clear there would be another enormous real deficit and a "full employment deficit" of around $8 billion. This would be inflationary indeed, but before the summer was over a price-wage freeze was imposed.

The White House correctly blamed cost overruns in uncontrollable federal programs and excessive, unasked spending by the Congress. But the economy's main ailment was the one they used to advertise little liver pills: It was nervous, rundown, weak.

Consumers who saw the values of paychecks, bank accounts and pensions still dwindling, after a 25 per cent attrition in five years, took a still firmer grip on their pocketbooks and postponed major outlays.

Not visible on any price tags but also a frighteningly real symptom of inflation was the U.S. balance of payments. It plunged in the second quarter to a $5.7 billion deficit, the worst on record. Soon even the balance of merchandise trade began running successive deficits, a situation unparalleled in modern history.

In May came a temblor, a transatlantic rumbling of earth-shocks to come. U.S. dollars already had piled up in Europe's central banks because Europeans were selling more of their goods in American markets, were buying fewer high-priced U.S. goods, and were accumulating unneeded dollars that Uncle Sam was spending on weapons, military aid and troop support.

Germany took emergency action. It floated the Deutschemark —cut the mark free from its fixed exchange parity with the dollar and let the mark's value be determined by day-to-day transactions in the money markets. Some other countries floated their currencies or revalued them upward.

France began presenting hundreds of millions worth of dollars to the Treasury to be redeemed in gold. Other countries—who held far more dollars than the U.S. had gold—seemed sure to line up with France at the "gold window," where Uncle Sam historically had doled out metal for dollars at $35 an ounce.

By mid-August, the gloom was thick in Wall Street and Washington. Inflation fever still ran high; with profits already in a squeeze, businessmen were dismayed by big wage settlements in key industries—42 per cent in 42 months for rail workers, 30 per cent over three years for steelworkers.

The early-year recovery was flattening out. A mid-summer steel strike was averted, but steel-using industries had stocked up so heavily in anticipation of a shutdown that they now stopped buying, for months to come. The stock market slumped 100 points below its April high. Both consumer confidence and investor confidence were frayed.

Congress renewed the standby authority it had given Nixon to impose mandatory controls on wages and prices. That was mainly a Democratic political ploy; nobody expected Nixon to use it, but Democrats could point out that they had done their part; they had given him the power.

Instead, brave statements on progress kept coming from the White House. The White House periodically issued an "Inflation Alert," highlighting some of the centers of inflationary pressure. But even though the Nixon game plan clearly had gone awry, the White House stuck to its steady course—no controls, no "incomes policy" of the European type, no voluntary guidelines,

not even any strong "jawboning" against price or wage excesses by individual companies, industries or unions.

On Aug. 12 a dozen high Administration staffers got quiet word from the White House to prepare for a working weekend at Camp David, Md., the presidential retreat in the Catoctin Mountains. On Aug. 13 helicopters settled down on the landing space among the rustic cabins. On Aug. 15 they flew back. That evening the President delivered a televised economic report to the people. Jaded reporters prepared for still another exhortation of industry and labor to practice moderation. But when the TV camera's red eye blinked on, the President began unfolding what he called his New Economic Policy.

It was instantly clear: Nixon had taken a big eraser, rubbed out the old game plan completely, and written a brand new blueprint for U.S. economic policy.

The bold actions affected every American family and business. Under peril of a collapsing dollar, Nixon and his Camp David team had swiftly updated a contingency plan for emergency. To a stunned world, Nixon ticked off his actions:

—A 90-day freeze of prices, wages and rents.

—A set of business-stimulating tax-relief proposals for Congress, including an increase in the personal income tax exemption, repeal of the 7 per cent excise tax on new cars, and revival of the 7 per cent investment credit to stimulate industry's outlays for new plant equipment and machinery. (It had been repealed in 1969 as an engine of inflation; now, with a lid on prices and wages, Nixon felt it could be restored).

—Sharp cuts in federal spending and employment. (This proved to be a weak link in Nixon's chain of austerity measures. Congress declined to go along; it refused to see the logic of cutting off jobs in government while trying to stimulate jobs in private industry).

—Two blockbusters in foreign economic policy. Nixon suspended the standing offer of the United States to take dollars from other governments and pay out gold in exchange. He repudiated, in effect, the pledge that made the dollar as good as

Above, AFL-CIO President George Meany, left, talking with Hunter Wharton, head of the Operating Engineers Union, and Joseph A. Bierne of the Communications Union. Below, C. Jackson Grayson, chairman of the Price Commission, answered questions before the Joint Economic Committee on Phase Two of President Nixon's economic program

gold. And, as a temporary protective move, he imposed a 10 per cent tariff surcharge on all dutiable imports.

By slamming shut the gold window, Nixon "floated" the dollar. It no longer had a fixed value in relation to gold. That in turn unglued the value of all other non-communist currencies, because their values were fixed in terms of dollars.

Everybody's currency floated—and stayed floating for a long and worrisome period of months, while Nixon's top economic spokesman, Secretary of the Treasury John B. Connally, pressed the other governments to revalue their currencies upward.

The effect would be the same as a devaluation of the dollar. It would make American goods cheaper in world markets and more competitive against imports in the home market. The fact that the dollar was overvalued was not in question; there had been at least 200 devaluations of other currencies since World War II, and each had left the dollar a bit more out of line with reality.

But the amount of devaluation wanted by Connally seemed excessive to the Europeans—enough to achieve a $13 billion swing in the U.S. balance of payments, from a big deficit to a surplus. A long power struggle ensued. There were threats of tariff and quota retaliation against U.S. farm and industrial products and, looming ahead, the larger hazard of a return to the 1930s-style economic warfare of trading blocs, protective barriers and regional currency systems.

The U.S. was accused of intransigeance and arrogance. Many foreigners believed, as the weeks became months, that Connally was being deliberately vague about U.S. demands and that the U.S. would be quite happy to keep its 10 per cent surcharge indefinitely—in effect, to return to the protective tariff.

At an International Monetary Fund meeting in September the 118 member nations agreed on an agenda for seeking an overall realignment of currency parities through negotiations of the "Group of Ten" richest nations. But the first followup session in November foundered. The other countries insisted that the U.S. should come part way by devaluing the dollar directly, by raising the price of gold.

It was December before Connally gave the hint that this was even thinkable. Meantime the average American citizen worried about the more immediately painful problems of inflation and unemployment.

The immediate reaction of Americans to Nixon's NEP package was one of vast relief. When the New York Stock Exchange opened on the morning after Nixon's bombshell, prices surged up. The dollar had been dethroned, the economy was in a straitjacket, yet businessmen, investors and consumers were jubilant.

If evidence had been needed of the psychological depth of public concern over the price-wage spiral, after five years in which inflation had stolen more than 25 cents out of every dollar bill, the response to Nixon's freeze was proof enough.

The freeze justified their hopes. It worked. The AFL-CIO rumbled its outrage at scheduled pay increases that were blocked, but gave grudging cooperation even while demanding that profits, dividends and interest rates be similarly frozen.

The price and pay ceilings leaked in spots. There were some violations, much early confusion inside and outside the government, many misunderstandings. There were some wide-open areas of exemption, including all unprocessed foods and all imports subject to the surcharge. The cost of living index, geared in some industries to trends and averages rather than spot markets, did not reflect the full clampdown.

Yet the living cost rise in September, the first full month of freeze, was held to 2.4 per cent—far from perfect, to be sure, but less than half the rate of consumer price increases in any recent year. The September wholesale price index showed the real impact—the biggest decline in 5 years.

Nixon had predicted that his drastic assault on inflation and unemployment would "lay the basis for renewed confidence; his economists expected business to pick up quick momentum.

But industry's response was cautious; business did not show the bounce the White House expected. Retail sales continued to improve strongly, but it would evidently require more than a 90-day freeze to make a big spender out of the American consumer after his five-year ordeal by inflation. He was still laying away an extraordinarily high amount of income as savings.

Congress moved slowly with Nixon's business-stimulating program. The Senate alone toyed with 119 amendments to his bill, including one irrelevant proposal permitting each taxpayer to earmark $1 of his tax as a political contribution. The Republicans filibustered against the scheme, which was clearly a device to help the Democratic party repair its fallen finances. Nixon threatened a veto.

President Nixon spoke as George Meany watched at AFL-CIO convention in Miami

The delays deferred the recovery. Corporations held back their outlays for new plant and equipment until the credit was actually back on the law books.

As the end of the freeze neared on Nov. 13, apprehensions and uncertainties clouded the preparations for Phase Two, the post-freeze period in which ways would have to be devised to preserve reasonable price-wage stability while correcting the thousands of inequities that were frozen into the economy by the Aug. 15 orders.

Herbert Stein, then vice chairman and later chairman of the President's Council of Economic Advisers, had foreseen the headache as he packed his books and papers for the momentous weekend at Camp David. "I knew immediately the problem would not be the freeze, but the unfreeze, the thaw," he said.

Stein knew and disliked controls. Like Nixon, he had worked in the World War II control bureaucracy. He was chosen to head the high-level task force to plan Phase Two.

They worked rapidly. Nixon was able to take to television on Oct. 8 to reassure the public the machinery had been designed to carry on the anti-inflation fight. There would be two, quasi-independent bodies, he said, a 15-member Pay Board made up of 5 members each from industry, labor and the public; and a Price Commission of 7 members, all public.

They would devise the guidelines needed to bring the inflation rate down to 2 to 3 per cent a year by the end of 1972, the President said. He would seek a one-year extension of the control law until April 30, 1973, along with standby authority to control interest rates and corporation dividends, although he did not intend to use that power. There would be no ceiling on profits, he emphasized, although the government would demand the cancellation of price increases that might result in windfall profits.

The controls would depend largely on "the voluntary cooperation of the American people," Nixon said. The Administration wished to leave elbow room for investment, venture and growth.

"We're not in the business of creating unemployment," explained one White House official. Another said: "It is important that we administer Phase Two in such a way that we don't short-circuit employment."

George Meany, the 77-year-old president of the AFL-CIO, listened in silence, but his union troops were busy laying the groundwork for a campaign to insure that all deferred pay increases which were contracted before the freeze were recognized, along with retroactive payment of wage boosts caught in the freeze. There were reports that labor would pull out of the Pay Board or boycott its rules if the AFL-CIO demands were ignored—including controls over profits, dividends and interest.

In the final week of the freeze the Pay Board announced its guidelines. They provided for a general standard of 5.5 per cent a year for new pay increases and full recognition of the deferred boosts except those "unreasonably disproportionate" to the basic guideline.

The Price Commission set not a guideline, but a goal. Prices could be increased to reflect increases in cost, less any gains in productivity, the commission said, with the aim of reducing the rise in the consumer price index to between 2 and 3 per cent a year by late 1972.

Profit margins could be increased, it was ruled, but only through stepped-up sales, cost-cutting, improved machinery or materials, increased output per worker or greater production volume—not through any increase in prices.

The use of profits as a control guideline, even to that limited extent, was a shocker to industry. Then came the first rulings, and they widened the shock waves.

The Pay Board voted to approve a first-year coal miners' wage package of at least 15 per cent. The Price Commission gave two steel companies price boosts on tinplate that exceeded 7 per cent. Most of the other early rulings dealt in unexpectedly large numbers.

It became clear that the ceilings were flexible indeed. And the AFL-CIO remained implacable on the issue of retroactivity. The federation met in Miami Beach in the first week of Phase Two and voted not to cooperate with the Pay Board if its rulings were not to its liking.

"If the President doesn't want our membership on the Pay Board on our terms, he knows what he can do," Meany told the delegates.

Nixon decided on the bold course of flying to Florida and addressing the labor convention. He told the unionists his anti-inflation plans would succeed with or without them and added:

"I know exactly what I can do. And I am going to do it."

The President said he wanted the participation of labor, but went on: "Whether we get that participation or not, it is my obligation as President of the United States to make this program of stopping the rise in the cost of living succeed, and to the extent that my powers allow it, I shall do exactly that."

Meantime the banking committees of both House and Senate inserted into Nixon's pending control bill provisions to give labor the retroactivity it demanded—even though it would be quite impossible to let employers go back and raise their prices retroactively to cover the cost.

By December the stock market was in another sinking spell. Administration aides admitted that a major cause of its wretched performance was the uncertainty of investors and consumers over how and whether Phase Two would really work, considering the loopholes, exemptions and exceptions provided.

Concern over NEP's international aspect was equally grave. "Instead of the improvement in psychology that had been hoped for—and counted on as a spur to consumer buying—apprehension is widespread," said the Morgan Guaranty Trust Company's November newsletter. It went on:

"And despite the frequent repetition by U.S. officials that there will be no international trade war and despite implications that there is no great urgency in getting international differences resolved, skeptics are legion here and abroad."

On December 1 a ray of light came from Rome to brighten the gloomy scene. At the close of a delayed meeting of the finance ministers of the Group of Ten, Secretary Connally dropped a little bombshell of his own.

The U.S. would indeed negotiate a direct devaluation of the dollar, possibly as much as 10 per cent, he told the Japanese and European ministers and bankers.

That left an enormous agenda of international business still unfinished—the dismantling of tariff barriers, the actual terms of devaluation, even the possible eventual displacement of gold as the basis of the world's currency values. Yet the task no longer looked totally hopeless.

Meantime, in less than three weeks of Phase Two, more than 500 of the 1,500 biggest corporations which were required to seek advance approval of price increases had applied for such consent. Most wanted increases larger than 2.5 per cent. The approvals exceeded denials by at least 20 to 1, and the applications were still pouring in.

The chances of success in Nixon's foreign economic policy, it appeared late in December, were at least as good as the chances that Phase Two would vanquish inflation.

British Foreign Secretary Sir Alec Douglas-Home (left) and Rhodesian Prime Minister Ian Smith after they reached agreement on terms for the white minority government's return to the Commonwealth

BRITAIN, RHODESIA PACT DRAWN

The members of Rhodesia's house of assembly fell silent as Prime Minister Ian Smith called for the floor.

For half an hour he spelled out the terms of an agreement with Britain aimed at settling the six-year-old dispute with the mother country that erupted when Smith's minority white regime made its unilateral declaration of independence in 1965. The pact would also turn the Rhodesian government into a lawful regime.

Agreement came Nov. 25, nearly two weeks after British Foreign Secretary Sir Alec Douglas-Home flew to Salisbury with a large team of negotiators in what many British and Rhodesians looked on as an empty gesture doomed to failure.

Rhodesian observers recalled that when Harold Wilson was Britain's Labor prime minister he had made a similar pilgrimage in 1966. But,

despite numerous concessions to Smith, Wilson had returned to Britain empty handed.

This time there was a key difference. Departing from his adamant stand in 1966, Smith began to make concessions, and Douglas-Home's advisors quickly urged him to accept.

However, Rhodesia had become a symbol of white supremacy for millions of blacks and the mere announcement that an agreement had been reached with Britain had an explosive effect. The Organization of African Unity angrily denounced the settlement even before its terms were known, calling it "an outright sellout for generations to come of five million Africans to 243,000 white Rhodesians committed to white rule and apartheid."

The terms, when they became known, were unclear in many cases, but they did not seem

designed to appease the angry blacks. The pact gave Rhodesia's whites the assurance of continuing political power. Provision was made for eventual growth in black parliamentary strength as African incomes increased. But the fact remained that the Africans could break through to a majority only if the whites withheld a veto.

On the other side of the coin, the pact guaranteed Rhodesia's blacks against a shift to South Africa's policy of apartheid or race segregation. The agreement also added to the constitution a bill of rights prohibiting any future discriminatory laws but did nothing about statutes already on the books. The pact showed, as had Rhodesia's successful defiance of economic sanctions imposed by the United Nations, that there was no way short of war to force a determined white minority to accept African majority rule.

DEATH PENALTY GIVEN MARTIN

Aubran W. "Buddy" Martin cut a modish figure as he stood in the courtroom in Washington, Pa., Nov. 12 clad in a gold shirt and green-striped pants. The 23-year-old defendant showed no emotion when the jury found him guilty in the slaying of United Coal Mine Workers official Joseph A. Yablonski and his wife and daughter.

The following day after 49 minutes delibera-

tion, the same jury sentenced Martin to death and again he sat emotionless.

During the trial, the prosecution had claimed that Martin, Claude Vealey, and Paul Gilly, all of Cleveland, Ohio, received $1,700 each for shooting the Yablonskis as they slept in their home in Clarksville, Pa. *(The World in 1970, 102).* Gilly's wife, Annette, and her father, Silous Huddleston, also faced charges in connection with the slaying.

The key prosecution witness against Martin was Vealey, who pleaded guilty to murder charges last summer. Vealey, a 27-year-old laborer, testified that he, Martin and Gilly, 38, a house painter, carried out the killings after stalking Yablonski for weeks.

Martin testified during the trial that he went to the home of Yablonski the night of the slayings but that his motive was to steal, not to commit murder.

JORDAN PREMIER ASSASSINATED

Jordan's prime minister, Wasfi Tell, was regarded by most of his countrymen as a symbol of the government's supremacy over the Palestinian guerrillas. But, to the commandos and Arabs of other nations, he was an arch villain.

Militant Palestinians waited for six months to get at 51-year-old Tell and finally saw their chance in November, when the prime minister went to Cairo to attend a meeting of the Arab League's Joint Defense Council.

Aware of the peril to their chief of government, security officials from Amman requested that all Jordanian subjects be removed from the Sheraton Hotel in Cairo where Tell was staying.

On Nov. 28 a reception clerk at the Sheraton noticed a man standing near the desk keeping a wary eye on the front door. But the stranger was well dressed, and the clerk assumed he was a guest.

A short while later, as Tell emerged from his limousine, the door watcher and two other men closed in on the prime minister. Witnesses gave this account of the action that followed:

One man waiting outside followed Tell to the door and the other two, waiting in the lobby, rushed out of the building toward him. All three drew guns and fired. Tell fell on his back amid a shower of broken glass from the door and nearby windows.

Jordan's foreign minister, Abdullah Salah, was grazed in the leg, and the hail of bullets wounded an Egyptian security man and one of the three gunmen.

The gunmen ran through the hotel waving their revolvers and fled by a rear exit into a parking lot overlooking the Nile River. Later the three were captured. They were identified as Ezzet Abdul Fatah, Gawad Baghady, and Monzie Khalifa. A fourth Palestinian with a Syrian passport, Zeyad Mahmoud Badran, was also picked up.

The accused made no attempt to deny responsibility for the assassination. They boasted that they had finally succeeded after waiting six months for an opportunity.

"We have taken revenge on a traitor," said Khalifa, making a V-for-victory sign with his fingers for photographers.

Egypt's official Middle East News Agency said Khalifa told interrogators that the assassination plot had been hatched in Beirut by the Black September organization, a movement formed to avenge the guerrillas killed in the Jordanian army's crackdown of September 1970 (*The World in 1970, 210–213*).

It was Tell who had played a major role in consolidating Jordan's sovereignty after government forces had suppressed the commandos during the bloody fighting of that September.

Visibly moved, King Hussein of Jordan went on the air to tell his people about the assassination and to condemn the killers as "the instrument of treachery and treason."

His voice breaking, Hussein eulogized "my brother Wasfi," as a "martyr who fell while serving his country."

The day after Tell's assassination, the king appointed Finance Minister Ahmed al-Lawzi, 46, as the new prime minister and gave him instructions to pursue the same policy as his predecessor.

Hours later Lawzi flew to Cairo to head his country's delegation to the Defense Council talks. The Egyptian government, which condemned Tell's slaying, tightened security measures around the Arab League headquarters and Cairo's major hotels.

Jordan's King Hussein sorrowfully attended funeral of his assassinated premier, Wasfi Tell

PROTESTS FAILED TO HALT TEST

On Nov. 6, the signal was given and the black cylinder on a mock Spartan anti-ballistic missile exploded 6,000 feet beneath little Amchitka Island in the Aleutians.

The blast, resulting from the most powerful underground nuclear test ever held by the United States, had the force of five million tons of TNT, or about 350 times the power of the A-bomb that devastated Hiroshima in 1945.

Half a second after the detonation, the earth heaved and aftershocks were felt nearly 25 miles away. The blast caused seismographs to register a shock of the magnitude of seven on the Richter scale.

But there was no environmental catastrophe as had been predicted by opponents of the test; Alaska suffered no damaging earthquake, Hawaii reported no tidal wave, and no cloud of radioactivity seeped up through the earthcracks from the explosion a mile underground, Atomic Energy Commission officials said.

The test, code-named Cannikin, achieved full-scale yield for the warhead prompting James Schlesinger, chairman of the AEC, to announce: "This proof test permits us to introduce the Spartan warhead into the inventory while minimizing the likelihood of a defective warhead."

Environmentalists had fought the test in the courts. Their protests had been the most vigorous ever lodged against nuclear testing in this country or abroad. Peace groups and environmentalists had demonstrated in front of the White House while others staged similar protests in Alaska and Canada. More than 30 U.S. senators had fired off a telegram to President Nixon urging him to call the test off, and the Japanese government had filed official reservations.

An appeal for a hearing to halt the test went to the Supreme Court, but the justices in an 11th-hour ballot, voted 4 to 3 to deny the injunction.

The AEC tried to stop the uproar by explaining that the test was necessary to provide a "thin-shield" defense against nuclear attack. The AEC agreed to quit the Amchitka test site, but made no promise to stop underground testing in Nevada, where over the past eight years the United States has averaged about 30 underground shots a year.

The uproar over Cannikin was another expression indicative of public discontent over the relative freedom with which nuclear weapons had been tested and deployed through the years in the United States. Since World War II about 500 atomic and hydrogen tests had been disclosed by the AEC.

STRIKE ENDED BY COAL MINERS

In a move to end a 44-day soft coal mine strike that had idled 100,000 miners in 25 states, the United Mine Workers Union and management teams agreed Nov. 14 on a new contract.

The three-year pact called for boosting wages of skilled workers from an average of $37 a day to $50 and doubling coal royalties over the term of the contract. The industry put a $1.2 million, or 39 per cent, price tag on the wage and benefit package.

The increase in royalties from 40 cents per ton to 80 cents at the end of the contract would add an estimated $382.5 million to the union's welfare fund for dispersement to miner's widows, disability benefits and miners' pensions.

The UMW struck mines of the Bituminous Coal Operators Association on Oct. 1. The strike caused related layoffs in railroads and threatened coal supplies of utilities and other industries.

Despite the agreement, many workers did not go back to work Nov. 15 as was ordered because the settlement had been reached subject to approval by the Pay Board. Thousands of miners in the Appalachian belt remained out of work, and Consolidation Coal Company, the second largest in the country, reported that only 4,000 of a force of 13,000 showed up.

Many miners continued the strike until the Pay Board approved the wage increase involving about 15 per cent of the nation's miners by a 10–3 vote on Nov. 19. The first-year provision of the contract was allowed despite a warning from public members that raises of such magnitude could impair the fight against inflation.

The mine settlement, reached only minutes before the freeze ended at midnight Nov. 14, had been classified earlier by the board as an "existing" contract and as such not subject to the 5.5 per cent guideline on new wage agreements signed during Phase Two.

SYNOD SESSION INCONCLUSIVE

After five weeks of often stormy debate, the World Synod of Catholic Bishops ended in Vatican City Nov. 6, leaving churchmen divided on the issue of whether married men should become priests. It also left them in doubt as to whether the parley had accomplished anything of substance.

The Synod gave solid support to the campaign of Pope Paul VI for social justice. But observers noted that it made only one major point that did not duplicate the speeches and writings of the pontiff: Urging church backing of conscientious objection to war.

A resolution stating that married men should not be considered for the priesthood, except in special cases allowed by the Pope, won a majority of 107 votes. But a surprisingly large number of delegates, totaling 87, voted in favor of an alternate statement encouraging Pope Paul to allow married men "of mature age and upright life" to become priests in some nations.

Neither resolution received the two-thirds majority needed for passage of any synod document and they were therefore incorporated into a final text covering the broad subject of the priesthood.

It was noted, however, that the document did not go into the wave of priestly defections in the West.

COURT UPHELD WOMEN'S RIGHTS

Advancement of women's rights was strengthened Nov. 22 when the Supreme Court unanimously overturned an Idaho state law giving men preference over the distaff side in administering the estates of deceased persons. It marked the first time that the nation's top tribunal had struck down a state law on grounds of sex discrimination.

The opinion rendered by Chief Justice Warren E. Burger declared that the Idaho statute denied women the equal protection of the law guaranteed by the 14th Amendment.

But despite a request by advocates of women's rights, Burger's ruling did not hold that all laws that treat women differently from men were inherently suspect under the Constitution.

By this omission the court stopped short of holding that laws which draw distinctions between the sexes should be presumed in violation of the Constitution, as were statutes which make distinctions based on race.

The ruling held that the Idaho legislature had rendered an "arbitrary" decision to favor men over women in order to spare trial judges from having to rule in each case which sex was best suited to administer a contested estate.

The high court declared that the result of this statute was to divide men and women into separate classes "on the basis of criteria wholly unrelated" to the objective of efficient distribution of estates.

The 14th Amendment, which went into effect in 1868, held that no state should "deny to any person within its jurisdiction the equal protection of the laws."

THAI REVOLT LED BY PREMIER

Field Marshal Thanom Kittikachorn, prime minister of Thailand, was an amiable man who said shortly after taking office: "I have become Americanized. I am rushing all the time." On Nov. 17, Thanom acted with dispatch, abolishing parliament, the constitution and the cabinet to seize absolute power for himself and eight high-ranking members of the government.

Thanom explained his move in a statement citing three main reasons:

—To forestall a small but growing movement among politicans to begin exploring new relations with China and keep a firm grip on the reins of foreign policy.

—To eliminate parliamentary inefficiency and the tendency among legislators to hold up government measures with disputes over details.

—To do away with restraints on police action that were embodied in the constitution and to give police a free hand to deal with crime and communist insurrection in northeast Thailand.

Thanom was clearly worried about the effect of the seating of Red China in the United Nations, and by the results which her emergence on the world scene might have on the three million ethnic Chinese dwelling in Thailand. This colony controlled much of Thailand's economy.

Economic problems apparently triggered the putsch. The Thai government had been trying since summer to get its tight budget passed by the Oct. 1 deadline, but Parliament had held it up.

Many members of Thanom's own United Thai People's party in Parliament were calling for a $16 million appropriation to be shared among members for projects in each constituency.

The government had argued that it needed all the money to push forward with its new five-year development program. When the legislators announced that they would still hold up the funds, Thanom staged his putsch.

It marked the ninth such coup in Thailand since the king's absolute rule was ended in 1932.

Tanks guarding revolutionary party headquarters following coup in Thailand

TOP DIPLOMATS TOURED WORLD, SEEKING INTERNATIONAL PACTS

It was a time of travel for many diplomats on both sides of the iron curtain, but the Russians led the field with a high-powered campaign of international diplomacy.

It began in September when Indian Prime Minister Indira Gandhi went to Moscow. Within the ensuing two months, Yugoslav President Tito visited Washington, Vice-President Spiro Agnew made a trip to his father's homeland in Greece and Emperor Hirohito of Japan met President Nixon in Alaska. Later, U.S. Presidential advisor Henry Kissinger went to Peking to make plans for Nixon's trip to Red China.

But the main interest centered on the globe trotting Russians. The flurry of activity by the Kremlin's three top leaders roused speculation whether the new U.S.-Chinese detente had sparked a Soviet peace offensive.

In November Leonid I. Brezhnev, Soviet Communist party chief, paid a visit to East Germany after a tour of France. On Nov. 1 he called for the East Germans to reach the "fastest possible" conclusion of their talks with West Germany on the practical arrangements for putting into effect the recent four-power accord on East-West Berlin (Page 180).

Brezhnev received a pledge of cooperation from the East German party leader, Erich Honecker, who said that if all sides showed good will the talks "could be concluded soon."

While in France for an eight-day visit Brezhnev and President Georges Pompidou had signed a ten-year trade agreement on Oct. 27. It sought primarily to increase trade by encouraging long-term contracts. The two countries also had called for the convening the following year of a European Security conference, a project the Soviets had been initiating.

Earlier Brezhnev had made a tour of Eastern Europe (Page 178) which included Yugoslavia, Hungary and Bulgaria.

The first of October, Soviet President Nikolai V. Podgorny embarked on a swing through Asia, stopping in India, Burma and North Vietnam. In India he urged that country not to engage in war with Pakistan and, to a degree, tightened the Soviet Union's ties with her. In August the two countries had signed a 20-year friendship treaty and in September Indira Gandhi had visited Moscow.

In North Vietnam Podgorny reaffirmed continued support for the North Vietnamese and the Viet Cong. The two countries on Oct. 10 set up a joint committee to would work out details of long-term economic, trade, cultural, scientific and technological relations between the two countries.

Premier Alexei N. Kosygin set out Oct. 4 on a tour of Northern Africa, with stops in Algeria and Morocco. After a four-day tour in Algeria, Kosygin promised to increase the large amount of aid Russia had given Algeria but declined to join in a belligerent stance in the Middle East. "The liberation of the territories occupied by the Zionists," he said, could be achieved "by political debate and not by the debate of war."

When he ended his three-day tour in Morocco Kosygin warned that African country that the Middle East situation was tense "and can degenerate into conflict" despite the good will of Egypt. The two countries issued a statement emphasizing the need for a rapid and peaceful solution of the Middle East problem.

Returning to Moscow Oct. 10, Kosygin and Podgorny met with Egyptian President Anwar Sadat and pledged to strengthen Russian aid to the Arabs.

Kosygin then began, on Oct. 17, an eight-day tour of Canada. On the second day of his tour a man shouting 'long live free Hungary' jumped on Kosygin as he and Canadian Prime Minister Pierre Elliott Trudeau were walking across parliament grounds. Kosygin was shaken but unhurt. Throughout his tour of Canada, Kosygin ran into demonstrations in which protesters asked that Jews in the Soviet Union be enabled to live as Jews or allowed to leave that country. The end of his visit was marked by disturbances in Toronto, where 6,000 demonstrators hurled lighted candles, rocks and sticks at police. At the close of Kosygin's stay a joint communique was issued which pledged that Canada and the Soviet Union would work together for disarmament measures, including a ban on underground nuclear tests.

From Canada the Soviet premier went to Cuba for a four-day visit.

During the period the Soviets were strengthening ties with other countries, Vice-President Agnew had embarked on a 13-day visit to Turkey, Iran and Greece. Agnew took part in a celebration marking the founding of the Persian Empire in 539 B.C. sponsored by Mohammed Reza Shah Pahlevi. In Greece he told Premier George Papadopoulos that the Nixon Administration wished to continue military support to Greece, to help that nation meet its Atlantic Alliance commitments.

For the first time in history a reigning Japanese emperor visited foreign soil on Sept. 27, when Emperor Hirohito met with Nixon in Anchorage, Alaska. After a brief talk with the President, Hirohito began an 18-day trip through Europe, his first in 50 years.

Tito visited Washington Oct. 27 for three days. During his stay he said that Brezhnev had told him all Soviet military personnel would be withdrawn from Egypt and other Arab countries once a Middle East settlement was reached. After leaving the United States Tito went to Canada for six days.

Indira Gandhi spent four days in the United States in November, talking with President Nixon about the India-Pakistan refugee problem.

Fidel Castro, Prime Minister of Cuba, wearing a hard hat when he visited workers during a tour of Chile

Soviet Premier Alexei N. Kosygin grimaced in alarm when he was attacked during visit to Canada

This is what remained of a bridge being built across Germany's Rhine River after it collapsed near Koblenz, killing 10 workers

ONLY SCATTERED VIOLENCE MARKED SCHOOL BUSING

The week before the public schools opened in Pontiac, Mich., last September, 10 school buses were set afire. As flames leaped 100 feet into the air, they illuminated one of the year's most deeply controversial national issues. For the vehicles were among a number assigned to bus black Pontiac children to white schools—for the sake of racial desegregation.

Six men identified as Ku Klux Klansmen later were indicted on federal charges in the destruction of the 10 buses.

Even so, in spite of misgivings by many citizens, Pontiac went ahead with the busing of one-third of its 24,000 public school pupils.

There were scattered incidents of violence elsewhere as the school year of 1971 began with massive busing programs mandated by the U.S. Supreme Court.

But all in all, the latest surge of school desegregation went off relatively smoothly if noisily in most cities. So much so that Asst. U.S. Atty. Gen. David Norman was able to announce that, despite the national furor, no federal intervention was needed.

As for pupils involved, a teacher in Pontiac's Madison junior high declared:

"Sure, we had a few fights. It's just that with all the attention focused on busing now, every time a kid gets busted in the mouth it is blown up all out of proportion. Things will work out."

Such was a nation in 1971 that was 17 years removed from the Supreme Court decree that classroom segregation in public schools was unconstitutional. Fourteen years had passed since President Eisenhower had sent federal troops into Little Rock, Ark., to escort nine black students into previously all-white Central High.

Over those years, in the 17 deep south and border states, all but 70 of 4,400 school districts had been adjudged in full compliance with school desegregation mandates. Most of the exceptions were in the larger cities.

Sorely but surely, classroom desegregation now was coming also to the big cities of the north and west, with their all-black ghetto schools. Its symbol was a time honored one in rural areas—the yellow school bus. Increasingly, it was being used to transfer black and white children to city schools outside their neighborhoods.

Actually, busing was not a new concept. Nearly 40 per cent of the nation's elementary school children already were being bused for reasons having nothing to do with desegregation. Distance was a determining factor in rural areas.

In addition, in a program dating back to 1964, New York City was transporting 18,000 ghetto children to largely white schools within the city. Boston was busing 1,600 black children to 30 different suburban school districts. Twenty-five suburban Connecticut towns were taking 2,100 Negro children from Bridgeport, Hartford, New Haven and Waterbury.

But for many years the brunt of school desegregation pressures had been directed against the south. Then on April 30 in a case involving the Charlotte, N.C. school system, the U.S. Supreme Court ruled that federal courts could order the busing of children as a legitimate means of desegregating schools.

The result was a spate of lawsuits demanding desegregation by busing. Many of them were filed in the north. With power to grant or withhold federal school aid, the Department of Health, Education and Welfare was involved in many of the cases.

However, the picture was complicated Aug. 3 when President Nixon announced he would "hold busing to the minimum required by law."

"I have consistently opposed the busing of our nation's school children to achieve a racial balance," he declared, "and I am opposed to the busing of children simply for the sake of busing."

Nixon's remarks were directed at a school desegregation plan drawn up by HEW for Austin, Tex. It involved extensive cross-busing of 89 per cent of that city's elementary pupils.

Complained a seemingly perplexed Dr. Mark Shedd, superintendent of Philadelphia's public schools: "The state Human Relations Commission tells us one thing. The Supreme Court another. Then HEW mandates still another policy and President Nixon promptly repudiates it. I feel like a quarterback trying to satisfy four different coaches."

In a statement Oct. 2, Michigan's Democratic state central committee endorsed school busing as a temporary measure, rather than a final solution, adding: "It is a crutch, not a cure. One day, hopefully soon, we can throw away the crutch."

What was the cure? One viewpoint came from federal court comment in relation to school busing in Atlanta: "Segregated housing . . . remains the unconquerable foe of the racial ideal of integrated public schools in the city."

But Roy Wilkins, head of the National Association for the Advancement of Colored People, wrote: "Housing may yet prove to be the most stubborn of the racial big three: Employment, education and housing."

School busing indeed had wrought controversy across the nation in the year 1971. And the end did not appear in sight. The NAACP's legal defense fund announced plans to bring busing suits in 12 more cities a year, for the next three years.

And there was every indication school busing might prove a vexatious issue in 1972's presidential campaigning.

December

The President in 1971:
A Year of Vital Change

Nixon's planned trips to Peking and Moscow, historic summit talks, drastic revision of monetary and economic programs were among dramatic U.S. and international occurrences

Nixon gesticulating after signing the budget message

For a decade, ever since John F. Kennedy journeyed to Vienna for a disappointing conference with Nikita Khrushchev, "summitry" had been a diplomatic art form practiced only infrequently, and then warily, by American presidents. Richard M. Nixon, like Lyndon B. Johnson before him, proclaimed early and often that superpower summit meetings were to be undertaken only if and when positive results seemed likely.

Against that backdrop, Nixon in 1971 put together all the pieces pointing toward unprecedented, indeed historic, summit talks in the capital cities of his country's two most implacable antagonists, Communist China and the Soviet Union. From Nixon's standpoint, the timing was fortuitous. The Peking and Moscow summits were scheduled for the first half of the 1972 election year, the very season for presidential primaries and pre-convention jockeying when, otherwise, the spotlight might have fallen by default to Nixon's potential Democratic challengers.

Moreover, the President added drama to the scenario—and did serious talking about serious issues—at a tightly-scheduled series of pre-summitry summit sessions with leaders of nations the White House classified as "major allies"—Canada, France, Great Britain, West Germany and Japan.

The advance round of conferences, which were unprecedented in their own way, found Nixon participating in a Summit-A-Week Club throughout December and during the earliest days of 1972.

Henry A. Kissinger, the President's ubiquitous assistant for national security affairs, summarized his view of the need for highest-level conversations with the allies:

"It was felt that so many things have happened since last year—the announcement of our trips to Peking and Moscow, the Berlin agreement, the ratification of the Okinawa reversion (to Japan), the whole economic negotiations, Britain's entry into the Common Market—that it was essential that the leaders at the highest level meet, to make sure that their basic direction was complementary and that they understood each other."

Kissinger added that "the meetings with our allies should be seen in the context of working visits brought about by a dramatic change in the international situation that has occurred in the last seven months."

The former Harvard University professor did not say it but, clearly, Richard Nixon contributed mightily to "dramatic change" in 1971.

At the start of the year Nixon was asked, in effect, if he were satisfied with his performance as 37th President of the United States as he approached the midway point of the term to which he had been narrowly elected in 1968.

"I hope I do better," he replied.

At that moment, Nixon had ample cause to seek an improved performance record. The war continued in Vietnam, inflation knew few checks, joblessness was mounting and crime statistics (once the problem of the Democrats) seemed to trend inexorably upward, if at a somewhat slackened pace. In the Democratic-controlled Congress, the chief executive's groundbreaking domestic initiatives were undergoing close, if not microscopic, scrutiny. And Nixon, still smarting after Senate rebuffs to Supreme Court nominees Clement Haynsworth and G. Harrold Carswell, had just emerged chastened from a 1970 off-year election campaign in which he had staked his personal prestige by taking to the stump from coast to coast. He proclaimed himself a campaign winner but the election returns indicated he had scant cause for joy (*The World in 1970*, 242–245).

Historians may one day view 1971 as the "do better" year, a time when the durable Nixon again picked himself up off the floor to transform impending defeat into victory. Although even a preliminary verdict must await that of the voters come November 1972, Nixon at least managed a turnaround in public opinion polls that, in mid-1971, strongly suggested he had not accumulated a loser's image in the early '60s entirely by happenstance.

Nixon, in fact, puts great stock by losing and, with inner spirit intact, coming back to win. He never tired of telling listeners he did exactly that himself. In late November, for example, he went to the training camp of the Washington Redskins and their new coach, George Allen. The Redskins, long a doormat of the National Football League, were enjoying a revival under Allen but had seemed less than impressive in their last three games. Nixon delivered an impromptu pep talk on the joys of overcoming adversity and the 'Skins promptly resumed their winning ways.

For all of this, 1971 was not a year of unalloyed joy for Nixon. His search, with Secretary of State William P. Rogers and others, for a Middle East peace, became stymied. And a new war broke out in December between India and Pakistan. The economic situation at home was heavily freighted with uncertainty.

If Nixon's July announcement that he would go to Peking was startling, the President was equally astonishing a month later, on August 15, when he made an equally abrupt departure from

Canadian Prime Minister Pierre Elliott Trudeau dined with the President

President and Mrs. Nixon greeting Japanese Emperor Hirohito and party in Anchorage, Alaska

post-World War II tradition and announced a "New Economic Program" that placed curbs on the domestic economy and placed major trading partners on notice that no longer could they fatten themselves on monetary windfalls from the United States.

Nixon, in a phrase, threw out the "free world" rulebook in 1971, economically and diplomatically.

Again his poll ratings climbed, just as a lot of Americans were wondering if they were destined to be served by a succession of one-term presidents.

The year 1971 brought Nixon a full measure of problems as well as successes. The conflict in Southeast Asia, receding from front pages as the year progressed, claimed center stage at the outset.

In February Nixon and wife Pat flew away from chilly Washington to the Virgin Islands. During their weekend stay in the Caribbean, the world press began publicizing unofficial reports of a new intervention in Laos, rekindling memories of Cambodia and the subsequent upheaval on the home front. Within a few days it was disclosed that hundreds of American aircraft and their crewmen—but no U.S. ground troops—were taking part in a "limited" South Vietnamese attack on enemy supply lines in Laos, near the demilitarized zone separating the two Vietnams.

Some widely-reported combat goals of the South Vietnamese forces were not met. And soon American TV-watchers and newspaper readers were greeted by photos of Saigon troops so eager to quit the combat that they escaped—or sometimes perished— by hanging to the landing skids of American-manned helicopters.

In early March Nixon tried to nail down public support for the Laotian maneuver during a televised news conference. The operation already had proven so successful, he stated, that the continued withdrawal of U.S. troops from South Vietnam had been assured into 1972. Barely three weeks later, in still another

TV appearance, Nixon argued the Laotian campaign had reduced the threat to the lives of American forces in South Vietnam. The 44-day campaign ended two days later.

On the day the operation ended, March 24, a peaceful crowd estimated variously at 200,000 to 500,000 massed in Washington to urge that Congress force a halt to American involvement in Vietnam. Quite possibly, in fact probably, it was the last of the huge Washington peace marches.

But it closely coincided with still another event that troubled the nation's conscience—and prompted two moves by Nixon that gained him some friends and alienated others. Four days after Army Lt. William Calley was found guilty of premeditated murder in the deaths of 22 Vietnamese civilians at My Lai in 1968, and just a day after Calley was sentenced by an Army court to life imprisonment (the only alternative was a death sentence), Nixon ordered the convicted officer released from the stockade and confined to his apartment pending a review of the case.

Nixon, sojourning at the time in Southern California, was acutely conscious of an extraordinary pro-Calley outpouring of mail and telegrams that reflected essentially conflicting trains of thought: (1) "hawks" argued that Calley was a conscientious officer who simply followed orders and did what he was trained to do, kill. (2) "doves" contended Calley was a scapegoat for higher officials ultimately responsible for what a nationwide majority was coming to regard as misguided American intervention in Vietnam.

Although many Americans could not claim membership in either camp, Nixon found it expedient to announce, with fanfare, his intervention on Calley's behalf. The public soon learned that the military, with no prompting from the White House, already had planned to do precisely what Nixon ordered done.

The President's second intervention in the Calley case followed.

He announced he would accord Calley a final review of his conviction and sentence, a step already carefully provided for by law.

Nixon's critics saw him trying to mount a bandwagon, taking a couple of "cheap shots." Calley's prosecutor, Army Capt. Aubrey M. Daniel III, of an old Virginia family, had his own complaint—and one that was not found unworthy by many in the Pentagon. In a widely-publicized letter to his commander-in-chief, Daniel argued that Nixon was toying, for political purposes, with the impartial administration of Army justice by suggesting, simply by his acts, that he favored clemency.

The Calley gambit presumably did nothing to drive a wedge between the chief executive and his most conservative supporters. However, in the early weeks of 1971, Nixon had prompted considerable concern from the political right wing by embracing the idea of a "full employment budget" in a time of sorry economic tidings. In other words, he contended, there is nothing bad about deficit spending at a time of economic slack, provided full blown prosperity would—using the same statistics—balance the budget were the country operating at full employment. It was an old Democratic argument, decked out in new nomenclature—and Nixon made his message more pointed by confessing that he had become a "Keynesian" in economic matters. He referred, of course, to the preachments of Englishman John Maynard Keynes, an economic underpinning for the red-ink budgets of Franklin D. Roosevelt—a name not likely to strike positive chords among the old stalwarts of Nixon's Grand Old Party.

The President had other problems, to be sure, in early 1971. The populace at large was not stirred, for example, by his 1971 domestic policy initiatives, which he equated with a "New American Revolution." Congress, controlled by the opposition party, seemed little moved by Nixon's appeals for governmental reorganization and the sharing of $16 billion of federal revenues with state, county and local governments on a few-strings-attached basis. Besides, some of the cabinet departments Nixon proposed for abolition under reorganization had strong parochial support among noteworthy GOP campaign contributors.

Congress then proceeded to underline its independence by voting to kill the Nixon-endorsed plan to build, with heavy federal subsidies, an American supersonic airliner.

Almost nothing turned up roses for Richard Nixon in the first half of 1971. And his poll standings turned noticeably downward.

But Nixon was nothing if not a practiced politician, schooled in adversity and ever ready to attempt self-resuscitation when his fortunes seemed most bleak.

Such a moment came on July 15, 1971.

Flying by helicopter from his home at San Clemente, Calif., to a television studio in Burbank, Nixon stunned the world with a four-minute broadcast announcement that he was accepting with pleasure an invitation to visit Communist China. He said:

"I have taken this action because of my profound conviction that all nations will gain from a reduction of tensions and a better relationship between the United States and the People's Republic of China."

The historic visit—no American president had ever gone to China—had been arranged a few days earlier by Henry Kissinger, who journeyed secretly to Peking during a seemingly routine global tour. Kissinger's negotiations were so hush-hush that even Vice President Spiro T. Agnew was kept in the dark.

In October Kissinger again went to Peking—this time after a public announcement—to nail down final details. After returning to Washington, Kissinger said the President and Mrs. Nixon would arrive in China on Feb. 21, 1972, and remain until Feb. 28—just before the first of the presidential primaries. They planned to visit Peking, Shanghai and Hang Chou.

The China announcement, while displeasing to many in the right wing of the Republican party, was greeted with approval by most Americans and by world leaders almost everywhere except in Moscow and Taipei.

Nixon, however, could not afford to get euphoric. The dollar, burdened by two decades of mounting deficits in the U.S. balance of international payments, was under heavy assault in world money markets. Moreover, the administration "game plan" for healing a troubled domestic economy had failed to produce

Nixon and his wife showing view from a White House balcony to India's Prime Minister Indira Gandhi

desired results. Prices kept moving upward and unemployment remained at an unacceptable rate of 6 per cent.

On Aug. 15 Nixon returned to the airwaves with another surprise, this one fully as significant as—and probably more so than—his China hat trick. Citing prosperity without war as his goal, Nixon said:

"The time has come for a New Economic Policy for the United States; its targets are unemployment, inflation and international speculation."

Wages and prices would be frozen for 90 days, a 10 per cent surcharge would be imposed on foreign imports pending international agreement on monetary and trade reforms, the United States was suspending its time-honored policy of selling gold to foreign governments and central banks at $35 an ounce.

These were but some of the highlights of what Nixon termed "the most comprehensive New Economic Policy to be undertaken by this nation in four decades."

Most Americans applauded; clearly they desired some kind of affirmative action on the economic front—and Nixon had given it to them. Many foreign leaders were surprised and perplexed; some of the more astute among them wondered why Uncle Sam had been so slow to act on an international monetary crisis that had been building for more than a decade.

The dog days of spring behind him, Nixon once again was a man on the move, heading into an election year with burnished image. In quick succession, he produced autumn announcements that U.S. force levels in Vietnam would be cut below 140,000 by Feb. 1, 1972—400,000 less than when he took office—and that in the late-May pre-convention season he would become the first American president to visit Moscow.

As his political stock began rising, Nixon was even aided by circumstances beyond his control. Within days of each other, two aging and ailing Supreme Court justices, Hugo L. Black and John M. Harlan, announced they were retiring. Nixon thus was given an opportunity to nominate his third and fourth members of the nine-man bench—sufficient to tilt the court in the conservative, "strict constructionist" direction he had envisioned during his 1968 campaign.

The lawyer-President stumbled and fumbled, however, as he searched for two new justices. The first names to be mentioned publicly bore much the same stamp of mediocrity that had doomed Nixon's earlier nomination of G. Harrold Carswell.

As public controversy mounted, Nixon reversed his field and submitted to the Senate the names of two distinguished lawyers: Asst. Atty. Gen. William H. Rehnquist of Arizona and Lewis F. Powell Jr. of Virginia.

Early in 1971, Nixon had promised to wear his presidential hat during the year and pay no mind to politics. He embraced the notion that good government automatically is good politics.

As the months went by, however, Nixon could not avoid some overt politicking. Exactly a year to the date before the 1971 balloting, he and wife Pat made flying trips to New York and Chicago to appear at $500-a-plate Republican fund-raising dinners. They were but two of 20 "Salute to the President" dinners designed to raise $5 million for the GOP campaign. They also marked the unofficial kickoff of Nixon's quest for votes, although his speeches to the big contributors seemed almost nonpartisan in tone.

In one area where Nixon had counted on support in 1972, the farm belt, trouble loomed as autumn leaves fell. A glut of feed grains saw corn prices plummet. The President acted: He abandoned a plan to abolish the Agriculture Department and announced he was getting himself a new secretary of agriculture: Indiana educator Earl Butz to replace Nebraska educator

Clifford Hardin. Again Nixon almost stumbled and fell. Because Butz was considered an advocate of corporate farming, his nomination drew widespread disapproval in sectors where the preservation of the family farm remained a potent political issue. Butz won Senate confirmation by a shaky 51–44 margin.

Fall brought Nixon other problems, too, and he mastered most of them. First there was the necessity of fashioning wage-price controls to follow the temporary freeze. Nixon set up a Pay Board and Price Commission, each representing management, labor and the public, to set policy on restraints. Big labor, personified by AFL-CIO president George Meany, threatened to scuttle the machinery. But just as it appeared that Meany might gain the upper hand, the aging union boss did some stumbling of his own and, unwittingly, came to the President's rescue.

On short notice, Nixon accepted a long-standing Meany invitation to address the AFL-CIO convention at Bal Harbour, Fla. At Meany's direction, the conventioneers gave the chief executive an icy reception. There were no booes or cheers, just a pattering of applause and sudden outbreaks of derisive laughter.

Meany might have carried it off, except for what came next. Nixon, his speech concluded, stepped onto the convention floor to chat and handshake with the delegates. The AFL-CIO president wielded his gavel and ordered the union men to take their seats; in other words, stop crowding around Nixon.

It is not often that a president of the United States is gaveled off the floor of a convention to which he has been invited. The spectacle, viewed by millions on TV news shows, provoked widespread expressions of public outrage. The 77-year-old Meany offered a feeble defense but no apology, then checked into a hospital with heart palpatations.

In December, Congressional Democrats gave Nixon still another opportunity to transform a potential setback into an impressive victory. As the Senate debated Nixon's legislative plan for furthering his economic stabilization program, Democrats tacked on more than $10 billion extra of tax cuts and, more important, added a rider that could have provided each of the major parties with $20.4 million for the 1972 presidential campaign. The GOP did not need the money but the debt-ridden Democrats did.

Nixon announced he would veto the bill unless it were stripped of the campaign financing proviso and the added tax cuts. It was a bold maneuver inasmuch as the basic legislation was essential to the furtherance of his economic program. The Democrats backtracked and chose not to make a fight of it. Nixon got the bill he wanted, and signed it promptly in mid-December.

The President produced another stroke before Christmas. Standing under the wing of the original Wright airplane in the Smithsonian Institution, he told a group of diplomats and reporters that the United States and other industrial countries had just made "the most significant economic agreement" in history.

After two days of hard bargaining, the finance ministers of the 10 major industrial countries had indeed agreed on a solution to one of the major economic problems of the world.

The roots of this problem went back to his Aug. 15 speech, when he cut the links between the dollar and gold, letting the dollar's value float freely. He also had imposed a 10 per cent extra tariff on most imports.

A preliminary meeting in Rome had produced some relaxation of positions on both sides, but the other countries insisted that the U.S. raise the price of gold, thereby devaluing the dollar. Nixon, after a meeting with President Pompidou of France, announced the United States would devalue as part of a general agreement.

This agreement was reached in Washington and announced at the Smithsonian. The United States agreed to remove the tariff surcharge; in exchange, the other countries raised the value of their currencies. This made it easier for the U.S. to export to them and harder for them to export to the United States.

The President also said the dollar would be devalued, by raising the price of gold from $35 per ounce to $38 IF—and it was a big if—other countries would remove some of their restrictions on U.S. trade. Negotiations on trade got under way within the week but at the end of the year they were still going on with no agreement.

Experts advised reporters to "read the fine print" in the communique issued after the meeting in Washington. When they did, they found that, although an agreement had been reached, the world's money problems were still around. Specifically, the gold agreement was only conditional; nobody knew whether the dollar would be exchanged for gold later; the problem of the Canadian dollar exchange rate had just been papered over, and the question of whether the United States could export enough to cancel its balance of payments deficit was still uncertain.

Nevertheless, the agreement reached after only two days of negotiation was a considerable achievement. For one thing, each of the new exchange rates had to be balanced, not only against the dollar, but against all the others. That meant that 90 new rates had to be agreed on. In a competitive world economy, that much agreement that quickly was unprecedented. The speed, if not the importance, of the Washington accord was indeed significant.

At year's end, the President had his ducks lined up pretty much where he wanted them to be—and he still was clinging to his presidential hat, off into a sunset that, at dawn, would spell Election 1972.

Above, the President and Israeli Prime Minister Golda Meir met in Washington. Below, the President strolling along the beach in front of his home in San Clemente, Calif.

Breaking its usual rule against pictures, the U.S. Senate posed for its official portrait

Congress Kept Busy by U.S. Economy Problems, Debates on War Abroad

But probably the 1971 session's best efforts were centered on 1972 elections, including voting rights for citizens over 18 and steps toward financing presidential campaigns

THE CONGRESS that spent much of 1971 debating issues of war abroad and the economy at home will leave its most lasting imprint not on those problems but on the elections of 1972 and beyond.

It had enlarged the American electorate by extending the vote to citizens over 18. It had begun the process of reforming political finances. And it had written into law, for elections beginning in 1976, a system of public financing of presidential campaigns.

The latter measure produced the most bitter partisan battle of the first session, 92nd Congress, and it was a struggle likely to be renewed in congresses to come.

President Nixon threatened to veto his own tax relief bill if it carried the campaign finance plan, in which the debt-plagued Democrats saw hope of quick financial rescue in 1972.

Had the Democrats made it stick, they might have managed an end run around their $9.3 million leftover debt, and gained some tax dollars to help bankroll the man they select to challenge for the White House in 1972.

But, in the end, it was Democrat Wilbur Mills of Arkansas, chairman of the House Ways and Means Committee, who backed down and agreed to a bill stripped of the 1972 campaign finance provision Nixon so bitterly opposed.

The $15.8 billion tax cut bill the President proposed as a spur to the lagging economy did carry the disputed plan, but provided that it would not take effect until the 1976 presidential election, when it could provide $25 million to the candidate of each major party.

It would create a system under which a taxpayer could check a box on his income tax return to donate $1 to the party of his choice.

But it would take additional legislation to implement it, even in 1976, and the Administration was almost certain to move again to block the plan. Vice President Spiro T. Agnew said Nixon never would have signed the bill unless he were sure he could act to jettison the system with a later veto.

On the other hand, political times could change. Who knows, by 1976 we could need the money, said Sen. Robert J. Dole of Kansas, the Republican national chairman and one of the leading GOP battlers against the checkoff plan which he called a Democratic treasury raid.

Another political feature of the tax bill would be felt in 1972, this one designed to encourage small campaign contributions by permitting tax credits of up to $12.50, or deductions of up to $50 a taxpayer, to cover half of a political donation. Congress also reached agreement, but did not finally enact, a campaign reform bill limiting candidate spending for most types of advertising to 10 cents for each eligible voter. It also would impose new requirements for fuller disclosure of political finances. That bill, due for a final House vote in 1972, would have the effect of limiting a 1972 presidential candidate to $8.4 million worth of radio and television advertising next year.

House Democrats had feared that Nixon, with the Republican party well bankrolled and in a position to spend far more than that, might veto the bill, but the White House sent word he would not.

The 18-year-old vote amendment swept through Congress and was approved by the required three-quarters of the states in record time, with Ohio becoming the 38th state to ratify on June 30.

"Some 11 million young men and women who have participated in the life of our nation through their work, their studies and their sacrifices for its defense, are now fully included in the electoral process of our country," said President Nixon. "I urge them to honor this right by exercising it."

Both political parties promptly set to work to recruit the newly enfranchised young voters. The 26th amendment to the Constitution took effect automatically upon ratification, but Nixon picked up a piece of the action by signing it anyhow.

The political controversies that did much to shape the session of 1971 were but a sampling of what was due in 1972, with House and Senate controlled by Democrats, Republican Nixon in the White House seeking a second term, and a corps of challengers based on Capitol Hill.

Over the course of the 1971 Congress, eight Senate Democrats were involved in presidential maneuvering, and Republican leaders delighted in pointing out their campaign-inspired absenteeism.

"The Democratic national convention will serve as an act of mercy," said Republican leader Hugh Scott.

Sen. Edmund S. Muskie of Maine, endorsed by a half-dozen colleagues as he sought to fashion a 1972 bandwagon, delayed his formal announcement of candidacy until Jan. 4, and went into the election year in what some politicans considered a commanding position for nomination. But there were primary elections and rivals to be faced. Sen. George McGovern of South Dakota, Sen. Henry M. Jackson of Washington were in the race and campaigning hard; Sen. Hubert H. Humphrey of Minnesota was looking for a 1972 rematch against Nixon; Sen. Edward M. Kennedy of Massachusetts remained potent in the polls for all his protestations of non-candidacy; former Sen. Eugene J. McCarthy said he was a candidate.

Sometimes ambition outreached finances. Sen. Fred R. Harris of Oklahoma announced his candidacy, then dropped it six weeks later for lack of money. Sens. Harold E. Hughes of Iowa and Birch Bayh of Indiana were in and out, too.

Sen. Vance Hartke of Indiana had presidential, or at least vice presidential, notions. He cultivated them on the speaking circuit and, at year's end, a committee was organized to promote his candidacy.

From the House side of the Capitol, Rep. Wilbur Mills of Arkansas, chairman of the Ways and Means Committee—and the man who gave in to Nixon on the campaign finance dispute —nourished longshot hopes of a presidential nomination. Rep. Shirley Chisholm of New York said she would enter some primaries in an effort to rally the black vote and guarantee its influence in 1972. Two House Republicans posted primary election challenges to Nixon, Rep. Paul N. McCloskey of California, from the anti-war left, and Rep. John M. Ashbrook of Ohio from the disenchanted right.

For all of that, Nixon fared well in the first session of the 92nd Congress. The measures he proposed as a "new American revolution" didn't get off the ground, but he got most of what he wanted in economic legislation, an area that is likely to provide one of the surpassing issues of the 1972 campaign.

The set of issues Congress left behind for its late summer recess, and the set it found waiting after Labor Day, were different things. For Nixon, on Aug. 15, froze prices and wages, announcing his new economic policy, which took some legislative doing in the months that followed.

In the waning weeks of the session, Congress sent the President his big tax cut bill. It wasn't as big as Democrats had tried to make it, with amendments offering more tax breaks to individual taxpayers. Its major features:

—Revival of the 7 per cent business tax credit for investments in new equipment and machinery, which the Administration called a job-producing measure.

—Repeal of the 7 per cent federal excise tax on automobiles, to spur car sales.

—A speedup in personal tax breaks already scheduled by law. These included a $100 increase in the personal income tax exemption and an increase to 15 per cent in the minimum standard income tax deduction.

In addition, Congress passed shortly before its Dec. 17 adjournment a bill extending until April 3, 1973, the President's authority to control wages, prices and rents in his campaign against inflation. But it included also a provision designed to require retroactive payment of most wage increases blocked by the wage freeze that was in effect from Aug. 15 until Nov. 14.

Congress also insisted that federal employes, civilian and military, get on Jan. 1 a pay raise Nixon had sought to postpone for six months. That cost the government $1.2 billion.

In matters of defense and foreign policy, the Administration had claimed new strength in the 92nd Congress, and on those issues Nixon indeed got his way.

The Senate struggled all year to write into law measures declaring it to be national policy for the United States to withdraw totally from Indochina within six or nine months, provided North Vietnam released American prisoners. The effort continued to the eve of adjournment—and failed, blocked by the House. Three times the Senate passed such amendments, three times the House blocked them.

Congress did approve one Vietnam war amendment, a mild one, which expressed congressional opinion in favor of total withdrawal and asked President Nixon to negotiate a timetable. Nixon signed the $21.3 billion military procurement bill carrying the amendment, but said he would ignore it. He said the amendment "is without binding force or effect and it does not reflect my judgment about the way the war should be brought to a conclusion."

If the war was deemed a fading issue in the country, it was a recurrent one in the Congress, particularly the Senate.

But, through the year, the Administration was withdrawing manpower, from more than 300,000 at the start of the year to about 158,300 at Christmas. And Senate Republican Leader Hugh Scott insisted that by the time Congress got around to legislating on troop withdrawals Nixon's withdrawal policy would have made the issue moot.

Controversy over Indochina added impetus to the drive for legislation to limit presidential warmaking powers, due to reach the Senate floor in 1972. It undermined the traditional effort of Senate liberals to change the rules and make it easier to cut off filibusters, as men like Sen. Frank Church, D Idaho, decided that unlimited debate could work for them, too, in efforts to prevent White House dominance of Congress. It stalled for nearly two months the two-year draft extension bill finally approved with provisions eliminating the system of local draft board quotas and automatic college deferments. The draft was extended to June 3, 1973.

That mood contributed to one of the year's most startling and dramatic votes when, on the night of Oct. 29, the Senate voted 41 to 27 to kill the foreign aid program. The White House called that irresponsible, and after weeks of controversy the program was reassembled temporarily, with a final settlement bequeathed to the second session of the 92nd Congress. The aid spending level was trimmed to about $2.8 billion, $800 million less than the Administration had sought.

Nixon got his way on another major foreign policy controversy, the effort of Senate Democratic Leader Mike Mansfield to cut by half, to 150,000, U.S. troop levels in western Europe. That proposal ignited the Administration's most intensive lobbying drive of the session, a campaign for which Nixon recruited past foreign policy makers of both parties.

Among the other major congressional decisions of 1971 were these measures:

—A 10 per cent increase in 1971 Social Security benefits, with the taxes to pay for it beginning in 1972. The House later added another 5 per cent increase, tied to the Administration's welfare overhaul and family assistance plan. That was stalled in the Senate Finance Committee, with action due in 1972.

—A $2.25 billion public service employment program to provide state and local work for the jobless. Nixon earlier had vetoed a bill providing $2 billion to provide jobs on public works projects, calling it a latter-day WPA.

—An extension, for 13 weeks, of unemployment compensation benefits in states where joblessness exceeded 6.5 per cent.

—The Senate approved a bill authorizing $14 billion for water pollution control plans and setting 1985 as the target date for a complete cleanup of the nation's rivers. The Administration criticized that bill, largely the handwork of presidential candidate Muskie, saying it would have too drastic an effect on industry. House action was put off until the next session of Congress.

—Congress rejected funds for the supersonic transport program, and it was shut down over Administration protests. "We will build it one day," Nixon said months later, after inspecting the British-French SST, the Concorde.

—In the health field, Congress approved a three-year $2.9 billion program to train new doctors, dentists and other health professionals; another $855 million for the training of nurses, and $1.6 billion over the same period to intensify the effort to combat cancer. But the biggest issue, the question of nationwide health insurance and the form it should take, was left for the next session.

On both sides of the Capitol the Democratic majorities had some new management. Senate Democratic Leader Mike Mansfield continued his record-long tenure, but the party switched deputy leaders in a surprise vote. Sen. Robert C. Byrd of West Virginia, a legislative technician dedicated to parliamentary detail, was elected Democratic whip, ousting Sen. Kennedy. The vote was 31 to 24.

As whip, Byrd spent almost all the Senate's working hours on the floor, scheduling votes, managing the day to day routine.

In the House, Carl Albert of Oklahoma was elected speaker to succeed the retired John W. McCormack. Rep. Hale Boggs of Louisiana became majority leader, and Rep. Thomas P. O'Neill Jr. of Massachusetts was elected Democratic whip.

Senate Majority Leader Mike Mansfield of Montana and Minority Leader Hugh Scott of Pennsylvania, left, telephoned the President in Key Biscayne, Fla., to inform him that Congress had adjourned

Gunfire in Middle East Minimal but Statesmen Found No Road to Peace

Al Fatah commando Abu Nar standing guard outside a cave near Jorasa in Jordan

FOR THE MOST PART the guns stayed silent, but the 23-year conflict between Israel and its Arab neighbors continued to defy all the resourcefulness of world statesmen seeking a solution that would bring permanent peace to the Middle East. More than 1,500,000 refugees from what once was Palestine still lived on international charity in camps around the fringes of their homeland and for them the year brought no fresh candleflame of hope.

Egypt's President Anwar Sadat, who last year succeeded the late President Nasser *(The World in 1970, 218–222),* declared an end March 7 to seven months of formal truce along the Suez Canal. But the antagonists, dug in behind massive defenses, held their fire.

"It is not possible to predict how long this quiet will last, but there can be little doubt that if the present impasse in the search for a peaceful settlement persists, new fighting will break out sooner or later," warned United Nations Secretary General U Thant.

Once the parties had taken advantage of the 1971 present lull to strengthen considerably their military capabilities, it was only too likely that the new round of fighting would be more violent and dangerous than the previous one, and there was always the danger that it might not be possible to limit it to the present antagonists and to the confines of the Middle East, Thant said.

His warning of the dangers of a wider conflict—behind it was the fear that the United States and the Soviet Union might be drawn into any new hostilities—brought no breakthrough in the protracted diplomatic exchanges which focused during much of the year on a partial agreement aimed at getting the Suez Canal reopened. The 100-mile waterway had been paralyzed since the 1967 war brought Israeli troops to its eastern bank. Sixteen ships, rusting and rotting, still rode at anchor where they were trapped by the battle.

When U.N. sponsored negotiations through Swedish diplomat Gunnar Jarring stalled early in the year, U.S. Secretary of State William P. Rogers took another personal hand in seeking a settlement with a springtime visit to Saudi Arabia, Jordan, Lebanon, Egypt and Israel. The Suez ceasefire had been Rogers' idea in the previous year and in 1971 he tried to take it a step further by proposing a partial Israeli withdrawal to permit the clearing and reopening of the canal.

Above, Israeli Defense Minister Moshe Dayan holding a news conference during a visit to the Allenby Bridge in Israeli-occupied Jordan. Right, Jordan's King Hussein trying out a new weapon on a visit to his troops in the Jordanian desert

Not for 18 years had an American secretary of state been in Cairo, and the last occasion was hardly auspicious. John Foster Dulles paid a visit in 1953, and relations between Egypt and the U.S. went rapidly downhill.

Washington refused to finance the building of the Aswan Dam and, as a result, Nasser seized the Suez Canal from its mainly British owners. The Russians gladly stepped in and quickly spread their influence through the Arab world. When the giant Aswan Dam was completed in January 1971 Soviet President Nikolai Podgorny was on hand for the ceremony.

The Rogers visit had no such disastrous consequences, even though it failed to break the deadlock, and it did succeed in clarifying the position of the two sides.

Israel demanded a permanent ceasefire as part of a Suez deal. Egypt wanted a time limit on any such truce. Israel was prepared for a limited withdrawal of up to 10 miles but insisted on maintaining military control of the evacuated area and the right to keep civilian technicians in the Bar-Lev Line, a formidable chain of blockhouses, bunkers and underground defensive positions running the length of the canal. Israel refused the Egyptian proposal that it should put troops across the waterway once the Israelis had withdrawn.

Most important of all, Egypt wanted a Suez deal that was recognized as being only the first part of an overall settlement based on the U.N. Security Council resolution of Nov. 22, 1967, calling for an Israeli withdrawal from occupied Arab territory.

Israel had said it would withdraw to "secure and recognized borders" only when these had been worked out as part of a peace agreement. Prime Minister Golda Meir was on record as having said there would be no pullback to the pre-1967 frontiers and she insisted Israel would keep the Syrian Golan Heights, all of the city of Jerusalem, and Sharm el Sheikh, the strategic southern tip of the Sinai desert which commanded Israel's outlet to the southern seas.

Rogers offered Israel international guarantees and U.S. participation in a peace-keeping force, but he failed to persuade Mrs. Meir's government to make further concessions. "If it is necessary to say no, we will say no to both our enemies and our friends," said Mrs. Meir. She was as good as her word. The deadlock continued.

No sooner was Rogers back in Washington than Egypt was rocked by a major political upheaval which may have had far-reaching effects on the course of Middle East events and from which Sadat eventually emerged with more personal power than ever. Communist-lining Aly Sabry, long regarded as Moscow's man in Cairo, was sacked May 2 from his post as Egypt's vice president. On May 14, in an impromptu 85-minute radio and television address, President Sadat announced he had foiled a conspiracy against his regime involving Sabry and six ministers, including the war minister and commander in chief, Lt. Gen. Mohammed Fawzi, together with two top leaders of the Arab Socialist Union, Egypt's only permitted political party, and the speaker of the National Assembly. All were placed under house arrest and subsequently charged with high treason. Sabry and two ministers were sentenced to life in prison. Fawzi drew a 15-year term. Scores of lesser officials were involved and within a week there were more than 100 arrests. Before the affair was over there were more than 1,500 arrests, sackings and demotions in the military, the ministries and the information media.

As Sadat told it, a young intelligence agent gave away the plot. He took to the president's house recordings of tapped telephone conversations revealing the Interior Minister Sharawi Gomaa had set a trap for Sadat's arrest. He had surrounded the Cairo radio station with plainclothes policemen to seize the president if he tried to speak to the nation after a heated meeting of the ruling party's central committee at which Sadat had been outvoted. But, to avert a crisis, Sadat had chosen not to broadcast. Gomaa was fired and his ministerial coplotters promptly resigned in an attempt to bring about Sadat's downfall. A secret organization within the Arab Socialist Union planned

demonstrations in Cairo which Fawzi would use as an excuse to bring in troops to seize power. Fawzi failed to get the backing of Egypt's senior army officers, and the coup never got off the ground.

Sadat, who revealed his own house had been bugged, proclaimed an immediate end to wiretapping and police measures infringing on the freedom of the individual—except where the security of the state was concerned. He swept away the existing structure of the ASU, which had proved of doubtful loyalty, and ordered fresh elections for party leaders at all levels.

Writing in Al Ahram newspaper, editor Mohammed Hassanein Heikal, a confidant of Sadat and Nasser before him and one of the most influential men in Egypt, reported the top plotters were pressing for an early battle with Israel in order to involve the Soviet Union and to "uncover rightwing forces" within Egypt. "Had they not been removed," wrote Heikal, "there might have been a bloodbath."

Sadat's relations with the Soviet Union apparently were unaffected by the purge of leftwingers for Soviet President Podgorny soon was back in Egypt to sign a 15-year treaty of friendship between the two countries. They would continue to cooperate in the military field, said the treaty. Russia would go on supplying Egypt with weapons and training facilities "with a view to strengthening its capacity to eliminate the consequences of the (Israeli) aggression." The treaty also provided for urgent consultations in the event of a renewed threat of war.

Addressing the Knesset, Israel's parliament, in Jerusalem, Prime Minister Golda Meir described the treaty as giving the Soviet Union control over Egyptian policies and introducing an era of "colonial servitude" for Egypt. She called on the United States to supply Israel with more planes and sophisticated equipment to counter the Soviet arms deliveries to Egypt.

There were other events in the Middle East during 1971 which had a bearing on the Arab-Israeli conflict. In Sudan a

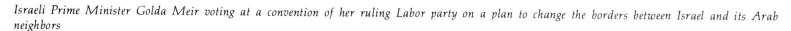

Israeli Prime Minister Golda Meir voting at a convention of her ruling Labor party on a plan to change the borders between Israel and its Arab neighbors

coup aimed at the overthrow of the premier, Maj. Gen. Gaafer al-Nimeiry, was smashed *(Page 135)*.

Meanwhile, the Palestinian guerrilla movement, which, with varying success, had courted Moscow's support since the end of the 1967 war, was being steadily decimated in Jordan. At the zenith of their power last year, exultant "fedayeen" brandishing Soviet-made Kalashnikov machineguns posed arrogantly on the charred wrecks of three western airliners they had hijacked to the Jordanian desert *(The World in 1970, 208–213)*. They seemed ready to take over the whole country from King Hussein.

From then on it was all downhill for the guerrillas. Hussein's tough Bedouin troops had routed them in last September's civil war and the guerrillas had been on the run ever since. Their few attacks in 1971 were directed more against the Jordan army than Israel. In March they were flushed out of the northern Jordanian town of Irbid, where, according to guerrilla spokesmen, 200 guerrillas and civilians were killed.

In a message to Premier Wasfi Tell broadcast over Amman Radio, Hussein accused the guerrillas June 2 of plotting to set up a breakaway Palestinian state and ordered Tell to take "bold, decisive and tough action against the handful of professional criminals and conspirators who use the commando movement to disguise their treasonable plots." Wasfi Tell, no lover of the guerrillas, needed no second urging, although it was a month before the army again swung into action.

This time it struck at the last remaining guerrilla strongholds in the wooded Ajloun hills and villages overlooking the town and Roman ruins of Jerash, 25 miles north of Amman. Against tanks and artillery, the 3,000 guerrillas never had a chance. Jordan valley farmers who witnessed the rout reported groups of them waving white flags were shot down as they attempted to surrender. More than 2,000 were captured, a couple of hundred escaped across the border to Syria and—most humiliating of all—55 fled across the Jordan river to surrender to the Israelis.

The Palestinian guerrillas "have finally ceased to be a problem," declared a triumphant King Hussein after four days of fighting. "We are not finished yet," declared guerrilla leader Yasser Arafat, but his defiant words had a hollow ring. Once the pride of the Arab world and a potent force standing against any compromise peace with Israel, Arafat's guerrillas found themselves confined ineffectually to a small corner of southern Lebanon and to Syria, where their activities were strictly watched over by the Damascus government. Syrian President Hafez Assad broke off diplomatic relations with Jordan to protest the crackdown and when he met in August with Egypt's Sadat and Libyan leader Col. Muammar Kadafi, the guerrilla question was on the agenda but nothing decisive came of it.

Their principal task was to approve a constitution linking the 43 million people of their three countries in a new Federation of Arab Republics. The federation was proclaimed Sept. 1 after 98 per cent of the voters approved it in a rubberstamp referendum. The three countries would have one flag, one national anthem and a federal capital but each would retain its own seat at the U.N. and its full sovereignty. Sadat was elected the federation's first president.

"As you march to the polls today," Kadafi told Libya's referendum voters, "you march to Golan and the West Bank, to the mosque of Al-Aqsa and to Jerusalem." Although the federation provided for a joint military command and the free movement of troops between member states, the new grouping was unlikely to affect the power balance in the Middle East. Egypt, Libya and Syria together in a federation were unlikely to be any stronger than they were on their own, concluded military analysts. The federation nevertheless gave its leaders some insurance against the sort of coup that nearly saw the end of Sudan's Nimeiry. The constitution provided that any two member states could intervene to maintain the status quo in the third.

Apart from the establishment of the federation, the scene was mainly of Arab disunity. Because of its crackdown on the Palestine guerrillas, Jordan was at odds with almost all the other Arab states and Libya's Kadafi called publicly for Hussein's assassination. Iraq had prematurely recognized the pro-communist rebels who briefly overthrew Nimeiry and the Sudan broke off diplomatic relations. Iraq also was still engaged in a longtime feud with Syria, which was ruled by a rival wing of the Arab Socialist Baath Party. Libya backed the army plotters who tried to kill King Hassan of Morocco and the two countries severed relations.

As the year drew to a close, war fever again was mounting in the Middle East. Israel downed an Egyptian Sukhoi-7 fighter bomber on the canal front Sept. 11 and six days later an Israeli air force stratocruiser was shot down by Egyptian missiles. Israel retaliated with a Phantom attack on Egyptian missile sites. Israeli Chief of Staff Lt. Gen. Haim Bar-Lev warned that if fighting broke out again "it will not be restricted to action by aircraft against aircraft. That will be one component of the fighting but not the exclusive one."

Speaking to the Egyptian nation on the first anniversary of President Nasser's death Sept. 28, Sadat said 1971 would be decisive for the Middle East conflict, either by peace or war. He later flew off to Moscow and returned with a Soviet promise to "further strengthen the military might of Egypt." Israel pressed Washington to resume the supply of Phantom fighter bombers, discontinued in June.

Egyptian War Minister Lt. Gen. Muhammad Sadek was named commander of all Egyptian and Syrian forces facing Israel. Syria claimed it had 250,000 men on the confrontation line. Sadek told his troops: "The battle is coming sooner than you imagine." In Cairo President Sadat donned army uniform, assumed direct command of all Egypt's armed forces, and moved his office to military headquarters.

Cairo's semi-official Al Ahram newspaper said that, although Egypt still was pursuing diplomatic efforts towards a settlement, this would not prevent it from preparing for the other alternative should these efforts fail. On Nov. 11 Sadat told his national assembly Egypt would take part in no further diplomatic negotiations until Israel committed itself to withdrawal from occupied Arab lands. Israel seemed unlikely to make any such move.

The U.S. State Department reported more Soviet aircraft were delivered to Egypt in November. They were said to be either supersonic fighter-bombers or TU-16 reconnaissance planes. According to Israeli information, at least 10,000 Soviet military personnel were stationed in Egypt. A forward interceptor force of upwards of four Russian-flown squadrons of improved Mig 21s was believed to augment Egypt's complex and formidable Sam II and Sam III missile systems. Shipments of additional Russian T-54 and T-55 tanks had enabled Egypt to raise another armored division.

As Cairo newspapers issued urgent civil defense warnings, Sadat toured frontline positions along the Suez Canal and told his troops Nov. 20:

"Egypt's decision is battle. There is no longer any hope of peaceful solutions. We were convinced that the battle was coming and now it has become certain to us that hope has died. Be ferocious in battle to prove to the world that we are fighting people who know how to defend our dignity and honor."

Ho Chi Minh Trail a Key Factor in Indochina War

President Nguyen Van Thieu cast his ballot in presidential election which saw him run unopposed

THE INDISPENSABLE LIFELINE in the Communist Command's relentlessly successful supply operation for their forces fighting in South Vietnam was known as the Ho Chi Minh Trail. It was not a trail in the usual sense, but a 4,000-mile maze of tangled routes ranging from footpaths to graveled highways. The system threaded westward out of three North Vietnamese passes through the Annamese Mountains into Laos, the Mu Gia, Ban Karai and Ban Raving. Then it looped south and east through Laos for 200 miles, reaching a spiderweb-like width of 50 miles at some points. Each tentacle was studded with lumpy hillocks and shielded from overhead view by dense, triple-canopied jungle growth.

Traffic down the trail always increased after the monsoon season ended in September or October. It reached a peak from February to April, the last months when supplies could leave North Vietnam and reach their southern destinations before the May rains again made the trail impassable. By foot, the trip took about four months. Soldiers wearing camouflage greenery marched single file at intervals of five yards and were almost impossible to detect. In addition, each night a fleet of about 1,000 trucks rolled out from hiding places in limestone caves and bunkers and threaded their way southward with supplies. Each driver traveled only a 15 to 40-mile stretch of the trail, night after night, over the same route when he knew it well enough to drive with his lights out. At the end of his run he passed his cargo to the next driver and went back for another load. Passed from truck to truck, and sometimes to bicycles and hand carts, a load of supplies took about two months to wend its way to supply dumps in the south.

In this antlike fashion the Communist Command, in the dry season of early 1971, was able to infiltrate as many as 17,000 men a month plus the tons of supplies needed to support them. Indeed, since the Cambodian port of Kompong Som (formerly Sihanoukville) was closed to them in May of 1970 by the U.S. incursion into that country (*The World in 1970, 234–241*), the enemy had to rely solely on the Ho Chi Minh Trail to move men and equipment into South Vietnam and Cambodia. Plainly, American commanders had longed to cut the trail ever since the United States entered the war, and in early 1971 American warplanes were flying up to 400 sorties a day toward that effort, often ducking fire from some 3,000 artillery emplacements along the trail. The raids were never able to reduce the supply flow by more than half. The only way to eliminate traffic completely, military authorities argued, was to sever the trail on the gound. It was a view strengthened by the reports of ARVN (Army of the Republic of Viet Nam) special-forces teams which had probed into the Laotian panhandle and found that many truck depots along the trail were too heavily fortified to be destroyed by anything less than an all-out ground assault.

As far as American forces were concerned, that was out of the question. Shortly after the Cambodian invasion of 1970, Congress had prohibited the use of American ground troops outside Vietnam. There were no strings, of course, on the ARVN, and early in February long columns of men and equipment began moving westward toward the Laotian border in the area known as Military Region I.

For three years Military Region I, formerly known as I Corps, a misty, mountainous area, had been a no man's land. Khe Sanh, where in 1968 a force of 6,000 Marines had endured a 77-day siege, was a rusting junkpile of twisted runway sheets and discarded shell casings. A few miles to the south, another old battleground known as the Rockpile was overrun with weeds. On a bluff overlooking the Laotian border the carcasses of Soviet-made tanks lay rusting at the Lang Vei Special Forces camp where 10 Americans and 225 South Vietnamese died in a single night of hand-to-hand combat.

Suddenly, in mid-February, all those old battlegrounds were alive with new activity. At Khe Sanh road graders patched up runways, and other long-disused combat bases were reopened. Farther west, Lang Vei was set up as an advance command post. In a matter of days 20,000 ARVN and 9,000 U.S. troops were massed in the region, plus a force of about 600 helicopters. The operation was given a code name: Dewey Canyon II. Though its purpose was cloaked in deepest secrecy, there was little doubt that a buildup of such massive proportions could mean anything less than a full blown invasion of Laos. Such suspicions were confirmed when a large sign was erected barely 200 yards from the Laotian border on Route 9: "Warning: No U.S. Personnel Beyond This Point."

The United States spared no effort in assuring the world that it would be a South Vietnamese operation. Before the order was issued sending troops across the border the code name was replaced with a Vietnamese name, Lam Son 719, and the announcement of the move-out came not from U.S. headquarters or from Washington but from South Vietnam's President Nguyen Van Thieu.

The attack got off at glacial pace. Not only were the ARVN troops slowed by mud and twisting terrain but they were well

U.S. wounded in South Vietnam

aware that 35,000 of the enemy were massed in the area, determined to hold their critical lifeline to the south. Nonetheless, first reports told only of success. After a week official reports claimed 269 enemy killed as against only 36 dead and 239 wounded on the ARVN side. Soon, however, truckload after truckload of ARVN corpses began returning from the battle-front and newsmen learned to discount official figures. After two weeks Maj. Gen. Frederick Weyland, the deputy U.S. commander in Saigon, admitted that the bloodshed was "worse than Tet," the large scale Communist offensive of 1968. Back in Washington, Pentagon spokesmen doggedly defended the operation, and the President, at a news conference, again referred to it as a "success."

His term might have been more hopeful than descriptive, for it was considered by many to be of utmost political importance to President Nixon that the military operation succeed. For one thing, it was the first major test of the combat effectiveness of ARVN troops, a key to his policy of Vietnamization. For another, it was aimed at blunting the opportunity for the Communist Command to mount a fall offensive that might hurt President Thieu's chances of reelection. It was also aimed at forestalling the chances of a Tet-style offensive in 1972, an election year in America.

In the rugged hills of Laos, however, it was obvious that the invasion was not going well at all. In fact, it was steadily turning into a full-scale rout. Just five weeks after the invasion began the ARVN effort was no longer a bold offensive to penetrate deep into Laos but rather a frantic, perilous and bloody battle to get out. Among the ARVN troops picked for the Lam Son operation were the army's toughest, battle-hardened units. Supporting them, locust swarms of American warplanes flew as many strike sorties every day as they ordinarily staged in all of

U.S. firebase on Laotian border supporting South Vietnamese troops

Indochina. Still, it was obvious that ARVN troops were being cut up badly and that their tenacious opponents were willing to sacrifice casualties by the thousands to keep their trail intact and to deal the South a physical and psychological mauling.

Indeed, the most precipitous retreat involved the ARVN's elite 1st Division. It had been assigned the job of manning fire bases overlooking the invasion route on Highway 9, which bored westward to Tchepone, a small town 25 miles inside Laos. American bombs blew the town to rubble and ARVN troops did triumphantly enter the town and quickly left it after heavy artillery barrages. Continued shelling and massed assaults also drove the 1st Division troops off their fire bases, and an ARVN armored column was stalled for five weeks on Highway 9. The 1st Division units eventually abandoned the fire bases, destroyed their own artillery and fought their way through the jungle until helicopters could reach them. Choppers that ordinarily carried eight men carried 14, some of them clinging in desperation to the skids. One of the 1st Division's three regiments returned with only 450 of its original 2,000 men still in fighting condition. One 1st Division battalion, of 500 men, was ordered to cover its comrades' retreat. Heavy ground fire kept supply helicopters from reaching the embattled men and soon they were out of artillery shells and critically short of rations and small arms ammunition. After six days without supplies and three days without sleep, the unit's one surviving officer radioed with such urgency that U.S. bombers at length blasted a rescue landing zone out of the jungle. Two of five rescue helicopters were shot down. Eventually all the survivors were picked up. Of the 500 men in the battalion, only 32 survived, a third of them wounded.

Other units suffered losses nearly as numbing. When the operation was finally declared ended, in the first week in April, Saigon officially admitted to 25 per cent casualties: 1,147 killed, 246 missing, 4,237 wounded. Unofficially, U.S. and South Vietnamese sources put the figure at closer to 50 per cent, with 3,000 dead or missing and 7,000 wounded. The U.S. toll included 66 helicopter pilots and crewmen dead, 28 missing and 83 wounded, and 94 helicopters destroyed. The official—and probably inflated—estimate of the enemy dead was 13,688.

However successful the Laotian invasion might have been in terms of enemy losses and even partial disruption of the Communist Command's supply system, the precipitous withdrawal and staggering casualties on the part of the ARVN were embarrassing and tragic. In 1971 in that tortured country, however, tragedy and embarrassment seemed commonplace. The next incidence of it involved not loss of life but of face and added to a prevailing mood of despair, cynicism and disgust. It centered on the election campaign for the South Vietnamese presidency.

The roots of that drama of South Vietnam politics went back to 1967 when Nguyen Cao Ky, the incumbent president, allowed Nguyen Van Thieu to become the presidential candidate and reluctantly, under American urging, accepted the vice-presidential nomination. In an 11-man contest the Thieu-Ky ticket won as expected, but with only 35 per cent of the vote. The less than overwhelming endorsement of his people had rankled Thieu ever since.

To make the 1971 election less of a free-for-all, Thieu backed a bill before the Vietnam House that would require a presidential candidate to obtain either 40 signatures from members of the Assembly or 100 signatures from among the 550 municipal and provincial councillors around the country, to be countersigned by the province chiefs. The Vietnam Senate favored a somewhat looser bill which American officials tried to persuade him to accept. Thieu was adamant. The House bill passed and

Thieu signed it on June 23. The very next day he issued a special decree subjecting the municipal and provincial councillors to a series of restrictions and permitting the premier to dismiss them on various grounds.

On July 26, a few days after Thieu had announced that he would run again, retired Gen. Duong Van Minh, key figure in the 1963 coup against Ngo Dinh Diem's regime, filed his declaration of candidacy for the presidency. Minh had reached a tacit agreement with Ky that they would join in attacking Thieu but would avoid cutting up each other in the process. He qualified for the nomination, in accordance with the new law, by obtaining signatures of 44 Assembly members. Minh also made it clear he would pull out of the race if he thought it was rigged.

Ky, in accordance with his agreement with Minh not to collide with each other, sought qualification to make the race not from members of the Assembly but from 100 councillors. He was too late. By June 20, even before signing the election law, Thieu had quietly obtained pledges of support from 450 councillors. As the Aug. 4 filing deadline drew nearer, Ky began soliciting Assembly signatures—only to discover that a local jurist named Tran Tam had suddenly announced his candidacy, obtained enough Assembly signatures to prevent Ky from doing likewise, and just as suddenly withdrew from the race. Ky could only head back to the hinterlands to solicit councillor pledges. He did, and succeeded in coralling 102 signatures on Aug. 4—however, only 62 of the signatures had been countersigned by province chiefs as the new law required. The following day, Aug. 5, four members of the nine-man Supreme Court ruled that Ky's candidacy was invalid. He filed a perfunctory appeal.

Meanwhile, Minh was whispering to friends in Saigon that he was becoming increasingly disillusioned about the possibility of a fair and open election. All along, American officials had been unimpressed by Minh's platform, which they considered a bit too chummy with the Communists, but with Ky barred from the race Minh's candidacy became essential if there were to be any semblance of a democratic election.

Between Aug. 9 and 19 Ambassador Elsworth Bunker was in Washington discussing the situation with President Nixon. While he was gone, on Aug. 12, Minh submitted to Deputy U.S. Ambassador Samuel Berger a sheaf of what Minh claimed to be documentary proof that Thieu had taken steps to rig the election.

The purported evidence was in the form of an order that Thieu allegedly had sent to province chiefs directing them to use government workers to intimidate and buy off voters, to infiltrate the ranks of opposition candidates, to transfer all "unfriendly civil servants to other jobs," and to take other steps including stuffing ballot boxes.

When Bunker returned to Saigon Aug. 19 he went to see Minh at the general's home. They talked in private but it was widely assumed that Minh sought American guarantees that the election would be conducted on the up and up. In any event, the next morning Minh withdrew from the race, declaring: "I cannot put up with a disgusting farce that strips away all the people's hope of a democratic regime and bars reconciliation of the Vietnamese people." He added, "I hope my warnings and those of others will make responsible people repent and realize fully the disastrous results a rigged election could bring to the country and to themselves."

The following day Bunker met privately with Ky. An hour after he left, the Supreme Court, sitting as a full body of nine, reversed itself and ruled that Ky's candidacy was valid and

Cambodian soldiers helping a wounded comrade outside beleaguered Phnom Penh

that his name would go on the ballot. As one Vietnamese commented, "our law is as slippery as an eel."

Ky spent the next 48 hours pondering his course. During this time one correspondent said Ky told him that he felt his own integrity was at stake and although he realized the danger to the country of letting Thieu run unopposed he could not let himself be used as a "clown" to satisfy anyone's desires to make it appear to be an honestly contested race. On Aug. 23 Ky announced his decision to drop out of the election, attacking Thieu as "the principal actor in the farce." To test Thieu's sincerity he proposed a solution: That the president of the Senate take over for 90 days, as the constitution provided, and that a presidential election be held after that period. Thieu did not respond to the offer. Instead, six days later, he announced that the Oct. 3 election would be held on schedule.

It was. The results were, according to the Thieu government figures, astounding. By those figures fully 87.7 per cent of the 7.4 million qualified voters went to the polls and only 5.5 per cent mutilated their ballots to indicate no confidence in the Thieu regime. On Oct. 31 Thieu was inaugurated with, officially, a 94.3 per cent vote of confidence, and Ky was out of a job.

Meanwhile, back at the war, as the year drew to a close only

158,000 American troops remained in Vietnam, under the President's "Vietnamization" policy of gradual withdrawal, from an early 1969 peak of 543,000 men. Meanwhile, the South Vietnamese armed forces had grown from 730,000 men during the 1968 Tet offensive to a well-equipped force of 1,100,000. It would seem, on the face, that Vietnamization was proceeding apace. Under the plan Nixon sought to strengthen the South Vietnamese army and administration to the point where it could—with help from U.S. air power and a residual American force of about 40,000 to 50,000 troops—hold the line against the North Vietnamese and the Viet Cong guerrillas. At a news conference in December 1970 he made clear he would accept no restrictions on the use of American air power to further this objective.

In the last five days of 1971 that declaration was brought awesomely to bear. During those five days American planes bombed North Vietnam in the heaviest assaults against the North since Nixon's predecessor, Lyndon B. Johnson, terminated the U.S. air war against the North a little more than three years earlier. Air Force and Navy jets flew about 1,000 attack sorties against fuel and supply depots, antiaircraft gun, missile and radar sites, and MIG fighter airfields. Most of the raids, officially described as "reinforced protective reaction" or "limited duration" air strikes, were concentrated on fuel and supply dumps near the three mountain passes leading out of North Vietnam down the Ho Chi Minh trail.

Despite the Laos invasion of February and March, by year's end the fact was that the North Vietnamese controlled more of Laos than they ever had and the air raids were clearly for the purpose of staving off a major military setback in Indochina.

A South Vietnamese soldier rode the skid of a helicopter carrying wounded as enemy troops drove Saigon forces out of Laos

'New' U.S. Army Marked by Leniency, Free Beer

A black soldier in Da Nang, South Vietnam giving black power salute

But conflicting comments by military personnel on efficiency included cases of racial unrest, officers' fear of GIs

"THE NEW ARMY is no army at all," complained a sergeant stationed in Korea. "Discipline's gone to hell."

"The Army isn't going to hell just because kids wear their hair long," argued a battle-tested company commander posted in Germany.

Those were samplings of the conflicting comments made in a global survey of U.S. Army posts by The Associated Press. Alarming changes had come over the U.S. armed services, raising problems of discipline and racial unrest. The changes had produced some startling results in terms of the old Army.

—Like the brigadier general in Vietnam who kept a loaded machinegun under his bed for fear of a fragging—grenade rolling—attack by his own troops, who had already killed two men they didn't like and wounded another 17.

—Or the reserve lieutenant who insisted that 90 per cent of the enlisted men in the service were as smart as he was, and who openly sought the company of GIs instead of fellow officers.

For months the armed forces had been scuttling time-honored traditions to introduce a new flexibility, remove some of the irritants of military life; to stress human relations and show a greater regard for individuality.

Instead of Kitchen Police and Saturday duty, the military featured beer in the barracks, polite drill instructors, courses in racial understanding and more passes.

But how did the new military affect the career man confronted with the problems of drugs, sideburns and psychedelic barracks? How did he feel about his life's work after My Lai and Calley?

Gen. Matthew B. Ridgway, allied supreme commander during the Korean War, reflected the feeling of the old soldier in an address to the West Point Society of Pennsylvania: "Not in my lifetime—and I was born into the Army in the 19th century—has the Army's public image suffered so many grievous blows and fallen to such low esteem in such wide areas of our society."

Gen. William C. Westmoreland, Army chief of staff, in an interview in his Pentagon office, agreed that drugs, race, discipline and a declining public image were major problems of modern military life. Westmoreland attributed them in part to the "unpopularity of the war in Vietnam" and the major problem of trying to wind down a war while it was still going on.

"It certainly is not surprising we have these problems," said the general, "because the Army is a reflection of our society. The ills of our society inevitably overlap into our ranks."

Westmoreland agreed that the image of the military had reached a low ebb, but he expressed doubt that an all-volunteer fighting force could come into being without a change in the public's attitude toward the service.

"The American public cannot have it both ways: It can't get rid of the draft and continue to degrade military service," he said.

First Lt. Gregg Hutch of Nutley, N.J., a forward observer with an airborne outfit in Vietnam, said he noticed the public shift against the military even before he went overseas.

"Four or five years of peace marches have gotten to the citizen soldier," he said. "I used to stuff my uniform in a locker as soon as I got to La Guardia airport. I didn't want anyone to associate me with what was going on in Vietnam."

Hutch, who regarded most fellow officers as Establishment, said that his closest friends were enlisted men. "Ninety per cent of the EMs (enlisted men) today are as smart as I am. If they don't like my orders, they just sit there. What can I do?"

In Hanau, Germany, Spec. 4 Lester Chadband, a medic from Trinidad, was painting a barracks building in the racially tense town.

"Somebody's gotta do it," he said. "Otherwise this place is gonna keep turning out racists and hooligans."

Hanau had been a hotbed since an 18-year-old black recruit from Virginia had been killed in a fall down a barracks stairwell in January. Blacks from the outfit had demanded to see the commanding general, invaded the orderly room, belted the officer of the day with a baseball bat and declared a "day of rage."

This black militancy touched off a white backlash that resulted in a wave of vandalism, rioting, interracial terrorism and vigilante action. To try to get the men's minds on something less dangerous and more constructive, Chadband had tried to interest both whites and blacks in painting and fixing up the venerable German barracks.

"We all got to work together or sure as hell this world is going to blow apart," declared Chadband, and he got the battalion commander and other officers to pay out of their own money for the paint, nails and other needed materials.

Five years earlier problems of race, rebellion against the Establishment and refusal to accept discipline were unheard of at the crisis level.

"We are a product of the society that put us there," said Maj. Gen. Harrison Hollis, personnel chief for the U.S. Army in Europe. "We cannot escape these problems, but maybe as a disciplined society we are in a little better position to seek solutions."

It was the same story in Vietnam, Thailand, Korea, Okinawa and Germany: Mounting resentment against the war and boredom with garrison life. The professional soldier could still take comfort, however, in the fact that the job was getting done. In Germany tanks still rumbled through the gate with the required 85 per cent of all hands aboard. In Berlin elite troops still rolled down the boulevards in their armored personnel carriers sometimes to be met with a barrage of rocks from students of the Free University. In the Gulf of Tonkin the 7th Fleet was still under steam, launching planes several times a day, swinging the supplies overside, patrolling the 600 miles of shoreline. In the depots of Japan, Taiwan and Okinawa, the bases in the Philippines and Korea, the trucks, planes and ships were still serviced. The pros had seen it all happen before, the pressure from the politicians who wanted the boys home by Christmas, or better still, by election day.

"I'm not running scared," said Capt. James Hampton of Los Angeles, who had lost an eye in combat and was commanding an armored company in Nuernberg. "I've seen the Army change three times since I've been in. I've seen it broke and had to make do with junk after Korea. Then the big Vietnam buildup. And now the big letdown into a peacetime Army.

"I'm glad the Old Army's gone," said Hampton. "In the old days, the toughest guy in the outfit was the first sergeant. That didn't mean he was the best man. Just the meanest."

Apparently some of the higher-ups agreed, because the Pentagon was clearly trying to make military life more attractive to the present generation by doing away with the old irritants like bed check, reveille, daily inspections and the drab rows of cots in even more drab rows of barracks. That Army was being replaced with one that operated on a five-day work week, allowed beer in the barracks and mess halls, individual living cubicles and a policy that gave the lowliest private the right to park outside the general's office with his gripes.

No army could function without some discipline, of course, but the effect of orders on many recruits was traumatic. Said Col. John Doody, an infantry commander at Augsburg, Germany: "For the Woodstock generation cultural shock is a big rawboned sergeant saying 'you will sweep that floor.' For some, it's the first time they've ever been told to do anything by anybody."

Sent off to war at a time when others were coming home, the GI with the peace symbol on his helmet and the love flower on his rifle butt wanted to know why he was asked to do or die. If the answer wasn't good enough, he sometimes sat out the next battle or left the next hill for somebody else to take.

The recruits from the teeming urban ghettos often had a unique idea who the enemy was.

"Some of the brothers tell you they can't wait for the Communists to come busting across that East German border so they can turn their guns the other way," said Capt. Curtis B. Smothers, a black military judge, working out of Frankfurt.

In Vietnam black militants often taunted their officers by confiding a new motivation to do battle: "We're learning all we can how to fight old Charlie, the Viet Cong, so when the time comes we'll be ready to take on Mr. Charlie, the white man."

Critics of the new relaxed military system argued that the easing of discipline and rules gave the anti-Establishment types a power vacuum in which to operate against the system. But veteran officers contended that infractions actually had not increased much.

"It's the same old 2 per cent who always got into trouble, only today they're more organized," said Brig. Gen. Harley Moore, provost marshal for the U.S. Army in Europe. He noted that the modern day recruit got into the same sort of trouble that his father did in World War II.

"Booze, broads and payday weekend are still his downfall," said Moore. The general noted, however, an "alarming increase in wilful, deliberate disobedience of orders. More and more kids are saying 'we don't want to.' Although, in their defense, I must admit we've got some pretty stupid orders, too."

Col. George S. Black, the Saigon provost marshal, found the present day soldier less violent and less aggressive toward women and rival units.

"In the 10 months I've been here," he said, "we haven't had a single old-fashioned barroom brawl, the kind that used to pit one unit against the other, or Marines against paratroopers. Today, if there's a big bust-up, it's invariably racial."

Many officers conceded that leading men was a far more complex task than ever before. Almost every outfit had a couple of college graduates in the ranks and a number of highly skilled specialists in radar or helicopter maintenance.

"The old saying 'Mister, the Navy doesn't pay you to think' just doesn't apply any more," said Lt. Cmdr. Russell Schultz of Milwaukee, career counseling chief on the carrier *Kitty Hawk*. "We've almost gone full turn from saying 'you will' to asking 'will you?' but the job still gets done. Maybe better now, because the kids are smarter all down the line."

The Army's noncoms regarded the new military system with mixed emotions.

"Can't tell a man to do something no more and expect it to get done," said Platoon Sgt. Wade Jackson, Columbia, S.C., a Vietnam veteran who had been transferred to Augsburg, Germany. "Gotta watch what you say. Everybody knows his rights, and the general's door is always open."

A quite different view was expressed by Sgt. Fred Murdock of Albany, N.Y., stationed in Nuernberg with an armored outfit. "The biggest problem today is that too many old sergeants want to run the new Army the old way," he declared. "If the guy is insubordinate and it reflects on his job, get on his back. But if he hasn't had time to get his fatigues out of the cleaners, and he's the only man in the outfit who can take a tank apart and put it together, why hassle him? Who cares what the book says?"

Said Gen. Hollis, the Army personnel chief in Europe: "The fortunes of our fighting forces are directly related to the esteem the public has for them."

"Lord knows," Hollis went on, "we've had our scandals and our mediocrities, but we've had our heroes too. Thousands of them; dedicated men. Not that the public gives a damn."

Gazing out of a window of his Heidelberg office, Hollis recalled the famous warning Gen. George Catlett Marshall, U.S. Army chief of staff, delivered to Congress when the fortunes of the American forces began to fall after World War II:

"You cannot have a political club and call it an army. Leave training and discipline to us. An undisciplined army is not only impotent; it is a menace to the state."

Spec. 4 Lester Chadband (right) of Trinidad and Tobago chatting with friend Spec. 4 Charles E. Harris of Shreveport, La., in barracks in the racially tense town of Hanau, Germany

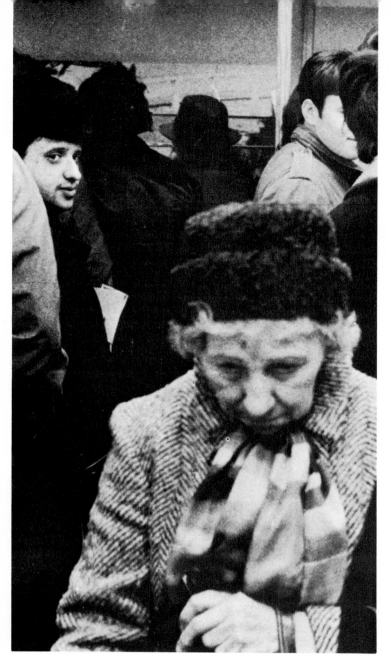

Offtrack Betting Made its Debut in New York

Wagering without visiting racecourses legalized by state

An elderly woman leaving offtrack betting parlor in New York City after placing a wager

T HE VERBAL BATTLE raged for three decades, until the New York state legislature enacted enabling legislation to legalize off-track parimutuel betting on horseracing, the first in the United States. In the spring of 1970 a bill cleared both houses and was signed by Gov. Nelson A. Rockefeller.

"Bonanza," cried New York City fiscal experts.

"Vicious vices," lamented those opposed to gambling.

"Our stands will be empty," moaned worried track owners.

As in the case of most legislative coups, there was a little something in the package for everyone:

—Any New York locality that could present a state agency with a feasible plan would be permitted to legalize offcourse horserace wagering, take bets and keep 15 per cent of the handle—the amount bet—for operating expenses and revenues, to be split 4-to-1 with the state.

—Moralists found their silver lining in a legislative mandate that legalized offtrack betting should "prevent and curb unlawful bookmaking and illegal wagering on horseraces," a stipulation clearly aimed at organized crime.

—The tracks also got a slice of the pie: One per cent of off-track handles from the top were to go to tracks and another one-half of 1 per cent to horsemen. The percentages, however, were to prove a continuously sticky problem in the early history of what came to be known universally as OTB.

New York City was the first locality—and at year's end re-mained so—to petition the State Parimutuel Offtrack Betting Commission, under Kent Brown, for authorization to make book. In July 1970, Mayor John V. Lindsay appointed Howard (Howie) J. Samuels chairman and president of OTB. Lindsay at that time said he hoped Samuels would turn a $53 million profit in the first year.

Samuels, who made a public reputation primarily through three unsuccessful attempts to become governor, had a better winning record as a businessman, having turned a small upstate company into a plastics empire. But it was his political savvy that put him at the reins of OTB. Samuels was the first Demo-crat to bolt his party and support Lindsay's successful Liberal and Independent campaign for reelection in 1969. In 1970 Lindsay appointed Democrat Samuels to the key OTB job and in 1971 the mayor switched parties.

Despite his business acumen, Samuels was unable to make good on the mayor's hopeful forecasts. But the fault was hardly his alone. Samuels began in mid-1970 to build what was to be-come, by November 1971, the country's 223rd largest business and the city's 80th. His major difficulties were:

1. Organizing instantaneously what within 15 months became a work force of 1,300; 2. developing a computer system that could take a full array of bets for decentralized betting parlors on at least two tracks and feed bet pool totals to participating tracks; 3. negotiating with track owners for "interfaces"—the specific

247

rights to tie pools into existing parimutuel fields; 4. settling wage and work rules for OTB clerks who worked year-round in the face of opposition from strong parimutuel clerk unions at tracks where work was seasonal, and 5. constantly monitoring all internal developments to ward off possible sabotage by OTB's only competitor, organized crime.

Clearly the obstacles were monumental. The combination prevented Samuels from accepting his first bet until April 8, 1971. Two shops with 15 windows opened that day and handled $62,000, a scant $52,000 more than Samuels had wishfully predicted.

By June the corporation had turned a $20,000 profit, miles short of Lindsay's $53 million figure. But, considering the impediments, a profit was a profit.

By the end of the first six months of bet-taking, Samuels had repaid $1.2 million of a $4.8 million city loan and said he thought he could restore the balance to city coffers by Jan. 1, 1972.

His handle at that time was a whopping $78 million from a total of 28 shops (301 windows) with a record one-day handle of $877,000. A survey indicated 75,000 individual bettors were playing OTB daily and Samuels confided he did not know if the 100 parlors he expected to have open by mid-1972 would be enough to service what Howie called "the fastest growing game in Fun City."

"The last thing I would say is that we're a great success," he commented, "but I am very proud of what we have accomplished in the short period we've been in business."

In Albany, Commissioner Brown had words of praise for the operation, with one qualification.

"In New York City, OTB is going like wildfire," he said. "With every monthly revenue statement, I grow more and more enthused. The one overbearing Damocles, however, is the legal requirement of reimbursing for on-track losses."

Brown referred to a legislative caveat by which, based on 1969 statistics, if track attendance, handle or taxes were lower at year's end, those hurt might apply to the state commission for reimbursements.

"On paper, the claims are running up monstrously, particularly at Yonkers Raceway," said Brown in November, admitting that he did not know "on what criteria the state commission would authorize reimbursements."

He said attendance drops could be attributed to weather, session date changes, offtrack betting or "stinking exactas." The last was a reference to a race at Yonkers in early summer which led to several investigations, after which attendance fell.

Where railroad commuters used to buy train tickets, crowds lined up at New York's Grand Central Terminal April 8 to place wagers

In any event, Samuels welcomed the approaching New Year, hoping he could turn $25 million over to the city before the end of the fiscal year in June 1972. But the goal of a $1 billion annual handle, which would net the city a neat $112 million profit, was far away.

Meanwhile, the competition in town continued to rake in the action. Bookies extended credit to some customers, allowed parlaying of bets and took wagers on all sports activity. Bookies also didn't depend on a complex, unpredictable computer. Samuels did.

During the Triple Crown races, before the computer was put on the line, OTB took bets manually and tabulated separate pools. Long lines and short tempers were the order of the day. At 11:30 p.m. the Friday before the Derby, fisticuffs almost erupted at New York's Grand Central Terminal, where OTB operatives tried to close windows half an hour early.

One harried OTB customer stood in line one hour to place 38 bets at the $10 window before the Belmont Stakes. Said he:

"It's ridiculous. When the place gets mobbed like this, the big bettors are just going to call the bookie. With the bookie, it's just one quick jump."

Samuels recognized the problem and advocated enlargement of OTB's legislative authorization so as to include all-sports betting. He was critical of legislative hostility to the idea, and charged "the hypocrisy concerning gambling is about as bad as it is with drugs."

"The public doesn't understand why you can go to the track and place a bet; why you can go to church and play bingo, and why you can't shoot craps on the corner. So they shoot craps on the corner and some get arrested and some don't."

Jimmy the Greek, the Las Vegas oddsmaker, for one, thought Samuels should be allowed to take all-sports action. "Then you could really knock the head off of organized crime." After all, as one bookie admitted, horse racing is only a small part of the underground gambling scene. "I handle horses for good customers strictly as an accommodation, and I don't know anyone who has big horse action."

But the law prohibited all-sports action. To change the law would have required two consecutive legislative sessions and a public referendum on the issue. So, for the time being, Samuels contented himself to dispatch lobbyists to Albany to beat his drum.

Meanwhile, he sought to maximize his profits, despite problems from the start. He had hoped to open his parlors in November 1970. That idea was scratched in favor of early January 1971, and the winter session at Yonkers. But management and the unions balked, and Samuels had to wait for April and the Roosevelt Raceway meet.

Not until two-and-a-half months later did he reach agreement with flat track operators, but from that date on the daily handle soared.

One month later, in late July, Samuels experienced the nightmare of businessmen tied to computers.

"Instead of talking about my eight kids," he was to reminisce about his days on the stump, "now I have to explain my damn computers (which is like a general trying to explain that victory is around the corner in Vietnam.)"

The adjective and Samuels' record as a dove adequately expressed the man's pique toward Computer Sciences Corp., the company that contracted to provide the sophisticated hub for the OTB operation.

The computer went on the line in late June 1971, seven months late and with only one-third the redundancy (or ver-

satility) it had promised to build into the machine-brain. When the computer went on the blink, OTB clerks were pressed back to manual duty. Lines lengthened again and bettors were enraged. Handles dipped 40 per cent.

As similar breakdowns became the norm rather than the exception through the summer, Samuels issued an ultimatum: Deliver the promised goods or get your machines out of the offices.

To lend credence to his threat, he ordered his five-man legal staff to prepare memoranda on contractual obligations, implied warranties and performance stipulations.

In early November, OTB announced Computer Sciences Corp. was "making steady progress" and had achieved "greater reliability." A contract renewal—good until July 1974—provided that CSC's equipment and that of Ticketron (supplied by Control Data Corp.) would work side by side in all OTB parlors as back-up units for one another.

All along, however, Samuels looked upon his basic business problem as one of finding an adequate marketing strategy. As he told it repeatedly:

"Horseracing is a stagnant sport. Only a small percentage of people are interested because it isn't brought to the masses. Some in the industry have vision and realize the need to market the sport. Others are slower to realize that basketball and football made the big-time through the medium of television."

And so he embarked on a campaign for a television show to air certain races daily. He failed to interest the New York City area tracks which feared a TV outlet for their product would reduce their attendance, and thus their handles. But Samuels found a welcome partner about 1½ hours from the city in Leon Greenberg, president of Monticello Raceway.

Both men were proud of their October deal to televise live a superfecta race (on which one bets the first four finishers in proper order) and broadcast tapes of the daily double. The idea behind the contract was to increase OTB's audience and its winter action, and up the business at Monticello—not regarded as a "big-time" track. The arrangement looked tailormade.

But Greenberg's fellow track operators felt differently. They petitioned the State Harness Racing Commission in the hope of either having the contract declared void or having Monticello's winter meet dates rescinded.

In the beginning of November, the situation was unclear. Brown said he didn't know how the racing commission would "rap the knuckles of Samuels and Greenberg" but expressed a personal interest in having a small test-marketing of a television show to determine its impact on the industry.

The Monticello controversy highlighted two of OTB's earliest and most deep-seated problems: The size of the racing industry's take from OTB proceeds and whether Samuels' marketing-through-TV approach would hinder or help the industry.

At year's end the OTB chief seemed reconciled to at least the horsemen's demands for a greater slice of the action, but he remained adamant against granting them "windfall profits."

"We have a responsibility to keep the industry healthy, but if you allow the horsemen 7 per cent of a $1 billion annual handle, amounting to $70 million, then that's a windfall profit that takes money away from areas of social concern" to which the government might allocate OTB-generated dollars.

At the year's end Samuels had a mixed track record: His revenues were a sensation viewed absolutely, but miniscule if compared to fantastic prognostications. OTB operations had made nary a dent in organized crime. Samuels still had major computer troubles. And his relations with trackmen were hardly conjugal.

Tribe Lost 1,000 Years?

*Anthropologist, linguists led by hunter to Tasaday people,
in Philippine forest where they had never seen the moon*

TALES OF lost tribes and hidden treasures had enriched the lore of the Philippines' rugged and exotic Mindanao Island, but facts rarely supported the legends. Skepticism colored Filipinos' initial reactions to the announcement that a group of people had been discovered in a Mindanao rain forest, cut off from the outside world for centuries and living in the style of the Stone Age.

There was no question that primitive people had been found in the wild country, but the extent of their supposed isolation verged on fantasy. It seemed incredible in an era when men walked on the moon to hear that one of these shy, G-string-clad people say they had never even seen the moon.

"We didn't know that was stuck up there," he told a team of

Members of the ancient Tasaday tribe turning away from the prop wash of a modern day helicopter

translators and interrogators, because the moon had been hidden by thick tropical growth and neither his tribe nor its ancestors had ever been outside the forest.

Doubt continued, but as the people revealed more details of their mountain universe, the anthropologists, linguists and other social scientists began nodding excitedly and using adjectives like "amazing," "remarkable" and "extraordinary."

The people—24 men, women and children in six families—called themselves the Tasaday, a name they said had been passed to them from their ancestors who had learned it in a dream "from the one who owns our forest."

Their most essential tools were made of stone, in the style of the Paleolithic and Neolithic prehistoric periods. They had never tasted rice, corn, sugar or salt and had no form of agriculture. They gathered their food, which mainly consisted of roots and plants. They had no knowledge of the sea or of wheels or of tobacco. Anthropologists speculated they were the only persons known who had never had contact with tobacco, sweet potatoes, corn or cassava—items of American Indian origin which swept the globe in the 17th century during The Age of Conquest and reached even remote peoples of Africa, South America and New Guinea.

Translators found no words for fighting or war in the Tasaday's unique dialect of Manubo, which like all Philippine tongues was in the Malayo-Polynesian family of languages. A linguist said their dialect indicated the Tasaday had been separated from other known Manubo peoples for at least 1,100 years. An anthropologist said their tool technology, their lack of a hunting or trapping tradition and lack of domesticated animals dated their separation many centuries before that.

After weeks of study, Manuel Elizalde Jr., the Harvard-educated Filipino responsible for finding them in 1971, and Dr. Robert B. Fox, an American anthropologist who worked closely with him wrote that the Tasaday "could provide one of the most fascinating chapters in man's history and development."

Elizalde first made contact with the Tasaday in June in a clearing at the edge of their forest that rolls over several hundred square miles of mountains 3,000 to 5,000 feet high in South Cotabato Province. The clearing is about 640 miles south of Manila and less than 10 miles inland from the Celebes Sea. It was no more than a one-minute helicopter flight from the nearest village outside the forest, but several hours' walk.

The 34-year-old Elizalde had gone there as head of PANAMIN, an organization dedicated to helping the Philippines' more than 60 minority groups deal with 20th Century problems. The minorities—many of them primitive—comprised about four million of the nation's 38 million persons which inhabited several hundred of the 7,100 Philippine islands.

PANAMIN was the acronym for Presidential Assistant on National Minorities, a cabinet-level position in the administration of President Ferdinand E. Marcos and for Private Association for National Minorities, a private, non-profit foundation.

For more than a year PANAMIN workers had heard of people living in this forest from a hunter named Dafal of the Manubo Blit tribe. Dafal, known among his people as "the man who walks the forest like the wind," had made a career of going deep into jungles and forests to catch animals for food and gather herbs for medicines.

The long-legged hunter's stories of a strange group intrigued the PANAMIN staff, but they were too busy with several projects to check the reports. Besides, Elizalde later observed, it sounded like so many other folk tales and myths. But then PANAMIN acquired its own helicopter and during a flight into the Manubo Blit settlement about April the pilot noticed smoke rising from the unexplored dark forest to the south. On closer inspection with Elizalde the expeditions by air reported something disturbing: Logging roads had been cut across mountains and were heading toward the rich stands of timber in the untouched wilds described as an unbelievably dense climax rain-forest.

If PANAMIN established the presence of native people it could be possible to convince the government to declare the forest a reserve forbidden to loggers, miners and other ambitious outsiders. Dafal was questioned more closely. He said he had chanced across the people, who wore only G-strings of leaves or were naked, about five years earlier, deep in the forest.

A member of the Tasaday tribe embracing a Filipino government official

They had fled in fear, but he pursued them, overcame their fright and won their friendship, he said. In several other meetings since then, he had given them bits of cloth, earrings, a few pieces of metal, a bow and arrows and other items he could not recall. In return they helped him set traps for wild pig, monkey and smaller jungle game.

In late May, Dafal was asked to hike into the forest, find the people and urge them to meet with PANAMIN. A few days later he returned, said it was arranged and went back in with a Taboli tribesman employed by PANAMIN to prepare a landing site for the helicopter. On June 7 the PANAMIN party flew to the small clearing. The helicopter's single engine and rotar blades shattered the stillness as the party walked toward a small lean-to constructed by Dafal. Within moments the hunter appeared, leading from the thicket four trembling men. "One was so terrified he almost collapsed," Elizalde recalled.

As the story later came out, not only the clearing and the strange roaring machine were making them nervous. Dafal had told them that if they would come out of their forest he would bring their long-awaited god named Diwata. He said he had learned of a legend handed down by their ancestors that Diwata, a Messiah-like diety, would some day come to help them.

In his favorite old battered yachting cap and several days' stubble of whiskers, Elizalde was accepted by them as Diwata.

As he patted the men and tried to befriend them, several women and children edged into the clearing. They squatted many yards away and stayed there, staring, throughout the first visit. PANAMIN offered bolos (long jungle knives), cloth, beaded necklaces, mirrors, arrows, a flashlight and sacks of salt and rice. The people accepted them without emotion. They gagged when they tried to sample salt and sugar. They nibbled the rice raw and wanted nothing to do with tobacco. On a later occasion cookies caused one man to vomit.

After two meetings with the people, Elizalde called for Fox, PANAMIN's director of research and chief anthropologist for the Philippines' National Museum. Fox, 54, who had spent most of the quarter-century since World War II in the Philippines, was unbelieving of the story that was unfolding.

"I tried every way I could think of to trip them up," he said later. "When they showed me some of their own cloth-like material, for example, I thought I had them. But no. They gave a classic description of obtaining it.

"They had done it by simply beating the trunk of a tree—unquestionably a wild fig—with a heavy stick. They tore the loosened bark away from the trunk by hand, then peeled the outer bark from the bast. The bast was dampened and pounded at the stream with any handy river cobble to make it pliable. They said they trimmed it with bamboo, sharpened to a knife's edge with a stone scraper," Fox recounted.

The use of stone to fashion secondary implements out of bamboo was considered a major feature of their technology. "It might be more accurate to describe them as living in a stone-bamboo period, rather than in a stone age," Fox observed. Bamboo was fashioned into blades adequate for cutting monkey meat and for instruments to pare and pierce.

Fox suggested that a study of the Tasaday could provide challenges to traditional approaches to classifying stages of prehistory. Perhaps, he said, prehistoric man's approach to agriculture and animals should be evaluated together with stone and metal technology, widely used standards of development. The care required in drawing conclusions about the Tasaday was dramatized in an incident involving a bamboo jew's harp. PANAMIN was excited when it found the instrument, carried by a young man named Balayam. The harp, historically, was one of the most widely distributed musical instruments in Asia and elsewhere in the Old World. Balayam's jew's harp, however, was later found by anthropologist Jesus T. Peralta of the National Museum to be made from a type of bamboo not found in the Tasaday's forest environment. It also appeared to have been shaped with a metal knife. On questioning, Balayam said Dafal had given him the instrument and taught him to play it. Dafal later recalled that was the case. It was the only musical instrument found throughout the initial series of contacts with the Tasaday.

After the first meetings, the Tasaday stopped trembling and showed a steadily increasing attitude of friendliness. They did not, however, like the clearing. It was too windy, too noisy and the sun was too bright, they said.

They became relatively accustomed to the helicopter, which they called the "big bird," and to rice and the large bolos. They remained quietly watchful of all that went on around them, smiled occasionally and found things they clearly wanted nothing to do with.

They consistently disdained tobacco or smoking and were leery of loud-talking or aggressive outsiders. Elizalde reported that, upon hearing themselves talk on a tape recorder, one Tasaday said: "We do not like the little black man (the recording machine)." Another commented with alarm: "He steals the voice of the Tasaday."

Fox and Elizalde's first 32-page report came out in July and was largely supported by following study. But, as both were later to say, they had not grasped at once the full importance of Dafal. Fox would note that a Dafal alone could provide a rich and unparalleled opportunity "to study how one man changed the lifeways of a small group of people."

The Tasaday's intimate knowledge of their universe (Fox remarked that they seemed to have hundreds of words just for varieties of plants) and apparent affection for their environment and each other indicated they had achieved unusual harmony in their lives. They were lithe and muscular, over five feet in height at maturity, and had well-defined features in an oval face with high cheekbones set off by dark, bright eyes. Their amber skin was lighter than that of other Mindanao people because their forest hid the sun. Their length of life was obviously short. The oldest man and woman were estimated to be from 45 to 50 years old.

Dr. Saturnino Rebong, PANAMIN's physician, was able to make only preliminary checks but he said the people generally appeared to be healthy. Goiters were rather common, however, and several children had skin infections. A dentist, Dr. Norton Winters, examined the teeth of three men and proclaimed that he found not a single cavity. The teeth of all adult Tasaday were stained red from chewing betel nut. The Tasadays' teeth were filed down, by river rock, nearly to the gums.

Among themselves, the Tasaday displayed warmth and affection and considerable gaiety, particularly when they felt comfortable in their surroundings. Parents continually nuzzled and sniffed—rather than kissed—their children. And the Tasaday obviously were fertile people. Thirteen of the 24 were believed to be less than 10 years old. There was, however, a woman shortage. All the adult women had mates and nine of the 13 children were boys.

Balayam—usually referred to as Ayam—was about 20 years old and one of the most talkative Tasaday. He expressed worry over his lack of a woman. The Tasaday said their custom dictated that once a man and woman became mates they stayed together the rest of their lives. There was no sharing of mates with others, as is done among many other Mindanao peoples.

The Tasaday apparently gathered food and slept in family units and made major decisions on a group level after open discussion in which opinions were freely expressed. Age and experience seemed to give added weight to opinions, and women had equal opportunity with men. There were no leaders in an organizational sense.

The Tasaday's shyness was illustrated by their reluctance to express their curiosity. They did not ask a question for weeks. Finally invited to do so, one murmured: "But would it be all right?" Assured that it would, questions came quickly: "Where do you come from? How far is it? Where do you get all your things (cameras, shoes, etc.)? What are their names?"

Child of the Philippine Stone Age Tasaday tribe sitting in a clearing

252

A "lost tribe" villager fashioning a stone ax

These were virtually the same questions the outsiders had asked the Tasaday.

Their forest life was glimpsed when Elizalde and Fox went less than two hundred yards into the forbidding growth with some invited newsmen. The hike took an hour over steep inclines clogged with trees and tangled by vines and roots. Underfoot, moist leaves and mud made the going oily slick. The outsiders, who had been comfortable in the clearing, sweated profusely in the humid air and puffed with exertion. The Tasaday, who had wrapped their arms about themselves to keep warm in the clearing, skimmed over the terrain. They dug their toes into the soil, juggled infants on their shoulders and stepped briskly through the undergrowth.

They stopped beside a rippling stream and built fires by twirling sticks together. It was here that Fox first saw their stone tools. "My God!" he exclaimed. "They've told us about these, but we've never seen them. This is incredible," he said as he pored over a stone the size of a chicken's egg laced to a wooden handle. A young man demonstrated with another stone tool that had a sharpened edge how to make a bamboo knife.

Rain poured into the forest, and the Tasaday scarcely moved. The eldest man reached up from a squatting position, grabbed the nearest frond of a palm and pulled it over himself and his woman. Another man sliced off a huge leaf with a bamboo knife and made a roof for himself and a half dozen others. The Tasaday sat peacefully for half an hour, appearing settled for all day, if necessary, until the rain stopped.

Light of the sun—which they called "the eye of the day"—sifted softly through the forest's three and four layers of dark green cover. Only tiny jagged patches of blue sky were visible among the leaves and branches that rose well above 100 feet at the forest's edge. Orange and yellow butterflies fluttered through the heavy atmosphere and pinhead-sized insects seemed to be everywhere.

The Tasaday later disclosed that their permanent place was a one-day walk—probably several days for outsiders—away from the stream. Nobody from the outside had ever been there, they told Elizalde, including Dafal.

Elizalde, who spent more time with the Tasaday than anybody else, said they described their permanent site as "beautiful, where the water flows from the mountain and they have shelters in lime stone ledges and in the buttressed roots of towering trees. . . . From their descriptions, they have learned to live there in harmony among themselves and nature."

A strong and active young man named Mahayag said that until Dafal taught the Tasaday to make bamboo traps for monkeys and other animals, "the largest animal I ever killed was a frog." The worst thing in their world, one Tasaday said, was "the big word"—thunder. Snakes also were feared. The most beautiful thing was "finding a big biking"—digging a particularly succulent wild root, like a yam, to eat. They said the souls of their dead ancestors lived in fine places in the tops of the highest trees.

PANAMIN and other authorities agreed that the best way to gather further accurate information about the Tasaday would be in their permanent homesite. A plan was devised for a small team of anthropologists, botanists, linguists and other social scientists to live with them through their seasons, perhaps through 1972.

In response to protests from various quarters that the Tasaday seemed happy and should be left alone, Elizalde proclaimed that the greatest care would be taken to help them live as they wished and that PANAMIN would not try to force the Tasaday to change. He argued that PANAMIN contacted them only because loggers and other outsiders with less concern for the Tasaday appeared certain to reach their forest soon.

Scientists were eager to follow up what Elizalde and Fox had said in an early report: "The discovery of the Tasaday provides an unparalleled opportunity in the 20th Century for us to more fully understand—and appreciate—man's culture and society before the appearance of agriculture and the domestication of animals."

They said they would "query again the basic stuff of man's nature," study the minimal requirements of human existence, development of technology and the process of social and cultural change for the individual and the group.

"The Tasaday," they wrote, "are a symbol of man's great variability and adaptability and also of his universality."

Left, Associate Justice John M. Harlan who retired at 72 and died three months later. Above, Associate Justice Hugo L. Black who died at 85 shortly after retirement.

TWO U.S. SUPREME COURT JUSTICES DIED SOON AFTER RETIREMENT

The nine-member U.S. Supreme Court lost two outstanding justices within six days, due to ill health.

Justice Hugo L. Black retired Sept. 17, after 34 years of service. Two days later he suffered a stroke which proved fatal Sept. 25. He was 85.

Justice John M. Harlan, 72, followed Justice Black into retirement Sept. 23, after serving 16 years. His physician said Justice Harlan was afflicted with bone cancer. Harlan's death came on Dec. 29.

Near year's end, the Senate approved the appointment of Lewis F. Powell, 64-year-old Virginia trial lawyer, and William Rehnquist, 47, an assistant attorney general, to fill the two vacancies on the tribunal.

* * * *   * * * *   * * * *   * * * *

Once a member of the Ku Klux Klan, Alabama's Justice Black took his seat on the Supreme Court in 1937, amid a storm of controversy. On advice from his mentor, President Franklin Roosevelt, he made a brief nationwide radio broadcast at the time in which he said: "I did join the Ku Klux Klan about 15 years ago. I later resigned. I never rejoined."

He never spoke of the incident again.

Black quickly made his reputation as one of the court's most liberal justices. The Constitution was his professional bible, particularly the First Amendment.

Since Aug. 28 he had been hospitalized for inflammation of the blood vessels. Had he been able to serve until March 1972 he would have been the justice with the longest tenure, exceeding Justice Stephen Field's record of 34 years, 6 months and 11 days, between 1863 and 1897.

After working his way through the University of Alabama, as a law student, Black served in World War I. He became United States Senator in 1927, an ardent supporter of Franklin Roosevelt's New Deal. When President Roosevelt made his controversial and abortive attempt to enlarge the Supreme Court so that more liberals could be expected to give majority support to New Deal programs, Black's loyalty won him a Supreme Court nomination in 1937.

"It is my belief," Black once wrote, "that there are 'absolutes' in our Bill of Rights and that they were put there on purpose by men who knew what the words meant, and meant their prohibitions to be 'absolutes'."

Black's last written opinion was a fiery defense of the right of the New York Times to publish the Pentagon Papers over the objections of the Nixon Administration. He also consistently voted against the suppression of pornography and subversive literature.

During his tenure he wrote some of the court's most profound decisions. In 1963 he made the landmark Gideon v. Wainwright decision, which extended the right of counsel to everyone accused of a felony. Black also wrote the decision that prayer in public schools was unconstitutional, and during the height of the McCarthy era in the 1950s he defended the right of an individual to refuse under the Fifth Amendment to answer questions by a congressional committee without risking citation for contempt.

* * * *   * * * *   * * * *   * * * *

Politically, Harlan was quite a contrast to Black. Noted in the legal profession for scholarly, well-instructed opinions, Harlan was a conservative who frequently opposed Black and other liberal members of the court.

During his years on the court he always main-tained the doctrine of *stare decisis*—strict adherence to prior judicial decisions. He held that political and social evils should be settled through the political process and not through the courts, and he believed that the federal judiciary should steer clear of state and local problems.

Harlan took issue with the majority on such questions as reappointment, the rights of criminal suspects, the legality of state poll taxes and the right of newspapers to publish classified material. He was one of the three dissenters from the Supreme Court decision that allowed the New York Times and the Washington Post to resume publication of their series on the Pentagon Papers. He said that the court was moving too fast, amid a "frenzied train of events," and that the issues deserved more deliberate consideration.

Upon hearing of Harlan's retirement, President Richard Nixon described him as "one of the great legal scholars in the history of the court."

Born of a distinguished legal family in Chicago, Harlan attended Princeton University and Oxford in England as a Rhodes scholar. He received his law degree from New York University. For more than 25 years he practiced with a prestigious Wall Street firm then called Root, Clark, Buckner and Howland.

He left the law firm briefly in 1925 to become assistant to U.S. Attorney Emory R. Bucher, for whom he served three years as chief of the prohibition division.

His only other excursion into public life came in 1951, when he was chief counsel for the New York Crime Commission.

In 1954 President Dwight D. Eisenhower named him to the United States Court of Appeals for the Second Circuit and less than a year later Eisenhower nominated him to the Supreme Court.

SARNOFF, DEVELOPER OF RADIO AND TELEVISION, DEAD AT 80

On the evening of April 14, 1912, a young telegrapher sat before a wireless receiver in New York City monitoring the rhythm of dots and dashes. Suddenly he was jolted by a terse message: "S.S. Titanic ran into iceberg. Sinking fast."

The clerk, whose name was David Sarnoff, alerted authorities and for the next 72 hours sat at his Morse key, telling the world about the disaster.

The catastrophe awakened the public and Congress to the important role that wireless could play in rescue operations. It helped to launch Sarnoff on a career that was to make him a driving force behind the development of the electronic media.

On Dec. 12, 1971 the National Broadcasting Company, which Sarnoff formed, interrupted their broadcast, Meet the Press, to tell listeners that Sarnoff, Chairman of RCA, had died at his six-story brownstone in New York City. He was 80 years old.

Born in a small Russian village, Sarnoff came to this country in 1900, the son of a poor, itinerant trader. When he was 15 he went to work for the Commercial Cable Co. as a messenger, saved enough money to buy a telegraph instrument and learned the Morse code.

He went to Marconi Wireless Telegraph Instrument Co. as a $5.50-a-week clerk and by 1917 had become American Marconi's commercial manager.

During World War I the British-owned American Marconi Company was absorbed by a new company called the Radio Corporation of America, jointly owned by General Electric and Westinghouse.

While an assistant traffic manager for Marconi, Sarnoff wrote a historic memo proposing a "radio music box." In part the memo read; "I have in mind a plan of development which would make radio a household utility in the same sense as a piano or phonograph. The idea is to bring music into the home by wireless."

Sarnoff estimated sales of a million sets at $75 each within three years. The actual RCA sales from 1922 to 1924 amounted to $83 million.

Neither the idea nor the practice of broadcasting radio music was original with Sarnoff. But he was the first to have the vision to urge mass production of the generally untried and crude home receiver.

Once radio started to catch on in 1923, Sarnoff wrote another famous memo saying: "I believe that television, which is the technical name for seeing as well as hearing by radio, will come to pass in the future."

In 1926, as vice-president and general manager of RCA, Sarnoff saw a dream come true: The formation of a central broadcasting organization through which RCA would feed programs to a number of interconnected radio stations. This was the National Broadcasting Company, which became America's first radio chain.

In 1930 Sarnoff became president of RCA and made it one of the 15 largest companies in the country.

In 1936, the British Broadcasting Corporation set up a working electronic TV operation in London. Then, in 1939 at the New York World's Fair, Sarnoff made the first television broadcast in this country.

During World War II Sarnoff went on duty as a colonel, serving as a communications consultant in the Pentagon and at the headquarters of General of the Army Dwight D. Eisenhower in Europe. In 1944 he became a brigadier general.

Sarnoff also pioneered in color TV, and turned to conquests such as electronic data processing.

In 1966 Sarnoff, who had served for 19 years as board chairman and chief executive officer of RCA, relinquished the post of chief executive but continued to have an active voice in the operation of RCA until his final illness.

CAREER OF RALPH BUNCHE, NOTED PEACEMAKER, ENDED

For the late Ralph J. Bunche the road to greatness and the Nobel Peace Prize had many obstacles. But, a man of many talents and a dedicated maker of peace, he cleared the hurdles.

For more than 20 years following his signal success in negotiating the difficult 1949 armistice between Israel and the Arab States, Bunche had served as a key diplomat at the United Nations and a top troubleshooter when the going got rough.

Born in Detroit, the son of a barber, he had been orphaned at the age of 14 and had gone to live with his grandmother whom he revered.

Bunche grew up in the era that preceded the great civil rights struggle in America, but friends said that he never stressed or played down his Negro blood.

A brilliant scholar, Bunche first turned to teaching, and in 1928 joined the faculty of Howard University in Washington. He soon broadened his field of studies in the realm of government, international and social relations.

From 1928–40, Bunche collaborated with Gunnar Myrdal of Sweden in researching "An American Dilemma." They raised questions about interracial sex relations that prompted a mob of incensed whites to chase them across Alabama one night.

During World War II Bunche served as an analyst of African and Far Eastern Affairs in the War Department. Later he moved to the State Department, where he soon found where his true interest lay. By the end of the war he was playing a key role in planning the United Nations.

In 1944 Bunche was at Dunbarton Oaks, helping to lay the groundwork for the world peace forum, and a year later he went to San Francisco to draw up the trusteeship sections of the U.N. Charter.

In 1947 Bunche quit the State Department to join the U.N. Secretariat, where he was to serve under three secretary-generals, starting with Trygve Lie.

Bunche went to Jerusalem in 1948 as an aide to Count Folke Bernadotte of Sweden to try to mediate the first Arab-Israeli war. On Sept. 17 of that year Bunche was en route to join Bernadotte but was detained a short distance from the scheduled meeting point.

A short time later Bernadotte was slain in an ambush and a French colonel occupying Bunche's regular seat in the count's car was also killed.

Bunche became acting mediator after the assassination and in 1949 secured an armistice between Egypt and Israel, the first step in a general cease-fire.

Both sides praised the American diplomat, and the Egyptians hailed him as "one of the world's greatest men." The following year Bunche received the Nobel Peace Prize.

Secretary-General Dag Hammarskjold sent Bunche to the strife-torn Congo in 1960 to set up a U.N. force. It was later used to suppress the secession of Katanga Province.

Under U Thant, Bunche served on a U.N. peace-keeping force in Cyprus when the Greek and Turkish Cypriots threatened to go to war.

In 1959 Bunche's teenage son was refused membership in the West Side Tennis Club, touching off a furor. The club president later resigned, and eventually both Bunche and his son were asked to join the fashionable club but they declined.

Ailments plagued Bunche, once a robust figure, in his latter years. He suffered from a kidney malfunction, diabetes, heart disease and near blindness. But he stayed on at his post as Under Secretary General for Special Political Affairs until June 1971.

After his death on Dec. 9, Israeli Prime Minister Golda Meir sent a cable to the Bunche family, saying: "His passing is a great loss to all who are interested in peace."

Ralph J. Bunche

INDIA, WINNER IN PAKISTAN, FRUSTRATED U.S., RED CHINA

For month after bloody month the military repression in East Pakistan rolled on. Perhaps one million died and another 9 million fled into neighboring India to escape the blood bath at the hands of West Pakistani troops and their allies among the non-Bengali people of the east.

In New Delhi the war hawks who wanted to dismember Pakistan and crush it forever as a rival power finally won the day. Anger in the world's second most populous nation reached the flash point and the third war between India and Pakistan was under way.

It was not nearly so bloody as some past battles (pp. 146–148). In another of history's cruel ironies, nearly all the dying was over before the first Indian army columns slashed across the East Pakistan border and later into West Pakistan a thousand miles away. In the two-week war some 30,000 soldiers and civilians on all sides died.

When Indian troops and the Mukti Bahini Bengali guerrillas seized the capital of Dacca, jubilant crowds kissed them and roared approval as the flag of the world's newest nation, Bangladesh, was set fluttering in the tropic breezes.

The newest clash of arms on the subcontinent was no mere neighborhood brawl. The repercussions in other capitals did not vanish with Pakistan's defeat and the ouster of its military strong man leader, Gen. Mohammed Yahya Khan. The United States and Communist China watched in helpless frustration as their ally Pakistan was defeated and suffered political humiliation and lessened influence in the area. On the other hand the Soviet Union championed India and greatly improved its prestige in India and elsewhere. It was a giant step forward for the men in the Kremlin who were seeking to become the dominant power in Asia. Besides furnishing arms

and cheering from the sidelines, the Soviets used their veto in the United Nations, blocking any effective action by the world body to halt the fighting until the Indians had scored their victory.

American influence in New Delhi tumbled to new lows first when Prime Minister Indira Gandhi decided Washington had taken a pro-Pakistan position and later when a U.S. naval force including the nuclear powered aircraft carrier *Enterprise* headed into the Bay of Bengal.

The fighting escalated from border skirmishes to serious war in December, when New Delhi decided to help the Bengalis to their freedom. In the east, Pakistani troops rapidly fell back to the capital city of Dacca, mostly without offering stiff resistance. From the Pakistani capital in the west came orders to hold Dacca at any cost. But local commanders surrendered when it became clear their forces had neither hope of reinforcement nor escape. A short time later a cease-fire was arranged in the west in Kashmir and to the south of that old Indo-Pakistani battleground.

Jubilation in East Pakistan soared while the West was pushed deep into gloom. Gen. Yahya Khan and other high officers were purged from the military and government for their part in the disaster. Civilian politicians said that, but for the military's "bloody mindedness," the East could have been saved. When Shiek Mujibur Rahman and his Awami League won the national elections in 1970 he wanted a measure of autonomy for his eastern provinces which had been discriminated against since Pakistan was born. The charismatic leader, who was considered the one man who could successfully lead Bengladesh, was jailed by Gen. Yahya Khan but Pakistan's new leader, Prime Minister Zulfikar Ali Bhutto, said Mujibur would be released soon. Bhutto, too, seemed a likely leader for what was left of

Pakistan. Bhutto was a long-time politician, and his party had won a majority of the seats in the West during the 1970 election. In the past he had been noted for his anti-American sentiments and warm friendship with Red China's leaders.

Shiek Mujibur, affectionately nicknamed Mujib, and the other new leaders of Bengladesh had their work cut out for them. Indeed, some western diplomats thought Bhutto's Pakistan was better off without the eastern provinces. Bengladesh's 55,126 square miles held 75 million persons who lived 1,300 to the square mile in a crushing poverty perhaps worse than any in Asia. Per capita income ran about $75 a year, and the nation routinely was ravaged by huge cyclones and famine. The country was visited by the former in 1970 and was in the throes of the latter as 1971 ended. The nation needed massive amounts of foreign aid. Its exports, which once provided 50 per cent of all Pakistan's foreign exchange, were in trouble. The country's tea was of poor quality and was losing foreign markets. Its jute was being replaced by synthetic fibers.

When the provisional government arrived in Dacca behind Indian tanks and paratroops, it proclaimed Bengladesh would have a socialist-style parliamentary government. A major worry to some foreign diplomats was whether the country would teeter on the brink of political chaos, even with Shiek Mujib. The Bengalis made up only 60 per cent of the population and the sub-continent had been known since the dawn of history to slip easily into communal strife.

And, despite victory, there were still worries for New Delhi. Its own Bengalis had been stirred by Bengladesh's independence and the Indian Bengalis' own dream of a separate state might become a problem.

Below, the bayonetting of an East Pakistani on the outskirts of Dacca during a wave of revenge killings that followed the fall of the city. Right, a Mukti Bahini soldier stomping a dying boy in Dacca

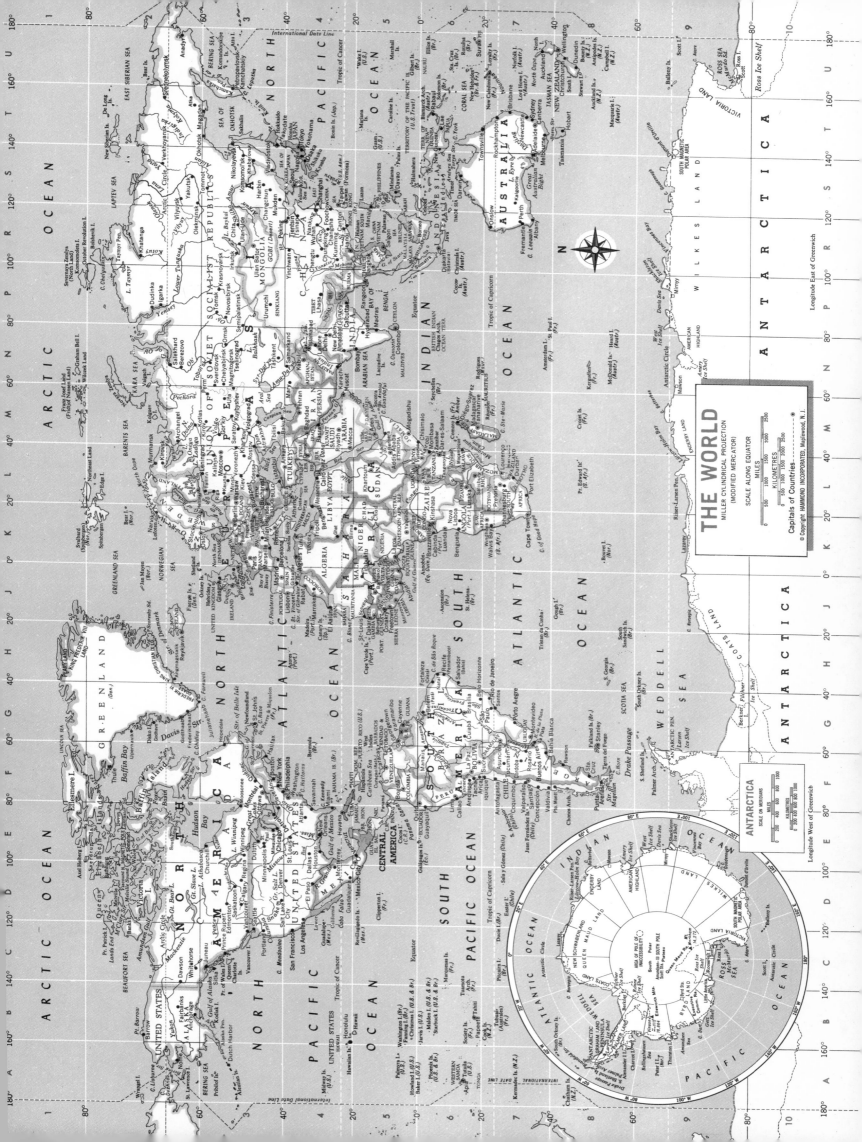

THE WORLD

MILLER CYLINDRICAL PROJECTION
(MODIFIED MERCATOR)

SCALE ALONG EQUATOR

MILES

KILOMETRES

● Capitals of Countries ....

© Copyright HAMMOND INCORPORATED, Maplewood, N.J.

ANTARCTICA

SCALE ON MERIDIANS

MILES

KILOMETRES

A passenger who removed her luggage from the liner Oceanic waited in vain on a New York pier for assistance during the dock strike

DOCK STRIKES HIT U.S. COASTS

It had been 23 years since Harry Bridges' 15,000-member independent International Longshoremen's and Warehousemen's Union had struck the West Coast docks. But out they went July 1, seeking a $1.60-an-hour increase in wages that averaged $2.29 an hour, plus jurisdiction over the Teamsters' Union in the handling of containerized cargo.

It had been less than two years since Thomas (Teddy) Gleason's 45,000-man AFL-CIO International Longshoremen's Association had staged the eighth of its post World War II strikes on the Atlantic and Gulf coasts. Out they too went Oct. 1, in a deadlock over continuation of a guaranteed annual wage for New York dockers.

Thus for the first time, the U.S. merchant marine found itself almost completely tied up on both coasts at the same time, a maritime crisis of record scope.

Farmers complained that millions of dollars in soybean, rice and other crops were in danger of spoiling. European shippers arranged to airfreight smaller items, to ship cars and the like to Canada for trucking into the United States.

Applications for food stamps rose 50 per cent in coastal areas.

With nearly 250 ships tied up in 24 ports from San Diego to Seattle, losses to the West Coast economy because of the ILWU strike were estimated at $1.7 billion. Thousands of workmen in dock-related industries were laid off.

For the first time since he took office, President Nixon on Oct. 4 invoked the Taft-Hartley law, with its 80-day cooling off period, extending the old Pacific Coast contract until Christmas. It was the 96th day of the strike. Longshoremen returned to their piers past cargo piled three times higher than their heads.

Meanwhile, the East and Gulf coast strike continued, except for 7,000 Texas dockers. They defied the ILA strike call on grounds the guaranteed wage issue pertained only to New York and had nothing to do with them.

More than 200 ships lay idle, 1.5 million tons of cargo in their holds. An estimated 30,000 members of other trades were laid off for lack of work because of the eastern pier tieup.

Bowing to the "impossibility of a timely settlement," Nixon for the second time invoked Taft-Hartley, on Thanksgiving day. The ILA strike had run 56 days, at an estimated cost to the economy just short of $1 billion.

Serenity returned to the docks at least temporarily. But in San Francisco the 69-year-old Bridges spoke darkly of massing his forces and those of the East coast ILA for a joint renewal of the strike after the Taft-Hartley cooling off periods had run their course.

ELLSBERG: FRESH INDICTMENTS

A federal grand jury which indicted Dr. Daniel Ellsberg in July for releasing the controversial Pentagon papers to the news media (pp. 182–185) acted again at year's end, leveling 12 criminal charges against him, including conspiracy.

The new charges issued against the 40-year-old Ellsberg in Los Angeles on Dec. 30 were more severe than the original ones. The December charges also included theft of government property and violation of espionage statutes.

Anthony J. Russo Jr., 35, a former colleague of Ellsberg at the Rand Corporation, had not been indicted earlier in the case, but he spent 47 days in jail for contempt after refusing to testify before the grand jury. In the December action he was named on four counts related to release of the papers.

The 25-page indictment named as co-conspirators Miss Lynda Sinay, a Los Angeles advertising woman, and Vu Van Thai, a former South Vietnamese ambassador to the United States.

At a news conference in New York, Ellsberg said that the charges against him were "false" and that he was not aware of having "violated any criminal statutes."

"I stole nothing and I did not commit espionage," Ellsberg said. "I violated no laws and I have not intended to harm my country."

Former Teamster Union president James Hoffa

5-YEAR TERM FOR AIR HIJACKER

Robert Lee Jackson—the man who hijacked a Braniff jetliner in the air over San Antonio, Tex., and forced its crews to fly it to Buenos Aires by way of Monterrey, Mex., Mexico City, Lima, Peru and Rio de Janeiro, Brazil—was sentenced Dec. 15 to serve five years in an Argentine prison.

The flight had originated at Acapulco, Mex. His accomplice, Lydia Lucrecia Sanchez, a native of Guatemala he had met in Mexico, drew a three-year term *(Page 130).*

Both penalties were stiffer than those recommended by prosecutors but were still well under the 15-year maximum provided by Argentina's air piracy law. The prosecution had asked that Jackson, 36, a U.S. Navy deserter, be given a four-year term and 23-year-old Miss Sanchez a two-year sentence.

COLONEL FREED BY ARMY COURT

Col. Oran K. Henderson stood at attention as Maj. Gen. Charles N. Mount Jr., president of the court-martial, informed him that he had won acquittal on all charges that he covered up the 1968 My Lai massacre.

The three charges against Henderson were:

—That he intentionally failed to carry out a thorough and proper investigation of atrocity reports and of the story of a confrontation between a helicopter pilot and Lt. William L. Calley over the safety of civilians.

—That he violated a Vietnam command regulation because he did not tell his commander, Brig. Gen. Samuel Koster, of the Americal Division, about incidents he thought were war crimes.

—That he lied to the Pentagon inquiry on Dec. 2, 1969, when he said he was positive that he had asked a helicopter unit commander to survey pilots about whether they had seen wild shooting at the Vietnamese village.

The jury of two generals and five colonels did not elaborate on its verdict, reached Dec. 17.

Originally, 13 U.S. soldiers were accused of covering up what a Pentagon inquiry had held to be the slaughter of 175 to 400 civilians. Henderson, however, was the only officer brought to trial by the Army on the coverup charge.

Five other servicemen had been tried on accusations related to the actual murders, but of these only Calley was convicted *(pp. 67–72).*

HOFFA FREED FROM U.S. PRISON

"Goodbye and Merry Christmas," called the graying man in the dark suit, pausing as he walked through the courtyard of the Federal Penitentiary in Lewisburg, Pa., and waving at the inmates watching him through a row of cell windows.

Thus on Dec. 23 James R. Hoffa, tough, energetic former president of the Brotherhood of Teamsters, walked out a free man after serving 4 years, 9 months and 16 days of a 13-year prison term.

Hoffa was released under a conditional commutation ordered by President Nixon. The former teamsters' boss himself had failed three times to win a parole from his sentences of eight years for jury tampering and five years for pension fund fraud.

As he strode through two electronically-controlled gates, Hoffa turned to newsmen and said grimly: "Anybody who tells you it's not tough to serve time should spend a day in there." He added, "I have no time to be bitter." But when reporters pressed him on his view of prison life, he said: "They're making criminals out of young people who were never criminals."

The terms of the commutation barred the 58-year-old former teamsters' chief from engaging in "the direct or indirect management" of any union until March 1980. But Hoffa was still a power to reckon with.

A Justice Department official disclosed that Hoffa had been given permission to renew his many friendships in the giant union and to speak out on issues affecting the union without violating the conditions of his commutation.

There was no doubt that Hoffa commanded the loyalty of the union rank and file, as evidenced by the five-inch buttons reading simply "Hoffa" that were worn at every convention since he had assumed high office.

Another thing was clear. Hoffa had no money problems. His lawyer, Morris Shenker, said that the former teamster leader had decided to take his pension of $1.7 million in a lump sum, and that he would get $1.2 million after taxes.

In granting the commutation, Nixon noted that Hoffa had been a model prisoner and that his wife was suffering from a heart condition.

NEWTON CLEARED IN GUN DEATH

"I feel this is a frustration of justice and would prefer to retry the case, but I am compelled to ask at this time for a dismissal," Atty. Gen. Lowell Jensen told the court in Oakland, Calif.

Thus, after nearly two years in prison and three trials, Black Panther leader Huey P. Newton won a dismissal Dec. 15 of charges that he had killed an Oakland policeman, John Frey *(Page 90).*

Newton himself made no comment on the dismissal, but his attorney Charles R. Garry declared that the action was "long overdue."

EXTORTIONIST ON PLANE GETS $200,000, THEN PARACHUTES

The middle-aged man in business suit and dark glasses summoned Stewardess Florence Schaffner shortly before Northwest Airlines' Flight 305 from Washington, D.C., was due to land at Seattle on the final leg of its trip. Wordlessly, he handed her a note.

"He was quite relaxed, sitting in the back seat on the starboard side," said another passenger, Robert Gregory of Sumner, Wash.

The 23-year-old Miss Schaffner thought the man was trying to make a date with her and stuffed the note casually in her purse.

"He motioned that I should take it out and read it," she recalled.

The note ordered instructions relayed to the ground that the 36 passengers aboard the Boeing 727 would be released upon payment of $200,000 in $20 bills. It also demanded that two parachutes be put aboard the jetliner when it landed.

As Miss Schaffner glanced at the man, he opened a brief case to display two wired cylinders that resembled dynamite.

The time was midafternoon of Nov. 24. The skyjacker had boarded Flight 305 at its next to last stop in Portland, Ore. He had given the name "D. B. Cooper," or "Dan Cooper."

For 2½ hours Capt. William Scott circled Seattle until he was informed the $200,000 ransom was on its way. He landed about 6 p.m.

The first parachutes produced were a military type, which were opened by static cords affixed to the airplane. The skyjacker rejected them. Two sports chutes then were rounded up. They could be opened by a parachutist at any stage of his descent.

With the parachutes and 10,000 $20 bills aboard, the passengers and two stewardesses, including Miss Schaffner, were allowed off the plane. Remaining aboard with the hijacker were Scott, first officer Robert Tataczak, second officer Harold Anderson and a third stewardess, Tina Mucklow, all based in Minneapolis.

The skyjacker directed that the plane be flown to Mexico City, but agreed to a refueling stop 500 miles away at Reno, Nev.

The captor ordered the crew to open the jetliner's rear door, keep an altitude of less than 10,000 feet and leave the landing gear and flaps down. The effect of this was to restrict the 727's speed to 200 m.p.h., while at that altitude no oxygen was required despite the open door.

It was about 7:30 p.m. when Flight 305 took to the air again, its crew members locked in their flight deck by the skyjacker, who turned off the lights in the cabin.

About 35 minutes later, over brushy, timbered foothills in the Cascade Mountains near Woodland, Wash., a flashing light on the flight deck indicated the plane's rear stairwell was being operated.

Seven hours after first reporting the aircraft hijacked, Scott landed at Reno. The 727's cabin was empty. The skyjacker apparently had jumped from the plane in flight.

A Boeing spokesman said the 727 was probably the only commercial airliner which a parachuter could leave successfully because, with its door in the tail, "he'd be away from the flaps and engines and go straight down."

Trailing the jetliner on its flight to Reno were three Air Force jets, but their pilots sighted no parachute. However, a free fall in a sports chute would have been almost impossible to detect in the darkness. A ground search of the Woodland area later was extended along a 500-mile corridor in Washington, Oregon, Nevada and northern California—corresponding to the air route Flight 305 took to Reno.

But nothing was found, and as November ended the hunt was called off.

Skyjackings and attempted skyjackings by extortionists had become a well nigh commonplace of the jet age, particularly in 1971 *(Pages 130–133)*. However, Dan Cooper, or whatever his name was, had set a record on Thanksgiving Eve. His was the first parachute escape by a skyjacker.

Soviet missiles were paraded through a blizzard in Red Square, Moscow, as part of a demonstration to mark the 54th anniversary of the Russian Revolution of 1917.

MARS FILMED BY MARINER 9

The 2,200-pound American spacecraft looked like a plump pear with four popsicles sticking from its sides. After swimming for five and a half months through the vast space gulf separating the Earth and Mars, it fired a maneuvering engine and went into Martian orbit, making the United States the first to achieve such a feat.

Mariner 9 arrived at Mars Nov. 13, more than three weeks ahead of two Soviet space probes, Mars 2 and 3.

On Dec. 7 the Soviet Union announced that Mars 3 had released a descent capsule equipped with television, making a soft landing Dec. 2 on the surface of Mars a record of its own.

After two hours in orbit, Mariner 9 began sending back television pictures stored in an onboard computer. The photos showed Mars filling the entire TV monitor, and scientists watching could see the South polar cap of frozen carbon dioxide through a haze of dust. At the time Mariner 9 went into orbit, Mars was undergoing a severe dust storm.

Despite the haze, Mariner did return some significant photographs. Its camera was able to spot a mysterious area that was warmer than its surroundings. It also returned data which indicated that materials containing silicates, common constitutents of earth rocks, were distributed over the planet.

Mariner 9, which orbited twice daily at approximately 865 miles from Mars, sent back close-up photographs of the Martian moons, Deimos and Phobos. "This is a historic first—the first time man has ever seen the disc of Deimos," said Dr. Bradford Smith of New Mexico State University after the first picture was transmitted to the California Institute of Technology's Jet Propulsion Laboratory in Pasadena, Calif.

Artists' concept of Mariner 9 in orbit around Mars

It also detected through an infrared spectrometer aboard the spacecraft the presence of water vapor over the south pole.

The Soviet mission, according to some scientists, gave the Russians a five-year start in planetary exploration over the United States, which planned it own soft landing on Mars with a Viking spacecraft for 1976.

BUTZ AGRICULTURE SECRETARY

"When the President told me this was the toughest job in Washington, I didn't realize what a master of understatement he was," said Earl L. Butz with a wry smile.

Butz made the remark after he was sworn in as Secretary of Agriculture Dec. 2 with President Nixon standing by his side. The President also had a comment:

"I think he will be a better secretary for the fight he has been through," Nixon declared. "I think he's going to do a great job."

A long bitter fight it had been on Capitol Hill before the Senate finally confirmed the nomination of Butz by a vote of 51–44. Opponents of Butz' candidacy had criticized his statements advocating corporate farming and opposing food stamp programs. He had insisted, however, that he would do all he could to raise farm prices and be a vigorous spokesman for farmers.

Both major parties saw the close vote in the Senate as the opening shot in 1972 the farm belt political campaigning of 1972.

The Republicans regarded their success in the hard-fought battle to confirm the 62-year-old Purdue University dean as a victory for Nixon. Democrats described the vote as a "cruel defeat" for American farmers.

Butz replaced Clifford M. Hardin, 56, whose resignation was announced by Nixon on Nov. 11. Hardin had said he was leaving to take "an exceptionally attractive offer" from a private firm.

Nixon originally had planned to abolish the Department of Agriculture and merge it with other agencies in a government reorganization, but he changed his mind. The proposal had met stiff opposition in Congress, particularly from farm advocates.

21 KILLED BY TUNNEL BLAST

Dusk had settled on the evening of Dec. 12 when the wives of miners building a tunnel in Port Huron, Mich., started their daily journey to pick up their husbands. As they approached the tunnel entrance they learned that an explosion had occurred 250 feet underground.

Fear and confusion mounted when officials led them to a construction shed, where they sat crying and trying to comfort one another.

Mrs. Rose Woolstenhulme talked about her husband, Vern, who was 62 and had been working on the tunnel for three years. "He started here," she said.

Shortly afterward St. Clair County undersheriff Norman Lundy walked into the shed and told her Vern was dead. Vern was one of 21 who lost their lives in the tunnel being built under Lake Huron to deliver lake water as a supplement to the supply for the Detroit metropolitan area.

Authorities estimated that about 40 workers had been in the six-mile tunnel when the explosion ripped through it at 3:11 p.m. At least 14 men escaped from the shaft on their own. Eight others rescued were taken to a hospital.

They also said that the force of the blast knocked a 15-ton piece of construction work back 40 feet.

One man who survived, Larry Vernor, 24, reported that "it picked me up and threw me about 10 feet through the air." He added that he grabbed onto "something" and thereafter rode an elevator to the surface. Vernor said his father and brother were trapped by the blast as they were working at the other end.

Michigan Gov. William G. Milliken announced the formation of an 18-member panel to probe the cause of the explosion. On Dec. 16 the panel reported that methane gas had caused the blast but that they had not been able to determine the source of the gas or the point of its ignition.

DEATH DECREED IN OHTA CASE

The young man's head was shaved of its once-long tresses, and his beard had been cut off. Sitting barefoot and impassive in the Redwood City, Calif., courtroom, John Linley Frazier listened to the reading of the jury's decision ordering him to die in the gas chamber for the killing of a wealthy surgeon and four others a year ago.

Frazier's only outward reaction was to smile at his court-appointed attorney, James Jackson, who merely shook his head. Jackson had contended that the 25-year-old former auto mechanic did not "know right from wrong" following a head injury received in an auto accident in May 1970.

Frazier had pleaded innocent and innocent by reason of insanity to the Oct. 19, 1970 shooting deaths of eye surgeon Dr. Victor Ohta, 45, his wife Virginia, 43, their sons Derrick, 12, and Taggart, 11, and Ohta's secretary, Dorothy Caldwallader, 38 (The World in 1970, 204). The court ruled that Frazier was sane.

A SHARON TATE CASE SEQUEL

The long, gruesome Sharon Tate murder trial was over, but the tangled tale of Charles Manson's hippie-type clan continued unraveling in the courtrooms of Los Angeles County.

By year's end, Manson and six young followers stood convicted of murder and were under death sentence (Pages 76–79). Manson also got a life sentence for two more killings. And two members of his "family" still faced trial for murder.

More charges piled up. Five clan members were arrested in a wild shootout at a suburban war surplus store, and a clan convert made a daring escape from jail but was recaptured. "Family" members were charged with aiding the escape.

There was barely a breather after Manson and three women codefendants were convicted and sentenced in April for the seven Tate murders. Soon Manson was in court again, charged with the killings of a musician and a movie stuntman.

A Manson henchman, Steve Grogan, also charged with the stuntman's death, went on trial separately. And, in a third courtroom, the Tate murders were retold for a jury trying Charles "Tex" Watson.

The Watson trial, postponed while the defendant fought extradition and then went to a mental hospital, was the first in which the defense contended a clan member was insane.

Defense attorneys Maxwell Keith and Samuel Bubrick conceded that Watson, 25, was a killer, but they said he was a youth driven to insanity by Manson's mesmerizing influence and hallucinogenic drugs.

"Watson had long before lost his own ego, becoming a psychotic extension of Manson, a robot," said Keith.

Watson's mother testified that Charles had been her "pride and joy," a good student and a high school football star. When Manson entered the son's life, she said, he became a different person.

Watson, a tall Texan who lived with Manson's group at suburban Spahn Ranch, sat emotionless throughout the trial. Midway through, he took the stand and calmly confessed that he had stabbed and shot Miss Tate and the others because "I was doing what Charlie told me to do."

Jurors found Watson guilty of first degree murder. A sanity trial followed at which psychiatrists testified. Doctors called by the defense said Watson was "a very sick person." But psychiatrists called by the state said Watson had feigned madness to escape punishment.

The jury decided that Watson was sane when he killed, and they returned a verdict of death in the gas chamber.

The trial of Grogan, 20, was complicated by the absence of the victim's body. Sheriff's deputies dug for weeks at the Manson clan's headquarters, Spahn Ranch, but found no trace of Donald "Shorty" Shea, 35, sometime movie stuntman and ranch hand, who disappeared in August 1969—the month of the Tate murders.

The state claimed that Grogan, following Manson's orders, decapitated Shea after other "family" members tortured the dying man. Young defectors from the Manson tribe testified that they heard Shea's screams and added that they had been told that women members had chopped the body up and disposed of it.

On a legal technicality, Grogan's case ended in a mistrial, but a second trial was quickly convened. After two months of testimony, the jurors took eight hours to decide that Grogan was guilty of first degree murder. They concluded that he should die in the gas chamber. But, on Dec. 23 the court reduced Grogan's sentence to life imprisonment.

More indictments were issued. Bruce Davis, 26, was charged with murder in the Shea and Gary Hinman killings. Mary Brunner, 27, a key witness against Robert Beausoleil in the slaying of Hinman, had been given immunity for her testimony, but then recanted what she said and was indicted herself for murder in the Hinman case. Hinman, 34, a musician, had been found slain at his Malibu home in July 1969, a few weeks before the Tate slayings. The death scene, with bloody scrawlings on the wall, was similar to that at the Tate murders. Beausoleil was sentenced to death row for Hinman's slaying.

After four months of testimony, the jury retired for two weeks to deliberate. Finally they found Manson guilty of first degree murder on both counts. This time they decreed life imprisonment.

Manson faced spectators in the courtroom and shouted, "You're in prison! You're in prison! You're in prison!"

A bailiff who hustled Manson off to his cell said of the clan leader's reaction: "He was a lot more pleased with this verdict than the last one."

A man jumping to his death from the blazing Taeyonkak Hotel in Seoul where more than 160 persons perished in the flames

TWO AMERICANS FREED BY CHINA

The young woman in pink slacks was smiling and exuberant, but the haggard-looking man by her side seemed cautious and withdrawn. Both apparently were stunned when they were suddenly freed from Community Chinese captivity.

The pair debarked Dec. 14 from a U.S. Air Force C141 at McGuire Base in New Jersey. They were Miss Mary Ann Harbert, 25, of Menlo Park, Calif., given up for dead by her parents after she disappeared in 1968 and Richard G. Fecteau, 43, of Lynn, Mass., who had spent much of his 19 years of confinement in solitary. He had been sentenced to 20 years.

Fecteau and John T. Downey, 41, of New Britain, Conn., both civilian employes of the Army, had been captured after a military plane on which they were passengers was shot down on a flight from Japan to South Korea during the Korean War in 1952.

Miss Harbert was aboard a yacht seized in Chinese territorial waters near Hong Kong three years ago. Peking authorities said that Gerald R. McLaughlin of California, owner of the yacht, committed suicide in captivity.

The Chinese had accused Fecteau and Downey of being operatives of the Central Intelligence Agency. They said Miss Harbert had "admitted her mistakes," which may have explained the different treatment the two received.

Leonard W. Johnson Jr., commander of the 9th Aeromedical Evacuation Group at Clark Air Force Base in the Philippines, related what the two captives had told him.

"Fecteau told me he spent a lot of time alone," he said. "He mentioned small walls and very small windows."

Johnson said Miss Harbert told him "she had been allowed to be outside. In fact, at one time, she was given a small garden."

Shortly after the release of Fecteau and Miss Harbert the White House said President Nixon had sent a personal appeal to Peking on behalf of American prisoners, including the two freed and Downey, whose life sentence had been reduced to five more years.

Richard G. Fecteau relaxing in the hospital following his release

Mrs. Jacqueline Kennedy Onassis smiled while her husband, Aristotle, looked dour at a party in the swank Club El Morocco

West German Chancellor Willy Brandt receiving the Nobel Peace Prize from Aase Lionaes, chairman of the Nobel Peace Prize Committee.

Veteran Austrian diplomat Kurt Waldheim, 53, who was chosen to succeed U Thant as secretary-general of the United Nations

263

Project Supervisor: Keith Fuller

Editor: Howard C. Heyn

Assistant Editor: Tom Hoge

Writer-Researcher: Marcia Henning

Photos: Sandy Colton

Promotion and Distribution: Dan Perkes; Jack Elcik

Feature Narratives
Peter Arnett, New York, and Horst
    Faas, Singapore
    U.S. cities and countryside
Howard Benedict, Cocoa Beach, Fla.
    Apollo 14
    Apollo 15
Fred Coleman, London
    British mail strike
    Britain in Common Market
Frank Cormier, Washington, D.C.
    The President's year
Linda Deutsch, Los Angeles
    Tate case sentences
Art Everett, New York
    Trial of Lt. Calley
Robert A. Fasce, Albany, N.Y.
    Thomas Dewey's death
Colin Frost, London
    Northern Ireland riots
Sterling Green, Washington, D.C.
    The new U.S. economy
G. Michael Harmon, Baton Rouge, La.
    Gulf tornadoes
Vern Haugland, Washington, D.C.
    The U.S. aircraft industry
Marcia Henning, New York
    Nostalgia
    Tricia Nixon wedding
    Louisiana rock festival
Howard C. Heyn, New York
    Igor Stravinsky dies
Tom Hoge, New York
    State of the U.N.
    The rich: Old and new
    U.N. seats Republic of China
Brian King, Albany, N.Y.
    Bloodshed at Attica
Jules Loh, New York
    Famine, fighting in Pakistan
    The Pentagon Papers
    The war in Vietnam
Bruce F. Lowitt, New York
    Frazier-Ali fight
Walter Mears, Washington, D.C.
    Congressional review
Syd Moody Jr., New York
    Louis Armstrong: King of Jazz
John E. Nance, Manila
    Philippine lost tribe
Dennis Neeld, Beirut
    A standoff in Middle East?
Charles Ragan, New York
    Offtrack betting launched
Mike Rathet, New York
    Super Bowl
    The World Series
William L. Ryan, New York
    China invites U.S. Ping Pong team
    Nikita Krushchev dies
Larry Stuntz, New York
    The dollar revalued
Jim Walters, Los Angeles
    Los Angeles earthquake

William J. Waugh, Washington, D.C.
    Problems in education
Jeannine Yeomans, San Francisco
    San Quentin escape attempt

Contributing Reporters
    Art Everett, New York
    Phil Thomas, New York
    John Wheeler, New York
    Saigon Staff:
        James Bourdier
        Richard Blystone
        George Esper
        Holger Jensen
        Robin Mannock
        Richard H. Pyle
        Nguyen Gia Thanh
        Robert Tuckman
        J. T. Wolkerstorfer

Photographs
(The illustrations in this volume
were selected for the most part
from the news photo reports of The
Associated Press and, except where
specifically credited, were taken
by staff photographers of The AP
and its member newspapers).

Staff Photographers
    Athens
        Aristotle Saricostas
    Beirut
        Henri Koundakjian
    Berlin
        Edwin Reichert
    Bonn
        Klaus Schlagman
    Buenos Aires
        Max Simon
        Domingo Zenteno Zeggara
    Copenhagen
        Henning Brink
        Mogens Holmberg
        Sigvard Holmer
        Poul Henrik Seifert
    Frankfurt
        Bernhard Frye
        Peter Hillebrecht
        Kurt Strumpf
    Hamburg
        Helmuth Lohmann
    Jakarta
        Cornelius Joost Katoppo
    Kuala Lumpur
        Tee Ee
    London
        Lawrence Harris
        Peter Kemp
        William F. Rider Rider
        Sidney Smart
        Edward S. Worth
    Madrid
        Leopoldo Gomez Gonzalez

Manila
    Alfonso del Mundo
Milan
    Raoul Fornezza
    Armando Trovati
Moscow
    Roger Leddington
Munich
    Dieter Endlicher
Oslo
    Tom Brauner Jensen
    Paul Oweson
Paris
    Phillipe Barbaud
    Spartaco Bodini
    Jean Pierre Etchegaray
    Pierre Godot
    Ernest Gacquere
    Michel Laurent
    Jean Jacques Levy
    Michel Claude Lipchitz
    Jacques Marqueton
    Michael Nash
    Georges Raulin Jr.
    Albert Roques
Rome
    Guiseppe Anastasi
    Giulio Broglio
    Giovanni Foggia
    Claudio Luffoli
    Massimo Sambucetti
    Mario Torrisi
Saigon
    James Bourdier
    Rick Merron
    Max Nash
    Dang Van Phuoc
    Carl D. Robinson
    Neal Ulevich
    Huynh Cong "Nick" Ut
    Hubert Van Es
Seoul
    Kim Chon-Kil
Singapore
    Horst Faas
Tel Aviv
    Brian Calvert
Tokyo
    Yuichi Ishizori
    Max Desfor
    Mitsunori Chigita
    Akira Sekiguchi
    Keiichi Mori
Albany
    Robert Schutz
Atlanta
    Horace W. Cort
    Charles E. Kelly
    Joe Holloway
Austin
    Ted Powers
Baltimore
    William A. Smith
Boston
    William Chaplis
    Francis C. Curtin
    J. Walter Green
    A. W. Maloof
Chicago
    John Filo
    Frederick H. Jewell
    Edward S. Kitch
    Charles E. Knoblock
    James Palmer
    Laurence E. Stoddard
Cincinnati
    Harvey E. Smith
Cleveland
    Julian C. Wilson
Columbia
    Louis Krasky
Columbus
    Gene E. Herrick
Dallas
    Charles Bennett

Ferd Kaufman
Dave Taylor
Harold Waters
Denver
    Robert D. Scott
Detroit
    James McKnight
    Rich Schweinwald
    Preston Stroup
Harrisburg
    Paul Vathis
Houston
    Edward F. Kolenovsky
Indianapolis
    Charles Robinson
Kansas City
    William P. Straeter Jr.
Los Angeles
    George Brich
    Harold F. Filan
    Wallace H. Fong Jr.
    Harry P. Matosian
    David F. Smith
    Edward C. Widdis
Miami
    Mark Foley
    James P. Kerlin
    Steven Starr
    Hal Valentine
Milwaukee
    Paul J. Shane
Minneapolis
    Robert J. Walsh
New Orleans
    Jack R. Thornell
New York
    Edward T. Adams
    Murray L. Becker
    Anthony Camerano
    Ron Frehm
    Daniel J. Grossi
    Harry L. Harris
    J. Spencer Jones
    Jack Kanthal
    Martin M. Lederhandler
    John J. Lent
    David Pickoff
    John P. Rooney
    Ray Stubblebine
    James Wells
Philadelphia
    Wilson G. Ingraham
    Ronald B. Kennedy
    Warren M. Winterbottom
Pittsburgh
    Harry Cabluck
Raleigh
    Perry Aycock
San Francisco
    Richard Drew
    Robert H. Houston
    Robert K. Klein
    Sal Veder
Sacramento
    Walter Zeboski
Seattle
    Barry R. Sweet
St. Louis
    Frederick O. Waters
Tallahassee
    William M. Hudson
Washington
    Henry D. Burroughs Jr.
    Robert A. Daugherty
    John A. Duricka
    Harvey W. Georges
    Charles P. Gorry
    Henry Giffin
    Charles W. Harrity
    Byron H. Rollins
    John H. Rous
    Charles B. Tasnadi

Almanac Editor
Dick Madden

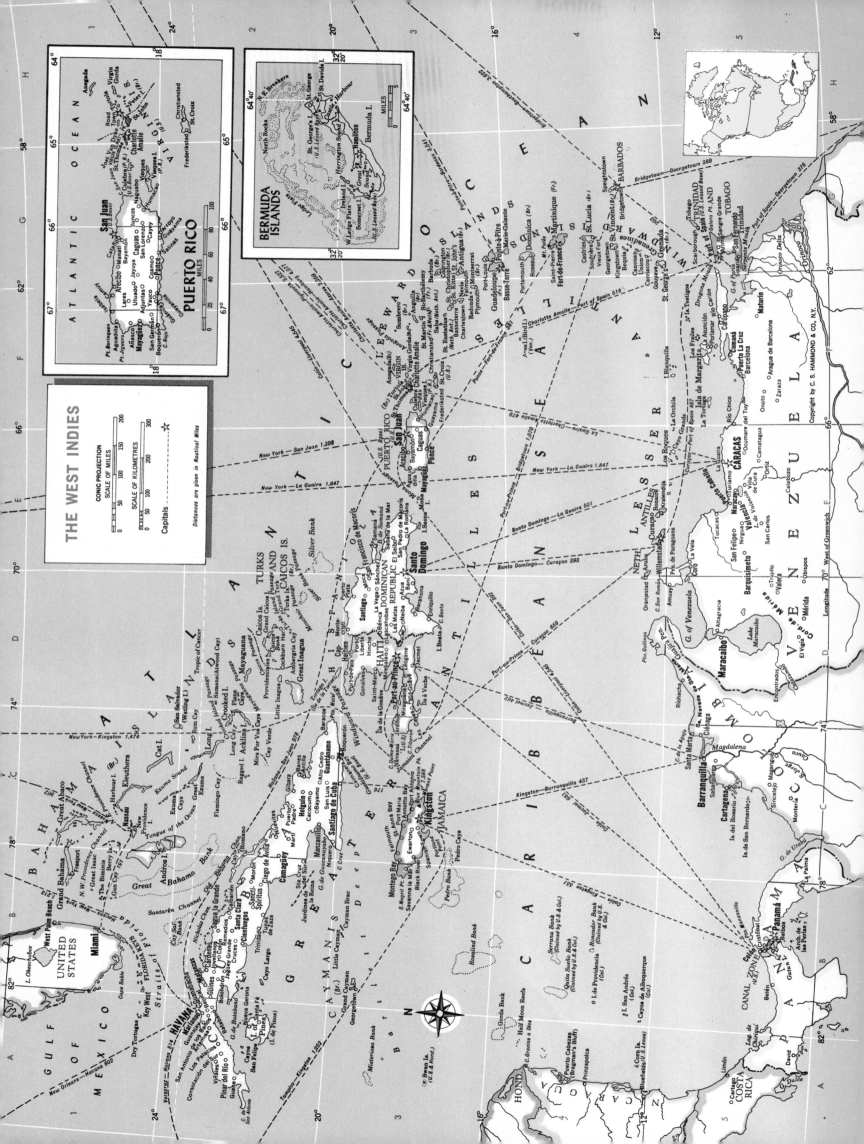

THE WEST INDIES

CONIC PROJECTION
SCALE OF MILES
0   50   100   150   200

SCALE OF KILOMETRES
0   50   100   200   300

★ Capitals

Distances are given in Nautical Miles

PUERTO RICO

ATLANTIC OCEAN

San Juan

Pt. Borinquen
Aguadilla
Pt. Jiguero
Añasco
Mayagüez
San Germán
Boquerón
C. Rojo

Arecibo Manatí
Utuado Jayuya
Adjuntas
Yauco

Bayamón
Juncos
Caguas Humacao
San Lorenzo
Arroyo
Coamo Guayama
Salinas

Naguabo

Vieques I. (P.R.)

MILES
0   20   40   60   80   100

BERMUDA ISLANDS

N.E. Breakers
North Rocks
St. George I. St. George
St. David's I.
Ireland I. Castle Harbour
Hamilton
Great Sound Harrington Sound
Somerset I. Bermuda I.
Long Bird I.
U.S. Leased Base

MILES
0   5

Key place names across the map

ATLANTIC OCEAN

LEEWARD ISLANDS

WINDWARD ISLANDS

LESSER ANTILLES

GREATER ANTILLES

CARIBBEAN SEA

BAHAMA ISLANDS

UNITED STATES

GULF OF MEXICO

MEXICO

CUBA

HAVANA

JAMAICA
Kingston

HAITI
Port-au-Prince

DOMINICAN REPUBLIC
Santo Domingo

PUERTO RICO (U.S.)
San Juan

VIRGIN ISLANDS

HISPANIOLA

TURKS AND CAICOS IS.

VENEZUELA
CARACAS
Maracaibo
Barquisimeto
Valencia

COLOMBIA
Barranquilla
Cartagena

PANAMA
CANAL ZONE

COSTA RICA
NICARAGUA
HONDURAS

Copyright by C. S. HAMMOND & CO., N.Y.

New York — San Juan 1,399
New York — La Guaira 1,847
New York — Kingston 1,474
Santo Domingo — La Guaira 501
Santo Domingo — Curaçao 393
Kingston — Barranquilla 437
Bridgetown — Georgetown 389
Port of Spain — Georgetown 378

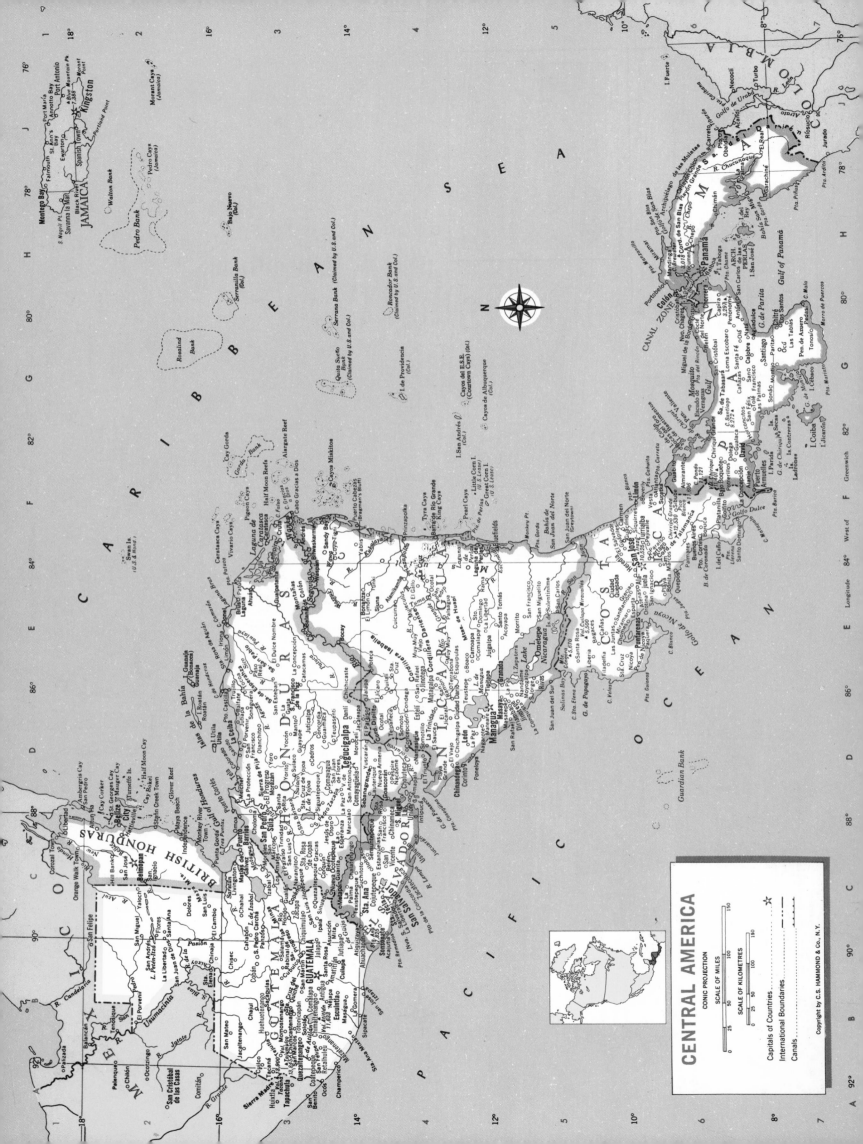

CENTRAL AMERICA

CONIC PROJECTION

SCALE OF MILES
0   25   50   100   150

SCALE OF KILOMETRES
0 25 50   100   150

Capitals of Countries............ ☆
International Boundaries............ ---
Canals............ ---

Copyright by C.S. HAMMOND & Co., N.Y.

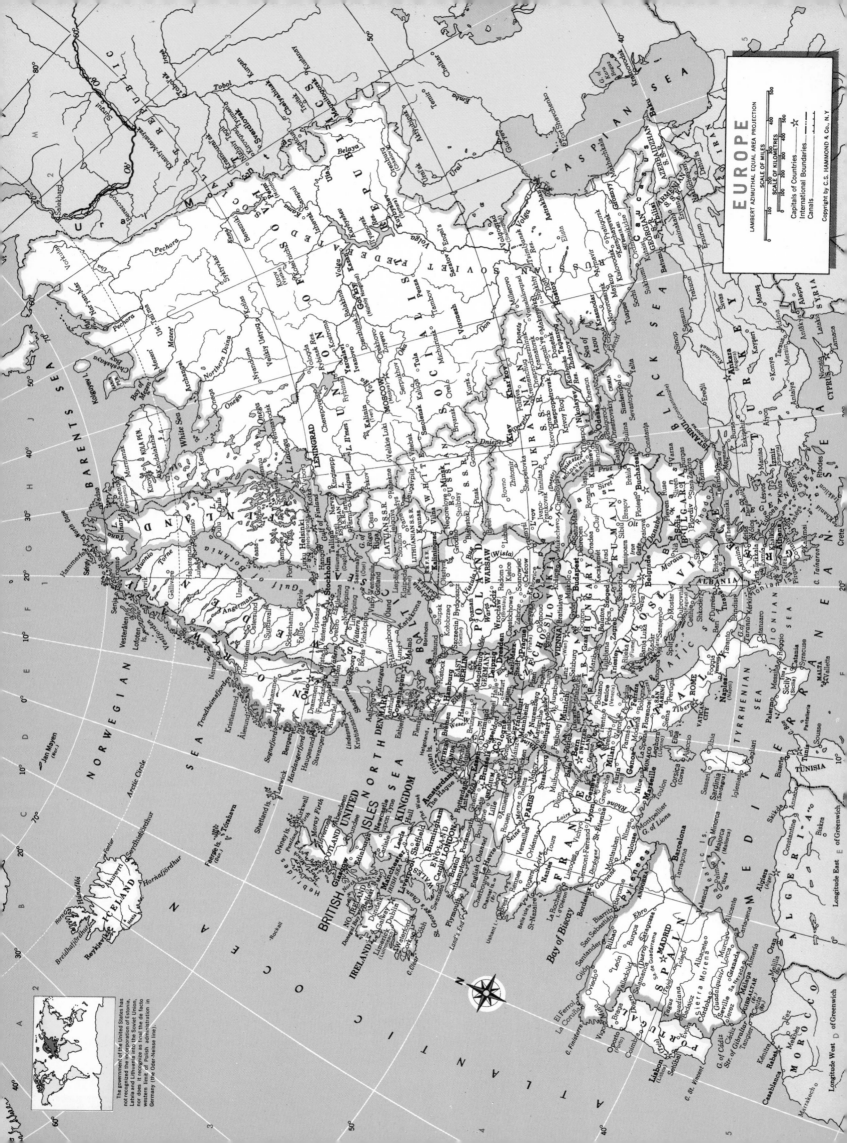

EUROPE

LAMBERT AZIMUTHAL EQUAL AREA PROJECTION

SCALE OF MILES

SCALE OF KILOMETRES

Capitals of Countries .... ★
International Boundaries .... ——
Canals .... ＝＝＝

Copyright by C.S. HAMMOND & Co., N.Y.

The government of the United States has not recognized the incorporation of Estonia, Latvia and Lithuania into the Soviet Union, nor does it recognize as lawful the de facto western limit of Polish administration in Germany (the Oder-Neisse line).

UNITED KINGDOM and IRELAND

BONNE PROJECTION

SCALE OF MILES

SCALE OF KILOMETRES

Capitals of Countries .... ★

Canals ....

SHETLAND ISLANDS
Same scale as main map.

GREATER LONDON

LONDON (inset)

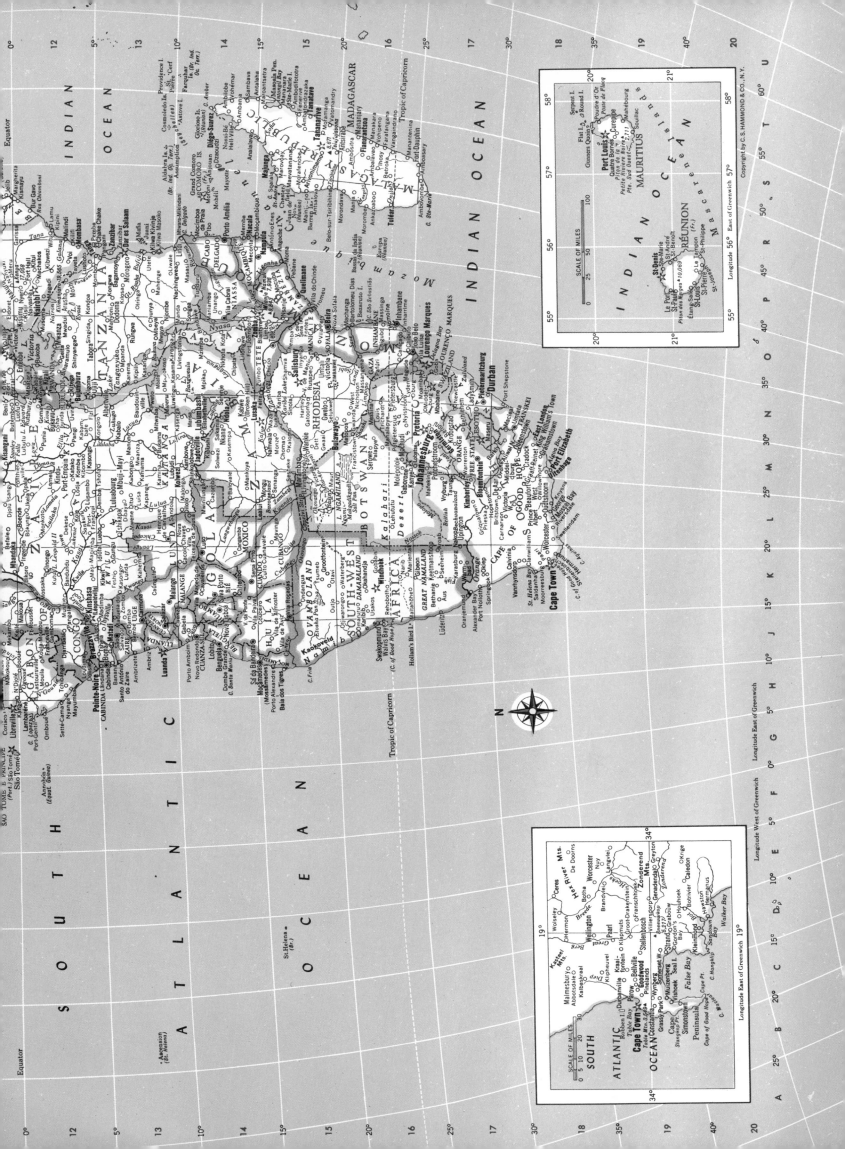

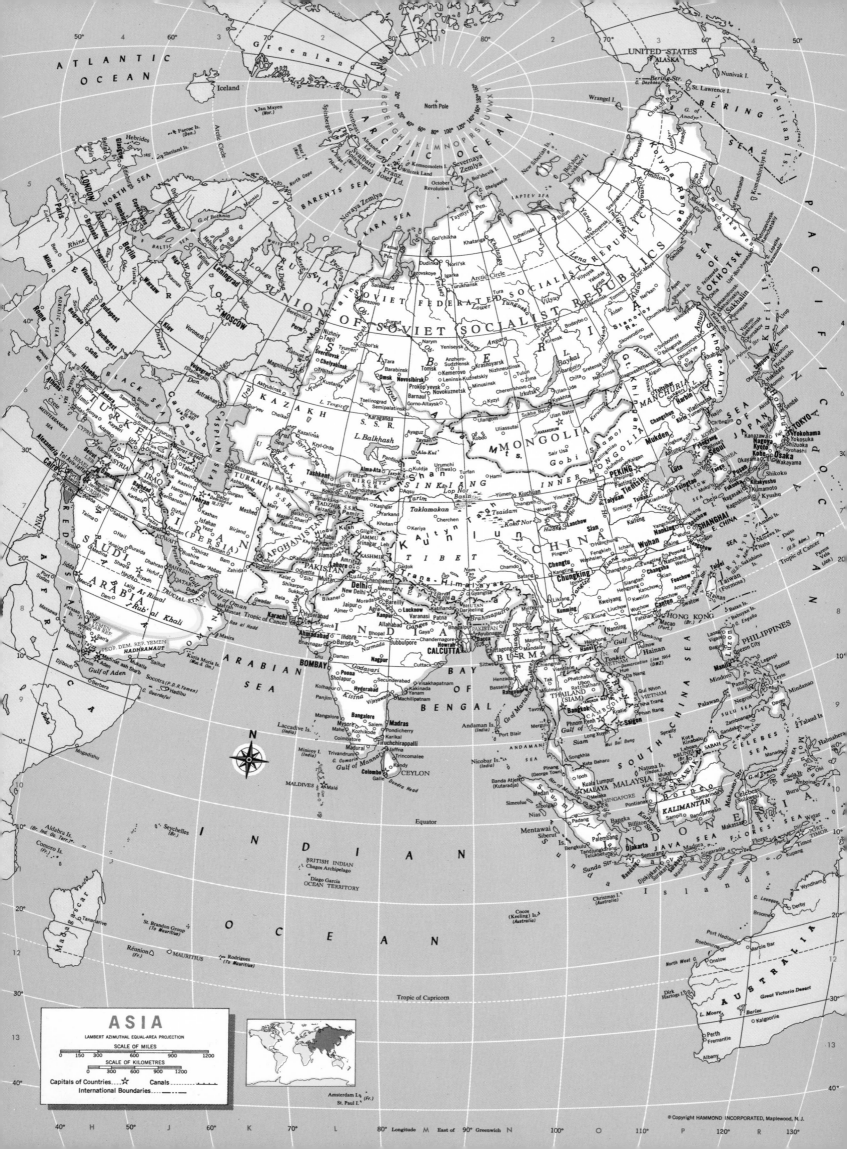

ASIA

LAMBERT AZIMUTHAL EQUAL-AREA PROJECTION

SCALE OF MILES

0 150 300   600   900   1200

SCALE OF KILOMETRES

0   300   600   900   1200

Capitals of Countries....☆   Canals ....
International Boundaries _____

® Copyright HAMMOND INCORPORATED, Maplewood, N.J.

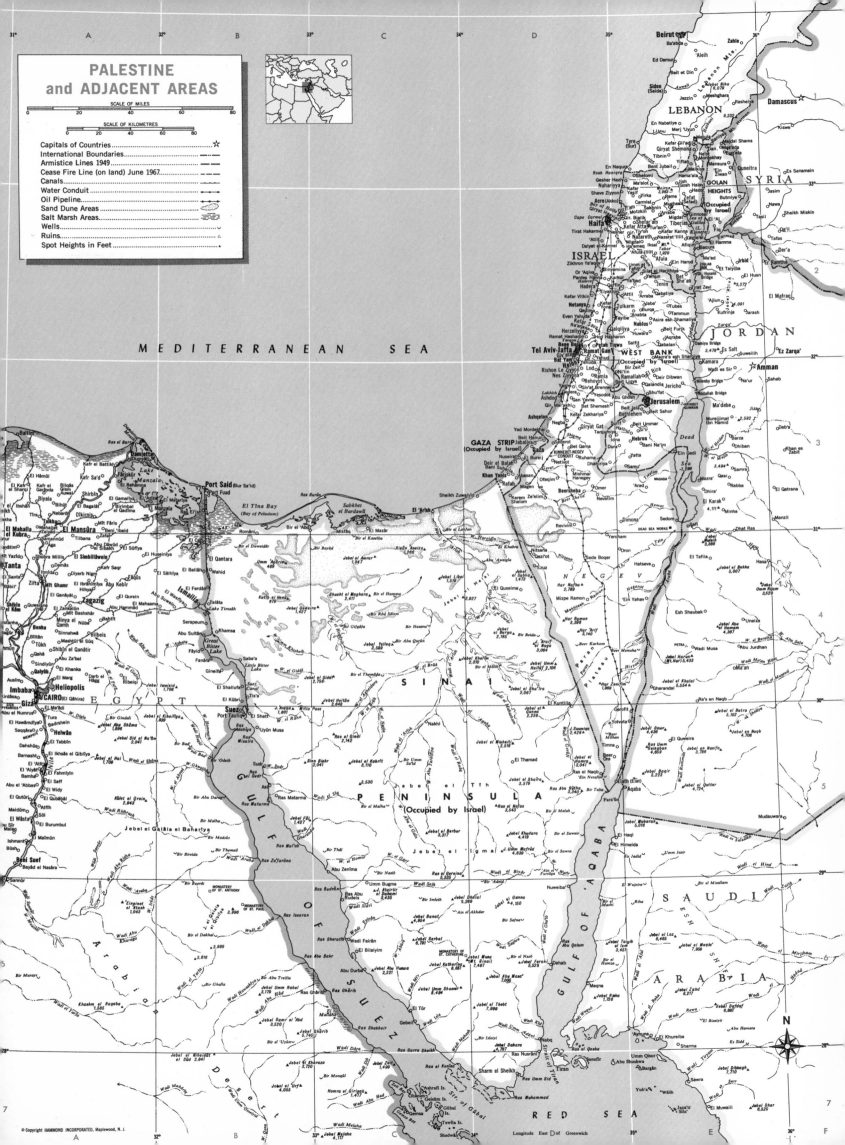

CHINA and MONGOLIA

CONIC PROJECTION

SCALE OF MILES
0 100 200 300 400 500

SCALE OF KILOMETRES
0 100 200 300 400 500

Capitals of Countries......☆
Provincial Capitals.........◉
Canals........................
International Boundaries....
Provincial Boundaries......
Walls.........................

Copyright by C.S. Hammond & Co., N.Y.

*Wuhan municipality consists of Hankow, Hanyang and Wuchang.

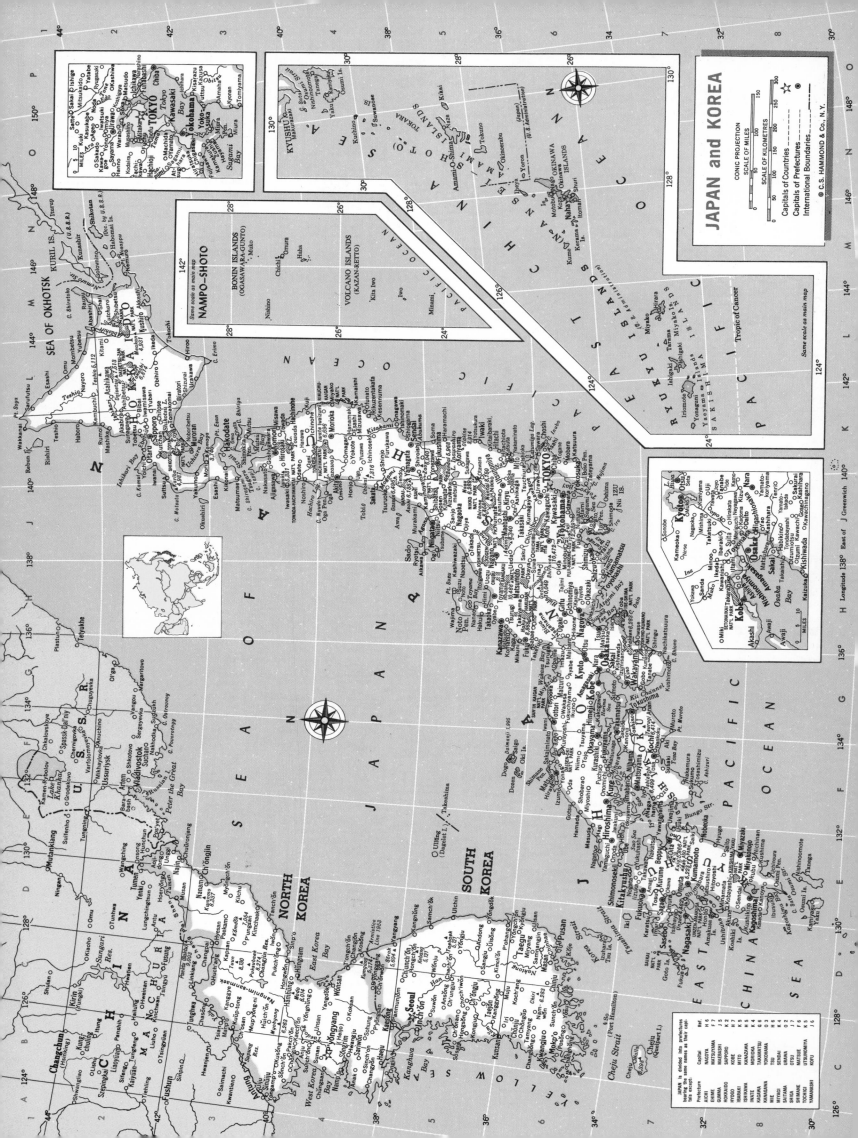

JAPAN and KOREA

CONIC PROJECTION

SCALE OF MILES

SCALE OF KILOMETRES

Capitals of Countries ☆
Capitals of Prefectures ⊛
International Boundaries

© C.S. HAMMOND & Co., N.Y.

NAMPO-SHOTO
Same scale as main map

BONIN ISLANDS
(OGASAWARA-GUNTO)

VOLCANO ISLANDS
(KAZAN-RETTO)

JAPAN is divided into prefectures bearing the same names as their capitals except:

Prefecture	Capital	Ref.
AICHI	NAGOYA	H 7
EHIME	MATSUYAMA	J 5
GUMMA	MAEBASHI	H 7
HOKKAIDO	SAPPORO	M 2
HYOGO	KOBE	H 7
IBARAKI	MITO	N 5
ISHIKAWA	KANAZAWA	H 6
IWATE	MORIOKA	O 3
KAGAWA	TAKAMATSU	H 6
KANAGAWA	YOKOHAMA	O 3
MIE	TSU	H 6
MIYAGI	SENDAI	N 4
SAGA	SAGA	J 7
SHIGA	OTSU	H 6
SHIMANE	MATSUE	J 6
TOCHIGI	UTSUNOMIYA	K 5
YAMANASHI	KOFU	J 6

AP News Almanac

CHRONOLOGY–1971

JANUARY

2—Sixty-six persons were killed when a barrier collapsed at Ibrox soccer stadium in Glasgow, Scotland, and resulted in a panic.

4—President Nixon said he would regard the servicing of Soviet "nuclear" submarines "either in Cuba or from Cuba" as a violation of a new understanding obtained from Moscow last October.

4—President Anwar el-Sadat of Egypt acknowledged that Soviet soldiers had been brought in to man Egyptian missile sites and said six of them had been killed in a raid on Dahshur, 20 miles south of Cairo.

5—The 91st Congress was ranked by President Nixon as one that would be remembered in history "not for what it did, but for what it failed to do." President Nixon complained that Congress had failed to act on welfare reform, Federal revenue sharing and a host of other "excellent proposals" before adjourning Jan. 2.

5—United Nations representatives from Israel, Jordan and the United Arab Republic resumed indirect peace talks in New York under the auspices of Dr. Gunnar V. Jarring of Sweden, Secretary-General U Thant's special United Nations representative for the Middle East.

7—The Federal Reserve Board lowered from 5.5 to 5.24 per cent the interest rate on loans to member banks in temporary need of funds. The action brought the discount rate to the lowest point since December 1968.

10—The United States protested to the Soviet Union over the harassing of United States citizens in Moscow. The protest demanded an end to the campaign begun by the Soviet government in retaliation against harassment of Soviet citizens by militant Jewish groups in the United States.

11—A Federal grand jury in Harrisburg, Pa., indicted six persons on charges of conspiring to kidnap a presidential adviser, Henry Kissinger, and to blow up heating systems of Federal buildings in Washington. Among the six was the Rev. Philip F. Berrigan, an antiwar priest serving a prison term for destroying draft cards.

14—Seventy Brazilian revolutionaries arrived in Chile and were granted political asylum. Their freedom had been demanded by the kidnapers of the Swiss Ambassador to Brazil, Giovanni Enrico Bucher.

14—A court-martial jury of six officers acquitted a former Louisiana farm hand, Sgt. Charles E. Hutto, who was accused of joining in the alleged slaughter of South Vietnamese civilians at My Lai.

16—Giovanni Enrico Bucher, the Swiss Ambassador to Brazil, who was kidnaped 40 days ago, was released in Rio De Janeiro.

16—The United States Steel Corp. announced price increases of about 6.8 per cent on major construction products.

19—New York City patrolmen ended their six-day walkout after union delegates voted return to duty. Unsettled were wage parity and possible penalities for the strike.

19—House Democrats chose Carl Albert of Oklahoma as speaker and Hale Boggs of Louisiana as majority leader. Both men were part of the Democratic leadership team under former Speaker John W. McCormack of Massachusetts in the 91st Congress.

21—The 92nd Congress convened in Washington with a suprise coup toppling Senator Edward M. Kennedy as assistant majority leader of the Senate. Sen. Robert C. Byrd of West Virginia won the post, 31 to 24.

22—President Nixon, in his second State of the Union message, proposed that state and local governments be given at least $16 billion a year in largely unrestricted federal funds. He proposed an intensive effort to conquer cancer, and said he would ask Congress for an extra $100-million to finance it.

26—The Soviet Union announced that its unmanned Venera 7 last month made the first soft landing on the torrid surface of Venus and sent back data for more than 20 minutes.

29—President Nixon sent to Congress a budget of $229.2 billion that he termed "expansionary but not inflationary" for the nation's economy. The President estimated revenues at $217.6 billion, leaving a deficit of $11.6 billion for the fiscal year of 1972.

29—Enemy supply and infiltration routes in southern Laos were bombed by American planes in what was described at Saigon as one of the most intensive aerial campaigns of the war.

29—All charges against Maj. Gen. Samuel W. Koster, division commander of the troops who allegedly participated in a massacre of civilians at the South Vietnamese hamlet of My Lai, were dismissed by the Army.

29—Rogers C. B. Morton was sworn in as Secretary of Interior, replacing Walter J. Hickel, who was dismissed by the President last November.

FEBRUARY

3—Twenty-four persons were fatally injured and 32 others were hospitalized when a blast and fire leveled a trap flares building at a Thiokol Chemical Corporation plant in Georgia.

4—The United States command announced that the Unites States and South Vietnam troops launched a major operation into the northwest corner of South Vietnam to clear the way toward the Ho Chi Minh Trail in Laos.

4—Rolls Royce, Ltd., the British manufacturer of automobiles and jet engines, declared bankruptcy. The company blamed losses in developing an engine for the Lockheed Aircraft Corp., and said it would not proceed with the engine under the present contract.

4—For the first time in seven months the unemployment rate declined two-tenths of a per cent point in the month of January, the Labor department reported.

5—Some 600 British troops were flown to Belfast, Northern Ireland, after a night of rioting in which four civilians and one soldier were killed.

6—The three astronauts of Apollo 14 started back to earth after Capt. Alan Shepard and Comdr. Edgar Mitchell completed two successful moon walks and collected moon samples.

7—In Switzerland, men voters reversed a decision made 12 years ago and approved a woman's suffrage amendment giving women the right to vote in federal elections and to hold federal office.

7—The Central Committee of Poland's Communist party suspended Wladyslaw Gomulka, the former party chief, from his membership on the committee because of his "serious mistakes in recent years."

8—The Senate confirmed the nomination of John B. Connally Jr., former Governor of Texas, to be Secretary of the Treasury.

9—The six Common Market countries agreed after months of argument to a plan to make their trade area into a single currency area over the next decade.

9—The Apollo 14 mission ended as the three astronauts rode their spacecraft capsule into the Pacific Ocean in a safe and precise splashdown.

9—A severe earthquake struck Southern California, killing at least 62 persons and causing damage estimated at more than $1 billion in Los Angeles and adjacent areas. Hardest hit were a large convalescent institution and a veterans' hospital where 80 persons were trapped when two buildings collapsed.

10—A helicopter carrying four news photographers was shot down in Laos. Those missing and presumed dead included two winners of the Robert Capa award—Larry Burrows of Life and Henri Huet of

The Associated Press; Kent Potter of United Press International, and Keisaburo Shimamoto of the Pan-Asia Newspaper Alliance.

11—A treaty banning nuclear weapons from the ocean floor was signed by the United States and Soviet Russia; President Nixon joined Soviet and British representatives in recommending a similar pact controlling such weapons on land areas.

14—Oil companies of 23 western nations agreed at Teheran to additional payments of more than $10 billion to six Persian Gulf states for a five-year agreement intended to stabilize the industry.

15—After using the metric system for hundreds of years, under which the pound was divided into 240 pence, the British currency was decimalized and the pound became 100 pence.

18—President Nixon, in a message to Congress, proposed a health care package he said would provide almost all Americans with better medical services, paid for largely with funds provided by employers.

22—President Nixon declared a major disaster for the state of Mississippi following a rash of tornadoes which raged through dozens of towns in the Mississippi and Louisiana delta areas. The number of dead in those two states reached more than 100, and the injured numbered 500.

22—President Thieu of South Vietnam listed a new reason for the incursion into Laos, stating that it successfully prevented a planned North Vietnamese drive to seize the five northern provinces of South Vietnam.

23—First Lieut. William Calley Jr. testified at his court-martial that he had shot some civilians in a ditch in the village of My Lai 4, adding he had been acting under orders and had no regrets.

24—Algeria took over majority control (51 per cent) of all French oil interests in that country and nationalized the French companies' assets in natural gas and gas pipelines.

25—A three-day conference in Brussels on the problems of Soviet Jews closed with an appeal by the leaders of world Jewish organizations that the Soviet Union be pressed by world opinion to give its Jewish citizens the right to their own cultural and religious life and the chance to emigrate.

26—The Army announced that Col. Oran K. Henderson, former commander of the Americal Division's 11th Brigade, would be tried by a general court-martial on charges of covering up the alleged massacre at the South Vietnamese hamlet of My Lai 4 in March 1968.

MARCH

1—A powerful bomb blasted a men's room and severely damaged adjoining rooms in the Senate wing of Washington's Capitol building; 30 minutes earlier a man warned by phone that the bombing would be retaliation for the American-backed movement into Laos.

2—The U.S. Supreme Court decreed that persons cannot be jailed solely because they are unable immediately to pay fines; in another ruling the court held that state divorce courts should be opened to persons too poor to afford the costs of their suits.

2—In Moscow, 30 Soviet Jews were granted permission to emigrate to Israel.

2—Held captive nearly seven months by Tupamaro guerrillas, Claude L. Fly, an American agronomist in Uruguay, was released in Montevideo after he suffered a heart attack.

4—Canada's Prime Minister Pierre Elliott Trudeau, 51-year-old bachelor, married Margaret Sinclair, 22, in a Roman Catholic ceremony at Vancouver, B.C.

8—A seven-month cease-fire along the Suez Canal ended, but neither Egypt nor Israel renewed hostilities at once; both appeared willing to cooperate in negotiations for a Middle East peace accord when the cease-fire deadline was not extended.

8—More than 1,000 U.S. planes attacked enemy forces in Laos and Cambodia, some in support of South Vietnamese who were consolidating their positions on the Ho Chi Minh trail, about 25 miles inside Laos.

8—Capt. Ernest L. Medina, as commander of an infantry company accused of over-running the hamlet of My Lai 4 and killing at least 100 South Vietnamese civilians, was ordered to stand court-martial on charges of premeditated murder and assault with a deadly weapon.

8—Heavyweight champion Joe Frazier won a 15-round decision over Muhammad Ali in New York's Madison Square Garden. Ali, also known as Cassius Clay, held the championship until 1967, when he lost his New York license and was stripped of the title for refusing induction to the armed forces on the exemption claim that he was a Moslem minister.

8—Draft exemptions cannot be granted to young men who claim they are conscientious objectors unless they oppose all wars, not just one—such as Indochina—which they consider "unjust." This was set out in an 8-to-1 ruling by the U.S. Supreme Court.

8—Four U.S. airmen kidnaped by Turkish leftists and held for $400,000 ransom were released in Ankara; they had been made captive five days earlier while leaving their U.S. radar base near that city.

10—Following serious erosion of his Liberal party's majority in parliament, John G. Gorton was deposed as Australia's prime minister and was replaced by William McMahon, minister of foreign affairs; the action was taken by party members in a secret ballot.

10—Tupamaro guerrillas in Montevideo kidnaped Uruguay's attorney general, Guido Berro Oribe, 59, at his home; there were rumors he was held for questioning about imprisoned Tupamaros.

12—Armed forces ousted the government of Turkey but made no immediate move to take over; they ordered Premier Suleyman Demirel to resign or face a military coup. Military officers demanded a government strong enough to halt what they called a state of anarchy.

13—Paul Rose, 27, was sentenced in Montreal to life imprisonment for his part in the slaying of Pierre Laporte, Quebec's minister of labor, on Oct. 16, 1970. Laporte was abducted Oct. 10 by members of the Front for Liberation of Quebec. Pending were trials of Rose and two accomplices on kidnaping charges.

14—Sheik Mujibur Rahman announced he was taking over East Pakistan, geographically separated from West Pakistan, seat of the central government. Seeking autonomy for East Pakistan, he based his right to control that area upon the Awami League's success last December in winning a majority of seats in both the eastern provincial assembly and the National Assembly in West Pakistan.

15—The fourth round of talks on limitation of strategic nuclear arms was opened in Vienna by American and Soviet Union delegations.

17—India's New Congress party reelected Prime Minister Indira Gandhi as their leader, following her landslide victory in a general election, and President V. V. Giri asked her to form a new cabinet.

17—President Nixon signed a bill increasing Social Security payments by 10 per cent, made effective Jan. 1, 1972 by congressional amendment of the legislation.

18—Federal police said in Lima, Peru that 400 to 600 persons died in an avalanche at Chungar, a mining camp 50 miles north of the capital.

19—Turkey's President Cevdet Sunay named Nihat Erim as premier to replace Suleyman Demirel, ousted a week earlier in a constitutional crisis.

20—Maj. James D. Chichester-Clark, prime minister of Northern Ireland, resigned in Belfast after resisting Protestant pressure for militant moves against Roman Catholics, two church groups long engaged in violent rioting.

22—The National Railroad Passenger Corporation announced routes and schedules of 184 daily trains to serve 114 U.S. cities, about half the service previously available; the corporation then known as Railpax, was created by Congress to relieve railroads of their expensive passenger responsibilities.

23—Argentina's three commanders of the armed forces took control as a junta after deposing Gen. Roberto Marcelo Levingston as president; the junta named Lt. Gen. Alejandro Agustin Lanusse of the army as its leader.

23—Tupamaro guerrillas freed Uruguay's attorney general, Guido Berro Oribe, who was kidnaped in Montevideo March 10.

23—A Protestant moderate, Brian Faulkner, was elected by the Union party as Northern Ireland's prime minister; he succeeded Maj. James D. Chichester-Clark, who resigned March 21 in a controversy over control of Roman Catholics seeking the union of Northern Ireland with the Republic of Ireland in continued armed violence between the two church groups.

24—The last South Vietnam troops in Laos—about 2,000—have withdrawn to their own border, ending a drive against enemy supply lines that began 44 days earlier; North Vietnam forces were close behind the departing troops. Nearly 20,000 South Vietnamese had been removed earlier, chiefly by helicopter.

24—Further funding of the controversial supersonic transport aircraft program was cut off by a 51 to 46 vote of the Senate; employes indicated the action reduced by about 7,000 the work force of Boeing Co., prime contractor, in Seattle.

26—A junta of three military officers who took over control of Argentina March 23, named Alejandro Agustin Lanusse, the junta's leader, as president.

28—The army of the central government in West Pakistan has taken control of Dacca, the capital of East Pakistan, in a drive to crush a nationalist movement there, an AP correspondent reported with Washington confirmation; other observers said East Pakistan tried to claim the majority political power it won in December, and the central government's forces moved in to forestall this after East-West Pakistan conferences collapsed.

29—President Nixon put into effect a system of restraints intended to curb the spiral of wages and prices in the construction industry; he termed the program largely self regulating. The order also reactivated the Davis-Bacon Act requiring contractors to pay union scale wages on federal projects.

29—In Los Angeles, death in the gas chamber was decreed for Charles Manson and three young women of his hippie "family" by the same jurors who two months ago found them guilty of the seven Tate-La Bianca murders.

30—Russia opened, in Moscow, the 24th Communist party congress at which the Soviet leader, Leonid I. Brezhnev, declared his country's peaceful intentions.

31—First Lt. William L. Calley Jr. was sentenced to life imprisonment for slaying at least 22 South Vietnamese civilians at My Lai 4 three years ago; Calley had been convicted March 29 by court-martial and could have received the death sentence.

APRIL

1—Newsmen returning to India reported that Sheik Mujibur Rahman's "liberation forces" in East Pakistan seized Jessore, forcing West Pakistani troops into a camp outside that city.

2—The Bureau of Labor Statistics in Washington reported the unemployment rate rose again to 6 per cent in March, after two months of decline.

2—In Tripoli, the Libyan government signed with western oil companies a five-year agreement raising the crude oil price from $2.55 a barrel to $3.45.

3—The White House announced that President Nixon would review personally the case of William L. Calley, convicted by court-martial of premeditated murder in the slayings of at least 22 civilians at My Lai 4; he was told he could appeal to the courts or ask the President to make a final decision. Calley, sentenced to life imprisonment, was released from the stockade at Ft. Benning, Ga., and confined to his apartment pending appeals.

6—Mayor Richard J. Daley of Chicago, a Democrat, won reelection for a fifth four-year term.

8—In South Vietnam, the U.S. Command reported that 88 American soldiers were killed the previous week, the highest weekly toll in nearly 10 months.

9—Members of the U.S. table tennis team crossed from Hong Kong into Communist China for a week of exhibition matches. They were the first Americans to visit China as a group since the mid-1950s.

10—Three American newsmen entered Red China to cover the visit of a U.S. table tennis team in a surprise reversal of the Communist policy of excluding American journalists. The three were John Roderick of The Associated Press and John Rich and Jack Reynolds of the National Broadcasting Company.

10—Administration officials in Washington reported that the Soviet Union airlifted into Egypt a small number of advanced jet fighters which allied officers said were capable of outperforming any other fighter in the world, including the U.S.-made F4 Phantom jet.

11—North Vietnamese elected a new 420-seat National Assembly in the first general elections since 1964. The official North Vietnam press agency said that, two hours before the polling booths closed, 95 to 97 per cent of the voters had cast their ballots.

12—Red Chinese Premier Chou En-lai warned India against any act of aggression against Pakistan, whose troops were endeavoring to put down an autonomy movement in East Pakistan.

13—A government scientist reported that rocks brought back by the Apollo 14 astronauts had dashed hopes that any life existed on the moon. Dr. Robin Brett, chief geochemist at the manned spacecraft center in Houston, told the American Geophysical Union in Washington that a chemical analysis of the rocks led to this conclusion.

13—Leaders of East Pakistan's secession movement announced the formation of a cabinet. Although their chief, Sheik Mujibur Rahman, was reportedly in prison in West Pakistan, the command group named him president of the breakaway province.

14—President Nixon announced a program designed to improve relations between the United States and Communist China. U.S. currency controls barring American dollars in dealings with Peking would be dropped. The United States would expedite visas or entry permits for visitors from China. Washington would prepare a list of nonstrategic goods which might be shipped to China without a specific license. Direct imports of specified items from China would be authorized.

16—Dr. Albert H. Bowker, chancellor of the City University in New York since 1963, was named chancellor of the University of California at Berkeley. The 51-year-old mathematician was chosen by the university's board of regents at a meeting in Los Angeles.

18—In Newark, the board of education and the Newark Teachers Union approved a contract proposed by Mayor Kenneth A. Gibson, ending a strike that kept half of the city's students—about 80,000—out of classes for 11 weeks.

19—The layoff of 8,250 New York state employes was announced by budget officials who detailed widespread reductions in such public services as health, higher education and recreation. The office of Budget Director Richard L. Dunham also announced the abolition of about 4,000 vacant state jobs.

20—The Supreme Court unanimously upheld the constitutionality of busing as a means to "dismantle the dual school systems" of the South, but made clear the decision did not apply to northern-style segregation based on neighborhood patterns. The ruling, as seen by lawyers, meant that most Southern cities would have to increase classroom integration considerably.

20—Bolivian painter Benjamin Mendoza was convicted in the Philippines of trying to stab Pope Paul VI during the Pontiff's visit there in November 1970. The court sentenced Mendoza to a minimum of two years, four months and one day in jail, but his counsel entered an appeal.

22—Tilman Durdin, a New York Times correspondent admitted to Red China, said doctors at a hospital in Shanghai claimed that they led the world in reconnecting severed hands, arms and fingers. The physicians cited one case in which a hand was successfully rejoined to an arm 36 hours after it had been severed.

25—When the Soviet spaceship Soyuz 10 docked with the huge orbiting space laboratory Salyut, it was "a little like a train entering a railroad terminal," one of the Soyuz crew members said at a news conference after the craft returned to the earth.

26—The Supreme Court voted 5-3 to uphold the constitutionality of state referendum laws that permit a majority of the voters in a community to block construction of low-rent housing for the poor.

28—Federal District Judge Gerhard A. Gessell ruled that the United Mine Workers of America, its multimillion-dollar welfare and retirement fund and the union-owned National Bank of Washington were jointly liable for millions of dollars in damages. Gessell held that the damages were payable to rank-and-file coal miners and miners' widows. The ruling grew out of a $75 million breach-of-trust civil suit filed in Washington in 1969 by a group of miners and widows.

29—President Nixon told a televised news conference that a residual force of U.S. troops would remain in South Vietnam indefinitely—"no matter how long it takes"—if Hanoi refused to release American prisoners of war. Nixon said he would not set a firm date for withdrawal until he received "not just the promise to discuss the release of our prisoners, but a commitment to release our prisoners."

MAY

1—The National Railroad Passenger Corporation known as Amtrak, officially went into business, bringing to the nation a new era of intercity rail service, but eliminating almost 200 trains, including some famous ones. The new quasi-government operator of the deficit-ridden rail passenger service promised to provide faster and more comfortable service on the lines that remained.

2—Washington, D.C. police ordered 30,000 antiwar protesters from their encampment on the banks of the Potomac in a sudden move that began just after dawn. City officials said the Nixon Administration had made the decision to disperse the Mayday Tribe, most of whom were sleeping or still listening to an all-night rock concert, when the order went out.

2—Cairo's official Middle East News Agency announced that Egyptian Vice President Aly Sabry had been relieved of his post. No explanation was given for the abrupt removal of the 50-year-old official who had played a role in the seizure of power from King Farouk in 1952.

3—Walter Ulbricht, the leader of the East German Communist party for the past 25 years, resigned; he cited old age and ill health. Erich Honecker, 58, was named as his successor.

5—Five major banks in West Germany, Switzerland, Belgium, the Netherlands and Austria withdrew their support of the U.S. dollar and closed down their foreign exchange markets.

5—A bronze statue by Edgar Degas, *La Petite Danseus de Quatorze Ans,* set a world price record for sculpture of $380,000 in a New York auction of 74 works of art from the collection of California industrialist Norton Simon.

7—The government announced that unemployment edged up to 6.1 per cent in April; among blacks the jobless rate reached 10 per cent, highest since 1962.

9—The West German Government decided to permit the mark to float within a limited range in relation to the United States dollar.

10—Former Maj. Gen. Carl C. Turner was sentenced to three years in prison for soliciting arms from the Chicago police, ostensibly for military use but actually put to his own use.

10—The U.S. command in Saigon announced the beginning of a 6,300 cut in American manpower; the Americal Division was withdrawn from combat south of Danang and prepared for deactivation.

10—In South Korea, a bus jammed with about 90 persons, missed a curve and plunged down a 50-foot cliff into a reservoir, killing 76 persons.

12—The Metropolitan Museum in New York announced acquisition of Velazquez's portrait of his Moorish assistant, Juan de Pareja, from Wildenstein and Co., the art dealership that paid more than $5.5 million for the painting in London.

13—In New York City, 13 Black Panthers were acquitted on all 12 counts of an indictment accusing them of conspiracy to bomb public places and to slay policemen; the jury, which included five blacks and one Puerto Rican, freed all the defendants, including two who fled to Algeria during the eighth-month trial.

16—President Anwar el-Sadat said the resignation a week earlier of six members of the Egyptian cabinet was part of an attempted coup. One cabinet member, Lieut. Gen. Mohammed Fawzi, who resigned as minister of war, and others were placed under house arrest. Sadat named a new cabinet.

18—Congress passed a bill requiring striking railroad signalmen to return to work and President Nixon signed it into law, ending the strike that had halted the nation's rail traffic May 17.

19—The Army demoted Maj. Gen. Samuel Koster to brigadier general on charges he failed to conduct a thorough investigation of the My Lai 4 incident and failed to report the civilian casualties to higher authority; Brig. Gen. George Young, Jr., a former assistant commander of Koster's division, was stripped of his Distinguished Service medal under similar charges.

19—The Senate defeated by a vote of 61-36 a bill by Senator Mike Mansfield, Democratic leader, to reduce the number of American troops in Europe; the Nixon Administration considered the vote a victory for the President's foreign policy.

19—Prime Minister Pierre Elliott Trudeau of Canada and Soviet Premier Alexei N. Kosygin signed an agreement calling for high-level talks to improve "friendships, good-neighborliness and mutual confidence" between Canada and the U.S.S.R.

19—Leslie Bacon, a 19-year-old antiwar activist, was cited for contempt of court and jailed for refusing to answer a federal grand jury's questions about the U.S. Capitol bombing.

20—Three news photographers, including Dennis Lee Royle of The Associated Press, were killed when a British naval helicopter crashed in the English Channel during an Atlantic alliance exercise.

21—The Consumer Price Index climbed 0.3 per cent, the largest rise in three months.

22—The $18.6 million Lyndon Baines Johnson Library complex was dedicated in a nationally televised ceremony. On behalf of the nation, President Nixon accepted the travertine marble building on the University of Texas campus.

23—Ephraim Elrom, the Israeli consul-general to Turkey, was found shot to death in an Istanbul apartment during a massive house-to-house search by 30,000 troops; he had been kidnaped by leftists May 17.

23—About 1,000 persons were killed in a severe earthquake which struck Bingol, in eastern Turkey. On May 12 a quake in Turkey's opium growing area near Burdur had taken 57 lives.

23—Seventy-five of 83 persons aboard a Soviet plane died when the aircraft crashed at Rijeka Airport in northwest Yugoslavia, the Belgrade radio reported.

25—Judge Harold M. Mulvey dismissed murder-

kidnaping charges against Black Panther Bobby Seale and Ericka Huggins after ruling that an unbiased jury would be impossible to select because of the "massive publicity" given the trial.

26—The Senate defeated, 42 to 31, a proposed massive rise in military pay allowances; the vote represented a victory for administration policy.

27—President Nikolai V. Podgorny of the Soviet Union and President Anwar el-Sadat of Egypt signed a 15-year treaty of friendship and cooperation. The treaty barred each from interference in the international affairs of the other country.

29—James E. Bennett Jr., a former New York policeman who hijacked an Eastern Airlines 727 to the Bahamas the day before, was captured in Nassau and arraigned in New York on charges of air piracy.

29—Gustav Husak was renamed head of the Czechoslovak Communist party at the final session of its 14th congress, amid shouts of "long live the Soviet Union."

30—Mariner 9 was successfully launched on a voyage to Mars, the mission which was aborted May 8 when Mariner 8 plunged into the Atlantic Ocean after the second stage of its booster rocket failed to function.

31—The United Steelworkers of America announced agreement on new three-year contracts with four major aluminum companies that gave 32,000 workers pay boosts totaling about 31 per cent over that period.

JUNE

1—Policemen wearing bulletproof vests stormed an apartment in Istanbul where the 14-year-old daughter of a Turkish army major was being held hostage by two leftist guerrillas wanted in connection with the kidnap-slaying of the Israeli consul general. The girl was rescued after a gunfight in which one of the guerrillas was killed and the other wounded.

1—In a sharp news conference exchange, President Nixon praised the behavior of District of Columbia police during the Mayday antiwar demonstration. He declared that charges that constitutional rights had been violated by the mass arrests were an "exaggeration." A few hours before the President made his comment, the Supreme Court ruled 5-4 that cities cannot make it a crime for small groups of citizens to loiter in an "annoying" manner in public places.

2—Brig. Gen. John W. Donaldson became the highest-ranking officer accused of war crimes in Indochina; the Army charged him with the murder of six Vietnamese civilians and with assaulting two others in My Lai 4 during the winter of 1968-1969.

4—The unemployment rate in May rose to 6.2 per cent of the labor force, from 6.1 per cent in April.

5—Sheriff's deputies in Yuba City, Calif., ended the grisly search of nearby orchards during which the bodies of 25 slain itinerant farm workers were found in shallow graves.

6—A DC 9 airliner, carrying 48 and a Navy F4 Phantom jet with a crew of two collided over the San Gabriel Canyon outside Los Angeles. All aboard the airliner and one of the Navy airmen were killed.

7—Twenty-eight persons were killed when an Allegheny Airlines passenger plane crashed through vacant beach cottages and into a swampy field as it attempted to land at Tweed-New Haven Airport in Connecticut; no one on the ground was injured.

8—Striking municipal workers accepted a settlement and agreed to end their walkout that had disrupted New York City for two days. The four-point formula put forward by the Office of Collective Bargaining called for resubmitting to the 1972 Legislature the controversial pension plan. The settlement came after a strike of municipal employes had spread to sewage, incineration and park agencies.

9—President Nixon ended a 21-year embargo on trade with Communist China, authorizing the export of 47 categories of nonstrategic items ranging from farm products to automobiles, lifting all controls on imports from China and suspending the shipping requirements that have inhibited the export of wheat and other grains to the Soviet Union, China and Eastern Europe.

9—The United States Commission on Civil Rights charged that, by delegating much of its responsibility in a home ownership program for low-income families to the private housing and home finance industry, the Federal Housing Administration was perpetuating segregation.

9—The City of New Orleans passenger train derailed in Southern Illinois at the speed of 90 miles an hour, killing 10 persons and injuring 94.

12—Tricia Nixon, daughter of President and Mrs. Nixon, was married to Edward Finch Cox in the Rose Garden of the White House. It was the first outdoor wedding in the history of the mansion.

13—Large stores of ammunition exploded in Cambodia's capital, Phnom Penh, ripping apart one building and causing fires in several others.

13—In Santiago, Chile, Ronald Rivera Calderon, 24, and his brother, Arturo, 20, died in a four-hour gun battle with police; they had been sought in the assassination of Edmondo Perez Zukovic, an ex-minister, on June 8.

14—Seven young people suspected of involvement in heroin traffic were found shot to death in a house in Detroit, Mich.

15—United States District Judge Murray I. Gurfein ordered The New York Times to halt publication of material from a secret Pentagon study of the Vietnam war for four days, pending hearing of an injunction petition.

15—Vernon E. Jordan Jr., 35, was named to succeed the late Whitney M. Young Jr., as executive director of the National Urban League.

16—Federal agents announced that they had recovered a painting by El Greco that was stolen from a mansion in Madrid during the Spanish Civil War. The Federal Bureau of Investigation said the painting had been recovered from a New York jeweler who was attempting to sell it privately.

16—Leslie Bacon, 19, was freed on $10,000 bail after she had spent four weeks in jail in Seattle, Wash., on charges arising from her refusal to answer jury questions and her alleged connection with the March 1 bombing of the Capitol.

16—The Senate, by a 55-42 vote, rejected the McGovern-Hatfield "end-the-war" amendment to the selective service bill that would have required withdrawal of all forces by the end of the year.

17—The House rejected all efforts to put it on record for a specific date to end the fighting in Indochina. The action represented a victory for the Nixon Administration's Vietnam policies.

17—President Nixon declared that drug abuse had "assumed the dimensions of a national emergency" and asked Congress for $155 million for a campaign of rehabilitation, research, education, enforcement and international controls. The President also named Dr. Jerome H. Jaffee, head of Illinois' drug abuse program, to head a new White House office on drug abuse.

19—Death took the last of the nonuplets born one week ago to Mrs. Leonard Brodrick in Sydney, Australia.

19—The White House acknowledged that President Nixon left a misleading impression the day before when he said that enactment of his general revenue-sharing plan by Congress would, in time, lead to a reduction of 30 per cent in local property taxes. Press Secretary Ronald L. Ziegler said that what Mr. Nixon had meant was that the measure, if approved, would give localities revenues equal to about 30 per cent of the "average annual increase in property taxes."

21—The U.S. Supreme Court ruled, 6 to 3, that juveniles do not have a constitutional right to a trial by jury. The decision went against 23 years of gradual extensions of Bill of Rights protections to juveniles facing court proceedings.

21—The International Court of Justice in The Hague said in an advisory ruling that South Africa was illegally occupying Namibia, also known as South-West Africa, and that it should end its administration of the territory at once.

21—The government reported the sharpest gain in living costs in five months, a rise of five-tenths of one per cent, for May.

21—In Miami Beach, Fla. The International Brotherhood of Teamsters accepted the resignation of James Hoffa as president and immediately named Vice President Frank Fitzsimmons their new president. Hoffa is serving a prison sentence for jury tampering.

22—The Boston Globe was enjoined from printing more stories on a secret Pentagon study, and appeal courts extended indefinitely the injunction against further publication by the New York Times and the Washington Post of similar information. The Chicago Sun-Times said it had top secret state department documents showing that the Kennedy Administration knew well in advance of the 1963 coup that toppled South Vietnamese President Ngo Dinh Diem, and that plans were under consideration to use force if necessary to prevent North Vietnam from interfering with the coup.

23—Claude E. Vealey, 27, one of five persons accused in the 1969 killing of Joseph A. Yablonski, a reform leader of the United Mine Workers of America, pleaded guilty in Washington, Pa., to a state charge of murder and threw himself on the mercy of the court. The guilty plea was accompanied by a confession.

23—The three-man Soviet crew of the Salyut orbital station broke the endurance record for man in space. At 12:54 a.m., Moscow time, the three cosmonauts aboard the craft broke the previous mark of 17 days 16 hours 58 minutes 50 seconds, set a year earlier by the two-man Soviet crew of the Soyuz 9.

24—Poland took the wraps off a new five-year economic plan that shifted priorities from investment in heavy industries to the needs of the nation's consumers.

25—Julius H. Weitzner, a London art dealer who often acted for American and European museums, paid $4,032,000 at a London auction for a Titian painting, *The Death of Actaeon*. The price was the second highest auction price for a work of art.

28—The Supreme Court declared unconstitutional state programs that reimburse Roman Catholic and other church-related schools for instruction in nonreligious subjects. With only Byron R. White dissenting, the eight other justices of the court ruled that direct financial aid of this type involved "excessive entanglement between government and religion."

29—President Nixon vetoed the $5.6-billion public works bill and the White House announced that he would continue his present economic policies. The announcement said that the President had decided not to seek a tax cut or increase spending as a means to stimulate the economy.

30—The Soviet Union's three Salyut astronauts, who had been in space for more than three weeks were found dead when their Soyuz-11 ferry craft landed, Tass, the Soviet press agency, announced.

30—District Attorney Jim Garrison of New Orleans was arrested by federal agents and charged with taking bribes to protect illegal pinball gambling in New Orleans.

30—By a vote of 6 to 3 the Supreme Court ruled that the New York Times and the Washington Post were free to publish articles based on a secret Pentagon study of Vietnam.

JULY

1—The semi-independent United States Postal Service assumed control of the nation's mail system amid labor difficulties, court challenges and the possibility of another rate increase for third class mail.

1—The House cleared, 343 to 14, and sent to the White House a $2.25-billion measure to create up to 200,000 emergency jobs in public service.

2—Secretary of Defense Melvin R. Laird ordered tighter security measures at the Rand Corp., following discovery by the Pentagon of "deficiencies" in the way the private research institute has safeguarded secret information.

3—Gov. Ronald Reagan cut California's budget by more than $500 million. Items for education, welfare and medical care were hardest hit.

5—Mayor Thomas J. Whelan of Jersey City and seven of his associates were convicted of extortion and conspiracy by a federal court in Newark. The eight men were charged with conspiring to collect kickbacks from city contractors.

7—The Food and Drug Administration and the Department of Agriculture ordered recall of all soups, sauces and other canned foods made by Bon Vivant Soups Inc., of Newark, N.J. The action followed discovery that at least five cans of Bon Vivant vichyssoise were contaminated with deadly botulinum toxin, the cause of botulism. Government officials also confirmed the link between the canned vichyssoise and the death of a Westchester County, N.Y., man.

7—The White House said it had ordered compilation of a list of all persons possessing authority to see top secret documents. The order was part of a review of the process of classification and declassification ordered by President Nixon six months earlier.

11—King Hassan II of Morocco said that four generals had clumsily mounted a "Libyan-style coup" against him and had failed.

11—Chile's congress approved a constitutional amendment permitting nationalization of the copper mining industry in which U.S. companies have a multimillion dollar investment.

12—The Soviet Union announced that the death of three cosmonauts aboard Soyuz 11 on June 30 apparently was caused by a rapid change of the air pressure within their capsule only minutes before it landed successfully.

12—President Nixon signed the $2.2-billion Emergency Employment Act of 1971, the first public employment legislation since the depression of the 1930s; the new law would finance jobs for 150,000 persons, ranging from Welfare recipients to unemployed professionals.

13—A proposed contempt citation against the Columbia Broadcasting System and its president was blocked by the House when it voted to send the citation back to the Commerce Committee.

13—Ten high-ranking officers of the Moroccan army, accused of plotting to assassinate King Hassan II, were executed by a firing squad.

14—A U.S. military court in Lakenheath, England, reprimanded Capt. Thomas S. Culver of the U.S. Air Force and fined him $1,000 for participating in a London antiwar demonstration; he could have been sentenced to four years' imprisonment, dishonorable discharge and forfeiture of pay.

14—About 400,000 communications workers of the Bell System began a nationwide strike for higher pay; company officials said administrative personnel maintained virtually unimpaired phone service.

15—The Federal Reserve Board approved an increase in the discount rate to 5 per cent from 4.75 per cent.

15—The Chilean Central Bank announced that two large foreign banks—the Bank of America and the Bank of London and South America—had agreed to sell their operations in Santiago to the nationalized banking system.

15—President Nixon announced that he would visit China before next May, at the invitation of Premier Chou En-lai, to "seek the normalization of relations between the two countries and to exchange views on questions of concern to the two sides."

16—Train crews struck the Union Pacific Railroad and the Southern Railway, halting traffic on both lines.

269

19—The South Vietnamese Government proposed a total cease-fire and the reunification of North and South Vietnam through general elections.

19—Jordan's Premier Wasfi Tai announced that the army had "rounded up" more than 2,000 Palestinian guerrillas and that only 200 remained at liberty in Jordan.

19—The Premier of Sudan, Maj. Gen. Gaafar al-Nimeiry, was deposed and replaced by a dissident group of officers, but by week's end the coup had collapsed; Nimeiry was restored to power, and execution of leading rebels followed.

20—The U.S. Postal Service and seven postal unions signed a contract covering more than 650,000 workers in the first collective bargaining agreement in the history of the post office. The contract provided an estimated pay boost of $1,710 over two years, bringing the average starting salary to $8,810 a year.

21—The Soviet newspaper Literaturnaya Gazeta published an assertion by the Bulgarian Telegraph Agency that President Nixon's planned trip to Peking was the result of anti-Soviet maneuvering by both the United States and Communist China. The criticism came three days after a Polish newspaper had hailed Nixon's decision as a long overdue reversal of U.S. attitudes toward Peking.

21—President Nixon accepted the resignation of Dr. Glenn T. Seaborg, the Nobel chemist who had been chairman of the Atomic Energy Commission for a decade. Seaborg stepped down in order to return to the University of California at Berkeley.

22—The Chicago & North Western Railway and the United Transportation Union reached agreement on a new contract, marking the first breakthrough in the lengthy dispute between the union and the nation's railroads. The North Western agreed to a wage increase of 42 per cent over 42 months.

23—At gunpoint, a former airline mechanic who had passed an arms check forced a jetliner to return to New York's LaGuardia Field. There he commandeered a truck to nearby Kennedy Airport, attempted to pirate another plane to Italy and was killed by an FBI sharpshooter.

23—The Consumer Price Index rose 0.5 per cent in June, a strong increase for the second consecutive month.

25—Dr. Christiaan N. Barnard and his pioneering heart graft team in South Africa transplanted both lungs and a heart to a 79-year-old man and said the patient was doing "as well as can be expected."

25—A firing squad executed Maj. Farouk Osman Hamadallah, chief aide to Lt. Col. Babakr al-Nur Osman, the man who would have led the Sudan if a coup July 19 had been successful.

26—Legislation to rescue the Lockheed Aircraft Corp. from bankruptcy and to authorize similar rescues of other large companies suffered two setbacks in the U.S. Senate. The Senate rejected a motion to cut off debate on the legislation. It also refused to vote down a proposal that would give Congress a second chance to deny government-backed loans to Lockheed even if it passed the measure granting general loans.

27—Three American astronauts aboard Apollo 15 soared toward the moon after a spectacular launching that was called the smoothest of any of the nation's lunar adventures.

28—The United States suspended flights over Red China to avoid any incident that might interfere with President's Nixon's visit to Peking, planned for sometime before May 1972.

28—British entry into the Common Market was solidly opposed by the Labor party's national executive body, on the terms so far negotiated.

28—A near record budget deficit of $23.2 billion was reported by the U.S. government for the fiscal year that ended June 30.

29—President Tito was unanimously reelected by the Yugoslav parliament to a five-year term. But he said he might retire before his mandate expired if the 22-man group elected to a new collective presidency of the republic under his chairmanship worked well together.

29—David K. E. Bruce retired as chief U.S. delegate to the Vietnam peace talks. The 73-year-old diplomat said he was withdrawing for health reasons and expressed hope that further deliberations would lead to "a just and lasting peace."

30—Two American astronauts, Col. David R. Scott and Lt. Col. James B. Irwin rode their lunar module from the Apollo 15 space craft to a smooth landing on the moon.

30—One hundred sixty-two persons died—the highest toll of any air disaster on record—when a Japanese Air Force fighter collided with a Japanese jetliner over the Japanese Alps.

31—The United States won the agreement of both Pakistan and the United Nations to station an international group of 153 civilian relief and rehabilitation experts in East Pakistan under United Nations sponsorship.

31—For hours of "exploration at its greatest," two American astronauts drove across the desolate surface of the moon in man's first motorized excursion among ancient lunar rocks, craters and rolling hills.

AUGUST

1—Agreement on a new three-year contract only hours before a strike deadline averted a shutdown of the nation's steel industry. Officials of the United Steelworkers of America described the terms as "the best ever."

2—Less than 24 hours after the steel industry reached a labor agreement calling for wage boosts of about 31 per cent over three years, most of the nation's major steel producers announced that they would raise prices by about 8 per cent. The price changes were the second round for 1971, bringing cumulative rise for the year to about 15 per cent.

2—Ending 20 years of resistance, the United States announced its support for seating Communist China in the United Nations. But it held out against expulsion of the Nationalist Chinese government, based on Taiwan.

2—The U.S. Senate, by a vote of 49-48, gave final Congressional approval to legislation aimed at saving the Lockheed Aircraft Corp. from bankruptcy. The bill was the same as the one passed by the House three days earlier by a vote of 192-189.

2—After three days of almost continuous bargaining negotiators for the United Transportation Union and the railroads signed a contract calling for a 42 per cent wage boost over 43 months. The new contract established some work rule changes that the railroads had sought for years.

2—After nearly three days spent exploring the moon, Apollo 15 Astronauts Col. David R. Scott and Lt. Col. James B. Irwin blasted off the lunar surface and rejoined their orbiting command ship two hours later. It marked the first televised launching from the moon.

5—Air Force Maj. Alfred M. Worden, Apollo 15 astronaut, became the first man to walk in interplanetary space, 196,000 miles from the earth; he spent 16 minutes outside the spacecraft, gripping handrails on the Endeavour and protected by a lifeline from the cabin, as the vehicle sped homeward from a visit to the moon.

5—The Labor Department in Washington reported a seven-tenths of one per cent increase in industrial wholesale prices during July, the largest gain in one month since late 1965, but food prices declined by one per cent after seasonal adjustment.

7—Apollo 15 returned safely from the moon despite failure of one of its three splashdown parachutes, and the astronauts were declared in good physical condition after their 12-day voyage of lunar exploration.

8—Soviet Foreign Minister Andrei A. Gromyko arrived in New Delhi for talks on shipments of arms to West Pakistan by the United States, which India opposed; the government of Prime Minister Indira Gandhi also was concerned by the massive influx of East Pakistan Bengali refugees into India.

9—A three-judge federal court in Buffalo, N.Y.,

declared unconstitutional a New York statute requiring one year's residence for welfare recipients.

9—In Northern Ireland, the government invoked emergency internment powers in an effort to quell violence between Protestants and Catholics which cost at least 12 lives in two days.

11—The Nixon Administration warned that government officials could lose their jobs if they insisted upon imposing widespread busing as a means of desegregating schools in the urban South; the U.S. Supreme Court had ruled April 20 that busing was proper unless distances threatened the health of pupils.

11—New York's Mayor John V. Lindsay announced he had switched his political allegiance from the Republican to the Democratic party.

11—Moscow officials reported that a Soviet airliner in route from Odessa to Vladivostok crashed on takeoff from Irkutsk, a routine stop in Siberia; all 97 persons aboard were killed.

12—Syria broke diplomatic relations with Jordan and barred Jordanian planes from Syrian airspace following reported border clashes between the two countries.

12—Australian Prime Minister William McMahon dismissed Defense Minister John G. Gorton, his predecessor as head of government, in a political controversy over a book containing allegations against Gorton's personal conduct during his tenure as chief of government.

13—Atty. Gen. John N. Mitchell announced that no federal grand jury investigation will be made in the fatal shooting of four Kent State University students by Ohio National Guardsmen in May 1970; he said there was no "credible evidence" of conspiracy and no likelihood of successful prosecution of individual guardsmen.

15—President Nixon ordered a 90-day freeze of wages and prices, requesting tax cuts and broad changes of domestic and international policies to strengthen the dollar; he added that the administration would cease to convert foreign-held dollars into gold.

16—In Los Angeles, Dr. Daniel Ellsberg pleaded innocent to charges that he illegally possessed and copied classified Pentagon papers.

18—After two days of heavy gains, the New York Stock Exchange plunged downward, the Dow Jones industrial average falling 13.73 points to 886.17 from its two-day rise of 43.88 points.

18—The Nixon Administration decided that state and local government employees—including firemen, policemen and civil servants—were subject to the 90-day wage freeze.

19—George Meany, A.F.L.-C.I.O. president, said in Washington that his organization had "absolutely no faith in the ability of President Nixon to successfully manage the economy of this nation" and added that the unions would refuse to cooperate with the wage-price freeze; Texas Gov. Preston Smith defied the wage freeze and was promptly rebuked by a Nixon spokesman.

20—In Saigon, Gen. Duong Van Minh, known as Big Minh, withdrew from the race for president of South Vietnam, leaving President Nguyen Van Thieu unopposed for reelection Oct. 3.

20—At Fort McPherson, Ga., Lt. Gen. Albert O'Connor, commanding general of the Third Army, reduced from life to 20 years the sentence of First Lt. William L. Calley Jr., convicted by court-martial in March of the murder of 22 persons in the South Vietnam village of My Lai 4 in 1968; the reduction made Calley eligible for parole in six to seven years.

20—Leaders of Egypt, Syria and Libya signed a constitution for the Federation of Arab Republics, dedicated to Arab socialism and liberation of territories occupied by Israel.

21—George Jackson, one of the Soledad Brothers, two other inmates and three guards were killed in what authorities said was an attempt by Jackson to escape from the maximum-security San Quentin Prison in San Rafael, Calif.; a prison spokesman said that the slayings involved 17 to 20 guards and inmates, and that Jackson possessed a revolver.

23—Civilian and military leaders took over the

left-wing government of Gen. Juan Jose Torres Gonzales in Bolivia and Col. Hugo Banzer Suarez assumed the presidency. Army and air force units bombarded the central tower of the University of San Andres, where leftist students had made a last stand against the anti-Marxist revolt. At least eight occupants of the tower were killed and 25 wounded.

23—European foreign exchange markets were re-opened for the first time since President Nixon's wage-price freeze of Aug. 15, and there was no rush to sell dollars. The Dow Jones industrial average in New York climbed 11.47 points to 892.38. In Texas, the state attorney general ruled that Gov. Preston E. Smith had no authority to exempt state employes from the national freeze order, and the governor said he would comply with the order.

23—An agreement on the future of West Berlin was reached by the United States, Britain, France and the Soviet Union after 16 months and 23 days of negotiations by envoys of the four powers on improving the situation in the isolated city.

26—Chemical Bank in New York, sixth largest in the nation, reduced its loan interest rates one point for consumer loans and one-half point for mortgages in cooperation with President Nixon's wage-price freeze.

26—Six prominent Israelis, all critics of Communist party policies, were welcomed to the Soviet Union, the first time such a group had been invited since Moscow broke diplomatic relations with Israel at the time of the 1967 Arab-Israeli war.

31—President Nixon refused to disclose to the Senate Foreign Relations Committee his long-range plans for foreign military aid; his action represented the second time he had exercised "executive privilege" in denying information to Congress, fore-stalling a threatened congressional stoppage of all foreign military assistance in the current year.

31—Murder charges were filed in San Rafael, Calif., against Stephen M. Bingham, 29-year-old lawyer, accused of smuggling a gun into San Quentin Prison and giving it to George Jackson, 29; authorities said Jackson used the weapon to start an escape attempt in which six persons were killed, including Jackson.

SEPTEMBER

1—Entrance to the United States by Joe Cahill, leader of the Irish Republican Army's militant "provisional" faction, was denied when he arrived at Kennedy International Airport in New York; immigration authorities said his visa was canceled at the request of the U.S. Department of State. Cahill's "provisionals" advocated open warfare with British troops in Northern Ireland in an effort to achieve a united Ireland.

1—Secretary of Defense Melvin Laird announced that the United States had agreed to furnish 175 Phantom jet fighter planes to West Germany for approximately $750 million.

1—The half-year wage freeze already imposed upon the armed forces and civil service government employes was extended by President Nixon to about 600,000 blue-collar federal workers.

2—The British bank rate was cut from 6 per cent to 5 per cent in a move to keep the pound from floating too high against the dollar.

2—Nearly unanimous endorsement of a loose union—Egypt, Syria and Libya—was established by referendums in the three countries comprising the Federation of Arab Republics; the union was the first since the United Arab Republic joined Egypt and Syria in 1958, a coalition that collapsed in 1961.

4—George Meany, 77-year-old president of the American Federation of Labor and Congress of Industrial Relations, said organized labor would cooperate in a voluntary plan of wage-price controls that were fair and equitable.

7—Terrorists pushed a bomb-laden bicycle into the path of a car carrying Emory C. Swank, U.S. ambassador to Cambodia, near his residence in Phnom Penh, but the explosive failed to go off. A spokesman said the riderless bicycle carrying a 13-pound plastic bomb concealed under the loaves

of bread brushed harmlessly against Swank's limousine.

8—The $70-million John F. Kennedy Center for the Performing Arts opened in Washington.

9—President Nixon told a joint session of Congress that he would not extend the wage-price freeze beyond the Nov. 13 expiration date, but he promised to invoke whatever steps were necessary "to see that America is not again afflicted by the virus of runaway inflation."

11—A Soviet effort to explore the moon's surface with a unmanned spacecraft ended in failure as Luna 18 lost contact with the earth upon landing.

13—After five straight days, a prison rebellion at the Attica Correctional Facility in New York ended as 1,000 state troopers, sheriff's deputies and prison guards stormed the prison under a pall of tear gas. The clash resulted in the death of 43 men.

15—Authoritative U.S. Administration officials said the United States had decided in principle to support actively the assignment of China's seat in the U.N. Security Council to the Peking government; they said this decision was intended to help the United States win adequate sponsorship for its effort to prevent explusion of Nationalist China from the United nations.

15—Federal officials, in a major reversal of environmental policy, told American housewives to return to the use of phosphate detergents. They said such detergents did cause ecological damage, but were less of an evil than cleaners containing caustic soda or the chemical NTA.

17—After 34 years of service spanning the administrations of six presidents, Associate Justic Hugo L. Black, 85, retired from the U.S. Supreme Court, citing health reasons.

18—President Agha Mohammad Yahya Khan of Pakistan agreed to demands that a new constitution would go to a national assembly for approval.

21—The Senate gave final congressional approval to the U.S. draft bill permitting a return to military conscription until June 1973.

21—The 26th General Assembly of the United Nations opened with the election of Indonesia's foreign minister, Adam Malik, as its president and the China question topping its agenda. Several thousand pro-Peking and pro-Taiwan Chinese staged rival rallies near the U.N. building.

22—Capt. Ernest L. Medina was acquitted of all charges of involvement in the killing of civilians at May Lai 4; the jury of five combat officers deliberated only 60 minutes.

23—Treasury Secretary John B. Connally was told by a group of savings and loan associations that they would not raise interest rates for home mortgages during the 90-day freeze nor during the "phase two" economic program following the freeze.

23—Associate Justice John M. Harlan resigned from the Supreme Court after 16 years of service, due to ill health.

24—Britain ordered 90 Soviet representatives to leave because of espionage activities and barred the return of 15 more temporarily away.

25—Leonid I. Brezhnev, the Soviet Communist party leader, and President Tito of Yugoslavia signed a new Belgrade declaration reaffirming Yugoslavia's political independence and her right to develop Communism in her own way.

25—Retired Associate Justice Hugo L. Black died at the age of 85.

26—Pope Paul VI celebrated his 74th birthday as the Italian press speculated that he might resign before his next birthday.

26—For the first time in history a President of the United States, Richard Nixon, met a ruler of Japan, Emperor Hirohito. The historic occurrence took place in a colorfully decorated airplane hangar at Anchorage in Alaska, where the two talked for 35 minutes. Although the White House said that nothing important was discussed, the President expressed hope that the meeting would provide some symbolic counterweight to his recent friendly overtures to Communist China.

28—The Soviet Union's foreign minister, Andrei

A. Gromyko, told the United Nations that his government favors "in principle" improvement of U.S.-China relations as a "natural development."

28—Chile nullified payments of $744 million to the United States companies for nationalization of three copper mines; Pres. Salvador Allende said he considered these payments to be excess profits.

28—Lady Fleming, Greek-born widow of penicillin's discoverer, was sentenced in Athens to 16 months in prison for her part in an attempt to free a would-be assassin from prison; her husband was Sir Alexander Fleming.

30—Treasury Secretary John B. Connally told the International Monetary Fund's annual meeting that the United States would remove the import surcharge if other leading nations would allow their currencies to float freely upward against the dollar and if some took "specific" measures to reduce American export barriers.

30—Oleg Lyalin was named by the British Foreign Office as the Soviet agent who defected early last September and gave the British evidence that led to the expulsion of 90 Soviet officials and a bar to the return of 15 to Britain.

OCTOBER

1—Some 45,000 longshoremen walked off the docks at East and Gulf Coast ports as the dockworkers in the Western ports continued their separate walkout into a fourth month.

1—The nation's production of soft coal was shut down by the strike of some 80,000 miners.

2—A British European Airways plane crashed near Ghent, Belgium, killing all 63 persons aboard. Six of the dead were reported to be Americans.

3—President Nguyen Van Thieu won a new four-year term as President of South Vietnam, in a one-candidate election marked by scattered protests, terrorism, intensified enemy shelling and the largest reported voter turnout in recent Vietnamese history.

6—President Nixon obtained Federal court injunctions ordering striking longshoremen to return to work on the Pacific Coast and in the port of Chicago.

7—President Nixon told the nation that the wage-price freeze would be followed by an indefinite period of close government supervision of the economy to limit prices, wages and rent without direct controls of profits. He made clear that the government would rely on compliance on guidelines for increases but that it would impose fines if necessary.

7—Even as the President spoke, the Labor Department announced that the Wholesale Price Index declined 0.4 per cent in September. The announcement said it was the first decline in the overall index since November 1970.

8—In retaliation for Britain's expulsion of 105 Soviet representatives, the Soviet Union ordered four British diplomats and three businessmen to leave the country. The Soviet government also canceled several high level visits, including that of the British foreign secretary, Sir Alec Douglas-Home.

8—After agreeing to support President Nixon's economic program on Thursday, organized labor withdrew its support, saying it had been misled by the Administration.

9—The Ford Foundation announced a six-year, $100-million program to improve the quality of a limited number of predominantly Negro private colleges and to provide various minority students with individual study awards at most types of institutions.

11—To help reduce the deficit in the American balance of payments with Japan, the government of Premier Eisaku Sato said it would be prepared to double its purchases of American military equipment.

12—President Nixon announced that he would make a trip to Moscow, "independent" of his planned journey to China, for a meeting with Soviet leaders.

12—Phase Two of President Nixon's program to fight inflation after the current 90-day wage and price freeze expired was given support by organized labor. The pledge was made after the President assured top labor leaders that the decisions of the Pay Board would not be subject to veto by the Cost of Living Council.

14—The 1971 Nobel Prize in physiology and medicine was awarded to Dr. Earl W. Sutherland Jr. of Nashville, professor of physiology at the Vanderbilt University School of Medicine for his work in discovering how hormones work.

15—Prof. Simon Kuznts, the 70-year-old American economist and statistician who developed the concept of using the gross national product as a measure of a nation's economic growth won the Alfred Nobel Memorial Prize in Economic Science.

16—H. Rap Brown, the fugitive black militant leader, and two policemen were wounded in a gun battle following the armed robbery of a West Side bar in New York City, police said.

17—The Pittsburgh Pirates defeated the favored Baltimore Orioles, 2-1, to win the 68th World Series in the seventh and final game.

18—Premier Aleksei N. Kosygin of the Soviet Union was assaulted by a man shouting "Long live free Hungary!" as he and Prime Minister Pierre Elliott Trudeau of Canada were walking across Parliament's grounds in Ottawa. Kosygin was uninjured.

20—The Nobel Peace Prize was awarded to Willy Brandt, West German chancellor, for his efforts to lessen East-West tensions.

20—The prime rate was lowered by several major banks from 6 per cent to 5¾ per cent under pressure from the Nixon Administration.

21—The 1971 Nobel Prize for literature was awarded to Pablo Neruda, the 67-year-old Chilean poet, diplomat and Communist leader who had his first poem published when he was 13.

21—President Nixon nominated Lewis F. Powell Jr. a former president of the American Bar Association, and William H. Renquist, an assistant attorney general, for appointment to the Supreme Court.

21—The Nixon Administration abruptly terminated its agreement to check the judicial qualifications of potential Supreme Court nominees with the American Bar Association before appointing them.

23—Prime Minister Indira Gandhi, on the eve of her departure on a three-week foreign tour, called on the Indian people to "stand united" and alerted because "our country is facing danger."

24—Charles F. (Chuck) Hughes of the Detroit Lions collapsed in the closing seconds of a National Football League game and died of a heart attack.

25—Communist China was admitted to the United Nations and Nationalist China was expelled by a 76-35 vote in the General Assembly; moments before the vote Lou Chieh, the Nationalist delegate, announced that his government would take no further part in the proceedings and left the hall.

25—The Pakistani government reported that its troops had killed 501 "enemy troops"—defined as "Indians and Indian agents"—in heavy fighting in East Pakistan.

27—Henry A. Kissinger said in Washington that President Nixon would visit China sometime after Jan. 1, and that Nixon hoped to restrict his conference there to issues concerning the two countries alone; the presidential aide had just returned from arrangement talks in Peking.

27—The government in Saigon announced that amnesty had been granted 3,000 Vietcong.

27—President Nixon authorized the Atomic Energy Commission to proceed with the underground test of a five-megaton nuclear warhead on an island in the Aleutian chain.

28—The Senate, by a three-vote margin, rejected a proposed amendment specifying that the President could not use funds in Indochina except to withdraw all American forces.

28—By a vote of 356 to 244, the House of Commons approved British membership in the European Common Market.

29—The Senate voted down 41-27 the Nixon Ad-

ministration's foreign aid authorization bill—the first time that a foreign aid bill requested by an administration had been rejected since 1948.

31—The South Vietnamese Government released the first of nearly 3,000 Vietcong prisoners under a recently announced amnesty.

NOVEMBER

1—Perhaps as many as 10,000 people were killed by a cyclone and tidal wave that hit the eastern coast of India. Tens of thousands of houses were destroyed or damaged in the delta area of Cuttack District in Orissa state, on the Bay of Bengal, about 250 miles southwest of Calcutta.

2—Prof. Dennis Gabor, a Hungarian-born scientist, was awarded the 1971 Nobel Prize in physics for his work in three-dimensional photography.

3—Secretary of State William P. Rogers announced that United States passports would be denied those Americans who refused to take an oath of allegiance to the Constitution.

5—The nation's unemployment rate edged downward from 6 per cent in September to 5.8 per cent in October; total employment continued to rise.

5—The Nixon Administration announced arrangements for the commercial sale of nearly $136 million worth of corn and other feed grains to Russia.

6—One hundred and seven of 200 bishops ended the third Synod of Bishops with a refusal to close the door on the possibility of ordaining married men as Roman Catholic priests.

6—The controversial Cannikin nuclear bomb test was conducted after the Supreme Court refused to order a delay in the experiment at Amchitka, Alaska, in the Aleutian Islands.

8—The Pay Board overrode unanimous labor objections and voted 10 to 5 to set a 5.5 per cent standard for wage increases during the Nixon Administration's economic stablization program.

10—Cheering crowds organized by the Socialist and Communist parties in Chile gave Premier Fidel Castro of Cuba an enthusiastic welcome in the streets of Santiago.

11—President Nixon announced the resignation of Clifford M. Hardin as Secretary of Agriculture, nominated Earl L. Butz, a Purdue University dean, for the post and declared that he would no longer seek to abolish the Department of Agriculture in his executive reorganization.

11—The Price Commission proclaimed a goal of limiting price increases to an average of 2.5 per cent a year and issued a comprehensive set of guidelines forbidding all price rises except those justified by higher costs. It also limited profit margins, but not total profits.

13—The Senate voted to repeal the 10 per cent excise tax on buses that were used by urban mass transit systems.

13—An unmanned American spacecraft, the television-equipped Mariner 9, rocketed into an orbit of Mars.

13—Twenty-three-year-old Aubran W. Martin, was sentenced to death in the electric chair for his part in the New Year's Eve slaying in 1969 of Joseph Yablonski, his wife and daughter.

15—Ernest L. Medina, who was acquitted of charges of killing South Vietnamese civilians at My Lai, told the court-martial of Col. Oran K. Henderson that he had lied to the colonel about the number of villagers killed during the assault.

16—Emperor Hirohito of Japan, in his first on-the-record meeting with foreign newsmen in his 45 years on the throne, defended his role before and during World War II as that of a constitutional monarch.

17—The Price Commission approved an immediate 2.5 per cent price increase for 1972 models of American Motors cars.

17—Citing "the dangers that have been threatening Thailand," Premier Thanom Kittikachorn and a group of other Thai leaders organized themselves into a "revolutionary" council, abolished the con-

stitution, dissolved parliament, disbanded the cabinet and instituted martial law.

18—A Federal Court ordered 23 companies in the Birmingham area of Alabama to halt production after air pollution climbed to twice the level of a danger alert.

19—The Pay Board by a vote of 10 to 3 approved a pay increase of at least 15 per cent for America's coal miners, despite a sharp warning from its public members that such boosts would endanger economic stabilization efforts.

19—President Nixon appealed to organized labor to cooperate with his Phase Two economic controls but declared that he would proceed with his program "whether we get that participation or not."

21—Workers at the General Motors Corporation's plants in Dayton, Ohio, agreed to give up future pay raises for two years.

22—The Supreme Court unanimously struck down an Idaho statute that gave men preference over women in administering deceased persons' estates. It marked the first time the court had invalidated a state law on grounds of sex discrimination.

23—Pakistani officials reported that large numbers of Indian troops pushed toward the nearby East Pakistani border. Pakistan declared a national emergency and charged that Indian forces had seized two villages and some border outposts in East Pakistan.

23—The Senate voted overwhelmingly in favor of providing $500 million in military credits for Israel, earmarking half the sum to cover the purchase of F-4 Phantom jet fighters. At the same time the Senate rejected a proposal for a 60,000-man reduction in the American forces in Western Europe.

24—Soviet Premier Alexei N. Kosygin presented his government's new five-year plan to the Supreme Soviet in Moscow and called on the United States to "give up its attempts to discriminate against the Soviet Union in trade, financing and shipping." U.S. Secretary of Commerce Maurice H. Stans was present when Kosygin spoke.

24—Paul W. McCracken announced he was resigning as chairman of the President's Council of Economic Advisors to return to teaching. Named as his successor was Herbert Stein, a member of the council.

25—A 24-hour rebellion by inmates of the Rahway State Prison in New Jersey ended with the release of the warden and five guards who had been held hostage; no serious injuries were reported.

25—Collecting a record $200,000 ransom from Northwest Airlines, a middle-aged hijacker parachuted from a jetliner somewhere northeast of Portland, Ore. He had collected the money by threatening to blow up the plane, carrying 36 passengers and six crew members, unless his demands were met.

25—The six-year struggle between Britain and her rebellious territory of Rhodesia neared an end as British Foreign Secretary Sir Alec Douglas-Home and Rhodesian Prime Minister Ian Smith signed a constitutional agreement. The pact offered new legal rights and economic possibilities for Rhodesia's black majority.

26—Saudi Arabia agreed to let Israeli Moslems visit Mecca on pilgrimages, a privilege denied them for 23 years.

28—Premier Wasfi Tell of Jordan was assassinated in Cairo, Egypt, by three gunmen reported to have entered Egypt with Syrian passports. The 51-year-old premier was shot when he was returning to his hotel from a meeting of the Arab League's Joint Defense Council.

29—Ahmed al-Lawzi, 46, who had served as finance minister, was named the new premier of Jordan, replacing Premier Wasfi, slain by assassins' bullets.

29—The White House announced that President Nixon's visit to China starting Feb. 21, 1972, would continue for perhaps a week and would include talks with officials of the People's Republic.

30—The Price Commission approved a request by the General Motors Corp. to raise the prices of its 1972 cars, trucks and equipment by an average of 2.5 per cent.

DECEMBER

2—The Democratic plan for financing the 1972 presidential campaign with federal tax revenue was dropped by a Senate-House conference committee at the suggestion of Rep. Wilbur D. Mills.

2—The Chilean army assumed control of public order in the capital of Santiago after more than 150 persons had been injured in violence set off by a woman's protest march against the government.

6—Prime Minister Pierre Elliott Trudeau of Canada and President Nixon conferred in Washington on tightening ties between the two nations; Nixon reassured Trudeau of continuing close relations on a series of international problems, including Canada's concern regarding the surtax on imports imposed by Nixon under his new economic policy.

6—The State Department suspended a large part of U.S. economic aid to India, mainly $87 million in development loans, on the ground that Prime Minister Indira Gandhi's government was the "main aggressor" in the conflict in Pakistan.

6—The Pakistan government in Rawalpindi severed international relations with India as the air battle between the two countries continued; India announced a similar break with West Pakistan and said India had recognized East Pakistani leaders in their revolt against the central Pakistan government.

6—In New York, the U.N. Security Council voted 11–0 to transfer to the General Assembly the debate on the India-Pakistan fighting; members who abstained from voting included the Soviet Union, which had earlier vetoed a cease-fire proposal in the Security Council.

7—The Price Commission in Washington granted U.S. Steel Corp., America's largest producer, an average price increase of 3.6 per cent; this, the company said, was considerably less than it expected, but it did not disclose how much.

7—A resolution urging India and Pakistan to halt hostilities was voted, 104–11, by the United Nations General Assembly; the United States and China favored the resolution and the Soviet Union was among the dissenters.

8—President Nixon asked Congress to help "self-reliant" Americans prepare for retirement by granting income tax deductions for pension contributions and by preserving the pension rights of workers who leave or change jobs.

8—President Salvador Allende of Chile announced that his left-wing government would take over full control of food distribution in Chile as part of an "offensive against Fascist sedition."

9—The Pay Board approved a contract under which railroad signalmen would receive wage increases far exceeding the board's general standard of 5.5 per cent annually.

9—The Vatican published a pronouncement by Pope Paul VI restating the Roman Catholic Church's prohibition against married priests.

9—The Pakistan government said it had "decided to accept" the General Assembly's call for a cease-fire and had so informed the United Nations, although India had indicated it would not accept the U.N. resolution; in Calcutta the commander of India's eastern forces said the retreat of Pakistani troops in East Pakistan had become a rout.

9—Death sentences were pronounced against four of nine former Egyptian officials accused of having conspired in May to seize power, but Egyptian President Anwar Sadat reduced the death sentences to life imprisonment at hard labor.

13—An American resolution calling for an immediate cease-fire and the withdrawal of Indian and Pakistani forces was vetoed by the Soviet Union in the U.N. Security Council.

13—An Egyptian-supported resolution calling for Israeli withdrawal from Egyptian territory occupied since 1967 was passed by the United Nations General Assembly; the United States abstained.

14—With Indian troops reporting they were within six miles of Dacca, East Pakistan's government resigned. Dr. A. N. Malik, governor of East Pakistan, wrote the resignation, which was sent to West Pakistan's President Agha Mohammad Yahya Khan in West Pakistan.

14—Presidents Nixon and Georges Pompidou of France, conferring in the Azores, issued a joint statement in which the United States announced it was prepared to devalue the dollar by a small but undetermined amount in an effort to resolve the world monetary crisis.

15—The Price Commission moved to cut in half the rate of increase in the cost of health care, imposing a 2.5 per cent limit on rises in doctor's fees and a 6 per cent ceiling on rises in hospital charges.

16—India ordered a complete cease-fire with East Pakistan following the seizure of Dacca, the eastern capital, and accepted surrender of Pakistani forces there; Indian commanders also ordered a cease-fire in West Pakistan, but President Agha Mohammad Yahya Khan declared the war was still on.

17—Pakistan accepted a cease-fire along the West Pakistan-India border, ending 15 days of war between the countries; India disclosed that during the fighting 2,307 Indians were killed and 6,163 wounded; 2.163 were missing.

17—A jury of two generals and five colonels cleared Col. Oran K. Henderson of charges that he covered up the killings at the hamlet of My Lai 4 by conducting an inadequate investigation of the incident.

18—President Nixon announced what he termed "the most significant monetary agreement in the history of the world;" the agreement, a new set of currency exchange rates, included devaluation of the dollar by 8.57 per cent and revaluations of the yen by 17 per cent and the mark by 5 per cent.

18—President Agha Mohammad Yahya Khan of Pakistan formally asked Zulfikar Ali Bhutto, Pakistan's foreign minister and deputy prime minister, to return home from the United States to form a new government.

21—President Nixon and Britain's Prime Minister Edward Heath ended more than nine hours of discussions in Bermuda with a joint pledge to set aside tactical differences and to work together for a strengthened Atlantic alliance.

22—Kurt Waldheim, Austrian career diplomat, was elected U.N. Secretary-General, succeeding U Thant, who was retiring. Waldheim was named to a five-year term by acclamation in the 132-member General Assembly.

23—President Nixon commuted the prison term of James R. Hoffa, former president of the International Brotherhood of Teamsters. Hoffa walked out of the federal penitentiary in Lewisburg, Pa., after serving 4 years, 9 months and 16 days of a 13-year term.

23—The Price Commission trimmed a rate increase on health and medical coverage for 1.6 million Federal workers from 34.1 per cent to 22 per cent.

24—Giovanni Leone, a Christian Democratic moderate and a conciliator, was elected the sixth president of Italy.

26—A fire in the Taeyunkak Hotel in Seoul, South Korea, killed 157 persons.

28—The Internal Revenue Service warned all retailers that they must post lists of base prices "prominently," for the convenience of customers, before Jan. 2.

28—Vietnam veterans barricaded inside the Statue of Liberty rejected a government compromise designed to reopen the historic monument to the public while allowing the veterans to continue their antiwar protest.

28—Secretary of Defense Melvin R. Laird warned North Vietnam that large-scale bombing raids might be repeated in an effort to protect American servicemen still in Vietnam.

28—President Nixon signed a bill requiring most able-bodied welfare recipients to register for jobs or job training and said the new law embodied the "workfare" provisions of his welfare reform plan.

30—The United States command announced the end of its intensified bombing of North Vietnam after five days of raids.

30—The United States announced the decision to resume the sale of F4 Phantom warplanes to Israel.

THE BIG STORIES OF 1971

(Selected by the news editors of Associated Press member newspapers and radio and television stations)

1. The China story.
2. President Nixon's wage-price freeze, of national and international effects.
3. Pentagon Papers.
4. Conviction of Lt. William L. Calley, Jr.
5. Successful Apollo 14 and Apollo 15 moon landings.
6. Attica Prison rioting took 43 lives.
7. Vietnam War, troop withdrawal and election of President Thieu.
8. School busing issue.
9. More than 60 died in California earthquake.
10. Senate voted down foreign aid authorization bill.

DEATHS—1971

JANUARY

Gabrielle (Coco) Chanel, 87, was a famed French fashion designer whose Chanel No. 5 perfume made her name known around the world. Beginning as a country dressmaker, she rose to fame in Paris' fashion circles. She opened her first Paris shop in 1910 and concentrated on selling hats. Two years later a customer asked her to design a dress for her small daughter. The mother was pleased with the result and asked for a duplicate of the dress that she could wear herself. Coco's climb to fame followed. A musical version of her life, *Coco,* ran on Broadway for eight months, closing in 1970. In Paris Jan. 10.

Harry F. Guggenheim, besides co-founding the country's largest suburban daily newspaper, Newsday, was a financier, philanthropist and horseman. He was the descendent of a wealthy mining family, and at one time became president of the Solomon R. Guggenheim Foundation established by his uncle. His chief business interest after 1941 was Newsday, which he and his third wife Alicia Patterson founded in Garden City, L.I. After his wife died Guggenheim became editor, publisher and president of the paper until he sold his stock in 1970 to the Times Mirror Co., publishers of the Los Angeles Times. Another of Guggenheim's interests was diplomacy. He served as United States ambassador to Cuba from 1929 to 1933. In 1951 he became the president of Guggenheim Brothers, which controlled mining operations throughout the world. A longtime attorney of Guggenheim's said a few years ago that "Harry just can't play, he has to convert even what other men consider play into work." His racing career was an example. He started by paying $400 for a yearling in 1934 and by 1953 his Dark Star defeated Native Dancer in the Kentucky Derby. Guggenheim was the prime mover in the establishment of the New York Racing Association. He died Jan. 22 at 80, at his home in Sands Point, Long Island.

Eric Hodgins, 71, was a writer and editor who in 1946 published his first novel, *Mr. Blandings Builds His Dream House,* and saw it become a best seller. The book told humorously of the ordeals of an advertising executive who built a home in the country and Hodgins later wrote it "made me pots of money; 20 years later it is still well remembered and will probably go on my tombstone. . . ." The novel also was made into a movie. Dec. 7, in New York City.

FEBRUARY

Adolf A. Berle Jr. was a lawyer, economist, law professor, diplomat and Liberal party leader who came into prominence as one of the original members of President Franklin D. Roosevelt's "Brain Trust." As counsel to the Reconstruction Finance Corporation during the New Deal, Berle had much to do with shaping legislation to reform banking, the stock market and railroading. At one point he was an assistant secretary of state, a position in which he became a leading authority on Latin American Affairs. On Feb. 18, of a stroke at 76, in New York.

Dr. Paul de Kruif, a bacteriologist and author of best selling books. Among them were *Microbe Hunters,* which was published in 1926 and which sold more than a million copies, and *Men Against Death,* published in 1932, in glorification of the American doctor. He also collaborated with Sinclair Lewis on *Arrowsmith,* the novel about a country doctor turned research scientist. Aside from his work as an author, De Kruif helped to develop a successful treatment of syphilis before the discovery of penicillin, and was instrumental in the discovery

of an antitoxin for gas gangrene. At 80, of a heart attack, Feb 28.

Fernandel, one of the most popular comedians of the French screen. At the age of 10 Fernandel followed his father as a cafe singer. He later performed as comic singer in Paris music halls and went on to films in 1930, starring in 150 productions. It was at this time that he won national and international acclaim as a comedian playing a little man of peasant origin. He also was a shrewd businessman, forming his own production company with Jean Gabin, another of France's biggest stars. At 67, of cancer, in Paris, Feb. 26.

Henri Huet, 43, Associated Press photographer, was believed to have had more experience than any other cameraman in photographing warfare in Indochina. His career was climaxed in 1967 when he was given the Capa award for "superlative still photography requiring exceptional courage and enterprise." Huet was born in South Vietnam of a French father and a Vietnamese mother. He had photographed the struggle in Indochina for nearly 22 years. He was a combat photographer with French forces in 1949–52, later joining the U.S. Economic Mission in Vietnam and for nine years doubling as a photographer for the U.S. Information Service. Huet joined the AP in 1963 and was later wounded and reassigned out of the war zone to Tokyo, but in a short time he asked to be returned to Saigon and war coverage. Huet and three other war photographers—Larry Burrows, 44, two-time winner of the Capa award and a Life staffer, and Kent Potter, 24, of United Press International—were killed Feb. 10 when their helicopter was shot down over the Ho Chi Minh trail in Laos. Huet was the 28th newsman to die in the war since 1965.

Robert Neal Manry, who once wrote to the Cleveland Plain Dealer: "Don't worry, I'll be back at 2 o'clock on Aug. 29." On June 1, 1965, Manry set sail from Falmouth, Mass., for Falmouth, England, in the smallest boat ever to make the voyage. *Tinkerbell,* a 13½ foot sailboat, was 36 years old, built in Maine as a whitecap class racing dinghy. Manry rebuilt the craft to make the 3,200-mile voyage that took him 78 days. After the trip he reported that he had been washed overboard six times, dodged sharks and dolphins and suffered hallucinations of ghosts. He never returned to the Cleveland Plain Dealer as a copy editor. Instead the fame of the trip turned him to magazine writing and lecture engagements. On Feb. 21, of a heart attack at 52.

James Cash Penney, one of a handful of 20th century merchant princes who created vast corporate edifices in their own image. He lived by the Golden Rule, part of which meant humane conduct to employes and customers. In 1902 he founded his first store, a few years later changed its name from the Golden Rule to the J.C. Penney Co., and by 1971 had built 1,659 others. The Penney chain became the country's fifth largest merchandising company, with sales of $4.1-billion. Until his death at 95, Penney worked three days a week, keeping five secretaries busy. On Feb. 12, of a heart attack.

G. Frederick Reinhardt, former United States ambassador to Italy and at the time of his death in charge of the Zurich headquarters of Stanford Research Institute. During World War II he served as a political advisor to military officials in Europe, on the staffs of General Dwight D. Eisenhower, Matthew B. Ridgway and Alfred M. Gruenther. Later he was deputy for civil affairs at the North Atlantic Treaty organization Defense College in Paris. In 1955 he held the post of ambassador to Vietnam for two years and in 1960 President Eisenhower appointed him ambassador to Italy. He served there until 1968. Feb. 22, of a heart attack at 59.

MARCH

Bebe Daniels, 71, who was extremely active in vaudeville, radio and television with her equally famous husband Ben Lyon. At the age of 14 Bebe landed her first adult film role with the Hal Roach Company and was later featured in the Lonesome Luke comedies. The star was Harold Lloyd, who died March 8. She starred in silent films and easily transferred her talents later to talkies. She and her husband moved to London in 1936 and starred in British films, including *Hi Gang,* a movie version of a radio program that ran 52 weeks on the BBC. As a team Daniels and Lyon also starred in *Return of Carol Deane* and *You Can't Escape Forever.* Bebe was survived by her husband and their two children. March 16, in London.

Charles Engelhard, 54, one of the richest men in the world, headed Engelhard Industries, an empire built on platinum, gold and silver that he inherited from his father. Because of his gold dealings he was sometimes identified as the inspiration for *Goldfinger,* a spy story written by his friend Ian Flemming. Besides being a friend of presidents, he was a substantial contributor to the Kennedy-Johnson ticket in 1960 and was a good friend of Lyndon Johnson. He was well known for his racehorses, the most successful of which was Nijinsky, the son of Native Dancer. Engelhard bought him for $84,000 and sold him to a syndicate in 1970 for a record $5.4 million. Nijinsky was the winner of the Epsom and Irish Derbies and was the front runner in all but two of his 14 starts. Engelhard died of a heart attack at his winter estate in Boca Grande, Fla. March 2.

Sherman Mills Fairchild, 74, photography and aviation pioneer, had the imagination and wealth to develop ideas into major industries. Founder of the Fairchild-Hiller Corp., designer of satellites, he was also chairman of Fairchild Camera and Equipment Company and a director of International Business Machines Corp., of which his father was a founder. In 1920 he founded the Fairchild Aerial Camera Corp., which manufactured cameras that he had developed. Fairchild was also an amateur cook, interested in gourmet food; a good dancer and tennis player, and was involved in music publishing. For his estate at Lloyd Neck, N.Y., he built an indoor tennis court with his own lighting system and no windows. On March 28, in New York's Roosevelt Hospital, after a long illness.

Leland Hayward, 68, a producer, aviator and agent who guided the careers of such stars as James Stewart, Judy Garland, Clark Gable, Katherine Hepburn and such writers as Ernest Hemingway and Edna Ferber. Flamboyant and fast talking, Hayward in the mid-1930s broke the gentlemen's agreement in which studios did not steal talent from other studios by offering more money even if the contract was about to expire. When Hayward convinced Warner Brothers to take three actors from Paramount by offering them double what they were getting he was disliked by some of the leading Hollywood figures. Shortly before the start of World War II Hayward started a flying school which later became Thunderbird Field in Phoenix, Ariz. For a time he served as a board member of Trans World Airlines and in 1946 co-founded Southwest Airways. His Broadway career began in 1944 with *A Bell for Adano.* An enormous hit, it was followed by others such as *South Pacific, Call Me Madam, Gypsy,* and *The Sound of Music.* Hayward, described as a tall and handsome man, was married five times, twice to the same woman. His widow was Mrs. Pamela Digby Churchill, divorced wife of Randolf Churchill, Sir Winston's son. March 18, in Yorktown Heights, N.Y.

Rockwell Kent, 88, internationally acclaimed artist whose run-ins with the Establishment made headlines, was a volatile and versatile figure. Kent distinguished himself in lithography, poetry, architecture, farming, exploring and the breeding of Great Danes as well as in painting. His rugged landscape paintings and book illustrations won him international renown, but his disputes with the authorities also attracted attention. Kent's paintings were in collections of the Metropolitan Museum of Art, the Chicago Art Institute and galleries in Washington, Pittsburgh, Los Angeles and San Francisco. He also caused a stir in 1967 when he went to Moscow to accept the Lenin Peace Prize, then donated the $10,000 prize money to North Vietnam. He wanted the money used, he said, to relieve "the suffering of women and children." Eight years earlier Kent's passport was lifted by U.S. authorities after he had addressed the Supreme Soviet in Moscow. However, he described the Communists as "my enemies." March 13 in Plattsburg, N.Y., after a long period of poor health.

Harold Lloyd, 77, one of the great comedians of both silent films and the talkies. Lloyd made an image for himself as the shy, innocent adolescent who narrowly escaped every hazard hoping to obtain something good in the end. Well known for his horn-rimmed glasses without lenses, Lloyd was the highest paid screen actor in the 1920s. Starting as a low-paid extra and a run-of-the mill slapstick comedian, he developed the character of Lonesome Luke. One of his best known films was *Safety Last,* in which Lloyd climbed up the face of a 14-story building and dangled from the hands of a giant clock, making him the most daring comedian in Hollywood. March 8, of cancer, in Hollywood.

Allan Nevins, 80, an author and historian who brought intrigue and liveliness to the subject of history. He was the winner of two Pulitzer prizes, one in 1933 for a biography of Grover Cleveland and another in 1937 for a study of Hamilton Fish. Nevins was acclaimed for his respect for the truth and his deep humanist approach. After working as editorial writer for several newspapers, Nevins joined the faculty at Columbia University in 1928 and stayed there until his retirement in 1958. In 1948 he set up an oral history program designed to aid future historians by preserving on tape and in typescript the opinions and recollections of hundreds of major contemporaries. At the time of his death he was the chairman of the American Heritage Magazine advisory board. In Menlo Park, Calif., March 5.

Dr. William Barry Wood Jr., 60, a teacher, physician and researcher, was credited with being the first to describe a phenomenon known as surface phagocytosis, a mechanism by which white blood cells fight bacteria and other invading organisms. He was also renowned for his work on the isolation of pyrogen, the substance that can contribute to the causes of fever. While attending Harvard Wood was an accomplished athlete in football, hockey, baseball and tennis. March 9, of a heart attack, in Boston.

APRIL

Robert J. Corbett, 65, Republican representative, was dean of Pennsylvania's congressional delegation. Corbett was first elected to the House in 1938 but was defeated in Franklin D. Roosevelt's third term sweep in 1940. He served as sheriff of Pennsylvania's Allegheny County until he was returned to Congress in 1944. In 1951, he joined in introducing a resolution asking that Formosa not be abandoned to Communist China or used as a bargaining element in peace negotiations. Corbett was the ranking Republican minority member of the House Committee on Post Office and Civil Service and also served on one of the Armed Services subcommittees. April 25, at Suburban General Hospital in Pittsburgh, Pa., after suffering a cerebral thrombosis.

William D. Eckert, 62, a former Air Force lieutenant general and commissioner of major league baseball, who was selected for baseball's highest post in 1965. Three years after he was chosen as commissioner, baseball officials bought up the remainder of Eckert's contract and named Bowie Kuhn as his successor. An expert in supply and logistics, he became part of the newly organized Air Force after World War II but retired in March 1961 after a mild heart attack. April 16, of a heart attack, while vacationing in the Bahamas.

Maj. George Fielding Eliot, 76, noted military analyst and author, was a military correspondent and analyst during World War II for the New York Herald Tribune and the Columbia Broadcasting System. He wrote a syndicated military affairs column until 1967 and was also military editor of Collier's Encyclopedia. Eliot was looked on as the dean of military analysts during World War II. His column appearing in the Herald Tribune and 34 other papers was said to have had 5 million readers. He saw infantry service during World War I with the Australian Imperial Force, was gassed once, wounded twice and was promoted to the rank of captain. He earned the rank of major during 10 years of service with the U.S. Military Intelligence Reserve from 1922–32. He was born in Brooklyn, but moved to Australia with his family before the first war. April 21 in Torrington, Conn., after a long illness.

S. Smith Griswold, 62, a pioneer in the fight against air pollution, was one of the most militant critics of the automobile industry. The federal law enacted in December 1970 setting a six-year-deadline for the auto industry to develop engines that were virtually pollution free was in a sense a monument to Griswold. He needled and heckled Detroit to reduce the fumes from cars, declaring that patent data showed that "automobile pollution controls were available as far back as 1909." Griswold took over direction of the Los Angeles Air Pollution Control District at a time when stationary smog sources, like industry, were still looked upon as the major cause of smog. He developed an agency with a budget of more than $5 million a year, persuaded the county government to ratify about 100 stringent restrictions on fume emission and battled some corporations all the way to the Supreme Court to make the ordinances stick. April 20, of cancer, in Bethesda Naval Hospital outside Washington, D.C.

Will Harridge, 86, served as president of baseball's American League for 27 years. Although he never played baseball, he devoted his life to the administrative aspect of the game. Serving the American League for more than three decades, he was its president from May 27, 1931, to Jan. 31, 1959, when he resigned. April 9, in Evanston, Ill.

Leonard George (Lennie) Hayton, 63, composer, conductor and arranger, received Academy awards for writing the scores of *Star* with Julie Andrews and for *On The Town.* Hayton began his career as a pianist and played with a number of jazz groups, including Red Nichols. He also was with Paul Whiteman's orchestra. Later he was heard on the *Hit Parade* programs on the radio. He had been a member of the American Society of Composers, Authors and Publishers since 1953. He was married to Lena Horne, the noted singer and actress, who once said "Lennie showed me how to do things with my voice that I had never been allowed to do in the movies." April 24, of a heart ailment in Desert Hospital, Palm Springs, Calif.

Viscount Portal of Hungerford, 77, as chief of Britain's air staff, played a major role in shaping the policy of the Royal Air Force during World War II. During his tenure, Britain saw a massive expansion of the Royal Air Force and the steady growth of the British air offensive against Germany. As a member of the chiefs of staff committee, Portal played a key role in presenting to the war cabinet the advice of the chiefs of staff on allied strategy and other

matters of policy. April 23, in Chichester, Sussex.

Paul Scott Mowrer, 83, served for many years as a leading foreign correspondent for the Chicago Daily News and as its editor for nearly a decade. He won the first Pulitzer Prize awarded for foreign correspondence in 1928, did a succession of books analyzing the European scene and managed to write several books of poetry. Mowrer was sent to Paris by the Chicago Daily News in 1910 and, while many correspondents were following the activities of fashionable Americans abroad, he began covering the Balkan wars that proved the curtainraiser for World War I. He served as editor of the Chicago paper from 1935–44, then switched to the New York Post until his retirement from newspaper work in 1947. He was married to the former Hadley Richardson, who was the first wife of Ernest Hemingway. On April 4 in Beaufort, S.C., while returning to his New Hampshire home from a Florida vacation.

Gen. Auguste Charles Nogues, 95, of France, resisted the allied landings in North Africa during World War II. After loyal service in Morocco during World War I, Nogues was charged with pacifying nationalistic and pro-labor forces there and was named resident general of Morocco in 1936. After the outbreak of World War II he was named commander in chief of all French forces in North Africa. When French resistance collapsed in 1940, a group of government deputies and other officials fled to Morocco and set up a resistance center. Nogues blocked their efforts to make contact with British agents. He was tried in 1947 and sentenced to 20 years at hard labor, but he was in Portugal and did not return to France until 1956, when he was arrested but later released. April 20 in Paris.

Cecil Parker, 73, the stage and movie actor, specialized in portrayals of the typical English gentleman. He made his first stage appearance at the age of 25 and established his reputation in 1941 with an appearance in Noel Coward's farce, *Blithe Spirit.* Parker made his New York debut in 1950 in *Daphne Laureola* with Edith Evans. Films in which he appeared included *Caesar and Cleopatra; The Man in the White Suit* and *The Detective.* April 20, at his home in Brighton.

Daniel F. Reeves, 58, was the principal owner of the Los Angeles Rams football team for 30 years. Reeves was the man who first brought a major professional team to the West Coast. He also paved the way for other successful franchise shifts to California, including baseball's Dodgers and Giants and basketball's Lakers. Reeves was the first owner to set up an extensive scouting system to find the college players with pro potential. After 25 years in pro football, Reeves gave the following formula for success: "There are only two things necessary. First you get the best players. Then you get the coach who can get the best out of them." April 15, of cancer, at his New York City apartment.

Elmo Roper, 70, acquired national fame for creating the scientific poll which was to become a 20th century phenomenon in political forecasting. Adapting sampling techniques he had developed as a marketing consultant, Roper predicted with remarkable accuracy the 1936 reelection of President Franklin D. Roosevelt. After that, Roper became an increasingly important figure in the world of politics. His technique consisted of using a public cross-section that was comparatively small but carefully picked to be as representative as possible. He had predicted a Roosevelt victory with 61.7 per cent of the popular vote. Roosevelt received 60.7 per cent. April 30 in Norwalk, Conn.

T. V. Soong, 77, longtime banking genius of the Nationalist Chinese regime, was the eldest son of the famous Shanghai family that included Mrs. Sun Yat-sen, Mrs. Chiang Kai-shek and Mrs. H. H. Kung. Beginning in the early 1930s, Soong was minister of finance and served several times as premier under his brother-in-law, President Chiang Kai-shek. For the final 20 years of the Republic of China, Soong dominated its financial affairs. In World War II, Soong was China's negotiator for western support. In 1940, he negotiated a loan of $100 million from the United States. In return, he promised that China would pin down one million Japanese troops while the United States prepared for the war with Japan that he felt was inevitable. Two weeks after the attack on Pearl Harbor, Soong was appointed foreign minister by Chiang. April 25, in San Francisco.

MAY

Gregory Cardinal Agagianian, 75, was one of the most scholarly members of the Sacred College of Cardinals. The Armenian-born prelate retired in October 1970 after 10 years as chief of the worldwide missions of the Roman Catholic Church. He lived much of his life in exile from his native Russia because of his work in the Catholic Church, yet served as spiritual leader for thousands of Armenian Catholics who continued to practice their faith in the southern areas of the Soviet Union. Pope Pius XII conferred the red hat of prince of the church on Msgr. Agagianian in February 1946, making him at 50 the youngest member of the sacred college. On May 16 at his Rome residence.

Col. Florence Blanchfield, 87, directed 60,000 nurses as head of the U.S. Army Nurse Corps during World War II. Col. Blanchfield was the first woman to receive a commission in the regular Army. Presenting her with the commission in 1947, Gen. Dwight D. Eisenhower paid tribute to the heroism of army nurses. She had argued for "full" rather than "relative" rank at hearings before a succession of Congressional committees. Col. Blanchfield also championed the right of army nurses to take a husband. During her years in the Nurse Corps she served in many countries, including China, the Philippines and a number of European installations. On May 12 at Walter Reed Hospital.

James Cox Brady, 63, financier and noted horseman, served for eight years as chairman of the New York Racing Association. He served in executive capacities in The Jockey Club and the Thoroughbred Racing Associations. When the Greater New York Racing Association was formed in 1954 to conduct racing in the state as a non-dividend-paying operation, Brady was one of the original members. In 1961 he was elected chairman of the organization, by then known as the New York Racing Association. Short of having a Kentucky Derby winner, Brady received virtually every other honor in the sport of kings. On May 24 at Overlook Hospital in Summit, N.J.

Frank Conniff, 57, former national editor of Hearst newspapers, was a co-winner of the Pulitzer Prize for 1955 when he participated in an interview with Nikita Khrushchev, then premier of the Soviet Union. Conniff, who began his career as a copy boy, became well known as a combat correspondent covering Allied operations in Africa, Italy and Germany in World War II. After the war he wrote a column, and in 1958 he was named general director of the Hearst Headline Service. Later he took up column writing again, first in Washington then New York. Conniff regarded as a high point of his reportorial career his coverage of Gen. Anthony McAuliffe's refusal to surrender American paratroopers to the Germans during the Battle of the Bulge in 1945. On May 25 in New York City.

Thomas J. Dodd, 64, former Democratic senator from Connecticut, was one of six men in the history of the U.S. Senate to be censured by that body. Dodd's public service career spanned more than a third of a century, beginning in the midst of the depression and ending when the new Congress was sworn in during January 1971. It reached a peak in 1964, when Dodd was mentioned as a vice presidential candidate. It hit bottom on June 23, 1967, when the Senate censured him for converting $116,083 in campaign funds to his personal use. Dodd claimed later that he had been vindicated. The Justice Department in December 1969 said it had examined Dodd's income tax records and could find no grounds for criminal prosecution. Dodd ran as an independent in 1970 for a third term in the Senate, but was defeated. He told supporters he was running to clear the blot from his record. On May 24, of a heart attack in Old Lyme, Conn.

Glenda Farrell, 66, appeared in 122 films and many plays on stage and television as the gum-chewing blonde who wisecracked her way through numerous rough and tumble scenes in the 1930s. Miss Farrell also starred in hard-boiled roles but refused to play any part that made her appear too tough. She last appeared on Broadway in 1969, as the mother of Julie Harris in the hit play *Forty Carats*. She became ill during the run of the show and never fully recovered. On May 1 in her New York apartment.

Leon (Goose) Goslin, 70, former hard-hitting American League outfielder, was elected to baseball's Hall of Fame in 1968. One of baseball's finest hitters, Goslin played left field from 1921 to 1938 for the Washington Senators, the St. Louis Browns and Detroit Tigers, compiling a lifetime average of .316. In five World Series his average was .287 with seven home runs. He received his nickname because of the odd way he chased fly balls. Opposing players said he resembled a bird, flapping its wings as he ran after the ball with his arms waving. On May 15 at Bridgeton Hospital in New Jersey.

Sir Tyrone Guthrie, 70, noted author and producer, dominated stages around the world for nearly half a century. His insistence on technical perfection became as much his trademark as the range of his productions which included Pirandello's *Six Characters in Search of an Author* and a modern dress *Hamlet*. Early in his career, he wrote plays for the British Broadcasting Corporation but he soon switched to directing. By the 1930s he was directing Shakespearean repertory for the Old Vic, a British Group he headed for 12 years. Guthrie demanded dedicated craftsmanship of his actors and his productions gained fame in Great Britain and the United States. On May 15 at his home in Newbliss, County Monaghan, Ireland.

William Brown Meloney, 69, theatrical producer, author, lawyer, publicist, editor and professor. In the 1930s he produced a number of plays, including *Soldier's Wife* and *Outrageous Fortune*. Among his books were *Call Back Love* and *Strange Victory*. He was the producer of *Claudia,* a radio series based on the character created by Rose Franken, his second wife. He was also a prolific contributor to magazines. On May 4 of a heart attack at his home in Kent, Conn.

Ogden Nash, 68, whose droll verse and unconventional rhymes made him one of the best known producers of humorous poetry in America. Looking back over his productive writing career that spanned 40 years, Nash remarked a few years before his death that he would probably be best recalled for his classic lines "Candy is dandy, but liquor is quicker."

Nash was a polished craftsman even if he did rhyme such words as "petunia" and "Pennsylvunia," or "parsley is gharsley."

Unlike most poets, Nash made a good living at his craft and put out 20 volumes of verse. After several frustrating years trying to sell bonds and write advertising copy, Nash dashed off a few lines of humorous verse and sent them to the New Yorker magazine. The poem was accepted and his career had begun. Nash also wrote the lyrics for the musical play *One Touch of Venus,* which became a smash hit of the 1943 Broadway season. On May 19 at Johns Hopkins Hospital in Baltimore.

Kenneth C. Royall, 66, the last U.S. Secretary of War and the first Secretary of The Army, served during the Truman Administration. Royall also served in uniform in both world wars, as an artillery lieutenant in the first and a colonel heading the legal division of the Army service forces in the second. Later he was named the War Department's deputy fiscal director and promoted to brigadier general in 1943. In April 1945 Royall was named assistant to the secretary of war and later under secretary. In 1947 he became secretary of the army and served until 1949, when he returned to civilian life, becoming a senior partner of a law firm in New York. On May 25 at a hospital in Durham, N.C.

Dennis Lee Royle, 49, Associated Press photographer, captured some of the great news pictures of the post-World War II years. Royle had faced danger countless times in wars in Africa and the East. In April 1960, he was on the spot at a South African country showground when a would-be assassin fired two bullets into Prime Minister Henrik Vervoerd. Royle's picture of the prime minister, blood streaming through fingers clutched to his head, went around the world. In 1952 Royle photographed one of the most remarkable maritime dramas ever to catch the imagination of the newspaper-reading public, the sinking of the American freighter *Flying Enterprise*. Through 13 days of winter weather in the eastern Atlantic, Capt. Kurt Carlsen defiantly stuck to the bridge of his listing ship, intent on getting her to port. With two AP reporters, Royle sat out the waiting hours aboard a pitching tug. They were the only news team there when, in the fading light of a January evening, Carlsen and his aide, Kenneth Dancey, jumped to safety and the *Flying Enterprise* finally slid beneath the waves. On May 20 in a helicopter crash while covering a naval exercise in the English Channel.

Allin Carrey Seward Jr., 62, played an important role in organizing the overseas operations of the United Nations. He had served with the U.N. truce supervision groups sent to the Middle East in 1948 and 1956, and he also assisted in arrangements for the U.N. peacekeeping force sent to the Congo in 1960. As chief of the U.N. field operations, he had a key role in expanding the field staff and the U.N. radio network and in developing the logistical support required by the peacekeeping forces of the world organization. In the 1930s Seward served with a number of U.S. government agencies before being assigned to the United States Navy Supply Service in 1942. In 1946 the United Nations borrowed him from the Navy to help set up the new organization's conference services. On May 20 at Norwalk Hospital in Connecticut.

Dr. Donald Dexter Van Slyke, 88, internationally known biological chemist, who had received 14 national and international scientific awards. He was recognized throughout the world for major discoveries in chemistry, physiology and medicine and was associated with the Rockefeller Institute for Medical Research from 1907 until his death. In 1951 a committee of the American Chemical Society named him as one of 39 Americans who had attained the greatest eminence in chemistry. He is perhaps best known for studies on acidosis which revolutionized the treatment of diabetes, for longterm studies in kidney diseases and for the textbook *Quantitative Clinical Chemistry,* which he coauthored. On May 4 of cancer in Garden City, N.Y.

JUNE

Herbert Biberman, 71, one of "The Hollywood 10," was a leading director of the Theater Guild whose films included the award-winning film *Salt of the Earth.* He was convicted of contempt of Congress in 1950 and served a six-month prison sentence in a Federal penitentiary in Texas. The conviction resulted from Biberman's refusal, at a session of the

House Committee on Un-American Activities in 1947, to answer the question: "Are you now, or have you ever been a member of the Communist Party?" Biberman based his refusal on the First Amendment. In 1954 he directed *Salt of the Earth,* a drama about striking New Mexico miners. In Europe it was voted the best picture of the year by the Motion Picture Academy of France. It also carried off a top prize of the Karlovy Vary Film Festival in Czechoslovakia. On June 30, in New York City.

Alexei Isayev, 62, described by the Soviet government as the man responsible for designing the nation's space engines. Isayev designed the engine units for the Vostok and Voshkhod rockets and the Soyuz manned spacecraft, said Tass news agency. Since 1934 Isayev had worked as a doctor of technical science in the nation's aviation industry and devoted much of his adult life to the development of aviation and rocket engines. He was one of the creators of the plane which on May 15, 1942, was reported to have made the world's first flight powered by jet engines. Soviet authorities had made no mention of Isayev's key role in the nation's space program until his death. On June 25.

Dr. Alvin Johnson, 96, was a founder of the New School for Social Research in New York and a leader in American education. He founded the school in 1919 with historian Charles A. Beard, philosopher John Dewey and other educators. Although he had retired from active work and had been president emeritus of the New School since 1945, Johnson continued writing, teaching and helping good causes. He was among the first American scholars to understand the anti-intellectual implications of Nazism. When Adolf Hitler seized power in Germany in 1933 and began persecuting non-Nazi intellectuals Johnson initiated a fund to rescue these scholars. Through the Rockefeller Foundation he brought more than 200 scholars to the United States. On June 7, at his home in Upper Nyack, N.Y.

Joe E. Lewis, 69, gravel-voiced nightclub comic, made a highly profitable career of joking about his hard drinking and heavy gambling. He sometimes told an audience, "I'm working under a terrible handicap tonight. I have no talent." In his nightclub routine, Lewis walked around the room, a microphone in one hand and a tumbler of whisky in the other, talking and drinking. In the late 1920s Lewis was slashed and bludgeoned by Chicago gangsters after playing in a rival club, and was left for dead. During his long recovery he had to learn how to talk all over again. On June 4, in a New York hospital after collapsing in his hotel suite.

The Rev. Reinhold Niebuhr, 78, was considered one of the greatest Christian thinkers the United States had produced. It was said that Dr. Niebuhr brought "original sin" back into fashion. He saw it in terms not just of individual self-adoration but in the whole web of collective forces that tend to become objects of idolatry, whether nationalism, scientism, pleasure cults, wealth or utopian social schemes. Dr. Niebuhr was ordained in 1915 in the Evangelical Synod of North America and became pastor of Bethel Evangelical Church in Detroit. From there he went to Union Theological Seminary in 1928. He retired from the seminary in 1960 after 32 years on the faculty, but continued his writings that included more than 20 books. On June 1, at his summer home in Stockbridge, Mass., after a long illness.

Lord Boyd Orr, 90, was the first director of the U.N. Food and Agricultural Organization and winner of the 1949 Nobel Peace Prize. An internationally known Scottish nutritionist before going to the FAO, Lord Boyd Orr worked for many years to relate health and agriculture and to raise the food standards of the world. During the depression years in the 1930s he experimented with 1,500 children of unemployed British miners by giving them skimmed milk thrown away by farmers. The results were favorable. Knighted in 1935 for his services to agriculture, Boyd Orr served during World War II on Ministry of Food commissions and was invited by the British Labor government to attend the Quebec conference in 1945 that set up the FAO. He resigned from the organization in 1949. On June 25, at his home at Edzell, Scotland.

Lord John Charles Walsham Reith, 81, the "Father of the British Broadcasting Corporation," whose austere personality shaped the character of the BBC for almost two decades. In 1923 he became managing director of BBC's forerunner, the British Broadcasting Company, and imposed ethical and intellectual standards on programs that exerted an influence for more than 30 years after his retirement in 1938. His programs were designed to encourage respect for national institutions, such as the Anglican Church, and the social systems and upper-class values. He was adamant about continuing the concept of dedicated public service but he also fought the Conservative and Labor governments to maintain BBC's freedom. After leaving the BBC he became the chairman of Imperial Airways, forerunner of the British Overseas Airways Corporation. June 16, in Edinburgh at the age of 81.

Michael Rennie, 62, was a smooth, debonair actor who attained fame as Harry Lime in the television series *The Third Man.* Rennie's portrayal of the romantic international spy was one of the most popular television series ever made. Born in England, he had been a U.S. citizen since 1960. Rennie made more than 50 films in Hollywood, including *Trio; The Day The Earth Stood Still; Seven Cities of Gold* and *Les Miserables.* On June 10, in Harrogate, Yorkshire, while visiting his mother.

Dr. Wendell M. Stanley, 66, a Nobel laureate who did pioneering work in viruses as well as serving as the director of the University of California Virus Laboratory, the largest research center of its kind. In the early 1930s, at a time when the nature of viruses were a dangerous mystery, Stanley solved the problem. After only two years of research he determined that viruses were creatures from a strange twilight zone between life and nonlife. His work on the tobacco mosaic virus, a "germ" that devastated tobacco crops, created a scientific sensation. In 1946 Stanley shared the Nobel Prize in chemistry with two other doctors who also did their research in viruses. He was asked to create the University of California Virus Laboratory at Berkeley and from the time it opened in 1948 to his retirement in 1969 he served as its director. June 15, in Salamanca, Spain.

John S. Sumner, 94, as executive secretary of the Society for the Suppression of Vice waged war for more than 35 years against what he regarded as the "forces of evil" in New York City. As unofficial guardian of public morals, Sumner kept up a constant search for signs of lewdness in books, pictures and records. Among books he went after were James Joyce's *Ulysses,* D. H. Lawrence's *Lady Chatterly's Lover* and *The Genius,* by Theodore Dreiser. He also played a part in having Mae West sent to jail for 10 days for directing the play called *Sex.* On June 20, at a nursing home in Floral Park, N.Y.

James Ramsey Ullman, 63, writer and mountain climber, wrote on a wide range of subjects and a variety of places, from the jungles of the Amazon to the Alps. He was most widely known for his books on mountains and mountain climbing. His first published novel, *The White Tower,* was a Book-of-the-Month selection in 1945 and received wide critical acclaim. Ullman was a member of the American expedition that scaled Everest in 1963, but he was unable to take part in the actual ascent because of a circulatory condition. He was in constant radio contact with the climbers and his account of their feat in 1964 became a best seller. On June 20, in Boston's University Hospital.

Kenny Washington, 52, was one of the greatest football players on the West Coast. As tailback for the University of California at Los Angeles, Washington was outstanding as a runner and passer in the 1930s. In a game with the University of Southern California in 1937, Washington lobbed a pass 62 yards, setting a UCLA record. Seven years after his college athletic career, Washington joined the professional ranks with the Los Angeles Rams and remained with them until 1949. Although plagued by bad knees, he set a club record of 859 yards. After retiring from football at the age of 31 he played professional baseball briefly with the New York Giants. On June 24 at U.C.L.A. Medical Center.

Garfield Arthur (Gar) Wood, 90, industrialist and powerboat racing enthusiast, was credited with inventing the lift for dump trucks. By investing 50 cents in a small polished cylinder, Wood began an intensive career struggling with the first hydraulic lift for dump trucks and built that investment into a $50 million personal fortune. In the 1930s he designed a high speed launch for the U.S. Navy which attracted the attention of President Franklin D. Roosevelt. It later became the hit-and-run PT boat of World War II. Wood, known as the "Gray Fox of Algonac," the Michigan town where he built his swift power craft, was one of the immortals of motorboat racing. The sport chose him in November 1953 as one of the 10 members of the American Power Boating Association's first "honor squadron." On June 19, in Miami.

JULY

Lord Constantine, 69, a former international cricket star, was Britain's first black peer. Once ambassador to London for Trinidad and Tobago, he had announced his retirement three weeks before his death. The grandson of a West Indian slave, he moved to England in 1929 after making a name as one of the most spectacular stars cricket had known. In recent years he had become an effective campaigner against color prejudice. He served on the Race Relations Board set up in 1966 to enforce Britain's anti-discrimination laws. On July 1, at his home in London.

Cliff Edwards, 76, the singer and performer, was widely known as Ukulele Ike. He gave Jiminy Cricket his squeaky voice in Walt Disney's 1940 *Pinocchio* and also sang the Oscar-winning song *When You wish Upon a Star.* Edwards was credited with selling more than 74 million records in his career, and he appeared in more than 100 films, introducing *Singin' in the Rain* in the *Hollywood Revue of 1929.* He also played prominent roles in Broadway musicals. On July 17, at a nursing home in Hollywood.

Edgar N. Eisenhower, 82, brother of the late president, who once criticized "Little Ike's" peacetime spending budget and made national news. A graduate of the University of Michigan Law School, Eisenhower settled in Tacoma, Wash., and acquired a legal practice of high repute in the Northwest. In 1957, shocked by the proposed $72-billion peacetime national budget, he told reporters: "I can't for the life of me understand what persuaded Dwight to go for that big budget this year! . . . I'd sure like to discover what influence is at work on my brother." Asked the next day about this dissension among brothers, President Eisenhower replied, "Edgar has been criticizing me since I was five years old." Nevertheless, the older brother of Dwight was a frequent visitor at the White House. July 12, in Tacoma.

Adm. Thomas C. Hart, 94, was commander in chief of the U.S. Asiatic Fleet at the time of Pearl Harbor. In 1936 he had been sent to Shanghai with the four stars of a full admiral to command the Asiatic Fleet, of which he had said: "All my ships were old enough to vote." Noting signs of coming conflict, Hart moved his headquarters to Manila. He was credited with dispositions that saved all his surface ships and more than 200,000 tons of merchant vessels in the initial Japanese attack. In February 1942, Hart was ordered home. Though a year overdue for retirement, he was immediately recalled to active duty and seated on the Navy's General Board, while Congress voted him permanent four-star rank. One of his duties was to collect depositions for the Navy's inquiry into the Pearl Harbor disaster before memories faded. In February 1945 he accepted appointment as Republican senator from Connecticut to fill the vacancy caused by the death of Francis T. Maloney. On July 4, at his home in Sharon, Conn.

Lord Astor of Hever, 85, was former publisher of the Times of London and regarded as the epitome of the British establishment although he was American by birth. Born John Jacob Astor V, he became a British subject after his father moved to England and was named the first Viscount Astor. Lord Astor became chairman and chief proprietor of the Times in 1922 and retained his chairmanship until 1959. Early in 1942, during World War II, he expressed the view shared by other British publishers that "except what may be useful to the enemy or endanger national security," nothing should be subjected to censorship. He was elevated to the peerage in 1956. In 1962 he left Britain and settled in Pegomas, Southern France, to escape inheritance taxes on the family trust fund. On July 19, at the hospital in Cannes.

Gerald P. Nye, 78, Republican senator from North Dakota, was known as an isolationist before World War II. From 1925-44 he assailed presidents, Wall Street bankers, munitions manufacturers and advocates of U.S. entry into the war. He also defended the farmer and the small merchant. Nye had made a name for himself in the Teapot Dome oil scandals of the 1920s, and by his inquiries into profiteering in munitions sales to the American military establishment in the 1930s. He decried what he believed to be steps toward American entry into the second world war and denounced Britain as an aggressor, but declared that Nazi propaganda was just as perilous to U.S. interests as that from Britain. The senator opposed war aid to the Soviet Union, which he depicted as a nation run by "thieves, human butchers and murderers of religion." On July 17, in Washington, D.C.

Norman Reilly Raine, 76, created the character known as Tugboat Annie in about 75 stories appearing in the Saturday Evening Post and also wrote many films. Raine won an Oscar in 1937 with his script for *The Life of Emile Zola,* but he was best known as creator of Tugboat Annie, the salty skipper of the tugboat *Narcissus.* Raine also wrote the famous film in 1933 in which Marie Dressler played Annie and Wallace Beery portrayed her tippling husband, Terry. Among the films he wrote were *The Adventures of Robin Hood* and *A Bell for Adano.* On July 19, at the Motion Picture Country Hospital in Woodland Hills, Calif.

AUGUST

Margaret Bourke-White, 67, was regarded as one of the world's greatest photographers. Her camera took her through a life of high adventure, including wars, dust bowls, communal riots, death camps and floods. She was torpedoed off North Africa in World War II, ambushed in Korea and toured the American Southland photographing poverty stricken workers. Many of the world's most famous figures posed for her, including Franklin D. Roosevelt, Winston Churchill, Josef Stalin and Pope Pius XI. More than 40 years ago, Miss Bourke-White began a career of photographing machinery

and—in the words of one critic—transforming the American factory "into a Gothic cathedral." She married novelist Erskine Caldwell and they toured the rural South, photographing sharecroppers and tenant farmers. One of her most famous series was made in 1945, when she toured liberated Nazi concentration camps and photographed stacks of dead bodies that brought a shudder of revulsion around the world. On Aug. 27 in Stamford, Conn.

Benett Cerf, 73, was one of the giants of the publishing world but best known as a television personality, author and joke teller. For 16 years, Cerf appeared weekly on TV screens as a panelist on the parlor game show *What's My Line?* The show, in which panelists attempted to guess the occupations of various guests, made Cerf a national celebrity. He also appeared, usually without fee, in advertisements endorsing a wide range of products from shoes to coffee. All these activities made people tend to forget that Cerf was a brilliant publisher with an ability for inspiring friendship with such diverse authors as John Hersey and John O'Hara. Cerf played a key role in developing the Modern Library series, a forerunner of the paperbacks and a pillar of Random House, which he headed for more than 40 years until December 1970. One of Cerf's biggest projects was *The Random House Dictionary of the English Language,* a 2,059-page volume issued in 1966 after 10 years of preparation and costing about $3 million. On Aug. 27 at his estate in Mount Kisco, N.Y.

Harvey Fergusson, 81, wrote novels about the American Southwest. His first book, *The Blood of the Conquerors,* appeared in 1921 and was hailed for opening a new vein of fiction. His *Wolf Song* was filmed in 1929 with Gary Cooper and his *Hot Saturday* was made into a movie with Cary Grant in 1932. His autobiographical work, *Home in the West,* was published in 1944. On Aug. 28 in Berkeley, Calif.

Joseph W. Frazer, 79, who after college took a job as a mechanic's helper at 16 cents an hour at the Packard Motor Car Company and later became a top executive in the automobile industry. Frazer pioneered in the manufacture of low-priced cars and served as president and general manager of Willys-Overland Motors, Inc., from 1939 to 1943. In 1945 he entered partnership with Henry J. Kaiser and co-founded the Kaiser-Frazer Corp., which produced the Kaiser and Frazer cars and was briefly the country's fourth largest producer of automobiles. Frazer served as president and then as vice chairman until the company halted production in 1953. In Newport, R.I., of cancer, Aug. 7.

Nathan F. Leopold, 66, shocked America in 1924 when he and Richard Loeb murdered a 14-year-old boy, Bobby Franks, for thrills and in a vain attempt to commit the perfect crime. It was, in the minds of many, the "crime of the century," a kidnaping and killing that had been planned by two sons of wealthy Chicagoans. The parents of the youths—Leopold was 19 and Loeb 18—hired Clarence Darrow, one of the most famous lawyers of the day, to defend the youths. On his advice the youths pleaded innocent, but later Darrow changed the plea to guilty. He explained thereafter that he had not wanted to risk a jury trial in view of the emotion and publicity surrounding the case. The two defendants were sentenced to life imprisonment in view of their youth, the judge explained. Loeb was slain in 1936 in a fight with another prisoner. But Leopold became a model inmate, helping set up a prison library and volunteering in medical tests. In 1958, on his fifth plea for parole, the Illinois Parole and Prison Board ruled that Leopold had earned a chance at rehabilitation. Released in the custody of the Church of the Brethren, Leopold left Stateville Prison in Joliet, Ill., and went to Puerto Rico to begin work as a $10-a-month assistant in a church medical mission. On Aug. 29 in San Juan.

Ted Lewis, 80, the entertainer with the slow drawl and battered top hat, began his act by shouting "Is ev'rybody happy?" Lewis became famous in the 1920s and 1930s by popularizing such songs as *Me and My Shadow; When My Baby Smiles at Me; On the Sunny Side of the Street* and *St. Louis Blues.* The rise of jazz made it possible for Lewis to get a job with a trio at Hammerstein's Theatre in 1911. About 10 years later he was making up to $7,000 a week, appearing in two or three nightclubs at a time, playing his clarinet and shuffling across stage crooning the lyrics of the songs he made famous. By the mid-1920s Lewis had gone to London with his band and was making up to $10,000 weekly introducing American jazz to the British at the London Hippodrome and the Kit Kat Club. Lewis made two films based on his life, *Is Ev-rybody Happy?* in 1929 and *Here Comes the Band* in 1931. On Aug. 25 at his home in New York City.

Paul Lukas, 76, veteran screen star, won an Academy Award as best actor in 1943 for his part in *Watch on the Rhine.* In more than 50 years of starring in films, stage plays and television shows, the tall, cultivated actor epitomized Continental suavity. When *Watch on the Rhine* appeared in New York in 1941, critics showered Lukas with praise for his performance. The actor recreated his stage role for Warner Brothers and was voted the best actor in 1943 by the New York film critics and by the Academy of Motion Picture Arts and Sciences, for which he was awarded the Oscar. Among the many films in which Lukas starred were *Address Unknown; The Lady Vanishes; Dodsworth;* and *Berlin Express.* On Aug. 15 in Tangier, Morocco.

Lord Oaksey, 90, as Sir Geoffrey Lawrence, was president of the international war crimes tribunal at Nuernberg and passed the death sentence on 11 leading Nazis, including Herman Goering. When he was chosen as president at Nuernberg, he was described as "thoroughly representative of all those values" which are associated, especially by foreigners, with the Victorian English gentleman. Lord Oaksey's scorn of eloquence was illustrated when the historic war crimes trials began on Nov. 20, 1945. His opening statement ran just 14 sentences. His maiden speech in the House of Lords in 1948 opposed a proposal to suspend the death penalty in Britain for five years. "I have the greatest horror of the capital sentence, but a greater horror of the crimes which have been perpetrated," he declared. On Aug. 28 at his home in Malmesbury, Wiltshire.

Spyros P. Skouras, 78, longtime motion picture magnate, retired from the movie business in 1969 and began concentrating on a new career. He gave up the chairmanship of 20th Century-Fox that year and became chairman of the Prudential-Grace Shipping Lines. Skouras got his start in the movie business in 1914 when he and his two brothers, Charles and George, bought a nickelodeon company. The theater prospered, and in 1926 the brothers had acquired 37 theaters in St. Louis as well as a large number in Kansas City and Indianapolis. The Skouras' profitable St. Louis theaters attracted the attention of Warner Brothers, which bought their holdings and appointed Spyros general manager of the theater circuit. In 1931, Spyros left to work for Paramount and the following year took over Fox Metropolitan Theaters in New York. Skouras brought the enterprise back from the brink of financial collapse and then proceeded to build the 20th Century-Fox empire. On August 16 at his home in Mamaroneck, N.Y.

SEPTEMBER

Spring Byington, 72, was noted as a character actress in scores of movies and in the television series

December Bride. Between 1924 and 1934, Miss Byington appeared in 20 Broadway plays, including *The Merchant of Venice; Tonight at Twelve,* and *Ladies Don't Lie*. She played the mother's role in the motion picture *Little Women* and had maternal roles in such films as *Way Down East* and *Ah Wilderness*. She also attained note with Charles Coburn in 1941 in *The Devil and Miss Jones,* starring Jean Arthur. Miss Byington had a supporting role in the television series *Laramie*. On Sept. 7 in Hollywood.

Billy Gilbert, 78, built a comic career on a sneeze. His roles embraced the legitimate stage, vaudeville, motion pictures, radio and television. But he was best remembered as the man with the funny sneeze; a talent that won him the part of Sneezy's voice in the Walt Disney cartoon film *Snow White and the Seven Dwarfs*. Gilbert made about 300 films, usually as a comedian, but occasionally he played such serious roles as the minister of war in Charlie Chaplin's the *Great Dictator*. Gilbert once recalled that he had not used the famous sneeze in more than five or six films. "But the way it sticks in people's memories, you'd think that was all I ever did" he added. On stage he appeared in *Fanny* and in the Straus operetta, *The Chocolate Soldier*. On Sept. 23 at a convalescent home in Hollywood.

Bourke B. Hickenlooper, 75, former Republican Senator from Iowa, was a co-sponsor of the Atomic Energy Act of 1954, which initiated the development of atomic energy for peaceful uses. In 1962 controversy arose over an amendment to the foreign aid bill which he successfully sponsored. It provided that the United States automatically deny aid to any foreign country that expropriated property or equity of a U.S. citizen holding valid contracts, unless that nation took appropriate steps within six months toward adequate compensation. Hickenlooper gained national attention in 1949 when he became chairman of the Joint Congressional Committee on Atomic Energy and conducted an investigation into President Harry S. Truman's appointment of David E. Lilienthal as chairman of the Atomic Energy Commission. Lilienthal was confirmed, however. Hickenlooper was elected chairman of the Senate Republican Policy Committee in 1962, and served on other senate committees. He decided not to run for re-election in 1968. On Sept. 4 in Shelter Island, N.Y.

Muriel Kirkland, 68, an actress, first achieved stardom in 1929 as a footloose southern belle in Preston Sturges' comedy *Strictly Dishonorable*. In 1930, she had a starring role in *The Greeks Had a Word for it* by Zoe Atkins. Among her other Broadway roles were Mary Todd Lincoln in *Abe Lincoln in Illinois* and Mrs. Brady in *Inherit the Wind*. In motion pictures she appeared in *Nana* with Anna Sten and *Little Man What Now?* among other films. On Sept. 26 in New York.

Dr. Paul Niehans, 89, Swiss surgeon, was known for his cellular therapy and treatment designed to arrest the aging process. From 1931 he had been treating patients with his "rejuvenation" injections containing the cells of young animals. A surgeon who had performed more than 50,000 operations in 40 years, Niehans developed his own rejuvenation treatment by injecting humans with the fetus of unborn lambs and other animals. The late Gen. Charles de Gaulle of France, Chancellor Konrad Adenauer of Germany, British author Somerset Maugham and many Middle East leaders were said to have been among his patients. On Sept. 1 at Montreux, Switzerland.

George Seferiadis, 71, veteran Greek diplomat, scholar and Nobel Prize-winning poet, wrote under the name of George Seferis. In the mid 1930s he wrote *Epiphany*, a collection of poetry from which, 20 years later, the Greek composer Mikis Theodorakis was to compose songs that became some of the most popular in Greece. First public recognition of Seferis' outstanding contribution to Greek poetry came in 1947, when he was awarded the Palamas Prize.

The announcement of the Nobel prize for his poetry came in October 1963, and Seferis received the prize personally in Athens that December. For the past four years, under Greek military rule, Seferis felt oppressed and refused to publish poetry under what he considered censorship. On Sept. 20 in Athens.

Sir Edgar Whitehead, 66, former prime minister of Rhodesia, whose fall nine years earlier had preceded the coming to power of the Rhodesian Front headed by Ian Smith. Weak eyes had forced him to abandon plans for a career in the British civil service. On the advice of doctors he settled in Rhodesia and bought a 2,000-acre farm in the highlands. He was elected to the legislative assembly in 1939, served in the Royal Army Service in World War II and later was named Rhodesia's high commissioner in London. In 1946 he was named minister of finance. In 1958, he became prime minister and spent the ensuing years trying to convince the blacks that they needed the white man to pull themselves out of poverty. He also urged the whites to accept multiracialism. Sir Edgar left Rhodesia in 1965, the year that the country declared unilateral independence. He spoke out against Rhodesia's split with Britain, and also criticized the British attempt to isolate the former colony. On Sept. 23 at a nursing home in Newbury, England.

OCTOBER

Dr. James E. Allen Jr., 60, served 18 months as U.S. Commissioner of Education under President Nixon. He resigned under pressure, he said, in June 1970, because of statements he had made advocating school desegregation and deploring U.S. military activities in Southeast Asia. Robert H. Finch, then Secretary of Health, Education and Welfare, said at the time that the President had been "generally disappointed" with Allen's performance. In his former post as New York State Commissioner of Education, Allen had gained a reputation as an urban-oriented innovator who could cut through educational red tape, often clashing with local political forces. On Oct. 16 in a plane crash in Arizona.

Chester Conklin, 83, was a pioneer movie comedian in the silent era and a member of the famed Keystone Kops. The actor with the walrus mustache appeared in scores of Mack Sennett shorts and at one time had amassed a considerable fortune. One of his pictures, *Dough and Dynamite* costarred Charlie Chaplin. With the advent of talkies, however, Conklin's career began to slide and for years he eked out a living playing bit parts in occasional films and working as a department store Santa Claus during Christmas holidays. On Oct. 11 in Hollywood.

Lt. Gen. Lewis B. (Chesty) Puller, 73, blunt, profane, cigar-chewing Marine, was the most decorated member of the Corps. The bantam-like general's courage and roughness were Marine Corps legends that had inspired soldiers for more than three decades—from Nicaragua to Wonsan. As a youth he entered Virginia Military Institute, a traditional path to a military career, but left when World War I broke out to enlist as a private in the Marine Corps. Between wars he sought assignments where the action was, including Haiti and Nicaragua. In World War II he commanded a battalion which landed on Guadalcanal and fought a stubborn battle against wave on wave of Japanese troops. Wounded in action and repeatedly under fire, he won the Navy Cross four times during the war, a record for the Corps. In the Korean War Puller commanded the 1st Marine Regiment at the famed Inchon landing in 1950. Later he served on training assignments in the United States, including command of the 2nd Marine Division at Camp Lejeune. On Oct. 11 at Hampton, Va.

Viliam Siroky, 69, was a former premier of Czechoslovakia, a founding member of the Czechoslovak Communist party and a member of its central committee for many years. A strict follower of the Moscow party line, he became premier in 1953 and served for 10 years. His party membership was suspended during the reform era of 1968, under Alexander Dubcek, but he was reinstated in 1971. As premier, Siroky directed Czechoslovakia's violent attacks on western propaganda. Siroky headed the Czechoslovak delegation to the United Nations General Assembly in 1950 and supported the Soviet resolution calling for the admission of North Korea to the world forum. On Oct. 6 in Prague.

J. David Stern, 85, was former publisher of the Philadelphia Record and the New York Post. As publisher of the Record, he signed, with the American Newspaper Guild, the first collective bargaining contract affecting newspaper editorial workers in the United States. Fifteen months later the Post, under his ownership, became the first paper in New York to sign a Guild contract. In 1947, after a series of disputes over labor relations, he sold three newspapers and a radio station, ending 36 years as a publisher. In 1962 his autobiography, *Memoirs of a Maverick Publisher,* was published, an account of his own shortcomings as reporter and publisher and problems of the industry as well. On Oct. 10 at Good Samaritan Hospital in Palm Beach, Fla.

Thomas More Storke, 94, firebrand editor and publisher, won the Pulitzer Prize for his crusade against the John Birch Society. He was a newspaper publisher from 1900 to 1964, with a brief absence from the Fourth Estate from 1909 to 1914. Storke attained his greatest fame in 1961, when his Santa Barbara News-Press carried an expose of the Birch Society which had begun branding many persons in the California city as Communists. The crusade won Storke the 1961 Lauterbach Award of the Nieman Foundation of Harvard University, a 1962 Pulitzer Prize for editorial writing and the 1962 Elijah Lovejoy Award for courageous journalism. In 1964 he sold the News-Press to Robert McLean, publisher of the Philadelphia Bulletin. On Oct. 12 at his home in Santa Barbara.

Philip Gordon Wylie, 69, a prolific and iconoclastic author, wrote 34 books that assailed everything from American motherhood to America's morals. Wylie was best known for the word "momism" which he used in his most noted book *Generation of Vipers* published in 1942. He used the word to describe what he felt was a uniquely American condition in which women dominated their sons, establishing a tyranny over their intellect and their wills. The American "mom", he said, was "a middle-aged puffin with an eye like a hawk that has just seen a rabbit twitch below." Ironically, the subject of "momism" took up only 19 pages in Wylie's 1942 book and he always insisted that the concept was a joke. He also castigated American society as hypocritical, lying, cheating, sex-crazed, advertising-doped and soft. In his latest book, *Sons and Daughters of Mom,* Wylie drew a bead on American youth describing them as dirty. He said that youth did not listen and added that he was upset by "girl-haired boys." On Oct. 25 in Miami, Fla.

NOVEMBER

Rudolf Ivanovich Abel, 68, was considered the most important Soviet spy ever captured in the United States. After nine years of working in America his downfall came about through the defection of an assistant, Reino Heyhanen. Heyhanen, reputedly a heavy drinker and an unreliable agent, defected after having been ordered back to Moscow by his superiors. In 1957 Abel received a 30-year prison sentence on espionage charges. During his trial Abel's direct involvement in specific cases of stolen defense secrets remained vague. But shortly after he was arrested in the Latham Hotel in New York City Allen W. Dulles, then the director of the Central Intelligence Agency, said, "I wish we had three or four (intelligence agents) like him inside Moscow right now." Abel, after serving only 4½ years of his sentence, was given back to the Soviet Union in exchange for Francis Gary Powers, the American pilot of a U-2 spy plane downed over the U.S.S.R. in 1960. At the time of his trial and during his jail term the Soviet Union contended that there had been no basis for Colonel Abel's arrest. But within three years of his release his role was officially acknowledged as part of a Soviet campaign glorifying the contributions of intelligence agents in the nation's defense. Of lung cancer, in Moscow, Nov. 16.

Walter Van Tilburg Clark, 62, was the author of the *Ox-Bow Incident,* one of the first books in Western fiction that did not glamorize the West. The story of a mob who killed three innocent men, Clark dealt respectfully with each man but created no heroes and no villains. Clark grew up in Nevada, the setting for all three of his novels. The other two were *The City of Trembling Leaves* and *The Track of the Cat. The Ox-Bow Incident* came out in 1940 and was made into a film in 1943, starring Henry Fonda, Dana Andrews and Anthony Quinn. Clark was born in Maine but when he was nine he moved to Reno, Nev., with his father who was named president of the University of Nevada. Clark, after getting his master's degree at the University of Nevada, became a teacher. Nov. 12 of cancer in Reno.

Gladys Cooper, 82, the actress who charmed three generations of theatergoers in New York and London. Miss Cooper's aristocratic beauty became the standard beside which British womanhood was judged. She was born in the unfashionable southeast London suburb of Lewisham, the daughter of a magazine editor, Charles Frederick Cooper, who founded The Epicure. Miss Cooper started her acting career at the age of 17 in provincial Colchester as Bluebell, in *Bluebell in Fairyland.* Two years later in 1906 she was in London at the Gaiety Theater as one of George Edward's famous "Gaiety Girls." In 1922 she gained dramatic status starring in London in Pinero's *The Second Mrs. Tanqueray.* From there she was in a long list of plays, some of which were the *The Shining Hour, Othello* and *Macbeth* in New York. Her best known work in American television was in the series *The Rogues.* She had planned to go on tour of Canada with *The Chalk Garden,* a play by Enid Bagnold, but she became ill with pneumonia. She had never planned to retire: "Retire," she said. "Whatever for? Who cares how old I am? Who cares how long it was since I first played Peter Pan?" In London, Nov. 17.

Sir Alan Patrick Herbert, 81, was a well known British author and humorist as well as a crusading reformer, a conservationist, a barrister who never practiced law, a member of parliament, and a writer of musical comedies. Herbert, who was knighted in 1945, was one of the most popular after-dinner speakers of his time. He wrote on an almost endless variety of subjects and was very much admired by his fellow Englishmen. He served in parliament from 1935 until 1950 as an independent member representing Oxford University. His most notable achievement while in the House of Commons came in 1937 when he pushed through the Matrimonial Causes Act, a radical revision of Britain's divorce laws. Herbert turned out more than 60 books, collections of verse and autobiographical volumes, in addition to collaborating on 17 musicals and revues. In London, Nov. 11.

Rabbi Yehuda Leib Levin, 76, was chief rabbi of Moscow's Central Synagogue. An imposing figure with a long white beard, he had been the spiritual leader of Moscow's Jewish religious community since 1957 and was regarded by some pro-Zionist dissidents as a spokesman for Soviet policy in opposition to Israel. In March 1970, Rabbi Levin signed a statement printed in the government newspaper Izvestia declaring that the Soviet Union was the "real motherland" of Soviet Jews. Early in 1971 he signed a petition handed to the U.S. embassy in Moscow accusing militant Jewish groups in the United States of "emulating Fascists" in their tactics and declaring that Soviet Jews did not want such "unsolicited protection." On his widely publicized visit to the United States in June 1968, the rabbi became the center of controversy between the American Council for Judaism, an anti-Zionist group that sponsored his visit, and pro-Zionist Jewish organizations. On Nov. 17 in Moscow.

Patrick J. McDonald, 54, a newsphoto executive of The Associated Press, planned the pictorial coverage of many of the nation's biggest political, scientific and sports events. As deputy newsphoto editor he was responsible for daily coverage of the New York headquarters photo department. He had also served as national assignments editor. McDonald had played a key role in arranging photo coverage for the national political conventions and presidential inaugurations in recent years and also directed coverage of the World Series, the Olympics and many world championship boxing matches. In 1965 McDonald was appointed newsphoto executive in charge of daily administration and in 1968 he was made deputy newsphoto editor. On Nov. 23, of a heart attack at his home in Hollis, N.Y.

Marjorie Hillis Roulston, 81, was the author of the best-selling book *Live Alone and Like it,* published in 1936. She joined the editorial staff of Vogue in 1918 and remained there until 1936, serving as an editor from 1932 to 1936. *Live Alone and Like it* was followed by *Orchids on Your Budget* in 1937 and *Work Ends at Nightfall* in 1938, among other works. In 1939 she married Thomas Henry Roulston of the grocery chain. He died in 1949 and a year later, Mrs. Roulston told an interviewer "I found there is a long period of adjustment you just have to accept. It's partly physical shock and partly grief." On Nov. 8 at her home, at 570 Park Avenue, New York City.

Joseph C. Wilson, 61, chairman of the Xerox Corporation, was head of the Presidential Committee on Health Education. His development and production of the xerography process of copying turned the Haloid Corporation, a modest-sized company in Rochester, N.Y., into Xerox, a $1.7 billion industrial giant. After graduating from the Harvard Business School in 1933, he joined Haloid, a business founded by his grandfather. Haloid, a manufacturer of photographic supplies, was doing a business of about $7 million a year when Wilson succeeded his father as president in 1946. He soon became interested in xerography, a dry-copying process invented by Chester Carlson. In 1947 he acquired the rights and spent 12 years developing the process. The Xerox 914 office copier finally emerged in 1960 and the Rochester firm swiftly became the center of an industrial empire. On Nov. 22, apparently of a heart attack while lunching with Gov. Rockefeller at the latter's New York City apartment.

DECEMBER

Andrei A. Andreyev, 76, was a close associate of Josef Stalin. From 1932 to 1952 he was a member of the powerful Soviet politburo. He and A. I. Mikoyan were the only surviving members of the Politburo who did not fall into disfavor during the regime of Nikita S. Khrushchev, who succeeded Stalin in 1953. As a party secretary in the North Caucasus, Andreyev carried out Stalin's program of forced collectivization from 1927 to 1930. As commissar for agriculture from 1943–46, he followed the more liberal policy toward the peasants that Stalin had adopted to enlist their support in the Soviet war effort. After the war, however, the wartime relaxation was abandoned, and Andreyev pursued the stringent restoration of the collective farm system. On Dec. 5, after a long illness.

Bobby Jones, 69, the master golfer, scored an unparalleled grand slam in 1930 by winning the United States and British Open and Amateur tournaments. Jones started golf at an early age. When he was 10 he shot a 90 for 18 holes, at 11 he was down to 80 and at 12 he shot a 70. His record, even aside from the grand slam, was magnificent. He won the United States Open championship four times, the British Open three times and the United States Amateur five times. Jones seemed cool and collected when he played in competition, but inwardly he seethed. He could never eat properly during a major tournament. The most his stomach would retain was dry toast and tea. After achieving the grand slam, Jones retired from golf. He said: "First come my wife and children. Next comes my profession—the law. Finally, and never as a life in itself, comes golf." On Dec. 18, at his home in Atlanta, Ga.

Gen. Emmett (Rosy) O'Donnell, 65, distinguished himself in aerial combat in the Pacific war theater in World War II. In September 1941, as a major, he commanded a squadron of nine B17s that moved from Hawaii to the Philippines. When Clark Field was attacked by the Japanese, O'Donnell led his squadron against Japanese naval vessels and won the Distinguished Flying Cross for pressing home the attack. With regular planes and fields out of action, O'Donnell and his squadron rehabilitated an old B16 to fly a general nonstop to Australia. He was aided by tail winds that let him bypass the scheduled refueling stop, which was already in Japanese hands. His next post was in Java, where he was operations officer for a bomber unit for 11 days until the Japanese arrived. Later in the war he was operations and training officer for the 10th Air Force, helping to evacuate Allied forces from Burma and flying the "hump" into China. He was promoted to brigadier general in 1944 and took over a wing of B29s training for bombing Japan from new bases in Saigon. He led the first major raid of superfortresses against Tokyo on Nov. 24, 1944. From 1953–59 he served as deputy chief of staff for personnel and in 1959 was promoted to four-star rank as commander of the Pacific Air Forces. He retired from the service in 1964. On Dec. 26, at his home in McLean, Va.

Ferdinand Pecora, 89, former New York State Supreme Court Justice, won nationwide fame for his investigation of Wall Street following the 1929 crash. In the Senate inquiry into the practices of American finance before the 1929 drop, a parade of financial giants passed before the committee for questioning by Pecora. The conditions that were revealed prompted the administration of Franklin D. Roosevelt to pass the Securities and Exchange Commission Act. Pecora served on the S.E.C. but resigned after six months to accept appointment to the Supreme Court. He ran unsuccessfully for the office of mayor of New York in 1950. On Dec. 7, in New York.

Arthur B. Spingarn, 93, was the president of the National Association of Colored People for 25 years. He was the last white president of the NAACP, serving from 1940 to 1965, when he was named honorary president. Spingarn became head of the organization's national legal committee and a vice president in 1911. As president he succeeded his brother, Joel E. Spingarn, a poet and professor of comparative literature. On Dec. 1, at his home in Manhattan.

PRIZES—AWARDS

PULITZER PRIZES 1971

Drama: Paul Zindel for "The Effect Of Gamma Rays on Man-in-the-Moon Marigolds."

Distinguished Criticism: Harold C. Schonberg, Music Critic, New York Times.

Meritorious Public Service: The Winston-Salem (N.C.) Journal & Sentinel for coverage of environmental problems that included blocking of proposed strip mining for aluminum ore, endangering thousands of acres of Blue Ridge mountain country.

General Local Reporting: The Akron (Ohio) Beacon Journal for the Kent State University Tragedy.

Spot News Photography: John Paul Filo for the Kent State University tragedy.

History: James McGregor Burns, Williams College professor of government, for "Roosevelt; The Soldier of Freedom."

Biography: Lawrance R. Thompson for "Robert Frost: The Years of Triumph, 1915-1938."

Poetry: William S. Merwin for "The Carrier of Ladders."

General Nonfiction: John Toland for "The Rising Sun."

Music: Mario Davidowsky, associate professor of music at City College for "Synchronisms No. 6 for Piano & Electronic Sound."

Special Local Reporting: William Hugh Jones of the Chicago Tribune for exposing bribery of policemen.

National Reporting: Lucinda Franks and Thomas Powers of United Press International for "The Making of a Terrorist."

International Reporting; Jimmie Lee Hoagland of the Washington Post for reporting on South Africa's apartheid system of racial separation and its effects.

Editorial Writing: Horance G. Davis Jr., professor at the University of Florida for more than 30 editorials for the Gainesville (Fla.) Sun in support of peaceful desegregation of Gainesville schools.

Cartooning: Paul Conrad of the Los Angeles Times.

Feature Photography: Jack Dykinga of the Chicago Sun-Times for pictures of children in the Lincoln and Dixon state schools for the retarded in Illinois.

Commentary: William A. Caldwell of the Record, Hackensack, N.J., for his daily column on local affairs, "Simeon Stylites."

Fiction: No award.

OSCARS

Best Actor—George C. Scott of "Patton."

Best Actress—Glenda Jackson of "Women in Love."

Best Movie—"Patton."

Best Supporting Performers—John Mills in "Ryan's Daughter", Helen Hayes in "Airport."

Best Director—Franklin J. Shaftner for "Patton."

Best Song—"For all we know" from "Lovers and Other Strangers."

Best Screen-writing—Ring Lardner Jr. for "M.A.S.H."

Sound—"Patton", Douglas Williams and Don Bassman.

Cinematography—"Ryan's Daughter."

Short subject (Live Action)—"The Resurrection of Broncho Billy." John Longenecker, Producer.

Cartoon short subjects—"Is it Always Right to be Right." Nick Bosutow, Producer; Lester A. Schoenfeld, films.

Original score—"Love Story." Francis Lai, Paramount.

Original song score—"Let it Be." Beatles—Apple Production, United Artists.

Special Visual effects—"Tora! Tora! Tora!". A. D. Flowers and L. B. Abbott, Twentieth Century-Fox.

Documentary short subjects—"Interviews with My Lai Veterans". Joseph Strick, Producer, Laser Film Corp.

Documentary features—"Woodstock", Bob Maurice, Producer; Wadleigh-Maurice Ltd.

Costume design—"Cromwell." Nino Novarese, an Irving Allen Ltd. Production, Columbia.

Art direction—"Patton." Urie McCleary and Gil Parrondo.

Set direction—"Patton." Antonio Mateos and Pierre-Louis Thevenet.

Foreign language film—"Investigation of a Citizen Above Suspicion." Vera Films S.P.A., Production. Italy.

NOBEL PRIZES

Peace—West German Chancellor Willy Brandt, because he had "stretched out his hand to reconciliation between countries that have long been enemies."

Physics—Prof. Dennis Gabor, Hungarian-born scientist, for his work in three-dimensional photography.

Chemistry—Prof. Gerhard Herzberg, National Research Council of Canada, for his research in the structure of the molecule.

Physiology and Medicine—Dr. Earl W. Sutherland Jr., Vanderbilt University for his work in unraveling the secrets of how hormones work.

Economics—Dr. Simon Smith Kuznets, developer of the measure of a nation's Gross National Product.

Literature—Pablo Neruda, poet, from Chile.

LASKER AWARDS

Dr. Edward D. Freis, senior medical investigator at the Veterans Administration Hospital, Washington, D.C., won the award in clinical research for his findings that "moderately high blood pressure, though it produces no symptoms, can be dangerous and that proper treatment can greatly reduce the otherwise high risk of stroke and heart failure."

The award in basic research was shared by Dr. Seymour Benzer of the California Institute of Technology, Dr. Sydney Brenner of England's University of Cambridge

and Dr. Charles Yanofsky of Stanford University. The three were pioneers in explaining how the blueprint for inherited characteristics in all living things was coded molecule by molecule along strands of DNA or chromosomes, and how the messages were decoded by the call to produce specific protein molecules.

THE COLLIER TROPHY

The Boeing Co.

FREEDOMS FOUNDATION AWARDS

George Washington Award—Bill Pierson, age 27, Arlington, Texas.

American Exemplar Medal—Maj. Wesley V. Geary, Army chaplain, Honolulu.

American Patriot Medal—John W. McCormack and Victor Riesel.

National Service Medal—John Wayne.

NATIONAL BOOK AWARDS

Fiction: Saul Bellow for "Mr. Sammler's Planet."

History and Biography: James McGregor Burns for "Roosevelt: The Soldier of Freedom."

Arts and Letters: Francis Steegmuller for "A Biography and Study of Jean Cocteau."

Translation: Shared by—Frank Jones for "Saint Joan of the Stockyards" and Edward G. Seidensticker for "The Sound of the Mountain."

Science: Raymond Phineas for "Science in the British Colonies of America."

Children's Book: Lloyd Alexander for "The Marvelous Misadventures of Sebastian."

TONY AWARDS

Best Play: "Sleuth" by Anthony Shaffer.

Best Musical: "Company" directed by Harold Prince.

Best Actor in a Play: Brian Bedford of "School for Wives."

Best Actress in a Play: Maureen Stapleton for "Gingerbread Lady."

Best Actor in a Musical: Hal Linden for "The Rothschilds."

Best Actress in a Musical: Helen Gallagher for "No, No Nanette."

Best Supporting Actor in a Play: Paul Sand for "Story Theater."

Best Supporting Actress in a Play: Rae Allen for "And Miss Reardon Drinks a Little."

Best Supporting Actor in a Musical: Keene Curtis for "The Rothschilds."

Best Supporting Actress in a Musical: Patsy Kelly for "No, No Nanette."

Best Director of a Play: Peter Brook for "A Midsummer Night's Dream."

Best Director of a Musical: Harold Prince for "Company."

Best Book for a Musical: George Furth for "Company."

Best Music for a Musical: Stephen Sondheim for "Company."

Best Lyrics for a Musical: Stephen Sondheim for "Company."

Best Scenic Design: Boris Aronson for "Company."

Best Lighting Design: R. H. Poindexter for "Story Theater."

Best Costume Design: Raoul Pene du Bois for "No, No Nanette."

Best Choreographer: Donald Saddler for "No, No Nanette."

BEAUTY CONTESTS

Miss America—Laurie Lee Schaefer, Bexley, Ohio.

Miss Universe—Georgian Rizk, Lebanon.

Miss World—Jennifer Hosten, British West Indies

Miss U.S.A.—Michele McDonald, Butler, Pa.

Miss Teen Age America, Mary Colleen Fitzpatrick, Columbus, Ohio.

NATIONAL ACADEMY OF RECORDING ARTS & SCIENCES (GRAMMY AWARDS)

Record of the Year: (Awards to the Artist and A & R Producer) "Bridge Over Troubled Water"—Simon and Garfunkel. A & R Producers: Paul Simon, Arthur Garfunkel, Roy Halee (Columbia).

Album of the Year: (Awards to the Artist and A & R Producer) "Bridge Over Troubled Water"—Simon and Garfunkel. A & R Producers: Paul Simon, Arthur Garfunkel, Ray Halee (Columbia).

Song of the Year: (A Songwriters' Award) "Bridge Over Troubled Water". Songwriter: Paul Simon (Columbia).

Best New Artist of the Year: Carpenters (A & M)

Best Contemporary Vocal Performance, Female: "I'll Never Fall in Love Again"—Dionne Warwick (Album) (Scepter).

Best Contemporary Vocal Performance, Male: "Everything is Beautiful"—Ray Stevens (Single) (Barn).

Best Contemporary Vocal Performance by a Group: "Close to You"—Carpenters (A & M).

Best Contemporary Instrumental Performance: "Theme from "Z" and other film music."—Henry Mancini (RCA).

Best Contemporary Song (A Songwriters' Award): "Bridge Over Troubled Water". Songwriter: Paul Simon (Columbia).

Best Rhythm & Blues Vocal Performance, Female: "Don't Play that Song"—Aretha Franklin (Single) (Atlantic).

Best Rhythm & Blues Vocal Performance, Male: "The Thrill is Gone" —B. B. King (Single) (ABC).

Best Rhythm & Blues Vocal Performance by a Duo or Group: "Didn't I (Blow Your Mind this Time)—The Delfonics (Philly Groove).

Best Rhythm & Blues Song: (A Songwriters' Award) "Patches". Songwriters: Ronald Dunbar and General Johnson (Atlantic).

Best Country Vocal Performance, Female: "Rose Garden"—Lynn Anderson (Single) (Columbia).

Best Country Vocal Performance, Male: "For The Good Times"—Ray Price (Single) (Columbia).

Best Country Performance by a Duo or Group: "If I were a Carpenter"—Johnny Cash & June Carter (Columbia).

Best Country Instrumental Performance: "Me & Jerry"—Chet Atkins & Jerry Reed (RCA).

Best Country Song: (A Songwriters' Award) "My Woman, My Woman, My Wife". Songwriter: Marty Robbins (Columbia).

Best Sacred Performance: (Non-Classical) "Everything is Beautiful"—Jake Hess (RCA).

Best Ethnic or Traditional Recording: (Including Traditional Blues) "Good Feelin' "—T-Bone Walker (Polydor).

Best Instrumental Composition: (A Composer's Award) "Airport Love Theme". Composer: Alfred Newman (Decca).

Best Original Score Written for a Motion Picture or a Television Special: (A Composer's Award) "Let it Be". Composers: John Lennon, Paul McCartney, George Harrison (Apple).

Best Score from an Original Cast Show Album: (Awards to the Composer and A & R Producer) "Company". Composer: Stephen Sondheim. A & R Producer: Thomas Z. Shepherd (Columbia).

Best Recording for Children: "Sesame Street"—Joan Cooney, Producer (Columbia).

Best Comedy Recording: "The Devil made me Buy this Dress"—Flip Wilson (Little David).

Best Spoken Word Recording: "Why I Oppose the War in Vietnam"

—Dr. Martin Luther King, Jr. (Black Forum).

Best Jazz Performance: Small group or soloist with small group. "Alone"—Bill Evans (MGM).

Best Jazz Performance: Large group or soloist with large group. "Bitches Brew"—Miles Davis (Columbia).

Album of the Year, Classical: (Awards to the Artist and A & R Producer). "Berlioz"—Les Troyens. Colin Davis Conducting Royal Opera House Orchestra and Chorus. A & R Producer: Erik Smith (Philips).

Best Classical Performance, Orchestra: (A Conductor's Award). Stravinsky: "Le Sacre du Printemps". Pierre Boulez conducting the Cleveland Orchestra (Columbia).

Best Chamber Music Performance: Beethoven: "The Complete Piano Trios". Eugene Istomin, Issac Stern, Leonard Rose (Columbia).

Best Classical Performance—Instrumental soloist or soloists (with or without orchestra): Brahms: "Double Concerto (Concerto in A Minor for Violin and Cello)". David Oistrakh & Mstislav Rostropovich (Angel).

Best Opera Recording: (Awards to the Conductor and A & R Producer) Belioz: "Les Troyens". Colin Davis conducting the Royal Opera House Orchestra and Chorus. A & R Producer: Erik Smith (Philips).

Best Choral Performance, (other than Opera) (Awards to the Conductor and Choral Director). Ives: "New Music of Charles Ives". Gregg Smith conducting the Gregg Smith Singers and Columbia Chamber Ensemble (Columbia).

Best Vocal Soloist Performance,: (Classical). Schubert: "Lieder" Dietrich Fischer-Dieskau (DGG-Polydor).

UNITED STATES GOVERNMENT

EXECUTIVE DEPARTMENT

President: Richard M. Nixon
Vice President: Spiro T. Agnew

WHITE HOUSE STAFF

Counsellors to the President:
  Robert H. Finch
  Donald Rumsfeld

Assistants to the President:
  John D. Ehrlichman—for Domestic Affairs
  Peter M. Flanigan
  H. R. Haldeman
  Dr. Henry A. Kissinger—for National Security Affairs
  Peter G. Peterson—for International Economic Affairs
  William E. Timmons—for Congressional Relations

Counsel to the President for Congressional Relations:
  Clark MacGregor

Science Advisor to the President:
  Dr. Edward E. David, Jr.

Special Consultants to the President:
  Leonard Garment
  Dr. Jerome H. Jaffe—for Narcotics and Dangerous Drugs
  William M. Magruder
  John A. Scali

Advisor to the President:
  Gen. Lewis B. Hershey, USA—on Manpower Mobilization

Director of Communications:
  Herbert G. Klein—for the Executive Branch

Special Assistants to the President:
  Desmond J. Barker, Jr.
  George T. Bell
  Patrick J. Buchanan
  Michael J. Farrell
  Max L. Friedersdorf
  William L. Gifford

  Mark I. Goode
  Jon M. Huntsman
  Roger E. Johnson
  Daniel T. Kingsley
  Mrs. Virginia H. Knauer—for Consumer Affairs
  Tom C. Korologos
  Frederic V. Malek
  Raymond K. Price, Jr.
  Jonathan C. Rose
  William L. Safire
  Robert L. Schulz—for Liaison with Former Presidents

Press Secretary to the President:
  Ronald L. Ziegler

Military Assistant to the President:
  Brig. Gen. James D. Hughes, USAF

Deputy Assistants to the President:
  Alexander P. Butterfield
  Dwight L. Chapin

Special Counsels to the President:
  Charles W. Colson
  Harry S. Dent
  Richard A. Moore

Counsel to the President:
  John Wesley Dean III

Deputy Assistants to the President:
  Brig. Gen. Alexander Meigs Haig, Jr.—for National Security Affairs
  Richard K. Cook—for Congressional Relations
  Eugene S. Cowen—for Congressional Relations
  John C. Whitaker
  Henry C. Cashen II

Deputy Press Secretaries:
  Neal Ball
  Gerald L. Warren

Personal Secretary to the President:
  Miss Rose Mary Woods

Staff Director for Mrs. Nixon:
  Mrs. Constance Stuart

Social Secretary:
  Mrs. Lucy Alexander Winchester

Physician to the President:
  Brig. Gen. Walter R. Tkach, USAF, MC

Chief Usher:
  Rex W. Scouten

EXECUTIVE OFFICES
Office of Management and Budget
  George P. Shultz, *director*

Council of Economic Advisers
  Paul W. McCracken, *chairman*

Central Intelligence Agency
  Richard Helms, *director*

Domestic Council
  John D. Ehrlichman, *executive director*

National Aeronautics and Space Council
  Spiro T. Agnew, *chairman*

Office of Economic Opportunity
  Phillip V. Sanchez, *director*

Office of Emergency Preparedness
  George A. Lincoln, *director*

Office of Science and Technology
  Edward E. David, Jr., *director*

Special Representative for Trade Negotiations
  William D. Eberle

Office of Intergovernmental Relations
  Spiro T. Agnew

Council on Environmental Quality
Russell E. Train, *chairman*

Office of Telecommunications Policy
Clay T. Whitehead, *director*

Office of Consumer Affairs
Virginia H. Knauer, *director*

**Special Action Office for Drug Abuse
Prevention**
Dr. Jerome H. Jaffe, *director*

Council on International Economic Policy
Peter G. Peterson, *executive director*

CABINET
Department of State
SECRETARY
William P. Rogers

UNDER SECRETARY
John N. Irwin 11

MISSION TO THE UNITED NATIONS
George Bush

PEACE CORPS
Joseph H. Blatchford, *director*

AGENCY FOR INTERNATIONAL DEVELOPMENT
Dr. John A. Hannah, *administrator*

Department of the Treasury
SECRETARY
John B. Connally, Jr.

UNDER SECRETARY
Charles E. Walker

UNDER SECRETARY FOR MONETARY AFFAIRS
Paul A. Volcker

INTERNAL REVENUE SERVICE
John M. Walters

BUREAU OF CUSTOMS
Myles J. Ambrose, *commissioner*

SECRET SERVICE
James J. Rowley, *director*

TREASURER OF THE UNITED STATES
Romana Acosta Banuelos

Department of Defense
SECRETARY
Melvin R. Laird

DEPUTY SECRETARY
Vacant

JOINT CHIEFS OF STAFF
Adm. Thomas H. Moorer, *chairman*
Gen. William C. Westmoreland, *chief of staff,
U.S. Army*
Adm. Elmo R. Zumwalt Jr., *chief of Naval
Operations*
Gen. John D. Ryan, *chief of staff, U.S. Air Force*
Gen. Leonard F. Chapman Jr., *commandant,
Marine Corps*

DEPARTMENT OF THE ARMY
Robert F. Froehlke, *secretary*

DEPARTMENT OF THE NAVY
John H. Chaffee, *secretary*

DEPARTMENT OF THE AIR FORCE
Dr. Robert C. Seamans Jr., *secretary*

Department of Justice
ATTORNEY GENERAL
John N. Mitchell

DEPUTY ATTORNEY GENERAL
Richard G. Kleindienst

SOLICITOR GENERAL
Erwin N. Griswold

BUREAU OF NARCOTICS AND DANGEROUS DRUGS
John E. Ingersoll, *director*

FEDERAL BUREAU OF INVESTIGATION
J. Edgar Hoover, *director*

Post Office Department
POSTMASTER GENERAL
Elmer Theodore Klassen

DEPUTY POSTMASTER GENERAL
Merrill A. Hayden

Department of the Interior
SECRETARY
Rogers C. B. Morton

UNDER SECRETARY
Dr. William T. Pecora

Department of Agriculture
SECRETARY
Earl L. Butz

UNDER SECRETARY
J. Phil Campbell

Department of Commerce
SECRETARY
Maurice H. Stans

UNDER SECRETARY
James T. Lynn

BUREAU OF THE CENSUS
George H. Brown, *director*

NATIONAL OCEANOGRAPHIC AND ATMOSPHERIC
ADMINISTRATION
Robert White, *acting administrator*

OFFICE OF EDUCATION
Dr. Sidney P. Marland, Jr.

Department of Housing and Urban Development
SECRETARY
George W. Romney

Department of Labor
SECRETARY
James D. Hodgson

UNDER SECRETARY
Laurence H. Silberman

Department of Health, Education, and Welfare
SECRETARY
Elliot L. Richardson

UNDER SECRETARY
John G. Veneman

PUBLIC HEALTH SERVICE
Dr. Jesse L. Steinfeld, *surgeon general*

SOCIAL SECURITY ADMINISTRATION
Robert M. Ball, *commissioner*

FOOD AND DRUG ADMINISTRATION
Dr. Charles C. Edwards, *commissioner*

UNDER SECRETARY
Richard C. Van Dusen

Department of Transportation
SECRETARY
John A. Volpe

UNDER SECRETARY
James M. Beggs

FEDERAL AVIATION ADMINISTRATION
John H. Shaffer, *administrator*

NATIONAL TRANSPORTATION SAFETY BOARD
John H. Reed, *chairman*

UNHTED STATES COAST GUARD
Adm. Chester R. Bender, *commandant*

MAJOR INDEPENDENT AGENCIES
ATOMIC ENERGY COMMISSION
Dr. James R. Schlesinger, *chairman*

FEDERAL RESERVE SYSTEM
Arthur S. Burns, *chairman*

CIVIL AERONAUTICS BOARD
Secor D. Browne, *chairman*

CIVIL SERVICE COMMISSION
Robert E. Hampton, *chairman*

FEDERAL COMMUNICATIONS COMMISSION
Dean Burch, *chairman*

FEDERAL POWER COMMISSION
John N. Nassikas, *chairman*

FEDERAL TRADE COMMISSION
Miles W. Kirkpatrick, *chairman*

GENERAL SERVICES ADMINISTRATION
Robert L. Kunzig, *administrator*

INTERSTATE COMMERCE COMMISSION
George M. Stafford, *chairman*

NATIONAL AERONAUTICS AND SPACE
ADMINISTRATION
Dr. James C. Fletcher, administrator

NATIONAL LABOR RELATIONS BOARD
Edward B. Miller, *chairman*

SECURITIES AND EXCHANGE COMMISSION
William J. Casey, *chairman*

SELECTIVE SERVICE SYSTEM
Dr. Curtis W. Tarr, director

SMALL BUSINESS ADMINISTRATION
Thomas S. Kleppe, *administrator*

UNITED STATES INFORMATION AGENCY
Frank J. Shakespeare Jr., *director*

VETERANS ADMINISTRATION
Donald E. Johnson, *administrator*

ENVIRONMENTAL PROTECTION AGENCY
William D. Ruckelshaus, *administrator*

LEGISLATIVE

92nd Congress
Second Session

SENATE

PRESIDENT PRO TEMPORE: Allen J. Ellender (D.-La.)
MAJORITY LEADER: Mike Mansfield (D.-Mont.)
MAJORITY WHIP: Robert C. Byrd (D.-W.Va.)
MINORITY LEADER: Hugh Scott (R.-Pa.)
MINORITY WHIP: Robert P. Griffin (R.-Mich.)
CHAPLAIN: Rev. Edward L. R. Elson

Members of the Senate

District	Party	District	Party	District	Party
ALABAMA		**IOWA**		**NEW JERSEY**	
John J. Sparkman	D	Jack Richard Miller	R	Clifford P. Case	R
James Browning Allen	D	Harold E. Hughes	D	Harrison A. Williams, Jr.	D
ALASKA		**KANSAS**		**NEW MEXICO**	
Ted Stevens	R	James B. Pearson	R	Clinton P. Anderson	D
Mike Gravel	D	Robert J. Dole	R	Joseph M. Montoya	D
ARIZONA		**KENTUCKY**		**NEW YORK**	
Paul Jones Fannin	R	John Sherman Cooper	R	Jacob K. Javits	R
Barry M. Goldwater	R	Marlow W. Cook	R	James L. Buckley	C–R
ARKANSAS		**LOUISIANA**		**NORTH CAROLINA**	
John L. McClellan	D	Allen J. Ellender	D	Sam J. Ervin, Jr.	D
J. W. Fulbright	D	Russell B. Long	D	B. Everett Jordan	D
CALIFORNIA		**MAINE**		**NORTH DAKOTA**	
Alan Cranston	D	Margaret Chase Smith	R	Milton R. Young	R
John Varick Tunney	D	Edmund S. Muskie	D	Quentin N. Burdick	D
COLORADO		**MARYLAND**		**OHIO**	
Gordon Llewellyn Allott	R	Charles McC Mathias, Jr.	R	William B. Saxbe	R
Peter H. Dominick	R	J. Glenn Beall, Jr.	R	Robert Taft, Jr.	R
CONNECTICUT		**MASSACHUSETTS**		**OKLAHOMA**	
Abraham A. Ribicoff	D	Edward M. Kennedy	D	Fred R. Harris	D
Lowell P. Weicker, Jr.	R	Edward W. Brooke	R	Henry L. Bellmon	R
DELAWARE		**MICHIGAN**		**OREGON**	
James Caleb Boggs	R	Philip A. Hart	D	Mark O. Hatfield	R
William V. Roth, Jr.	R	Robert P. Griffin	R	Bob Packwood	R
FLORIDA		**MINNESOTA**		**PENNSYLVANIA**	
Edward John Gurney	R	Walter F. Mondale	D–F–L	Hugh Scott	R
Lawton Mainor Chiles, Jr.	D	Hubert H. Humphrey	D–F–L	Richard S. Schweiker	R
GEORGIA		**MISSISSIPPI**		**RHODE ISLAND**	
Richard B. Russell	D	James O. Eastland	D	John O. Pastore	D
Died 1-21-71		John C. Stennis	D	Claiborne Pell	D
David H. Gambrell	D				
Sworn in 2-2-71		**MISSOURI**		**SOUTH CAROLINA**	
Herman Eugene Talmadge	D	Stuart Symington	D	Strom Thurmond*	R
		Thomas F. Eagleton	D	Ernest F. Hollings	D
HAWAII		**MONTANA**		**SOUTH DAKOTA**	
Hiram L. Fong	R	Michael J. Mansfield	D	Karl E. Mundt	R
Daniel K. Inouye	D	Lee Metcalf	D	George McGovern	D
IDAHO		**NEBRASKA**		**TENNESSEE**	
Frank Church	D	Roman L. Hruska	R	Howard H. Baker, Jr.	R
Len B. Jordan	R	Carl T. Curtis	R	William E. Brock, III	R
ILLINOIS		**NEVADA**		**TEXAS**	
Charles H. Percy	R	Alan Bible	D	John G. Tower	R
Adlai E. Stevenson, III	D	Howard W. Cannon	D	Lloyd M. Bentsen, Jr.	D
INDIANA		**NEW HAMPSHIRE**		**UTAH**	
Vance Hartke	D	Norris Cotton	R	Wallace F. Bennett	R
Birch Bayh	D	Thomas J. McIntyre	D	Frank E. Moss	D

District	Party
VERMONT	
George D. Aiken	R
Winston L. Prouty	R
Died 9-10-71	
Robert T. Stafford	R
Sworn in 9-17-71	
VIRGINIA	
Harry F. Byrd, Jr.	I
William B. Spong, Jr.	D

District	Party
WASHINGTON	
Warren G. Magnuson	D
Henry M. Jackson	D
WEST VIRGINIA	
Jennings Randolph	D
Robert C. Byrd	D
WISCONSIN	
William Proxmire	D
Gaylord Nelson	D

District	Party
WYOMING	
Gale W. McGee	D
Clifford P. Hansen	R

*Served prior, noncontinuous term in the Senate.

HOUSE OF REPRESENTATIVES

SPEAKER: Carl B. Albert (D.-Okla.)
MAJORITY LEADER: Hale Boggs (D.-La.)
MAJORITY WHIP: Thomas P. O'Neill (D.-Mass.)
MINORITY LEADER: Gerald R. Ford (R.-Mich.)
MINORITY WHIP: Leslie C. Arends (R.-Ill.)
CHAPLAIN: Rev. Edward G. Latch

Members of the House of Representatives

District	Party
ALABAMA	
1—Jack Edwards	R
2—William L. Dickinson	R
3—George W. Andrews	D
4—William Nichols	D
5—Walter Flowers	D
6—John Buchanan Jr.	R
7—Tom Bevill	D
8—Robert E. Jones	D
ALASKA	
AL—Nicholas J. Begich	D
ARIZONA	
1—John J. Rhodes	R
2—Morris K. Udall	D
3—Sam Steiger	R
ARKANSAS	
1—William Alexander	D
2—Wilbur D. Mills	D
3—John P. Hammerschmidt	R
4—David Pryor	D
CALIFORNIA	
1—Don H. Clausen	R
2—Harold T. Johnson	D
3—John E. Moss	D
4—Robert L. Leggett	D
5—Philip Burton	D
6—William S. Mailliard	R
7—Ronald V. Dellums	D
8—George P. Miller	D
9—Don Edwards	D
10—Charles S. Gubser	R
11—Paul N. McCloskey Jr.	R
12—Burt L. Talcott	R
13—Charles M. Teague	R
14—Jerome R. Waldie	D
15—John J. McFall	D
16—B. F. Sisk	D
17—Glenn M. Anderson	D
18—Robert B. Mathias	R
19—Chet Holifield	D
20—H. Allen Smith	R
21—Augustus F. Hawkins	D
22—James C. Corman	D

District	Party
23—Del Clawson	R
24—John H. Rousselot	R
25—Charles E. Wiggins	R
26—Thomas M. Rees	D
27—Barry M. Goldwater Jr.	R
28—Alphonzo Bell	R
29—George E. Danielson	D
30—Edward R. Roybal	D
31—Charles H. Wilson	D
32—Craig Hosmer	R
33—Jerry L. Pettis	R
34—Richard T. Hanna	D
35—John G. Schmitz	R
36—Bob Wilson	R
37—Lionel Van Deerlin	D
38—John V. Tunney	D
COLORADO	
1—James D. McKevitt	R
2—Donald G. Brotzman	R
3—Frank E. Evans	D
4—Wayne N. Aspinall	D
CONNECTICUT	
1—William R. Cotter	D
2—Robert H. Steele	R
3—Robert N. Giaimo	D
4—Stewart B. McKinney	R
5—John S. Monagan	D
6—Ella T. Grasso	D
DELAWARE	
AL—Pierre S. DuPont IV	R
FLORIDA	
1—Robert L. F. Sikes	D
2—Don Fuqua	D
3—Charles Bennett	D
4—Bill Chappell Jr.	D
5—Louis Frey Jr.	R
6—Sam M. Gibbons	D
7—James A. Haley	D
8—C. W. Bill Young	R
9—Paul G. Rogers	D
10—J. Herbert Burke	R
11—Claude Pepper	D
12—Dante B. Fascell	D

District	Party
GEORGIA	
1—G. Elliott Hagan	D
2—M. Dawson Mathis	D
3—Jack Brinkley	D
4—Ben B. Blackburn	R
5—Fletcher Thompson	R
6—John J. Flynt Jr.	D
7—John W. Davis	D
8—William S. Stuckey Jr.	D
9—Phil M. Landrum	D
10—Robert G. Stephens Jr.	D
HAWAII	
AL—Spark M. Matsunaga	D
AL—Patsy T. Mink	D
IDAHO	
1—James A. McClure	R
2—Orval Hansen	R
INDIANA	
1—Ray J. Madden	D
2—Earl F. Landgrebe	R
3—John Brademas	D
4—J. Edward Roush	D
5—Elwood Haynes Hillis	R
6—William G. Bray	R
7—John T. Myers	R
8—Roger H. Zion	R
9—Lee H. Hamilton	D
10—David W. Dennis	R
11—Andrew Jacobs Jr.	D
ILLINOIS	
1—Ralph H. Metcalfe	D
2—Abner J. Mikva	D
3—Morgan Francis Murphy	D
4—Edward J. Derwinski	R
5—John C. Kluczynski	D
6—George W. Collins	D
7—Frank Annunzio	D
8—Dan Rostenkowski	D
9—Sidney R. Yates	D
10—Harold R. Collier	R
11—Roman E. Pucinski	D

285

District	Party
12—Robert McClory	R
13—Philip M. Crane	R
14—John N. Erlenborn	R
15—Charlotte T. Reid	R
Resigned 10-8-71	
Vacant 10-8-71—end of year	
16—John B. Anderson	R
17—Leslie C. Arends	R
18—Robert H. Michel	R
19—Tom Railsback	R
20—Paul Findley	R
21—Kenneth J. Gray	D
22—William L. Springer	R
23—George E. Shipley	D
24—Charles Melvin Price	D

IOWA

District	Party
1—Fred Schwengel	R
2—John C. Culver	D
3—H. R. Gross	R
4—John Kyl	R
5—Neal Smith	D
6—Wiley Mayne	R
7—William J. Scherle	R

KANSAS

District	Party
1—Keith G. Sebelius	R
2—Chester L. Mize	R
3—Larry Winn Jr.	R
4—Garner E. Shriver	R
5—Joe Skubitz	R

KENTUCKY

District	Party
1—Frank A. Stubblefield	D
2—William N. Natcher	D
3—Romano L. Mazzoli	D
4—M. G. Snyder	R
5—Tim Lee Carter	R
6—John Clarence Watts	
died 9-24-71	
Wm. P. Curlin, Jr.	D
Sworn in 12-6-71	
7—Carl D. Perkins	D

LOUISIANA

District	Party
1—F. Edward Hebert	D
2—Hale Boggs	D
3—Patrick T. Caffery	D
4—Joe D. Waggonner Jr.	D
5—Otto E. Passman	D
6—John R. Rarick	D
7—Edwin W. Edwards	D
8—Speedy O. Long	D

MAINE

District	Party
1—Peter N. Kyros	D
2—William D. Hathaway	D

MARYLAND

District	Party
1—Rogers C. B. Morton	R
Resigned 1-29-71	
William O. Mills	R
Sworn in 5-27-71	
2—Clarence D. Long	D
3—Edward A. Garmatz	D
4—Paul S. Sarbanes	D
5—Lawrence J. Hogan	R
6—Goodloe Edgar Byron	D
7—Parren J. Mitchell	D
8—Gilbert Gude	R

MASSACHUSETTS

District	Party
1—Silvio O. Conte	R
2—Edward P. Boland	D
3—Robert F. Drinan, S.J.,	D
4—Harold D. Donohue	D
5—F. Bradford Morse	R
6—Michael Harrington	D
7—Torbert H. Macdonald	D
8—Thomas P. O'Neill Jr.	D
9—Louise Day Hicks	D
10—Margaret M. Heckler	R

District	Party
11—James A. Burke	D
12—Hastings Keith	R

MICHIGAN

District	Party
1—John Conyers Jr.	D
2—Marvin L. Esch	R
3—Gary Brown	R
4—Edward Hutchinson	R
5—Gerald R. Ford	R
6—Charles E. Chamberlain	R
7—Donald W. Riegle Jr.	R
8—James Harvey	R
9—Guy Vander Jagt	R
10—Elford A. Cederberg	R
11—Philip E. Ruppe	R
12—James G. O'Hara	D
13—Charles C. Diggs Jr.	D
14—Lucien N. Nedzi	D
15—William D. Ford	D
16—John D. Dingell	D
17—Martha W. Griffiths	D
18—William S. Broomfield	R
19—Jack H. McDonald	R

MINNESOTA

District	Party
1—Albert H. Quie	R
2—Ancher Nelson	R
3—Bill Frenzel	R
4—Joseph E. Karth	D-F-L
5—Donald MacKay Fraser	D-F-L
6—John M. Zwach	R
7—Bob Selmer Bergland	D-F-L
8—John A. Blatnik	D-F-L

MISSISSIPPI

District	Party
1—Thomas G. Abernethy	D
2—Jamie L. Whitten	D
3—Charles Griffin	D
4—Gillespie V. Montgomery	D
5—William M. Colmer	D

MISSOURI

District	Party
1—William Clay	D
2—James W. Symington	D
3—Leonor K. Sullivan	D
4—William J. Randall	D
5—Richard Bolling	D
6—W. R. Hull Jr.	D
7—Durward G. Hall	R
8—Richard H. Ichord	D
9—William L. Hungate	D
10—Bill D. Burlison	D

MONTANA

District	Party
1—Richard G. Shoup	R
2—John Melcher	D

NEBRASKA

District	Party
1—Charles Thone	R
2—John Y. McCollister	R
3—David T. Martin	R

NEVADA

District	Party
AL—Walter S. Baring	D

NEW HAMPSHIRE

District	Party
1—Louis C. Wyman	R
2—James C. Cleveland	R

NEW JERSEY

District	Party
1—John E. Hunt	R
2—Charles W. Sandman Jr.	R
3—James J. Howard	D
4—Frank Thompson Jr.	D
5—Peter H. B. Frelinghuysen	R
6—Edwin B. Forsythe	R
7—William B. Widnall	R
8—Robert A. Roe	D
9—Henry Helstoski	D
10—Peter W. Rodino Jr.	D
11—Joseph G. Minish	D
12—Florence P. Dwyer	R

District	Party
13—Cornelius E. Gallagher	D
14—Dominick V. Daniels	D
15—Edward J. Patten	D

NEW MEXICO

District	Party
1—Manuel Lujan Jr.	R
2—Harold L. Runnels	D

NEW YORK

District	Party
1—Otis G. Pike	D
2—James R. Grover Jr.	R
3—Lester L. Wolff	D
4—John W. Wydler	R
5—Norman Frederick Lent	R
6—Seymour Halpern	R
7—Joseph P. Addabbo	D
8—Benjamin S. Rosenthal	D
9—James J. Delaney	D-C
10—Emanuel Celler	D
11—Frank J. Brasco	D
12—Shirley Chisholm	D
13—Bertram L. Podell	D
14—John J. Rooney	D
15—Hugh L. Carey	D
16—John M. Murphy	D
17—Edward I. Koch	D-L
18—Charles B. Rangel	D-R
19—Bella S. Abzug	D
20—William F. Ryan	D-L
21—Herman Badillo	D
22—James H. Scheuer	D
23—Jonathan B. Bingham	D-L
24—Mario Biaggi	D-C
25—Peter A. Peyser	R
26—Ogden R. Reid	R
27—John Goodchild Dow	D
28—Hamilton Fish Jr.	R
29—Samuel S. Stratton	D
30—Carleton J. King	R
31—Robert C. McEwen	R
32—Alexander Pirnie	R
33—Howard W. Robison	R
34—John H. Terry	R
35—James Michael Hanley	D
36—Frank J. Horton	R
37—Barber B. Conable Jr.	R
38—James F. Hastings	R
39—Jack F. Kemp	R-C
40—Henry P. Smith III	R
41—Thaddeus J. Dulski	D-L

NORTH CAROLINA

District	Party
1—Walter Jones	D
2—L. H. Fountain	D
3—David N. Henderson	D
4—Nick Galifianakis	D
5—Wilmer Mizell	R
6—Richardson Preyer	D
7—Alton A. Lennon	D
8—Earl B. Ruth	R
9—Charles R. Jonas	R
10—James T. Broyhill	R
11—Roy A. Taylor	D

NORTH DAKOTA

District	Party
1—Mark Andrews	R
2—Arthur A. Link	D
-Nonpartisan Leaguer	

OHIO

District	Party
1—William J. Keating	R
2—Donald D. Clancy	R
3—Charles W. Whalen Jr.	R
4—William M. McCulloch	R
5—Delbert L. Latta	R
6—William H. Harsha	R
7—Clarence J. Brown Jr.	R
8—Jackson E. Betts	R
9—Thomas L. Ashley	D
10—Clarence E. Miller	R
11—J. William Stanton	R
12—Samuel L. Devine	R
13—Charles A. Mosher	R

District	Party		District	Party		District	Party
14—John F. Seiberling	D		26—Thomas E. Morgan	D		**UTAH**	
15—Chalmers P. Wylie	R		27—James Grove Fulton			1—K. Gunn McKay	D
16—Frank T. Bow	R		died 10-6-71			2—Sherman P. Lloyd	R
17—John M. Ashbrook	R		vacant 10-6-71—on				
18—Wayne L. Hays	D					**VERMONT**	
19—Charles J. Carney	D		**RHODE ISLAND**			AL—Robert Theodore Stafford	R
20—James Vincent Stanton	D		1—Fernand J. St. Germain	D		resigned 9-17-71	
21—Louis Stokes	D		2—Robert O. Tiernan	D		vacant 9-17-71—on	
22—Charles A. Vanik	D						
23—William E. Minshall	R		**SOUTH CAROLINA**			**VIRGINIA**	
24—Walter E. Powell	R		1—Mendel J. Davis	D		1—Thomas N. Downing	D
			2—Floyd Davidson Spence	R		2—G. William Whitehurst	R
OKLAHOMA			3—W. J. Bryan Dorn	D		3—David E. Satterfield III	D
1—Page Belcher	R		4—James R. Mann	D		4—Watkins M. Abbitt	D
2—Ed Edmondson	D		5—Tom S. Gettys	D		5—W. C. (Dan) Daniel	D
3—Carl B. Albert	D		6—John L. McMillan	D		6—Richard H. Poff	R
4—Tom Steed	D					7—J. Kenneth Robinson	R
5—John Jarman	D		**SOUTH DAKOTA**			8—William L. Scott	R
6—John N. Camp	R		1—Frank Edward Denholm	D		9—William C. Wampler	R
			2—James G. Abourezk	D		10—Joel T. Broyhill	R
OREGON							
1—Wendell Wyatt	R		**TENNESSEE**			**WASHINGTON**	
2—Al Ullman	D		1—James H. Quillen	R		1—Thomas M. Pelly	R
3—Edith Green	D		2—John J. Duncan	R		2—Lloyd Meeds	D
4—John Dellenback	R		3—LaMar Baker	R		3—Julia B. Hansen	D
			4—Joe L. Evins	D		4—Mike McCormack	D
PENNSYLVANIA			5—Richard H. Fulton	D		5—Thomas S. Foley	D
1—William A. Barrett	D		6—William R. Anderson	D		6—Floyd V. Hicks	D
2—Robert N. C. Nix	D		7—Ray Blanton	D		7—Brock Adams	D
3—James A. Byrne	D		8—Ed Jones	D			
4—Joshua Eilberg	D		9—Dan Kuykendall	R		**WEST VIRGINIA**	
5—William J. Green	D					1—Robert H. Mollohan	D
6—Gus Yatron	D		**TEXAS**			2—Harley O. Staggers	D
7—Lawrence G. Williams	R		1—Wright Patman	D		3—John Slack	D
8—Edward G. Biester	R		2—John Dowdy	D		4—Ken Hechler	D
9—John H. Ware III	R		3—James M. Collins	R		5—James Kee	D
10—Joseph M. McDade	R		4—Ray Roberts	D			
11—Daniel J. Flood	D		5—Earle Cabell	D		**WISCONSIN**	
12—J. Irving Whalley	R		6—Olin E. Teague	D		1—Leslie Aspin	D
13—R. Lawrence Coughlin	R		7—Bill Archer	R		2—Robert W. Kastenmeier	D
14—William S. Moorhead	D		8—Bob Eckhardt	D		3—Vernon W. Thomson	R
15—Fred B. Rooney	D		9—Jack Brooks	D		4—Clement J. Zablocki	D
16—Edwin D. Eshleman	R		10—J. J. (Jake) Pickle	D		5—Henry S. Reuss	D
17—Herman T. Schneebeli	R		11—W. R. Poage	D		6—William Steiger	R
18—Robert J. Corbett			12—James C. Wright Jr.	D		7—David R. Obey	D
died 4-25-71			13—Graham Purcell	D		8—John W. Byrnes	R
H. John Heinz	R		14—John Young	D		9—Glenn R. Davis	R
Sworn in 11-4-71			15—Eligio de la Garza	D		10—Alvin E. O'Konski	R
19—George A. Goodling	R		16—Richard C. White	D			
20—Joseph M. Gaydos	D		17—Omar Burleson	D		**WYOMING**	
21—John H. Dent	D		18—Robert D. Price	R		AL—Teno Roncalio	D
22—John P. Saylor	R		19—George H. Mahon	D			
23—Albert W. Johnson	R		20—Henry B. Gonzalez	D		**DISTRICT OF COLUMBIA**	
24—Joseph P. Vigorito	D		21—O. C. Fisher	D		Delegate Walter E. Fauntroy	D
25—Frank M. Clark	D		22—Bob Casey	D		Sworn in 4-19-71	
			23—Abraham Kazen Jr.	D			

*Served prior, noncontinuous term in the House.

JUDICIARY

SUPREME COURT

CHIEF JUSTICE OF THE UNITED STATES

	Home State	Date of Birth	Date took Court seat	Appointed By
Warren E. Burger	Minn.	Sept. 17, 1907	Oct. 6, 1969	Nixon

ASSOCIATE JUSTICES OF THE SUPREME COURT

	Home State	Date of Birth	Date took Court seat	Appointed By		Home State	Date of Birth	Date took Court seat	Appointed By
Hugo L. Black	Ala.	Feb. 27, 1886	Oct. 4, 1937 retired Sept. 17, 1971 died Sept. 25, 1971	Roosevelt		William J. Brennan	N.J.	Apr. 25, 1906	Oct. 16, 1956	Eisenhower
						Potter Stewart	Ohio	Jan. 23, 1915	Oct. 14, 1958	Eisenhower
						Byron R. White	Colo.	June 8, 1917	Apr. 16, 1962	Kennedy
						Thurgood Marshall	Md.	July 2, 1908	Oct. 2, 1967	Johnson
						Harry A. Blackmun	Ill.	Nov. 12, 1908	June 9, 1970	Nixon
William O. Douglas	Wash.	Oct. 16, 1898	April 17, 1939	Roosevelt						
John M. Harlan	N.Y.	May 20, 1899	March 28, 1955 retired Sept. 23, 1971 died Dec. 29, 1971	Eisenhower						
						Lewis F. Powell Jr.		Senate approves nomination Dec. 6, 1971		
						William H. Rehnquist		Senate approves nomination Dec. 10, 1971		

THE SECRETARIAT

SECRETARY-GENERAL

U Thant   Burma

UNDER-SECRETARIES-GENERAL

I. H. Abdel-Rahman	U.A.R.	Executive Director, U.N. Industrial Development Organization.
Philippe de Seynes	France	Under-Secretary-General for Economic & Social Affairs.
Issoufous S. Djermakoye	Niger	Under-Secretary-General for Trusteeship & Non-Self-Governing Territories.
Roberto E. Guyer	Argentina	Under-Secretary-General for Special Political Affairs.
Leonid N. Kutakov	U.S.S.R.	Under-Secretary-General for Political and Security Council Affairs.
C. V. Narasimhan	India	Chef de Cabinet.
Jiri Nosek	Czechoslovakia	Under-Secretary-General for Conference Services.
Manuel Perez Guerrero	Venezuela	Secretary-General, U.N. Conference on Trade and Development.
Horatio K. Matthews	U.K.	Under-Secretary-General for Administration and Management.

Constantin A. Stavropoulos	Greece	Under-Secretary-General for General Assembly Affairs and Legal Counsel.
Vittorio Winspeare Guicciardi	Italy	Director-General, U.N. Office at Geneva, Switzerland.

GENERAL ASSEMBLY

Country	Year of Admission	Permanent Representative
Afghanistan	1946	Abdur-Rahman Pazhwak
Albania	1955	Sami Baholli
Algeria	1962	Abdellatif Rahal
Argentina	1945	Dr. Carlos Oritiz de Rozas
Australia	1945	Laurence McIntyre
Austria	1955	Kurt Waldheim
Barbados	1966	Waldo E. Waldron-Ramsey
Belgium	1945	Edouard Longerstaey
Bolivia	1945	Walter Guevara Arze
Botswana	1966	T. J. Molefhe
Brazil	1945	Sergio Armando Fražao
Bulgaria	1955	Guero Grozev
Burma	1948	H. E. Ulwin
Burundi	1962	Nsanze Terence
Byelorussian S.S.R.	1945	Vitaly Stepanovich Smirnov
Cameroon	1960	Michel Njine
Canada	1945	Yvon Beaulne
Central African Republic	1960	Michel Adama-Tamboux
Ceylon	1955	Hamilton Shirley Amerasinghe
Chad	1960	Vacant
Chile	1945	Dr. Humberto Diaz Casanueva
China, People's Republic of	1971	Huang Hua
Colombia	1945	Dr. Augusto Espinosa
Congo, Dem. Rep. of	1960	André Fernand Mandi
Costa Rica	1945	José Luis Molina
Cuba	1945	Richardo Alarcon Quesada
Cyprus	1960	Zenon Rossides
Czechoslovakia	1945	Dr. Zdeněk Černik
Dahomey	1960	Wilfrid de Souza
Denmark	1945	Otto R. Borch
Dominican Republic	1945	Fernándo Amiama-Tio
Ecuador	1945	Lepoldo Benites
Egypt	1945	Dr. Mohammed Hassan el-Zayyat
El Salvador	1945	Reynaldo Galindo Pohl
Equatorial Guinea	1968	Primo José Esono Mica
Ethiopia	1945	Yohannes Tseghe

State	Rank in Population	Population (Latest Estimate or Local Census)	Capital	Population of Capital
Alabama	21	3,444,165	Montgomery	133,386
Alaska	50	302,173	Juneau	6,050
Arizona	33	1,772,482	Phoenix	581,562
Arkansas	32	1,923,295	Little Rock	132,483
California	1	19,953,134	Sacramento	256,127
Colorado	30	2,207,259	Denver	514,678
Connecticut	24	3,032,217	Hartford	158,017
Delaware	46	548,104	Dover	17,488
Florida	9	6,789,443	Tallahassee	71,763
Georgia	15	4,589,575	Atlanta	496,973
Hawaii	40	769,913	Honolulu	324,871
Idaho	42	713,008	Boise	74,990
Illinois	5	11,113,976	Springfield	91,753
Indiana	11	5,193,669	Indianapolis	744,624
Iowa	25	2,825,041	Des Moines	200,587
Kansas	28	2,249,071	Topeka	125,011
Kentucky	23	3,219,311	Frankfort	20,054
Louisiana	20	3,643,180	Baton Rouge	165,963
Maine	38	993,663	Augusta	22,104
Maryland	18	3,922,399	Annapolis	28,042

NATIONS

Country	Year of Admission	Permanent Representative	Country	Year of Admission	Permanent Representative
Fiji	1970	Semesa K. Sikivou, M.B.E.	New Zealand	1945	John Vivian Scott
Finland	1955	Max Jakobson	Nicaragua	1945	Guillermo Sevilla-Sacasa
France	1945	Jacques Kosciusko-Morizet	Niger	1960	Georges Mahamane Condat
Gabon	1960	Jean Davin	Nigeria	1960	Edwin Ogebe Ogbu
Ghana	1957	Richard Maximilian Akwei	Norway	1945	Edvard Hambro
Greece	1945	Dimitri S. Bitsois	Pakistan	1947	Agha Shahi
Guatemala	1945	Rafael E. Castillo-Valdés	Panama	1945	Aquilino E. Boyd
Guinea	1958	Dr. El Hadj Abdoulaye Toure	Paraguay	1945	Miguel Solano Lopez
Guyana	1966	Frederick H. Talbot	People's Dem. Rep. of Yemen	1967	Abdul Malek Ismail
Haiti	1945	Jean Coradin	People's Rep. of the Congo	1960	Nicolas Mondjo
Honduras	1945	Señora de Jimenez Manguia (Deputy)	Peru	1945	Javier Peréz de Cuellar
Hungary	1945	Károly Szarka	Philippines	1945	Narciso G. Reyes
Iceland	1946	Hannes Kjartansson	Poland	1945	Eugeniusz Kulaga
India	1945	Samar Sen	Portugal	1955	Antonio A. de Medeiros Patricio
Indonesia	1950	J. B. P. Maramis (Deputy)	Romania	1955	Gheorghe Diaconescu
Iran	1945	Fereydoun Houeyda	Rwanda	1962	Fidèle Nkundababagenzi
Iraq	1945	Talib el-Shibib	Saudi Arabia	1945	Jamil M. Baroody (Deputy)
Ireland	1955	Cornelius C. Cremin	Senegal	1960	Médoune Fall
Israel	1949	Yosef Tekoah	Sierra Leone	1961	Ismael Byne Taylor-Kamara
Italy	1955	Piero Vinci	Singapore	1965	Shunmugam Jayakumar
Ivory Coast	1960	Siméon Ake	Somalia	1960	Abdulrahim Abby Farah
Jamaica	1962	Keith Johnson	South Africa	1945	Carl F. G. von Hirschberg
Japan	1956	Toru Nakagawa	Spain	1955	Don Jaime de Pinies
Jordan	1955	Baha Ud-Din Toukan	Sudan	1956	Kamal Mustafa (Deputy)
Kenya	1963	Joseph Odero-Jowi	Swaziland	1968	Mboni Naph Dlamini
Khmer Republic	1954	Truong Cang	Sweden	1946	Olof Rydbeck
Kuwait	1963	Abdalla Yaccoub Bishara	Syrian Arab Rep.	1945	George J. Tomeh
Laos	1955	Prince Khammao	Thailand	1946	Anand Panyarachun (Acting)
Lebanon	1945	Edouard Ghorra	Togo	1960	Michel Eklo
Lesotho	1966	Mooki V. Molapo	Trinidad and Tobago	1962	Eustace E. Seignoret
Liberia	1945	Nathan Barnes	Tunisia	1956	Rachid Driss
Libyan Arab Republic	1955	Mahmood Suleiman Maghribi	Turkey	1945	Umit Haluk Bayulken
Luxembourg	1945	Andre Philippe	Uganda	1962	Grace S. Ibingira
Madagascar	1960	Blaise Rabetafika	Ukrainian S.S.R.	1945	Mikhail Deonisovich Polyanichko
Malawi	1964	Nyemba Wales Mbekeani	Union of Soviet Socialist Republic	1945	Yakov Aleksandrovich Malik
Malaysia	1957	H. M. A. Zakaria	United Kingdom of Great Britain	1945	Sir Colin Crowe
Mali	1960	Seydou Traore	United Republic of Tanzania	1964	Salim Ahmed Salim
Malta	1964	Joseph Attard Kingswell	United States	1945	George H. Bush
Mauritania	1961	Moulaye el Hassen	Upper Volta	1960	Tensoré Paul Rouamba
Mauritius	1968	Radha Krishna Ramphul	Uruguay	1945	Dr. Augusto Legnani
Mexico	1945	Dr. Alfonso Garcia Robles	Venezuela	1945	Dr. Andrés Aguilar M.
Mongolia	1961	Mangalyn Dugersuren	Yemen	1947	Yahya H. Geghman
Morocco	1956	Mehdi Mrani Zentar	Yugoslavia	1945	Lazar Mojsov
Nepal	1955	Padma Bahadur Khatri	Zambia	1964	Vernon Johnson Mwaanga
Netherlands	1945	Robbert Fack			

THE UNION

Largest City	Population of Largest City	Governor	Party	Term Expires
Birmingham	300,910	George C. Wallace	D	1975
Anchorage	48,029	William A. Egan	D	1974
Phoenix	581,562	John R. Williams	R	1975
Little Rock	132,483	Dale Bumpers	D	1973
Los Angeles	2,816,061	Ronald Reagan	R	1975
Denver	514,678	John A. Love	R	1975
Hartford	158,017	Thomas J. Meskill	R	1974
Wilmington	80,386	Russell W. Peterson	R	1973
Jacksonville	528,865	Reuben O'Daskew	D	1975
Atlanta	496,973	Jimmy Carter	D	1975
Honolulu	324,871	John A. Burns	D	1974
Boise	74,990	Cecil D. Andrus	D	1975
Chicago	3,366,957	Richard B. Ogilvie	R	1973
Indianapolis	744,624	Edgar D. Whitcomb	R	1973
Des Moines	200,587	Robert R. Day	R	1973
Wichita	276,554	Robert B. Docking	D	1973
Louisville	361,472	Louie B. Nunn	R	1971
New Orleans	593,471	John J. McKeithen	D	1972
Portland	65,116	Kenneth M. Curtis	D	1975
Baltimore	905,759	Marvin Mandel	D	1971

State	Rank in Population	Population (Latest Estimate or Local Census)	Capital	Population of Capital
Massachusetts	10	5,689,170	Boston	641,071
Michigan	7	8,875,083	Lansing	131,546
Minnesota	19	3,805,069	St. Paul	309,980
Mississippi	29	2,216,012	Jackson	153,968
Missouri	13	4,677,399	Jefferson City	51,921
Montana	43	694,409	Helena	22,730
Nebraska	35	1,483,791	Lincoln	149,418
Nevada	47	488,738	Carson City	15,264
New Hampshire	41	737,681	Concord	30,022
New Jersey	8	7,168,164	Trenton	104,638
New Mexico	37	1,016,000	Santa Fe	41,167
New York	2	18,190,740	Albany	113,988
North Carolina	12	5,082,059	Raleigh	121,577
North Dakota	45	617,761	Bismarck	34,703
Ohio	6	10,652,017	Columbus	539,677
Oklahoma	27	2,559,253	Oklahoma City	366,481
Oregon	31	2,091,385	Salem	68,296
Pennsylvania	3	11,793,909	Harrisburg	65,828
Rhode Island	39	949,723	Providence	179,213
South Carolina	26	2,590,516	Columbia	113,542
South Dakota	40	680,514	Pierre	9,732
Tennessee	17	3,924,164	Nashville	447,877
Texas	4	11,196,730	Austin	246,904
Utah	36	1,059,273	Salt Lake City	175,885
Vermont	48	444,732	Montpelier	9,102
Virginia	14	4,648,494	Richmond	249,621
Washington	22	3,409,169	Olympia	22,143
West Virginia	30	1,744,237	Charleston	71,505
Wisconsin	16	4,417,933	Madison	173,258
Wyoming	49	332,416	Cheyenne	40,914
District Of Columbia		756,510		
Commonwealth Of Puerto Rico		2,712,033	San Juan	440,952

ECONOMICS

EMPLOYMENT

Year	Civilian Labor Force	Un-employed	Percent-age Unemployed
1929	49,180,000	1,550,000	3.2
1933	51,590,000	12,830,000	24.9
1940	55,640,000	8,120,000	14.6
1944	54,630,000	670,000	1.2
1960	70,612,000	3,931,000	5.6
1961	71,603,000	4,806,000	6.7
1962	71,854,000	4,007,000	5.6
1963	72,975,000	4,166,000	5.7
1964	74,233,000	3,876,000	5.2
1965	75,635,000	3,456,000	4.6
1966	75,770,000	2,875,000	3.8
1967	77,348,000	2,975,000	3.8
1968	78,737,000	2,816,000	3.6
1969	80,733,000	2,831,000	3.5
1970	82,715,000	4,088,000	4.9

1971 by month (seasonally adjusted)

January	83,897,000	5,033,000	6.0
February	83,384,000	4,847,000	5.8
March	83,475,000	5,000,000	6.0
April	83,783,000	5,085,000	6.1
May	84,178,000	5,217,000	6.2
June	83,132,000	4,689,000	5.6
July	83,829,000	4,888,000	5.8
August	84,312,000	5,115,000	6.1
September	84,598,000	5,073,000	6.0
October	84,783,000	4,938,000	5.8
November	85,172,000	5,150,000	6.0

(Source: Department of Labor)

GROSS NATIONAL PRODUCT

(The total output of goods and services in the United States measured in terms of expenditures by which they were acquired)

Year	GNP
1929	$103,100,000,000
1933	55,600,000,000
1940	99,700,000,000
1945	211,900,000,000
1950	284,800,000,000
1960	503,700,000,000
1961	520,100,000,000
1962	560,300,000,000
1963	590,500,000,000
1964	632,400,000,000
1965	683,900,000,000
1966	743,300,000,000
1967	789,663,000,000
1968	865,700,000,000
1969	931,400,000,000 ·
1970	974,100,000,000
1971 (estimated)	1,045,000,000,000

(Source: Department of Commerce)

U.S. TOTAL GROSS PUBLIC DEBT

Year	Total	Per capita
1860	$65,000,000	$2
1900	1,263,000,000	17
1920	24,299,000,000	228
1930	16,185,000,000	132
1940	42,968,000,000	325
1945	258,682,000,000	1,849
1960	286,331,000,000	1,585
1961	288,971,000,000	1,573
1962	298,201,000,000	1,598
1963	305,860,000,000	1,615
1964	311,713,000,000	1,622
1965	317,274,000,000	1,631
1966	319,907,000,000	1,625
1967	326,221,000,000	1,638
1968	347,578,000,000	1,727
1969	353,720,000,000	1,741
1970	370,919,000,000	1,811
1971	398,130,000,000 (preliminary)	1,923

(Source: Department of the Treasury)

PER CAPITA PERSONAL INCOME

1950	$1,496	1966	2,978
1960	2,215	1967	3,159
1961	2,264	1968	3,421
1962	2,368	1969	3,687
1963	2,455	1970	3,921
1964	2,586	1971 (estimated)	4,140
1965	2,765		

(Source: Department of Commerce)

Largest City	Population of Largest City	Governor	Party	Term Expires
Boston	641,071	Francis W. Sargent	R	1975
Detroit	1,511,482	William G. Milliken	R	1975
Minneapolis	434,400	Wendell R. Anderson	D	1975
Jackson	153,968	John Bell Williams	D	1972
St. Louis	622,236	Warren E. Hearnes	D	1973
Billings	61,581	Forrest H. Anderson	D	1973
Omaha	347,328	J. James Exon	D	1975
Las Vegas	125,787	D. N. O'Callaghan	D	1975
Manchester	87,754	Walter Peterson	R	1973
Newark	382,417	William T. Cahill	R	1974
Albuquerque	243,751	Bruce King	D	1975
New York	7,895,563	Nelson A. Rockefeller	R	1975
Charlotte	241,178	Robert W. Scott	D	1973
Fargo	53,365	William L. Guy	D	1973
Cleveland	750,903	John J. Gilligan	D	1975
Oklahoma City	366,481	David Hall	D	1975
Portland	382,619	Tom McCall	R	1975
Philadelphia	1,948,609	Milton J. Shapp	D	1975
Providence	179,213	Frank Licht	D	1973
Columbia	113,542	John C. West	D	1975
Sioux Falls	72,488	Richard F. Kneip	D	1973
Memphis	623,530	Winfield Dunn	R	1975
Houston	1,232,802	Preston Smith	D	1971
Salt Lake City	175,885	Calvin L. Rampton	D	1973
Burlington	38,633	Deane C. Davis	R	1973
Norfolk	307,951	Linwood Holton	R	1974
Seattle	530,831	Daniel J. Evans	R	1973
Huntington	74,315	Arch A. Moore Jr.	R	1973
Milwaukee	717,099	Patrick J. Lucey	D	1975
Cheyenne	40,914	Stanley K. Hathaway	R	1975
San Juan	440,952	Luis A. Ferré		1973

CONSUMER PRICE INDEX (Living Costs)

Year	All Items	Food	Apparel	Housing	Rent	Medical Care	Transportation
1913	34.5	33.6	33.8	--	55.7	--	--
1920	69.8	70.8	98.0	--	72.9	--	--
1929	59.7	55.6	56.2	--	85.4	--	--
1933	45.1	35.3	42.8	--	60.8	--	--
1940	48.8	40.5	49.6	--	63.2	--	--
1945	62.7	58.4	71.2	--	66.1	--	--
1950	83.8	85.8	91.5	83.2	79.1	73.4	79.0
1960	103.1	101.4	102.1	103.1	103.1	108.1	103.8
1961	104.2	102.6	102.8	103.9	104.4	111.3	105.0
1962	105.4	103.6	103.2	104.8	105.7	114.2	107.2
1963	106.7	105.1	104.2	106.0	106.8	117.0	107.8
1964	108.1	106.4	105.7	107.2	107.8	119.4	109.3
1965	109.9	108.8	106.8	108.5	109.8	122.3	111.6
1966	113.1	114.2	109.6	111.1	110.4	127.7	112.7
1967	116.3	115.2	114.0	114.3	112.4	136.7	115.9
1968	121.2	119.3	120.1	119.1	115.1	145.0	119.6
1969	127.7	125.5	127.1	126.7	118.8	155.0	124.2
1970	135.3	132.4	132.2	135.9	123.7	164.9	130.6

1971 by month	All Items	Food	Apparel	Housing	Rent	Medical Care	Transportation
January	119.2	115.5	117.6	122.7	112.9	124.9	117.5
February	119.4	115.9	118.1	122.6	113.6	125.8	117.5
March	119.8	117.0	118.6	122.4	113.4	126.8	117.8
April	120.2	117.8	119.1	122.5	114.4	127.5	118.1
May	120.8	118.2	120.2	123.2	114.7	128.1	118.8
June	121.5	119.2	120.1	124.0	115.2	128.6	119.6
July	121.8	119.8	124.5	124.5	115.4	129.3	119.5
August	122.2	120.0	119.0	125.1	115.8	130.0	120.1
September	122.4	119.1	120.6	125.5	116.1	130.4	119.8
October	122.6	118.9	121.6	125.9	116.4	129.6	120.6

(Source: Department of Labor)

SPORTS
BASEBALL
FINAL MAJOR LEAGUE STANDINGS

AMERICAN LEAGUE

EASTERN DIVISION	W.	L.	Pct.	G.B.	WESTERN DIVISION	W.	L.	Pct.	G.B.
Baltimore	101	57	.639	—	Oakland	101	60	.627	—
Detroit	91	71	.562	12	Kansas City	85	76	.528	16
Boston	85	77	.525	18	Chicago	79	83	.488	22½
New York	82	80	.506	21	California	76	86	.469	25½
Washington	63	96	.396	38½	Minnesota	74	86	.463	26½
Cleveland	60	102	.370	43	Milwaukee	69	92	.429	32

Baltimore defeated Oakland 3 games to 0 to win American League Championship.

NATIONAL LEAGUE

EASTERN DIVISION	W.	L.	Pct.	G.B.	WESTERN DIVISION	W.	L.	Pct.	G.B.
Pittsburgh	97	65	.599	—	San Fran.	90	72	.556	—
St. Louis	90	72	.556	7	Los Angeles	89	73	.549	1
Chicago	83	79	.512	14	Atlanta	82	80	.506	8
New York	83	79	.512	14	Cincinnati	79	83	.488	11
Montreal	71	90	.441	25½	Houston	79	83	.488	11
Philadelphia	67	95	.414	30	San Diego	61	100	.379	28½

Pittsburgh defeated San Francisco 3 games to 1 to win National League Championship.

WORLD SERIES

First Game

PITTSBURGH	ab.	r.	h.	rbi.	BALTIMORE	ab.	r.	h.	rbi.
Cash, 2b	4	0	1	1	Buford, lf	4	2	2	1
Clines, cf	4	0	0	0	Blair, lf	0	0	0	0
Clemente, rf	4	0	2	0	Rettenm'd, cf	4	1	1	3
Stargell, lf	3	0	0	0	Powell, 1b	3	0	0	0
Robertson, 1b	3	1	0	0	F. Rob'son, rf	4	1	2	1
Sanguillen, c	4	1	0	0	Hendricks, c	4	0	1	0
Pagan, 3b	4	0	0	0	B. Rob'son, 3b	4	0	1	0
Hernandez, ss	2	1	0	1	Johnson, 2b	4	0	1	0
Oliver, ph	1	0	0	0	Belanger, ss	4	1	2	0
Ellis, p	1	0	0	0	McNally, p	3	0	0	0
Moose, p	1	0	0	0	Total	34	5	10	5
Mazeroski, ph	1	0	0	0					
Miller, p	0	0	0	0					
Total	32	3	3	2					

Pittsburgh Pirates		0 3 0	0 0 0	0 0 0	0—3			
Baltimore Orioles		0 1 3	0 1 0	0 0 0	x—5			

Errors—Belanger 2, Hendricks. Left on base—Pittsburgh 5, Baltimore 6. Two-base hit—Clemente. Three-base hit—Belanger. Home runs—F. Robinson (1), Rettenmund (1), Buford (1). Sacrifice—Hernandez. Wild pitch—McNally. Time of game—2:06. Attendance—53,229.

	IP.	H.	R.	ER.	BB.	SO.
Ellis (L, 0–1)	2⅓	4	4	4	1	1
Moose	3⅔	3	1	1	0	4
Miller	2	3	0	0	0	1
McNally (W, 1–0)	9	3	3	0	2	9

Second Game

PITTSBURGH	ab.	r.	h.	rbi.	BALTIMORE	ab.	r.	h.	rbi.
Cash, 2b	5	0	0	0	Buford, lf	5	0	0	1
Hebner, 3b	3	1	1	3	Rettenm'd, cf	5	1	2	1
Clemente, rf	5	0	2	0	Powell, 1b	5	1	1	0
Stargell, lf	3	0	1	0	F. Rob'son, rf	4	2	3	0
Glusti, p	0	0	0	0	Blair, cf	1	1	1	0
Oliver, cf	5	0	1	0	Hendricks, c	3	2	2	1
Robertson, 1b	3	0	0	0	B. Rob'son, 3b	3	2	3	3
Sanguillen, c	5	0	1	0	D. Johnson, 2b	5	1	2	2
Hernandez, ss	2	1	1	0	Belanger, ss	3	1	0	0
May, ph	1	0	0	0	Palmer, p	2	0	0	2
B. Johnson, p	2	0	0	0	Hall, p	0	0	0	0
Kison, p	0	0	0	0	Total	36	11	14	10
Moose, p	0	0	0	0					
Veale, p	0	0	0	0					
Sands, ph	1	0	0	0					
Miller, p	0	0	0	0					
Davalillo, lf	1	1	1	0					
Total	36	3	8	3					

Pittsburgh Pirates		0 0 0	0 0 0	0 3	0—3
Baltimore Orioles		0 1 0	3 6 1	0 0	x—11

Errors—Oliver, Belanger. Double plays—Pittsburgh 2. Left on base—Pittsburgh 14, Baltimore 9. Two-base hit—Clemente. Home run—Hebner (1). Save—Hall. Hit by pitcher—by B. Johnson (Hendricks). Time of game—2:55. Attendance—53,239.

	IP.	H.	R.	ER.	BB.	SO.
B. Johnson (L, 0–1)	3⅓	4	4	4	2	1
Kison	0	0	0	0	2	0
Moose	1	5	5	5	0	0
Veale	⅔	1	1	1	2	0
Miller	2	3	1	1	0	1
Glusti	1	1	0	0	1	0
Palmer (W, 1–0)	8	7	3	3	8	10
Hall	1	1	0	0	0	0

Third Game

BALTIMORE	ab.	r.	h.	rbi.	PITTSBURGH	ab.	r.	h.	rbi.
Buford, lf	4	0	0	0	Cash, 2b	4	1	1	0
Rettenmund, cf	4	0	0	0	Oliver, cf	4	0	0	0
Powell, 1b	4	0	0	0	Clemente, rf	4	1	1	1
F. Robinson, rf	4	1	2	1	Stargell, lf	1	1	0	0
Hendricks, c	3	0	0	0	Robertson, 1b	4	1	1	3
B. Robinson, 3b	3	0	1	0	Sanguillen, c	4	1	2	0
D. Johnson, 2b	3	0	0	0	Pagan, 3b	4	0	2	1
Belanger, ss	3	0	0	0	Alley, ss	2	0	0	0
Cuellar, p	1	0	0	0	Hernandez, ss	1	0	0	0
Dukes, p	0	0	0	0	Blass, p	4	0	0	0
Shopay, ph	1	0	0	0	Total	32	5	7	5
Watt, p	0	0	0	0					
Total	30	1	3	1					

Baltimore Orioles		0 0 0	0 0 0	1 0	0—1
Pittsburgh Pirates		1 0 0	0 0 1	3 0	x—5

Errors—Powell, B. Robinson, Cuellar. Double play—Baltimore 1. Left on base—Baltimore 4, Pittsburgh 9. Two-base hits—Cash, Pagan, Sanguillen. Home runs—F. Robinson (1), Robertson (1). Time of game—2:20. Attendance—50,403.

	IP.	H.	R.	ER.	BB.	SO.
Cuellar (L, 0–1)	6	7	5	4	6	4
Dukes	1	0	0	0	0	0
Watt	1	0	0	0	0	1
Blass (W, 1–0)	9	3	1	1	2	8

Fourth Game

BALTIMORE	ab.	r.	h.	rbi.	PITTSBURGH	ab.	r.	h.	rbi.
Blair, cf	4	1	2	0	Cash, 2b	4	1	1	0
Belanger, ss	4	1	1	0	Hebner, 3b	5	1	1	0
Rettenmund, lf	4	1	1	0	Clemente, rf	4	0	3	0
F. Robinson, rf	2	0	0	0	Stargell, lf	5	1	2	1
B. Robinson, 3b	3	0	1	1	Oliver, cf	4	0	2	2
Powell, 1b	3	0	0	1	Robertson, 1b	4	1	1	0
D. Johnson, 2b	3	0	0	0	Sanguillen, c	4	0	2	0
Etchebarren, c	2	0	0	0	Hernandez, ss	3	0	1	0
Dobson, p	2	0	0	0	Davalillo, ph	1	0	0	0
Jackson, p	0	0	0	0	Giusti, p	0	0	0	0
Shopay, ph	1	0	0	0	Walker, p	0	0	0	0
Watt, p	0	0	0	0	Kison, p	2	0	0	0
Richert, p	0	0	0	0	May, ph	1	0	1	1
Total	28	3	4	2	Alley, ss	0	0	0	0
					Total	37	4	14	4

Baltimore Orioles		3 0 0	0 0 0	0 0	0—3
Pittsburgh Pirates		2 0 1	0 0 0	1 0	x—4

Errors—Blair. Double plays—Baltimore 1, Pittsburgh 1. Left on base—Baltimore 4, Pittsburgh 13. Two base hits—Stargell, Oliver, Blair. Stolen bases—Sanguillen, Hernandez. Sacrifice fly—B. Robinson, Powell. Save—Giusti. Hit by pitch—by Kison (Johnson), (F. Robinson), (Etchebarren). Passed ball—Sanguillen. Time of game—2:48. Attendance—51,378.

	IP.	H.	R.	ER.	BB.	SO.
Dobson	5⅓	10	3	3	3	4
Jackson	⅔	0	0	0	1	0
Watt (L, 0-1)	1⅓	4	1	1	0	1
Richert	⅔	0	0	0	0	1
Walker	⅔	3	3	3	1	0
Kison (W, 1-0)	6⅓	1	0	0	0	3
Giusti	2	0	0	0	0	1

Fifth Game

BALTIMORE

	ab.	r.	h.	rbi.
Buford, lf	3	0	0	0
Blair, cf	4	0	0	0
Powell, 1b	3	0	1	0
F. Robinson, rf	3	0	0	0
Hendricks, c	2	0	0	0
B. Robinson, 3b	3	0	1	0
Johnson, 2b	3	0	0	0
Belanger, ss	3	0	0	0
McNally, p	1	0	0	0
Leonhard, p	0	0	0	0
Shopay, ph	1	0	0	0
Dukes, p	0	0	0	0
Rettenmund, ph	1	0	0	0
Total	27	0	2	0

PITTSBURGH

	ab.	r.	h.	rbi.
Cash, 2b	4	0	0	0
Clines, cf	3	2	1	0
Clemente, rf	4	0	1	1
Stargell, lf	4	0	1	0
Robertson, 1b	3	1	1	1
Sanguillen, c	4	1	1	0
Pagan, 3b	4	0	1	0
Hernandez, ss	3	0	2	0
Briles, p	2	0	1	1
Total	31	4	9	3

Baltimore Orioles	0 0 0 0 0 0 0 0 0—0
Pittsburgh Pirates	0 2 1 0 1 0 0 0 x—4

Error—B. Robinson. Double plays—Pittsburgh 2. Left on base—Baltimore 2, Pittsburgh 9. Three-base hit—Clines. Home run—Robertson (2). Stolen bases—Clines, Sanguillen. Sacrifices—Briles (2). Hit by pitch—by Dukes (Hernandez). Wild pitch—McNally. Time of game—2:16. Attendance—51,377.

	IP.	H.	R.	ER.	BB.	SO.
McNally (L, 1-1)	4	7	4	3	2	3
Leonhard	1	0	0	0	1	0
Dukes	3	2	0	0	0	1
Briles (W, 1-0)	9	2	0	0	2	2

Sixth Game

PITTSBURGH

	ab.	r.	h.	rbi.
Cash, 2b	5	0	1	0
Hebner, 3b	4	0	0	0
Clemente, rf	4	1	2	1
Stargell, lf	4	0	0	0
Oliver, cf	5	1	1	0
Miller, p	0	0	0	0
Robertson, 1b	4	0	2	1
Sanguillen, c	4	0	3	0
Hernandez, ss	4	0	0	0
Moose, p	1	0	0	0
B. Johnson, p	1	0	0	0
Giusti, p	0	0	0	0
Davalillo, cf	1	0	0	0
Total	37	2	9	2

BALTIMORE

	ab.	r.	h.	rbi.
Buford, lf	4	1	3	1
D. Johnson, 2b	5	0	1	1
Powell, 1b	5	0	1	0
F. Robinson, rf	4	1	0	0
Rettenmund, cf	5	0	1	0
B. Robinson, 3b	4	0	1	1
Hendricks, c	4	0	0	0
Belanger, ss	1	1	1	0
Palmer, p	2	0	0	0
Shopay, ph	1	0	0	0
Dobson, p	0	0	0	0
McNally, p	0	0	0	0
Total	35	3	8	3

Pittsburgh Pirates	0 1 1 0 0 0 0 0 0 0—2
Baltimore Orioles	0 0 0 0 0 1 1 0 0 1—3

Error—Hebner. Double play—Pittsburgh 1. Left on base—Pittsburgh 9. Baltimore 10. Two-base hits—Oliver, Buford. Three base hit—Clemente. Home runs—Clemente (1), Buford (2). Stolen bases—Belanger, Cash. Sacrifice—Moose, Palmer. Sacrifice fly—B. Robinson. Time of game—2.59. Attendance—44,174.

	IP.	H.	R.	ER.	BB.	SO.
Moose	5	4	1	1	2	3
B. Johnson	1⅔	1	1	1	1	2
Giusti	2⅓	2	0	0	1	3
Miller (L, 0-1)	*⅔	1	1	1	1	0
Palmer	9	8	2	2	1	5
Dobson	⅔	1	0	0	1	1
McNally (W, 2-1)	⅓	0	0	0	1	0

*Two out when winning run was scored.

Seventh Game

PITTSBURGH

	ab.	r.	h.	rbi.
Cash, 2b	4	0	0	0
Clines, cf	4	0	0	0
Clemente, rf	4	1	1	1
Robertson, 1b	4	0	1	0
Sanguillen, c	4	0	2	0
Stargell, lf	4	1	1	0
Pagan, 3b	3	0	1	1
Hernandez, ss	3	0	0	0
Blass, p	3	0	0	0
Total	33	2	6	2

BALTIMORE

	ab.	r.	h.	rbi.
Buford, lf	3	0	1	1
D. Johnson, 2b	4	0	0	0
Powell, 1b	4	0	0	0
F. Robinson, rf	4	0	0	0
Rettenmund, cf	4	0	0	0
B. Robinson, 3b	2	0	0	0
Hendricks, c	3	1	2	0
Belanger, ss	3	0	1	0
Cuellar, p	2	0	0	0
Shopay, ph	0	0	0	0
Dobson, p	0	0	0	0
McNally, p	0	0	0	0
Total	29	1	4	1

Pittsburgh Pirates	0 0 0 1 0 0 0 1 0—2
Baltimore Orioles	0 0 0 0 0 0 0 1 0—1

Error—Robertson. Double play—Pittsburgh 1. Left on base—Pittsburgh 4, Baltimore 4. Two-base hits—Hendricks, Pagan. Home run—Clemente (2). Sacrifice—Shopay. Time of game—2:10. Attendance—47,291.

	IP.	H.	R.	ER.	BB.	SO.
Blass (W, 2-0)	9	4	1	1	2	5
Cuellar (L, 0-2)	8	4	2	2	0	6
Dobson	⅔	2	0	0	0	1
McNally	⅓	0	0	0	0	0

Pittsburgh defeated Baltimore 4 games to 3 to win World Series.

World Series Composite Box Score

PITTSBURGH PIRATES

	G	AB	R	H	2B	3B	HR	RBI	SO	BB	Avg.	PO	A	E	Avg.
Cash, 2b	7	30	2	4	1	0	0	1	1	3	.133	20	24	0	1.000
Clines, cf	3	11	2	1	0	1	0	0	1	1	.091	6	0	0	1.000
Hebner, 3b	3	12	2	2	0	1	0	3	3	3	.167	1	3	1	.800
Clemente, rf	7	29	3	12	2	1	2	4	2	2	.414	16	0	0	1.000
Stargell, lf	7	24	3	5	1	0	0	1	9	7	.208	11	1	0	1.000
Robertson, 1b	7	25	4	6	0	0	2	5	8	4	.240	64	4	1	.986
Sanguillen, c	7	29	3	11	1	0	0	3	0	0	.379	37	0	0	1.000
Pagan, 3b	4	15	0	4	2	0	0	2	1	0	.267	2	8	0	1.000
Hernandez, ss	7	18	2	4	0	0	0	0	6	2	.222	9	15	0	1.000
Alley, ss	2	2	0	0	0	0	0	0	0	1	.000	1	4	0	1.000
May, ph	2	2	0	1	0	0	0	1	0	0	.500	0	0	0	.000
Oliver, cf	5	19	1	4	2	0	0	2	5	2	.211	11	0	1	.917
Ellis, p	1	1	0	0	0	0	0	0	1	0	.000	1	0	0	1.000
Moose, p	3	2	0	0	0	0	0	0	0	0	.000	0	3	0	1.000
Mazeroski, ph	1	1	0	0	0	0	0	0	0	0	.000	0	0	0	.000
Miller, p	3	0	0	0	0	0	0	0	0	0	.000	1	1	0	1.000
Giusti, p	3	0	0	0	0	0	0	0	0	0	.000	0	0	0	.000
B. Johnson, p	2	3	0	0	0	0	0	0	2	0	.000	2	0	0	1.000
Kison, p	2	2	0	0	0	0	0	0	2	1	.000	0	1	0	1.000
Veale, p	1	0	0	0	0	0	0	0	0	0	.000	0	1	0	1.000
Sands, ph	1	1	0	0	0	0	0	0	1	0	.000	0	0	0	.000
Davalillo, lf	3	3	1	1	0	0	0	0	0	0	.333	1	0	0	1.000
Blass, p	2	8	0	0	0	0	0	0	1	0	.000	2	4	0	1.000
Walker, p	1	0	0	0	0	0	0	0	0	0	.000	0	0	0	.000
Briles, p	1	2	0	1	0	0	0	1	1	0	.500	0	1	0	1.000
Total	7	238	23	56	9	2	5	20	47	26	.235	185	70	3	.988

BALTIMORE ORIOLES

	G	AB	R	H	2B	3B	HR	RBI	SO	BB	Avg.	PO	A	E	Avg.
Buford, lf	6	23	3	6	1	0	2	4	3	3	.261	13	1	0	1.000
Blair, cf	4	9	2	3	1	0	0	1	0	0	.333	6	2	1	.889
Rettenmund, cf	7	27	3	5	0	0	1	4	4	0	.185	17	0	0	1.000
Powell, 1b	7	27	1	3	0	0	1	3	1	1	.111	52	4	1	.982
F. Robinson, rf	7	25	5	7	0	0	2	2	8	2	.280	12	0	0	1.000
Hendricks, c	6	19	3	5	0	0	1	3	2	2	.263	40	4	1	.978
B. Robinson, 3b	7	22	2	7	0	0	0	5	1	1	.318	6	16	2	.917
D. Johnson, 2b	7	27	1	4	0	0	0	3	1	0	.148	19	12	0	1.000
Belanger, ss	7	21	4	5	0	1	0	0	2	5	.238	10	20	3	.909
Etchebarren, c	1	2	0	0	0	0	0	0	0	0	.000	5	0	0	1.000
McNally, p	4	4	0	0	0	0	0	0	3	0	.000	0	2	0	1.000
Palmer, p	2	4	0	0	0	0	0	2	2	2	.000	2	1	0	1.000
Hall, p	1	0	0	0	0	0	0	0	0	0	.000	1	0	0	1.000
Cuellar, p	2	3	0	0	0	0	0	0	2	1	.000	0	3	1	.750
Dukes, p	1	0	0	0	0	0	0	0	0	0	.000	0	0	0	.000
Shopay, ph	5	4	0	0	0	0	0	0	0	0	.000	0	0	0	.000
Watt, p	2	0	0	0	0	0	0	0	0	0	.000	0	0	0	.000
Dobson, p	3	2	0	0	0	0	0	0	0	0	.000	1	3	0	1.000
Jackson, p	1	0	0	0	0	0	0	0	0	0	.000	0	0	0	.000
Richert, p	1	0	0	0	0	0	0	0	0	0	.000	0	0	0	.000
Leonhard, p	1	0	0	0	0	0	0	0	0	0	.000	0	0	0	.000
Total	7	219	24	45	2	1	5	22	35	20	.205	183	70	9	.965

Two out when winning run was scored in 10th inning of 6th game.

COMPOSITE SCORE BY INNINGS

Pittsburgh	3	6	3	1	1	1	4	4	0		0—23
Baltimore	3	2	3	3	7	2	2	1	0		1—24

Pitching Summary
PITTSBURGH

	G	CG	IP	H	R	BB	SO	HB	WP	W	L	Pct.	ER	ERA
Ellis	1	0	2⅔	4	4	1	1	0	0	0	1	.000	4	15.43
Moose	3	0	9⅔	12	7	2	7	0	1	0	0	.000	7	6.52
Miller	3	0	4⅔	7	2	1	2	0	0	0	1	.000	2	2.25
B. Johnson	2	0	5	5	5	3	3	1	0	0	1	.000	5	3.86
Kison	2	0	6⅓	1	0	2	3	3	0	1	0	1.000	0	0.00
Veale	1	0	⅔	1	1	2	2	0	0	0	0	.000	1	13.50
Giusti	3	0	5⅓	3	0	2	4	0	0	0	0	.000	0	0.00
Blass	2	2	18	7	2	4	13	0	0	2	0	1.000	2	1.00
Walker	1	0	⅔	3	3	1	0	0	0	0	0	.000	3	40.50
Briles	1	1	9	2	0	2	2	0	0	1	0	1.000	0	0.00
Total	7	3	61⅔	45	24	30	35	4	1	4	3	.571	24	3.50

BALTIMORE

	G	CG	IP	H	R	BB	SO	HB	WP	W	L	Pct.	ER	ERA
McNally	4	1	13⅔	10	7	5	12	0	1	2	1	.667	3	1.98
Palmer	2	0	17	15	5	9	15	0	0	1	0	1.000	5	2.65
Hall	1	0	1	1	0	0	0	0	0	0	0	.000	0	0.00
Cuellar	2	0	14	11	7	6	10	0	0	0	2	.000	6	5.86
Dukes	2	0	4	2	0	0	1	0	0	0	0	.000	0	0.00
Dobson	3	0	6⅔	13	3	4	6	0	0	0	0	.000	3	4.05
Jackson	1	0	⅔	0	0	1	0	0	0	0	0	.000	0	0.00
Watt	2	0	2⅓	4	1	0	2	0	0	0	1	.000	1	6.75
Richert	1	0	⅔	0	0	0	1	0	0	0	0	.000	0	0.00
Leonhard	1	0	1	0	0	1	0	0	0	0	0	.000	0	0.00
Total	7	1	61	56	23	26	47	0	1	3	4	.429	18	2.66

DP—Pittsburgh 7, Baltimore 2. LOB—Pittsburgh 63, Baltimore 39. S—Hernandez, Briles 2, Moose, Palmer, Shopay. SF—B. Robinson 2, Powell. SB—Sanguillen 2, Hernandez, Clines, Belanger. Save—Hall, Giusti. U—Chylak (AL), Sudol (NL), Rice (AL), Vergo (NL), OF—Odom (AL), Kibler (NL). T—2:06 (1st game), 2:55 (2d game), 2:20 (3d game), 2:42 (4th game), 2:16 (5th game), 2:59 (6th game), 2:10 (7th game). A—53,229 (1st game), 53,239 (2d game), 50,403 (3d game), 51,378 (4th game), 51,377 (5th game), 44, 174 (6th game), 47,291 (7th game).

PRO FOOTBALL

Final Standings

AMERICAN CONFERENCE

Eastern

	W	L	T	Pct.	PF	PA
*Miami	10	3	1	.769	315	174
×Baltimore	10	4	0	.714	313	140
JETS	6	8	0	.429	212	299
New England	6	8	0	.429	238	325
Buffalo	1	13	0	.071	184	394

Central

	W	L	T	Pct.	PF	PA
*Cleveland	9	5	0	.643	285	273
Pittsburgh	6	8	0	.429	246	292
Houston	4	9	1	.308	251	330
Cincinati	4	10	0	.286	284	265

Western

	W	L	T	Pct.	PF	PA
*Kansas City	10	3	1	.769	302	208
Oakland	8	4	2	.667	344	278
San Diego	6	8	0	.429	311	341
Denver	4	9	1	.308	203	275

NATIONAL CONFERENCE

Eastern

	W	L	T	Pct.	PF	PA
*Dallas	11	3	0	.786	406	222
×Washington	9	4	1	.692	276	190
Philadelphia	6	7	1	.462	221	302
St. Louis	4	9	1	.308	231	279
GIANTS	4	10	0	.286	228	362

Central

	W	L	T	Pct.	PF	PA
*Minnesota	11	3	0	.786	245	139
Detroit	7	6	1	.538	341	286
Chicago	6	8	0	.429	185	276
Green Bay	4	8	2	.333	274	298

Western

	W	L	T	Pct.	PF	PA
*San Francisco	9	5	0	.643	300	216
Los Angeles	8	5	1	.615	313	260
Atlanta	7	6	1	.538	274	277
New Orleans	4	8	2	.333	266	347

*Clinched Division title
×-Clinched Playoff spot

N.F.L. Playoffs

Semifinal Round

NFC—San Francisco 24, Washington 20
Dallas 20, Minnesota 12

AFC Baltimore 20, Cleveland 3
Miami 27, Kansas City 24

Final

AFC Baltimore 0, Miami 21
NFC San Francisco 3, Dallas 14

Dallas wins NFC championship.
Miami wins AFC championship.

Dallas and Miami
meet in the Super Bowl in
New Orleans, Jan. 16.

COLLEGE FOOTBALL

Ratings

The top 20, with points figured on a 20-18-16-14-12-10-9-8-7-6-5-4-3-2-1 basis for first through 15th places (first-place votes in parentheses) and won-lost-tied records.

	W.	L.	T.	Pts.
1—Nebraska (48)	12	0	0	1,086
2—Alabama (4)	11	0	0	954
3—Oklahoma	10	1	0	880
4—Michigan (3)	11	0	0	797
5—Auburn	9	1	0	581
6—Georgia	10	1	0	480
7—Colorado	9	2	0	432
8—Arizona State	10	1	0	394
9—Tennessee	9	2	0	385
10—Penn State	10	1	0	334

Intercollegiate Champions

National—Nebraska.
Eastern (Lambert Trophy)—Penn State.
Eastern (Lambert Cup)—Delaware.
Eastern (Lambert Bowl)—Alfred.
Ivy League—Dartmouth-Cornell (tie).
Big Ten—Michigan.
Yankee Conference—Connecticut-Massachusetts (tie).
Southeastern Conference—Alabama.

Atlantic Coast Conference—North Carolina.
Southern Conference—Richmond.
Mid-American Conference—Toledo.
Big Eight—Nebraska.
Missouri Valley—Memphis.
Pacific Eight—Stanford.
Ohio Valley—Western Ky.
Southwest Conference—Texas.
Big Sky—Idaho.
Pacific Coast A.A.—Long Beach St.
Western Athletic—Arizona St.

ALL-AMERICAS

Offense

Pos.	Player	College
TE—	Doug Kingsriter,	Minnesota
WR—	Terry Beasley,	Auburn
T—	Jerry Sisemore,	Texas
T—	John Uella,	Southern California
G—	Reggie McKenzie,	Michigan
G—	Royce Smith,	Georgia
C—	Tom Brahaney,	Oklahoma
QB—	Pat Sullivan,	Auburn
RB—	Ed Marinaro,	Cornell
RB—	Lydell Mitchell,	Penn State
RB—	Greg Pruitt,	Oklahoma

Defense

Pos.	Player	College
E—	Smylie Gebhart,	Georgia Teck
E—	Walt Patulski,	Notre Dame
T—	Larry Jacobson,	Nebraska
T—	Mel Long,	Toledo
G—	Rich Glover,	Nebraska
LB—	Dave Chaney,	San Jose State
LB—	Jeff Siemon,	Stanford
LB—	Mike Taylor,	Michigan
B—	Clarence Ellis,	Notre Dame
B—	Bobby Majors,	Tennessee
B—	Tom Myers,	Syracuse

Bowl Games

Liberty Bowl—Tennessee 14, Arkansas 13.
Peach Bowl—Mississippi 41, Georgia Tech 18.
Gator Bowl—Georgia 7, North Carolina 3.
Sugar Bowl—Oklahoma 40, Auburn 22.
Cotton Bowl—Penn St. 30, Texas 6.
Orange Bowl—Nebraska 38, Alabama 6.
Astra-Blue Bonnet—Colorado 29, Houston 17.
Fiesta Bowl—Arizona St. 45, Florida St. 38.
Sun Bowl—Louisiana St. 33, Iowa St. 15.
Tangerine Bowl—Toledo 28, Richmond 3.

TENNIS

International Team Champions

Davis Cup—United States.
Wightman Cup (Women)—United States.
Federation Cup (Women)—Australia.

Wimbdledon Champions

Men—John Newcombe—Australia.
Women—Evonne Goolagong—Australia.
Men's Doubles—Roy Emerson—Rod Laver—Australia.
Women's Doubles—Mrs. Billie Jean King, Calif., Rosemary Casals, Calif.

U.S. Open Champions

Men—Stan Smith—Calif.
Women—Mrs. Billie Jean King—Calif.
Men's Doubles—John Newcombe—Roger Taylor.
Women's Doubles—Rosemary Casals—Judy Dalton.

U.S. Clay Court Champions

Men—Zelko Franulovic, Yugoslavia.
Women—Mrs. Billie Jean King.
Men's Doubles—Jan Kodes—Czechoslovakia—Zelko Franulovic, Yugoslavia.
Women's Doubles—Judy Dalton—Billie Jean King.

U.S. Indoor Champions

Men—Clark Graebner
Women—Billie Jean King
Men's Doubles—Juan Gisbert—Manuel Orantes.

GOLF

U.S. OPEN—Lee Trevino
P.G.A.—Jack Nicklaus
MASTERS—Charles Coody
U.S. AMATEUR—Gary Cowan
BRITISH OPEN—Lee Trevino
BRITISH AMATEUR—Steve Melnyk
NCAA (Team)—Texas
NCAA (Individual)—Ben Crenshaw
WORLD CUP—United States
WOMEN'S OPEN—JoAnne Gunderson Carner
WOMEN'S PGA—Kathy Whitworth
WOMEN'S AMATEUR—Laura Baugh
RYDER CUP—United States

BOXING

World Professional Champions

Heavyweight—Joe Frazier, Philadelphia.
Light-Heavyweight—Bob Foster, Wash. D.C.
Middleweight—Carlos Monzon, Argentina.
Welterweight—Jose Napoles, Mexico City.
Jr. Welterweight—Nicolino Loche, Argentina.
Lightweight—Ken Buchanan, Scotland.
Jr. Lightweight—Alfredo Marcano, Venezuela.
Featherweight—Kuniaki Shibata, Japan.
Bantamweight—Ruben Olivares, Mexico.
Flyweight—Erbito Salvarria, Philippines.

TRACK & FIELD

AAU Champions

Hammer throw, George Frenn, Pacific Coast Club.
Discus throw, Tim Vollmer, U.S. Army.
100-yard dash, Dr. Delano Meriwether, Baltimore Olympic Club.
120-yard high hurdles, Rod Milburn, Southern Univ.
Long jump, Arnie Robinson, San Diego Track Club.
Three-mile run, Steve Prefontaine, Oregon.
440-yard dash, John Smith, Southern California Striders.
440-yard intermediate hurdles, Ralph Mann, Southern California Striders.
880-yard run, Juris Luzins, U.S. Marines.
One-mile run, Marty Liquori, N.Y. Athletic Club.

220-yard dash, Don Quarrie, Southern California Striders.
3,000-meter steeplechase, Sid Sink, Bowling Green.
Shot-put, Karl Salb, Mid-America Track Club.
Two-mile walk, Larry Young, Mid-America Track Club.
Javelin throw, Bill Skinner, N.Y. Athletic Club.
Six-mile run, Frank Shorter, Florida Track Club.
Triple jump, John Craft, Chicago Track Club.
Pole vault, Jan Johnston, Chicago Track Club.

NCAA Champions

100 yards, Harrington Jackson, Texas-El Paso.
220 yards, Larry Black, North Carolina Central
440 yards, John Smith, UCLA
880 yards, Mark Winzenried, Wisconsin
One mile, Marty Liquori, Villanova
Three miles, Steve Prefontaine, Oregon
Six Miles, Garry Bjorklund, Minnesota
120 yard high hurdles, Rod Milburn, So. Univ.
440 yard hurdles, Ralph Mann, Brigham Young
3000 meter steeplechase, Sid Sink, Bowling Green
440 yard relay, Southern California
One mile relay, UCLA
High jump, Reynaldo Brown, Calif. Poly.
Pole vault, Dave Roberts, Rice
Long jump, Bouncy Moore, Oregon
Triple jump, Mohinder Gill, Calif. Poly.
Shot put, Karl Salb, Kansas
Discus throw, Mike Louisiana, Brigham Young
Javelin throw, Cary Feldmann, Washington
Hammer throw, Jacques Accambray, Kent State
Decathlon, Ray Hupp, Ohio State
Team champion, UCLA

HOCKEY
NATIONAL HOCKEY LEAGUE
Final Standing Of The Teams

East Division

	GP	W	L	T	PTS.	GF	GA
Boston	78	57	14	7	121	399	207
New York	78	49	18	11	109	259	177
Montreal	78	42	23	13	97	291	216
Toronto	78	37	33	8	82	248	211
Buffalo	78	24	39	15	63	217	291
Vancouver	78	24	46	8	56	229	296
Detroit	78	22	45	11	55	209	308

West Division

Chicago	78	49	20	9	107	277	184
St. Louis	78	34	25	19	87	223	208
Philadelphia	78	28	33	17	73	207	225
Minnesota	78	28	34	16	72	191	223
Los Angeles	78	25	40	13	63	279	303
Pittsburgh	78	21	37	20	62	221	240
California	78	20	53	5	45	199	310

STANLEY CUP PLAYOFFS

East Preliminaries—
Montreal defeated Boston 4 games to 3. N.Y. defeated Toronto 4 games to 2.
Semi-Finals
Chicago defeated N.Y. 4 games to 3.

West Preliminaries—
Chicago defeated Philadelphia 4 games to 0. Minnesota defeated St. Louis 4 games to 2.
Semi-Finals
Montreal defeated Minnesota 4 games to 2.
Championship Final
Montreal defeated Chicago 4 games to 3.

INDIVIDUAL SCORING

	G.	A.	PTS.
Esposito, Boston	76	76	152
Orr, Boston	37	102	139
Bucyk, Boston	51	65	116
Hodge, Boston	43	62	105
Hull, Chicago	44	52	96
Ullman, Toronto	34	51	85
Cashman, Boston	21	58	79
McKenzie, Boston	31	46	77
Keon, Toronto	38	38	76
Beliveau, Montreal	25	51	76
Stanfield, Boston	24	52	76
Thaczuk, N.Y.	26	49	75

ALL-STAR TEAM

Goal—Ed Giacomin, N.Y., Defense—Bobby Orr, Boston—Defense—J.C. Tremblay, Montreal—Center—Phil Esposito, Boston—Right Ving, Ken Hodge, Boston—Left Wing, John Buyck, Boston.

Second Team

Goal—Jacques Plante, Toronto—Defense—Brad Park, N.Y.—Defense—Pat Stapelton, Chicago—Center—Dave Keon, Toronto—Right Wing—Yuan Cournoyer, Montreal, Left Wing—Bobby Hull, Chicago.

TROPHY WINNERS

Hart Memorial Trophy (Most Valuable Player), Bobby Orr, Boston.
Lady Byng Memorial Trophy (Gentlemanly Conduct), Johnny Bucyk, Boston
James Norris Memorial Trophy (Best Defenseman), Bobby Orr, Boston.
Calder Memorial Trophy (Outstanding Rookie), Gil Perreault, Buffalo.
Ross Trophy (Leading Scorer), Phil Esposito, Boston.
Venzina Trophy (Leading Goalie), Shared by Ed Giacomin and Gilles Villemure, New York.

PRO BASKETBALL

NATIONAL BASKETBALL ASSOCIATION

Final Standings
Eastern Conference
Atlantic Division

	W	L	PCT.	GB.
New York	52	30	.634	—
Philadelphia	47	35	.573	5
Boston	44	38	.537	8
Buffalo	22	60	.268	30

Central Division

Baltimore	42	40	.512	—
Atlanta	36	46	.439	6
Cincinnati	33	49	.402	9
Cleveland	15	67	.183	27

Western Conference
Midwest Division

Milwaukee	66	16	.805	—
Chicago	48	34	.585	18
Phoenix	48	34	.585	18
Detroit	45	37	.549	21

Pacific Division

Los Angeles	48	34	.580	—
San Francisco	41	41	.500	7
San Diego	40	42	.488	8
Seattle	38	44	.463	10
Portland	29	53	.354	19

Playoffs

Eastern Semi-finals N.Y. defeated Atlanta 4 games to 1.
Eastern Semi-finals Baltimore defeated Philadelphia 4 games to 3.
Eastern Final Baltimore defeated N.Y. 4 games to 3.
Western Semi-finals Milwaukee defeated San Francisco 4 games to 1.
Western Semi-finals Los Angeles defeated Chicago 4 games to 3.
Western Final Milwaukee defeated Los Angeles 4 games to 1.
Championship Final Milwaukee defeated Baltimore 4 games to 0.

MOST VALUABLE PLAYER

Lew Alcindor, Milwaukee

ROOKIE OF THE YEAR

Shared by Dave Cowens, Boston, and Geoff Petrie, Portland.

ALL-STAR TEAM (FIRST)
Forward—Billy Cunningham, Philadelphia
Forward—John Havlicek, Boston
Center—Lew Alcindor, Milwaukee
Guard—Jerry West, Los Angeles
Guard—Dave Bing, Detroit

ALL-STAR TEAM (SECOND)
Forward—Gus Johnson, Baltimore
Forward—Bob Love, Chicago
Center—Willis Reed, N.Y.
Guard—Oscar Robertson, Milwaukee
Guard—Walt Frazier, N.Y.

ALL-STAR GAME
Jan. 13 at San Diego
West 108, East 107

INDIVIDUAL SCORING

	FG.	FT.	PTS.	AVG.
Alcindor, Milwaukee	1,063	470	2,596	31.7
Havlicek, Boston	892	554	2,338	28.9
Hayes, San Diego	948	454	2,350	28.7
Bing, Detroit	799	615	2,213	27.0
Hudson, Atlanta	829	381	2,039	26.8
Loue, Chicago	765	513	2,043	25.2
Petrie, Portland	784	463	2,031	24.8
Maravich, Atlanta	738	404	1,880	23.2
Cunningham, Phila.	702	455	1,859	23.0
VanArsdale, Cincinnati	749	377	1,875	22.9

AMERICAN BASKETBALL ASSOCIATION
Final Standings

Eastern Division

	W	L	PCT.	GB.
Virginia	55	29	655	—
Kentucky	44	40	524	11
N.Y.	40	44	476	15
Floridians	37	47	440	18
Pittsburgh	36	48	429	19
Carolina	34	50	405	21

Western Division

	W	L	PCT.	GB.
Indiana	58	26	690	—
Utah	57	27	679	.1
Memphis	41	43	488	17
*Texas	30	54	357	28
Denver	30	54	357	28

*Texas defeated Denver in playoff for 4th place.

Playoffs
Eastern Div. Semi-finals—Virginia defeated N.Y. 4 games to 2. Kentucky defeated Floridians 4 games to 2.

Eastern Div. Final—Kentucky defeated Virginia 4 games to 2.

Western Div. Semi-finals—Indiana defeated Memphis 4 games to 0. Utah defeated Texas 4 games to 0.

Western Div. Final—Utah defeated Indiana 4 games to 3.

Championship Final—Utah defeated Kentucky 4 games to 3.

MOST VALUABLE PLAYER
Mel Daniels, Indiana

ROOKIE OF THE YEAR
Dan Issel, Kentucky and Charlie Scott, Virginia (Tie)

ALL-STAR TEAM (FIRST)
Forward—Rick Barry, N.Y.
Forward—Roger Brown, Indiana
Center—Mel Daniels, Indiana
Guard—Charlie Scott, Virginia
Guard—Mack Calvin, Florida

ALL-STAR TEAM (SECOND)
Forward—John Brisker, Pittsburgh
Forward—Joe Caldwell, Carolina
Center—Zelmo Beaty, Utah, Dan Issel, Kentucky (Tie)
Guard—Larry Cannon, Denver
Guard—Don Freeman, Texas

ALL-STAR GAME
Jan. 23, at Greensboro, N.C.
East 126, West 122.

INDIVIDUAL SCORING

	FG.	FT.	PTS.	AVG.
Issel, Kentucky	938	604	2,480	29.88
Barry, N.Y.	613	451	1,734	29.39
Brisker, Pittsburgh	809	430	2,315	29.30
Calvin, Floridians	727	696	2,201	27.17
Scott, Virginia	886	456	2,276	27.10
Cannon, Denver	733	606	2,126	26.57
Jones, Floridians	719	471	2,044	24.33
Freeman, Texas	596	367	1,559	23.62
Caldwell, Carolina	679	302	1,678	23.31
Beaty, Utah	659	420	1,744	22.95

COLLEGE BASKETBALL

NCAA Tournament

East
Villanova 90, Pennsylvania 47

Mideast
Western Kentucky 81, Ohio State 78

Midwest
Kansas 73, Drake 71

Far West
UCLA 57, Long Beach State 55

Semi-fianls
Villanova 92, Western Kentucky 89
UCLA 68, Kansas 60

Third Place
Western Kentucky 77, Kansas 75

Championship
UCLA 68, Villanova 62

College Division—Championship
Evansville 97, Old Dominion 82

National Invitation Tournament—Championship
North Carolina 84, Georgia Tech 66

Leading Scorers

Player, College	G	FG	FT	Pts.	Avg.
Neumann, Mississippi	23	366	191	923	40.1
Carr, Notre Dame	29	430	241	1101	38.0
Humés, Idaho St.	24	287	203	777	32.4
McGinnis, Indiana	24	283	153	719	30.0
McDaniels, Western Ky.	30	357	164	878	29.3
Rinaldi, St. Peter's	24	260	167	687	28.6
Mengelt, Auburn	26	265	208	738	28.4
Phillips, SMU	26	262	213	737	28.3
Meely, Colorado	26	282	165	729	28.0
Brown, Iowa	24	268	126	662	27.6

Rankings

	W	L
1—UCLA	25	1
2—Marquette	27	0
3—Penn	27	0
4—Kansas	25	1
5—Southern California	24	2
6—South Carolina	23	4
7—Western Kentucky	21	5
8—Kentucky	22	4
9—Fordham	25	2
10—Ohio State	19	5

Major Conference Champions
IVY LEAGUE—Penn
PACIFIC EIGHT—UCLA
BIG EIGHT—Kansas
BIG TEN—Ohio State
MISSOURI VALLEY—
SOUTHWEST—T.C.U.
SOUTHERN—Davidson
WESTERN ATHLETIC—Brigham Young
WEST COAST ATHLETIC—Pacific
OHIO VALLEY—Western Kentucky
YANKEE—Mass.
SOUTHEASTERN—Kentucky
MID-AMERICAN—Miami
ATLANTIC COAST—North Carolina
BIG SKY—Weber State

All-American

Player	College
Artis Gilmore	Jacksonville
Jim McDaniels	Western Kentucky
Dean Meminger	Marquette
Austin Carr	Notre Dame
Sidney Wicks	UCLA

Horse Racing

Kentucky Derby
Churchill Downs, Ky.

$145,500

HORSE	JOCKEY	OWNER	MARGIN
1—Canonero II	Avila	E. Caibett	3¾ Lengths
2—Jim French	A. Cordero Jr.	E. J. Caldwell	
3—Bold Reason	Cruget	W. A. Levin	

Preakness
Pimlico, Md.

$137,400

HORSE	JOCKEY	OWNER	MARGIN
1—Canonero II	Avila	E. Caibett	1½ Lengths
2—Eastern Fleet	Maple	Calumet Farms	
3—Jim French	A. Cordero Jr.	E. J. Caldwell	

Belmont Stakes
Belmont Park, N.Y.

$97,710

HORSE	JOCKEY	OWNER	MARGIN
1—Pass Catcher	Blum	October House Farm	¾ Length
2—Jim French	A. Cordero Jr.	E. J. Caldwell	3½ Lengths
3—Bold Reason	Cruget	W. A. Levin	Nk.

Awards
Horse of the Year—Ack Ack.
Older Horse—Ack Ack.
Three-Year-Old—Canonero II.
Three-Year-Old Filly—Turkish Trousers.
Two-Year-Old Colt—Riva Ridge.
Two-Year-Old Filly—Numbered Account.
Steeplechase—Shadow Brook.
Turf Horse—Run the Gantlet.
Best Sprinter—Ack Ack.

THE WORLD IN 1971 – INDEX